BLACKSTONE'S GUIDE TO

The Human Rights Act 1998

SIXTH EDITION

John Wadham, Helen Mountfield QC,
Elizabeth Prochaska, Christopher Brown

OXFORD
UNIVERSITY PRESS

OXFORD

UNIVERSITY PRESS

Great Clarendon Street, Oxford OX2 6DP

Oxford University Press is a department of the University of Oxford.
It furthers the University's objective of excellence in research, scholarship,
and education by publishing worldwide in

Oxford New York

Auckland Cape Town Dar es Salaam Hong Kong Karachi
Kuala Lumpur Madrid Melbourne Mexico City Nairobi
New Delhi Shanghai Taipei Toronto

With offices in

Argentina Austria Brazil Chile Czech Republic France Greece
Guatemala Hungary Italy Japan Poland Portugal Singapore
South Korea Switzerland Thailand Turkey Ukraine Vietnam

Oxford is a registered trade mark of Oxford University Press
in the UK and in certain other countries

Published in the United States
by Oxford University Press Inc., New York

Sixth edition first published 2011

British Library Cataloguing in Publication Data

Data available

Library of Congress Cataloging-in-Publication Data

Data available

Typeset by Cenveo, Bangalore, India
Printed in Great Britain
on acid-free paper by
CPI Antony Rowe,
Chippenham, Wiltshire

ISBN 978-0-19-969700-7

1 3 5 7 9 10 8 6 4 2

Preface to the Sixth Edition

It is now over a decade since the Human Rights Act 1998 came into force. There can be no doubt that it has had a profound effect on domestic law, substantially improving the protection afforded to human rights in the United Kingdom. Where citizens once had 'negative' liberties—no more than the residue of rights left over after the law had been obeyed—they now enjoy positive freedoms and the power to enforce them. The Human Rights Act has held the Government and public authorities to account in a multitude of contexts—preventing the indefinite detention of foreign terrorist suspects,[1] broadening the ambit of procedural justice,[2] recognizing the rights of transsexuals to marry someone of their original gender,[3] protecting the right to freedom of speech, even when it offends,[4] ensuring that the state does not retain the DNA records of innocent people.[5] If it was ever a matter of doubt, it is now plain that the Human Rights Act can no longer be regarded as just another statute. Lord Justice Laws placed it in a category of 'constitutional statutes' which include the Magna Carta and the European Communities Act 1972,[6] and the previous Government accepted its status as a 'received part of our constitutional arrangements'.[7] However the number of cases going to the Strasbourg Court has not yet been stemmed (see Chapter 9 for more details), and the decisions of appeal courts in the United Kingdom are regularly 'overturned' by the European Court of Human Rights, so it would appear that our judges have not yet got it quite right.[8]

And yet attacks on the Human Rights Act continue unabated. The Act is condemned by the popular press as a 'villains' charter' that privileges the rights of unpopular minorities over the law-abiding majority, while the judiciary is damned for its usurpation of democratic power. These accusations are unwarranted. Despite common misconceptions to the contrary, the Human Rights Act does not allow courts to strike down legislation that violates fundamental rights. Instead, the Act strikes a careful balance between parliamentary sovereignty and judicial oversight that enables the courts only to issue a declaration of incompatibility where a legislative provision is incapable of being read compatibly with Convention rights. Ministers make the final decision whether to amend errant legislation. Though it is under no legal obligation to do so, the evidence so far is that governments respond to declarations of incompatibility by changing legislation

---

[1] *A and ors v Secretary of State for the Home Department* [2004] UKHL 56, [2005] 2 AC 68.

[2] For example, for Iraqi families of those killed in detention by British troops (*R (Al-Skeini) v Secretary of State for Defence* [2007] UKHL 26, [2008] 1 AC 153); for those placed on 'safeguarding' registers (*R (F and Thompson) v Secretary of State for the Home Department* [2010] UKSC 17, [2011] AC 331).

[3] *Bellinger v Bellinger* [2003] UKHL 21, [2003] 2 AC 467.

[4] *Livingstone v Adjudication Panel for England* [2006] EWHC 2533 (Admin), [2006] LGR 799.

[5] *R (GC) v Commissioner of the Police for the Metropolis* [2011] UKSC 21.

[6] *Thoburn v Sunderland City Council* [2002] EWHC 195 (Admin), [2002] 3 WLR 247.

[7] JCHR, *A Bill of Rights for the UK?* 29th Report (2007–2008), HL 165-I, HC 150-I, vol II, Jack Straw Ev 78.

[8] *S and Marper v UK* (2008) 25 BHRC 557; *Kay v UK* [2010] ECHR 1322 (21 September 2010); *Hirst v UK* (2006) 42 EHRR 41.

(albeit generally after an appeal and some delay). Rather than judicial usurpation, this model of rights protection ought to be characterized as healthy democratic dialogue.[9] The late Lord Bingham summed up the position in his powerful and eloquent speech in the *Belmarsh* case concerning detention of terrorist suspects:

I do not in particular accept the distinction between democratic institutions and the courts. It is of course true that the judges in this country are not elected and are not answerable to Parliament. It is also of course true that Parliament, the executive and the courts have different functions. But the function of independent judges charged to interpret and apply the law is universally recognised as a cardinal feature of the modern democratic state, a cornerstone of the rule of law itself. The Attorney General is fully entitled to insist on the proper limits of judicial authority, but he is wrong to stigmatise judicial decision-making as in some way undemocratic. It is particularly inappropriate in a case such as the present in which Parliament has expressly legislated in section 6 of the 1998 Act to render unlawful any act of a public authority, including a court, incompatible with a Convention right, has required courts (in section 2) to take account of relevant Strasbourg jurisprudence, has (in section 3) required courts, so far as possible, to give effect to Convention rights and has conferred a right of appeal on derogation issues.[10]

In any event, contrary to some press accusations, the application of the Human Rights Act by the judiciary has been cautious.[11] The approach to section 2 of the Act, which demands that Strasbourg cases are 'taken into account' in interpreting Convention rights, illustrates the restraint with which the judiciary has approached its new powers. In an attempt to avoid being labelled judicial activists, the House of Lords has developed the 'no more, no less' approach to Strasbourg cases and arguably frustrated the creation of a progressive domestic rights jurisprudence.[12] It is necessary only to look at those decisions of the House of Lords and Supreme Court that have been overturned on appeal to the Strasbourg Court to see that English courts are adopting a narrow interpretation of the Convention rights.[13]

Despite the judiciary's responsible application of the Human Rights Act, its future is far from assured. The Conservative Party went into the 2010 general election vowing to abolish the Human Rights Act and to substitute it with a 'Bill of Rights'. The Liberal Democrat Party's manifesto promised to: 'Ensure that everyone has the same protections under the law by protecting the Human Rights Act.'[14] The Coalition Government resolved these contradictions in the Coalition Agreement by promising to establish a Commission to investigate the creation of a Bill of Rights that incorporates and builds on the European Convention.

The Commission was not originally due to be established until December 2011. However, in early 2011 fury over the Human Right Act reached fever pitch as a result of the long-delayed legislation brought forward to give prisoners the right to vote in

---

[9] See ch 1, para 1.28.

[10] *A and ors v Secretary of State for the Home Department* [2004] UKHL 56, [2005] 2 AC 68 at [42].

[11] See the careful analysis in Leigh and Masterman, *Making Rights Real: The Human Rights Act in its First Decade* (London: Hart Publishing, 2009).

[12] See *R (Ullah) v Special Adjudicator* [2004] UKHL 26, [2004] 2 AC 323.

[13] See *Hirst v UK (No 2)* (2006) 42 EHRR 41; *S and Marper v UK* App Nos 30562/04 and 30566/04, 4 December 2008; *Kay v UK* App No 37341/06, 21 September 2010.

[14] Liberal Democrat Manifesto 2010, 94.

line with the decision of the European Court in *Hirst v UK (No 2)* in 2006.[15] The media and many politicians denounced the Convention and called for the United Kingdom to remove itself from the jurisdiction of the European Court. The Coalition Government responded by committing itself to working with its Council of Europe partners to reform the Court to 'rebalance' its relations with national courts when the United Kingdom takes over the chairmanship of the Council of Europe in November 2011. The establishment of the Commission on a Bill of Rights was rushed forward to March 2011. Its terms of reference limit it to proposing a Bill of Rights that 'incorporates and builds on all our obligations' under the Convention and its membership balances supporters and critics of the Human Rights Act. This suggests that there will be little opportunity for the Convention's detractors formally to rid English law of the Convention rights. Some critics have suggested that the duty to take Strasbourg judgments into account could be reworded to give domestic courts greater leeway to develop a distinctive national human rights jurisprudence (changing 'must' to 'may' in section 2). This is, in fact, what many human rights advocates have long called for in the hope that English law may fill in some of the gaps in the Convention's protection. However the real danger is that the more conservative approach to human rights sometimes taken by the House of Lords and Supreme Court will create a schism with the jurisprudence from Strasbourg. What is also at risk is the mechanisms for robust incorporation and redress provided by the Act (sections 3, 6, 7, 8, and 9) which may be compromised rather than enhanced.

Unfortunately the Government's approach to the rights provided by the European Court of Human Rights itself is not as positive as we would wish it to be, and it appears that the Government is to use the fact that the United Kingdom is Chair of the Council of Europe from November 2011 to promote a more hands-off approach. The Secretary of State for Justice at the last international conference on the reform of the Court stated that:

The UK has always been a strong supporter of the European Court of Human Rights. But at times the Court has been rather too ready to substitute its own judgment for that of national courts, without giving enough weight to the strength of the domestic legal system, or allowing for genuine differences of national approach.[16]

The authors hope that the recent frenzy about human rights leads to a free and informed debate that enhances rather than hinders the development of the law.

The law is up to date to 1 June 2011 but, where possible, we have included some later material.

Any mistakes in the text—of course—are ours.

John Wadham, Helen Mountfield QC, Elizabeth Prochaska, and
Christopher Brown
June 2011

---

[15] (2006) 42 EHRR 41.
[16] 26 April 2011, Izmir, Turkey (Ministry of Justice website).

Acknowledgements

Since the first edition of this Guide, the list of acknowledgements we ought to make has grown. We remain enormously grateful to everyone with whom we have discussed the Human Rights Act and incorporation of the Convention into domestic law over the past decade. The thanks which we have accorded to those names in previous editions still stand. We owe particular debts, however, to Anna Edmundson who jointly authored the third and fourth editions and to Caoilfhionn Gallagher who was a joint author on editions four and five.

In addition, for this edition we wish to thank Martin Crick from the Equality and Human Rights Commission, Clare Ovey, a lawyer from the Court, and Professor Philip Leach for their help with Chapter 9. At Oxford University Press Eleanor Walter, Faye Judges and Fiona Stables have given us assistance and encouragement throughout the writing, copy-editing, and proofing process, and we are very grateful to them.

Contents

TABLE OF CASES   xv

TABLE OF INTERNATIONAL INSTRUMENTS   xlix

TABLE OF EUROPEAN LEGISLATION   liii

TABLE OF STATUTES   lv

TABLE OF STATUTORY INSTRUMENTS   lix

1. INTRODUCTION

   A. Introduction   1.01

   B. Human Rights in the United Kingdom before the Human Rights Act   1.06

   C. The Incorporation of the Convention   1.17

   D. The Human Rights Act as a Constitutional Instrument   1.26

   E. The Institutional Framework—Creating a Culture of Respect for
Human Rights   1.37

   F. The Future of Human Rights Protection in the United Kingdom   1.49

2. THE FRAMEWORK OF THE EUROPEAN CONVENTION ON
HUMAN RIGHTS

   A. Introduction   2.01

   B. Interpreting the Convention   2.07

   C. The Scope of Convention Rights   2.25

   D. Restricting Convention Rights   2.40

   E. The Margin of Appreciation   2.77

3. THE FRAMEWORK OF THE HUMAN RIGHTS ACT

   A. Introduction   3.01

   B. Summary of the Effects of the Human Rights Act   3.07

   C. Overview of the Key Provisions of the Human Rights Act   3.08

   D. The Human Rights Act Mechanism in Detail   3.28

   E. Public Authorities and the Human Rights Act: Meaning of
'Public Authority' and 'Functions of a Public Nature'   3.57

   F. Private Parties and the Human Rights Act   3.72

   G. Exceptions and Special Cases   3.75

4. ENFORCING THE HUMAN RIGHTS ACT

   A. Introduction   4.01

   B. The Appropriate Forum for an Argument under the Human Rights Act   4.07

   C. Standing: Who May Bring Proceedings under the Human Rights Act?   4.16

   D. Limitation Periods: Are There Time Limits for Bringing a
       Claim under the Human Rights Act?   4.29

   E. Retrospectivity   4.33

   F. Interventions in Human Rights Act Cases   4.35

   G. Other Means of Enforcement by the Equality and
       Human Rights Commission   4.43

   H. Remedies   4.53

   I. Key Convention Concepts in the Domestic Courts   4.100

   J. Enforcement of the Human Rights Act in Summary   4.131

5. THE INTERACTION BETWEEN CONVENTION
   PRINCIPLES AND EUROPEAN UNION LAW

   A. Introduction   5.01

   B. The Developing Doctrine of Fundamental Rights in EU Law   5.03

   C. The EU Charter of Fundamental Rights   5.11

   D. Accession to the Convention   5.17

   E. The Interaction of EU Law and Convention Principles in UK Courts   5.18

   F. Conclusion   5.27

6. THE CONVENTION RIGHTS: ABSOLUTE RIGHTS

   A. Introduction   6.01

   B. Article 1: Jurisdiction   6.04

   C. Article 2: Right to Life   6.09

   D. Article 3: Prohibition of Torture   6.55

   E. Article 4: Prohibition of Slavery and Forced Labour   6.115

7. THE CONVENTION RIGHTS: LIMITED AND
   QUALIFIED RIGHTS

   A. Introduction   7.01

   B. Article 5: Right to Liberty and Security   7.03

   C. Article 6: Right to a Fair Trial   7.74

   D. Article 7: No Punishment Without Lawful Authority   7.172

   E. Article 8: Right to Respect for Private and Family Life   7.217

   F. Article 9: Freedom of Thought, Conscience, and Religion   7.299

   G. Article 10: Freedom of Expression   7.349

H. Article 11: Freedom of Assembly and Association   7.408

I. Article 12: Right to Marry and Found a Family   7.459

J. Article 13: Right to an Effective Remedy   7.490

K. Article 14: Prohibition on Discrimination   7.504

L. Article 15: Exceptions in Time of War   7.547

M. Article 16: Restrictions on Political Activity of Aliens   7.579

N. Article 17: Prohibition of Abuse of Rights   7.587

O. Article 18: Limitation on Use of Restrictions on Rights   7.591

8. THE CONVENTION PROTOCOLS

A. Introduction   8.01

B. Protocol 1, Article 1: Protection of Property   8.02

C. Protocol 1, Article 2: Right to Education   8.60

D. Protocol 1, Article 3: Right to Free Elections   8.88

E. Protocol 4   8.113

F. Protocol 6   8.127

G. Protocol 7   8.129

H. Protocol 12   8.159

I. Protocol 13   8.161

9. BEYOND THE DOMESTIC COURTS: TAKING A CASE TO STRASBOURG

A. Introduction   9.01

B. The Structure and Jurisdiction of the Court   9.08

C. Making an Application   9.10

D. Admissibility and Merits   9.18

E. Funding for Cases in Strasbourg   9.55

F. Implementation of Judgments   9.62

10. RESEARCHING HUMAN RIGHTS JURISPRUDENCE

A. Introduction   10.01

B. Convention Jurisprudence   10.03

C. Finding Convention Case Law   10.10

D. Finding Human Rights Act Materials   10.20

APPENDIX 1. Human Rights Act 1998   335

APPENDIX 2. Convention for the Protection of Human Rights and Fundamental Freedoms   359

INDEX   385

Table of Cases

A and A v Netherlands (1992) 72 DR 251 . . . . 7.270
A, B and C v Ireland App No 25579/5 . . . . 6.18, 7.231
A and C, Re [2010] EWHC 978 (Fam), [2010] 2 FLR 1363 . . . . 7.19, 7.71
A (Children) (conjoined twins: surgical separation), Re [2001] Fam 147 . . . . 6.30
A v B [2002] EWCA Civ 237, [2003] QB 195 . . . . 7.261
A v Croatia, App No 55164/08, 14 October 2010 . . . . 7.231
A v Essex County Council [2008] EWCA Civ 364, [2008] ELR 321 . . . . 8.73, 8.74
A v Essex County Council [2010] UKSC 33, [2011] 1 AC 280 . . . . 4.32
A v Hoare [2006] EWCA Civ 395, [2006] 1 WLR 2320 . . . . 4.31
A v Netherlands (1988) 59 DR 274 . . . . 8.125
A v Scottish Ministers 2002 SC (PC) 63 . . . . 7.595
A v Secretary of State for the Home Department [2004] UKHL 56, [2005] 2 AC 68 . . . . . . 4.83,
        7.09, 7.15, 7.312, 7.504, 7.531, 7.553, 7.555, 7.558, 7.571, 7.586
A v Secretary of State for the Home Department [2005] UKHL 71, [2006] 2 AC 95 . . . . . . 4.38,
        4.92, 6.60, 6.74, 7.47
A v UK (1998) 5 BHRC 137 . . . . 6.94, 6.95
A v UK (2009) 26 BHRC 1 . . . . 4.120, 7.09, 7.20, 7.44, 7.65, 7.133, 7.144, 7.578
AB v Netherlands (2003) 37 EHRR 48 . . . . 7.297
ADT v UK (1981) 4 EHRR 149 . . . . 7.235
A-G's Reference (No 4 of 2002) [2004] UKHL 43, [2005] 1 AC 264 . . . . 3.31
AL (Serbia) v Secretary of State for the Home Department [2008] UKHL 42, [2008]
        4 All ER 1127 . . . . 7.507, 7.520
AS (Somalia) v Secretary of State for the Home Department [2009] UKHL 32, [2009]
        1 WLR 1385 . . . . 3.41, 7.522, 7.539
AT (Pakistan) v Secretary of State for the Home Department [2010] EWCA Civ 567,
        [2010] NLJR 806 . . . . 7.200
Abdul v DPP [2011] EWHC 247 (Admin) 7.392
Abdulaziz, Cabales and Balkandali v UK (1985) 7 EHRR 471 . . . . 7.225, 7.283, 7.508,
        7.510, 7.511, 7.523, 7.539
Aberdeen Bon-Accord Loyal Orange Lodge 701 v Aberdeen City Council 2002
        SLT (Sh Ct) 52 . . . . 7.428
Abnee v DPP [1999] 2 AC 294 . . . . 4.90
Abrams v US 250 US 616 (1919) 7.349
Abu-Hamza (No 1) v UK, App No 31411/07, 18 January 2011 . . . . 7.121
Acar v Turkey [2005] ECHR 36088/97 . . . . 6.54
Achour v France (2007) 45 EHRR 2 . . . . 7.204, 7.205, 7.209, 7.210
Acquaviva v France App No 19248/91 . . . . 7.87
Adams and Benn v UK (1997) 23 EHRR CD 160 . . . . 7.88
Adams v Khan v UK (1967) 10 YB 478 . . . . 7.467
Adamson v UK, App No 42293/98, 26 January 1999 . . . . 7.195, 7.196
Ademyilmaz v Turkey, App No 41496/98, 21 March 2006 . . . . 7.444
Adetoro v UK [2010] All ER (D) 109 (Apr) 7.139

Adolf v Austria (1982) 4 EHRR 313 . . . . 7.79
Agee v UK (1976) 7 DR 164 . . . . 8.139
Agneesens v Belgium (1998) 58 DR 63 . . . . 8.10
Ahmed v R [2011] EWCA Crim 184 . . . . 6.77
Ahmad v UK (1981) 4 EHRR 126 . . . . 7.302, 7.324
Ahmed v UK (1995) 20 EHRR CD 72 . . . . 4.21
Ahmed v UK (2000) 29 EHRR 1 . . . . 7.354
Ahmut v Netherlands (1996) 24 EHRR 62 . . . . 7.276
Air Canada v UK (1995) 20 EHRR 150 . . . . 8.30, 8.53
Airey v Ireland (1979) 2 EHRR 305, (1977) 8 DR 42 . . . . 2.02, 3.54, 7.26, 7.105,
7.107, 7.221, 7.506
Akdas v Turkey, App No 41056/04, 16 February 2010 . . . . 7.382, 7.403
Akkus v Turkey [1997] ECHR 19263/92 . . . . 2.64
Aksoy v Turkey (1996) 23 EHRR 553 . . . . 7.52, 7.492, 7.493, 7.551
Akta v Turkey [2003] ECHR 24351/94 . . . . 6.09
Al Khawaja and Tahery v UK (2009) 49 EHRR 1 . . . . 3.51, 7.168
Al-Adsani v UK (2001) 34 EHRR 273 . . . . 2.20, 7.110, 7.112
Al-Jedda v UK, App No 27021/08, 7 July 2011 . . . . 3.10
Al-Rawi v Security Service [2010] EWCA Civ 482 . . . . 7.144, 7.166
Al-Saadoon v UK, App No 61498/08, 2 March 2010 . . . . 2.20, 6.07, 6.10, 6.71, 9.14
Al-Skeini v UK, App No 55721/07, 7 July 2011 . . . . 2.23, 2.24, 3.10, 6.06, 9.23
Albert and Le Compte v Belgium (1983) 5 EHRR 533 . . . . 7.81, 7.85, 7.158
Aldemir v Turkey, App No 32124/02, 18 December 2007 . . . . 7.429, 7.430
Ali v Birmingham City Council [2010] UKSC 8 . . . . 7.89, 7.93, 7.148
Ali v Head Teachers and Governors of Lord Grey School [2004] EWCA Civ 382,
[2006] UKHL 14 . . . . 8.71
Ali v UK (2011) 30 BHRC 44 . . . . 8.72, 8.74
Allard v Sweden (2004) 39 EHRR 14 . . . . 8.41, 8.48
Allen v UK [2011] Crim LR 147 . . . . 7.54, 7.64
Allenet de Ribemont v France (1995) 20 EHRR 557 . . . . 7.150
Allgemeine Gold und Silberscheideanstalt v UK (1986) 9 EHRR 1 . . . . 8.53
Allison v Her Majesty's Advocate [2010] UKSC 6 . . . . 7.143
Amuur v France (1996) 22 EHRR 533 . . . . 7.20
Anderson v UK, App No 33689/96, 27 October 1997 . . . . 7.420
Andersson and Kullman v Sweden (1986) 46 DR 251 . . . . 7.487
Andrews v Reading Borough Council [2005] EWHC 256 (QB) 7.251
Andronicou v Cyprus (1997) 25 EHRR 491 . . . . 6.50
Angelova v Bulgaria (2007) 23 BHRC 61 . . . . 6.37
Anheuser-Busch v Poland (2007) 23 BHRC 307 . . . . 8.15
Anufrijeva v Southwark London Borough Council [2003] EWCA Civ 1406,
[2004] QB 1124 . . . . 4.55, 4.57, 4.59, 4.63, 7.224
Appleby v UK (2003) 37 EHRR 38 . . . . 7.369, 7.436, 7.437
Application 10295/82 v UK (1983) 6 EHRR 558 . . . . 7.315
Arrowsmith v UK (1978) 3 EHRR 218 . . . . 7.305, 7.316
Arslan v Turkey, App No 41135/98, 23 February 2010 . . . . 7.328
Artico v Italy (1980) 3 EHRR 1 . . . . 2.11, 3.54, 7.156, 7.164
Ashdown v Telegraph Group [2001] EWCA 1142, [2002] 1 Ch 149, [2001]
3 WLR 1368 . . . . 3.80, 7.351
Ashingdane v UK (1985) 7 EHRR 528 . . . . 2.29, 7.05, 7.11, 7.12, 7.72, 7.108, 7.109

Ashworth Hospital Authority v MGN [2002] UKHL 29, [2002] 1 WLR 2033 . . . . 7.361
Asmundsson v Iceland (2005) 41 EHRR 42 . . . . 8.51
Assenov v Bulgaria (1998) 28 EHRR 652 . . . . 6.56, 6.89
Associated Provincial Picture Houses Ltd v Wednesbury Corp [1948]
    1 KB 223 . . . . 4.112, 4.115, 7.496
Association of General Practitioners v Denmark (1989) 62 DR 226 . . . . 8.10
Aston Cantlow and Wilmcote with Billesley Parochial Church Council v Wallbank
    [2003] UKHL 37, [2004] 1 AC 546 . . . . 3.59, 3.64, 3.65, 3.68, 4.22, 8.28
Attorney General v Scotcher [2005] UKHL 36, [2005] 1 WLR 1867 . . . . 7.351
Attorney General's Reference (No 2 of 2001) [2001] 1 WLR 1869 . . . . 7.129, 7.130
Austin v Commissioner of Police for the Metropolis [2009] UKHL 5, [2009]
    2 WLR 372 . . . . 7.10, 7.17, 7.411
Austria v Italy (1961) 4 YB 116 . . . . 2.09
Autotronic AG v Switzerland (1990) 12 EHRR 485 . . . . 2.67, 7.353
Axen v Germany (1984) 6 EHRR 195 . . . . 7.122
Ayder v Turkey [2004] ECHR 23656/94 . . . . 7.218
Aydin v Turkey (1998) 25 EHRR 251 . . . . 4.58, 6.63
Aziz v Cyprus App No 69949/01 22 December 2004 . . . . 7.506

B and L v UK, App No 36536/02, 29 June 2004 . . . . 7.500
B, Re [2008] UKHL 35, [2009] 1 AC 11 . . . . 6.93
B v France (1992) 16 EHRR 1 . . . . 7.236
B v Secretary of State for Work and Pensions [2005] EWCA Civ 929, [2005]
    1 WLR 3796 . . . . 8.12
B v UK (1988) 10 EHRR 87 . . . . 7.276
B v UK (2002) 34 EHRR 19 . . . . 7.124
BB v UK App No 53760/00, 10 February 2004 . . . . 7.539
BBC, In re [2009] UKHL 34, [2009] 3 WLR 142 . . . . 7.261, 7.263
BJ (Incapacitated Adult), Re [2009] EWHC 3310 (Fam), [2010] 1 FLR 1373 . . . . 7.66
Baczkowski v Poland, App No 1543/06, 3 May 2007 . . . . 7.418, 7.421
Balani v Spain (1995) 19 EHRR 566 . . . . 7.135
Balfour v UK App No 30976/96 . . . . 7.94
Balyemez v Turkey App No 3245/03 . . . . 6.114
Bangs v Connex South Eastern [2001] UKHL 67, [2002] 2 AC 357 . . . . 7.129
Bank Mellat v HM Treasury [2011] EWCA Civ 1 . . . . 5.24, 8.25
Bankovic v Belgium (2007) 44 EHRR SE5 . . . . 2.23, 4.101, 4.103, 9.23
Bankovic v UK (2001) 11 BHRC 435 . . . . 6.05, 6.06
Barberà v Spain (1988) 11 EHRR 360 . . . . 4.58, 7.150
Barnfather v Islington Education Authority [2003] EWHC 418 (Admin), [2003]
    1 WLR 238 . . . . 7.154
Barrett v Enfield London Borough Council [2001] 2 AC 550 . . . . 7.111, 7.112
Barrow v UK [2006] ECHR 42735/02 . . . . 7.537, 7.544, 8.51
Barthold v Germany (1985) 7 EHRR 383 . . . . 2.43, 7.357
Batasuna and Batasuna v Spain, App Nos 25803/04 and 25817/04,
    30 June 2009 . . . . 7.452
Bayatyan v Armenia [2009] ECHR 23459/03 . . . . 7.311
Beaulane Properties v Palmer [2005] EWHC 817 (Ch), [2006] Ch 79 . . . . 8.43
Beckles v UK (2003) 36 EHRR 13 . . . . 7.139
Beet v UK [2006] RA 384 . . . . 7.27

Begum v Tower Hamlets [2003] UKHL 5, [2003] 2 AC 430 . . . . 2.15, 7.92, 7.148
Belgian Linguistics (No 2) (1968) 1 EHRR 252 . . . . 7.106, 7.511, 7.516, 7.521, 7.523,
                                   7.530, 7.534, 8.62, 8.64, 8.68, 8.86
Belilos v Switzerland (1988) 10 EHRR 466 . . . . .2.72, 7.114
Bellinger v Bellinger [2003] UKHL 21, [2003] 2 AC 467 . . . . .3.41, 4.78, 4.80, 7.237, 7.473
Bendenoun v France Series A No 284, 24 February 1994 . . . . 7.97
Benes v Austria (1992) 72 DR 271 . . . . 7.269
Benham v UK (1996) 22 EHRR 293, 10 June 1996 . . . . 7.27, 7.97, 7.99, 7.163
Benjamin and Wilson v UK (2003) 36 EHRR 1 . . . . 7.57
Bensaid v UK (2001) 33 EHRR 205 . . . . 6.106, 7.231, 7.497
Bentham v Netherlands (1986) 8 EHRR 1 . . . . 7.85
Berrehab v Netherlands (1988) 11 EHRR 322 . . . . 7.278
Beyeler v Italy (2001) 33 EHRR 52 . . . . 8.20
Bezicheri v Italy (1989) 12 EHRR 210 . . . . 7.62
Bickel (Case C-274/96) [1998] ECR I-7637 . . . . 5.09
Blood and Tarbuck v Secretary of State for Health [2003] UKHL 21, [2003] 2 AC 467 . . . . . 4.80
Blum v Director of Public Prosecutions [2006] EWHC 3209 (Admin) 7.431
Boddaert v Belgium (1993) 16 EHRR 242 . . . . 7.128
Boiceno v Moldova [2006] ECHR 41088/05 . . . . 6.89
Bönisch v Austria (1987) 9 EHRR 191 . . . . 7.143
Booker Acquaculture Ltd (t/a Marine Harvest McConnell) v Scottish Ministers
    (Case C-20/00) [2003] ECR I-7411 . . . . .5.06, 5.07
Booth-Clibborn v UK (1985) 43 DR 236 . . . . 8.93
Boškoski v Former Yorkshire Republic of Macedonia, App No 11676/04,
    2 September 2004 . . . . 8.95
Boso v Italy, App No 50490/99, ECHR 2002-VII 6.11, 7.461
Bosphorus Hava Yollari Turizm Ve Ticaret AS v Ireland (2006)
    42 EHRR 1 . . . . 5.20
Botta v Italy (1998) 26 EHRR 241 . . . . 7.222, 7.510, 7.513
Boughanumi v France (1996) 22 EHRR 228 . . . . 7.276
Bowman v UK (1998) 26 EHRR 1 . . . . 7.350, 7.352, 7.357
Boyle and Rice v UK (1988) 10 EHRR 425 . . . . .3.76, 7.490
Bozana v France (1986) 9 EHRR 297 . . . . 7.03
Bozano v France (1984) 39 DR 119 . . . . 7.593
Brady v UK (1979) 3 EHRR 297 . . . . 7.88
Bramelid and Malmstrom v Sweden (1982) 29 DR 64 . . . . 8.10
Brannigan v McBride v UK (1993) 17 EHRR 297 . . . . 7.548, 7.557, 7.562, 7.568
Brasserie du Pêcheur SA v Germany (Joined Cases C-46 and 48/93) [1996]
    ECR I-1029 . . . . 5.24
Brecknell v UK (2008) 46 EHRR 957 . . . . 6.34, 6.37, 6.53
Brennan v UK (2002) 34 EHRR 18 . . . . 7.162
Brind and McLaughlin v UK (1994) 7-A DR 42 . . . . 7.382
Briody v St Helen's and Knowsley Health Authority [2001] EWCA Civ 1010,
    [2002] QB 856 . . . . 7.479
British Airways Plc v Unite the Union [2010] EWCA Civ 669, [2010] IRLR 423 . . . . 7.449
Brogan v UK (1988) 11 EHRR 117 . . . . .7.04, 7.30, 7.52, 7.73, 7.568
Brolly (Anne), Re [2004] NIQB 69 . . . . 7.149
Broniowski v Poland (2004) 15 BHRC 573 . . . . 8.10, 8.19, 9.42
Brooks v Commissioner for Police for the Metropolis [2005] UKHL 2, [2005] 2 AC 176 . . 7.112

Brown v Rwanda [2009] EWHC 770 (Admin) 7.80
Brown v Stott [2001] 2 WLR 817, [2003] 1 AC 681 . . . . 1.36, 7.77, 7.502
Brown's Application, Re [2003] NIJB 168 . . . . 7.149
Broziecek v Italy (1989) 12 EHRR 371 . . . . 7.157
Bruckmann v Germany (1974) 17 YB 458 . . . . 8.123
Bryan v UK (1995) 21 EHRR 342 . . . . 7.149
Bryant v Commissioner of Police for the Metropolis [2011] EWHC
    1314 (Admin) 4.106, 7.223
Bubbins v UK App No 50916/99, 17 March 2005 . . . . 6.51
Buckley v UK [2008] UKHL 64, (1996) 23 EHRR 101 . . . . 7.288, 7.506
Budayeva v Russia, App No 15339/02, 20 March 2008 . . . . 6.22, 8.23
Bukta v Hungary, App No 25691/04, 17 July 2007 . . . . 7.430
Bullock v UK (1996) 21 EHRR CD 85 . . . . 7.515
Bulut v Austria (1997) 24 EHRR 84 . . . . 7.131
Bulves AD v Bulgaria, App No 3991/03, 22 January 2009 . . . . 8.08
Burden & Burden v UK (2008) 24 BHRC 709 . . . . 4.85, 7.500, 8.51
Burden v UK, App No 13378/05, 12 December 2006, [2006] ECHR 1064 . . . . 9.21, 9.27

C v DPP [1996] AC 1, 28 . . . . 7.190
C v UK (1983) 37 DR 142 . . . . 7.310
CG v Bulgaria, App No 1365/07, 24 April 2008 . . . . 8.136
CNR v Canada (Human Rights Commission) [1987] 1 SCR 1114 . . . . 7.528
CTB v News Group Newspapers and Imogen Thomas [2011] EWHC 1232 (QB) 3.80
Caballero v UK (2000) 30 EHRR 643 . . . . 7.55, 7.73
Cadder v HM Advocate [2010] UKSC 43, [2011] 1 WLR 2601 . . . . 3.49, 7.140
Caisse Regionale de credit Agricole Mutuel v France 19 Oct 2004 . . . . 8.21
Cameron v Network Rail Infrastructure Ltd [2006] EWHC 1133 (QB), [2007]
    1 WLR 728 . . . . 3.67, 4.29
Campbell and Cosans v UK (1982) 4 EHRR 293 . . . . 4.20, 6.64, 6.94, 7.306, 8.77, 8.79
Campbell and Fell v UK (1985) 7 EHRR 165 . . . . 7.96, 7.99, 7.100, 7.114, 7.158
Campbell v MGN Ltd [2004] UKHL 22, [2004] 2 AC 457 . . . . . 3.72, 3.73, 3.79, 7.259, 7.350,
    7.3516
Campbell v MGN Ltd (Costs) [2005] UKHL 61, [2005] 1 WLR 3394 . . . . 7.398
Campbell v South Northamptonshire District Council [2004] EWCA Civ 409,
    [2004] 3 All ER 387 . . . . 7.320, 8.12
Campbell v UK (1992) 15 EHRR 137 . . . . 2.53, 2.64
Can v Austria (1985) 8 EHRR 14121 . . . . 7.158
Canea Catholic Church v Greece (1999) 27 EHRR 521 . . . . 7.109, 7.533
Cantoni v France 1996-V, 1614 . . . . 5.20, 7.181, 7.185
Cardot v France (1991) 13 EHRR 853 . . . . 9.26
Carlin v UK, App 27537/95 . . . . 8.16
Carpenter v Secretary of State for the Home Department (Case C-60/00) [2002]
    ECR I-6279 . . . . 5.07, 5.19
Carson v UK, App No 42184/05, 16 March 2010 . . . . 7.512, 7.515, 7.519, 8.17, 9.27
Case v Minister of Safety and Security (1996) 3 SA 617 . . . . 7.361
Cassell and Co Ltd v Broom [1972] AC 1027 . . . . 7.351
Catholic Care v Charity Commission [2010] EWHC 520 (Ch), [2010]
    4 All ER 1041 . . . . 7.314, 7.343
Ceylan v Turkey (2000) 30 EHRR 73 . . . . 7.382

Chahal v UK (1996) 23 EHRR 413 . . . . 2.27, 2.80, 4.83, 6.04, 6.57, 6.100, 6.101, 7.44,
7.57, 7.512, 7.570, 8.136, 9.23
Chapman v UK (2001) 33 EHRR 399 . . . . 2.52, 2.53, 7.224
Chassagnou v France (1999) 29 EHRR 615 . . . . .7.308, 7.411, 7.414, 7.450, 8.47
Chassagnou v France [2007] UKHL 52, [2008] 1 AC 719 . . . . 7.308
Chauvy v France [2004] ECHR 64915/01 . . . . .7.185, 7.399
Cheall v UK (1985) 42 DR 178 . . . . 7.440
Chikwamba v Secretary of State for the Home Department [2008] UKHL 40,
[2008] 1 WLR 1420. . . . . 7.286
Christian Democratic People's Party v Moldova, App No 28793/02, 14 February 2006 . . . . 7.411
Christians Against Racism and Facism v UK (1983) 21 DR 138 . . . . 7.418, 7.420, 7.427
Church of Jesus Christ of Latter Day Saints v Gallagher [2008] UKHL 56,
[2008] 1 WLR 1852. . . . . 7.312
Church of Jesus Christ of Latter Day Saints v Price [2004] EWHC 3245 (Admin). 7.340
Ciorap v Moldova [2007] ECHR 12066/02 . . . . 6.62
Clayton v Clayton [2006] EWCA Civ 878 . . . . 3.80
Collins v Imtrat Handelsgesellschaft mbH (Case C-92/92) [1993] ECR I-5145 . . . . 5.22
Colman v UK (1993) 18 EHRR 119 . . . . 7.357
Commission for Equality and Human Rights v Griffin [2010] EWHC 3343 (Admin). 4.28
Commission v Germany (Case C-427/85) [1989] ECR I-1263. . . . . 5.09
Condron v UK (2001) 31 EHRR 1. . . . . 7.139
Connolly v DPP [2007] EWHC 237 (Admin), [2008] 1 WLR 276. . . . . 7.362
Connor's Application for Judicial Review, Re [2004] NICA 45 . . . . 7.488
Connors v UK (2005) 40 EHRR 9 . . . . 2.39, 7.217, 7.293
Copland v UK (2007) 25 BHRC 216 . . . . 7.296
Copsey v Devon Clays Ltd [2005] EWCA Civ 932, [2005] IRLR 811. . . . . 7.302
Cossey v UK (1990) 13 EHRR 622 . . . . .2.19, 7.236, 7.272, 7.471, 7.474
Costello-Roberts v UK (1995) 19 EHRR 112. . . . . .3.63, 6.94
Council of Civil Service Unions v Minister for the Civil Service [1985] AC 375 . . . . 4.112
Council of Civil Service Unions v UK (1987) 50 DR 228 . . . . 7.455
Cream Holdings v Banerjee [2004] UKHL 44, [2005] 1 AC 253 . . . . .3.79, 7.406
Croissant v Germany (1993) 16 EHRR 135 . . . . 7.164
Crosbie v Secretary of State for Defence [2011] EWHC 879 (Admin) 7.79
Cudak v Lithuania (2010) 51 EHRR 15 . . . . .7.94, 7.110
Cumpana and Mazare v Romania, App No 33348/96, 17 December 2004 . . . . 7.371
Curley v UK (2001) 31 EHRR 14. . . . . 7.73
Cuscani v UK (2003) 36 EHRR 2. . . . . 7.170
Cyprus v Turkey (1976) 4 EHRR 482. . . . . 6.72, 7.07, 7.12
Czekalla v Portugal [2002] ECHR 657 . . . . 7.164

D v UK (1997) 24 EHR 423. . . . . 6.106, 6.107, 6.108
DEES v Hungary, App No 2345/06, 9 November 2010 . . . . 7.249
DH v Czech Republic (2007) 23 BHRC 526 . . . . 7.504, 7.505, 7.517, 7.527, 7.529, 7.539
DP and JC v UK (2003) 36 EHRR 14 . . . . 7.495
DPP v Collins [2006] UKHL 40, [2006] 1 WLR 2223. . . . . 7.293, 7.362, 7.590
Dahlab v Switzerland [2001] ECHR 42393/98. . . . . 7.327, 7.331, 7.338
Daltel Europe Ltd (in liquidation) v Hassan Ali Makki [2006] EWCA Civ 94 . . . . 7.98
Damnjanovic v Serbia [2009] 1 FLR 339 . . . . 7.128
Danilenkov v Russia, App No 67336/01, 30 July 2009 . . . . 7.458

Darby v Sweden (1990) 13 EHRR 774 . . . . 7.300, 7.303, 7.310, 7.515
Darnell v UK (1993) 18 EHRR 205 . . . . 7.128
De Becker v Belgium (1958) 2 YB 214 . . . . 7.593
De Boucherville v Mauritius [2008] UKPC 37 . . . . 6.79
De Cubber v Belgium (1984) 7 EHRR 236. . . . . 7.147
De Freitas v Permanent Secretary of Ministry of Agriculture, Fisheries,
    Lands and Housing [1999] 1 AC 69 . . . . 4.114, 4.116
De Haes v Belgium (1997) 25 EHRR 1. . . . . 7.358, 7.362
De Wilde, Ooms and Versyp v Netherlands (1971) 1 EHRR 373 . . . . 7.51, 7.178
Dehal v DPP [2005] EWHC 2154 (admin), (2005) 169 JP 581 . . . . 7.351, 7.382, 7.391
Delcourt v Belgiumn (1970) 1 EHRR 355 . . . . 7.74
Demades v Turkey [2003] ECHR 16219/90. . . . . 7.290
Demicoli v Malta, Series A No 2010, 27 August 1991 . . . . 7.99
Demir v Turkey (2001) 33 EHRR 43 . . . . 2.21, 7.438, 7.448, 7.557
Denev v Sweden (1989) 59 DR 127 . . . . 8.32
Denmark v Greece (1969) 12 YB 1 . . . . 6.64
Dennis v Ministry of Defence [2003] EWHC 793 (QB), [2003] Env LR 34 . . . . 7.251
Department of Work and Pensions v M [2006] UKHL 11, [2006] 2 AC 91. . . . . 2.16, 4.106,
                                                                                      7.271, 7.274
Derbyshire County Council v Times Newspaper Ltd [1992] QB 770,
    [1993] AC 534. . . . . 1.15, 7.351
Deumeland v Germany (1986) 8 EHRR 448 . . . . 7.89
Devaseelan v Secretary of State for the Home Department [2002] UKIAT 702 . . . . 7.287
Deweer v Belgium (1980) 2 EHRR 439 . . . . 2.11, 7.81, 7.95, 7.103, 7.123
DH v Czech Republic (2007) 23 BHRC 526 . . . . 7.505, 8.87
Dickson v UK (2007) 24 BHRC 19, (2006) 46 EHRR 419 . . . . 2.64, 7.240, 7.481,
                                                                      7.482, 7.483, 7.486, 7.487
Diennet v France (1995) 21 EHRR 554 . . . . 7.122
Dobson v Thames Water Utilities [2007] EWHC (QB) 2021 . . . . 4.29, 4.56
Dodds v UK, App No 59314/00, 8 APril 2003 . . . . 7.500
Dodov v Bulgaria App No 59548/00. . . . . 6.25
Doherty v Birmingham City Council [2008] UKHL 57, [2008] 3 WLR 636 . . . . . . 7.294, 7.295
Donald v Ntuli [2010] EWCA Civ 1276, [2011] 1 WLR 294. . . . . 7.264
Donoghue v Poplar Housing [2001] EWCA Civ 595, [2002] QB 48 . . . . 3.32, 3.65
Doorson v Netherlands (1996) 22 EHRR 330 . . . . 7.137, 7.166
Douglas v Hello! Ltd [2001] QB 96 . . . . 7.351, 7.590
Douglas v Hello! (No 3) [2005] EWCA Civ 595, [2006] QB 125 . . . . 7.258
Doustaly v France 70 Rep Judg & Dec 1998 11 850 . . . . 4.58
Draper v UK (1980) 24 DR 72. . . . . 7.487
Dudgeon v UK (1981) 4 EHRR 149 . . . . 2.58, 2.59, 2.64, 4.20, 7.228, 7.235,
                                                                                      7.506, 9.21
Dunn v Parole Board [2008] EWCA Civ 374, [2009] 1 WLR 728 . . . . 4.29, 4.31
Duplex Printing Press Co v Deering 254 US 443 (1921). 7.446
Duport Steels Ltd v Sirs [1980] 1 WLR 142 . . . . 1.31

E, Re [2008] UKHL 66, [2008] 3 WLR 1208. . . . . 4.38, 4.39, 4.116, 6.73, 6.97
E v UK (2003) 36 EHRR 519. . . . . 6.96
EB (Kosovo) v Secretary of State for the Home Department [2008] UKHL 41,
    [2008] 3 WLR 178. . . . . 7.286

EB v France (2008) 47 EHRR 21 . . . . 7.235, 7.268, 7.282, 7.478, 7.538, 7.540
EM (Lebanon) v Secretary of State for the Home Department [2008] UKHL 64,
    [2009] 1 All ER 559 . . . . 3.49, 7.266, 7.276, 7.287
ETK v News Group Newspapers [2011] EWCA Civ 439 . . . . 3.79, 7.265
East African Asians v UK (1981) 3 EHRR 76 . . . . 1.11, 6.61, 6.70, 7.03, 7.540
Eckle v Federal Republic of Germany (1983) 5 EHRR 1 . . . . 7.128
Editions Plon v France [2004] ECHR 58148/00 . . . . 7.255
Edwards v UK (1992) 15 EHRR 417 . . . . 7.77, 7.132, 7.147, 7.156
Edwards v UK (2002) 12 BHRC 190 . . . . 6.20, 6.34, 6.36, 6.37, 6.39, 7.493
Eerikainen v Finland [2009] ECHR 3514/02 . . . . 7.255
Ekbatani v Sweden (1991) 13 EHRR 504 . . . . 7.142
Ekinci v London Borough of Hackney [2001] EWCA Civ 776, [2002] HLR 2 . . . . 7.225
Elgafaji v Saatssecretaris van Justitie (Case C-465/07) [2009] WLR (D) 59 . . . . 5.10, 5.15
Elliniki Radiophonia Tileorassi (ERT) v Dimotiki Etairia Pliroforissis (DEP)
    (Case C-260/89) [1991] ECR I-2925 . . . . 5.07, 5.18
Emesa Sugar (Free Zone) NV v Aruba (Case C-17/98) [2000] ECR I-665 . . . . 5.09
Enerji v Turkey, App No 68959/01, 21 April 2009 . . . . 7.448
Engel v Netherlands (1976) 1 EHRR 647 . . 2.29, 7.04, 7.10, 7.79, 7.96, 7.97, 7.99, 7.382, 7.515
English v Emery Reimbold & Strick [2002] EWCA Civ 605 . . . . 7.136
Enhorn v Sweden (2005) 41 EHRR 633 . . . . 7.34, 7.41
Eren v Turkey [2006] ELR 155 . . . . 8.70
Eskelinen v Finland (2001) 31 EHRR 651 . . . . 7.94
European Parliament v Council (Case C-540/03) [2006] ECR I-5769 . . . . 5.11
Evans v Amicus Healthcare Ltd [2004] EWCA Civ 727, [2005] Fam 93 . . . . 6.12
Evans v UK (2007) 22 BHRC 190 . . . . 6.13, 7.240
Evans v UK (2008) 46 EHRR 34 . . . . 7.222, 7.239, 7.480
Ewing v UK (1988) 10 EHRR 141 . . . . 7.128
Ezeh and Connors v UK (2004) 39 EHRR 1 . . . . 7.96, 7.97, 7.99, 7.100
Ezelin v France (1991) 14 EHRR 362 . . . . 7.412

F v Switzerland (1987) 10 EHRR 411 . . . . 7.464, 7.485
Factortame (Case C-213/89) [1990] ECR I-2433 . . . . 5.22
Fadeyeva v Russia [2005] ECHR 55723/00 . . . . 2.36, 7.250
Family H v UK (1984) 37 DR 105 . . . . 8.67
Farhri v France (2009) 48 EHRR 34 . . . . 7.119
Fatullayev v Azerbaijan (2011) 52 EHRR 2 . . . . 7.150
Fayed v UK (1994) 18 EHRR 393 . . . . 2.62, 7.82
Feldbrugge v Netherlands (1986) 8 EHRR 425 . . . . 7.89
Férét v Belgium, App No 15615/07, 16 Ju;y 2009 . . . . 7.363
Ferrazzini v Italy (2002) 34 EHRR 1068 . . . . 7.85, 7.88
Findlay v UK (1997) 24 EHRR 221 . . . . 7.114, 7.116, 7.147
Fischer v Austria [2002] ECHR 33382/96 . . . . 7.122, 7.131
Fitt v UK (2000) 30 EHRR 480 . . . . 7.144
Fitzpatrick v Sterling Housing Association Ltd [2001] 1 AC 27 . . . . 7.220, 7.273
Fogarty v UK (2002) 34 EHRR 302 . . . . 7.110, 7.112
Foka v Turkey, App No 28940/95, 24 June 2008 . . . . 7.370
Foldes v Hungary [2006] ECHR 41463/02 . . . . 8.117
Folgero v Norway (2007) 23 BHRC 227 . . . . 8.76, 8.81, 8.82
Foster v British Gas plc (Case C-188/89) [1990] ECR I-3313 . . . . 5.26

Foucher v France (1998) 25 EHRR 234 . . . . 7.143
Fox v UK (1990) 13 EHRR 157 . . . . 7.29, 7.73
France 2 v France, App No 30262/96, 15 January 1997 . . . . 8.14
Francovich v Italy (Case C-6/90) [1991] ECR I-5357 . . . . 5.24
Frankowicz v Poland, App No 53025/99-16 December 2008 . . . . 7.354
Freda v Italy (1980) 21 DR 250 . . . . 7.07, 7.26
Fredin v Sweden (1991) 13 EHRR 784 . . . . 7.516
Freedom and Democracy Party (OZDEP) v Turkey (2001) 31 EHRR 27 . . . . 7.453
Fretté v France (2004) 38 EHRR 21 . . . . 7.282, 7.478
Frodl v Austria (2011) 52 EHRR 5 . . . . 8.100
Fuentes Bobo v Spain (2000) 31 EHRR 1115 . . . . 7.367
Funke v France (1993) EHRR 297 . . . . 5.08, 7.138, 7.155

G v E [2010] EWCA Civ 822, [2011] 1 FLR 239 . . . . 7.21, 7.39
G v Germany (1989) 60 DR 256 . . . . 7.418, 7.420
G v Netherlands (1993) 16 EHRR CD 38 . . . . 7.277
G v United Kingdom 35 DR 75 . . . . 7.138
G, Re [2008] UKHL 38, [2009] 1 AC 173 . . . . 3.49
GHB v UK [2000] EHRLR 545 . . . . 7.280
GOC v Poland App No 48001/99 . . . . 7.127
GS and RS v UK, App No 17142/90, 10 July 1991 . . . . 7.481
Gabarri Moreno v Spain, App No 68066/01, 22 July 2003 . . . . 7.201
Gäfgen v Germany, App No 22978/05, 3 June 2010 . . . . 6.57, 6.62, 6.64, 7.138
Gaganus v Turkey, App No 39335/98, 5 June 2001 . . . . 8.59
Ganchev v Bulgaria, App No 28858/95, 25 November 1996 . . . . 8.102
Garaudy v France App No 65831/01, 24 June 2003 . . . . 7.399, 7.589
Garcia Alva v Germany (2001) 37 EHRR 335 . . . . 7.144
Gardel v France, App No 16428/05, 17 December 2009 . . . . 7.196
Garyfallou AEBE v Greece Reports of Judgments and Decisions 1996-III,
    10 June 1996 . . . . 7.97, 7.99
Gaskin v UK (1990) 12 EHRR 36 . . . . 3.22, 7.280, 7.364
Gast and Popp v Germany (2001) 33 EHRR 37 . . . . 7.127
Gasus-Dosier and Fordertechnik v Netherlands (1995) 20 EHRR 403 . . . . 8.31, 8.52
Gatt v Malta, App No 28221/08, 27 July 2010 . . . . 7.27
Gault v UK (2008) 46 EHRR 1202 . . . . 7.54
Gaunt v OFCOM [2010] EWHC 1756, [2010] NLJR 1045 . . . . 7.363
Gaweda v Poland (2004) 39 EHRR 4 . . . . 7.380
Gaygusuz v Austria (1996) (1997) 23 EHRR 364 . . . . 8.16
Georgian Labour Party v Georgia [2008] ECHR 9103/04 . . . . 8.90
Georgiev v Bulgaria, App No 4551/05, 24 February 2011 . . . . 7.127
Ghaidan v Godin-Mendoza [2004] UKHL 30, [2004] 2 AC 557 . . . . . . 3.17, 3.36, 3.38, 4.130,
                                                                        7.220, 7.273, 7.504, 7.511
Gillan and Quinton v UK App No 4158/05 . . . . 2.47, 4.109
Gillan v UK (2010) 28 BHRC 420 . . . . 7.14, 7.227, 7.229
Gillow v UK (1986) 11 EHRR 335 . . . . 7.290, 7.537
Gitonas v Greece (1980) 21 DR 211 . . . . 8.109
Glimmerveen & Hagenbeek v Netherlands, (1979) 18 DR 187 . . . . 7.363, 7.589
Golder v UK (1975) 1 EHRR 524 . . . . 2.09, 2.12, 2.15, 2.29, 7.74, 7.105, 7.106,
                                                                                7.108, 7.109

Goodwin v UK (2002) 35 EHRR 18 . . . . .2.19, 2.37, 4.80, 7.236, 7.237, 7.272,
7.472, 7.473, 7.485, 7.489
Gorzelik v Poland, App No 44158/98, 17 February 2004 . . . . 7.442, 7.450, 7.451, 7.453
Gough v Chief Constable of Derbyshire [2002] EWCA Civ 351, [2002] QB 1213 . . . . 7.199
Govell v UK, App No 27237/95, 14 January 1998 . . . . .2.45, 7.501
Granger v UK (1990) 12 EHRR 469 . . . . 7.163
Grant v South-West Trains [1998] 1 CR 449. . . . . 7.474
Grant v UK (2007) 44 EHRR 1 . . . . 7.237
Greek Case (1969) 11 YB 501. . . . . 6.62, 7.12, 7.554
Green Corns Ltd v Clavery Group [2005] EWHC 958 (QB) 3.79
Greens v UK, App No 60041/08, 23 November 2010 [2010] ECHR 1826. . . . . .8.101, 9.52
Gregory v United Kingdom (1998) 25 EHRR 577 . . . . .7.119, 7.120
Grieves v United Kingdom (2004) 39 EHRR 2. . . . . .7.115, 7.117
Grigoriades v Greece (1997) 27 EHRR 464 . . . . 7.354
Grobbelaar v News Group Newspapers Ltd [2002] UKHL 40, [2002] 1 WLR 3024 . . . . . . 7.362
Groppera Radio AG v Switzerland (1990) 12 EHRR 321 . . . . 2.43, 7.353, 7.355, 7.375
Guardian News and Media, Re [2010] UKSC 1 . . . . 7.246, 7.263, 7.364
Guérin Automobiles v 15 Members of the EC, App No 5157/99, 4 July 2000 . . . . 5.17
Guerra v Italy (1998) 26 EHRR 357. . . . . 2.36
Guja v Moldova [2008] ECHR 14277/04. . . . . .7.354, 7.382
Gül v Switzerland (1996) 22 EHRR 93. . . . . 7.283
Gül v Turkey (2002) 34 EHRR 28 . . . . 6.34, 6.49
Guliyeu v Azerbaijan, App No 355584/02, 27 May 2004 . . . . 8.95
Gunduz v Turkey, App No 35071/97, 4 December 2003. . . . . 7.387
Gunes v Turkey, App No 28490/95, 19 June 2003. . . . . 7.142
Gürbüz v Turkey, App No 26050/04, 10 November 2005 . . . . 6.114
Gurguchiani v Spain (1995) 20 EHRR 247. . . . . .7.198, 7.200
Gusinski v Russia (2004) 16 BHRC 427. . . . . .7.592, 7.593
Gustaffson v Sweden (1996) 22 EHRR 409 . . . . .7.448, 7.458
Güvec v Turkey, App No 70337/01, 20 January 2009 . . . . 6.83
Guzzardi v Italy (1980) 3 EHRR 333 . . . . .7.11, 7.33

H & K v UK (1983) 34 DR 218. . . . . 7.356
H v Finland, App No 37359/09, not yet decided. 7.272
H v France (1990) 12 EHRR 74 . . . . 7.128
H v UK (1992) 16 EHRR CD 44. . . . . 7.305
HC (Malaysia) v Secretary of State for the Hime Department [2010]
    EWCA Civ 1014 . . . . 7.274
HL v UK (2004) 40 EHRR 761 . . . . 7.12, 7.21, 7.39
HM (Iraq) v Secretary of State for the Home Department [2010] EWCA Civ 1322. . . . . . . 7.284
HM v Switzerland [2002] ECHR 39187/98. . . . . 7.10
Hackett v UK (2005) 5 EHRLR 543 . . . . 6.39
Hadjianastassiou v Greece (1992) 16 EHRR 219 . . . . .7.135, 7.158
Hakansson and Sweden v Sweden (1991) 13 EHRR 1. . . . . .7.123, 7.490
Halford v UK (1997) 24 EHRR 523. . . . . 3.76, 7.247, 7.296
Hall v Mayor of London [2010] EWCA Civ 817. . . . . 7.432
Hamer v UK (1979) 24 DR 5. . . . . .7.464, 7.487
Hammerton v Hammerton [2007] EWCA Civ 248 . . . . .7.98, 7.163
Hammond v DPP [2004] EWHC 69 (Admin), (2004) 168 JP 601. . . . . 7.390

Han v Commissioners of Customs and Excise [2001] EWCA Civ 1040, [2001] 4 All ER 687 2.16
Handyside v UK (1976) 1 EHRR 737 . . . . 2.09, 2.55, 2.56, 2.58, 2.78, 7.349, 7.362,
7.400, 7.401, 8.53
Hasan and Chaush v Bulgaria (2002) 34 EHRR 55. . . . . .7.304, 7.313
Hashman and Harrup v UK (2000) 30 EHRR 241. . . . . 2.48, 7.350, 7.381, 7.411
Hassan-Daniel v HMRC [2010] EWCA Civ 443 . . . . .6.57, 6.113
Hatton v UK (2002) 34 EHRR 1 . . . . 2.83, 4.112, 7.249, 7.250, 7.496, 7.499, 9.08,
9.46, 10.06, 10.11
Heaney and McGuinness v Ireland (2001) 33 EHRR 12. . . . . 7.77, 7.81, 7.139
Helle v Finland (1997) 26 EHRR 159. . . . . 7.135
Hentrich v France (1994) 18 EHRR 440 . . . . 8.38
Herczegfalvy v Austria (1992) 15 EHRR 437 . . . . 6.88
Hermi v Italy (2008) 46 EHRR 46 . . . . 7.142
Hertel v Switzerland (1998) 28 EHRR 534. . . . . 7.351, 7.358, 7.360, 7.400
Hess v UK (1975) 2 D & R 72 . . . . 4.103
Hickling v Baker [2007] EWCA 287, [2007] 1 WLR 2386. . . . . 7.26
Hilbe v Liechtenstein, App No 31981/96-ECHR 1999, VI. 8.98
Hilton v UK (1998) 57 DR 108 . . . . 9.28
Hirst v UK (No 2) (2006) 42 EHRR 41 . . . . 1.53, 2.64, 2.68, 2.81, 4.86, 7.350, 8.62,
8.91, 8.98, 8.100, 8.101, 9.01, 9.52, 9.63
Hoang v France (1993) 16 EHRR 53 . . . . 7.163
Hodgson and Woolf v UK (1987) 51 DR 136. . . . . 7.354
Hoffer and Annen v Germany (2011) 29 BHRC 654 . . . . 7.388
Hogben v UK (1986) 46 DR 231 . . . . 7.178
Hokkanen v Finland [1996] 1 FLR 289 . . . . 7.128
Holy Monasteries v Greece (1997) 23 EHRR 387. . . . . 7.304, 8.09, 8.58
Hood v UK (2000) 29 EHRR 365 . . . . 7.116
Huang v Secretary of State for the Home Department [2007] UKHL 11, [2007]
2 AC 167 . . . . 4.116, 7.285, 7.286
Huber v France (1998) 26 EHRR 457 . . . . 7.94
Hussain v UK (1996) 22 EHRR 1. . . . . 7.63
Hyde Park v Moldova (No 4) App No 18491/07, 7 April 2009 . . . . 7.418

Imbrioscia v Switzerland (1993) 17 EHRR 441. . . . . 7.161, 7.164
Incal v Turkey (2000) 29 EHRR 449. . . . . 7.114, 7.116
Independent News and Media Limited v A [2010] EWCA Civ 343, [2010]
3 All ER 32. . . . . 7.365
Informationsverein Lentia v Austria (1994) 17 EHRR 93 . . . . 7.374
Interfact v Liverpool City Council [2005] EWHC 995 (Admin), [2005] 1 WLR 3118 . . . . 7.362
International Transport Roth GmbH v Secretary of State for the Home
Department [2002] EWCA Civ 158, [2002] 3 WLR 344 . . . . 4.122, 4.124
Inze v Austria (1987) 10 EHRR 394. . . . . 7.511, 7.537, 7.540
Inzunza v USA [2011] EWHC 920 (Admin) 6.104
Ireland v UK (1978) 2 EHRR 413 . . . . 6.58, 6.59, 6.60, 6.62, 6.69, 6.72, 7.49, 7.556, 9.09
Isak v Turkey, App No 21924/05, 2 February 2010 . . . . 7.309
Ismoilov v Russia [2008] ECHR 2947/06. . . . . 7.207

JM v UK, App No 37060/06, 28 September 2010. . . . . .2.16, 2.19, 4.42, 7.267, 7.271, 7.272,
7.274, 7.506, 7.510, 7.538, 8.13, 8.16

JR17's Application for Judicial Review, Re [2010] UKSC 27 . . . . 8.72, 8.74
JR1, Re Judicial Review [2011] NIQB 5 . . . . 4.19
JT [2003] EWCA Crim 111 . . . . 7.210
Jablonski v Poland (2003) 36 EHRR 27 . . . . 7.128
Jain v Trent Strategic Health Authority [2009] UKHL 4, [2009] 2 WLR 248 . . . . 7.87
Jakóbski v Poland (2010) 30 BHRC 417 . . . . 7.305, 7.318
Jalloh v Germany (2007) 44 EHRR 32 . . . . 7.138
Jameel v Wall Street Journal Europe [2006] UKHL 44, [2007] 1 AC 359 . . . . 7.372
James v London Electricity plc [2004] EWHC 3226 (QB) 3.67
James v UK (1986) 8 EHRR 123 . . . . 8.07, 8.08, 8.40
Jamil v France (1995) 21 EHRR 65 . . . . 7.195
Jankauskas v Lithuania [2005] ECHR 59304/00 . . . . 7.297
Janovwskiv v Poland (1999) 29 EHRR 705 . . . . 7.358
Jersild v Denmark (1995) 19 EHRR 1 . . . . 2.67, 7.362, 7.363, 7.372, 7.387
Jespers v Belgium (1981) 27 DR 61 . . . . 7.143, 7.158
Jevremovic v Serbia [2007] 2 FCR 671 . . . . 7.279
Jewish Liturgical Association Cha'are Shalom Ve Tesedek v France (2000) 9 BHRC 27 . . . . 7.323
Johansen v Norway (1985) 44 DR 155 . . . . 7.26
Johnson v UK (1999) 27 EHRR 296 . . . . 4.60, 7.36, 7.41
Johnston v Chief Constable of the Royal Ulster Constabulary (Case 222/84) [1987] QB 129 1.15
Johnston v Ireland (1986) 9 EHRR 203 . . . . 2.17, 4.20, 7.476
Jokela v Finland (2003) 37 EHRR 26 . . . . 8.08
Jones v Saudi Arabia [2006] UKHL 26, [2007] 1 AC 270 . . . . 6.66, 7.110
Jordan v UK (2003) 37 EHRR 2 . . . . 7.524
Jorgic v Germany (2008) 47 EHRR 207 . . . . 7.115, 7.172, 7.187
Jussila v Finland (2007) 45 EHRR 38 . . . . 7.98, 7.101

K v UK (1986) 50 DR 199 . . . . 7.267
KB v NHS Pensions Agency Case C-117/01 [2004] ECR I-541 . . . . 7.489
KH (Afghanistan) v Secretary of State for the Home Department [2009] EWCA
    Civ 1354 . . . . 6.108
KH v Slovakia, App No 32881/04, 28 April 2009 . . . . 7.242, 7.364
Kadi v Council and Commission (Case T-315/01)[2005] ECR II-3649 . . . . 5.09
Kafkaris v Cyprus [2008] ECHR 21906/04, 25 BHRC 591, 25 BHRC 591 . . . . . 6.79, 7.178, 7.206
Kalashnikov v Russia (2002) 36 EHRR 34 . . . . 6.81, 6.84
Kamasinski v Austria (1991) 13 EHRR 36 . . . . 7.157, 7.164, 7.169
Kamma v The Netherlands (1974) 1 DR 4 . . . . 7.591
Karaduman v Turkey (1993) 74 DR 93 . . . . 7.322
Karakó v Hungary, App No 39311/05, 28 July 2009 . . . . 7.246
Karner v Austria, App No 40016/98, 24 July 2003 . . . . 7.539
Katsaros v Greece (2003) 36 EHRR 58 . . . . 8.08
Kay v Lambeth London Borough Council [2006] UKHL 10, [2006] 2 AC 465 . . . . . . 3.51, 7.294
Kay v UK, App No 37341/06, judgment of 21 September 2010 . . . . 2.39, 7.220, 7.295
Kaya v Turkey (1998) 28 EHRR 1 . . . . 6.93, 7.518, 7.593
Kaye v Robertson [1991] FSR 62 . . . . 7.219
Kazmierczak v Poland, App No 4317/04, 10 March 2009 . . . . 7.151
Keegan v Ireland (1994) 18 EHRR 342 . . . . 7.222, 7.277
Keenan v UK (2001) 33 EHRR 913 . . . . 6.19, 6.20, 6.26, 7.493
Kennedy v UK, App No 26839/05, 18 May 2010 . . . . 2.47

Kerimova v Azerbaijan, App No 20799/06, 30 September 2010 . . . . 8.112
Khan v UK (1986) 48 DR 253 . . . . 7.247, 7.463
Khan v UK (2000) 31 EHRR 45. . . . . 7.501
Khider v France, App No 39364/05, 9 July 2009. . . . . 6.83
Kimlya v Russia [2009] ECHR 76836/01 . . . . 7.304
King v United Kingdom [2004] STC 911. . . . . 7.88
Kingsley v United Kindom (2002) 35 EHRR 10. . . . . 4.57
Kingston v UK App No 27837/95, 9 April 1997. . . . . 7.181
Kiss v Hungary, App No 38832/06, 20 May 2010. . . . . 8.98
Kjeldsen, Busk Madsen and Pedersen v Denmark (1979) 1 EHRR 711 . . . . 2.09, 7.515, 8.80
Klamecki v Poland (2003) 39 EHRR 7 . . . . 7.52, 7.64
Klass v Germany (1978) 2 EHRR 214 . . . . 2.09, 4.19, 4.20, 7.492
Kleyn v Netherlands (2004) 38 EHRR 14. . . . . 7.115
Klip and Kruger v Netherlands (1997) 91 A-DR 66 . . . . 7.468
Knudsen v Norway, 42 DR 247 . . . . 7.316
Kokkinakis v Greece (1994) 17 EHRR 397. . . . . 7.174, 7.191, 7.299, 7.300, 7.336, 7.337
Konig v Germany (1978) 2 EHRR 170. . . . . 7.79, 7.81, 7.85, 7.87
Kononov v Latvia (2009) 25 BHRC 317. . . . . 7.187
Konstantinidis v Stadt Altensteig-Standesamt (Case C-168/91) [1993] ECR I-1191 . . . . 5.07
Kopecky v Slovakia (2005) 41 EHRR 43. . . . . 8.22
Kopp v Sweden (1999) 27 EHRR 91 . . . . 2.44
Korbely v Hungary (2008) 25 BHRC 382. . . . . 7.127, 7.172, 7.187
Kosieck v Germany (1986) 9 EHRR 328 . . . . 7.94
Kostovski v Netherlands (1989) 12 EHRR 434. . . . . 7.137, 7.166
Kovach v Ukraine [2008] ECHR 39424/02 . . . . 8.112
Kramelius v Sweden, App No 210062/92, 17 January 1996 . . . . 8.68
Krcmar v Czech Republic (2001) 31 EHRR 41. . . . . 7.143
Kremzow v Austria (Case C-299/95) [1997] ECR I-2629 . . . . 5.09
Kröchen and Möller v Switzerland (1984) 6 EHRR 345 . . . . 7.158
Krone Verlag GmbH and Co KG v Austria [2002] ECHR 34315/96. . . . . 7.255
Kroon v Netherlands (1994) 19 EHRR 263 . . . . 7.270, 7.281
KRS v UK, App No 32733/08, 2 December 2008. . . . . 6.105
Krzycki v Germany (1978) 13 DR 57 . . . . 7.23
Kücükdeveci v Swedex GmbH (Case C-555/07) [2010] ECR I-365 . . . . 5.15
Kudeshkina v Russia, App No 29492/05, 26 February 2009 . . . . 7.350, 7.354
Kudla v Poland (2002) 35 EHRR 11. . . . . 6.68
Kulkarni v Milton Keynes NHS Hospital Trust [2009] EWCA Civ 789,
    [2009] IRLR 829 . . . . 7.104, 7.134
Kurt v Turkey (1998) 27 EHRR 373. . . . . 7.04
Kurucay v Turkey App No 24040/04 . . . . 6.114
Kurup v Denmark (1986) 8 EHRR CD 93 . . . . 7.158
Kuznetsov v Ukraine [2003] ECHR 39042/97 . . . . 7.326
Kyprianou v Cyprus (2007) 44 EHRR 27. . . . . 7.388

L v Human Fertilisation and Embryology Authority [2008] EWHC 2149 (Fam),
    [2008] 2 FLR 1999. . . . . 7.239
LK (Serbia) v Secretary of State for the Home Department [2007] EWCA Civ 1554 . . . . . . 7.285
Labita v Italy, App No 2677/95, 6 April 2000 . . . . 8.98
Ladele v London Borough of Islington [2009] EWCA Civ 1357, [2010] IRLR 211. . . . . . . 7.314

Ladent v Poland, App No 11036/03, 18 March 2008 . . . . 7.28
Lamy v Belgium (1989) 11 EHRR 529 . . . . 7.132
Langborger v Sweden (1989) 12 EHRR 416 . . . . 7.115
Lauko v Slovenia (2001) 33 EHRR 40 . . . . 7.97
Lautsi v Italy, App No 30814/06, 18 March 2011 . . . . 2.82, 8.82
Lavents v Latvia, App No 58442/00, 28 November 2002 . . . . 7.115
Lawless v Ireland (No 3) (1961) 1 EHRR 15 . . . . 2.79, 7.17, 7.30, 7.178, 7.552, 7.562, 7.588
Le Compte v Belgium (1981) 4 EHRR 1 . . . . 7.445
Le Pen v France, App No 18788/09, 20 April 2010 . . . . 7.363
Leander v Sweden (1987) 9 EHRR 433. . . . . 2.60
Lebbink v Netherlands [2004] 3 FCR 59 . . . . 7.267
Leeds City Council v Hall [2011] UKSC 8 . . . . 7.295
Lehideux v France (1998) 5 BHRC 540 . . . . 7.387
Lenzing AG v UK [1999] EHRLR 132 . . . . 8.14
Letellier v France (1991) 14 EHRR 83 . . . . 7.55
Liberal Party v UK (1980) 4 EHRR 106 . . . . 8.109
Liberty v UK (2009) 48 EHRR 1 . . . . 2.47, 7.227
Lindon, Otchakovsky-Laurens and July v France (2008) 46 EHRR 35 . . . . 7.254, 7.373,
. . . . 7.378, 7.382
Lindon v Austria (2008) 46 EHRR 35 . . . . 7.359
Lingens v Austria (1981) 26 DR 171 . . . . 7.153, 7.350, 7.357
Lingens v Austria (1986) 8 EHRR 407 . . . . 7.358
Lithgow v UK (1986) 8 EHRR 329 . . . . 7.516, 8.07, 8.59
Litster v Forth Dry Dock and Engineering Co Ltd [1990] 1 AC 546 . . . . 3.34
Livingstone v Adjudication Panel for England [2006] EWHC 2533 (Admin),
   [2006] LGR 799. . . . . 7.362, 7.392
Lizarraga v Spain, App No 62543/11, 27 April 2004 . . . . 2.09
Loizidou v Turkey (1996) 23 EHRR 513 . . . . 4.103, 9.23
London Borough of Harrow v Qazi [2003] UKHL 43, [2004] 1 AC 983. . . . 7.220, 7.288, 7.294
London Borough of Hounslow v Powell [2011] UKSC 8 . . . . 7.295
London Borough of Islington v Ladele [2009] ICR 387 . . . . 3.81, 7.342, 7.590
London Quadrant Housing Trust v Weaver [2009] EWCA Civ 58, [2010] 1 WLR 363 . . . . . 3.71
Lopez Ostra v Spain (1995) 20 EHRR 27 . . . . 7.249
Loutchansky v Times Newspapers Ltd [2001] EWCA Civ 1805, [2002] QB 783 . . . . 7.351
Luedicke, Belkacem and Koc v Germany (1979–1980) 2 EHRR 149 . . . . 7.169
Luordo v Italy [2003] ECHR 32190/96 . . . . 8.49
Lustig-Prean and Beckett v UK (1999) 29 EHRR 548. . . . . 2.67
Lutz v Germany Series A No 123, 25 August 1987 . . . . 7.97
Lynas v Switzerland (1976) 6 DR 141 . . . . 7.43
Lynch v DPP [2001] EWHC 882 (Admin), [2003] QB 137 . . . . 7.154

M v Germany (2009) 28 BHRC 521 . . . . 7.30, 7.178, 7.196
M v Secretary of State for Work and Pensions [2006] UKHL 11, [2006] 2 AC 91 . . .7.221, 7.267
M v United Kingdom (1987) 52 DR 269 . . . . 7.110
MA v Finland (2003) 37 EHRR CD. 8.21
MAK and RK v UK [2010] 2 FLR 451 . . . . 7.231done, 7.495
MB v Secretary of State for the Home Department [2007] UKHL 46, [2008]
   1 AC 440 . . . . 7.96, 7.102
MGN v UK, App No 39401/04, 18 January 2011 . . . . 7.259, 7.350, 7.352, 7.398

MH v UK, App No 11577/06, 19 February 2008 . . . . 7.40, 7.137
MK (Iran) v Secretary of State for the Home Department [2009] EWHC 3452
    (Admin) 7.94
MS v Sweden (1999) 28 EHRR 313 . . . . 7.242
McCann v UK (1995) 21 EHRR 97 . . . . 4.57, 6.09, 6.33, 6.49, 6.50, 6.52, 7.293
McCartan Turkington Breen v Times Newspaper Ltd [2001] 2 AC 277 . . . . 7.349, 7.351
McCaughey, In re [2011] UKSC 20 . . . . 4.33, 6.36
McClintock v Department of Constitutional Affairs [2008] IRLR 29 . . . . 7.308
McElhinney v Ireland (2002) 34 EHRR 13 . . . . 7.112
McFarlane v Ireland [2010] ECHR 1272 . . . . 7.127
MacFarlane v Relate [2010] EWCA Civ 771, [2010] IRLR 872 . . . . 7.314, 7.348
McGinley v Egan v UK (1999) 27 EHRR 1 . . . . 2.36, 7.135
McGonnell v UK (2000) 30 EHRR 289 . . . . 7.115
McGuinness v UK, App No 39511/98, 8 June 1999 . . . . 7.305, 7.337, 8.105
McInnes v Her Majesty's Advocate [2010] UKSC 7 . . . . 7.143
McKay v UK (2006) 24 BHRC 471 . . . . 7.51
McKennitt v Ash [2006] EWCA Civ 1714, [2007] 3 WLR 194 . . . . 7.259
McKeown v UK, App No 6684/05, 11 January 2011 . . . . 7.143
McKerr, Re [2004] UKHL 12, [2004] 1 WLR 807 . . . . 4.33, 6.36
MacLeod v Secretary of State for Communities and Local Government
    [2008] EWHC 384 (Admin) 6.123
McMichael v UK (1995) 20 EHRR 205 . . . . 2.66
McShane v UK (2002) 35 EHRR 23 . . . . 6.29, 6.31, 6.32, 6.38, 6.40, 6.47, 6.53, 7.524
Maestri v Italy, App No 39748/98, 17 February 2004 . . . . 7.450
Magee v UK (2001) 31 EHRR 822 . . . . 7.161
Magill v Porter (1993) 18 EHRR 205 . . . . 7.129
Mahmud v Galloway and McKay [2006] EWHC 1286 (QB), [2006] EMLR 26 . . . . 3.83
Malarde v France App No 46813/99, 5 September 2000 . . . . 8.92
Malhous v Czech Republic [2001] ECHR 33071/96 . . . . 8.18
Malone v Metropolitan Police Commissioner [1979] Ch 344 . . . . 1.03, 7.219
Malone v UK (1984) 7 EHRR 14 . . . . 1.14, 7.296
Manchester City Council v Pinnock [2010] UKSC 45, [2010]
    3 WLR 1441 . . . . 3.21, 3.22, 3.53, 4.116, 7.295
Mangouras v Spain, App No 12050/04, 28 September 2010 . . . . 7.54
Manole v Moldova [2009] ECHR 13936/02 . . . . 7.369
Manoussakis v Greece Reports of Judgments and Decisions 1996-IV 7.313
Marais v Governor of HMP Brixton [2001] EWHC 1051 (Admin) 7.178
Marcic v Thames Water Utilities [2003] UKHL 66, [2004] 2 AC 42 . . . . 7.251, 8.24, 8.55
Marckx v Belgium (1979) 2 EHRR 330 . . . . 2.11, 4.20, 7.221, 7.477, 7.534, 7.536
Markovic v Italy (2007) 44 EHRR 52 . . . . 7.110
Markt Intern Verlag v Germany (1989) 12 EHRR 161 . . . . 7.360
Marleasing SA v La Comercial Internacional de Alimentacion
    (Case C-106/89) [1990] ECR I-4135 . . . . 5.01, 5.22
Marlow v UK, App No 42015/98, 5 December 2000 . . . . 7.382
Marshall v Southampton and South West Hampshire Area Health Authority
    (Teaching) (Case 152/84) [1986] QB 401 . . . . 5.22
Marshall v Southampton and South West Hampshire Area Health Authority
    (Teaching) (No 2) (Case C-271/91) [1993] ICR 893 . . . . 5.23
Martin v United Kingdom (2007) 44 EHRR 31 . . . . 7.116

Martins v Commissioners of Customs and Excise [2001] EWCA Civ 1040, [2001]
        4 All ER 687. . . . . 2.16
Marzari v Italy (1999) 28 EHRR CD 175 . . . . 7.224
Mastromatteo v Italy [2002] ECHR 3770397. . . . . 6.24
Matadeen v Pointu [1999] AC 98 . . . . 7.504
Mathieu-Mohin v Belgium (1987) 10 EHRR 1. . . . . 8.88, 8.89, 8.92, 8.110
Matthews v Ministry of Defence [2002] EWHC 13 (QB), [2003] UKHL 4,
        [2003] 1 AC 1163 . . . . 7.110
Matthews v UK (1999) 28 EHRR 36 . . . . 5.20, 8.93
Mattoccia v Italy (2003) 36 EHRR 47 . . . . 7.157
Matveyev v Russia, App No 26601/02, 3 July 2008. . . . . 8.147
Mayeka v Belgium [2006] N3 FCR 637 . . . . 6.73, 7.05, 7.12, 7.72
Mayor of London v Haw [2011] EWHC 585 (QB) 7.432
Medicaments and Related Classes of Goods (No 4), Re [2001] EWCA Civ 1217,
        [2002] 1 WLR 269. . . . . 4.21, 4.24
Medvedyev v France, App No 3394/03, 29 March 2010 . . . . 7.20
Megadat.com SRL v Moldova App No 21151/04, 8 April 2008 . . . . 8.25
Mellacher v Austria (1989) 12 EHRR 391 . . . . 8.10, 8.33
Melnychenko v Ukraine (2006) 42 EHRR 39. . . . . 8.98, 8.104
Menson v UK [2003] ECHR 47916/00 . . . . 6.34
Mentes v Turkey [1998] ECHR 23186/94 . . . . 7.218
Metropolitan Church of Bessarabia v Moldova [2001] ECHR 45701/99. . . . . 7.313
Michalak v Wandsworth LBC [2002] EWCA Civ 271, [2002] 1 WLR 617. . . . . 7.545
Mikulic v Croatia [2002] 1 FCR 720 . . . . 7.279
Minelli v Switzerland (1983) 5 EHRR 554 . . . . 7.150
Mirolubous v Latvia, App No 798/05, 15 September 2009 . . . . 7.313
Miss Behavin' Ltd v Belfast City Council [2007] UKHL 19, [2007] NI 89 . . . . 7.360, 7.362,
                                                                                    7.382, 8.06
Mitchell v Glasgow City Council [2009] UKHL 11, [2009] AC 874. . . . . 6.24
Mizzi v Malta [2006] 1 FCR 256 . . . . 7.281
Moldovan v Romania (2007) 44 EHRR 16. . . . . 7.105
Monnell and Morris v United Kingdom (1988) 10 EHRR 205 . . . . 7.122
Monteiro da Costa Noqueira v Portugal, App No 4035/08, 11 January 2011. . . . . 7.388
Moore v UK, App No 37841/97, 30 May 2000. . . . . 8.99
Moreira de Azevedo v Portugal (1990) 13 EHRR 721 . . . . 7.74
Morris v UK (2002) 34 EHRR 52. . . . . 3.51
Moscow Branch of the Salvation Army v Russia (2006) 44 EHRR 912 . . . . 7.313
Moser v Austria [2007] 1 FLR 702 . . . . 7.124
Mosley v Newsgroup Newspaper Ltd [2008] EWHC 1777 (QB), [2008] NLJR 1112. . . . . 7.256,
                                                                                            7.382
Mosley v UK, App No 48009/08, 10 May 2011 . . . . 2.39, 2.80, 2.82, 7.256, 7.350, 7.404
Moss v HM Coroner for North and South Districts of Durham and Darlington
        [2008] EWHC 2940 (Admin) 6.46
Motais de Narbonne v France, App No 48161/99, 2 July 2002 . . . . 2.64
Moustaquim v Belgium (1991) 13 EHRR 802 . . . . 7.283
Müller v Austria (1975) 3 DR 25 . . . . 8.16, 8.17
Müller v Switzerland (1988) 13 EHRR 212 . . . . 2.49, 7.357, 7.362
Multiplex v Croatia, App No 58112/00, 10 July 2003. . . . . 7.74
Murphy v Ireland (2003) 38 EHRR 212. . . . . 7.387, 7.403

Murray v Express Newspapers plc [2008] EWCA Civ 446, [2008] 3 WLR 1360 . . . . 7.260
Murray v UK (1994) 18 EHRR CD1 . . . . .7.138, 7.139
Murray v UK (1994) 19 EHRR 193 . . . . .7.29, 7.155
Murray v UK (1996) 22 EHRR 29 . . . . .7.155, 7.161
Mustafa and Armag an Akn v Turkey, App No 4694/03, 6 April 2010 . . . . 7.280

N v Secretary of State for the Home Department [2005] UKHL 31, [2005]
    2 AC 296 . . . . 3.49, 6.107, 6.108
N v Switzerland (1983) 34 DR 208 . . . . 7.356
N v UK, App No 4239/08, 27 May 2008 . . . . 6.126
NHS Trust v M [2001] Fam 348 . . . . 6.27
Nachova v Bulgaria [2005] ECHR 43577/98 . . . . 6.37, 6.52, 7.524, 7.525
Napier v Scottish Ministers [2002] UKHR 308, 1 SC 229 . . . . 6.81, 6.84
National Panasonic (UK) Ltd v Commission (Case 136/79) [1980] ECR 2033 . . . . 5.09
National and Provincial Building Society v UK (1997) 25 EHRR 127 . . . . .7.516, 8.52
National Union of Belgian Police v Belgium (1975) 1 EHRR 578 . . . . 7.447, 7.448, 7.509
Neigel v France [1997] EHRLR 424 . . . . 7.94
Nerva v UK (2003) 36 EHRR 4 . . . . 8.21
Nesibe Haran v Turkey App No 28299/95, 6 October 2005 . . . . 7.593
Neumeister v Austria (1968) 1 EHRR 91 . . . . 7.51
New York Times v Sullivan (1964) 376 US 254 . . . . 7.358
New Zealand Maori Council v Attorney General of New Zealand [1994] 1 AC 466 . . . . 4.90
News Verlags GmbH and Co KG v Austria (2000) 9 BHRC 625 . . . . 7.255
Niemietz v Germany (1992) 16 EHRR 97 . . . . .7.229, 7.291
Nnyanzi v UK, App No 21878/06, 8 April 2008 . . . . 6.108
Norris v Ireland (1988) 13 EHRR 186 . . . . 4.20
Northern Ireland Commissioner for Children and Young Peoples' Application
    [2007] NIQB 115 . . . . 6.95
Norwood v DPP [2003] EWHC 1564 (Admin), (2005) 169 JP 581 . . . . 7.382, 7.390, 7.399
Norwood v UK (2004) 40 EHRR SE 111, [2003] Crim LR 888 . . . . .7.587, 7.589

OOO v Commissioner of Police of the Metropolis [2011] EWHC 1246 (QB) 4.68,
                                                                                            4.105, 6.127
OSH v Austria, App No 57813/00, 1 April 2010 . . . . 7.240
Oates v Poland, App No 35036/97, 11 May 2000 . . . . 7.592
Oberschlick v Austria (1997) 25 EHRR 357 . . . . .7.356, 7.358
Observer v UK (1991) 14 EHRR 153 . . . . .7.371, 7.382
Öcalan v Council of the European Union (Case C-229/05) [2007] ECR I-439 . . . . . . .5.09, 5.25
Öcalan v Turkey (2005) 41 EHRR 45 . . . . .7.52, 7.158
O'Carroll v UK App No 35557/03, 15 March 2005 . . . . .7.181, 7.186
Odievre v France (2003) 14 BHRC 526 . . . . 7.279
O'Donoghue v UK, App No 34848/07, 14 December 2010 . . . . .2.64, 7.470
Officer L, Re [2007] UKHL 36, [2007] 1 WLR 2135 . . . . .6.21, 7.166
Ofulue v Bossert [2008] EWCA Civ 7, [2008] 3 WLR 1253 . . . . 8.43
Ogur v Turkey (2001) 31 EHRR 40 . . . . 6.31
O'Halloran and Francis v UK (2008) 46 EHRR 21 . . . . .7.103, 7.141
O'Hara v UK (2002) 34 EHRR 32 . . . . 7.29
Öllinger v Austria, App No 76900/01, 29 June 2006 . . . . 7.424, 7.425, 7.433, 7.437
Olsson (No 1) (1998) 11 EHRR 259 . . . . 2.67

Olujic v Croatia (2011) 52 EHRR 26 . . . . 7.115
Omoregie v Norway, App No 265/07, 31 July 2008 . . . . 7.283
Omwenyeke v Germany, App No 44294/04, 20 November 2007 . . . . 8.116
Öneryildiz v Turkey (2004) 18 BHRC 145 . . . . 2.36, 6.22, 8.09, 8.23
Open Door Counselling and Dublin Well Woman v Ireland (1992)
    15 EHRR 244 . . . . 4.21, 7.354, 7.355, 7.382
Opinion 2/94 on Accession by the Community to the ECHR [1996] ECR I-1759 . . . . 5.03, 5.06
Opuz v Turkey (2009) BHRC 159 . . . . 6.23, 6.33, 6.34, 6.89, 7.506, 7.517, 7.546
Orkem v Commission (Case 374/87), [1989] ECR 3283 . . . . 5.08
Orobator v Governor of HMP Holloway [2010] EWHC 58 (Admin) 7.80
O'Rourke v UK App No 39022/97, 26 June 2001. 6.109, 6.110, 7.224
Orr v Norway, App No 31283/04, 15 May 2008. . . . . 7.152
Oršuš v Croatia (2010) 28 BHRC 558 . . . . 8.87
O'Shea v MCN [2001] EMLR 40. . . . . 7.351
Osman v UK (1998) 29 EHRR 245 . . . . . . 2.35, 6.19, 6.20, 6.21, 6.24, 6.32, 6.53, 7.108, 7.111
Otto-Preminger Institute v Austria (1994) 19 EHRR 34 . . . . 7.350, 7.362, 7.382, 7.402
Özgur Gündem v Turkey (2001) 31 EHRR 49 . . . . 7.367
Ozturk v Germany Series A No 73, 21 February 1984. . . . . 7.97

P, C and S v UK (2002) 35 EHRR 31 . . . . 7.460
P and Q v Surrey County Council [2011] EWCA Civ 190 . . . . 7.18
PF and EF v UK, App No 28326/09, 23 November 2010 . . . . 6.97
PG and JH v UK [2001] ECHR 44787/98. . . . . 7.141
PG v UK [2001] ECHR 44787/98. . . . . 7.229, 7.248
PG v UK, App No 10822/84, 7 June 1987 . . . . 7.481
PS v Germany (2003) 36 EHRR 61 . . . . 7.166
Pabla Ky v Finland (2006) 42 EHRR 34 . . . . 7.115
Padovani v Italy, App No 13396/87, 26 February 1993 . . . . 7.113
Papageorgiou v Greece (2004) 38 EHRR 30 . . . . 7.165
Papon v France (2004) 39 EHRR 10. . . . . 7.213
Paton v UK (1980) 19 DR 244. . . . . 6.11
Paturel v France, App No 54968/00, 22 December 2005. . . . . 7.301
Patyi v Hungary, App No 5529/05, 7 October 2008 . . . . 7.418
Pearson v UK, App No 8374/03, 27 April 2004 . . . . 7.500
Peck v UK (2003) 35 EHRR 41 . . . . 7.229, 7.247, 7.252, 7.496, 7.499
Peers v Greece (2001) 33 EHRR 51 . . . . 6.68, 6.81
Peev v Bulgaria [2007] ECHR 64209/01 . . . . 7.290
Pellegrin v France (1998) 26 EHRR 457. . . . . 7.94
Péllisier and Sassi v France (2000) 30 EHRR 715 . . . . 7.127, 7.157
Pendragon v UK, App No 3146/96, 19 October 1998. . . . . 7.427
Pentiacova v Moldova, App No 14462/03, 4 January 2005 . . . . 7.225
Pepper v Hart [1993] AC 593. . . . . 10.27, 10.28
Perdigáo v Portugal, App No 24768/06, 16 November 2010. . . . . 8.50
Perez and Gomez (Joined Cases C-570/07 and C-571/07) [2010] ECR I-000. . . . . 5.14
Perks v United Kingdom (2000) 30 EHRR 33 . . . . 7.163
Perry v Latvia [2007] ECHR 30273/03. . . . . 7.335
Persey v Secretary of State for Environment, Food and Rural Affairs [2002] EWCA 371
    (Admin), [2003] QB 794 . . . . 7.351
Petropoulou-Tsakisi v Greece, 6 December [2007] ECHR 44803/04 . . . . 7.546

Petrov v Bulgaria, App No 15197/02, 22 May 2008 . . . . 7.297
Petrovic v Austria (2001) 33 EHRR 307 . . . . 7.510, 7.511, 7.538
Pfeifer v Austria (2009) 48 EHRR 8 . . . . 7.254
Phillips v UK (2001) 11 BHRC 280 . . . . 7.151, 8.53
Pichon v France App No 49853/99, 2 October 2001 . . . . 7.317
Piera Giacomelli v Italy [2006] ECHR 59909/00 . . . . 7.250
Piermont v France (1995) 20 EHRR 301 . . . . 7.382, 7.579, 7.580, 7.581, 7.585, 8.120
Pierre-Bloch v France (1998) 26 EHRR 202 . . . . 7.88
Pine Valley Developments Ltd v Ireland (1992) 14 EHRR 319 . . . . 8.19, 8.31
Pini v Romania, App Nos 78028/01, 22 June 2004 . . . . 7.280
Pla v Andorra (2004) 42 EHR 522 . . . . 7.540
Plattform 'Artze fur das Leben' v Austria (1988) 13 EHRR 204 . . . . 3.16, 7.424, 7.457
Podkolzina v Latvia [2002] ECHR 46726/99 . . . . 8.104
Poirrez v France (2005) 40 EHRR 2 . . . . 8.16
Poltoratskiy v Ukraine [2003] ECHR 38812/97 . . . . 7.326, 7.335
Powell & Rayner v UK (1990) 12 EHRR 355 . . . . 7.85
Powell v Ireland, App No 15404/89, 16 April 1991 . . . . 7.354
Powell v UK (2000) 30 EHRR CD 362 . . . . 6.25
Prager and Oberschlick v Austria (1995) 21 EHRR 1 . . . . 7.385, 7.388
Pressos Compania Naviera SA v Belgium (1995) 21 EHRR 301 . . . . 8.10
Pretto v Italy (1983) 6 EHRR 182 . . . . 7.122, 7.125
Pretty v UK (1998) 26 EHRR 241 . . . . 7.230, 7.233
Pretty v UK (2002) 35 EHRR 1 . . . . 6.27, 6.55, 6.98, 9.13
Price v UK (2002) 34 EHRR 53 . . . . 6.81, 6.82
Procunier v Martinez 416 US 396 (974) 7.349
Pudas v Sweden (1988) 10 EHRR 380 . . . . 7.81, 7.86, 7.88
Pullar v UK (1996) 22 EHRR 391 . . . . 7.120
Punzelt v Czech Republic (2000) 33 EHRR 1159 . . . . 7.51
Pupino (Case C-105/03) [2005] ECR I-5285 . . . . 5.06, 5.09
Pye v UK (2008) 46 EHRR 34 . . . . 2.65, 8.07, 8.08, 8.29, 8.40, 8.42, 8.43, 8.316

Quinn v Ireland [2000] ECHR 36887/97 . . . . 7.81

R (A) v Director of Establishments of the Security Service [2010] UKSC 12,
    [2010] 2 WLR 1 . . . . 3.21
R (A) v London Borough of Croydon [2009] UKSC 8, [2009]
    1 WLR 2557 . . . . 2.16, 7.88, 7.93
R (A) v Partnerships in Care Ltd [2002] EWHC 529 (Admin), [2002] 1 WLR 2610 . . . . 3.65
R (AB) v Secretary of State for Justice [2009] EWHC 2220 (Admin) 7.238
R (AC) v Berkshire West Primary Care Trust [2011] EWCA Civ 247 . . . . 7.225, 7.236
R (Adams) v Secretary of State for Justice [2011] UKSC 18 . . . . 7.152, 8.150
R (Al-Jedda) v Secretary of State for Defence [2005] EWHC 1809, aff'd [2006]
    EWCA Civ 327, [2006] 3 WLR 954 . . . . 3.50
R (Al-Jedda) v Secretary of State for Defence [2007] UKHL 58, [2008]
    1 AC 332 . . . . 3.10, 3.49, 7.07
R (Al-Sadoon) v Secretary of State for Defence [2009] EWCA Civ 7,
    [2010] 1 QB 486 . . . . 4.102, 6.07, 9.14
R (Al-Skeini) v Secretary of State for Defence [2007] UKHL 26, [2008]
    1 AC 153 . . . . 3.10, 4.102, 4.103, 6.06, 6.07, 7.512

R (Alconbury Developments Ltd) v Secretary of Sate for Environment, Transport and
the Regions [2001] UKHL 23, [2003] 2 AC 295. . . . . 7.90
R (AM) v Secretary of State for the Home Department [2009] EWCA Civ 219 . . . . 6.90
R (Amicus) v Secretary of State for Trade and Industry [2004] EWHC 860 (Admin),
[2004] ELR 31 . . . . 3.81, 7.348
R (Amin) v Secretary of State for the Home Department [2003] UKHL 51, [2004]
1 AC 653 . . . . 4.105, 6.41
R (Anderson) v Secretary of State for the Home Department [2002] UKHL 46, [2003]
1 AC 837 . . . . 3.39, 3.49, 4.80, 9.01
R (Animal Defenders International) v Secretary of State for Culture, Media &
Sport [2008] UKHL 15, [2008] 1 AC 1312 . . . . 3.43, 3.44, 7.350, 7.351, 7.356,
7.377, 7.387
R (B) v Ashworth Hospital Authority [2005] UKHL 20, [2005] 2 AC 278 . . . . 6.88, 7.39
R (B) v DPP [2009] EWHC 106 (Admin) 4.105
R (B) v Head Teacher and Governing Body of Alperton Community School [2001]
EWHC 299 (Admin) 7.93
R (Bagdanavicius) v Secretary of State for the Home Department [2005] UKHL 38
[2005] 2 AC 668 . . . . 6.102
R (Baiai) v Secretary of State for the Home Department [2008] UKHL 53, [2008]
3 All ER 1094. . . . . .7.468, 7.469, 7.470, 7.485, 7.486
R (Bancoult) v Secretary of State for Foreign & Commonwealth Affairs [2008]
UKHL 61, [2009] 1 AC 453. . . . . 3.10
R (Barclay) v Secretary of State for Justice and the Lord Chancellor [2008]
EWCA Civ 1319 . . . . 7.115, 8.96, 8.106
R (Bary) v Secretary of State for Justice [2010] EWHC 587 (Admin). 6.87
R (Beer) v Hampshire County Council [2003] EWCA Civ 1056, [2004] 1 WLR 233 . . . . . . 3.67
R (Bernard) v London Borough of Enfield [2002] EWHC 2282 (Admin), (2003)
UKHRR 148 . . . . 4.59, 4.63
R (Binyam Mohamed) v Secretary of State for Foreign and Commonwealth Affairs
[2010] EWCA Civ 65, [2010] 3 WLR 554 . . . . 6.92, 7.364
R (Black) v Secretary of State for Justice [2009] UKHL 1, [2009] 2 WLR 282 . . . . 7.69
R (Brehony) v Chief Constable of Greater Manchester (2005) EWHC 640 (Admin) 7.437
R (British American Tobacco) v Secretary of State for Health [2004] EWHC 2493
(Admin), [2005] ACD 27. . . . . 7.351, 7.360, 7.382
R (British Gurkha Welfare Society) v Ministry of Defence [2010] EWCA Civ 1098 . . . . 7.16
R (Burke) v General Medical Council [2005] EWCA Civ 1003, [2005]
3 WLR 1132 . . . . 4.20, 4.25, 6.27
R (C) v Sevenoaks Youth Court [2009] EWHC 3088 (Admin) 7.142
R (Carson) v Secretary of State for Work and Pensions [2005] UKHL 37. . . . 7.513, 7.520, 7.545,
8.12
R (Cart) v Upper Tribunal [2009] EWHC 3052 (Admin) 7.65
R (Cawser) v Secretary of State for the Home Department [2003] EWCA Civ 1522 . . . . 7.72
R (Chester) v Secretary of State for Justice & Wakefield Metropolitan Borough Council
[2009] EWHC 2923 (Admin) 4.86, 8.101
R (Clift) v Secretary of State for the Home Department [2006] UKHL 54, [2007]
1 AC 484 . . . . 4.80, 4.81, 4.90
R (Condliff) v North Staffordshire PCT [2011] EWHC 872 (Admin) 7.225
R (Countryside Alliance) v Attorney General [2007] UKHL 52, [2007] QB 305,
[2008] 1 AC 719 . . . . .4.113, 4.117, 5.25, 7.233, 7.308, 7.439,
8.06, 8.10, 8.29, 8.34, 8.44, 8.56

R (Craven) v Secretary of State for the Home Department [2001] 2 Cr App R 181 . . . . 2.52
R (D) v Secretary of State for the Home Department [2006] EWCA Civ 143,
    [2006] 3 All ER 946 . . . . 6.37, 6.45
R (Daly) v Secretary of State for the Home Department [2001] 2 WLR 1622 . . . . . . 4.115, 7.298
R (Degainis) v Secretary of State for Justice [2010] EWHC 137 (Admin) 7.73
R (E) v The Governing Body of JFS [2009] UKSC 15, [2010] 1 All ER 319 . . . . 7.314, 7.539
R (Equality and Human Rights Commission) v Government Equality Office
    [2010] EWHC 147 (Admin) 4.28
R (EW) v Secretary of State for the Home Department [2009] EWHC 2957
    (Admin) 6.110
R (F) v Secretary of State for the Home Department [2010] UKSC 17, [2010]
    2 WLR 267 . . . . 3.47, 4.80, 4.116, 7.245
R (Farrakhan) v Secretary of State for the Home Department [2002] EWCA Civ 606,
    [2002] QB 1391. . . . . 7.352, 7.362, 7.363, 7.393, 7.582
R (Faulkner) v Secretary of State for Justice [2009] UKHL 1, [2009] 2 WLR 282 . . . . 7.69
R (G) v Governors of X School [2009] EWHC 504 (Admin), [2009] ELR 206 . . . . 7.161
R (G) v Governors of X School [2011] UKSC 30, [2011] 3 WLR 237. . . . . 4.42, 7.83, 7.96,
    7.102, 7.134
R (G) v Governors of X School [2010] UKSC (nyr) 7.83, 7.147
R (Gabaji) v First Secretary of State [2005] EWCA Civ 1184, [2006] 1 WLR 505 . . . . . 4.80, 4.91
R (GC and C) v Commissioner of Police of the Metropolis [2011] UKSC 21,
    [2011] WLR 1230 . . . . 3.17, 3.37, 4.37, 4.42, 4.74, 7.244
R (Gentle) v Prime Minister [2008] UKHL 20, [2001] 1 AC 1356 . . . . 4.102, 6.28
R (Ghai) v Newcastle upon Tyne City Council [2009]
    EWHC 978 (Admin) 7.321, 7.340
R (Giles) v Parole Board [2003] UKHL 42, [2004] 1 AC 1 . . . . 7.67
R (Gillan) v Commissioner of Police for the Metropolis [2006] UKHL 12, [2006]
    2 WLR 537 . . . . 2.42, 4.109, 7.13, 7.422
R (Goodson) v HM Coroner for Bedfordshire and Luton [2004] EWHC 2931
    (Admin) 6.46
R (Green) v Police Complaints Authority [2004] UKHL 6, [2004] 1 WLR 725. . . . . . . 6.39, 6.56
R (Greenfield) v Secretary of State for the Home Department [2005] UKHL 14,
    [2005] 1 WLR 673. . . . . 4.59, 4.64, 4.65
R (Guardian News and Media) v City of Westminster Magistrates' Court [2010]
    EWHC 3376 (Admin) 7.365
R (H) v Mental Health Review Tribunal [2001] EWCA Civ 415, [2001]
    3 WLR 512 . . . . 4.69, 4.80, 4.98, 7.40
R (Heather) v Leonard Cheshire Foundation [2002] EWCA Civ 366, [2002]
    2 All ER 936. . . . . 3.66, 3.68
R (Hirst) v Secretary of State for the Home Department [2002] EWHC 602
    (Admin), [2002] UKHRR 758. . . . . 7.351
R (Hirst) v Secretary of State for the Home Department [2006] EWCA Civ 945,
    [2006] 1 WLR 3083. . . . . 7.24
R (Hooper) v Secretary of State for Work and Pensions [2003] EWCA Civ 813,
    [2005] UKHL 29, [2005] 1 WLR 1681 . . . . 3.17, 3.46, 4.20, 7.536
R (Humberstone) v Legal Services Commission [2010] EWCA Crim 1479,
    (2010) 118 BMLR 79. . . . . 6.25, 6.46
R (Husain) v Asylum Support Adjudicator [2001] EWHC 852 (Admin). 7.92
R (Imran Bashir) v Independent Adjudicator [2011] EWHC 1108 (Admin) 7.318, 7.326
R (Jackson) v Attorney-General [2005] UKHL 56, [2006] 1 AC 262 . . . . 3.38, 7.504

R (JL) v Secretary of State for Justice [2008] UKHL 68, [2008] 3 WLR 1325 . . . . 1.47, 4.42,
4.105, 6.20, 6.34, 6.41, 6.45, 6.54
R (Johns) v Derby City Council [2011] EWHC 375 (Admin). 7.314, 7.343
R (Johnson and Maggs) v Professional Conduct Committee of the Nursing
and Midwifery Council [2008] EWHC 885 (Admin) 7.159
R (KB) v Mental Health Review Tribunal [2003] EWHC 193, [2003]
1 MHLR 28. . . . . .4.68, 7.73
R (Kebilene) v DPP [2000] 2 AC 326. . . . . .4.121, 7.154
R (Kehoe) v Secretary of State for Work and Pensions [2005] UKHL 48,
[2006] 1 AC 42 . . . . 7.92
R (Klimas) v Prosecutors General Office of Lithuania [2010] EWHC 2076 (Admin). 6.105
R (Kurdistan Workers Party) v Secretary of State for the Home Department
[2002] EWHC 644 (Admin), [2002] ACD 99 . . . . 3.21
R (Laporte) v Chief Constable of Gloucestershire [2006] UKHL 55, [2007]
2 AC 105 . . . . .4.110, 4.116, 7.31, 7.350, 7.351, 7.411, 7.412, 7.415, 7.425, 7.426
R (L and ors) v Manchester City Council [2001] EWHC 707 (Admin). 7.529
R (LG) v Board of Governors of Tom Hood School [2010] EWCA Civ 142,
[2009] EWHC 369 (Admin) 7.96
R (Limbuela) v Secretary of State for the Home Department [2005] UKHL 66,
[2006] 1 AC 396 . . . . 2.02, 4.107, 6.73, 6.110
R (Lumba and Mighty) v Secretary of State for the Home Department [2011]
UKSC 12, [2011] 2 WLR 671 . . . . .7.42, 7.46
R (M) v Lambeth London Borough Council [2008] EWCA Civ 1445 . . . . .7.88, 7.93
R (McCann) v Crown Court at Manchester [2002] UKHL 39, [2003] 1 AC 787 . . . . .7.87, 7.96
R (Macdonald) v Royal Borough of Kensington and Chelsea [2010] EWCA Civ 1109 . . . . 7.225
R (Mdlovu) v Secretary of State for the Home Department [2008] EWHC 2089
(Admin). 8.73
R (Middleton) v HM Coroner for Weston District of Somerset [2004] UKHL 10,
[2004] 2 AC 182 . . . . 7.595
R (Moos and McClure) v Commissioner of Police of the Metropolis [2011]
EWHC 957 (Admin) 4.110, 7.426
R (Morgan Grenfell and Co Ltd) v Special Commissioner of Income Tax [2002]
UKHL 21, [2003] 1 AC 563. . . . . 7.74
R (Morris) v Westminster City Council and First Secretary of State [2005]
EWCA Civ 1184, [2006] 1 WLR 505. . . . . .4.80, 4.82
R (Mousa) v Secretary of State for Defence [2010] EWHC 3304 (Admin). 6.91
R (Mullen) v Secretary of State for the Home Department [2004] UKHL 18,
[2005] 1 AC 1 . . . . 8.150
R (Mullin) v Jockey Club Appeal Board (No 1) [2005] EWHC 2197 (Admin),
[2006] ACD 2 . . . . 3.67
R (Munjaz) v Mersey Care NHS Trust [2005] UKHL 58, [2006] 2 AC 148 . . . . .6.86, 7.39
R (N) v Secretary of State for the Home Department [2003] EWHC 207 (Admin) 4.57
R (Nadarajah) v Secretary of State for the Home Department [2003] EWCA
Civ 840, [2004] INLR 139. . . . . 7.46
R (Naik) v Secretary of State for the Home Department [2010] EWHC 2825
(Admin). 7.393
R (Nasseri) v Secretary of State for the Home Department [2009] UKHL 23,
[2010] 1 AC 1 . . . . 3.28

R (National Union of Journalists) v Central Arbitration Committe [2005]
EWCA Civ 1309 . . . . 7.448
R (Neilson) v Secretary of State for the Home Department [2004]
EWCA Civ 540, [2005] 1 WLR 1028. . . . . 7.351
R (New London College) v Secretary of State for the Home Department
[2011] EWHC 856 (Admin) 8.10, 8.30
R (Noorkoiv) v Home Secretary and Parole Board [2002] HRLR 36 . . . . 7.68
R (North Cyprus Tourism Centre Ltd) v Transport for London [2005]
EWHC 1698 (Admin) 7.360
R (O) v Crown Court at Harrow [2006] UKHL 42, [2007] 1 AC 249. . . . . 7.56
R (Parminder Singh) v Chief Constable of West Midlands Police [2006]
EWCA Civ 1118, [2006] 1 WLR 3374. . . . . 7.411, 7.420
R (Petsafe Ltd) v Welsh Ministers [2010] EWHC 2908 (Admin). 8.57
R (Playfoot) v Governing Body of Millais School [2007] EWHC 698 (Admin),
[2007] ELR 484 . . . . 7.331
R (Pretty) v DPP [2001] UKHL 61, [2002] 1 AC 800. . . . . 4.104, 6.27
R (ProLife Alliance) v BBC [2002] EWCA Civ 297, [2003]
3 WLR 1080 . . . . 2.49, 4.126, 4.128, 7.351, 7.362, 7.376
R (Purdy) v DPP [2009] UKHL 45, [2010] 1 AC 345. . . . . 3.52, 6.27, 7.230, 7.232
R (Puri) v Bradford Teaching Hospitals NHS Foundation Trust [2011]
EWHC 970 (Admin) 7.87
R (Q) v Secretary of State for the Home Department [2003] EWCA Civ 364,
[2004] QB 36. . . . . 6.110
R (Quark Fishing Ltd) v Foreign Secretary [2005] UKHL 57, [2005] 3 WLR 837. . . . 3.10, 4.101
R (R) v Durham Constabulary [2005] UKHL 21, [2005] 2 All ER 369. . . . . 7.102, 7.103
R (Razgar) v Secretary of State for the Home Department [2004] UKHL 27,
[2004] 2 AC 368 . . . . 7.232, 7.285
R (Reynolds) v IPCC [2008] EWCA Civ 1160 . . . . 6.45
R (RJM) (FC) v Secretary of State for Work and Pensions [2008] UKHL 63,
[2008] 3 WLR 1023, [2009] 1 AC 311. . . . . 3.51, 4.42, 7.512, 7.541, 8.12
R (Royal College of Nursing) v Secretary of State for the Honme Department
[2010] EWHC 2761 (Admin) 7.223
R (Rusbridger) v Attorney General [2003] UKHL 38, [2004] AC 357 . . . . 3.33, 4.78,
4.132, 7.370
R (S and Marper) v Chief Constable of South Yorkshire Police [2004] UKHL 39,
[2004] 1 WLR 2196. . . . . 3.37
R (Saadi) v Secretary of State for the Home Department [2002] UKHL 41, [2002]
1 WLR 3131 . . . . 7.46
R (Sacker) v West Yorkshire Coroner [2004] UKHL 11, [2004] 1 WLR 796 . . . . 6.34
R (Saunders) v Independent Police Complaints Commission [2008] EWHC 2372
(Admin). 6.40
R (SB) v Governors of Denbigh High School [2006] UKHL 15, [2007]
1 AC 100 . . . . 7.302, 7.329, 7.331, 8.85
R (Singh) v Chief Constable of West Midlands Police [2006] EWCA Civ 1118,
[2007] 2 All ER 297 . . . . 7.301
R (SL) v Commissioner of Police for the Metropolis [2008] EWHC 1442
(Admin). 4.59, 4.65
R (Smith) v Oxfordshire Assistant Deputy Coroner [2009] EWCA Civ 441 . . . . 4.102, 6.08

R (Smith) v Parole Board [2005] UKHL 1, [2005] 1 WLR 350 . . . . 4.31
R (Smith) v Secretary of State for Defence [2010] UKSC 29, [2011] 1 AC 1 . . . 3.10, 4.42, 4.103,
6.08, 6.28, 6.46
R (Sunder) v Secretary of State for the Home Department [2001] EWHC 252
(Admin), [2001] All ER (D) 55. . . . . 7.100
R (Suppiah) v Secretary of State for the Home Department [2011] EWHC 2
(Admin) 6.87, 7.05, 7.18
R (T and ors) v London Borough of Haringey [2005] EWHC 2235 (Admin) 7.225
R (Tabernacle) v Secretary of State for Defence [2009] EWCA Civ 23 . . . . 7.395, 7.418,
7.424, 7.429
R (Thompson) v Secretary of State for the Home Department [2008] EWHC 3170 (QB). 4.90
R (Trailer and Marina Level Ltd) v Secretary of State for the Environment, Food
and Rural Affairs [2004] EWCA Civ 1580, [2005] 1 WLR 1267. . . . . 8.54
R (Ullah) v Special Adjudicator [2004] UKHL 26, [2004] 2 AC 323. . . . 3.49, 6.124, 7.80, 7.287
R (Uttley) v Secretary of State for the Home Department [2003] EWHC 950
(Admin) 7.210
R (V) v Independent Appeal Panel for Tom Hood School [2010] EWCA Civ 142 . . . . 7.96, 7.102
R (Wright) v Secretary of State for Health [2009] UKHL 3, [2009] 1 AC 739 . . . . 3.47
R v A (No 2) [2001] UKHL 25, [2002] 1 AC 45 . . . . 3.31, 3.35, 3.36, 3.39,
3.44, 4.73, 6.77, 7.77
R v Advertising Standards Authority Ltd, ex p Vernons Organization Ltd
[1992] 1 WLR 1289. . . . . 7.351
R v Alden and Wright [2001] EWCA Crim 296, [2001] 2 Cr App Rep 275. . . . . 7.208
R v Alexander [2004] EWCA CRim 2341. . . . . 7.119
R v Bajwa [2007] EWCA Crim 1618 . . . . 7.120
R v Bamber [2009] EWCA Crim 962 . . . . 7.211
R v Bao [2007] EWCA Crim 2871 . . . . 7.208
R v Beckles [2004] EWCA Crim 2766, [2005] 1 All ER 705. . . . . 7.139
R v Benjafield [2002] UKHL 2, [2003] 1 AC 1099 . . . . .7.151, 8.59
R v Bieber [2008] EWCA Crim 1601 . . . . 6.80
R v Bow Street Magistrate, ex p Pinochet (No 2) [2000] 1 AC 119 . . . . 4.18
R v Briggs-Price [2009] UKHL 19, [2009] 1 WLR 1101. . . . . 2.16, 7.87, 7.151
R v Budimir and Rainbird [2010] EWCA Crim 1486, [2010] 3 CMLR 1377 . . . . 7.193
R v Byers [2004] NIQB 23 . . . . 7.340
R v C [2004] EWCA Crim 292, [2004] 1 WLR 2098. . . . . .7.184, 7.216
R v Camberwell Green Youth Court, ex p D [2005] UKHL 4, [2005] 1 WLR 393 . . . . 7.166
R v Coroner for Western District of Somerset, ex p Middleton [2004] UKHL 10,
[2004] 2 AC 182 . . . . .4.105, 6.33, 6.41, 6.43, 6.46
R v Crown Prosecution Services, ex p Hogg [1994] COD 237. . . . . 3.63
R v Davis [2008] UKHL 36, [2008] 1 AC 1128 . . . . .7.166, 7.167
R v Department of Health, ex p Source Information [2002] 2 WLR 940. . . . . 4.18
R v Dimsey [2001] UKHL 46, [2002] 1 AC 509. . . . . 7.155
R v Director of Public Prosecutions, ex p Kebilene [2002] 2 AC 326 . . . . 3.22, 3.28, 3.31
R v Disciplinary Committee of the Jockey Club, ex Aga Khan [1993] 1 WLR 909. . . . . 4.08
R v East Berkshire Health Authority, ex p Walsh [1985] QB 152. 3.63
R v Field [2002] EWCA Crim 2913, [2003] 1 WLR 882 . . . . 7.199
R v G [2008] UKHL 37, [2009] 1 AC 92 . . . . 7.153
R v Galfetti [2002] EWCA Civ 1916, [2002] MHLR 418. . . . . 4.54
R v Governor of Durham Prison, ex parte Hardial Singh [1984] 1 WLR 704. . . . . 7.46

R v Governor of Frankland Prison, ex p Russell [2000] 1 WLR 2027 . . . . 6.81
R v Grant [2001] EWCA Crim 2611, [2002] QB 1030. . . . . 7.39
R v H [2004] UKHL 3, [2004] 2 AC 134 . . . . .7.77, 7.144
R v HM Advocate [2002] UKPC D3, [2004] 1 AC 462 . . . . .7.129, 7.130
R v Horncastle [2009] EWCA Crim 964, [2010] 2 WLR 47 . . . . 3.51, 7.49, 7.168
R v James and Karimi [2006] EWCA Crim 14, [2006] 1 All ER 759 . . . . 3.56
R v Jones and Ayliffe [2006] UKHL 16, [2007] 1 AC 136. . . . . 7.215
R v Kansal (No 2) [2001] 3 WLR 1562. . . . . 4.33
R v Kearns [2002] EWCA Crim 748, [2002] 1 WLR 2815 . . . . 7.138
R v Kerry Rena Young [2005] EWCA Crim 2963 . . . . 8.153
R v Khan [1996] 3 WLR 162 . . . . 1.15
R v Lambert [2001] UKHL 37, [2002] 2 AC 545 . . . . 3.37, 3.39, 4.33
R v Lichniak and Pyrah [2002] UKHL 47, [2003] 1 AC 903. . . . . 6.80
R v Lyons [2002] UKHL 44, [2003] 1 AC 976 . . . . 4.33
R v Ministry of Agriculture, Fisheries and Food, ex p First City Trading Ltd [1997]
    1 CMLR 250 . . . . 5.18
R v Ministry of Agriculture, Fisheries and Food, ex p Hamble Fisheries (Offshore)
    Ltd [1995] 1 CMLR 553 . . . . 5.18
R v Ministry of Defence, ex p Smith [1996] QB 517 . . . . 4.112
R v Mirza [2004] UKHL 2 . . . . 7.120
R v Misra [2004] EWCA Crim 2375, [2005] 1 Cr App R 328. . . . . 7.188
R v Muhamad [2001] EWCA Crim 1856, [2003] QB 1031 . . . . 7.193
R v North and East Devon District Health Authority, ex p Coughlan [2001]
    QB 213 . . . . .7.290, 7.293
R v Offen [2001] 1 WLR 253 . . . . 3.01, 6.80, 7.209
R v OKZ [2010] EWCA Crim 2272. . . . . 7.120
R v Panel on Take-overs and Mergers, ex p Datafin plc [1987] QB 815 . . . . 5.26
R v Parole Board, ex p West [2005] UKHL 4, [2005] 1 All ER 755 . . . . 7.104
R v Perrin [2002] EWCA Crim 747 . . . . 7.351
R v Qureshi [2001] EWCA Crim 1807, [2002] 1 WLR 518 . . . . 7.120
R v R [1992] 1 AC 599. . . . . 7.183
R v R (B) [2003] EWCA Crim 2199, [2004] 1 WLR 490 . . . . 7.210
R v Rezvi [2002] UKHL 1 . . . . .7.151, 8.59
R v Rimmington [2005] UKHL 63, [2006] 1 AC 459 . . . . .7.188, 7.192
R v S [2010] EWCA Crim 1579 . . . . 7.77
R v Secretary of State for Employment, ex p Equal Opportunities Commission
    [1995] 1 AC 1 . . . . 4.113
R v Secretary of State for the Environment, ex p Friends of the Earth [1996]
    Env LR 198 . . . . 5.25
R v Secretary of State for Health, ex p Wagstuff and Associated Newspapers
    [2001] 1 WLR 292. . . . . 7.351
R v Secretary of State for the Home Department, ex p Anderson and Taylor [2002]
    UKHL 46, [2003] 1 AC 837. . . . . 3.39
R v Secretary of State for the Home Department, ex p Brind [1991] 1 AC 696. . . . . 1.15
R v Secretary of State for the Home Department, ex p Holub [2001] 1 WLR 1359 . . . . 4.20, 8.73
R v Secretary of State for the Home Department, ex p Mellor [2001] EWCA Civ 472,
    [2002] QB 13. . . . . 7.483
R v Secretary of State for the Home Department, ex p Simms [2002]
    2 AC 115 . . . . .3.22, 7.349, 7.350, 7.351

R v Sellick (Santino) [2005] EWCA Crim 651, [2005] 1 WLR 3257. . . . . 7.77
R v Shayler [2002] UKHL 11, [2003] 1 AC 247 . . . . .4.108, 7.351, 7.382, 7.394, 7.595
R v Spear [2002] UKHL 31, [2003] 1 AC 73 . . . . .3.51, 7.117
R v Taylor [2001] EWCA Crim 2263, [2002] 1 Cr App R 519 . . . . 7.340
R v Thoron [2011] EWCA Crim 1797 . . . . 7.120
R v Twomey (No 2) [2011] EWCA Crim 8 . . . . 7.87
R v UK (1988) 10 EHRR 74 . . . . 7.223
R v UK (2007) 44 EHRR SE17 . . . . 7.103
R v Yam [2008] EWCA Crim 269. . . . . 7.123
R v Young [2002] EWCA Crim 2913, [2003] 1 WLR 882 . . . . 7.199
R v Z [2005] UKHL 35, [2005] 2 AC 645 . . . . 7.191
R (Vovk) v Secretary of State for the Home Department [2006] EWHC 3386 (Admin). 7.42
R (W) v Lambeth London Borough Council [2002] EWCA Civ 613, [2002]
    2 FLR 327 . . . . 7.225
R (Watkins-Singh) v Governing Body of Aberdare Girls' School [2008]
    EWHC 1865 (Admin), [2008] ELR 561 . . . . .7.315, 7.529
R (Wellington) v Secretary of State for the Home Department [2008] UKHL 72,
    [2009] 2 WLR 48. . . . . 6.80, 6.103, 7.17
R (West) v Lloyds of London [2004] EWCA Civ 506, [2004] 3 All ER 251. . . . . 3.67
R (Westminster City Council) v Mayor of London [2002] EWHC (Admin) 2440. . . . . 4.22
R (Wilkinson) v Inland Revenue Commissioners [2003] EWCA Civ 814, [2003]
    1 WLR 2683 . . . . 4.80
R (Williamson) v Secretary of State for Education and Skills [2002] EWCA
    Civ 1926, [2003] QB 1300. . . . . .3.81, 7.347
R (Williamson) v Secretary of State for Education and Skills [2005] UKHL 15,
    [2005] 2 AC 246 . . . . 2.21, 7.307, 7.315, 7.319, 7.340, 8.78
R (Wood) v Metropolitan Police Commissioner [2008] EWHC 1105 (Admin),
    (2008) HRLR 34 . . . . .7.220, 7.248, 7.411, 7.422, 7.442
R (Woolas) v Election Court [2010] EWHC 3168 (Admin), [2010] NJLR 1756. . . 7.397, 7.399,
    8.107
R (Wright) v Secretary of State for Health [2007] EWCA Civ 999, [2008] 2 WLR 536 . . . . . 4.90
R (Wright) v Secretary of State for Health [2009] UKHL 3, [2009] 2 WLR 267 . . . . . 3.40, 3.41,
    3.47, 4.79, 4.90, 7.83, 7.148
R (Wright) v Secretary of State for Health and Secretary of State for Education
    and Skills [2006] EWHC 2886 (Admin). 4.81, 7.83
R (Wright) v Secretary of State for the Home Department [2006] EWCA Civ 67 . . . . 7.73
R (X) v The Headteacher of Y School [2007] EWHC 298 (Admin), [2007] ELR 278 . . . . . 7.331
RB (Algeria) v Secretary of State for the Home Department [2009] UKHL 10,
    [2009] 2 WLR 512. . . . . .2.27, 4.125, 6.78, 6.104, 7.80
RJW & SJW v Guardian Group News and Media Ltd, 11 September 2009. . . . . 3.80
RK and AK v UK [2009] 1 FLR 274. . . . . 7.495
RMT v Serco Ltd [2011] EWCA Civ 226, [2011] IRLR 399 . . . . 7.449
RP v UK, App No 38245/08, not yet decided 4.40, 9.46
RSPCA v Attorney General [2002] 1 WLR 448 . . . . 7.441
Rabone v Penine Care NHS Trust [2010] EWCA Civ 698. . . . . .4..20
Raimondo v Italy (1994) 18 EHRR 237 . . . . .7.12, 8.117
Raja v Van Hoogstraten [2004] EWCA Civ 968, [2004] 4 All ER 793. . . . . 7.98
Ramsahai v Netherlands [2007] ECHR 52391/99 . . . . .6.37, 6.40
Rasmussen v Denmark (1984) 7 EHRR 371. . . . . 7.537

Rassemblement Jurassien and Unite Jurassienne v Switzerland (1979) 17 DR 93 . . . . 7.418, 7.429
Rayner v UK (1986) 47 DR 5 . . . . 7.249, 10.13
Rees v UK (1987) 9 EHRR 56 . . . . 2.18, 2.19, 7.236, 7.272, 7.471, 7.474
Refah Partisi (The Welfare Party) v Turkey (2003) 37 EHRR 1 . . . . 2.53, 2.60, 7.350, 7.378,
7.452, 7.453, 8.84
Reid v UK [2003] ECHR 94 . . . . 7.37, 7.59
Reinprecht v Austria [2005] ECHR 67175/01 . . . . 7.64
Rekevenyi v Hungary (2000) 30 EHRR 519 . . . . 7.350, 7.354, 7.411
Remli v France (1996) 22 EHRR 253 . . . . 7.113, 7.114
Renolde v France, App No 5608/05, 16 October 2008 . . . . 6.25
Reynolds v Times Newspapers Ltd [1999] 4 All ER 609 . . . . 7.351, 7.358
Reynolds v Times Newspapers Ltd [2001] 2 AC 127 . . . . 7.358
Riad and Idiab v Belgium, App Nos 29787/03 and 2981/03, 24 January 2008 . . . . 6.85, 7.45
Rieg v Austria [2005] ECHR 184 . . . . 7.103
Ringeisen v Austria (1971) 1 EHRR 466 . . . . 7.81, 7.114
Roberts v Nottingham Healthcare NHS Trust [2008] EWHC 1934 (QB) 7.132
Roberts v Parole Board [2005] UKHL 45, [2005] 2 AC 738 . . . . 7.66
Robins v UK (1998) 26 EHRR 527 . . . . 7.84
Roche v United Kingdom (2006) 42 EHRR 30 . . . . 7.85
Roemen and Schmit v Luxembourg [2003] ECHR 102 . . . . 7.361
Rowe and Davis v UK (2000) 30 EHRR 1 . . . . 7.132, 7.144, 7.147
Rowe v Kingston upon Hull City Council [2003] EWCA Civ 1281 . . . . 4.31
Rowland v Environment Agency [2003] EWCA Civ 1885, [2005] Ch 1 . . . . 8.12, 8.54
Ruiz Torija v Spain (1995) 19 EHRR 55 . . . . 7.131
Ruiz-Mateos v Spain (1993) 16 EHRR 505 . . . . 7.131, 7.143
Rusbridger and Toynbee v Attorney-General [2003] UKHL 38, [2004] 1 AC 357 . . . . 4.25
Rutili v Ministre de l'Intérieur (Case 36/75) [1975] ECR 1219 . . . . 5.06

S (a child) (identification: restrictions on publication), Re [2004] UKHL 47,
    [2005] 1 AC 593 . . . . 3.30, 3.78, 7.261
S (FC), In re [2002] UKHL 10, [2002] 2 AC 291 . . . . 7.502
S and Marper v UK (2008) 48 EHRR 1169 . . . . 2.21, 2.64, 2.80, 2.220, 3.37, 4.37, 4.42,
7.242, 7.244, 7.423, 7.515, 9.61
S and Marper v UK [2008] ECHR 1582, App Nos 30562/04 and 30566/04,
    4 December 2008 . . . . 9.01, 9.46
S, Re (care order: implementation of care plan) [2002] UKHL 10, [2002] 2 AC 291 . . . . 3.31,
3.40, 3.41, 3.77, 4.76, 4.106
S v Airedale NHS Trust [2003] EWCA Civ 1036, [2004] QB 395 . . . . 7.05, 7.595
S v London Borough of Lambeth [2007] 1 FLR 152 . . . . 7.279
S v Switzerland (1991) 14 EHRR 670 . . . . 7.162
S v UK (1986) 47 DR 274 . . . . 7.273
SC v UK (2004) 40 EHRR 226 . . . . 7.142
SD v Greece, App No 53541/07, 11 June 2009 . . . . 6.85
SK (Zimbabwe) v Secretary of State for the Home Department [2011] UKSC 23 . . . . . 7.42, 7.46
SN v Sweden (2004) 39 EHRR 13 . . . . 7.166
SW v UK (1995) 21 EHRR 363 . . . . 7.184
Saadi v Italy (2008) 24 BHRC 123 . . . . 2.27, 6.101, 9.46
Saadi v UK (2008) 47 EHRR 427 . . . . 6.55, 7.04, 7.42, 7.45, 7.50
Sabeh el Leil v France (2008) 24 BHRC 327 . . . . 7.94

Sadak v Turkey (2003) 36 EHRR 23 . . . . 8.102
Sahin v Germany (2003) 36 EHRR 43 . . . . 7.515
Sahin v Turkey (2005) 41 EHRR 8 . . . . 7.328, 7.330, 7.350
Sahin v Turkey (2007) 44 EHRR 5 . . . . 2.29, 7.302, 7.313, 8.69, 8.70, 8.83, 8.84, 8.85
Saïdi v France (1994) 17 EHRR 251 . . . . 7.166
Sakik v Turkey (1998) 26 EHRR 662 . . . . 7.52, 7.560
Sala v Freistaat Bayern (Case C-85/96) [1998] ECR I-2691 . . . . 5.09
Salabiaku v France (1988) 13 EHRR 379 . . . . 2.09, 7.152
Salduz v Turkey (2009) 49 EHRR 19 . . . . 7.140, 7.161
Salesi v Italy (1998) 26 EHRR 187 . . . . 7.91
Sampanis v Greece, App No 32526/05, 5 June 2008 . . . . 8.87
Sanchez Navajas v Spain, App No 57442/00, 21 June 2001 . . . . 7.447
Sanchez-Reisse v Switzerland (1986) 9 EHRR 71 . . . . 7.64
Sander v UK (2001) 31 EHRR 44 . . . . 7.120
Sanders v France (1996) 87 B-DR 160 . . . . 7.462, 7.468
Sannino v Italy (2009) 48 EHRR 25 . . . . 7.164
Sanoma Uitgevers B.V. v Netherlands [2010] ECHR 38224/03 . . . . 7.361, 7.368, 7.380
Saunders v UK (1996) 23 EHRR 313 . . . . 7.138, 7.155
Saunders v UK (1997) 23 EHRR 10 . . . . 4.58
Savage v South Essex Partnership NHS Foundation Trust [2008] UKHL 74,
    [2009] 2 WLR 115 . . . . 4.105, 6.25, 6.26, 6.27, 6.53
Saygili v Turkey App No 19353/03 . . . . 7.361
Schalk and Kopf v Austria, App No 30141/04, 24 June 2010 . . . . 2.19, 2.21, 7.271, 7.274, 7.474
Scharsach v Austria (2005) 40 EHRR 22 . . . . 7.388
Schimanek v Austria, App No 32307/96, 1 February 2000 . . . . 7.589
Schmid v Austria (1985) 44 DR 195 . . . . 8.117
Schmidberger v Austria (Case C-112/00) [2003] ECR I-5659 . . . . 5.06
Schmidt and Dahlstrom v Sweden (1976) 1 EHRR 632 . . . . 7.448
Schmidt v Germany (1994) 18 EHRR 513 . . . . 7.511
Schuler-Zgraggen v Switzerland, Series A No 263, 24 June 1993 . . . . 7.539
Scoppola v Italy, App No 126/05, 18 January 2011 . . . . 8.100
Scottish National Party v BBC [2010] SC 395 (Court of Session) 7.406
Seal v Chief Constable of South Wales [2007] UKHL 31, [2007] 1 WLR 1910 . . . . 7.110
Seal v UK (2010) ECHR 1976 . . . . 7.110
Šečić v Croatia (2007) 23 BHRC 24 . . . . 6.56, 6.89
Secretary of State for Defence v Elias [2006] EWCA Civ 1293, [2006] 1 RLR 934 . . . . 4.113
Secretary of State for the Foreign Office and Commonwealth Affairs v Maftah
    [2011] EWCA Civ 350 . . . . 7.88, 7.90, 7.93
Secretary of State for the Home Department v AF [2007] UKHL 46, [2008]
    1 AC 440 . . . . 7.144
Secretary of State for the Home Department v AF (No 3) [2009] UKHL 28, [2010]
    2 AC 269 . . . . 3.49, 3.52, 7.65, 7.74, 7.87, 7.104, 7.106, 7.133, 7.144
Secretary of State for the Home Department v AH [2008] EWHC 1018 (Admin) 7.16
Secretary of State for the Home Department v E [2007] UKHL 47, [2008] 1 AC 499 . . . . . . 7.16
Secretary of State for the Home Department v Hindawi [2006] UKHL 54,
    [2007] 1 AC 484 . . . . 4.80
Secretary of State for the Home Department v JJ [2007] UKHL 45, [2008]
    1 AC 385 . . . . 4.84, 7.155

Secretary of State for the Home Department v M [2006] UKHL 11, [2006]
2 AC 91 . . . . 7.510, 7.513, 7.527, 8.13
Secretary of State for the Home Department v MB [2006] EWCA Civ 1140, [2008]
1 AC 440 . . . . 3.46, 7.16, 7.144
Secretary of State for Justice v James [2009] UKHL 22, [2010] 1 AC 553 . . . . 7.25, 7.69
Segerstedt-Wilberg v Sweden (2007) 44 EHRR 2 . . . . 7.411, 7.419
Segi v 15 Members of the EC, App No 6422/02, 16 May 2002 . . . . 5.17
Sejdic and Finci v Bosnia and Herzegovina, App Nos 27996/06 and 34836/06,
22 December 2009 . . . . 2.22
Sekanina v Austria (1994) 17 EHRR 221 . . . . 7.152
Selçuk and Asker v Turkey (1998) 26 EHRR 477 . . . . 7.218
Selim v Cyprus Friendly Settlement, App No 47293/99, 16 July 2002 . . . . 7.467
Selmouni v France (2000) 29 EHRR 403 . . . . 6.60, 6.63
Sentges v Netherlands [2003] ECHR 715; 7.225
Senthuran v Secretary of State for the Home Department [2004] EWCA Civ 950 . . . . 7.280
Sepet v Secretary of State for the Home Department [2003] UKHL 15, [2003]
3 All ER 304 . . . . 6.123
Serif v Greece App No 38178/97, ECHR 1999-IX 7.313
Serious Organised Crime Agency v Gale [2010] EWCA Civ 759, [2010]
1 WLR 2881 . . . . 7.87
Shara and Rinia v The Netherlands (1985) 8 EHRR 307 . . . . 7.464
Sheffield and Horsham v UK (1998) 27 EHRR 163 . . . . 2.19, 7.236, 7.471
Sheldrake v DPP [2004] UKHL43, [2005] 1 AC 264 . . . . 7.154
Shelley v UK (2008) 46 EHRR SE16 . . . . 9.26
Shevchenko v Ukraine, App No 32478/02, 4 April 2006 . . . . 6.09
Sibson v UK (1993) 17 EHRR 193 . . . . 7.444
Sidabras v Lithuania [2004] ECHR 55480/00 . . . . 2.02, 7.515
Sidiropolous v Greece, 10 July 1998 RJD 1998-IV 7.442
Sigurdur A Sigurjonsson v Iceland (1993) 16 EHRR 462 . . . . 7.445
Siliadin v France (2005) 20 BHRC 654 . . . . 6.116, 6.117, 6.121, 6.125
Silih v Slovenia [2009] ECHR 571 . . . . 4.33, 6.35, 6.36
Silver v UK (1983) 5 EHRR 347 . . . . 2.46, 7.494
Simpson v UK (1989) 64 DR 188 . . . . 8.65
Sinclair Collis Ltd v Secretary of State for Health [2010] EWHC 3112
(Admin) 8.06, 8.34, 8.57
Singh v Entry Clearance Officer [2004] EWCA Civ 1075, [2005] QB 608 . . . . 7.267
Sitaropoulos v Greece, App No 42202/07, 8 July 2010 . . . . 8.98
Smith and Grady v UK (2000) 29 EHRR 33 . . . . 2.67, 4.112, 7.235, 7.499, 7.506
Smith Kline and French Laboratories Ltd v Netherlands (1990) 66 DR 70 . . . . 8.14
Smith v Scott [2007] CSIH 9 . . . . 4.98, 8.100, 8.101
Socialist Party v Turkey 1998-III 7.450
Sociètè Levage Prestations v France (1996) 24 EHRR 351 . . . . 7.109
Soering v UK (1989) 11 EHRR 439 . . . . 2.09, 2.23, 2.61, 6.65, 6.71, 6.99, 6.103,
6.106, 7.80, 7.497
Somerville v Scottish Ministers [2007] UKHL 44, [2007] 1 WLR 2734 . . . . 4.32
Somjee v UK (2003) 36 EHRR 16 . . . . 7.128
Sommerfeld v Germany (2003) 36 EHRR 33 . . . . 7.105
Sommerfeld v Germany (2004) 38 EHRR 35 . . . . 7.105

Sorenson and Rasmussen v Denmark, App No 52562/99, 11 January 2006. . . . . . . .7.444, 7.458
Spadea v Italy (1995) 21 EHRR 514. . . . . 8.45
Spiers v Ruddy and HM Advocate General [2005] EWCA Civ 14, [2005]
　　2 All ER 316. . . . . 7.130
Spiller v Joseph [2010] UKSC 53, [2011] 9 All ER 947. . . . . .7.246, 7.351
Sporrong and Lonnroth v Sweden (1982) 5 EHRR 35 . . . . 7.87, 8.07, 8.27, 8.46
Stafford v UK (2002) 35 EHRR 32. .4.80, 7.24, 7.63, 7.499, 7.538
Stankov and the United Macedonian Organisation Illinden v Bulgaria,
　　Apps No 29221/95 and 29225/95, ECHR 2001-IX 7.424, 7.428, 7.453
Stec v UK (2006) 43 EHRR 1017, (2006) 20 BHRC 348. . . . . .7.91, 7.505, 7.512,
　　　　　　　　　　　　　　　　　　　　7.521, 7.543, 7.544, 8.10, 8.12, 8.16, 8.17, 8.51
Stedmand v UK (1997) 23 EHRR 168 . . . . 7.324
Steel and Morris v UK (2005) 41 EHRR 22 . . . . .2.64, 7.105, 7.143, 7.352, 7.386
Steel v UK (1998) 26 EHRR 603 . . . . .2.48, 7.26, 7.381, 7.382, 7.435
Steindel v Germany, App No 29878/07, 14 September 2010. . . . . 6.121
Stevens v UK (1986) 46 DR 245. . . . . 7.356
Stewart v UK (1984) 38 DR 162. . . . . 6.48
Stockholms Forsakrings-och Skadestandjuridik AB v Sweden [2004] BPIR 218 . . . . 8.49
Stôgmüller v Austria (1969) 1 EHRR 155. . . . . .7.55, 7.126
Stoichkov v Bulgaria (2007) 44 EHRR 14. . . . . 7.22
Storck v Germany (2006) 43 EHRR 6 . . . . 7.70
Stran Greek Refineries v Greece (1994) 19 EHRR 293 . . . . 8.35
Streletz, Kessler and Krenz v Germany (2001) 33 EHRR 751 . . . . 7.214
Stretch v UK (2004) 38 EHRR 12 . . . . 8.20
Stretford v Football Association [2007] EWCA Civ 238 . . . . 7.123
Stubbings v UK (1996) 23 EHRR 213 . . . . 7.519
Sud Fondi Srl v Italy, App No 75909/01, 20 January 2009 . . . . 8.38
Sunday Times v UK (1979) 2 EHRR 245 . . . . 1.14, 2.10, 2.43, 2.44, 2.48, 2.56, 2.57,
　　　　　　　　　　　　　　　　　7.334, 7.350, 7.353, 7.355, 7.371, 7.378, 7.379, 7.381,
　　　　　　　　　　　　　　　　　　　　　　　　　　　　7.382, 7.391, 7.393, 7.413
Sunday Times v UK (No 2) (1991) 14 EHRR 229 . . . . .7.371, 7.382
Supreme Holy Council of the Muslim Community v Bulgaria [2004]
　　ECHR 39023/97. . . . . 7.313
Surayanda v Welsh Ministers [2007] EWCA Civ 893 . . . . .3.81, 7.340
Swedish Engine Drivers' Union v Sweden (1979) 1 EHRR 617. . . . . 7.448

T and KM v UK (2002) 34 EHRR 2. . . . . 7.223
T v Italy [1992] ECHR 14104/88. . . . . 7.157
T and V v UK (1999) 30 EHRR 121 . . . . .2.21, 7.63
Takoushis v HM Coroner for Inner London [2005] EWCA Civ 1440. . . . . 6.46
Tammer v Estonia (2001) 10 BHRC 543 . . . . 7.255
Tanase v Moldova [2008] ECHR 7/08 . . . . .8.102, 8.104
Tangney v Governor of Elmley Prison and Secretary of State for the Home
　　Department [2005] EWCA Civ 1009. . . . . 7.96, 7.97, 7.101
Tarariyeva v Russia, App No 4353/03 . . . . 6.25
Tariq v Home Office [2010] EWCA Civ 465 . . . . 7.144
Tarsasag a Szabadsajogokert v HUngary [2009] ECHR 37374/05. . . . 7.353, 7.364, 7.365, 7.366
Taskin v Turkey (2006) 42 EHRR 50 . . . . .2.36, 7.249
Taxquet v Belgium, App No 926/05, 16 November 2010 . . . . 7.135

Taylor v Lancashire County Council [2005] EWCA Civ 284 . . . . 4.25, 4.78
Taylor v UK (2007) 45 EHRR 2 . . . . 7.202, 7.204
Taylor-Sabori UK (2003) 36 EHRR 17 . . . . 7.501
Teixeira de Castro v Portugal (1999) 28 EHRR 101 . . . . 7.137
Ternovszky v Hungary, App No 67545/09, 14 December 2010 . . . . 7.241
Terry v Persons Unknown [2010] EWHC 119 (QB) 3.80, 7.264
Teteriny v Russia [2005] ECHR 11931/03 . . . . 8.10
Thlimmenos v Greece (2000) 31 EHRR 411 . . . . 7.336, 7.515, 7.517, 7.521, 7.524, 7.525
Thoburn v Sunderland City Council [2002] EWHC 195 (Admin),
    [2002] 3 WLR 247 . . . . 1.36, 3.01
Thoma v Luxembourg (2001) 36 EHRR 359 1 . . . . 7.385
Thorgeirson v Iceland (1992) 14 EHRR 843 . . . . 7.358
Thynne v UK (1990) 13 EHRR 666 . . . . 7.63
Times Newspapers Ltd v UK (Nos 1 and 2) [2009] ECHR 3002/03 . . . . 7.389
Timishev v Russia [2005] ECHR 55762/00 . . . . 8.70
Tinnelly & Sons Ltd v Mcelduff v UK (1999) 27 EHRR 249 . . . . 7.110
Togher v Revenue and Customs Prosecutions Office [2007]
    EWCA Civ 686, [2008] QB 476 . . . . 7.212
Tolstoy Miloslavky v UK (1995) 20 EHRR 442 . . . . 7.372, 7.381, 10.11
Tomlinson v Birmingham City Council [2010] UKSC 8, [2010] 2 WLR 471 . . . . 3.51
Toth v Austria (1991) 14 EHRR 551 . . . . 7.55
Tovey v Ministry of Justice [2011] EWHC 271 (QB) 8.101
Traynor [2007] ScotCS CSOH 78 (Scottish Court of Session) 4.86, 8.101
Tre Traktörer AB v Sweden (1989) 13 EHRR 309 . . . . 8.10
Triggiani v Italy [1991] ECHR 20 . . . . 7.127
Tsfayo v UK (2009) 48 EHRR 18 . . . . 7.148
Tsonev v Bulgaria App No 45963/99, 13 July 2006 . . . . 7.442
Tum Haber Sen and Cinar v Turkey, App No 28602/95, 21 February 2006 . . . . 7.450, 7.455
Twaite, Re [2010] EWCA Crim 2973, [2011] 1 Cr App R 249 . . . . 7.118
Tyrer v UK (1978) 2 EHRR 1 . . . . 2.17, 6.68, 6.94
Tysiac v Poland (2007) 22 BHRC 155 . . . . 6.17, 7.231

Ucar v Turkey [2006] ECHR 52392/99 . . . . 7.222
Unal Tekeli [2004] ECHR 29865/96 . . . . 7.538
Üner v Netherlands (2007) 45 EHRR 14 . . . . 7.233, 7.284
United Christian Broadcasters Ltd v UK, App No 44802/98, 7 November 2000 . . . . 7.400
United Communist Party of Turkey v Turkey, Reports of Judgments and
    Secisions 1998-I, 30 January 1998 . . . . 7.450
United Macedonian Organization Ilinden v Bulgaria (1998) 26 EHRR
    CD 103 . . . . 7.442, 7.453, 7.454
Ure v UK, App No 28027/95, 27 November 1996 . . . . 7.292
Üstïn v Turkey [2007] ECHR 37685/02 . . . . 7.382
Uyan v Turkey, App No 7454/04, 10 November 2005 . . . . 6.114

V (a child) (Care proceedings; human rights claims) [2004] EWCA Civ 54 . . . . 4.11
Vajnai v Hungary, App No 33629/06, 8 July 2008 . . . . 7.356
Valsamis v Greece (1996) 24 EHRR 294 . . . . 8.80
Van Colle v Chief Constable of Hertfordshire Police [2008] UKHL 50,
    [2008] All ER 977 . . . . 6.24

Van de Hurk v Netherlands (1994) 18 EHRR 481 . . . . 7.135
Van de Leer v Netherlands (1990) 12 EHRR 567 . . . . 7.49
Van der Mussele v Belgium (1983) 6 EHRR 163. . . . . 6.120, 6.122, 7.511, 7.519
Van Droogenbroeck v Belgium Case B44 (1980). 6.118, 6.119, 7.24
Van Marle v The Netherlands (1986) 8 EHRR 483. . . . . 8.10
Van Mechelen v Netherlands (1997) 25 EHRR 647 . . . . 7.106, 7.137, 7.166
Van Oosterwijck v Belgium (1979) 3 EHRR 581 . . . . 7.478
Van Raalte v Netherlands (1997) 24 EHRR 503 . . . . 7.539
Varec SA v Belgium (Case C-450/06) [2008] ECR I-581 . . . . 5.09
Vaudelle v France (2001) 37 EHRR 16. . . . . 7.157
Venables and Thompson v Newsgroup Newspapers and Associated Newspapers Ltd
    [2001] 2 WLR 1038. . . . . 3.73
Vereinigung Bildender Kunstler v Austria (2008) 47 EHRR 5 . . . . 7.357, 7.359, 7.362
VgT Verein Gegen Tierfabriken v Switzerland (2002) 34 EHRR 4 . . . . . 2.52, 3.43, 7.377, 7.400
Vilvarajah v UK (1991) 14 EHRR 248 . . . . 7.497
Vo v France [2004] 2 FCR 577 . . . . 6.11, 6.14
Vogt v Germany (1995) 2 EHRR 205. . . . . 2.67, 7.354, 7.455
Von Hannover v Germany (2006) 43 EHRR 7 . . . . 7.222, 7.254, 7.255, 7.258
Von Maltzan v Germany (2006) 42 EHRR SE11 . . . . 8.21
Vördur Ölafsson v Ireland, App No 20161/06, 27 April 2010 . . . . 7.443
Vriend v Alberta [1998] 1 SCR 495 . . . . 1.35

W and B (Children: care plan) [2001] EWCA Civ 757, [2001] 2 FLR 582 . . . . 4.106
W v UK (1987) 10 EHRR 29. . . . . 7.87, 7.223, 10.09
WP v Poland, App No 42264/98, 2 September 2004. . . . . 7.589
Wainwright v Home Office [2003] UKHL 53, [2004] 2 AC 406. . . . . 7.219
Wainwright v UK (2006) 42 EHRR 41. . . . . 6.61, 7.219
Waite v UK (2003) 36 EHRR 54 . . . . 7.24
Wakefield v UK (1990) 66 DR 251. . . . . 7.269
Walker v UK, App No 37212/02, 16 March 2004. . . . . 7.500
Ward, Re; BBC v CAFCASS Legal [2007] EWHC 616 (Fam). 3.80
Wasilewski v Poland (2004) 38 EHRR 10. . . . . 7.297
Waters v Public Transport Corporation (1991) 173 CLR 349 . . . . 7.528
Weber and Saravia v Germany [2006] ECHR 54934/00 . . . . 2.46
Weber v Switzerland Series A No 177, 22 May 1990 . . . . 7.99
Weeks v UK (1987) 10 EHRR 293. . . . . 7.23, 7.58, 7.63, 7.64
Weir v Secretary of State for Transport [2004] EWHC 2772 (Ch),
    [2005] UKHRR 154 . . . . 4.29
Welch v UK (1995) 20 EHRR 247. . . . . 7.195, 7.197, 7.199
Wemhoff v Germany (1968) 1 EHRR 55 . . . . 2.10, 7.55
Wendenburg v Germany (2003) 36 EHRR CD 154 . . . . 8.11
Wessels-Bergevoert v Netherlands [2002] ECHR 34462/97 . . . . 8.16
Whaley v Lord Advocate [2007] UKHL 53, [2007] SLT 1209. 7.439
Whittaker v Watson (t/a P & M Watson Haulage) [2002] ICR 1244. . . . . 4.12
Wickramisinghe v UK, [1998] EHRLR 338. . . . . 7.87
Wieser and Bicos Beteiligungen v Austria (2008) 46 EHRR 54. . . . . 7.217
Wilkinson v Kitzinger [2006] EWHC 2002 (Fam), [2007] 1 FLR 295 . . . . 7.475
Wille v Lichtenstein (1999) 30 EHRR 558. . . . . 7.354
Willis v UK (2002) 35 EHRR 21 . . . . 8.16

Wilson and Palmer v UK (2002) 35 EHRR 20 . . . . 7.448, 7.457, 7.458
Wilson v First County Trust (No 2) [2003] UKHL 40, [2004] 1 AC 816. . . . . . . 3.73, 3.42, 4.33,
7.75, 7.108, 8.22, 10.27
Windisch v Austria (1990) 13 EHRR 281. . . . . 7.137
Wingrove v UK (1997) 24 EHRR 1 . . . . 2.49, 7.357, 7.402
Winterwerp v Netherlands (1979) 2 EHRR 387. . . . . 7.20, 7.64
Wood v UK (1997) 24 EHRR CD 69. . . . . 7.292

X & Y v Persons Unknown [2007] EMLR 290 . . . . 3.79
X and Church of Scientology v Sweden (1979) 16 DR 68 . . . . 7.304
X v Austria (1972) 42 CD 145 . . . . 7.143
X v Austria (1974) 46 CD 214 . . . . 8.123
X v Austria (1979) 18 DR 154 . . . . 7.12
X v Austria (1987) 11 EHRR 112. . . . . 7.22
X v Belgium (1981) 24 DR 198 . . . . 8.117
X v Denmark (1976) 5 DR 157 . . . . 7.310
X v Germany (1974) 17 YB 148 . . . . 6.121
X v Germany 3 YB 254. . . . . 7.178
X v Germany (1971) 14 YB 692 . . . . 8.115
X v Germany (1974) 1 DR 64. . . . . 7.467
X v Germany (1975) 3 DR 92. . . . . 7.26, 8.94
X v Germany (1987) 11 EHRR 84 . . . . 7.137
X v Germany (1997) 9 DR 190. . . . . 8.120
X v Germany (1981) 24 DR 158. . . . . 7.11
X v Netherlands (1976) 6 DR 184 . . . . 7.178, 8.16
X v Switzerland 28 DR 127. . . . . 7.166
X v UK 3 Digest 211 (1973). 7.177
X v UK (1975) 2 DR 50. . . . . 8.68
X v UK (1975) 3 DR 165 . . . . 8.94
X v UK (1976) 4 DR 115 . . . . 7.137
X v UK (1978) 14 DR 26 . . . . 7.103
X v UK (1980) 19 DR 244 . . . . 7.277
X v UK (1982) 4 EHRR 188 . . . . 7.48, 7.63
X v UK (1987) 11 EHRR 48 . . . . 7.283
X v UK (1992) 15 EHRR CD 113 . . . . 7.137
X v Y [2004] EWCA Civ 662 . . . . 3.72
X and Y v Sweden (1977–1978) 7 DR 123 . . . . 7.12
X and Y v UK (1977) 12 DR 32 . . . . 7.478
X, Y and Z v UK (1997) 24 EHRR 143. . . . . 7.272
X, Y and Z v UK, App No 32666/10, not yet decided 6.96

Y v Secretary of State for the Home Department, SC/36/2005 . . . . 6.66
YL v Birmingham City Council [2007] UKHL 27, [2008] 1 AC 95 . . . . 3.07, 3.68, 3.69,
3.71, 4.37
Yaman v Turkey, App No 32446/96, 2 November 2004. . . . . 7.60, 7.559
Yankov v Bulgaria (2005) 41 EHRR 854. . . . . 7.358
Yasa v Turkey (1999) 28 EHRR 408 . . . . 6.53
Yazar v Turkey, App No 22723/93, 9 April 2002 . . . . 7.453
Yildiz v Turkey App No 22913/04, 10 November 2005. . . . . 6.111

Young, James and Webster v UK (1982) 4 EHRR 38. . . . . 2.09, 7.443, 7.450, 7.458
Younger v UK (2003) 33 EHRR CD 252 . . . . 6.24
Yumak v Sadak v Turkey (2009) 48 EHRR 1 . . . . 8.90

Z v Finland (1998) 25 EHRR 371 . . . . 7.242
Z v UK (2002) 34 EHRR 3 . . . . 2.35, 6.93, 6.96, 7.112, 7.495
ZH (Tanzania) v Secretary of State for the Home Department [2011] UKSC 4 . . . . . . 1.55, 7.286
Zagorski v Secretary of State for Business, Innovation and Skills [2010]
 EWHC 3110 (Admin) 5.16
Zambrano (Case 34/09) [2011] ECR I-0000 . . . . 5.14
Zamir v UK (1983) 40 DR 42 . . . . 7.42, 7.61
Zand v Austria [1981] ECC 50 . . . . 7.115
Zarb Adami v Malta (2006) 20 BHRC 703 . . . . 6.122, 7.511, 7.526, 7.537, 7.538
Zdanoka v Latvia (2007) 45 EHRR 17 . . . . 7.587, 8.90, 8.103
Ziegler v Switzerland [2002] ECHR 33499/96 . . . . 7.84
Zimmerman and Steiner v Switzerland (1984) 6 EHRR 17 . . . . 7.128

Table of International Instruments

Canadian Charter of Fundamental
  Rights and Freedoms 1.22, 1.29
Convention for the Elimination of
  All Forms of Discrimination
  Against Women 9.32
Convention on the Rights of People
  with Disabilities 9.32
European Convention for the
  Protection of Human Rights and
  Fundamental Freedoms 2.01, 3.01,
    4.01, 5.03, 5.15, 5.16, 5.18, 7.408,
    7.414, 8.129, 8.130, 9.03, 9.07,
    9.14, 9.24, 9.33, 9.35, 10.02,
    10.03, 10.08, 10.19
  Preamble 2.09, 2.42
  Art 1. . . . . .2.23, 2.24, 2.33, 3.09,
    3.77, 4.103, 6.01, 6.04, 6.05,
    6.06, 6.89, 7.31, 7.503
  Art 2. . . . . .2.26, 2.35, 2.38, 2.74,
    3.73, 4.19, 4.20, 4.42, 4.43,
    4.103, 4.104, 4.105, 6.01, 6.09,
    6.10, 6.11, 6.14, 6.15, 6.16,
    6.17, 6.18, 6.19, 6.21, 6.22,
    6.24, 6.26, 6.27, 6.28, 6.29, 6.31,
    6.33, 6.36, 6.37, 6.39, 6.41, 6.42,
    6.44, 6.45, 6.46, 6.49, 6.50, 6.52,
    6.53, 6.54, 6.55, 6.56, 6.89, 6.90,
    6.127, 7.80, 7.166, 7.493, 7.546,
    7.550, 8.127
  Art 2(2) 2.55, 6.29, 6.32, 6.48,
    6.49, 6.50
  Art 3. . . . . 2.26, 2.35, 2.38, 2.74, 3.73,
    4.10, 4.66, 4.82, 4.83, 4.92, 4.103,
    4.105, 4.107, 5.15, 6.01, 6.07, 6.10,
    6.33, 6.55, 6.57, 6.58, 6.59, 6.61, 6.62,
    6.66, 6.69, 6.70, 6.72, 6.73, 6.75, 6.79,
    6.80, 6.81, 6.82, 6.83, 6.84, 6.85, 6.86,
    6.87, 6.89, 6.90, 6.92, 6.94, 6.95, 6.96,
    6.100, 6.101, 6.102, 6.103, 6.105, 6.106,
    6.108, 6.109, 6.110, 6.111, 6.112, 6.124,
    6.125, 6.127, 7.17, 7.23, 7.77, 7.80, 7.112,
    7.203, 7.224, 7.495, 7.497, 7.498, 7.546,
    7.550, 7.551, 7.569, 7.592, 9.13

Art 4. . . . . 6.115, 6.116, 6.122,
    6.123, 6.124, 6.125, 6.127, 7.511
Art 4(1) 2.26, 2.74, 6.115, 7.550
Art 4(2) 6.115, 6.122
Art 4(3) 6.115
Art 5. . . . . .2.28, 4.10, 4.65, 4.68,
    4.80, 4.83, 4.92, 7.01, 7.03, 7.04, 7.05,
    7.06, 7.07, 7.08, 7.09, 7.10, 7.12, 7.14,
    7.15, 7.16, 7.17, 7.18, 7.21, 7.31, 7.39,
    7.40, 7.64, 7.70, 7.73, 7.176, 7.178,
    7.179, 7.207, 7.411, 7.570, 7.571,
    7.575, 7.594
Art 5(1) 7.13, 7.17, 7.19, 7.20,
    7.555, 7.558
Art 5(1)(a) 7.21, 7.23, 7.24, 7.25, 7.67
Art 5(1)(a)–(f) 7.05
Art 5(1)(b) 7.26
Art 5(1)(c) 7.17, 7.28, 7.29, 7.30, 7.51
Art 5(1)(d) 7.32
Art 5(1)(e) 7.33, 7.34, 7.35, 7.38,
    7.39, 7.41
Art 5(1)(f) 7.09, 7.42, 7.44, 7.45,
    7.46, 7.47, 7.570
Art 5(2) 7.06, 7.48, 7.49, 7.50, 7.157
Art 5(3) 7.126, 7.128, 7.06, 7.51,
    7.52, 7.54, 7.55, 7.56, 7.551, 7.568
Art 5(4) 4.31, 7.06, 7.35, 7.40, 7.58,
    7.59, 7.61, 7.63, 7.64, 7.65,
    7.66, 7.67, 7.68, 7.69, 7.72,
    7.145, 7.490
Art 5(5) 3.24, 7.06, 7.73
Art 6. . . . . 1.15, 2.12, 2.15, 2.21, 2.28,
    2.29, 3.73, 4.05, 4.16, 4.42, 4.80,
    5.09, 7.01, 7.8, 7.16, 7.22, 7.23,
    7.64, 7.65, 7.74, 7.76, 7.77, 7.78,
    7.80, 7.81, 7.82, 7.88, 7.90, 7.94,
    7.95, 7.97, 7.98, 7.100, 7.106,
    7.110, 7.112, 7.115, 7.116, 7.118,
    7.122, 7.123, 7.132, 7.134, 7.136,
    7.138, 7.139, 7.140, 7.148, 7.155,
    7.159, 7.163, 7.168, 7.171, 7.179,
    7.398, 7.501, 8.139, 8.140,
    8.142, 9.53

European Convention for the
  Protection of Human Rights and
  Fundamental Freedoms (*cont.*)
Art 6(1) 2.12, 2.29, 2.55, 4.58, 4.80,
  7.59, 7.64, 7.65, 7.74, 7.76, 7.77,
  7.79, 7.94, 7.102, 7.103, 7.104,
  7.105, 7.106, 7.107, 7.108, 7.110,
  7.111, 7.113, 7.115, 7.117, 7.122,
  7.126, 7.129, 7.130, 7.132, 7.134, 7.135,
  7.137, 7.138, 7.139, 7.140, 7.141, 7.142,
  7.143, 7.144, 7.147, 7.151, 7.155, 7.156,
  7.163, 7.165, 7.490
Art 6(2) 7.76, 7.104, 7.137, 7.150,
  7.151, 7.152, 7.154, 7.155
Art 6(3) 7.76, 7.137, 7.143, 7.156,
  7.161
Art 6(3)(a) 7.157
Art 6(3)(b) 7.158, 7.159
Art 6(3)(c) 2.32, 7.140, 7.158, 7.160,
  7.163
Art 6(3)(d) 7.142, 7.165, 7.167, 7.168
Art 6(3)(e) 7.169, 7.170
Art 7. . . . . .2.74, 7.01, 7.172, 7.174,
  7.176, 7.177, 7.178, 7.179, 7.181,
  7.184, 7.187, 7.189, 7.192, 7.193,
  7.195, 7.196, 7.197, 7.199, 7.200,
  7.201, 7.202, 7.205, 7.207,
  7.208, 7.210, 7.212, 7.550
Art 7(1) 2.26, 7.173, 7.175, 7.180,
  7.182, 7.188, 7.194, 7.201, 7.213,
  7.214, 7.216
Art 7(2) 7.175, 7.194, 7.213, 7.214,
  7.215, 7.216
Art 8. . . . . 1.14, 1.48, 2.16, 2.18,
  2.19, 2.30, 2.36, 2.37, 2.38, 2.39,
  2.52, 2.53, 2.63, 2.66, 3.22, 3.37,
  3.47, 3.73, 3.75, 3.78, 3.80, 4.34,
  4.42, 4.80, 4.82, 4.91, 4.104, 4.105,
  4.106, 4.116, 5.09, 6.17, 6.61, 6.93,
  7.01, 7.106, 7.217, 7.218, 7.220,
  7.221, 7.223, 7.224, 7.225, 7.226,
  7.227, 7.228, 7.229, 7.230, 7.233,
  7.235, 7.236, 7.238, 7.239, 7.241,
  7.242, 7.244, 7.245, 7.246, 7.248,
  7.249, 7.250, 7.253, 7.254, 7.255,
  7.256, 7.257, 7.258, 7.261, 7.262,
  7.263, 7.266, 7.267, 7.268, 7.271,
  7.276, 7.279, 7.281, 7.285, 7.292,
  7.293, 7.295, 7.296, 7.297, 7.397,
  7.411, 7.413, 7.419, 7.423, 7.460,
  7.461, 7.475, 7.478, 7.480, 7.481,
  7.482, 7.485, 7.487, 7.493, 7.494,
  7.499, 7.513, 7.534, 8.48, 8.56,
  8.63, 8.908.118, 9.01
Art 8(1) 3.81, 7.220, 7.233, 7.234,
  7.243, 7.247, 7.283, 7.285, 7.294
Art 8(2) 2.31, 6.48, 7.220, 7.226,
  7.228, 7.230, 7.260, 7.283, 7.284,
  7.285, 7.292, 7.294, 7.423, 7.461
Art 9. . . . . .2.26, 2.30, 2.52, 2.63,
  3.75, 3.81, 7.01, 7.106, 7.299,
  7.300, 7.301, 7.302, 7.303, 7.304,
  7.305, 7.306, 7.307, 7.310, 7.311,
  7.312, 7.317, 7.318, 7.320, 7.326,
  7.329, 7.330, 7.331, 7.332, 7.333,
  7.336, 7.339, 7.342, 7.343, 7.345,
  7.347, 7.348, 7.411, 7.412, 7.413,
  7.439, 7.467, 7.485, 7.493, 7.521,
  7.534, 7.590, 8.56, 8.76, 8.90, 8.118
Art 9(1) 2.26, 7.301, 7.319, 7.329,
  7.330, 7.340, 7.341, 7.343
Art 9(2) 6.48, 7.300, 7.319, 7.327,
  7.331, 7.333, 7.334, 7.335,
  7.336, 7.340, 7.341, 7.343
Art 10. . . . . .1.15, 2.30, 2.52, 2.63,
  2.64, 3.22, 3.43, 3.73, 3.75, 3.78,
  3.80, 4.21, 5.07, 7.01, 7.106,
  7.176, 7.253, 7.254, 7.255, 7.256,
  7.258, 7.261, 7.262, 7.263, 7.301,
  7.302, 7.306, 7.349, 7.350, 7.351,
  7.352, 7.353, 7.355, 7.357, 7.358,
  7.359, 7.361, 7.362, 7.363, 7.364,
  7.367, 7.371, 7.383, 7.388, 7.389,
  7.393, 7.395, 7.396, 7.397, 7.398,
  7.399, 7.400, 7.404, 7.406, 7.411,
  7.412, 7.413, 7.424, 7.425, 7.426,
  7.435, 7.436, 7.439, 7.485, 7.534,
  7.585, 7.589, 7.590, 8.63, 8.90,
  8.107, 8.111, 8.118
Art 10(1) 2.49, 7.301, 7.356, 7.357,
  7.360, 7.373, 7.374, 7.379, 7.394
Art 10(2) 2.31, 2.49, 6.48, 7.246,
  7.350, 7.363, 7.373, 7.374, 7.378,
  7.379, 7.381, 7.382, 7.385, 7.394
Art 11. . . . . .2.30, 2.52, 2.63, 3.16,
  3.73, 4.10, 7.01, 7.31, 7.106, 7.176,
  7.301, 7.304, 7.350, 7.395, 7.408,
  7.409, 7.410, 7.411, 7.412, 7.413,

7.417, 7.419, 7.420, 7.421, 7.422,
7.423, 7.424, 7.426, 7.429, 7.433,
7.434, 7.435, 7.436, 7.439, 7.440,
7.441, 7.443, 7.444, 7.446, 7.447,
7.448, 7.449, 7.452, 7.457, 7.458,
7.485, 7.534, 7.585, 8.90,
8.114, 8.118
Art 11(1) 7.413, 7.414, 7.420,
7.442, 7.455
Art 11(2) 6.48, 7.413, 7.420, 7.450,
7.455, 7.456
Art 12. . . . . . 2.19, 2.28, 4.80, 7.01, 7.268,
7.272, 7.459, 7.461, 7.462, 7.463,
7.465, 7.470, 7.471, 7.474, 7.475,
7.476, 7.477, 7.478, 7.480, 7.481,
7.482, 7.483, 7.484, 7.485,
7.486, 7.487, 7.488, 7.489,
7.492, 8.158
Art 13. . . . . . 70503, 1.15, 2.33, 3.09, 3.75,
3.76, 3.77, 4.06, 4.69, 4.85,
4.87, 4.112, 6.47, 7.01,
7.490, 7.491, 7.493, 7.494,
7.495, 7.497, 7.498, 7.499,
7.501, 7.502, 7.512, 9.02, 9.27
Art 14. . . . . . . 1.25, 2.63, 3.46, 4.16, 4.20,
4.80, 4.82, 4.83, 4.91, 7.01, 7.09,
7.91, 7.268, 7.271, 7.274, 7.279,
7.282, 7.301, 7.312, 7.320, 7.336,
7.475, 7.504, 7.505, 7.507, 7.508,
7.509, 7.510, 7.511, 7.512, 7.513,
7.514, 7.515, 7.516, 7.518, 7.519,
7.520, 7.521, 7.529, 7.530, 7.534,
7.537, 7.546, 7.558, 7.571, 7.576,
7.589, 8.05, 8.12, 8.16, 8.51,
8.86, 8.159
Art 15. . . . . . 2.26, 2.74, 6.01, 6.09, 6.115,
7.01, 7.08, 7.47, 7.172, 7.547,
7.549, 7.552, 7.556, 7.559, 7.563,
7.567, 7.570, 7.574
Art 15(1) 2.55, 2.73, 7.556, 7.561
Art 15(2) 7.550
Art 15(3) 7.561
Art 16. . . . 2.76, 7.01, 7.579, 7.582, 7.583,
7.584, 7.585, 7.586
Art 17. . . . 2.76, 7.01, 7.363, 7.399, 7.420,
7.587, 7.588, 7.589, 7.590
Art 18. . . . . 2.53, 2.76, 7.01, 7.591, 7.592,
7.593, 7.594, 7.595
Art 18(2) 7.591

Art 23(4) 7.417
Art 25. . . . . .4.19
Art 30. . . . . .9.08
Art 34. . . . . . . 4.16, 4.19, 4.20, 4.22, 6.11,
6.53, 7.354, 9.19
Art 35. . . . . .9.18, 9.26, 9.37
Art 35(2) 9.29
Art 35(3) 9.29
Art 35(3)(b) 9.35
Art 36. . . . . .9.46
Art 38(1)(b) 9.41
Art 41. . . . . .4.57, 4.63, 9.51
Art 43. . . . . 9.08, 9.46, 9.50, 10.06
Art 46. . . . . .9.62
Art 46(2) 10.07
Art 57. . . . . .2.69
Art 57(2) 2.72
Protocol 1. . . . . 1.18, 2.02, 8.60
Art 1. . . . . 2.16, 2.30, 2.63, 3.73, 4.10,
4.117, 7.91, 7.274, 7.291, 8.02,
8.05, 8.06, 8.07, 8.08, 8.11, 8.12,
8.14, 8.16, 8.20, 8.22, 8.23, 8.24,
8.28, 8.38, 8.40, 8.43, 8.44, 8.45,
8.50, 8.51, 8.52, 8.54, 8.57
Art 1(2) 8.29
Art 2. . . . . . . 2.28, 2.29, 2.32, 2.71, 7.301,
7.306, 7.339, 8.60, 8.61, 8.62, 8.64,
8.68, 8.69, 8.71, 8.73, 8.74, 8.75,
8.76, 8.78, 8.79, 8.80, 8.82
Art 3. . . . . . . 2.28, 2.32, 5.20, 7.350, 8.62,
8.88, 8.89, 8.91, 8.92, 8.93, 8.94, 8.96,
8.97, 8.98, 8.100, 8.101, 8.102, 8.103,
8.104, 8.111, 9.63
Protocol 4. . . . . 8.113, 8.126, 9.24
Art 2. . . . . .7.10, 8.117, 8.121
Art 2(3) 8.117, 8.118
Art 2(4) 8.117, 8.119
Art 3. . . . . 8.121, 8.122
Art 4. . . . . .8.125
Art 5. . . . . 8.121, 8.124
Protocol 6. . . . . . 6.10, 8.127, 8.128, 8.162
Protocol 7. . . . . .7.171, 8.129, 8.130,
8.131, 8.132, 8.153, 9.24
Art 1. . . . . 7.171, 8.133, 8.137, 8.139
Art 2. . . . . .7.171, 8.140, 8.148
Art 2(2) 8.143
Art 3. . . . . 8.146, 8.149, 8.150, 8.151
Art 4. . . . . 8.151, 8.155
Art 4(2) 8.152, 8.153

European Convention for the
  Protection of Human Rights and
  Fundamental Freedoms (*cont.*)
  Art 5 . . . . .8.156
  Art 6 . . . . .8.155
  Protocol 11 . . . . . .2.05, 4.19, 10.05, 10.06
  Protocol 12 . . . . . .1.25, 7.508, 8.160, 9.24
  Protocol 13 . . . . .6.09, 6.10, 8.128,
                   8.161, 8.162
  Art 1 . . . . .8.162
  Art 2 . . . . .8.161
  Art 3 . . . . .8.161
  Protocol 14 . . . . . . .2.05, 9.06, 9.35, 9.44
International Covenant on Civil and
  Political Rights 1.04, 1.55, 2.22,
                 8.02, 8.130, 8.131
  Art 26 . . . . .7.508
International Covenant on Economic,
  Social and Cultural Rights 1.04,
                     8.02, 8.129
Rules of Procedure of the European
  Court of Human Rights 9.07, 10.06
  r 6 . . . . .9.62
  r 32 . . . . .9.30
  r 36 . . . . .9.16
  r 36(2) 9.16
  r 39 . . . . .9.13
  r 41 . . . . .9.13
  r 44 . . . . .9.46

  r 44(1)(b) 9.46
  r 47 . . . . 9.11, 9.17
  r 47(5) 9.12
  r 49 . . . . 9.37, 9.45
  r 61 . . . . .9.42
  r 73 . . . . .9.50
Slavery Convention 1926 . . . . .6.117
UN Convention against Torture 1.04
UN Convention on the Elimination
  of all Forms of Racial
  Discrimination 2.22
UN Convention on the Rights of a
  Child 1.55, 2.21, 7.286
UN Universal Declaration on Human
  Rights (1948) 1.04, 2.02, 7.408,
                         10.02
  Art 16 . . . . .7.476
  Art 20 . . . . .7.409
  Art 23(4) 7.409
Vienna Convention on the Law of
  Treaties 1969 . . . . .2.20
  Preamble 2.09
  Art 31 . . . . .2.08
  Art 31(1) 2.08, 2.69
  Art 31(2) 2.09
  Art 31(3)(c) .2.20
  Art 32 . . . . .2.08
  Art 33 . . . . .2.08
  Art 33(4) 2.08

Table of European Legislation

Charter of Fundamental Rights of the
    European Union 2.21, 5.03, 5.05,
                  5.11, 5.13, 5.15, 5.21
  Chap I 5.12
  Chap II. 5.12
  Chap III 5.12
  Chap IV 5.12
  Chap V. 5.12
  Chap VI 5.12
  Chap VII 5.12
  Preamble 5.12
  Art 9. . . . . .7.474
  Art 24. . . . . .5.13
  Art 25. . . . . .5.13
  Art 35. . . . . .5.13
  Art 39. . . . . .5.13
  Art 51. . . . . .5.14
  Arts 51–54 . . . . .5.14
  Art 51(1) 5.13
  Art 52(3) 5.16
  Art 52(5) 5.13
  Art 52(7) 5.13

  Art 53. . . . . .5.15
  Art 54. . . . . .5.15
Directive 2000/43/EC Equal Treatment
    Directive .5.05
Directive 2000/78/EC Framework
    Employment Directive 5.05
European Social Charter 2.21, 7.448
  Art 5. . . . . .7.456
  Art 6. . . . . .7.448
  Art 28. . . . . .7.447
Lisbon Treaty 5.11
  Protocol 8. . . . . .5.17
Treaty of Amsterdam 5.05
Treaty on European Union
  Art 4(3) 5.01
  Art 6(1) 5.11
  Art 6(2) 5.03
  Art 6(3) 5.03
Treaty on the Functioning of the
    European Union. 5.11
  Art 19. . . . . .5.05
  Art 56. . . . . .5.19

Table of Statutes

Access to Justice Act 1999
   s 19 . . . . .9.56
Anti-Terrorism, Crime and Security
    Act 2001 . . . . . . 1.42, 7.09, 7.65, 7.555
   Pt IV 6.74, 7.570
   s 23 . . . . .4.83
Armed Forces Act 1996. . . . . .7.117
Bill of Rights (1689) 1.06
British Nationality Act 1981 . . . . .8.124
Care Standards Act 2000. . . . . 3.47, 4.80
Child Support Act 1991 . . . . .7.92
Children Act 1989 . . . . .3.40, 7.93, 7.124
Children Act 2004
   s 58 . . . . .6.95
Civil Partnership Act 2004 . . . . .7.275, 7.344,
                               7.475
   s 6(1)(b) .7.344
Commonwealth Immigrants Act 1968 . . .1.11
Communications Act 2003. . . . . .7.590
   s 319 . . . . .3.43
   s 321 . . . . .3.43
Companies Act 1985 . . . . .7.155
Contempt of Court Act 1981 . . . . .1.14
Coroners Act 1988
   s 11(5) 6.43, 6.44
Coroners and Justice Act 2009 . . . 6.45, 6.126
   ss 86–97. .7.167
   Sch 1 . . . . .6.46
Crime and Justice Act 2008 . . . . .7.384
Crime (Sentences) Act 1997 . . . . .4.80
Criminal Evidence (Witness
    Anonymity) Act 2008. . . . . .7.167
Criminal Justice Act 1988
   s 133 . . . . .8.150
Criminal Justice Act 1991. . . .4.80, 4.81, 4.90
   s 33(2) 4.89
   s 35 . . . . .4.89
   s 35(1) 4.89
   s 37(4)(a) 4.89
   s 39 . . . . .4.89
   s 46(1) 4.80
   s 50(2) 4.80

Criminal Justice Act 2003. . . . . . . .4.80, 7.53,
                        7.168, 7.211, 8.155
   ch 7 . . . . .4.80
   s 78 . . . . .8.155
   sch 21. . . . . .4.80
   sch 22. . . . . .4.80
Criminal Justice and Immigration
    Act 2008
   s 27 . . . . .4.80
Criminal Justice and Public Order
    Act 1994 . . . . 1.11, 7.139
   s 25 . . . . 7.55, 7.56
Criminal Procedure and Investigations
    Act 1996
   ss 54–56. . . . . .8.154
Crown Proceedings Act 1947
   s 10 . . . . .4.89
Drug Trafficking Act 1994 . . . . . . 7.212, 8.53
Equality Act 2006. . . . . 1.44, 1.45, 1.46, 4.25,
                        4.26, 4.41, 4.44
   s 1 . . . . .1.45
   s 3 . . . . .1.45, 4.42, 4.44
   s 7 . . . . .1.47
   s 8 . . . . 1.45, 4.42, 4.44, 4.45
   s 8(1) 4.53
   s 8(2) 4.54
   s 9 . . . . .1.45, 4.42, 4.45
   s 9(1) 4.45
   s 9(2)(b) 4.45
   s 9(3) 4.45
   s 10 . . . . 1.45, 3.81, 4.42, 4.44, 4.45
   s 11 . . . . 1.45, 4.42
   s 11(1) 4.46
   s 11(2) 4.46, 4.132
   s 12 . . . . .3.81
   s 16 . . . . .1.46
   s 16(1) 4.50
   s 20(1) 4.52
   s 28 . . . . .1.47
   s 30 . . . . .1.47, 4.25, 4.41
   s 30(1) 1.47, 4.26
   s 30(3) 4.26

Equality Act 2010
Pt 15 . . . . 8.131, 8.156
s 4 . . . . .7.342
s 202 . . . . .7.344
European Communities Act 1972. . . . . .1.27
s 2 . . . . 5.01, 5.22
European Parliamentary Elections Act 2002 . .
9.52
Gender Recognition Act 2004 . . . . 4.80,
7.237, 7.473
Health Act 2009. . . . . .8.34
Housing Act 1996 . . . . 7.93, 7.148
s 185(4) 4.80
Housing and Regeneration Act 2008. . . . .4.91
sch 15. . . . . .4.80
Human Fertilisation and Embryology
Act 1990
s 28(6)(b) 4.80
Human Fertilization and Embryology
(Deceased Fathers) Act 2003. . . . . . .4.80
Human Rights Act 1998. . . . . .1.01, 1.02,
1.05, 1.13, 1.14, 1.18, 1.19, 1.20, 1.24,
1.25, 1.26, 1.30, 1.31, 1.34, 1.35, 1.36,
1.37, 1.38, 1.39, 1.45, 1.49, 1.50, 2.06,
2.16, 2.24, 3.01, 3.02, 3.03, 3.04, 3.05,
3.06, 3.07, 3.08, 3.09, 3.11, 3.12, 3.20,
3.21, 3.22, 3.25, 3.27, 3.28, 3.32, 3.36,
3.43, 3.44, 3.51, 3.56, 3.58, 3.71, 3.74,
3.75, 3.76, 3.81, 4.01, 4.02, 4.06, 4.07,
4.09, 4.12, 4.13, 4.16, 4.17, 4.18, 4.23,
4.24, 4.25, 4.28, 4.31, 4.33, 4.34, 4.36,
4.37, 4.43, 4.55, 4.56, 4.57, 4.59, 4.62,
4.64, 4.65, 4.67, 4.69, 4.71, 4.72, 4.76,
4.79, 4.88, 4.91, 4.94, 4.98, 4.100,
4.101, 4.102, 4.103, 4.108, 4.111,
4.112, 4.113, 4.122, 4.123, 4.124,
4.131, 4.132, 5.22, 5.23, 5.24, 6.02,
6.066.36, 6.113, 7.02, 7.10, 7.47,
7.183, 7.219, 7.220, 7.257, 7.298,
7.405, 7.415, 7.418, 7.495, 7.496,
7.497, 7.499, 7.500, 7.565, 8.01,
8.126, 9.01, 9.03, 9.57, 10.22,
10.23, 10.26, 10.27
s 1 . . . . .3.09
s 1(2) 3.09, 3.27, 7.563
s 2 . . . . 3.11, 3.28, 3.48, 3.49, 3.51,
3.52, 3.54, 3.55, 3.56, 4.06,
5.10, 6.03, 7.503, 7.512
s 2(1) 3.07, 3.10, 3.11
s 3 . . . . . 1.28, 1.31, 3.03, 3.07, 3.12, 3.28,

3.31, 3.32, 3.35, 3.36, 3.37, 3.38,
3.40, 3.45, 3.46, 3.47, 3.55, 3.56,
3.73, 4.25, 4.31, 4.33, 4.73,
5.01, 7.154
s 3(1) 3.31, 3.33, 3.41, 3.54
s 3(2)(b) 3.07, 3.14, 5.22
s 3(2)(c) 3.07, 3.14, 5.22
s 4 . . . . 1.28, 3.07, 3.14, 3.28, 3.45,
3.46, 4.05, 4.13, 4.25, 4.69,
4.72, 4.92, 7.500
s 4(2) 4.71
s 4(5) 4.11
s 4(6)(b) 4.71
s 5 . . . . .3.14
s 6 . . . . 3.05, 3.15, 3.28, 3.57, 3.73,
4.37, 4.62, 4.87, 5.01, 5.26
s 6(1) 3.07, 3.17, 3.18, 3.24,
3.29, 3.57, 4.03, 4.04, 4.10,
4.34, 4.130
s 6(2) 3.07, 3.17, 4.130
s 6(2)(a) 3.17
s 6(2)(b) 3.17
s 6(3) 1.28, 3.07, 3.18, 3.73, 4.130
s 6(3)(a) 3.12, 3.19, 3.29
s 6(3)(b) 3.58, 3.60, 3.62, 3.69
s 6(4) 3.19
s 6(5) 3.58, 3.60
s 6(6) 3.15
s 6(6)(a) 3.18
s 7 . . . . 3.05, 3.07, 3.21, 3.72, 4.02,
4.03, 4.07, 4.19, 4.35, 4.62,
4.78, 5.25
s 7(1) 4.16
s 7(1)(a) 3.21, 3.24, 4.04, 4.07, 4.30
s 7(1)(b) 3.21, 4.07, 4.26, 4.30, 4.34
s 7(3) 3.21, 4.16, 4.24, 4.26
s 7(4) 4.26
s 7(5) 3.21, 4.04, 4.29
s 7(5)(a) 4.32
s 7(5)(b) 4.30
s 7(7) 3.07, 3.21, 4.04, 4.19
s 7(9) 3.21
s 7(10) 3.21
s 7(11) 3.21, 3.23
s 7(12) 3.21
s 7(13) 3.21
s 7(14) 3.21
s 8 . . . . 4.05, 4.06, 4.50, 4.61, 4.87,
4.93, 4.131
s 8(1) 3.23, 4.05

s 8(3) 3.23, 4.56
s 8(4) 4.57, 4.64
s 9 . . . . 3.2, 3.24, 4.50, 4.68, 7.73
s 9(3) 4.13, 4.68
s 9(3)–(5) 7.73
s 9(4) 4.68
s 10 . . . . 1.28, 1.41, 3.07, 3.14, 4.50,
        4.69, 4.72, 4.85, 4.92, 4.93,
        4.94, 4.96, 4.99
s 11 . . . . 3.07, 3.25, 3.56, 4.61
s 12 . . . . 3.26, 3.75, 3.78, 3.79, 3.80,
        7.264, 7.406
s 12(1) 3.79, 7.405
s 12(2) 3.79, 7.405, 7.407
s 12(3) 3.79, 7.371, 7.405, 7.406
s 12(4) 3.79
s 13 . . . . . . 3.26, 3.75, 3.81, 7.345, 7.347,
        7.348
s 14 . . . . .3.27, 7.563, 7.564
s 14(5) 7.564
s 15 . . . . .3.27
s 16 . . . . .3.27, 4.49, 7.564
s 17 . . . . .3.27
s 19 . . . . 1.33, 3.13, 3.43, 3.44,
        3.47, 4.132
s 19(1)(a) 3.13, 3.43
s 19(1)(b) 3.13, 3.43
s 20 . . . . .4.49
s 21(1) 3.10
s 22(4) 3.21, 4.33, 4.34
s 30(2) 4.26
s 31 . . . . .4.49
sch 1 . . . . .3.09, 3.77, 8.128
sch 2 . . . . 1.41, 3.07, 3.14, 3.27,
        4.50, 4.93
   para 1(3) .4.95
   para 2(a) 4.94, 4.96
   para 2(b) 4.94, 4.98
   para 3 . . . . .4.96
   para 4 . . . . .4.98
   para 5 . . . . .4.96
sch 3 . . . . 3.27, 7.564
   pt II 2.71, 8.61
Hunting Act 2004 . . . . 7.233, 8.44
Immigration Act 1971 . . . . .7.569
Interceptions of Communications
   Act 1985 .1.14
Limitation Act 1980 . . . . .4.31
   s 2 . . . . .4.31

Magna Carta (1215) 1.01, 1.06
Marriage Act 1949 . . . . .7.466
Matrimonial Causes Act 1973
   s 11(c) 4.80, 7.473
Mental Capacity Act 2005 . . . . .7.39
Mental Health Act 1983 . . . . 3.65, 9.52
Nationality, Immigration and Asylum
   Act 2002
   s 55 . . . . .6.110
Northern Ireland (Emergency Provisions)
   Act 1978 .7.29
Obscene Publications Act 1959 . . . . .2.78
Official Secrets Act 1989 . . . . .7.394
Police and Criminal Evidence
   Act 1984 .7.53
   s 64 . . . . 7.243, 7.244
   s 64(1A) 3.37
   s.78 . . . . .1.15
Police and Justice Act 2006 . . . . .7.103
Prevention of Terrorism Act 2005 . . . . . . 3.46,
        4.83, 7.15
Prevention of Terrorism (Temporary
   Provisions) Act 1989 . . . . .7.568
Public Order Act 1986 . . . . .7.384
Public Order Act 2008
   Pt 3A 7.384
   s 29J 7.384
   s 29JA 7.384
Race Relations Act 1976 . . . . 7.331, 7.539
Registered Homes Act 1984 . . . . .3.65
Regulation of Investigatory Powers
   Act 2000 .1.14
Representation of the People Act 1983 . . .8.99
   s 3(1) 8.101
Safeguarding Vulnerable Groups
   Act 2006 .4.80
Scottish Human Rights Commission
   Act 2006 .1.47
Serious Organised Crime and Police
   Act 2005 .7.431
Sexual Offences Act 2003 . . . . 3.47, 4.80
Social Security (Contributions and
   Benefits) Act 1992 . . . . .3.46
Terrorism Act 2000 . . . . 2.47, 3.21, 4.109,
        7.13, 7.53, 7.191, 7.227, 7.568
   s 44 . . . . .7.422
Terrorism Act 2005 . . . . .4.92
Terrorism Act 2006 . . . . 1.42, 7.53

Table of Statutory Instruments

Civil Procedure (Amendment No 4) Rules
 2000, SI 2000/2092 . . . . 3.21, 4.09
Civil Procedure Rules
 r 7.11 . . . . .3.21
 pt 16 PD
  para 15 . . . . .4.13
 r 19.4A(1) 4.14
 pt 19 . . . . .4.14
 pt 19 PD 4.14
 r 19.4A. 4.67
 pt 30 . . . . .4.11
 pt 30 PD 3.21
 pt 33 . . . . .3.21
 pt 54 . . . . 4.05, 4.16, 4.30, 4.36
Criminal Appeals (Amendment)
 Rules 2000, SI 2000/2036 . . . . .3.21
Employment Equality (Religion or
 Belief) Regulations 2003,
 SI 2003/1660 . . . . .7.342
Family Proceedings (Amendment)
 Rules 2000, SI 2000/2267 . . . 3.21, 4.09

Human Rights Act 1998 (Designated
 Derogation) Order 2001,
 SI 2001/3644 . . . . .7.570
Human Rights Act (Amendment)
 Order 2004, SI 2004/1574
 Art 2(3) 8.162
Human Rights Act (Designated
 Derogation) Order 2001,
 SI 2001/3644 . . . . .4.83
Mental Health Act 1983 (Remedial)
 Order 2001, SI 2001/3712 . . . . .4.98
Prescribed Organisations Appeal
 Commission (Human Rights
 Act Proceedings) Rules 2006,
 SI 2006/2298 . . . . .3.21
Supreme Court Rules 2009,
 SI 2009/1603 . . . . .4.09
 pt 9 PD 3.21
 r 40 . . . . .3.21

1

INTRODUCTION

A. Introduction   1.01

B. Human Rights in the United Kingdom before
   the Human Rights Act   1.06
   1. Rights in English common law before the Human Rights Act   1.06
   2. European Convention rights in the United Kingdom
      before the Human Rights Act   1.12

C. The Incorporation of the Convention   1.17

D. The Human Rights Act as a Constitutional Instrument   1.26
   1. Parliamentary sovereignty and entrenchment   1.27
   2. Politicizing the judiciary?   1.31

E. The Institutional Framework—Creating a Culture of
   Respect for Human Rights   1.37
   1. A human rights culture in Parliament?   1.40
   2. The Equality and Human Rights Commission   1.43

F. The Future of Human Rights Protection in the United Kingdom 1.49

A. INTRODUCTION

The Human Rights Act 1998 has been in force for over a decade, but the notion of   1.01
rights has an historic pedigree. Legal philosophers have grappled with the complex
implications of the concept ever since rights first emerged in the Magna Carta.[1] Despite
different perspectives on the debate, however, common threads are discernible in
the theorists' writings. It is generally accepted that rights contain both a positive
('claim-right') and a negative ('liberty-right') aspect:

The status of a right entails that a person is both entitled to stand on his own right *and* to require
others to be duty bound to respect it. It means, for example, that when a person asserts his right
to privacy, he has a claim right which others are duty bound to respect; and also that he has a
liberty right to privacy which entitles him to insist on an entitlement to be let alone.[2]

---

[1] Detailed discussions can be found in: Hart, *The Concept of Law* (Oxford: Clarendon Press, 1961);
Dworkin, *Taking Rights Seriously* (London: Duckworth, 1978); Tuck, *Natural Rights Theories: Their Origins
and Development* (Cambridge: Cambridge University Press, 1979); Finnis, *National Law and Natural Rights*
(Oxford: Clarendon Press, 1979); Raz, *The Morality of Freedom* (Oxford: Clarendon Press, 1986).

[2] Clayton and Tomlinson, *The Law of Human Rights*, 2nd edn (Oxford: Oxford University Press, 2009) 22,
citing Dworkin, *Taking Rights Seriously* (London: Duckworth, 1977) ch 7.

1.02   Equally, it is accepted that rights and responsibilities are inextricably linked. In *Rights of Man* Thomas Paine asserted that 'a Declaration of Rights is, by reciprocity, a Declaration of Duties also . . . whatever is my right as a man, is also the right of another; and it becomes my duty to guarantee, as well as to possess'.[3] For Paine, rights were not purely the preserve of the 'selfish' individual but were vital to a healthy civil society. As we discuss below, the relationship between rights and responsibilities has become a central feature of the debate over the future of the Human Rights Act.

1.03   English lawyers were traditionally sceptical of the idea of human rights as a positive concept. They preferred instead to focus on the negative conception of liberties in which 'freedom' consisted of the residual leftovers after the law had been obeyed.[4] While there was no recognized right of free expression, for example, everyone was free to write or say what they like provided it was not libelous or slanderous, or in breach of confidence, or contrary to the Official Secrets Act, or in contempt of court, or in breach of statute. However, without positive guarantees of rights enshrined in a written constitution or a human rights instrument, this negative liberty offered little protection against the acts or omissions of public bodies that harmed fundamental rights. When the former Prime Minister John Major proclaimed 'we have no need of a Bill of Rights because we have freedom',[5] he failed to appreciate that government may show 'a more mundane but still corrupting insensitivity to liberty, a failure to grasp its force and place in democratic ideals'.[6]

1.04   English lawyers' perspective on the legal protection of liberty began to change during the rapid development of international human rights in the second half of the twentieth century. After the horrors of World War Two and the Holocaust, the international community framed new covenants explicitly enshrining universal human rights to try to ensure that such atrocities would never occur again. The first major convention that dealt with human rights, the Universal Declaration on Human Rights (1948), recognized civil and political rights as well as economic, social, and cultural rights. In 1966, the UN-sponsored International Covenant on Civil and Political Rights (ICCPR) was opened for signature. In the same year, the International Covenant on Economic, Social and Cultural Rights (ICESCR) was drawn up, but, unlike the ICCPR, the rights contained within it are subject to the availability of resources and the obligations are to be 'progressively realized'. Doubts about the universality and practicability of economic and social rights have been expressed and the nature of the ICESCR accommodates these concerns.[7] A range of other legal instruments aimed at securing key human rights for specified groups of people (including women, ethnic groups, children, and refugees) and at protecting particular thematic rights (for example, the UN Convention against Torture) have since become an integral part of international law. These treaties and conventions articulate a range of different rights that combine the twin concepts of 'positive' and 'negative' rights, and strive to achieve a balance between individuals' rights and their responsibilities.

---

[3] Paine, *The Rights of Man*, 1791 (Oxford: Oxford University Press, 1995) 165.

[4] See *Malone v Metropolitan Police Commissioner* [1979] CL 344.

[5] Quoted by Lord Irvine, 'The Development of Human Rights in Britain under an Incorporated Convention on Human Rights', Tom Sargant Memorial Lecture, London, 16 December 1997.

[6] Dworkin, 'Devaluing Liberty' (1988) 17(8) Index on Censorship 7.

[7] See Steiner and Alston, *International Human Rights in Context*, 2nd edn (Oxford: Oxford University Press, 2000).

The development with the most profound impact on English law and, indeed, on international human rights jurisprudence more broadly, has been the European Convention for the Protection of Human Rights and Fundamental Freedoms (Convention). Although British lawyers were responsible for much of the drafting of the Convention[8] and the United Kingdom was among the first signatories in 1950, it was nearly half a century before the Government was willing to 'bring rights home' by incorporating Convention rights into domestic law in the Human Rights Act 1998. The explanation for this reticence lies in part in the constitutional and common law traditions that, many judges and politicians believed, already accorded human rights adequate protection.

B. HUMAN RIGHTS IN THE UNITED KINGDOM BEFORE THE HUMAN RIGHTS ACT

1. Rights in English common law before the Human Rights Act

Prior to the enactment of the Human Rights Act, Britain was almost alone amongst western democracies in not having a positive guarantee of rights. However, various historic constitutional texts offered the English limited guarantees of particular rights. The Magna Carta, drafted in 1215, introduced the concepts of habeas corpus and trial by jury. The Bill of Rights of 1689 contained some provisions that later appeared in other human rights covenants, including a prohibition on cruel and unusual punishment, but it was principally a part of a political settlement limiting the power of the monarch and did not purport to protect the basic rights of the citizen.

In the eighteenth and early nineteenth centuries, many ideas that we regard as central to the rule of law—such as a philosophy of liberty and the notion of the freedom of the press—were developed by English thinkers such as Tom Paine, John Locke, and JS Mill. But despite their political writings and contemporary events such as the French Revolution and the American Declaration of Independence, Britain did not adopt a comparable 'Declaration of the Rights of Man'.

Instead, the English relied upon 'negative' liberty, the most influential exposition of which is contained in Dicey's nineteenth-century theory of residual rights.[9] Dicey's theory holds that individuals may say or do whatever they please provided they do not transgress the substantive law or infringe the legal rights of others. In other words, 'we are free to do everything except that which we are forbidden to do by law'. Further, the Crown and other public authorities may not do anything unless they are so authorized by a rule of common law (including the royal prerogative) or statute, and thus may not interfere with individuals' liberties.

As well as these residual freedoms, Dicey and others (including Blackstone in his *Commentaries on the Laws of England*)[10] identified a separate body of fundamental rights in English common law including those to personal security and liberty, private property, freedom of discussion, and assembly. These were protected by the presumption of

1.05

1.06

1.07

1.08

1.09

---

[8] See Simpson, *Human Rights and the End of Empire: Britain and the Genesis of the European Convention* (Oxford: Oxford University Press, 2004).

[9] Dicey, *Law of the Constitution*, 1885, 9th edn (London: Macmillan, 1950).

[10] (1765–1769).

legality, which holds that rights cannot be removed by Parliament except by express words. These rights were recognized by the courts as part of the compact between monarch and Parliament and the birthright of the people. Dicey argued that this system worked well, as Parliament, elected by the people, was the only body which could legislate rights out of existence. Dicey's confidence in residual rights has not been borne out by experience.

1.10 The enormous growth in the power of public and quasi-public bodies over the lives of individuals during the twentieth century has diluted the ability of Parliament to scrutinize legislation—if, indeed, it ever had such omnipotence. Since Dicey was writing, the way in which power is distributed in modern society has altered fundamentally. It is no longer accurate to talk of constitutional power being shared between the legislature, executive, and judiciary alone. The imposition of strict parliamentary party-political discipline has meant that the executive's power within the legislature is often unchallenged, and the growth of quasi-public bodies performing privatized functions of government has led to a reallocation of public power among a variety of different constitutional actors.

1.11 In any case, as JS Mill observed in *On Liberty*,[11] democracy is not in itself a guarantee against the tyranny of the majority over unpopular minorities. In the notorious *East African Asians Case*[12] the European Commission of Human Rights (ECmHR) found that the Commonwealth Immigrants Act 1968, passed to stop British passport holders in East Africa who were fleeing persecution in their home countries coming to the United Kingdom, was motivated by racism. Parliament is also prone to legislating to remove fundamental rights as, for example, in the Criminal Justice and Public Order Act 1994, when the newly created offence of 'trespassory assembly' limited individuals' common law right to assemble (one of the fundamental rights identified by Dicey). In a fast-changing society, relying on the incremental development of the common law to protect rights proved unsatisfactory.

2. European Convention rights in the United Kingdom before the Human Rights Act

1.12 The Convention was drafted with significant input from English lawyers.[13] The United Kingdom ratified the Convention in 1951 and recognized the individual right of petition in 1966. Ironically, in light of the UK's contribution to the Convention, the positive guarantees of fundamental rights contained in the international Convention have been found by the European Court of Human Rights (ECtHR) to have been violated by successive British governments in a surprising number of cases.[14] One reason for this was the judiciary's inability to develop English law consistently with the Convention. Under the dualist principles of English law, international treaties ratified by the UK Government, such as the Convention, do not have direct legal effect in domestic courts until they are incorporated into domestic law by an Act of Parliament.

[11] (Oxford: Oxford University Press, 1869).
[12] (1981) 3 EHRR 76.
[13] See n 8 above.
[14] See the partial list of (pre-incorporation) violations in Hunt, *Using Human Rights Law in English Courts* (London: Hart Publishing, 1997) app 1.

However, before the Human Rights Act came into force—indeed, even before the Bill   1.13
was drafted—it was possible for Convention principles to have an impact on domestic
law either indirectly (through judgments against the United Kingdom in Strasbourg that
were then implemented by changes in the law), or directly (by developing the common
law through legal arguments based on the Convention).

Over the five decades preceding the enactment of the Human Rights Act, the   1.14
Convention indirectly had an increasing impact on the development of the English law.
Findings of violations against the United Kingdom led to several changes being made to
primary legislation. The Strasbourg Court's judgment in *Sunday Times v UK (No 1)*[15]
was an important factor leading to the reform of the law of contempt by the Contempt
of Court Act 1981. The violation of the right to respect for private life in Article 8 found
by the ECtHR in the telephone-tapping case of *Malone v UK*[16] led to the enactment of
the Interception of Communications Act 1985 (provisions now contained in the
Regulation of Investigatory Powers Act 2000).

The judiciary was also able to directly consider the provisions of the Convention in   1.15
cases before the domestic courts. The most important pre-Act uses of the Convention
were as follows:

(a) as an aid to the construction of legislation in cases of ambiguity, for example in *R v
     Secretary of State for the Home Department, ex p Brind*.[17] There is a presumption that
     Parliament does not intend to act in breach of international law (and the specific
     treaty obligations the UK Government has committed to on behalf of the Crown),
     so where there is ambiguity in a statute the courts will construe the law consistently
     with these international treaty obligations;

(b) to establish the scope of the common law where it is developing and uncertain, or
     where it is certain but incomplete. For example, in *Derbyshire County Council v
     Times Newspapers Ltd*[18] Article 10 informed the House of Lords' decision that a
     local authority could not bring an action for libel as it would offend against the
     freedom of expression protections in the Convention;

(c) to inform the exercise of judicial (as opposed to administrative) discretion. For
     example, in *R v Khan*[19] the House of Lords held that a trial judge may have regard
     to the Convention as a material consideration in exercising the discretion conferred
     by section 78 of the Police and Criminal Evidence Act 1984 as to whether to exclude
     evidence; and

(d) to inform decisions on EU law taken by the domestic courts. For example, in
     Johnston v Chief Constable of the Royal Ulster Constabulary[20] the European Court of
     Justice (ECJ) took Articles 6 and 13 into account in determining that the applicant
     did not have an effective remedy in her sex discrimination case. The ECJ has declared
     that the general principles of EU law include the protection of fundamental rights.
     This means that not only should English judges have regard to the Convention

---

[15] (1980) 2 EHRR 245.
[16] (1984) 7 EHRR 14.
[17] [1991] 1 AC 696.
[18] [1992] QB 770.
[19] [1996] 3 WLR 162.
[20] [1987] QB 129.

when dealing with questions of fundamental rights in EU law, but also that ECJ judgments involving fundamental rights are to be regarded as authoritative when domestic courts grapple with questions of EU law. These issues are discussed in detail in Chapter 5.

1.16　　These techniques continue to be important, and are still used in relation to other international treaties that have not been incorporated into English law.[21]

C. THE INCORPORATION OF THE CONVENTION

1.17　The initial justifications advanced by Parliament for not giving full effect to the provisions of the Convention included concerns that the constitutional doctrines of parliamentary sovereignty and separation of powers would be irreparably harmed. In particular, commentators were worried that judges would wield too much power and that difficult societal questions and conflicts of interests would be resolved by judges rather than through political debate by elected MPs. Opponents also argued that it was an unnecessary step given that rights were already adequately protected by the common law, and indeed the incorporation of the 'vague', general principles of the Convention would be a retrograde step for the protection of rights in the United Kingdom as the 'flexibility' of the unwritten constitution would be constrained.

1.18　　Over the past 50 years, those views on the incorporation of the Convention into domestic law slowly changed, culminating in the Human Rights Act. Supporters of a Bill of Rights had long argued that the common law safeguards for rights were inadequate and open to attack by politicians in the grip of party politics. They pointed out that the strict party discipline imposed on the parliamentary political parties did not allow for a fully independent legislature, and so a Bill of Rights was needed to deal with what Lord Hailsham called an 'elective dictatorship'. Supporters relied, too, on the unavoidable facts that the United Kingdom was one of a handful of western democracies that did not have a written Bill of Rights and that British citizens were forced to undertake a lengthy and expensive route to enforcing their Convention rights in Strasbourg. The debate on a Bill of Rights during this period was not the preserve of one political party or political philosophy. In the late 1940s, the main British protagonists of what became the Convention were Conservatives such as Winston Churchill and Harold Macmillan. Equally, it was the Labour Attlee Government that ratified the Convention in 1951, the Churchill Government that ratified the First Protocol in 1953, and the Labour Government of Wilson that accepted the right of individual petition to the ECtHR in 1966.

1.19　　In 1968, the publication of the pamphlet *Democracy and Individual Rights* by Anthony Lester (now the Liberal Democrat peer Lord Lester QC) marked the beginning of the debate that led eventually to the Human Rights Act. Lester suggested that incorporating the Convention was only a first step for enshrining human rights guarantees but would be no more than an interim measure. In subsequent years, the issue of incorporating the Convention was debated a number of times from a variety of political perspectives.

---

[21] For a more detailed analysis, see Hunt, *Using Human Rights Law in English Courts* (London: Hart Publishing, 1997); Fatima, *Using International Law in Domestic Courts* (London: Hart Publishing, 2005).

An important step forward was made in 1974, when Sir Leslie Scarman (later the cross-bench peer Lord Scarman) wrote of the need for an instrument to challenge the sovereignty of Parliament and to protect basic human rights which could not be adequately protected by the legislature alone. Scarman was in favour of entrenchment. He believed that only by making a Bill of Rights superior to the machinations of Parliament could such fundamental rights be protected.[22]

The Labour Party National Executive Committee unveiled a *Charter of Human Rights* in 1975. This document advocated an unentrenched Human Rights Act. This proposal was regarded as insufficient by many who considered that such an Act would offer inadequate protection to individual interests against the growing power of the state. In particular, many Conservatives (including Sir Geoffrey Howe (now Lord Howe), Lord Brittan and Roy Jenkins (the late Lord Jenkins)) preferred the concept of a Bill of Rights with entrenched clauses that would prevent even Parliament from granting the executive excessive power over the lives of individuals.   1.20

In 1976, the Liberal Democrat Lord Wade moved a Bill in the House of Lords which proposed to entrench the Convention as a part of all existing legislation and to make it an entrenched part of all subsequent enactments unless Parliament specifically legislated otherwise. Lord Wade and Lord Harris continued to be the chief advocates for a Bill of Rights in the Lords. In 1978, a House of Lords Select Committee examined the arguments for and against legislation to incorporate the Convention and create a Bill of Rights. However, traditional constitutional views prevailed, particularly a concern about the idea of judges deciding 'human rights' cases. The fear was that this would remove the judiciary from its traditionally impartial role, supposedly beyond politics, and embroil it in (party) political questions.   1.21

After John Smith became leader of the Labour Party in 1992, there was a clear shift in Labour Party policy. The Labour Party Conference in October 1993 adopted a two-stage policy supporting the incorporation of the European Convention of Human Rights to be followed by the enactment of a domestic Bill of Rights. The Labour Party planned to entrench Convention rights by the use of a 'notwithstanding clause' procedure. This was similar to the Canadian Charter of Rights and Freedoms, and would have led to the Convention overriding domestic law unless Parliament expressly provided for it to apply notwithstanding that it would violate the instrument. The conference also advocated the establishment of a human rights commission to monitor and promote human rights. Tony Blair MP (shortly before he became leader of the Labour Party) set out his views in the *Guardian* and reaffirmed the need for strengthened incorporation and the idea of a 'notwithstanding clause'.[23]   1.22

Lord Lester of Herne Hill continued his human rights work in the Lords by introducing a Bill in November 1994. The Bill did not receive support from the Conservative Government. Particular aspects of the proposed Bill were criticized by the Law Lords, but significantly they supported incorporation in so far as it allowed UK judges to interpret human rights domestically.   1.23

In December 1996, Jack Straw MP and Paul Boateng MP published a Consultation Paper, *Bringing Rights Home*, setting out the Labour Party's plans to incorporate the   1.24

---

[22] Lord Scarman, *English Law—The New Dimension*, Hamlyn Lectures, 26th Series (London: Stevens, 1974).
[23] 16 July 1994.

7

Convention if it won the election due in 1997. Whereas the 1993 policy had advocated incorporation to be followed by a second stage in the form of a home-grown Bill of Rights, the Consultation Paper deferred the second stage, and the five key issues posed by the paper concerned only the incorporation of the Convention. In May 1997, Labour won a landslide victory on a manifesto which included a commitment to incorporate the Convention into domestic law. The debate then turned to how the Convention should be incorporated, and in particular to whether it should be permitted to override statutes, subject to a 'notwithstanding' clause. The unique solution adopted in the Human Rights Act is the subject of Chapters 3 to 4 of this book.

1.25   The incorporation of the Convention is not the end of the story. The Convention is by no means a perfect human rights treaty and there remain gaps in the protection of human rights in the United Kingdom. The Convention was drafted in the aftermath of the Second World War and, although it is a 'living instrument', the values it embodies are those of a different generation. If the Convention were to be drafted today, a number of rights might be included that are not currently found within its scope. For example, the Convention does not contain a right to freedom of information;[24] the anti-discrimination provision is 'parasitic' in that it applies only where another Convention right has been violated;[25] there is little specific recognition of children's rights or environmental rights; and it does not contain an absolute prohibition against self-incrimination for criminal defendants.[26] In addition, the types of Convention rights are limited in range compared with the nature of rights more broadly, and offer little protection to social and economic rights. In contrast, the Charter of Fundamental Rights of the European Union contains more wide-ranging rights, including employment, equality, and children's rights.[27] The Convention's deficiencies are replicated in the Human Rights Act, which simply incorporated the Convention in English law.

D. THE HUMAN RIGHTS ACT AS A CONSTITUTIONAL INSTRUMENT

1.26   In the lead-up to the enactment of the Human Rights Act, some commentators expressed concern about the relationship between the new statute and the existing constitutional arrangements. The flashpoint for many was the perceived tension between the English tradition of regarding the sovereignty of the democratic Parliament as being the cornerstone of its (unwritten) constitution and the fact that the Convention was to be enforceable in the courts.[28] Similar concerns have resurfaced in recent attacks on the Human Rights Act, with detractors claiming that it gives the judiciary the power to override the will of the democratically elected Parliament and draws judges into societal debates in a

---

[24] See ch 7, para 7.366.
[25] See discussion of Art 14 and Protocol 12 in ch 8, para 8.159.
[26] For further discussion, see Wadham, 'Why Incorporation of the European Convention on Human Rights is Not Enough', in Gordon and Wilmot-Smith (eds), *Human Rights in the United Kingdom* (Oxford: Oxford University Press, 1996); and Wadham and Taylor, 'Bringing More Rights Home' [2002] EHRLR 713.
[27] The Charter is discussed in ch 5.
[28] See, eg Ewing, 'The Human Rights Act and Parliamentary Democracy' [1999] MLR 79.

manner that is alien to the UK's constitutional settlement. To gauge the strength of these criticisms, each of the claims is examined below.

1. Parliamentary sovereignty and entrenchment

The idea that Parliament is the supreme legal power has been a consistent theme in English law as reflected in the writings of Coke, Blackstone, and Dicey. The doctrine has several elements. According to the theory, the sovereign legislature (the Queen, the House of Lords, and the House of Commons) can make and repeal any legislation whatsoever, so that no Parliament can bind its successors. As a result, it is impossible to 'entrench' particular legislation (for example, a Bill of Rights) by specifying that it would be repealable only under some specially safeguarded process. A corollary is that no act of the sovereign legislature can be invalid in the eyes of a court, because Parliament alone has the legal and political power to make laws. The potency of the parliamentary sovereignty theory has been diluted by the changes to the domestic legal system effected by the European Communities Act 1972, but it still carries some force. A strict adherence to the doctrine would be problematic. It would limit the ability of courts to uphold human rights and could mean that a future Parliament could legislate such rights out of existence. To protect fundamental rights, some form of 'entrenchment' is necessary.

The solution adopted in the Human Rights Act is a complex one, reflecting a delicate political compromise between 'incorporating' Convention rights and retaining parliamentary sovereignty. The rule of construction in section 3 of the Human Rights Act places courts under a strong interpretative obligation to read and give effect to all legislation, whether primary or secondary, old or recent, in a way which is compatible with Convention rights 'so far as it is possible to do so'. Section 4 makes it clear that if a conflict between the provisions of a piece of legislation and Convention rights cannot be overcome, higher courts will have to make a declaration of incompatibility. The court cannot 'strike down' the offending Act, and so it remains operative after such a declaration. The scheme of the Human Rights Act means that the only legal effect of a declaration of incompatibility is to permit (but not oblige) a minister to amend the impugned legislation by a 'remedial order' under section 10. If the declaration of incompatibility is not accepted by the Government, and there is no overwhelming parliamentary pressure to change the law, there is no domestic legal obligation to change the law. Further, section 6(3) excludes Parliament from the definition of 'public authority' so that it is not bound by the provisions of the Human Rights Act.

This form of legislation for human rights is not as strong as the Canadian model, which gives courts the power to strike down primary legislation but allows the legislature to enact measures for a limited period 'notwithstanding' its contravention of provisions in the Charter of Fundamental Rights and Freedoms. It is, however, much stronger than the New Zealand model, which imposes only a weak obligation upon courts to 'prefer' an interpretation of legislation that is consistent with the Bill of Rights Act over an inconsistent one if possible.

Ultimately, the Human Rights Act protects the principle of parliamentary sovereignty because it does not permit the Convention to be used so as to override primary legislation: if a statute is clear in its terms, and clearly incompatible with the Convention, courts must give effect to it. Equally, if the terms of the primary legislation require subordinate legislation made under it (which will usually be in a statutory instrument) to be

1.27

1.28

1.29

1.30

interpreted in a way that means that the subordinate legislation is incompatible with the Convention, it must still be given effect even though this may result in a breach of a Convention right.[29]

2. Politicizing the judiciary?

1.31   Before the Human Rights Act came into force, some legal and academic commentators[30] warned that it would infringe the basic constitutional tenet that 'Parliament makes the laws, the judiciary interpret them'.[31] The strong approach to statutory construction required by section 3 would lead to a politicization of the judiciary and an encroachment on Parliament's constitutional sphere. However, English courts reviewing controversial issues is not a new phenomenon. The Human Rights Act may have brought about a more intense degree of judicial scrutiny of executive and parliamentary action, but not scrutiny of a different kind. Indeed, one of the important effects of the Human Rights Act has been to focus public attention and debate on the proper nature and scope of the judicial function.

1.32   In response to criticisms of judicial activism, the former Lord Chief Justice Lord Woolf has pointed out that:

> . . . judges are only doing what they have to swear to do on appointment and that is to give a judgement according to law. The law now includes the HRA. By upholding the HRA the courts are not interfering with the will of Parliament. On the contrary, when they interfere, the judges are protecting the public by ensuring that the Government complies with the laws made by Parliament. The courts are therefore acting in support of Parliament and not otherwise.[32]

1.33   The Human Rights Act itself provides a mechanism for balancing the role of the executive, Parliament, and the courts in the form of section 19. It presumes that new legislation is to be (and can be) read compatibly with the Convention. When legislation is introduced into Parliament for a second reading, the introducing minister must make a statement that, in his or her view, the legislation is compatible with the Convention, or make a statement that, although the legislation is not compatible with the Convention, the Government still wishes to proceed. It is unlikely that governments will often wish to state publicly that they are acting incompatibly with an internationally binding human rights instrument, though they have been prepared to do so on occasion. Where a 'section 19' statement is made, Parliament has the opportunity to thoroughly examine the minister's assertion before the Bill is passed. Reports of the Joint Parliamentary Committee on Human Rights (see para 1.42 below) demonstrate that section 19 statements have the potential to be powerful democratic tools for scrutinizing Bills, when Parliamentarians press for detailed reasoning behind statements of compatibility from the Government, rather than accepting generalized, uninformative statements that Bills are Convention compliant. A section 19 statement of compatibility also gives a strong indication to the judiciary that the Government intended its new legislation to be human

---

[29] For more details, see Bamforth, 'Parliamentary Sovereignty and the Human Rights Act 1998' [1998] PL 572.

[30] See n 28 above. See also Griffith, *The Politics of the Judiciary*, 5th edn (London: Fontana Press, 1997).

[31] Lord Diplock in *Duport Steels Ltd v Sirs* [1980] 1 WLR 142.

[32] 'The Impact of Human Rights', speech at Oxford Lyceum, 6 March 2003.

rights compliant and that the judges are able to proceed with their judicial scrutiny with that intention in mind.

Despite some commentators' claims, since the Human Rights Act came into force 1.34 judges have erred on the side of caution rather than judicial activism.[33] They have developed the concept of a 'discretionary area of judgment' (sometimes called 'deference') which considers when it is appropriate (and when it is not) for courts to defer to decisions made by other constitutional bodies such as the legislative, executive, or administrative branches. The appropriateness and breadth of the discretionary area of judgment that should be applied have been hotly debated by Law Lords, practitioners, and academics alike and is considered in more detail in Chapter 4.[34]

The notion of 'democratic dialogue' is the most helpful for evaluating the interaction 1.35 between Parliament, the executive, and the judiciary under the new constitutional arrangement ushered in by the Human Rights Act.[35] This 'dialogue' takes place when a court, in reviewing legislative and executive action, scrutinizes the justification for laws or actions which limit fundamental human rights within the framework of the Convention, and seeks to make the law compatible with the Convention, by interpretation, if possible, or to declare the fact of incompatibility, if not. The final word on the content of law, however, still rests with Parliament. In the leading Canadian Supreme Court case of *Vriend v Alberta*[36] Iacobucci J concluded:

. . . a great value of judicial review and this dialogue among the branches is that each of the branches is made somewhat accountable to the other. The work of the legislature is reviewed by the courts and the work of the court in its decisions can be reacted to by the legislature in the passing of new legislation . . . This dialogue between and accountability of each of the branches has the effect of enhancing the democratic process, not denying it.

Despite the ongoing concerns about parliamentary sovereignty and judicial activism, 1.36 both the judiciary and government have acknowledged the place of the Human Rights Act in the UK constitution. Lord Bingham has called the Human Rights Act 'an important constitutional instrument'.[37] As Lord Justice Laws has explained, this is so because the Act conditions the legal relationship between citizen and state and determines the scope of what we now regard as fundamental constitutional rights.[38]

E. THE INSTITUTIONAL FRAMEWORK—CREATING A CULTURE OF RESPECT FOR HUMAN RIGHTS

Many commentators, including the authors, hoped that as well as transforming the legal 1.37 landscape, the 1998 Act would have a broad impact on our political and social culture.

---

[33] See Leigh and Masterman, *Making Rights Real: The Human Rights Act in its First Decade* (London: Hart Publishing, 2009).

[34] See ch 4, paras 4.119–4.130.

[35] See, eg Clayton, 'Judicial Deference and "Democratic Dialogue": the Legitimacy of Judicial Intervention under the Human Rights Act 1998' [2004] PL 33; Hickman, 'Constitutional Dialogue, Constitutional Theories and the Human Rights Act 1998' [2005] PL 306.

[36] [1998] 1 SCR 495.

[37] *Brown v Stott* [2003] 1 AC 681, 703.

[38] See Laws LJ in *Thoburn v Sunderland City Council* [2002] 3 WLR 247.

There are two dimensions to this new culture—ethical and institutional. The ethical dimension involves individual members of society developing an understanding that they enjoy certain rights by virtue of being human (not merely as a contingent gift of the state); *and* that with these rights comes the responsibility to respect the human rights of other individual citizens. Developing an institutional human rights culture involves mainstreaming fundamental principles into the design and delivery of policy, legislation, and public services so that decisions taken by public authorities such as schools and hospitals are proportionate, rational, and respectful of fundamental rights. The obligation on public authorities imposed by the Human Rights Act goes beyond non-interference with rights and requires such bodies to take active steps to protect people's rights against interference by others.[39]

1.38   The Act's aim of creating an institutional human rights culture has not been entirely successful. Research undertaken on the effect of the Human Rights Act has demonstrated that public bodies have not taken advantage of the benefits a human rights culture could offer for improved decision-making by using the framework of the Act to inform best practice. Instead, public bodies have confined human rights to their legal compliance departments, adopting a minimalist approach to protecting people's fundamental rights by 'Strasbourg-proofing' their policies and procedures to avoid litigation.[40]

1.39   The Human Rights Act is also widely misunderstood and mistrusted by the public, caricatured by the popular press as a 'charter for criminals and terrorists'. As we discuss below, the future of the Act is uncertain. The failure to set up a body at the Human Rights Act's inception to promote understanding and awareness of the benefits of human rights left it vulnerable to these attacks because it was without a powerful, institutional champion to defend the benefits of human rights. This failure was belatedly remedied by the creation of the Equality and Human Rights Commission.[41]

1. A human rights culture in Parliament?

1.40   Both the Labour Party Consultation Paper, *Bringing Rights Home*, and the White Paper, *Rights Brought Home*, stated that 'Parliament itself should play a leading role in protecting the rights which are at the heart of parliamentary democracy'.[42] A Human Rights Committee has proved to be a fundamental part of this. The idea of a Human Rights Committee in Parliament originated in Francesca Klug's *A People's Charter: Liberty's Bill of Rights*.[43] Klug's suggestion was that the new Committee could conduct inquiries on a range of human rights issues, produce reports to assist the Government and Parliament in deciding what action to take, and range more widely, examining issues relating to the other international obligations of the United Kingdom.

---

[39] See ch 2, para 2.39.

[40] British Institute of Human Rights, 'Something for Everyone: The Impact of the Human Rights Act and the Need for a Human Rights Commission' (2002); Audit Commission, 'Human Rights: Improving Service Delivery' (2003); EHRC, 'Human Rights Inquiry' (2009).

[41] See para 1.45 below.

[42] Straw and Boateng, 'Bringing Rights Home: Labour's Plans to Incorporate the ECHR into UK Law: A Consultation Paper' (1997); White Paper, 'Rights Brought Home: The Human Rights Bill' (Cm 3782, 1997). See app 2.

[43] London: National Council for Civil Liberties, 1991.

The Joint Committee on Human Rights (JCHR) (a Select Committee consisting of 1.41 members of both Houses of Parliament) was appointed in January 2001. Its terms of reference are to consider:

(a) matters relating to human rights in the United Kingdom (excluding consideration of individual cases);

(b) proposals for remedial orders, draft remedial orders, and remedial orders made under section 10 of, and laid under Schedule 2 to, the Human Rights Act; and

(c) in respect of draft remedial orders and remedial orders, whether the special attention of the House should be drawn to them on any of the grounds specified in Standing Order 73 (Joint Committee on Statutory Instruments).

The JCHR carries out important work, including prolific scrutiny of important bills, 1.42 and, in the future, intends to expand its pre-legislative scrutiny work (to draw the attention of Parliament and the Government to any potential pitfalls in relation to a proposed policy course) and include a new strand of work related to post-legislative scrutiny (to assess whether the implementation of new laws has produced unwelcome human rights implications).[44] It has had an important influence on Parliament and, in particular, on controversial and human rights sensitive pieces of legislation such as the Anti-Terrorism, Crime and Security Act 2001 and the Terrorism Act 2006.[45]

2. The Equality and Human Rights Commission

One of the initial tasks the JCHR undertook was an inquiry into whether a Human 1.43 Rights Commission was needed. It concluded that the case for setting up a Commission for Human Rights was compelling.[46] Without it, the development of a 'culture of understanding of rights and responsibilities' envisaged by the original proposals was stalled.

After a series of consultation papers between 2002 and 2004, the Government con- 1.44 firmed that it would set up a new, single Commission for Equality and Human Rights and brought forward legislation to establish that body.[47] There were good reasons for establishing an integrated body. Not only have other countries demonstrated the practical benefits of linking human rights and equality work (for example in the Australian Human Rights and Equal Opportunity Commission), but, conceptually, human rights and equality are inextricably linked. Equality is treated as a fundamental human right in the core international human rights treaties, and human rights and equality derive from the same fundamental principle: equal respect for the inherent dignity of all.

---

[44] For accounts and assessments of the work of the JCHR to date, see JCHR, *The Committee's Future Working Practices* 23rd Report (2005–2006) (available at <http://www.parliament.uk>); Lester, 'Parliamentary Scrutiny of Legislation under the Human Rights Act 1998' [2002] EHRLR 432; Feldman, 'The impact of human rights on the UK legislative process' (2004) 25(2) Stat LR 91; Hiebert, 'Parliament and the Human Rights Act: can the JCHR help facilitate a culture of rights?' (2006) 4(1) IJCL 1; Leigh and Masterman, *Making Rights Real: The Human Rights Act in its First Decade* (London: Hart Publishing, 2009).
[45] For a detailed analysis, see JCHR, *The Committee's Future Working Practices* 23rd Report (2005–2006) app 5 (available at <http://www.parliament.uk>).
[46] JCHR, *The Case for a Human Rights Commission* 6th Report (2002–2003), HL 67-I, HC 489-I.
[47] Equality Act 2006 (EA 2006).

1.45   The Equality and Human Rights Commission[48] started work in October 2007. The Equality Act 2006 set out specific legal duties for the Commission, including a duty to promote understanding of the importance of human rights and to encourage compliance with the Human Rights Act.[49]

1.46   In order to carry out its duties the Equality Act provided the Commission with a range of legal powers. In particular, it can conduct formal inquiries into any matters relating to its duties,[50] intervene in litigation,[51] bring judicial review in its own name,[52] and provide legal assistance to individuals in proceedings concerning the equality enactments.[53] In June 2009 the Commission published the results of its Inquiry to assess the effectiveness and enjoyment of a culture of respect for human rights in Great Britain.[54] The Inquiry found that while the vast majority of people want to see human rights embedded in national law, there were significant misunderstandings and misconceptions about human rights. Where a human rights approach has been adopted, the Inquiry found that it led to speedy positive resolution of problems and systemic changes in service delivery by public authorities.

1.47   The Scottish Parliament has also set up the Scottish Human Rights Commission, which set out its first strategic plan in December 2008.[55] This Commission has its own powers and duties but these are restricted to devolved matters—matters within the competence of the Scottish Parliament.[56]

1.48   The creation of these Commissions represented an important opportunity to kick-start the development of a culture of respect for human rights in the United Kingdom. However, the Coalition Government has proposed reforms to the remit of the Equality and Human Rights Commission, and its future role is under consideration in the Public Bodies Bill currently before Parliament. The Bill has been subject to serious criticism for the manner in which it proposes reform of statutory bodies without sufficient parliamentary scrutiny.[57]

F. THE FUTURE OF HUMAN RIGHTS PROTECTION IN THE UNITED KINGDOM

1.49   Since the Human Rights Act came into force it has been the focus of intense political debate. The Act is widely blamed for administrative and judicial decisions that have been caricatured as privileging the rights of criminals and terrorists. In particular, the Convention prohibition on deporting individuals to countries where there is a real risk that they will be tortured has attracted the scorn of the press and calls by politicians to

---

[48] EA 2006, s 1 establishes the 'Commission for Equality and Human Rights' but the body has adopted the name 'Equality and Human Rights Commission'.

[49] EA 2006, ss 3, 8, 9, 10, and 11.

[50] EA 2006, s 16.

[51] EA 2006, s 30. See, eg *R (JL) v Secretary of State for Justice* [2008] UKHL 68, [2008] 3 WLR 1325.

[52] EA 2006, s 30(1).

[53] EA 2006, s 28.

[54] Equality and Human Rights Commission, 'Our Human Rights Inquiry' (June 2009), available at: <http://www.equalityhumanrights.com/human-rights/our-human-rights-inquiry/>.

[55] EA 2006, s 7; and see <http://www.scottishhumanrights.com>.

[56] Scottish Human Rights Commission Act 2006.

[57] See, eg Liberty's Report Stage Briefing on the Public Bodies Bill in the House of Lords (March 2011).

're-balance' the Act in favour of 'security'.[58] Recently, the Act has received ferocious criticism from media organizations for enabling the judiciary to create a law of privacy unsanctioned by Parliament.[59] Amongst human rights advocates, there is a consensus that the Government 'failed to explain the basic philosophy of the Human Rights Act to the people'.[60] As the Equality and Human Rights Commission found in its Human Rights Inquiry, there is a general lack of public awareness of the positive role that human rights can play in individual lives.

Reform of the Human Rights Act has been under consideration since former Prime Minister Gordon Brown published a Green Paper[61] and a statement[62] exploring the possibility of a British Bill of Rights as part of a wider programme of constitutional reform. The JCHR contributed to the debate by undertaking a formal inquiry into a Bill of Rights, which reported in August 2008.[63] It found that the case for a Bill of Rights had been made out, but emphasized that the Bill could not be a vehicle for diluting the protections of the Human Rights Act; rather, it should add to those rights already protected.   1.50

In March 2009, the Labour Government formally launched the consultation process into a Bill of Rights in the publication by the Ministry of Justice of its long-awaited Green Paper, *Rights and Responsibilities: Developing our Constitutional Framework*.[64] The Green Paper set out preliminary proposals for a 'Bill of Rights and Responsibilities', but the 2010 general election intervened before the consultation was completed.   1.51

In the Coalition Agreement between the Conservatives and Liberal Democrats it was stated: 1.52

We will establish a Commission to investigate the creation of a Bill of Rights that incorporates and builds on all our obligations under the European Convention on Human Rights, ensures that these rights continue to be enshrined in British law, and protects and extends British liberties. We will seek to promote a better understanding of the true scope of these obligations and liberties.[65]

The Commission on a Bill of Rights was established in March 2011, earlier than planned, after a political frenzy over prisoners' voting rights during which Parliament refused to sanction giving certain categories of prisoners the right to vote as required by the decision of the European Court judgment in *Hirst v UK*.[66]   1.53

As a result of negotiations between the Coalition parties, the Commission's terms of reference limit it to proposing a Bill of Rights that 'incorporates and builds on all our obligations' under the Convention. It therefore appears predisposed to favour using the Convention rights as an explicit starting point, though at the time of writing it is too early to predict exactly what the Commission's Bill of Rights may contain. The Green   1.54

---

[58] See Home Office Report, *Rebalancing the Criminal Justice System in favour of the law-abiding majority* (July 2006).
[59] Equality and Human Rights Commission, 'Our Human Rights Inquiry' (June 2009), available at: <http://www.equalityhumanrights.com/human-rights/our-human-rights-inquiry/>, 104.
[60] JCHR, *A Bill of Rights for the UK?* 29th Report (2007–2008), HL 165-I, HC 150-I, vol II, Klug Ev 1.
[61] *The Governance of Britain* (Cm 7170, 2007).
[62] Prime Minister's statement on constitutional reform, HC, col 819 (3 July 2007).
[63] JCHR, *A Bill of Rights for the UK?* 29th Report (2007–2008), HL 165-I, HC 150-I.
[64] Cm 7577, 2009.
[65] Cabinet Office, 'The Coalition: our programme for government' (May 2010), available at: <http://www.cabinetoffice.gov.uk/sites/default/files/resources/coalition_programme_for_government.pdf>, 11.
[66] (2005) 19 BHRC 546.

Paper published by the Labour Government focused on including 'responsibilities' as well as rights in a Bill of Rights, and the Commission is likely to consider whether to include reference to responsibilities. The notion of responsibility is already embedded within the qualifications to Convention rights which permit consideration of the rights of others and the public interest in the proportionality analysis, and any exposition of responsibilities in a Bill of Rights should be approached with caution. In particular, if the Bill of Rights contains an interpretative imperative to take 'responsibilities' into account, courts may mistakenly require that rights, or remedies for their breach, be made contingent on the exercise of responsibility.

1.55   The Commission is due to report no later than the end of 2012. In the meantime, the greatest domestic developments in human rights may come from increasing awareness of, and recourse to, the other international human rights treaties that the United Kingdom has ratified and the diverse range of protections that they offer. There is no doubt that incorporation of the Convention has opened the eyes of English lawyers and judges to the creative ways in which international legal obligations interact with domestic laws. Although treaties such as the ICCPR and the Convention on the Rights of the Child are not directly enforceable in the English courts, they are increasingly likely to offer interpretative guidance to courts and to inspire new developments in similar ways to those in which the Convention was used by the judiciary prior to its incorporation.[67]

---

[67] See, eg the use of the Convention on the Rights of the Child in *ZH (Tanzania) v Secretary of State for the Home Department* [2011] UKSC 4.

2

THE FRAMEWORK OF THE EUROPEAN
CONVENTION ON HUMAN RIGHTS

A. Introduction	2.01
B. Interpreting the Convention	2.07
1. 'Object and purpose'	2.08
2. Effectiveness principle	2.11
3. Autonomous concepts	2.14
4. Dynamic interpretation	2.17
5. Recourse to other human rights instruments	2.20
6. Jurisdiction	2.23
C. The Scope of Convention Rights	2.25
1. Absolute, limited, and qualified rights	2.25
2. Positive obligations	2.32
D. Restricting Convention Rights	2.40
1. Legality	2.42
2. Legitimate aim	2.50
3. 'Necessary in a democratic society'	2.54
4. Restrictions specifically provided for by reservations and derogations	2.69
5. Restrictions under Articles 16, 17, and 18	2.76
E. The Margin of Appreciation	2.77

A. INTRODUCTION

The European Convention for the Protection of Human Rights and Fundamental   2.01
Freedoms (Convention) is an international human rights treaty agreed by states that
are members of the Council of Europe. The Council of Europe was established in 1949
as part of the Allies' programme to 'reconstruct durable civilization on the mainland of
Europe'.[1] Today it has 46 members with a wide variety of political traditions, including
many former Communist states from Eastern Europe. The Convention came into force
on 3 September 1953.

The rights guaranteed by the Convention are modelled on those contained in the   2.02
UN Universal Declaration of Human Rights (1948), but the content of the rights and

---

[1] *Rights Brought Home: The Human Rights Bill* (Cm 3782, 1997) para 1.1.

qualifications to them are more specific, reflecting the states' intention that the rights be legally enforceable. The Convention's provisions are mostly civil and political in nature (with the notable exceptions of the right to property and the right to education in Protocol 1). However, the interpretation of Convention rights may extend into the sphere of social and economic rights[2] in order to 'safeguard the individual in a real and practical way'.[3] As well as allowing states to bring proceedings against one another, individuals are able to enforce their Convention rights against states that have accepted the right of 'individual petition'.

2.03   The United Kingdom ratified the Convention in 1951 but, unlike many of the other signatories, did not set about incorporating the Convention rights into domestic law. Incorporation was thought to be unnecessary, as it was believed that the rights safeguarded by the Convention already flowed from English common law.

2.04   In 1966, the United Kingdom accepted the right of individual petition. This has meant that, even before its incorporation into domestic law, the Convention offered individual litigants in Britain the possibility of redress in international law where their civil liberties had been infringed by the state, and where no adequate remedy could be provided by the domestic courts. (It is important to appreciate that, as a matter of international law, the Convention creates rights against states, not against private individuals.)

2.05   The Convention originally established three bodies to monitor human rights within the countries that had ratified it: the European Commission of Human Rights (ECmHR),[4] the European Court of Human Rights (ECtHR),[5] and the Committee of Ministers. All three were based in Strasbourg. Until November 1998, the ECmHR and the ECtHR heard complaints from individuals about violations of their rights. The ECmHR exercised a 'screening' function, and could refer cases to the ECtHR for a final determination. However, Protocol 11 to the Convention brought major changes to the Strasbourg system. From November 1998, the ECmHR ceased to exist. Instead, a one-tier system was introduced in which all cases are dealt with by different chambers of the ECtHR. Decisions of the ECtHR are binding on the country concerned.[6]

2.06   The Convention is unlike a UK statute. Its broad provisions cannot be interpreted according to the traditional English 'black-letter' approach that closely defines the scope and content of a power. The ECtHR, and latterly the UK courts under the Human Rights Act 1998, have developed a sophisticated jurisprudence built upon underlying principles and interpretative techniques which 'flesh out' the scope of the rights to give them meaning in the context of individual cases. The domestic approach to the principles discussed below is considered in Chapter 4.

---

[2] See, eg *Sidabras v Lithuania* [2004] ECHR 55480/00; *R (Limbuela) v Secretary of State for the Home Department* [2005] UKHL 66, [2006] 1 AC 396.

[3] *Airey v Ireland* (1979) 2 EHRR 305, para 26.

[4] Established in 1954.

[5] Established in 1959.

[6] Note that Protocol 14 to the Convention, which came into force on 1 June 2010, empowers the Committee of Ministers to ask the ECtHR to interpret a final judgment if it encounters difficulties in doing so when supervising its execution. In order to further the aim of rapid execution of judgments, Protocol 14 also allows the Committee of Ministers to decide, in exceptional circumstances and with a two-thirds majority, to initiate proceedings of non-compliance in the Grand Chamber of the ECtHR in order to make the state concerned execute the Court's initial judgment.

B. INTERPRETING THE CONVENTION

The interpretative principles set out below should not be treated in isolation, with one   2.07
given more importance than another—they are part of a single, complex jurisprudential
exercise to ensure that the 'object and purpose' of the Convention are fulfilled.

1. 'Object and purpose'

The Convention is an international treaty and as such should be interpreted in accord-   2.08
ance with Articles 31–33 of the Vienna Convention on the Law of Treaties 1969 (the
Vienna Convention). Article 31(1) states:

A treaty shall be interpreted in good faith in accordance with the ordinary meaning to be given to
the terms of the treaty in their context and in light of its object and purpose.[7]

The Convention is intended to be interpreted purposively, that is, to give effect to its   2.09
central purposes. The text, preamble, annexes, and related agreements and instruments
of the contracting states are relevant to determining what these are.[8] The ECtHR has
held that the 'objects and purpose' of the Convention include:

(a) the 'maintenance and further realization of human rights and fundamental free-
    doms'[9] and the 'protection of individual human rights'.[10] The effective protection of
    the rights of the individual has been described by the ECtHR as the 'overriding
    function of this Convention';[11]

(b) the promotion of the ideals and values of a democratic society,[12] which supposes
    'pluralism, tolerance and broadmindedness'[13] so as to achieve a balance between
    individual and group interests which 'ensures the fair and proper treatment of
    minorities and avoids any abuse of a dominant position';[14]

(c) the rule of law.[15]

As the essence of the Convention is to protect the fundamental rights of persons from   2.10
violation by contracting parties, limitations or qualifications of the rights set out in the
Convention are to be narrowly construed.[16] The ECtHR will try to:

. . . seek the interpretation that is most appropriate in order to realize the aim and achieve the
object of the treaty; not that which would restrict to the greatest possible degree the obligations
undertaken by the parties.[17]

---

[7] See also Vienna Convention, Art 33(4).
[8] Vienna Convention, Art 31(2).
[9] Preamble to the Convention.
[10] *Soering v UK* (1989) 11 EHRR 439.
[11] *Austria v Italy* (1961) 4 YB 116, para 138.
[12] *Kjeldsen, Busk Madsen and Pedersen v Denmark* (1979) 1 EHRR 711.
[13] *Handyside v UK* (1976) 1 EHRR 737.
[14] *Young, James and Webster v UK* (1982) 4 EHRR 38.
[15] Preamble to the Convention; *Golder v UK* (1979) 1 EHRR 524, para 35; *Klass v Germany* (1978)
2 EHRR 379, para 55; *Salabiaku v France* (1988) 13 EHRR 379, para 28; *Gorraiz Lizarraga v Spain* App
No 62543/00, 10 November 2004, para 64.
[16] *Sunday Times v UK* (1979) 2 EHRR 245, para 65.
[17] *Wemhoff v Germany* (1968) 1 EHRR 55, para 8.

2. Effectiveness principle

2.11   The Convention is intended to guarantee rights that are not merely 'theoretical and illusory' but 'practical and effective'.[18] The ECtHR is concerned with the reality of the individual's position and will 'look behind appearances and examine the realities of the procedure in question'.[19]

2.12   In order for some rights to provide 'effective' protection in accordance with the 'object and purpose' of the Convention, it may be necessary to read an element into a right that is not expressly provided for. An example of reading in these 'implied rights' can be found in the ECtHR's interpretation of Article 6 in *Golder v UK*.[20] In that case a prisoner complained that he could not get to court at all—a right not expressly contained in the text of Article 6. The ECtHR considered that to interpret Article 6 as merely providing procedural guarantees in the course of existing proceedings would enable contracting parties to remove the jurisdiction of the courts in relation to certain claims and thus undermine the protection of the right. To correct this, the ECtHR held that the right of access to the courts constituted 'an element which is inherent in the right stated by Article 6(1)'.[21]

2.13   The ECtHR has also recognized that in order to secure truly effective protection, certain rights must be read as imposing obligations on the state to take action to ensure that they are protected. This doctrine of positive obligations is considered more fully at paras 2.32 to 2.39 below.

3. Autonomous concepts

2.14   Some specific Convention terms are 'autonomous', in the sense of having a particular meaning defined by the ECtHR, and the concepts they contain may go beyond their ordinary or domestic meaning. This is necessary both so that there is uniformity of meaning and understanding across the different national legal systems of the parties to the Convention, and to protect human rights from the possibility of being undermined by manipulation of terms by contracting states.

2.15   Examples of these autonomous concepts include the free-standing definitions of 'criminal charge' and 'civil rights and obligations' under Article 6. The ECtHR has created its own classification criteria for these concepts. These criteria are not solely dependent on the classification determined by the domestic law of the respondent country. Without this 'autonomous concepts' doctrine a state could, without breaching Article 6, exercise arbitrary power and act in a manner repugnant to the rule of law: it could 'do away with its courts, or take away their jurisdiction to determine certain classes of civil actions and entrust to it organs dependent on the Government'.[22] Other concepts, such as 'private life' and 'family life', have developed incrementally since 1950 to ensure that the protection offered by the Convention is 'effective'. Further consideration of these terms is found in Chapter 6.

---

[18] *Marckx v Belgium* (1979) 2 EHRR 330, para 31; *Artico v Italy* (1981) 3 EHRR 1, para 33.
[19] *Deweer v Belgium* (1980) 2 EHRR 439.
[20] (1979) 1 EHRR 524.
[21] Ibid, para 35.
[22] *Golder v UK* (1979) 1 EHRR 524, para 35; cited by Lord Hoffmann in *Runa Begum v Tower Hamlets* [2003] UKHL 5, [2003] 2 AC 430 at [29].

The 'autonomous concepts' doctrine has become important in English law, some-   2.16
times in stopping domestic courts from artificially cutting down the scope of a
Convention article.[23] However, the 'autonomous concepts' doctrine has also been used
to prevent the Human Rights Act from becoming a mechanism for a more expansive
interpretation of the scope of Convention rights than that afforded by the Strasbourg
organs.[24]

4. Dynamic interpretation

The Convention is not to be interpreted as it would have been by those who drafted it   2.17
60 years ago. It is a 'living instrument which must be interpreted in the light of present-
day conditions'.[25] As such its meaning will develop over time and new case law will
develop in an organic way without old case law being specifically overruled. Thus, when
an English court is considering the meaning and effect of a decision of the ECmHR
or the ECtHR, it must nevertheless interpret the Convention by the standards of society
today, and not those when the Convention was drafted or when older cases were
decided.

The case law surrounding the Article 8 rights of transsexuals provides a good example   2.18
of the 'growth' of the Convention to accommodate changing social attitudes. In *Rees v
UK*[26] the ECtHR considered that the rule that a transsexual could not alter her birth
certificate to reflect her gender reassignment did not, by the standards of the mid-1980s,
contravene Article 8. But it was conscious of the seriousness of the problems and distress
faced by people in that situation and stated:

> The Convention has always to be interpreted and applied in the light of the current circumstances.
> The need for appropriate legal measures should therefore be kept under review having regard
> particularly to the scientific and societal developments.[27]

Having followed its decision in *Rees* in a number of cases,[28] the ECtHR changed tack   2.19
in *Goodwin v UK*[29] and held that in present conditions, the lack of legal recognition of
the applicant's new gender did result in a violation of Article 8. The ECtHR stated
that:

> It is of crucial importance that the Convention is interpreted and applied in a manner which
> renders its rights practical and effective, not theoretical and illusory. A failure by the Court to

---

[23] See, eg *Han v Commissioners of Customs and Excise; Martins v Commissioners of Customs and Excise* [2001]
EWCA Civ 1040, [2001] 4 All ER 687.
[24] *Secretary of State for Work and Pensions v M* [2006] UKHL 11, [2006] 2 AC 91 (though note that
the ECtHR subsequently disagreed with the House of Lords on what the ambit of Art 1 of Protocol 1 and
Art 8 were in *JM v UK* App No 37060/06, 28 September 2010); *R v Briggs-Price* [2009] UKHL 19, [2009]
1 WLR 1101. See, to the same effect, *R (A) v London Borough of Croydon* [2009] UKSC 8, [2009] 1 WLR
2557 at [64].
[25] *Tyrer v UK* (1978) 2 EHRR 1, para 31; *Johnson v Ireland* (1986) 9 EHRR 203, para 53.
[26] (1987) 9 EHRR 56.
[27] Ibid, para 47.
[28] See *Cossey v UK* (1990) 13 EHRR 622; *Sheffield and Horsham v UK* (1998) 27 EHRR 163.
[29] (2002) 35 EHRR 18.

maintain a dynamic and evolutive approach would indeed risk rendering it a bar to reform or improvement.[30]

There are, however, limits to the extent to which the ECtHR is willing to interpret the Convention in the light of changing social attitudes. In *Schalk and Kopf v Austria*,[31] for instance, the ECtHR refused to accept that Article 12 protected the right to same-sex marriage.

5. Recourse to other human rights instruments

2.20   In interpreting the Convention, account is to be taken of 'any relevant rules of international law applicable in the relations between the parties'.[32] The ECtHR has regularly cited the Vienna Convention, holding that the Convention 'cannot be interpreted in a vacuum' and 'should, so far as possible be interpreted in harmony with other rules of international law of which it forms part'.[33]

2.21   Increasingly, the ECtHR takes into account relevant international law rules when interpreting the Convention. For example, in *T and V v UK*[34] the ECtHR relied in part on the UN Convention on the Rights of the Child (UNCRC) and the Standard Minimum Rules for the Administration of Juvenile Justice ('Beijing Rules') to find that the UK's procedures for trying children charged with serious crimes did not enable the defendants to participate fully and effectively in the trial process and so violated their Article 6 rights to a fair trial. Similarly, in *S and Marper v UK*, the ECtHR drew on the UNCRC in condemning the indefinite retention of children's DNA on the UK police database.[35] The ECtHR has begun to cite the EU Charter of Fundamental Rights,[36] and it has also referred to the European Social Charter, which enshrines a right to strike.[37]

2.22   Broadly, Council of Europe instruments such as Conventions and Resolutions of the Parliamentary Assembly, the European Social Charter, and separate European Union materials may be relevant.[38] In addition, UN human rights instruments such as the International Covenant on Civil and Political Rights, the Convention on the Elimination of all Forms of Racial Discrimination, and other standards and 'general comments' from the human rights bodies of the UN have been used to help determine the scope of fundamental human rights.[39]

---

[30] Ibid, para 74. For a more sceptical view of the Convention as a 'living instrument', see Baroness Hale, 'The Limits of the Evolutive Interpretation of the Convention', speech given at the opening of the ECtHR's judicial year, 28 January 2011: <http://www.echr.coe.int/NR/rdonlyres/D4E2008C-FBAE-432A-AF4D-BF862D69035A/0/20110128_SEMINAIRE_Discours_Baroness_Hale_EN.pdf>.

[31] App No 30141/04, 24 June 2010.

[32] Vienna Convention, Art 31(3)(c).

[33] *Al-Adsani v UK* (2001) 34 EHRR 273, para 55; *Al-Saadoon v UK* App No 61498/08, 2 March 2010, para 126.

[34] (2000) 30 EHRR 121.

[35] (2008) 25 BHRC 557, para 124. For an example of the domestic courts referring to the UNCRC, see *R (Williamson) v Secretary of State for Education and Employment* [2005] UKHL 15, [2005] 2 WLR 590 at [80] per Baroness Hale.

[36] See, eg *Schalk and Kopf v Austria* (cited above).

[37] *Demir and anor v Turkey* [2009] IRLR 766.

[38] For a detailed examination of the interrelationship between EU law and the Convention, see ch 5.

[39] See, eg *Sejdic and Finci v Bosnia and Herzegovina* App Nos 27996/06 and 34836/06, 22 December 2009, paras 19 and 43.

6. Jurisdiction

The basis for the jurisdictional scope of the Convention is found in Article 1, which   2.23
provides that states 'shall secure to everyone within their jurisdiction the rights and freedoms defined in Section 1 of this Convention'. The meaning of the phrase 'within their
jurisdiction' has been considered by the Grand Chamber of the ECtHR in the leading cases
of *Bankovic v Belgium*,[40] and, very recently, *Al-Skeini v UK*.[41] The Court considered that
jurisdiction should be interpreted in accordance with the principles of public international
law, which holds that states are ordinarily only responsible for acts and omissions in their
national territory. However, it accepted that there were certain, limited situations in which
a state may be responsible for acts or omissions occurring outside its territory. The first is
where a contracting state, through its agents, exercises control and authority over an individual.[42] The second situation is where one contracting state is occupied by the armed
forces of another: the occupying state should be held accountable for breaches of human
rights within the occupied territory, for otherwise there would be a 'vacuum' of protection
within the 'Convention legal space'. This does not mean, however, that jurisdiction under
Article 1 can never exist outside the territory covered by the Council of Europe Member
States.[43] The third situation, confirmed to exist in *Al-Skeini*, concerns acts carried out in the
territory of a non-contracting state which is under the 'effective control' of a contracting
state as a consequence of military action. In *Al-Skeini*, the Court held that the Convention
was engaged in relation to the killing of Iraqi citizens by UK army personnel in security
operations near Basra, which was part of Iraq over which the UK had assumed responsibility
for the maintenance of security following the removal from power of the Ba'ath regime.[44]

Notably, Article 1 is not incorporated into English law under the Human Rights Act.   2.24
The domestic approach to extraterritoriality (which now needs to be read in the light of
Al-Skeini v UK) is considered in Chapter 4[45] and Chapter 6.[46]

C. THE SCOPE OF CONVENTION RIGHTS

1. Absolute, limited, and qualified rights

In broad terms, Convention rights may be placed into three categories: 'absolute' rights   2.25
capable of no derogation; rights which are expressly or impliedly limited; and rights
which are expressly qualified. This is not a precise taxonomy but a way of understanding
the nature and structure of the Convention rights.

(a) *Absolute rights*

Absolute rights under the Convention include the right to life under Article 2 (except in   2.26
respect of deaths resulting from lawful acts of war), the prohibition on torture under
Article 3, the prohibition on slavery and servitude under Article 4(1), and the right not

---

[40] (2007) 44 EHRR SE5.
[41] App No 55721/07, 7 July 2011.
[42] See, eg *Soering v UK* (1989) 11 EHRR 439.
[43] *Al-Skeini v UK*, App No 55721/07, 7 July 2011, para 142.
[44] Ibid, para 149.
[45] See ch 4, paras 4.101–4.103.
[46] See ch 6, paras 6.04–6.08.

to be subjected to retrospective criminal offences under Article 7(1).[47] No derogations from these articles are permitted under Article 15 and there are no circumstances in which infringements of these rights can be justified in the public interest.

2.27 The power of absolute rights was illustrated in *Chahal v UK* in which the ECtHR was asked to consider the UK's attempt to expel a suspected Sikh terrorist despite the real risk of his being subjected to torture in the receiving country.[48] The ECtHR held that, despite the national security threat posed by the applicant, 'the Convention prohibits in absolute terms torture or inhuman or degrading treatment or punishment irrespective of the victim's conduct'.[49] If a claimant can prove on the balance of probabilities that the state has acted in violation of an absolute right, the state is not entitled to mount a justification of its conduct. This principle has come under sustained attack from the British Government (and the tabloid press). The Government intervened in *Saadi v Italy* to attempt to change the ECtHR's view of absolute rights, but the ECtHR reiterated the traditional principles in forceful terms.[50]

(b) *Limited rights*

2.28 Limited rights include Article 5 (right to liberty and security of the person), Article 6 (fair trial rights), Article 12 (right to marry and found a family), Protocol 1, Article 2 (right to an education), and Protocol 1, Article 3 (right to free elections). These rights can be restricted in explicit and finite circumstances as set out in the article itself, or may be subject to restrictions implied by the ECtHR.[51]

2.29 Restrictions have been implied into the right to education under Article 2 of Protocol 1[52] and into fair trial rights (in addition to the express limitations set out in Article 6).[53] However, any limitations are to be construed narrowly, as a wide interpretation 'would entail consequences incompatible with the notion of the rule of law from which the whole Convention draws its inspiration'.[54] In *Ashingdane v UK* the ECtHR held that the right of access to the court may be subject to restrictions, but that any limitation 'will not be compatible with Article 6(1) if it does not pursue a legitimate aim and if there is not a reasonable relationship of proportionality between the means employed and the aim sought to be achieved'.[55] Thus, implied restrictions will be subject to the general principles applicable to the qualified rights (discussed below at para 2.41).

(c) *Qualified rights*

2.30 The 'qualified rights' are those that include a general qualification provision in the second paragraph of the article. They are the rights that most obviously raise the conflicts with

---

[47] The right to hold a religion or belief under Art 9(1) is sometimes considered absolute, but Art 9 can be derogated from under Art 15. See ch 7, para 7.547.

[48] (1996) 23 EHRR 413.

[49] Ibid, para 78.

[50] (2008) 24 BHRC 123. The Government's response to the ECtHR's case law has been to seek assurances concerning deportees from states where torture is known to be endemic. These assurances have been challenged before the domestic courts: see in particular *RB (Algeria) v Secretary of State for the Home Department* [2009] UKHL 10, [2009] 2 WLR 512.

[51] See the discussion of the controversial 'inherent limitations' doctrine in Clayton and Tomlinson, *The Law of Human Rights*, 2nd edn (Oxford: Oxford University Press, 2009) 377–81.

[52] See, eg *Sahin v Turkey* (2007) 44 EHRR 5, para 154.

[53] See, eg *Golder v UK* (1975) 1 EHRR 524.

[54] *Engel v Netherlands* (1976) 1 EHRR 647, para 69.

[55] (1985) 7 EHRR 528.

the overall interests of society or the rights of others—for example, the right to respect for private life (Article 8), freedom of thought, conscience, and religion (Article 9), freedom of expression (Article 10), freedom of assembly and association (Article 11), and the right to the enjoyment of possessions (Protocol 1, Article 1).

'Qualified rights' are usually set out in two parts in the text of the Convention. The   2.31
first paragraph of the article sets out the substantive right, and it is then qualified in the second paragraph. The precise terms of the limitations vary (contrast, for example, Article 10(2) with Article 8(2)), but a restriction will be compatible with the Convention only if it meets the general principles applicable to all restrictions on rights, namely it is 'in accordance with the law'; the interference is directed towards an identified legitimate aim; and the aim is 'necessary in a democratic society' (which encompasses the test of 'pressing social need' and proportionality). These general principles are considered in detail at paras 2.40–2.68 below.

2. Positive obligations

The principal purpose of the Convention is to protect individual rights from infringe-   2.32
ment by states, and this is achieved by the imposition of so-called 'negative' obligations on the states, which require them to refrain from interference with the rights in question. However, the wording of certain articles also imposes positive duties on the state, such as the obligation under Protocol 1, Article 3 to hold free elections. In addition to these express positive obligations, the ECtHR has recognized that there is a broader need for positive steps to be taken by the state to provide the legal or institutional structures or resources to protect human rights—for example, to provide laws which prevent private parties from infringing individual rights, to provide proper institutional protection from domestic violence, or to provide free legal assistance in criminal cases under Article 6(3)(c), or to enable access to institutions to provide education under Protocol 1, Article 2.

The ECtHR has expressly declined to develop any 'general theory' of positive obliga-   2.33
tions, and thus attempts to extract key principles from the jurisprudence of the ECtHR in order to locate positive obligations in a coherent legal framework have been subject to some controversy.[56] It is, however, accepted that the legal basis for reading the Convention in a way which imposes positive obligations is found in a combination of: the overarching duty on states in Article 1 'to secure to everyone within their jurisdiction' the rights and freedoms set out in the Convention; express wording in some articles (for example, the right to life 'shall' be protected by law); the principle set out in Convention case law that protection of rights is intended to be 'practical and effective' not merely theoretical; and the right to an adequate remedy for arguable breaches of Convention rights under Article 13.

Starmer has argued that there are five main positive duties under the Convention: 2.34

(a) a duty to have in place a legal framework which provides effective protection for Convention rights;

(b) a duty to prevent breaches of Convention rights;

---

[56] See Mowbray, *The Development of Positive Obligations under the European Convention on Human Rights by the European Court of Human Rights* (London: Hart Publishing, 2004).

(c) a duty to provide information and advice relevant to a breach of Convention rights;

(d) a duty to respond to breaches of Convention rights; and

(e) a duty to provide resources to individuals to prevent breaches of their Convention rights.[57]

2.35   The types of legal and administrative measures that the ECtHR has held are necessary to fulfil these duties vary according to the article in issue. For example, Article 2 provides that the right to life 'shall be protected by law', and this has been interpreted as an obligation on the state to:

> . . . secure the right to life by putting in place effective criminal law provisions to deter the commission of offences against the person, backed up by law enforcement machinery for the prevention, suppression and sanctioning of breaches of such provisions.[58]

Although the ECtHR has drawn back slightly from this position in recent cases, it is still accurate to say that not only is the state required to adopt an adequate system of law to deter and punish individuals guilty of violating the Convention rights of others, but it is also recognized that the police[59] and other relevant public bodies[60] can be under a positive obligation to take reasonable operational measures to prevent a violation of individuals' rights under Articles 2 and 3.

2.36   In cases under Article 8, the ECtHR recognizes that access to relevant information can help individuals to protect their Convention rights. In *Guerra v Italy*[61] the ECtHR established that, on the specific facts of the case, the respondent state was under a positive obligation to provide information to the applicants who lived near a 'high risk' chemical factory and were very likely to be adversely affected by environmental pollution. In *McGinley and Egan v UK*[62] the ECtHR held that when a government engages in hazardous activities, such as nuclear testing, which might have hidden adverse effects on the health of those involved, 'Article 8 requires that an effective and accessible procedure be established which enables persons to seek all relevant and appropriate information'.[63]

2.37   When determining whether or not a positive obligation exists, the ECtHR will have regard to 'the fair balance that has to be struck between the general interest of the community and the interests of the individual, the search for which balance is inherent in the whole of the Convention'.[64]

2.38   A number of factors may have a bearing on the extent of any positive obligation, including whether the right in question is broadly or narrowly defined; whether essential aspects of a right are at issue; the extent of any burden that may be imposed on the state;

---

[57] Starmer, 'Positive Obligations under the Convention', in Jowell and Cooper (eds), *Understanding Human Rights Principles* (London: Hart Publishing/JUSTICE, 2001).

[58] *Osman v UK* (2000) 29 EHRR 245.

[59] Ibid.

[60] See, eg local authorities in *Z v UK* (2002) 34 EHRR 3.

[61] (1998) 26 EHRR 357.

[62] (1999) 27 EHRR 1.

[63] Ibid, para 101. See also *Taskin v Turkey* (2006) 42 EHRR 50; *Fadeyeva v Russia* [2005] ECHR 55723/00; *Öneryildiz v Turkey* (2004) 18 BHRC 145.

[64] *Goodwin v UK* (2002) 35 EHRR 18.

and the uniformity of views or practices in other contracting states.[65] However, one of the most important factors taken into consideration by the ECtHR is the severity of the effect of the omission on the applicants' rights (particularly their fundamental rights such as those protected by Articles 2 and 3, or their intimate rights such as those of 'private and family life' protected under Article 8). The more serious the effect, the more likely it is that the state will be obliged to prevent or remedy it.

In a series of recent cases, the ECtHR has developed a duty under Article 8 in certain circumstances not to deprive a person of the home he or she already has, even where in domestic law no duty to supply him/her with one exists.[66] In *Mosley v UK*, however, the ECtHR found that the United Kingdom was not under a positive obligation to put in place a system requiring the pre-notification of articles to the subject of them.[67] Much therefore depends on the facts and on the margin of appreciation given to the state in any particular case.[68] 2.39

D. RESTRICTING CONVENTION RIGHTS

The Convention seeks to balance the rights of the individual against other public inter- 2.40 ests, but the object of human rights jurisprudence in democratic systems is not simple majoritarian rule. The rule of law is also required to ensure that democracy does not mean that the tyranny of the majority causes disproportionate interference with the rights of minorities. Once a complaint has been shown to infringe a limited or qualified right, the Strasbourg institutions consider the justification advanced by the state in order to determine whether there has been a violation.

The Convention seeks to ensure that the limitations placed upon an individual's pro- 2.41 tected rights, in the name of the common or competing interests, are imposed only if they are:

(a) prescribed by law; and

(b) intended to achieve a legitimate objective; and

(c) 'necessary in a democratic society' (which incorporates the vital requirement of proportionality).

These general principles govern all restrictions on rights, regardless of precise terms of the article and whether it is limited or qualified.

1. Legality

The rule of law is at the heart of the Convention. It is described in the Preamble as 2.42 part of the 'common heritage' that the signatories share, and is one of the 'fundamental

---

[65] See the discussion in Clayton and Tomlinson, *The Law of Human Rights*, 2nd edn (Oxford: Oxford University Press, 2009), 364–9.

[66] *Connors v UK* (2005) 40 EHRR 9; *McCann v UK* (2008) EHRR 47; *Kay v UK* App No 37341/06, 21 September 2010.

[67] *Mosley v UK* App No 48009/08, 10 May 2011.

[68] See chs 6, 7, and 8 for a more detailed discussion of positive obligations arising under particular articles of the Convention.

principles of a democratic society'.[69] No interference with a right protected under the Convention is permissible unless the citizen is able to ascertain the legal basis for the interference. In the absence of such detailed authorization by the law, any interference, however justified, will violate the Convention. In Strasbourg jurisprudence, a derogation must also have an ascertainable legal basis.

2.43   The legal basis for a measure naturally includes statute law, but the ECtHR has ruled that secondary legislation,[70] applicable rules of EU law,[71] the common law,[72] and even rules of a professional body[73] may be sufficient if validly made and available to those bound by them.

2.44   In addition to being formally prescribed by law, the law itself must fulfil the substantive requirement that it have the appropriate 'qualities' to make it compatible with the rule of law.[74] The ECtHR explained this concept in *Sunday Times v UK*:

> Firstly, the law must be adequately accessible: the citizens must be able to have an indication that is adequate in the circumstances of the legal rules applicable to a given case. Secondly, a norm cannot be regarded as a 'law' unless it is formulated with sufficient precision to enable the citizen to regulate his conduct.[75]

2.45   The accessibility rule is intended to counter arbitrary power by providing that a restriction cannot be justified, even if it is authorized in domestic law, unless the applicable law is published in a form accessible to those likely to be affected by it. Internal guidelines from government departments or agencies probably do not fulfil the accessibility requirement unless they are published or their content made known.[76]

2.46   The certainty rule is intended to enable individuals likely to be affected by a restriction on their rights to understand the circumstances in which any such restriction may be imposed, and to enable such individuals to foresee with a reasonable degree of accuracy the consequences of their actions.[77] Where the state covertly monitors its citizens it is still required to adhere to minimum safeguards to ensure that it does not wield its power arbitrarily.[78]

2.47   For instance, in *Liberty v UK* the Court found that the law regulating the system of interception of telephone calls between the United Kingdom and Ireland did not 'indicate with reasonable clarity the scope and manner of exercise of the relevant discretion conferred on the public authorities'.[79] And in *Gillan and Quinton v UK*, the Court found that the 'stop and search' powers under the Terrorism Act 2000, which gave the police extremely broad discretion both to authorize searches and to decide to carry them

---

[69] *Iatridis v Greece* App No 31107/96, 25 March 1999, para 62. See also *R (Gillan) v Commissioner of the Police for the Metropolis* [2006] UKHL 12, [2006] 2 AC 307 at [34].
[70] *Barthold v Germany* (1985) 7 EHRR 383.
[71] See *Groppera Radio AG v Switzerland* (1990) 12 EHRR 321.
[72] *Sunday Times v UK* (1979) 2 EHRR 245.
[73] *Barthold v Germany* (1985) 7 EHRR 383.
[74] See *Kopp v Sweden* (1999) 27 EHRR 91, paras 55 and 64.
[75] (1979) 2 EHRR 245, para 49.
[76] *Govell v UK* [1999] EHRLR 121.
[77] *Silver v UK* (1983) 5 EHRR 347.
[78] *Weber and Saravia v Germany* [2006] ECHR 54934/00.
[79] (2009) 48 EHRR 1, para 69; see also *Kennedy v UK* App No 26839/05, 18 May 2010, paras 155–170.

out, were neither sufficiently circumscribed nor subject to adequate legal safeguards against abuse; they were therefore not 'in accordance with the law'.[80]

The degree of certainty required will depend on the facts of the case, but it is clear that the ECtHR does not require absolute certainty. In *Sunday Times v UK* the ECtHR said that: 2.48

> Whilst certainty is highly desirable, it may bring in its train excessive rigidity and the law must be able to keep pace with changing circumstances. Accordingly, many laws are inevitably couched in terms which, to a greater or lesser extent, are vague and whose interpretation and application are questions of practice.[81]

Applying this principle, the ECtHR accepted that the common law relating to contempt of court was formulated with sufficient precision to satisfy the requirements of the Convention.[82]

In *Wingrove v UK*[83] and *Müller v Switzerland*,[84] cases involving freedom of expression, the ECtHR accepted that the concepts of blasphemy and obscenity were not capable of precise definition, emphasizing 'the impossibility of attaining absolute precision in the framing of laws . . . in fields in which the situation changes according to the prevailing views of society'.[85] The requirement of legal certainty is thus more flexible in relation to laws whose subject matter touches 'areas of sensitive judgment where public opinion may shift'.[86]   2.49

2. Legitimate aim

Any interference by a public authority with a Convention right capable of limitation must be directed towards an identified legitimate aim. Without such a legitimate aim there can be no justification for the interference.   2.50

To establish that an aim exists, the state must show that it was genuinely seeking to advance one or more of the objectives identified in the qualifying paragraphs to the qualified articles, or, in relation to other limited rights, that it was pursuing an acceptable policy goal with regard to the context of the case. In general, the ECtHR and domestic courts accept the aim put forward by the state without a great deal of scrutiny, and it has been suggested that the question of whether there is a 'legitimate aim' for an interference with rights has been dealt with too cursorily.[87]   2.51

In Articles 8, 9, 10, and 11 the legitimate aims are set out in the second part of each article. Examples of aims which are considered 'legitimate' under the Convention are the interests of public safety, national security, the protection of health and morals, and the economic well-being of the country, or the protection of the rights and freedoms of others.   2.52

---

[80] App No 4158/05, 12 January 2010.
[81] (1979) 2 EHRR 245, para 49.
[82] See also *Steel v UK* (1998) 26 EHRR 603. Cf *Hashman and Harrup v UK* (2000) 30 EHRR 241.
[83] (1997) 24 EHRR 1.
[84] (1991) 13 EHRR 212.
[85] Ibid, para 29.
[86] Per Laws LJ in *R (ProLife Alliance) v BBC* [2002] EWCA Civ 297, [2002] 3 WLR 1080 at [24] (the Court of Appeal's decision was reversed by the House of Lords, their Lordships finding that Art 10(1) was not engaged and therefore expressing no opinion on the Court of Appeal's approach to Art 10(2): [2003] UKHL 23, [2004] 1 AC 185).
[87] Gordon, 'Legitimate Aim: A Dimly Lit Road' [2002] EHRLR 421.

The notion of the 'rights and freedoms of others' (in Articles 8, 9, and 11) and the 'reputation and rights of others' (Article 10) is not limited to the rights contained under the Convention. These phrases are capable of including other 'rights' and 'freedoms', including rights enshrined only in national law and rights which are not even known to national law.[88] However, the nature of the right that the state is aiming to protect may go to the separate question of the proportionality of the interference.

2.53   The legitimate aims set out under the qualified rights should be read with Article 18 of the Convention, which provides that 'The restrictions permitted under this Convention to the said rights and freedoms shall not be applied for any purpose other than those for which they have been prescribed'.[89] This is effectively a good faith provision. It is very difficult for applicants to establish that an interference was not in reality pursued for the reason claimed by the state. For example, in *Campbell v UK*[90] a prisoner complained about the authorities opening his correspondence with his lawyer. He argued that the real reason was to assess the contents. The Government claimed that the interference was for the purposes of the prevention of disorder or crime. While finding that there had been an interference of Article 8, the ECtHR saw no reason to doubt that there had been a legitimate aim for the interference.

3. 'Necessary in a democratic society'

2.54   Where the Convention allows restrictions on rights it not only requires them to be in accordance with law and justified by a legitimate aim, it also requires the interference to be 'necessary in a democratic society'. This phrase incorporates the proportionality standard that determines all permissible restrictions on rights.

2.55   The ECtHR has made clear that the term 'necessary' is not synonymous with 'indispensable', and it is certainly a less stringent test than those that appear elsewhere in the Convention: in Article 2(2) ('absolutely necessary'); Article 6(1) ('strictly necessary'); and Article 15(1) ('to the extent strictly required by the exigencies of the situation').[91]

2.56   Nevertheless, 'necessary in a democratic society' is a rigorous test. In *Handyside v UK* and *Sunday Times v UK* the ECtHR established that the term 'necessary' does not have the 'flexibility of such expressions as "admissible", "ordinary", "useful", "reasonable" or "desirable" [and] it implies the existence of a "pressing social need"'.[92]

2.57   The ECtHR has not developed a consistent set of principles that it uses to assess necessity in every case. However, it set out a three-fold test in *Sunday Times v UK* that is now generally applied in relation to the qualified rights:

(a) whether the interference complained of corresponded to a 'pressing social need'; and

(b) whether it was 'proportionate to the legitimate aim pursued'; and

---

[88] *VgT Verein Gegen Tierfabriken v Switzerland* (2001) 34 EHRR 159, paras 59–62; *Chapman v UK* (2001) 33 EHRR 399, paras 80–82; see *also R (Craven) v Secretary of State for the Home Department* [2001] 2 Cr App R 181.

[89] See, eg *Refah Partisi (The Welfare Party) v Turkey* (2003) 37 EHRR 1.

[90] (1992) 15 EHRR 137.

[91] *Handyside v UK* (1976) 1 EHRR 737, para 48.

[92] *Handyside v UK* (1976) 1 EHRR 737, para 48; *Sunday Times v UK* (1979) 2 EHRR 245, para 59.

(c) whether the reasons given by the national authority to justify it were 'relevant and sufficient'.[93]

When addressing limited rights, the Court may apply this test in full or simply ask whether the measures taken by the state were proportionate. Each aspect of the *Sunday Times* test is considered in turn below.

(a) *Pressing social need*

A 'pressing social need' must accord with the requirements of a democratic society, which supposes 'pluralism, tolerance and broadmindedness'.[94] In assessing whether there is a 'pressing social need' in play, the ECtHR pays close regard to the importance of the relevant right. A very powerful need will be required if there is an interference with a right—or an aspect of a right—which the ECtHR considers to be particularly important. The 'pressing social need' that the state must show in order to justify an interference with an intimate aspect of private life, for example, will be particularly strong.[95]   2.58

A 'pressing social need' is distinct from a legitimate aim. Thus, in *Dudgeon v UK* the ECtHR recognized that one of the purposes of the legislation criminalizing homosexual behaviour was 'to afford safeguards for vulnerable members of society, such as the young, against the consequences of homosexual practices' and accepted that this was then a legitimate aim. However, it went on to say that: 2.59

It cannot be maintained in these circumstances that there is a 'pressing social need' to make such acts criminal offences, there being no sufficient justification provided by the risk of harm to vulnerable sections of society requiring protection or by the effects on the public.[96]

In contrast, the ECtHR will generally accept the existence of a pressing social need where the state asserts national security considerations[97] or threats to the stability of its democratic institutions of the state.[98]   2.60

(b) *Proportionality*

Proportionality is at the heart of the necessity test. Indeed, it has been called the 'dominant theme underlying the whole of the Convention'.[99] As the ECtHR put it in *Soering v UK*:   2.61

Inherent in the whole of the Convention is a search for the fair balance between the demands of the general interest of the community and the requirements of the protection of the individual's human rights.[100]

Proportionality is a principle that helps strike that 'fair balance'. It requires a reasonable relationship between the goal pursued and the means the state has chosen to achieve   2.62

---

[93] *Sunday Times v UK* (1979) 2 EHRR 245, para 59.
[94] *Handyside v UK* (1976) 1 EHRR 737.
[95] *Dudgeon v UK* (1981) 4 EHRR 149.
[96] Ibid, para 60.
[97] See, eg *Leander v Sweden* (1987) 9 EHRR 433.
[98] See, eg *Refah Partisi (The Welfare Party) v Turkey* (2003) 37 EHRR 1.
[99] Reid, *A Practitioner's Guide to the European Convention on Human Rights*, 3rd edn (London: Sweet & Maxwell, 2008), para I-066.
[100] (1989) 11 EHRR 439, para 89.

that goal.[101] This means that even if a policy which interferes with a Convention right might be aimed at securing a legitimate aim of social policy, for example the prevention of crime, this will not in itself justify the violation if the means adopted to secure the aim are excessive in the circumstances. In other words, the state must not use a sledgehammer to crack a nut.

2.63   Proportionality arises in a number of different contexts. It is most commonly associated with the balancing exercise the ECtHR adopts in determining claims under Articles 8, 9, 10, and 11—as one element of the 'necessary in a democratic society' test. However, it also arises in other discrete ways in the Convention. It is the yardstick by which the scope of restrictions on implied rights are measured;[102] it is used when determining whether a positive obligation should be imposed on a contracting state;[103] it is the central mechanism for determining whether interferences with property are justified under Protocol 1, Article 1;[104] and it is relevant to the prohibition of discrimination under Article 14.[105]

2.64   Proportionality is not an exact science, and different writers have produced varying formulations of the test.[106] However, it is clear from the case law of the ECtHR that certain general factors are relevant to the ECtHR's proportionality exercise. These include:

(a) the extent to which the interference impairs the 'very essence' of a right, which effectively means a very serious interference.[107] The ECtHR will distinguish between different types of rights arising under the same Convention article. For example, the state will need to adduce particularly weighty reasons to justify an interference with political speech. In contrast, the ECtHR gives greater latitude to the state when assessing interference with commercial speech;[108]

(b) whether the state has adopted a blanket policy that does not permit examination of the merits of individual cases. Thus, in *S and Marper* the ECtHR was particularly concerned by the 'blanket and indiscriminate nature of the power of retention' of the DNA of all those arrested for criminal offences, no matter how minor and regardless of whether the individual was ever charged.[109] A policy that only permits assessment of individual circumstances in 'exceptional' cases may also prove disproportionate;[110]

(c) whether a less-restrictive alternative, yet equally effective, measure is available to the state to achieve the legitimate aim pursued. For example, in *Campbell v UK* the ECtHR held that the blanket opening of all prisoners' mail was disproportionate

---

[101] *Fayed v UK* (1994) 18 EHRR 393, para 71.
[102] See para 2.29 above.
[103] See para 2.38 above.
[104] See ch 8, paras 8.45–8.57.
[105] See ch 7, paras 7.535–7.536.
[106] See the comparison of different approaches in Rivers, 'Proportionality and Variable Intensity of Review' (2006) CLJ 174. See also Hickman, 'The Substance and Structure of Proportionality' (2008) PL 694.
[107] See, eg *Dudgeon v UK* (1981) 4 EHRR 149.
[108] See ch 7, para 7.360.
[109] App Nos 30562/04 and 30566/04, 4 December 2008. See also *O'Donoghue and ors v UK* App No 34848/07, 14 December 2010 (successful challenge to the scheme designed to prevent 'sham' marriages).
[110] *Dickson v UK* (2008) 24 BHRC 19.

because the less intrusive measure of opening only those letters reasonably considered to contain prohibited material would have achieved the same aim;[111]

(d) whether there are any effective safeguards or legal controls over the measures in
question. This includes the adequacy of compensation or legal remedies for those
affected by the measures.[112] In Article 10 cases, the ECtHR will also examine the
opposite question: whether an award of damages for defamation is excessive taking
into account all of the circumstances.[113]

The intensity of the proportionality inquiry will vary according to the right at stake.   2.65
For example, where property rights are in issue the ECtHR will apply less exacting
scrutiny than where there is an interference with the right to privacy or freedom of
expression.[114]

Proportionality also incorporates a concept of procedural fairness. An infringement of   2.66
a qualified right is less likely to be a proportionate response to a legitimate aim if the
person affected by the action was not consulted, or not given the right to a hearing, than
if he or she was given such opportunities. The ECtHR has stated that, 'whilst Article 8
contains no explicit procedural requirements, the decision-making process leading to
measures of interference must be fair and such as to afford due respect to the interests
safeguarded by Article 8'.[115] However, in some cases this guarantee may be redundant as
the stronger procedural protections of Article 6 will apply.

(c) *Relevant and sufficient reasons*

The final element of the 'necessary in a democratic society' test involves the ECtHR's   2.67
assessment of whether the state's reasons for interfering with the right are 'relevant and
sufficient'.[116] This is an objective test. It is not enough that the respondent state has
acted 'reasonably, carefully and in good faith'.[117] The ECtHR will examine the reasons
for the state's actions and determine whether they are adequate. In *Smith and Grady v
UK*[118] and *Lustig-Prean and Beckett v UK*,[119] for example—cases involving a ban on
homosexuals serving in the army—it was not enough for the respondent state simply to
assert that the reason for the ban was 'operational effectiveness' or 'threat to morale'.
Cogent evidence was needed, and the state could not provide it. Where no evidence is
adduced in support of the reasons given for a restriction, a breach of the Convention is
almost inevitable.[120]

The ECtHR adopted a particularly strong approach to reason-giving in *Hirst v UK*,   2.68
in which it held that the state's reasons for banning convicted prisoners from voting were
inadequate.[121] This was despite the lack of consensus in other Member States on this

---

[111] (1992) 15 EHRR 137. See also *Hirst v UK* (2006) 42 EHRR 41.
[112] See, eg *Motais de Narbonne v France* App No 48161/99, 2 July 2002; *Akkus v Turkey* [1997] ECHR
19263/92.
[113] *Steel and Morris v UK* (2005) 41 EHRR 22.
[114] See, eg *Pye v UK* (2008) 46 EHRR 34.
[115] *McMichael v UK* (1995) 20 EHRR 205, para 87.
[116] *Jersild v Denmark* (1995) 19 EHRR 1.
[117] *Olsson (No 1)* (1988) 11 EHRR 259, para 58; *Vogt v Germany* (1995) 21 EHRR 205, para 52.
[118] (1999) 29 EHRR 493, paras 71–112.
[119] (1999) 29 EHRR 548, paras 64–105.
[120] *Autronic AG v Switzerland* (1990) 12 EHRR 485.
[121] (2006) 42 EHRR 41.

issue, and the fact that Parliament had voted for an express ban in a piece of primary legislation. The Grand Chamber stated:

There is no evidence that Parliament has ever sought to weigh the competing interests or to assess the proportionality of a blanket ban on the right of a convicted prisoner to vote . . . [It] cannot be said that there was any substantive debate by members of the legislature on the continued justification in light of modern day penal policy and of current human rights standards for maintaining such a general restriction on the right of prisoners to vote.[122]

4. Restrictions specifically provided for by reservations and derogations

(a) *Reservations*

2.69   Article 57 entitles states to make reservations in respect of rights contained in the Convention. A reservation to an international treaty is a device used by a signatory state to reserve particular policies or law in order to exempt them from challenge under the instrument. They are often used as a temporary measure, which gives states time to bring their laws into line with the requirements of the Convention. Reservations can be made only at the time of signing or ratification and must comply with Article 31(1) of the Vienna Convention on the Law of Treaties, which states:

A treaty shall be interpreted in good faith in accordance with the ordinary meaning to be given to the terms of the treaty in their context and in the light of its objects and purpose.

2.70   A reservation is likely to be invalid if it seeks to circumvent key terms or underlying principles contained within the treaty in question.

2.71   There is currently one reservation by the United Kingdom to the Convention, which pertains to the second sentence of Protocol 1, Article 2 (which requires education to be provided in conformity with parents' religious and philosophical convictions). The United Kingdom has accepted this provision only so far as it is compatible with the provision of efficient instruction and training and the avoidance of unreasonable public expenditure.[123]

2.72   Any reservation must meet the requirements of Article 57(2) of the Convention and not be couched in terms that are too vague or broad for it to be possible to determine their exact scope and meaning.[124]

(b) *Derogations*

2.73   Article 15(1) of the Convention states:

In time of war or other public emergency threatening the life of the nation any High Contracting Party may take measures derogating from its obligations under this Convention to the extent strictly required by the exigencies of the situation, provided that such measures are not inconsistent with its obligations under international law.

---

[122] Ibid, para 79.

[123] The full text of the reservation is set out in Part II of Sch 3 to the Human Rights Act 1998; see App 1.

[124] *Belilos v Switzerland* (1988) 10 EHRR 466. It has been suggested that the reservation might not withstand challenge, given the language used by the United Kingdom: Emmerson and Simor, *Human Rights Practice* (London: Sweet & Maxwell, 2000) para 1.024.

This enables states to restrict the exercise of some of the rights and freedoms without   2.74
violating the Convention. Any derogation must be proportionate to the threat and must
be necessary to deal with the emergency. As a matter of international law, a state, by
lodging a derogation in Strasbourg, can, to the extent that the derogation is lawful under
Article 15, avoid a particular obligation in particular circumstances. Article 15 does not
allow derogations from Article 2 (the right to life), Article 3 (freedom from torture),
Article 4(1) (slavery and servitude), and Article 7 (retrospective criminal penalties).

At the time of writing the United Kingdom has no derogations in place.[125]   2.75

5. Restrictions under Articles 16, 17, and 18

The rights contained in the Convention are subject to express restrictions in three   2.76
specific areas:

(a) Article 16 (restrictions on the political activities of aliens);

(b) Article 17 (restrictions on activities aimed at the destruction of Convention rights);
and

(c) Article 18 (prohibition on using Convention restrictions for an improper
purpose).

The exact scope of these articles is considered in detail in Chapter 7.

E. THE MARGIN OF APPRECIATION

The meaning of the term 'margin of appreciation' is not immediately apparent, originat-   2.77
ing as it does from French administrative law. It has recently been described by Lord
Hoffmann as an 'unfortunate Gallicism'.[126] In essence, it refers to the freedom that a
state is permitted in the manner in which it observes Convention rights.

As Clayton and Tomlinson point out, it fulfils two functions in Convention jurispru-   2.78
dence.[127] First, it establishes 'an interpretative obligation' to respect the varying cultural
traditions of the contracting states. As the Convention is an international human rights
instrument, policed by an international court, the Strasbourg institutions have to be
sensitive to the need for 'subsidiarity', that is, to ensuring that the Member States' own
political and cultural traditions are respected. For example, actions that may offend
religious sensitivities in one country may be a recognized act of free speech in another.
Secondly, the margin of appreciation functions as a standard of review that enables the
ECtHR to take a 'hands-off' approach to certain issues where national authorities are
better placed to make an assessment of proportionality.

The doctrine was developed by the ECtHR in *Handyside v UK*, which concerned the   2.79
publication in England in 1971 of the *Little Red School Book*, which was intended for
children and included a section on sex.[128] The police seized the books and a forfeiture

---

[125] See the discussion of previous derogations in ch 7, paras 7.567–7.578.
[126] 'The Universality of Human Rights', Judicial Studies Board Annual Lecture 2009, available at <http://www.judiciary.gov.uk/training-support/judicial-college/Annual+Lectures>.
[127] *The Law of Human Rights*, 2nd edn (Oxford: Oxford University Press, 2009) 315.
[128] (1976) 1 EHRR 737 (following the ECmHR in *Lawless v Ireland* (1961) 1 EHRR 15).

order was obtained on the grounds that the books contravened the Obscene Publications Act 1959. The applicant claimed a violation of the right to freedom of expression and the Government argued that the restriction was necessary for the purpose of the 'protection of morals'. The Court accepted that the limitation was 'prescribed by law' and thus had to decide whether the limitation in question was proportionate and 'necessary in a democratic society'. The Court stated:

> By reason of their direct and continuous contact with the vital forces of their countries, state authorities are in principle in a better position than the international judge to give an opinion on the extent of these requirements as well as on the 'necessity' of a 'restriction' or 'penalty' intended to meet them.

2.80   Nevertheless, this power of appreciation is not unlimited. Over the years, the Court has developed its case law in this area such that it can be said that the margin of appreciation has become a central element of the ECtHR's method of reasoning. The case law was recently summarized in *S and Marper v UK*[129] as follows:

> A margin of appreciation must be left to the competent national authorities . . . The breadth of this margin varies and depends on a number of factors including the nature of the Convention right in issue, its importance for the individual, the nature of the interference and the object pursued by the interference. The margin will tend to be narrower where the right at stake is crucial to the individual's effective enjoyment of intimate or key rights . . . Where a particularly important facet of an individual's existence or identity is at stake, the margin allowed to the State will be restricted . . . Where, however, there is no consensus within the Member States of the Council of Europe, either as to the relative importance of the interest at stake or as to how best to protect it, the margin will be wider.

2.81   In recent cases, however, this final factor appears to have held less sway. In *Hirst v UK* the ECtHR made clear that the lack of a common European approach to the problem was not in itself determinative of the issue[130] and indicated that certain forms of blanket interference with rights could fall outside the margin of appreciation altogether:

> such a general, automatic and indiscriminate restriction on a vitally important Convention right must be seen as falling outside any acceptable margin of appreciation, however wide that margin might be . . . While the Court reiterates that the margin of appreciation is wide, it is not all-embracing.[131]

2.82   It might be said that the Court often uses the 'margin of appreciation' concept to avoid ruling on acutely sensitive issues which involve an element of political controversy. In *Lautsi v Italy*, for instance, the Grand Chamber (overturning an earlier Chamber decision) held that the decision whether crucifixes should be present in state-school classrooms was, in principle, a matter falling within the margin of appreciation of the respondent state, and that in light of this, the decision did not lead to a form of indoctrination such as to violate Article 2 of Protocol 1 to the Convention.[132] And in *Mosley v UK*, the Court found that whether or not a pre-notification requirement should be

---

[129] (2008) 25 BHRC 557, para 102; for a fuller exposition, see *Mosley v UK* App No 48009/08, 10 May 2011, paras 108–111.
[130] (2006) 42 EHRR 41, para 81.
[131] Ibid, para 82. See also *Dickson v UK* (2008) 24 BHRC 19.
[132] App No 30814/06, 18 March 2011.

imposed on the press to protect a person's privacy fell within the state's margin of appreciation.[133]

In its use as a standard of review, the margin of appreciation is controversial. Many   2.83
commentators consider that the doctrine is applied carelessly and without clear guiding
principles, and suggest that it may be a means of avoiding the proportionality analysis in
difficult cases.[134] A former judge of the Court trenchantly criticized the doctrine for
allowing the Court to evade its responsibility to articulate the reasons why its intervention in particular cases may or may not be appropriate.[135] Lord Hoffmann suggested that
while the ECtHR has failed to enunciate the principles on which the margin of appreciation is based, it has not taken it 'nearly far enough'.[136] According to Lord Hoffmann, it
is 'constitutionally inappropriate' for an international court to determine domestic questions such as the proportionality of landing regulations at Heathrow,[137] and the margin
of appreciation should be enthusiastically employed to delegate proportionality decisions
to national authorities.

As discussed in Chapter 4, the margin of appreciation should not be employed by the   2.84
domestic courts.[138]

---

[133] App No 48009/08, 10 May 2011.
[134] See, eg Lord Lester of Herne Hill QC, 'Universality Versus Subsidiarity: A Reply' [1998] EHRLR 73;
Clayton and Tomlinson, *The Law of Human Rights*, 2nd edn (Oxford: Oxford University Press, 2009)
319–20.
[135] See Macdonald, 'The Margin of Appreciation', in Macdonald, Matscher, and Petzold (eds), *The
European System for the Protection of Human Rights*, 3rd edn (The Hague: Kluwer Law International, 1993).
[136] 'The Universality of Human Rights', Judicial Studies Board Annual Lecture 2009, available at <http://
www.judiciary.gov.uk/training-support/judicial-college/Annual+Lectures>.
[137] *Hatton v UK* (2003) 37 EHRR 28.
[138] See ch 4, paras 4.119–4.130.

3

THE FRAMEWORK OF THE HUMAN RIGHTS ACT

A. Introduction   3.01

B. Summary of the Effects of the Human Rights Act   3.07

C. Overview of the Key Provisions of the Human Rights Act   3.08
    1. Section 1 and Schedule 1—definition of Convention rights   3.09
    2. Section 2—interpretation of Convention rights   3.11
    3. Section 3—interpretation of legislation   3.12
    4. Section 19—statements of compatibility   3.13
    5. Sections 4, 5, 10, and Schedule 2—incompatibility
       of legislation   3.14
    6. Section 6—acts of public authorities   3.15
    7. Section 7—proceedings against public authorities   3.21
    8. Section 8—judicial remedies   3.23
    9. Section 9—judicial acts   3.24
    10. Section 11—safeguard for existing human rights   3.25
    11. Sections 12 and 13—respect for freedoms   3.26
    12. Designated derogations and reservations   3.27

D. The Human Rights Act Mechanism in Detail   3.28
    1. Section 6   3.29
    2. Section 3   3.31
    3. Interplay of sections 3 and 19   3.43
    4. Interplay of sections 3 and 4   3.45
    5. Section 2   3.48
    6. Interplay of sections 2 and 3   3.54

E. Public Authorities and the Human Rights Act: Meaning of
   'Public Authority' and 'Functions of a Public Nature'   3.57
    1. 'Core' public authorities   3.59
    2. 'Functional' public authorities   3.60

F. Private Parties and the Human Rights Act   3.72

G. Exceptions and Special Cases   3.75
    1. Article 13   3.76
    2. Section 12   3.78
    3. Section 13   3.81

A. INTRODUCTION

3.01   The Human Rights Act is a special statute imbued with constitutional significance. It is described in its long title as an Act to give 'further effect' to the rights and freedoms guaranteed under the European Convention for the Protection of Human Rights and Fundamental Freedoms (Convention). The special status of the Human Rights Act has been recognized judicially,[1] academically,[2] and by parliamentarians.[3]

3.02   Since the Human Rights Act came into force it has altered the interpretation and use of the common law and all other legislation in cases involving human rights issues. The overriding objective of the Act is to weave the Convention into the existing legal system, so that all courts will consider Convention arguments, and rights which could have been obtained in Strasbourg can be secured in national courts, while minimizing disruption to the existing legal system. The method adopted, however, is a complex one, reflecting a delicate political compromise between 'incorporating' Convention rights and retaining parliamentary sovereignty.

3.03   The Human Rights Act created a general statutory requirement that all legislation, primary or secondary, whenever enacted, must be read and given effect in a way which is compatible with Convention rights *whenever possible*. This principle of construction, contained in section 3 of the Human Rights Act, requires generous and progressive interpretation to give effect to the purpose of this constitutional statute. If it is not possible to interpret legislation in a compliant way then the higher courts may declare the legislation to be incompatible with the Convention.

3.04   This principle of construction applies to all litigation, whether or not a public authority is involved. It can, therefore, affect the rights of private persons between themselves. But the Human Rights Act does not directly create a new cause of action for 'breach of the Convention' against private bodies.

3.05   However, by virtue of section 6, the Human Rights Act requires public authorities—including courts—to act compatibly with the Convention unless they are prevented from doing so by statute. This means that the courts have their own primary statutory duty to give effect to the Convention unless positively prevented from doing so. Section 7 gives the 'victim' of any act of a public authority which is incompatible with the Convention power to challenge the authority in court using the Convention to found a cause of action or a defence.

3.06   This chapter explains the mechanism of the Human Rights Act, and the effect it has had in proceedings involving public and private authorities. It starts with a very brief summary of the Human Rights Act mechanism, followed by an overview of the key provisions of the Act. The next part contains a more detailed analysis of the main operative provisions of the Act and how they interact. No further explanation of the Act can proceed without the discussion in the following section of what the Act means by the terms 'public authority' and 'functions of a public nature'. The chapter then examines some of the ways in which the Act has been applied in litigation involving private parties.

---

[1] See, eg *R v Offen* [2001] 1 WLR 253, 275 per Lord Woolf; *Thoburn v Sunderland City Council* [2002] EWHC 195 (Admin), [2002] 3 WLR 247 per Laws LJ.

[2] See Jowell and Cooper (eds), *Delivering Rights: How the Human Rights Act is Working* (London: Hart Publishing, 2003) 2.

[3] Constitution Committee, Sixth Report, Session 2006–2007, para 8.

The final section concerns statutory 'special cases'. Procedural issues concerning bringing a claim under the Human Rights Act, key Convention concepts in domestic law, and the remedies available under the Act are discussed in Chapter 4.

B. SUMMARY OF THE EFFECTS OF THE HUMAN RIGHTS ACT

In summary, the wide-reaching effects of the Human Rights Act are as follows.   3.07

(a) In *all* cases in which Convention rights are in question, the Human Rights Act gives 'further effect' to the Convention, whether the litigants are private persons or public authorities. It does this in three ways:
    (i) by obliging courts to decide all cases before them (whether brought under statute or the common law) compatibly with Convention rights unless prevented from doing so either by primary legislation or by provisions made under primary legislation which cannot be read compatibly with the Convention;[4]
    (ii) by placing an obligation upon courts to interpret existing and future legislation in conformity with the Convention wherever possible;[5]
    (iii) by requiring courts to take Strasbourg case law into account in all cases, in so far as they consider it is relevant to proceedings before them.[6]

(b) The Human Rights Act does not make Convention rights *directly* enforceable against a private litigant, nor against a functional public authority (that is, a body which is not obviously public in form but which has some functions of a public nature) if it is acting in a private capacity.[7] But in cases against a private litigant, or functional public authority acting in exercise of its private law functions, the Human Rights Act may still have an effect on the outcome, because the court:
    (i) is obliged to interpret legislation in conformity with the Convention wherever possible;
    (ii) must exercise any judicial discretions compatibly with the Convention; and
    (iii) must ensure that its application of common law or equitable rules is compatible with the Convention.

(c) Section 7 of the Human Rights Act creates directly enforceable rights against public bodies. First, it has introduced a new ground of illegality into proceedings brought by way of judicial review, namely, a failure to comply with the Convention rights protected by the Human Rights Act, subject to a defence that there is a clear statutory obligation to act incompatibly with the Convention. Secondly, it has created a stand-alone cause of action against public bodies that fail to act compatibly with the Convention. Thirdly, Convention rights are available via the Human Rights Act as a ground of defence or appeal in cases brought by public bodies against private persons (in both criminal and civil cases). However, the scope and meaning of 'public

---

[4] Section 6(1)–(3).
[5] Section 3.
[6] Section 2(1).
[7] See paras 3.60–3.71 below.

authority' remains in doubt following the decision of the House of Lords in *YL v Birmingham City Council*.[8]

(d) Section 7 can be used only by 'victims' of violations of the Convention, the term 'victim' being defined in section 7(7). However, even a litigant who is not defined as a 'victim', and so cannot challenge a public authority's decision directly using the provisions of the Human Rights Act, is able to rely on the court's obligation under section 3 of the Human Rights Act to interpret legislation compatibly with the Convention where possible, and to use Convention arguments in the circumstances in which this was possible before the Human Rights Act was brought into force.[9]

(e) The Human Rights Act does not permit the Convention to be used so as to override primary legislation: if a statute is clear in its terms, and clearly incompatible with the Convention, courts must give effect to it. Equally, if the terms of the primary legislation require subordinate legislation made under it (which will usually be in a statutory instrument) to be interpreted in a way which means that the subordinate legislation is incompatible with the Convention, it must still be given effect even though this may result in a breach of a Convention right. To that extent, parliamentary sovereignty is preserved.[10] But if legislation cannot be read so as to comply with the Convention, the higher courts have the power to issue 'declarations of incompatibility', and a fast-track procedure exists whereby the Government can legislate to remedy such incompatibility.[11]

C. OVERVIEW OF THE KEY PROVISIONS OF THE HUMAN RIGHTS ACT

3.08 The Human Rights Act is a short and elegantly drafted piece of legislation. It is nonetheless helpful to approach it schematically rather than simply reading the sections in the order in which they appear.

1. Section 1 and Schedule 1—definition of Convention rights

3.09 After the long title, which states that the Act gives 'further effect' to the rights and freedoms guaranteed under the Convention, section 1 and Schedule 1 define the 'Convention rights', which have been incorporated, subject to any designated derogations or reservations.[12] Article 1 (the obligation on contracting states to the Convention to 'secure' Convention rights to 'everyone within their jurisdiction') and Article 13 (the right to an effective remedy in a national court) are not specifically designated as 'Convention rights' within this definition.

3.10 'The Convention' in this context means 'the Convention . . . as it has effect for the time being in relation to the United Kingdom'.[13] The House of Lords has held that this

---

8 [2007] UKHL 27, [2008] 1 AC 95.
9 Section 11.
10 Section 3(2)(b) and (c).
11 Sections 4, 10, and Sch 2.
12 Section 1(2).
13 Section 21(1).

means that the Convention does not have effect if it is limited or extinguished by some other, overriding provision of international law, such as a UN Security Council Resolution.[14] The effect of the Convention is usually, but not always, territorially limited, so (for example) it covers British military bases but not soldiers when on active service abroad.[15]

2. Section 2—interpretation of Convention rights

Section 2 requires any court or tribunal determining a question that has arisen in connection with a Convention right to 'take into account' the jurisprudence of the Strasbourg organs (the European Court of Human Rights, the Commission of Human Rights, and the Committee of Ministers). This jurisprudence must be considered 'so far as, in the opinion of the court or tribunal, it is relevant to the proceedings in which that question has arisen', whenever the judgment, decision, or opinion to be taken into account was handed down.[16] Section 2 is considered in detail below at para 3.48.

3.11

3. Section 3—interpretation of legislation

Section 3 is the lynchpin of the Act, 'pivotal to [its] operation'.[17] It requires primary and subordinate legislation to be read and given effect in a way which is compatible with Convention rights, 'so far as it is possible to do so', whether the legislation in question was enacted before or after the Human Rights Act. Section 3 is a general requirement, addressed to any person reading the legislation, not just to the courts. This strong interpretative obligation is one of the key provisions in the Human Rights Act. It has had an impact on all types of cases, civil or criminal, public or private, where a Convention right is at stake, because all domestic courts and tribunals are defined as 'public authorities' (under section 6(3)(a)) and must interpret statutory provisions and the common law compatibly with Convention rights wherever possible regardless of other, perhaps more literal, interpretations or precedents to the contrary. Section 3 is dealt with in more detail below at para 3.31.

3.12

4. Section 19—statements of compatibility

Section 19 requires the minister with conduct of any Bill,[18] before its second reading, to either make and publish a 'statement of compatibility',[19] or openly make a statement

3.13

---

[14] *R (Al-Jedda) v Secretary of State for Defence* [2007] UKHL 58, [2008] 1 AC 332 (although see now *Al-Jedda v UK*, App No 27021/08, 7 July 2011). See also *R (Quark Fishing Ltd) v Foreign Secretary* [2005] UKHL 57, [2006] 1 AC 529 at [25], [32], [87], and [97]; and *R (Al-Skeini) v Secretary of State for Defence* [2007] UKHL 26, [2008] 1 AC 153 (although see now *Al-Skeini v UK*, App No 55721/07, 7 July 2011).

[15] *R (Bancoult) v Secretary of State for Foreign and Commonwealth Affairs* [2008] UKHL 61, [2009] 1 AC 453; *R (Smith) v Secretary of State for Defence* [2010] UKSC 29, [2011] 1 AC 1. Although *Smith* is binding in domestic law until overturned by the Supreme Court, its authority is placed in doubt in the light of the ECtHR's very recent judgment in *Al-Skeini v UK*, App No 55721/07, 7 July 2011, discussed at para 4.103.

[16] Section 2(1).

[17] Bradley, 'The Sovereignty of Parliament—Form or Substance?', in Jowell and Oliver (eds), *The Changing Constitution* (Oxford: Oxford University Press, 2007) 37.

[18] There is no such requirement for Private Members' Bills.

[19] Section 19(1)(a).

that although he or she is unable to state that the legislation is compatible with the Convention rights, the Government nevertheless wishes to proceed with the Bill.[20] Section 19 is dealt with in more detail below at para 3.43.

5. Sections 4, 5, 10, and Schedule 2—incompatibility of legislation

3.14 If it is *not* possible to read legislation so as to give effect to the Convention, then that legislation remains in force. The courts cannot, as in some constitutional structures, 'strike it down' as being incompatible with Convention principles. Section 3(2)(b) and (c) of the Act expressly provide that if legislation cannot be read compatibly, this does not affect its validity, continuing operation, or enforcement. Instead, in such circumstances, section 4 empowers the higher courts to express their view that the legislation is not compatible with the Convention by making a 'declaration of incompatibility'. If such a declaration is to be sought, the Crown has a right to be notified, and to intervene, under section 5 of the Act. In circumstances where a court has made a declaration of incompatibility, the Act provides a 'fast track' legislative procedure, by which the executive can act to cure the incompatibility, which is contained in section 10 of, and Schedule 2 to, the Act. These provisions are described in more detail below.

6. Section 6—acts of public authorities

3.15 Section 6 makes it unlawful in most circumstances for a public authority to act in a way which is incompatible with a Convention right. A public authority may only do so if it is required to by primary legislation, or by secondary legislation made under it, which cannot be interpreted compatibly with the Convention. 'Act' in section 6 includes failure to act.[21] This general obligation is very wide, and means that in the exercise of any power or duty, any public body must act in such a way as to give effect to the Convention.

3.16 'Giving effect to the Convention' means more than simply requiring the public authority to avoid violating Convention rights itself. Where a public authority has positive obligations under the Convention, that is, a duty to act in such a way as to protect people from having their Convention rights violated by third parties, then section 6 will also require the public authority to give effect to these.[22] For example, a public authority could violate the right to freedom of association under Article 11 of the Convention, not only by prohibiting a demonstration, but also by failing to police it so as to ensure that demonstrators are not assaulted by violent counter-demonstrators.[23]

3.17 Section 6(1) is limited only in so far as is necessary to preserve the concept of parliamentary sovereignty. First, section 6(2)(a) provides that the duty under section 6(1) to give effect to Convention rights does not apply if the public authority *could not* have acted differently as a result of one or more provisions of primary legislation. Section 6(2)(b) provides that section 6(1) does not apply if the authority was acting to give effect to or to enforce one or more provisions made under primary legislation which cannot be read or given effect in a way which is compatible with the Convention rights.

---

[20] Section 19(1)(b).
[21] Section 6(6).
[22] See ch 2.
[23] *Plattform Artze für das Leben v Austria* (1988) 13 EHRR 204.

Plainly there is some overlap between section 6(2)(a) and (2)(b), both in effect amounting to a 'primary legislation defence', and the House of Lords has recognized this.[24] In practice, section 6(2) is rarely applied.[25] Most powers or duties *can* be read in a way which is compatible with the Convention: and if public authorities do not themselves comply with section 6(1) by reading their powers and duties in a Convention-compliant way, the courts (as public authorities themselves) are under their own duties to find a reading of the legislation which permits the public authority to comply with the Convention if at all possible.

The second limit on the effect of section 6(1) is that Parliament in its legislative capac-   3.18
ity is not a 'public authority'[26] and so is not bound by section 6(1).[27] Thus, even if Parliament has failed to enact legislation which is arguably required in order to give effect to Convention principles, that is not a matter which can be challenged in domestic courts. Though the 'act' of a public authority which can be challenged includes an omission, it does not include a failure to legislate.[28]

Section 6(3)(a) makes courts and tribunals (including the House of Lords in its judi-   3.19
cial capacity)[29] public authorities, and so subject to their own primary duty to act compatibly with the Convention. This is important when considering the effect of the Convention in private litigation, because the courts are themselves subject to a duty to 'give effect' to the Convention in reaching their decisions, if they can.

Public authorities are in a special position under the Human Rights Act, because   3.20
the Convention rights scheduled to the Act can be directly enforced against them. The Convention has also been relevant in determining some cases between private individuals, as well as those between an individual and the state, because as a 'public authority' a court is obliged to act in a way which is compatible with the Convention. This 'horizontal' impact of the Human Rights Act is considered below at paras 3.72–3.74.

7. Section 7—proceedings against public authorities

Section 7 deals with proceedings under the Human Rights Act, both free-standing and   3.21
other proceedings in which the Act is relevant. It may be used only by a person who is or would be a 'victim' of the unlawful act,[30] a term which is analysed in Chapter 4. A 'victim' may rely on Convention rights in two ways in legal proceedings. First, under section 7(1)(a) he or she may bring free-standing proceedings against a public authority which infringes a Convention right 'in the appropriate court or tribunal'. The appropriate forum is determined by the subject matter of the claim and rules made by the Secretary of State concerned or the Lord Chancellor (which also deal with other

---

[24] *R (Hooper) v Secretary of State for Work and Pensions* [2005] UKHL 29, [2005] 1 WLR 1681, where Lord Hoffmann and Lord Hope held that the appropriate defence was s 6(2)(b) and Lord Scott and Lord Brown held that it was s 6(2)(a).

[25] As to the extent and effect of s 6(2), see *Ghaidan v Godin-Mendoza* [2004] UKHL 30, [2004] 2 AC 557; see also *R (GC and C) v Commissioner of Police of the Metropolis* [2011] UKSC 21, [2011] 1 WLR 1230 at [19]–[44].

[26] Section 6(3).

[27] Ibid.

[28] Section 6(6)(a).

[29] Section 6(4).

[30] Section 7(3) and (7).

jurisdictional matters, such as remedies).[31] Section 7(5) imposes a limitation period for bringing free-standing proceedings. Secondly, section 7(1)(b) permits a person to rely on the Convention right or rights concerned in 'any legal proceedings'. Section 22(4) provides that section 7(1)(b) can be used as a defence whenever the act in question took place, but proceedings may be instigated under section 7(1)(a) only in relation to acts committed after the Human Rights Act came into force on 2 October 2000.

3.22   The Human Rights Act creates three ways in which Convention rights can be directly enforced against public authorities:

(a) as a cause of action for breach of statutory duty where a public authority has not acted compatibly with the Convention. For example, a person might argue that a social services authority is in breach of statutory duty because it has violated Article 8 of the Convention (the right to respect for private and family life) in failing to give access to his or her file;[32]

(b) as a head of illegality in judicial review proceedings. For example, it could be argued that a decision to refuse to allow a journalist access to a prisoner was ultra vires because rules contravened Article 10 of the Convention and the primary legislation did not require them to be read or given effect in that form, so founding a judicial review;[33]

(c) as a defence in any proceedings that a public authority might itself bring against an individual which are themselves contrary to the Convention or founded on a breach of the Convention. For example, a defendant in criminal proceedings might raise a violation of the Convention by the prosecution in his or her defence.[34]

8. Section 8—judicial remedies

3.23   Section 8(1) gives a court a wide power to grant such relief, remedies, or orders as it considers just and appropriate, provided they are within its existing powers.[35] The different remedies that may be granted by courts are discussed in Chapter 4. Briefly, damages may be awarded, but only if necessary to afford 'just satisfaction' to the claimant.[36]

---

[31] Section 7(2) and (9)–(14); Civil Procedure (Amendment No 4) Rules 2000, SI 2000/2092, concerning human rights issues in the Administrative Court; Family Proceedings (Amendment) Rules 2000, SI 2000/2267, for family courts; CPR Pt 33 and Practice Direction 30 concerning transfer between courts; Criminal Appeals (Amendment) Rules 2000, SI 2000/2036, concerning human rights issues in criminal courts; and in the Supreme Court, Supreme Court Rules 2009, r 40 and Practice Direction 9 (the Human Rights Act 1998); and for matters related to the proscription of a terrorist organization under the Terrorism Act 2000, the appropriate forum is the Proscribed Organization Appeals Commission: *R (Kurdistan Workers Party) v Secretary of State for the Home Department* [2002] EWHC 644 (Admin), [2002] ACD 99; Proscribed Organisations Appeals Commission (Human Rights Act Proceedings) Rules 2006, SI 2006/2298. CPR 7.11 says that a direct claim under s 7(1)(a) in respect of a judicial act may only be brought in the High Court: see *R (A) v Director of Establishments of the Security Service* [2010] UKSC 12, [2010] 2 WLR 1. However, a county court is an appropriate court or tribunal to read down a statute: see *Manchester City Council v Pinnock* [2010] UKSC 45, [2010] 3 WLR 1441.

[32] *Gaskin v UK* (1990) 12 EHRR 36.

[33] *R v Secretary of State for the Home Department, ex p Simms* [2000] 2 AC 115.

[34] *R v Director of Public Prosecutions, ex p Kebilene* [2000] 2 AC 326. See also, in a civil law context, *Manchester City Council v Pinnock* [2010] UKSC 45, [2010] 3 WLR 1441.

[35] The powers of existing courts or tribunals may be enlarged by order: s 7(11).

[36] Section 8(3).

If another remedy or exercise of the court's power could achieve this effect, damages should not be awarded.

9. Section 9—judicial acts

Section 9 focuses on how the 'public body' provisions operate against courts which have 3.24 allegedly acted contrary to the Convention. Although courts are public authorities, proceedings may not be brought directly against them for failure to comply with section 6(1) during the course of their determinations. Proceedings in respect of judicial acts under section 7(1)(a) may be brought only by exercising a right of appeal or as prescribed by rules. However, awards of damages may be made against the Crown if they are necessary to compensate a person as required by Article 5(5) of the Convention.

10. Section 11—safeguard for existing human rights

Section 11 of the Act provides, for the avoidance of doubt, that reliance on Convention 3.25 rights does not restrict reliance on other legal rights, or procedural methods of enforcing them. This has two important effects. First, it cannot be argued that any pre-existing right (for example under an existing discrimination statute) is impliedly limited by reference to Strasbourg jurisprudence: the Convention rights are a floor, not a ceiling. Secondly, litigants are not required to pursue alternative remedies before relying on the Convention. A Human Rights Act argument can be run at the same time as any other arguments a litigant may have, without any requirement first to exhaust alternative remedies.

11. Sections 12 and 13—respect for freedoms

Sections 12 and 13 provide specific assurances as to the respect that will be afforded 3.26 to freedom of expression and freedom of thought, conscience, and religion: these are 'comfort clauses' for sections of the press and certain religious organizations.[37]

12. Designated derogations and reservations

The Human Rights Act provides for limited 'designated derogations and reservations' 3.27 from the effect of the Convention under sections 1(2), 14–17, and Schedules 2 and 3. The provisions in the Convention which allow the protection of human rights to be limited are considered in Chapter 2, paras 2.40–2.76.

D. THE HUMAN RIGHTS ACT MECHANISM IN DETAIL

The key Human Rights Act mechanism is the interplay between sections 6, 3, 4, and 2, 3.28 which—though they preserve parliamentary sovereignty—have fundamentally altered

---

[37] See the discussion at paras 3.78–3.81 below.

both the manner in which courts can scrutinize legislation and the ways in which judges must interpret common law.[38]

1. Section 6

3.29 As outlined above, section 6(1) provides that it is unlawful for a 'public authority' to act in a way which is incompatible with a Convention right. As courts and tribunals are defined as public authorities they have their own primary duty to act compatibly with the Convention.[39] Parliamentary sovereignty is preserved by section 6(2), which limits the section 6(1) duty in circumstances where the court or tribunal could not have acted differently as a result of a statutory obligation which *cannot* be read to give effect to it in a way which is compatible with the Convention rights, notwithstanding the obligation in section 3 to do so if possible. This clever device places courts and tribunals themselves under a primary obligation to give effect to Convention rights except where they are prevented from doing so by statute.

3.30 The obligation upon courts to give effect to the Convention wherever possible applies to all cases. The consequence is that Convention questions are pivotal in cases where courts or tribunals are deciding the scope of a statutory provision (even one which regulates the behaviour of one private individual to another); where they are determining what the common law is (in so far as this is within their jurisdiction); or when they are exercising a judicial discretion—for example, the exercise of judicial discretion as to whether to grant an injunction to give effect to Articles 8 and 10.[40]

2. Section 3[41]

3.31 The interpretative obligation in section 3(1) of the Human Rights Act is a strong one. The requirement that courts and tribunals *must* read primary and subordinate legislation and give it effect in a way which is compatible with Convention rights 'so far as it is possible to do so' has been held to mean 'unless it is plainly impossible'.[42] The Government rejected amendments proposed during the passage of the Human Rights Bill to reduce this to 'so far as it is *reasonable* to do so' precisely because it wished to preserve the strong obligation to find all 'possible' interpretations of a provision which were compatible with the Convention. Section 3 has been characterized as a 'strong interpretative obligation',[43] not an 'optional canon of construction'.[44]

---

[38] *R v DPP, ex p Kebilene* [2000] 2 AC 326 per Lord Hope. See also *Nasseri v Secretary of State for the Home Department* [2009] UKHL 23, [2010] 1 AC 1 at [19] per Lord Hoffmann.

[39] Section 6(3)(a).

[40] *Re S (a child) (identification: restrictions on publication)* [2004] UKHL 47, [2005] 1 AC 593.

[41] See further Gearty, 'Reconciling Parliamentary Democracy and Human Rights' (2002) 118 LQR 248; Gearty, 'Revisiting s 3(1) of the Human Rights Act' (2003) 119 LQR 551; Sales, 'A comparison of the principle of legality and section 3 of the Human Rights Act 1998' (2009) 125 LQR 598.

[42] *R v A (No 2)* [2001] UKHL 25, [2002] 1 AC 45.

[43] See Lord Steyn and Lord Cooke in *R v Director of Public Prosecutions, ex p Kebilene* [2000] 2 AC 326; see also Lord Bingham in *A-G's Reference (No 4 of 2002)* [2004] UKHL 43, [2005] 1 AC 264 ('the interpretative obligation under section 3 is a very strong and far reaching one').

[44] Lord Nicholls in *Re S (care order: implementation of a care plan)* [2002] UKHL 10, [2002] 2 AC 291 at [37].

The interpretative obligation applies to both primary and secondary legislation when-   3.32
ever it was enacted, that is, whether before or after the enactment of the Human Rights
Act so 'it is as though legislation which predates [the Human Rights Act] and conflicts
with the Convention has to be treated as being subsequently amended to incorporate the
language of section 3'.[45]

The interpretative obligation in section 3(1) is a general one: a claimant seeking a   3.33
declaration as to the meaning of legislation under section 3(1) need not be a 'victim'—it
is sufficient that he or she has an interest and standing.[46]

The purposive approach to statutory construction is similar to that adopted by   3.34
the Court of Justice of the European Union in giving effect to EU law,[47] and to those
adopted by Strasbourg bodies to provide for effective, not merely theoretical, guarantees
of protection for human rights.[48]

When applying section 3 in practice the courts first, using ordinary principles of   3.35
statutory construction, decide whether the primary legislation is compatible with a
Convention right. If there is an incompatibility they will then go on to consider the
application of section 3. In doing this, courts try to isolate and identify the precise
word or phrase in the legislation which is incompatible. Claimants must identify 'with
precision' the particular statutory provision which is said to contravene Convention
rights.[49]

The House of Lords has confirmed that section 3 may require legislation to be given   3.36
a Convention-compliant meaning even where there is no ambiguity in the statute which
would lead to doubt about its alternative 'natural' meaning.[50] Additionally, the obligation under section 3 may sometimes require the courts to adopt a linguistically strained
interpretation of legislation.[51] As well as potentially modifying both the meaning and
effect of primary and secondary legislation, it has been accepted that this exercise may
also require the court to depart from the parliamentary intention behind the Act.[52]

Courts may comply with the interpretative obligation by 'reading in' additional words   3.37
so as to give effect to the presumed intended effect of the Convention, or by 'reading
down' so as to apply a narrow interpretation of the legislation and enable the court to
render it compatible with Convention rights. For example, in *R (GC) v Commissioner of
Police of the Metropolis*, section 3 was applied so as to read down section 64(1A) of the
Police and Criminal Evidence Act 1984 (which provides that fingerprints and DNA
samples 'may be retained after they have fulfilled the purposes for which they were taken');
it did not give the police the power to retain such data from all suspects indefinitely.[53] In
this way, the domestic provision was consistent with Article 8 of the Convention.[54]

---

[45] Lord Woolf in *Donoghue v Poplar Housing* [2001] EWCA Civ 595, [2002] QB 48.
[46] *R (Rusbridger) v Attorney General* [2003] UKHL 38, [2004] 2 AC 357 per Lord Steyn.
[47] eg *Litster v Forth Dry Dock and Engineering Co Ltd* [1990] 1 AC 546.
[48] See ch 2, paras 2.07–2.19.
[49] *R v A (No 2)* [2001] UKHL 25, [2001] 1 AC 45 at [110] per Lord Hope.
[50] Lord Nicholls in *Ghaidan v Godin-Mendoza* [2004] UKHL 30, [2004] 2 AC 557 at [29].
[51] *R v A (No 2)* [2001] UKHL 25, [2001] 1 AC 45 at [4]–[45] and [67]–[68] per Lord Steyn.
[52] Lord Nicholls in *Ghaidan v Godin-Mendoza* [2004] UKHL 30, [2004] 2 AC 557 at [30].
[53] [2011] UKSC 21, [2011] 1 WLR 1230.
[54] In this way, the Supreme Court gave effect to the ECtHR judgment in *S and Marper v UK* (2008) 48
EHRR 1169 and departed from its earlier decision in *R (S) v Chief Constable of the South Yorkshire Police*
[2004] UKHL 39, [2004] 1 WLR 2196.

Another technique the courts may use involves clarifying what the effect of the provision is without altering the ordinary meaning of the words used.[55]

3.38   In *Ghaidan v Godin-Mendoza*[56] the House of Lords stressed that the strong interpretative obligation in section 3 is crucial to the working of the Human Rights Act, that it should provide the main remedy, and that 'in practical effect there is a strong rebuttable presumption in favour of an interpretation consistent with Convention rights'. A broad approach to interpretation is necessary to fulfil the 'core remedial purpose' of section 3. Arguments based on parliamentary sovereignty, though a significant consideration, should not be used to limit the interpretative obligation in section 3 or the constitutional purpose of the Human Rights Act to protect Convention rights.[57] During the passage of the Human Rights Bill, the Lord Chancellor said that 'in 99% of all cases that will arise, there will be no need for judicial declarations of incompatibility because of the intended impact of s 3'.[58] Despite occasional reminders by the House of Lords that parliamentary sovereignty is a judge-made doctrine, potentially capable of judicial limitation, the supremacy of Parliament 'is still the *general* principle of our constitution'.[59] Ultimately, the structure of the Human Rights Act preserves parliamentary sovereignty. If Parliament disagrees with the courts' interpretation of a statute in line with the Convention it is free to override their decision by amending the legislation and expressly reinstating the provision that conflicts with fundamental rights[60]—although 'the courts will of course decline to hold that Parliament has interfered with fundamental rights unless it has made its intentions crystal clear'.[61]

3.39   However, though stronger than any previous rule of interpretation, section 3 is still:

> only a rule of interpretation. It does not entitle the judges to act as legislators . . . The compatibility is to be achieved only so far as this is possible. Plainly this will not be possible if the legislation contains provisions which expressly contradict the meaning which the enactment would have to be given to make it compatible.[62]

Similarly, when reading words into legislation, the courts have stressed that these words must be consistent with the scheme and essential principles of the legislation.[63]

3.40   The leading case on the limits of section 3 is *Re S (care order: implementation of care plan)*.[64] The House of Lords held the Court of Appeal's attempt to construe the Children Act 1989 as compatible with the Convention departed too far from the scheme of the legislation and key principles of the Children Act: 'a meaning which departs substantially from a fundamental feature of an Act of Parliament is likely to have crossed the

---

[55] Lord Hope in *R v Lambert* [2001] UKHL 37, [2002] 2 AC 545.

[56] [2004] UKHL 30, [2004] 2 AC 557 at [50].

[57] Ibid at [106] per Lord Rodger.

[58] *Hansard*, HL, col 840 (5 February 1998).

[59] See Lord Steyn in *R (Jackson) v Attorney-General* [2005] UKHL 56, [2006] 1 AC 262 at [102]; also Lord Hope at [107] and Baroness Hale at [159].

[60] Cf Gearty, 'Reconciling Parliamentary Democracy and Human Rights' (2002) 118 LQR 248.

[61] *R (Jackson) v Attorney-General* [2005] UKHL 56, [2006] 1 AC 262 at [159] per Baroness Hale.

[62] *R v A (No 2)* [2001] UKHL 25, [2001] 1 AC 45 at [108]. See also *R v Lambert* [2001] UKHL 37, [2002] 2 AC 545 at [79] per Lord Hope; *R v Secretary of State for the Home Department, ex p Anderson and Taylor* [2002] UKHL 46, [2003] 1 AC 837.

[63] Lord Bingham in *R v Secretary of State for the Home Department, ex p Anderson and Taylor* [2002] UKHL 46, [2003] 1 AC 837 at [70].

[64] [2002] UKHL 10, [2002] 2 AC 291.

boundary between interpretation and amendment'.[65] Similarly, in *R (Wright) v Secretary of State for Health*, the statute could not properly be read in a compatible manner. Baroness Hale declined to set out how she would 'right' the problem, emphasizing that it was not for their Lordships 'to attempt to rewrite the legislation'.[66]

Compatible interpretation through section 3(1) is also impossible where the legisla- 3.41
tion in question has wide-ranging implications and raises policy issues which it would be inappropriate or impossible for courts to determine, or would require the construction of a wide-ranging new extra-statutory scheme.[67]

When examining the rationale which underlies legislation and determining the policy 3.42
objective of particular provisions, courts can refer to sources outside the statute such as white papers, *Hansard*, and explanatory notes. However, resort to materials such as *Hansard* should be rare and the court should be careful to use them only as background material, not treat the ministerial or other statement as indicative of the objective intention of Parliament, and assess the proportionality of any statutory measure by reference to the facts of the case before the court alone.[68]

3. Interplay of sections 3 and 19

Section 19 requires the minister introducing a piece of legislation to express an opinion 3.43
as to the compatibility of the legislation with the Convention. It is intended to encourage the executive to address the issue of whether proposed legislation is compatible with the Convention at a formative stage. A statement of compatibility under section 19(1)(a) is also intended to act as evidence that a Convention-compliant interpretation of the legislation is intended by Parliament, and to be 'a strong spur to the courts to find means of construing statutes compatibly with the Convention'.[69] Cabinet Office guidance says that if, after further debate or amendment, a minister considered that the provisions of a Bill no longer met the standards required for a section 19(1)(a) statement, 'it would be a breach of the Ministerial Code to proceed towards Royal Assent without either amending the provisions or informing Parliament of the issue'.[70] It is only in very rare circumstances that a minister has made a statement under section 19(1)(b) that, although he cannot be sure that legislation may be incompatible with the Convention, the Government wishes to pass it anyway.[71]

---

[65] Ibid at [40].

[66] [2009] UKHL 3, [2009] 1 AC 739 at [39].

[67] *Re S (care order: implementation of a care plan)* [2002] UKHL 10, [2002] 2 AC 291; *Bellinger v Bellinger* [2003] UKHL 11, [2003] 2 AC 467; *R (Wright) v Secretary of State for Health* [2009] UKHL 3, [2009] 2 WLR 267 at [39]; *AS (Somalia) v Secretary of State for the Home Department* [2009] UKHL 32, [2009] 1 WLR 1385.

[68] See Lord Nicholls in *Wilson v Secretary of State for Trade and Industry* [2003] UKHL 40, [2004] 1 AC 816 at [61]–[67].

[69] Lord Irvine of Lairg, Tom Sargant Memorial Lecture, 16 December 1997.

[70] Cabinet Office, *Guide to Making Legislation: ECHR*, 6 May 2009, available at <http://www.cabinetoffice.gov.uk>.

[71] See the s 19(1)(b) statement made in respect of the ban on the broadcasting of political advertising in ss 319 and 321 of the Communications Act 2003, made in the light of *Vgt Verein gegen Tierfabriken v Switzerland* (2001) 34 EHRR 159. The House of Lords in fact held the ban to be compatible with Art 10 in *R (Animal Defenders International) v Secretary of State for Culture, Media and Sport* [2008] UKHL 15, [2008] 1 AC 1312.

3.44   In practice, a statement under section 19 has not had a significant effect upon courts.[72] Lord Hope described it as 'no more than expressions of opinion by the minister . . . they are not binding on the court, nor do they have any persuasive authority'.[73] When Whitehall assesses whether a particular provision complies with the Convention, it applies the traditional 'Strasbourg-proofing' test, which existed before the Human Rights Act—that is, whether, on the balance of probabilities, the provisions of the Bill would be found compatible with Convention rights if challenged in court.[74] In addition, ministers seem to assume that all those public authorities that have to implement the provision will act in compliance with the Convention if they have the power to do so. So, for instance, a Bill that gave wide discretion to the police to act in ways which would clearly violate the Convention would still be assessed as complying with the Convention because the discretion would be constrained by the Human Rights Act.[75]

4. Interplay of sections 3 and 4[76]

3.45   The dividing line between interpreting and legislating under section 3 of the Human Rights Act has an important impact upon the power conferred on higher courts to make 'statements of incompatibility' under section 4. Section 4 states that, where legislation cannot be read compatibly with the Convention, courts are empowered to make a declaration of incompatibility. Logically, if courts find it impossible to construe primary legislation compatibly with the Convention under section 3 then, as 'a measure of last resort',[77] they should declare it incompatible under section 4.

3.46   In *Secretary of State for the Home Department v MB*[78] the Court of Appeal applied section 3 to achieve a Human Rights Act-compatible construction of the 'control order' provisions in the Prevention of Terrorism Act 2005, and reversed the declaration of incompatibility made by the High Court.[79] However, in *R (Hooper) v Secretary of State for Work and Pensions*[80] the provisions of the Social Security (Contributions and Benefits) Act 1992 relating to 'widows' could not be read under section 3 to include 'widowers'. As a result, the court held that the discriminatory provisions (on the grounds of sex within Article 14 read with Article 8) were incompatible with the Convention, and the court made a declaration of incompatibility under section 4 of the Human Rights Act.

3.47   When the whole scheme of the legislation is inconsistent with Convention rights (or where it contains several incompatibilities) it is unlikely that section 3 can be used to remedy the defect in the statute. Therefore, the courts will need to turn to section 4 and consider making a declaration of incompatibility. For example, in *R (Wright and ors) v Secretary of State for Health* the House of Lords considered it impossible to use section 3 to interpret the 'provisional blacklisting' provisions for care workers in the Care Standards

---

[72] Though see Lord Bingham in *Animal Defenders* at [33] explaining why the s 19(1)(b) statement in fact gave Parliament's judgment on the importance of the legislation particular weight.

[73] *R v A (No 2)* [2001] UKHL 25, [2002] 1 AC 45 at [69] per Lord Hope.

[74] Home Office evidence to the Joint Committee on Human Rights (as set out in para 15 of JCHR Report 2000–2001, HL 66, HC 332).

[75] *R v A (No 2)* [2001] UKHL 25, [2002] 1 AC 45.

[76] See Sales, 'Rights—consistent interpretation and the Human Rights Act 1998' (2011) 127 LQR 217.

[77] Lord Steyn in *Ghaidan v Godon-Mendoza* [2004] UKHL 30, [2004] 2 AC 557.

[78] [2006] EWCA Civ 1140, [2007] QB 415.

[79] See also the appeal to the House of Lords: [2007] UKHL 46, [2007] 3 WLR 681.

[80] [2003] EWCA Civ 813; and upheld by the House of Lords at [2005] UKHL 29, [2005] 1 WLR 1681.

Act 2000 in a Human Rights Act-compliant manner, and therefore declared the relevant provisions incompatible.[81] And in *R (F) v Secretary of State for the Home Department* the Supreme Court likewise held that the indefinite requirements imposed on those convicted of sexual offences to notify the authorities of their travel plans by virtue of the Sexual Offences Act 2003 were incompatible with Article 8 of the Convention; a declaration of incompatibility was therefore made.[82]

5. Section 2[83]

Section 2 is the provision by which Convention rights have been 'brought much more   3.48
fully into the jurisprudence of the courts throughout the United Kingdom and their interpretation . . . far more subtly and powerfully woven into our law'.[84] It provides that a court or tribunal determining a question which has arisen under any statute in connection with a Convention right *must* take account of any judgment, decision, declaration, or advisory opinion of the ECtHR, opinion or decision of the Commission, or decision of the Committee of Ministers, whenever made or given, so far as, in the opinion of the court or tribunal, it is relevant to the proceedings in which that question has arisen. The decisions of the different Strasbourg organs carry different weights, and decisions of the Court sitting as a Grand Chamber take precedence.[85]

Section 2 requires a court only to take a Strasbourg judgment into account, not to   3.49
follow it.[86] However, the authority of a considered statement of the Grand Chamber is such that our courts have no option but to accept and apply it.[87] The House of Lords has explained that, although the section 2 obligation requires courts to take the Convention case law into account (not to follow it), the purpose of section 2 is to ensure that the same Convention rights are enforced under the Human Rights Act as would be enforced by the Strasbourg Court. It is not intended to provide Convention rights with an autonomous domestic meaning.[88] As Lord Bingham said in *R (Ullah) v Special Adjudicator*:[89]

It is of course open to member states to provide for rights more generous than those guaranteed by the Convention, but such provision should not be the product of interpretation of the Convention by national courts, since the meaning of the Convention should be uniform throughout the states party to it. The duty of national courts is to keep pace with the Strasbourg jurisprudence as it evolves over time: no more, but certainly no less.[90]

---

[81] [2009] UKHL 3, [2009] 1 AC 739.

[82] [2010] UKSC 17, [2010] 2 WLR 992.

[83] Klug and Wildbore, 'Follow or Lead? The Human Rights Act and the European Court of Human Rights' [2010] EHRLR 621.

[84] See *Rights Brought Home: The Human Rights Bill* (Cm 3782, 1997) para 1.14.

[85] See ch 8.

[86] *R v Horncastle* [2009] UKSC 14, [2010] 2 AC 373 (a seven-judge court).

[87] *Home Secretary v AF (No 3)* [2009] UKHL 28, [2010] 2 AC 269. See also *R (Anderson) v Secretary of State for the Home Department* [2002] UKHL 46, [2003] 1 AC 837 at [18] and *Cadder v HM Advocate* [2010] UKSC 43, [2011] 1 WLR 2601 at [46].

[88] *N v Secretary of State for the Home Department* [2005] UKHL 31, [2005] 2 AC 296; *R (Ullah) v Special Adjudicator* [2004] UKHL 26, [2004] 2 AC 323; *R (Al Jedda) v Secretary of State for Defence* [2007] UKHL 58, [2008] 1 AC 332.

[89] [2004] UKHL 26, [2004] 2 AC 323.

[90] See also Lord Hope in *N v Secretary of State for the Home Department* [2005] UKHL 31, [2005] 2 AC 296 at [25]. This case has been consistently followed on numerous occasions by the House of Lords and Supreme Court.

On the other hand, where Member States have a margin of appreciation or where the ECtHR jurisprudence is not well developed, the Supreme Court has occasionally gone further than is strictly required by that jurisprudence.[91]

3.50　　The circumstances in which domestic courts will not follow Strasbourg case law are rare, however. The 'less than imperative' terms in which the Convention was drafted were necessary to allow a distinction to be drawn between the Strasbourg approach and that of domestic courts, for example, where domestic courts have a narrower area of discretion.[92]

3.51　　One circumstance in which domestic courts may decline to follow Strasbourg case law is in circumstances where the decision is based on a clear misunderstanding of domestic law or procedure.[93] In *Kay v Lambeth London Borough Council*, the House of Lords held that the doctrine of precedent was not in some way displaced by section 2 of the Act, so that lower courts remained bound to follow higher domestic authority in preference to Strasbourg case law, save in wholly exceptional cases where the previous domestic decision was reached without reference to the Convention, before the Human Rights Act was in force and led to a finding against the United Kingdom in the European Court of Human Rights.[94]

3.52　　The Supreme Court is, however, free to depart from its own previous decisions following a conflicting decision of the ECtHR, and will do so in a case in which the United Kingdom was a party even if it does not necessarily agree with the conclusion.[95]

3.53　　Likewise, '[w]here . . . there is a clear and constant line of decisions whose effect is not inconsistent with some fundamental substantive or procedural aspect of our law, and whose reasoning does not appear to overlook or misunderstand some argument or point of principle, we consider that it would be wrong for this Court not to follow that line'.[96]

6. Interplay of sections 2 and 3

3.54　　Strasbourg case law requires *effective* protection of the Convention rights, ensuring rights that are not 'theoretical or illusory but . . . practical and effective'.[97] Accordingly, to comply with their obligation under section 3(1) of the Human Rights Act, UK courts have to interpret statutory provisions so as to give real and effective protection to the rights that the Convention was intended to safeguard.

---

[91] See, eg *Re G* [2008] UKHL 38, [2009] 1 AC 173; *EM (Lebanon) v Secretary of State for the Home Department* [2008] UKHL 64, [2009] 1 AC 1198.

[92] *R (Al-Jedda) v Secretary of State for Defence* [2005] EWHC 1809 (Admin); affirmed by the Court of Appeal at [2006] EWCA Civ 327, [2006] 3 WLR 954.

[93] *R v Spear* [2002] UKHL 31, [2003] 1 AC 73 at [12]–[13]; declining to follow *Morris v UK* (2002) 34 EHRR 1253; see *R v Horncastle* [2009] UKSC 14, [2010] 2 AC 373; declining to follow *Al Khawaja and Tahery v UK* (2009) 49 EHRR 1 (the latter case is currently pending before the Grand Chamber), and *Tomlinson and ors v Birmingham City Council* [2010] UKSC 8, [2010] 2 WLR 471.

[94] [2006] UKHL 10, [2006] 2 AC 465. Where a Court of Appeal decision is inconsistent with a later decision of the ECtHR, the Court of Appeal may, but is not obliged, to depart from its previous decision: *R (RJM) (FC) v Secretary of State for Work and Pensions* [2008] UKHL 63, [2008] 3 WLR 1023.

[95] *R (Purdy) v DPP* [2009] UKHL 45, [2010] 1 AC 345, and *Secretary of State for the Home Department v AF (No 3)* [2009] UKHL 28, [2010] 2 AC 269.

[96] *Manchester City Council v Pinnock* [2010] UKSC 45, [2010] 3 WLR 1441 at [48].

[97] *Artico v Italy* (1980) 3 EHRR 1, para 33; *Airey v Ireland* (1979) 2 EHRR 305.

Under sections 2 and 3 of the Human Rights Act, the Convention must be given   3.55
effect wherever possible. Because Strasbourg case law must be taken into account, the
Strasbourg method of judicial reasoning has gradually entered UK legal practice over the
past decade. Where there is potentially a Convention question in play, the domestic
court or tribunal first has to identify the right in question, including the positive aspects
of the right (that is, the obligations of the court, as a public body, to take positive steps
to protect the right). Then it must identify the alleged interference with the right and
look to see whether it is prescribed by law. It must then decide what objectives are said
to be served by the interference, and whether the interference is necessary in a democratic society for the purposes of achieving those objectives. This involves a careful application of the principles of proportionality, and in certain circumstances an explicit
balancing of the rights of individuals against the rights and freedoms of others and the
general public interest.

Section 2 limits the effect of section 3 to the extent required to give effect to the doc-   3.56
trine of precedent. However, in the criminal context, the courts have shown themselves
willing to depart from the strict principles of *stare decisis* when faced with a conflict
between a binding House of Lords' decision and a more recent decision of the Privy
Council.[98] Should the courts fail to follow an ECtHR decision by application of the
principle of *stare decisis*, this leaves the United Kingdom open to an adverse judgment in
Strasbourg. The effects of sections 2 and 11, the common law power of the courts to
develop free-standing human rights principles, and the right of individual petition to
Strasbourg, ought to mean that the Strasbourg jurisprudence is a long-stop or bottom
line for human rights protection, but not a barrier to the development of free-standing
domestic law human rights principles. It should be treated as a floor, not a ceiling.[99]

E. PUBLIC AUTHORITIES AND THE HUMAN RIGHTS ACT: MEANING OF 'PUBLIC AUTHORITY' AND 'FUNCTIONS OF A PUBLIC NATURE'

Section 6 of the Human Rights Act imposed a new statutory duty upon all public   3.57
authorities to act compatibly with the Convention, and section 7 created new causes of
action through which these 'vertically effective' obligations can be enforced. In other
words, if a body is a public authority, then individuals have *direct* statutory remedies
against them for breach of section 6(1), either by way of judicial review or for breach
of statutory duty. As a result, the question of which types of bodies come within the
definition of a 'public authority' for the purposes of the Act is a very important one, not
only for individual litigants seeking to ascertain whether they have a cause of action, but
for the overall ambit of the Act.

'Public authorities' that are subject to the direct 'vertical' effect of the Human Rights   3.58
Act include core public authorities, which are 'obviously' public in nature, in respect
of all their functions, whether the nature of those functions is public or private.[100]

---

[98] *R v James and Karimi* [2006] EWCA Crim 14, [2006] 1 All ER 759.
[99] For a recent example of the common law providing protection in circumstances where the HRA did not
do so, see *HM Treasury v Ahmed (Nos 1 and 2)* [2010] UKSC 2, [2010] 2 AC 534.
[100] Section 6(3)(a).

However, section 6(3)(b) and (5) also deem to be public authorities any person certain of whose functions are functions of a public nature *in respect of the performance of those public functions*, but not in respect of acts *the nature of which is private*. The concepts of 'functions of a public nature' and acts 'the nature of which is private' are therefore critical to understanding the ambit of the Act. The case law on this subject is complex and controversial.

1. 'Core' public authorities

3.59 'Core' public authorities include all bodies that are obviously public in nature, such as government departments and ministers, local authorities, NHS Trusts, coroners, police, prisons, bodies such as the Parole Board, Legal Services Commission, and the General Medical Council. The House of Lords has favoured a relatively narrow test for core public authority status.[101] Core public authorities must act in conformity with the Convention whether exercising functions governed by public law (for example, assessment to tax) or private law (for example, employment).

2. 'Functional' public authorities

3.60 'Functional' or 'hybrid' public authorities in section 6(3)(b) include any person 'certain of whose functions are functions of a public nature', but only in relation to public functions. Section 6(5) provides that 'In relation to a particular act, a person is not a public authority by virtue only of subsection (3)(b) if the nature of the act is private'.

3.61 The Government which introduced the Human Rights Act intended it to apply to 'a wide rather than a narrow range of public authorities'[102] and to encompass:

... a realistic and modern definition of the state so as to provide a correspondingly wide protection against the abuse of human rights.[103]

3.62 The Lord Chancellor said that:

[section 6(3)(b)] is there to include bodies which are not manifestly public authorities, but some of whose functions are only of a public nature . . . Railtrack would fall into that category because it exercises public functions in its role as a safety regulator, but it is acting privately as a property developer. A private security company would be exercising public functions in relation to the management of a contracted out prison but would be acting privately when, for example, guarding commercial premises. Doctors in general practice would be public authorities in relation to their National Health Service functions, but not in relation to their private patients.[104]

3.63 The intention was to reflect the line of Strasbourg case law which holds that a state cannot escape liability under the Convention by delegating essentially public functions to private bodies.[105] The effect is that a direct cause of action is available against functional public authorities for acting in breach of the Convention, and hence unlawfully,

---

[101] *Aston Cantlow and Wilmcote with Billesley Parochial Church Council v Wallbank* [2003] UKHL 37, [2004] 1 AC 546.
[102] *Hansard*, HL, col 1232 (3 November 1997).
[103] Jack Straw, *Hansard*, HC, cols 405–408 (17 June 1998).
[104] *Hansard*, HL, vol 583, col 811 (24 November 1997).
[105] *Costello-Roberts v United Kingdom* (1995) 19 EHRR 112.

when the act under challenge is of a public nature, and in contexts where its functions would be amenable to judicial review; but not when they are acting within the scope of their *private* law activities. For example, in general, employment law questions are questions of private law.[106] However, they may be questions of public law if they relate to policy questions.[107]

The extent to which private organizations performing delegated public functions should be regarded as functional public authorities has proved controversial.[108] In *Aston Cantlow Parochial Church Council v Wallbank*[109] the determining factor was said to be whether the nature of the function performed was public.[110] It was held that there should be a 'generously wide' interpretation of public function but that there was 'no single test of universal application . . . given the diverse nature of governmental functions and the variety of means by which these functions are discharged today'.[111] 3.64

However, although the House of Lords in *Aston Cantlow* appeared to lay down a broad functional approach, it did not expressly overrule the decisions in earlier cases in which courts had taken rather narrower approaches to what factors were relevant to deciding whether a body was a 'functional' public authority. Those cases focused more narrowly on the institutional features of the situation, rather than the nature of the functions being performed, and their place in public service provision.[112] Relevant features, in rendering a function which would otherwise be private, public, had been held to include, for example, whether the body was exercising statutory authority not available to private persons,[113] and the proximity of the relationship between the private body and the delegating public authority. 3.65

The Joint Committee on Human Rights (JCHR) expressed concern about the 'deficit' in protection resulting from the *Leonard Cheshire* decision[114] for those who received public services on a contracted-out basis.[115] 3.66

Since then, a number of cases in the lower courts examined the issue of which bodies are 'functional public authorities' for the purposes of the Human Rights Act.[116] 3.67

---

[106] *R v East Berkshire Health Authority, ex p Walsh* [1985] QB 152.

[107] *R v Crown Prosecution Service, ex p Hogg* [1994] COD 237.

[108] See JCHR Report, 'The Meaning of Public Authority under the Human Rights Act', 7th Report (2003–04), HL 39, HC 382, February 2004); Sunkin, 'Pushing Forward the Frontiers of Human Rights Protection: The Meaning of Public Authority under the Human Rights Act' [2004] PL 643; Oliver, 'Functions of a Public Nature under the Human Rights Act' [2004] PL 329; Craig, 'Contracting Out, the Human Rights Act, and the Scope of Judicial Review' (2002) 118 LQR 551.

[109] [2003] UKHL 37, [2004] 1 AC 546.

[110] Ibid at [41] per Lord Hope.

[111] Ibid at [12] per Lord Nicholls.

[112] Eg *Donoghue v Poplar Housing Association* [2001] EWCA Civ 595, [2002] QB 48 at [58]; *R (Heather) v Leonard Cheshire Foundation* [2002] EWCA Civ 366, [2002] 2 All ER 936.

[113] See *R (A) v Partnerships in Care Ltd* [2002] EWHC 529 (Admin), [2002] 1 WLR 2610, where the decision of managers of a private psychiatric hospital to alter the care and treatment of a patient was an act of a public nature, susceptible to judicial review, and the hospital managers were, by virtue of the statutory regime and regulations under the Registered Homes Act 1984 and the Mental Health Act 1983, a public authority for the purposes of the Human Rights Act.

[114] *R (Heather) v Leonard Cheshire Foundation* [2002] EWCA Civ 366, [2002] 2 All ER 936.

[115] JCHR, 'The Meaning of Public Authority under the Human Rights Act', 7th Report (2003–2004), HL 39, HC 382, February 2004.

[116] See, eg *Cameron v Network Rail Infrastructure Ltd* [2006] EWHC 1133 (QBD); *R (Mullin) v Jockey Club Appeal Board (No 1)* [2005] EWHC 2197 (Admin), [2006] ACD 2; *R (Beer) v Hampshire County Council* [2003] EWCA Civ 1056, [2004] 1 WLR 233; *R (West) v Lloyds of London* [2004] EWCA Civ 506, [2004] 3 All ER 251, supply of electricity; *James v London Electricity plc* [2004] EWHC 3226 (QB).

They sometimes appeared to focus closely on the legal nature of the *body* in question, and inadequately on the reality of the functions that particular bodies are performing, notwithstanding that Jack Straw (then Home Secretary) had said, when introducing the Bill:

... as we are dealing with public functions and with an evolving situation, we believe that the test must relate to the substance and nature of the act, not to the form and legal personality.[117]

3.68   The law therefore took a serious, and, in our view, wrong turn when, in 2007, the House of Lords considered the point of principle in *Leonard Cheshire* and, by a bare majority of 3–2, endorsed it in what is now the leading case on the meaning of 'functions of a public nature', *YL v Birmingham City Council*.[118] In that case, the House of Lords held that a privately owned care home which provided accommodation and care for an elderly and vulnerable resident which was both arranged and paid for by the local authority nonetheless did not perform a 'function of a public nature' in doing so. Although the House of Lords endorsed the list of factors it had earlier set out in *Aston Cantlow*, the judges in the majority and the minority afforded significantly different weight to the various factors in that balance.

3.69   The majority of the House of Lords in *YL* (Lord Scott, Lord Mance, and Lord Neuberger) held that there was a distinction between the council's function in arranging and paying for the care and accommodation pursuant to its statutory duty, and that of the private company in providing the care and accommodation under contract, on a commercial basis (albeit paid for by public money), rather than on the basis of a direct subsidy from public funds. They focused heavily on the company's commercial purposes:

It is neither a charity nor a philanthropist ... It receives no public funding, enjoys no special statutory powers, and ... charge[s] whatever fees in its commercial judgment it thinks suitable.[119]

In a strongly worded dissent, Lord Bingham and Baroness Hale disagreed. Lord Bingham said:

When the 1998 Act was passed, it was very well known that a number of functions formerly carried out by public authorities were now carried out by private bodies. Section 6(3)(b) of the 1998 Act was clearly drafted with this well-known fact in mind. The performance by private body A by arrangement with public body B, and perhaps at the expense of B, of what would undoubtedly be a public function if carried out by B, is in my opinion, precisely the case which section 6(3)(b) was intended to embrace. It is, in my opinion, this case.[120]

Baroness Hale attached importance to the public interest in the provision of such care, the fact that there was public funding for such care, and the coercive powers of the state,[121] and concluded:

Taken together, these factors lead inexorably to the conclusion that the company, in providing accommodation, health and social care for [YL], was performing a function of a public nature.

---

[117] *Hansard*, HC, cols 409–410 (17 June 1998).
[118] [2007] UKHL 27, [2008] 1 AC 95.
[119] Ibid at [26] per Lord Scott.
[120] Ibid at [20].
[121] Ibid at [67]–[69].

This was a function performed for [YL] pursuant to statutory arrangements, at public expense and in the public interest.[122]

With respect, we agree with the minority in that case that the decision of the majority 3.70 does not reflect the clear intention of Parliament in adopting a 'functional' approach to the concept of a 'public authority', but, rather, places an erroneous focus on the nature of the provider and its commercial motivation.[123]

The consequence of *YL* has been considerable uncertainty as to the ambit of the 3.71 Human Rights Act. For example, the Court of Appeal recently held that housing management functions performed by a registered social landlord were 'public functions'.[124] It has also led to a serious protection gap for vulnerable individuals in relation to public services procured from the private sector. As the JCHR pointed out following its inquiry into this issue, the consequence is that 'a central provision of the Human Rights Act has been compromised in a way which reduces the protection it was intended to give to people at some of the most vulnerable moments in their lives'.[125]

F. PRIVATE PARTIES AND THE HUMAN RIGHTS ACT

The Convention is not 'directly effective' against private litigants. In litigation concern- 3.72 ing purely private bodies, or 'functional public authorities' in pursuit of their 'functions of a private nature', there is no stand-alone cause of action for 'breach of the Convention' under section 7 of the Act.[126] It is not therefore possible for one private individual to sue another private legal person for a tort of 'breach of the Convention'.

The Convention is, however, indirectly enforceable against a private legal person in 3.73 the following ways:

(a) Where the effect of a statutory provision is in question in a dispute between private individuals, the courts—as 'public authorities' for the purposes of the Act—are under an obligation to interpret the legislation so as to accord with the Convention (under section 3 in conjunction with section 6(3) of the Human Rights Act). For example, in *Wilson v First County Trust (No 2)*[127] both parties were 'private' individuals. This did not prevent the Court of Appeal deciding that the bar against enforcing a credit agreement breached the pawnbroker's right of access to a court under Article 6 of the Convention and the right to property under Article 1 of Protocol 1.[128]

---

[122] Ibid at [73].

[123] See also the criticisms of Baroness Hale (one of the minority) in her speech to the Salford Human Rights Conference, 4 June 2010: <http://www.supremecourt.gov.uk/docs/speech_100604.pdf>.

[124] *London Quadrant Housing Trust v Weaver* [2009] EWCA Civ 58, [2010] 1 WLR 363.

[125] JCHR, 'The Meaning of Public Authority under the Human Rights Act', 7th Report (2003–2004), HL 39, HC 382, February 2004.

[126] *Campbell v MGN Ltd* [2004] UKHL 22, [2004] 2 AC 457; and the Court of Appeal in *X v Y* [2004] EWCA Civ 662 at [58]. See also the rationale advanced by Murray Hunt in 'The "Horizontal Effect" of the Human Rights Act' [1998] PL 423 and Lord Steyn in '2000–2005: Laying the Foundations of Human Rights Law in the United Kingdom' [2005] EHRLR 349.

[127] [2001] EWCA Civ 633, [2002] QB 74.

[128] See also the House of Lords' decision at [2003] UKHL 40, [2004] 1 AC 816 (reversed on other grounds).

(b) Similarly, where there is a judicial discretion to be exercised, section 6 requires it to be exercised so as to give effect to a Convention right (for example, in civil proceedings between private parties when the court has a discretion regarding the admission of evidence obtained in breach of a Convention right).

(c) Where the rights in question touch upon positive obligations under Articles 2, 3, 8, 10, or 11, the court is itself under a positive obligation to protect individuals from the violation of their rights by other private individuals. For example, in *Venables and Thompson v Newsgroup Newspapers and Associated Newspapers Ltd*[129] the two children who had been convicted of the murder of James Bulger were granted permanent injunctions preventing publication of further information about them on the basis that the Court of Appeal was under a positive obligation to secure their right to life (Article 2) and right to respect for private life (Article 8).

(d) Where the courts are dealing with cases involving the common law they are under an obligation to develop the common law to be compatible with Convention rights (by virtue of section 6(3)). The 'horizontal' effects of the Human Rights Act in private litigation have been most marked in this area.

3.74   Although the common law previously recognized some fundamental rights (and the Convention could be used in some circumstances to give clarity to English law), since the Human Rights Act came into force the common law has been 'reinvigorated'.[130] The effects of the Convention on evolving the common law have most clearly been seen in a series of cases concerning the privacy of public figures, in which the boundaries of common law torts have been transformed, analysed further in Chapter 7. It has now become clear that a litigant, A, who wishes to use a Convention argument in a case brought against a private opponent, B, will certainly be able to do so if A finds an existing private law argument on which to 'hang' the Convention argument (for example, breach of confidence in tort in relation to an infringement of the right to respect for private life). A could also focus the action on a public body, C, which has failed to protect A's rights from being violated by B. In this way Convention standards have infiltrated, influenced, and even created new common law rights, and will continue to do so.

G. EXCEPTIONS AND SPECIAL CASES

3.75   The Human Rights Act is principally a constitutional instrument of general application. However, one important omission from the Schedule to the Act (Article 13) and two specific provisions (sections 12 and 13) about particular interest groups (the press and religious organizations) require brief explanation.[131]

---

[129] [2001] 2 WLR 1038; and *Campbell v MGN Ltd* [2004] UKHL 22, [2004] 2 AC 457.

[130] Lord Irvine, 'The Impact of the Human Rights Act' [2003] PL 308; and English and Havers (eds), *An Introduction to Human Rights and the Common Law* (Oxford: Hart Publishing, 2000).

[131] For a full discussion of the scope and content of Arts 8, 9, 10, and 13 of the Convention, see ch 7.

1. Article 13

Article 13 imposes a duty on the state to provide the opportunity to test at a national   3.76
level whether a Convention right has been violated. It guarantees in general terms that
there is a suitable national avenue of redress capable of providing a remedy in an appropriate case. However, it does not mean that states have to ensure that a *particular* result
is secured. So, for example, the right will be breached where the victim has no right of
recourse in the domestic courts[132] or where primary legislation excludes any such challenge. Article 13 is not a free-standing right (that is, a claim cannot be founded on the
article alone and must be brought in connection with an alleged breach of another
Convention right), but it is not necessary to show a breach of another Convention right
before the court can consider its application—it is enough to show that the complaint
in relation to the other right is 'arguable' but cannot be argued because there is no means
for this to be done before a national court.[133]

Although Article 13 is not one of the rights included in the Schedule to the Human   3.77
Rights Act, it was intended that the Act itself would give effect to Articles 1 and 13 by
securing the rights and freedoms of the Convention. In other words, Article 13 is given
effect by establishing a scheme under which Convention rights can be raised and remedied before UK courts. In *Re S (FC) and ors* Lord Nicholls said:

Article 13 guarantees the availability at the national level of an effective remedy to enforce the
substance of Convention rights. Sections 7 and 8 seek to provide that remedy in this country.
The object of these sections is to provide in English law the very remedy article 13 declares is the
entitlement of everyone whose rights are violated.[134]

2. Section 12

The object of section 12 is to emphasize that the courts must pay due regard to Article   3.78
10 and the right to freedom of expression contained in that article. It was a response to
lobbying by some sections of the press during the passage of the Human Rights Bill
which argued that the judiciary might interpret Article 8 of the Convention (right to
respect for private and family life) in a way which unacceptably limited the freedom of
the press. In practice, those concerns are not justified[135] and section 12 has had little
effect.

Section 12 has a number of components. First, it prevents 'gagging injunctions' being   3.79
granted *ex parte* except in the rarest of circumstances. It provides that if a court is considering whether to grant any relief that might affect the exercise of the Convention right
to freedom of expression *ex parte*, there is a presumption against the grant of such relief.
'No such relief is to be granted' unless the court is satisfied that the person seeking the
relief has taken all practicable steps to notify the defendant, or there are compelling

---

[132] *Halford v United Kingdom* (1997) 24 EHRR 523.
[133] *Boyle and Rice v United Kingdom* (1988) 10 EHRR 425.
[134] [2002] UKHL 10, [2002] 2 AC 291 at [61].
[135] See *Re S (A child) (identification) restrictions on publication* [2004] UKHL 47, [2005] 1 AC 593, in
which Lord Steyn explained the 'balancing exercise' that needs to take place in order to balance the competing
demands of respect for private life and freedom of expression.

reasons why the defendant should not be notified.[136] Secondly, the merits of the claimant's case must be tested before any such restraint is made. Section 12(3) provides that no relief is to be granted so as to restrain publication before trial unless the court is satisfied that the applicant is likely to establish that publication should not be allowed.[137] Thirdly, section 12(4) provides that the court must have 'particular regard' to the right to freedom of expression, and that where the proceedings relate to material which the respondent claims is, or which appears to the court to be, journalistic, literary, or artistic material, the court must have regard to the extent to which the material has, or is about to, become available to the public, or it is, or would be, in the public interest for the material to be published.[138] It must also have regard to any relevant privacy code such as the code issued by the Press Complaints Commission.

3.80   Perhaps because Article 10 itself requires 'particular regard' to be given to the right to freedom of expression, in practice, domestic courts have made clear that section 12 adds little to existing domestic or Strasbourg jurisprudence[139] and the court will need to form its own view on the balance between Articles 8 and 10 on the facts of a particular case. This topic has been one of acute public controversy (and considerable public misunderstanding) recently, fuelled by the granting of the first 'super-injunction' in the *Trafigura* case[140] and a number of anonymized injunctions.[141] Whilst it is fairly clear that super-injunctions have been applied for only rarely, and have normally been granted (if at all) only for a limited period, it has recently been stressed that 'such injunctions [should] only be granted following intense scrutiny by the court in the individual case, and only when it is strictly necessary as a means to ensure that justice is done'.[142]

3. Section 13

3.81   During the passage of the Human Rights Bill, fears were expressed on behalf of the Church of England, for example, that the Human Rights Act might lead to questions about whether they could refuse to marry gay couples, or dismiss church schoolteachers who had lost their faith. To address these fears, section 13 provides that if the court's determination of any question under the Act might affect the exercise by a religious

---

[136] Section 12(1) and (2). Note that in *X & Y v Persons Unknown* [2007] EMLR 290 Eady J concluded that its ambit covered not only the parties to the proceedings but also non-parties who in practice are likely to have their Art 10 right constrained by an injunction. The recent Report of the Committee on Super-Injunctions, chaired by Lord Neuberger, emphasized that a failure to provide advance notice is only justifiable in exceptional circumstances: para 3.22.

[137] See *Cream Holdings v Banerjee* [2004] UKHL 44, [2005] 1 AC 253 where the House of Lords considered the test under s 12(3) and accorded it a relatively limited effect. See also *Campbell v MGN Limited* [2004] UKHL 22, [2004] 2 AC 457 at [55] per Lord Hoffmann and at [141] per Baroness Hale; and, recently, *ETK v News Group Newspapers* [2011] EWCA Civ 439 at [10(6)].

[138] See *Green Corns Ltd v Clavery Group* [2005] EWHC 958 (QB), where the fact that the information in question was available to the public did not justify withholding an injunction under s 12 because the information was not so widely in the public domain, and re-publication could have an effect and was likely to impact on Art 8 rights.

[139] For the courts' general approach, see *Ashdown v Telegraph Group* [2001] EWCA Civ 1142, [2001] 3 WLR 1368; *Clayton v Clayton* [2006] EWCA Civ 878; and *Re Ward; BBC v CAFCASS Legal* [2007] EWHC 616 (Fam).

[140] *RJW & SJW v The Guardian News and Media Ltd*, Order of Maddison J of 11 September 2009.

[141] See, in particular, *CTB v News Group Newspapers and Imogen Thomas* [2011] EWHC 1232 (QB) (injunction granted) and *Terry v Persons Unknown* [2010] EWHC 119 (QB) (injunction refused).

[142] Report of the Committee on Super-Injunctions, para 2.37; see also para 2.28.

organization, whether as an organization or by its members collectively, of the Convention right to freedom of thought, conscience, and religion, it must have particular regard to the importance of that right. This is something that is inherent in the structure of Article 9 of the Convention, which is where that guarantee is to be found. Since the whole scheme of the Convention is to give particular regard to a prima facie right, permitting derogations from it only if they are necessary, proportionate, and so on, the effect of this section is really to add political comfort to religious interests rather than to add anything in terms of practical effect.[143] In most cases where a dispute about the meaning of section 13 might arise, the question is now one governed by the provisions protecting people from discrimination on the grounds of religion or belief,[144] or on the grounds of sexual orientation.[145]

---

[143] See per Richards J (as he then was) in *R (Amicus) v Secretary of State for Trade and Industry* [2004] EWHC 860 (Admin), [2004] ELR 31 at [41]: 'section 13 of the 1998 Act does not give greater weight to [Art 9] rights than they would otherwise enjoy under the Convention'; see too *R (Williamson) v Secretary of State for Education* [2002] EWCA Civ 1926 (for s 13 discussion, not overruled by House of Lords); and *R (Surayanda) v Welsh Ministers* [2007] EWCA Civ 893. Ordinarily, the courts do not refer to s 13 when applying Art 9 of the Convention: see, eg *London Borough of Islington v Ladele* UKEAT/453/08, [2009] ICR 387.

[144] Equality Act 2010, s 10.

[145] Equality Act 2010, s 12.

4

ENFORCING THE HUMAN RIGHTS ACT

A. Introduction   4.01

B. The Appropriate Forum for an Argument Under
   the Human Rights Act   4.07

C. Standing: Who May Bring Proceedings Under
   the Human Rights Act?   4.16
   1. Victims   4.19
   2. Standing of public interest groups   4.23
   3. Standing of the Equality and Human Rights Commission   4.26

D. Limitation Periods: Are There Time Limits for Bringing a
   Claim Under the Human Rights Act?   4.29

E. Retrospectivity   4.33

F. Interventions in Human Rights Act Cases   4.35
   1. Interventions by public interest groups   4.36
   2. Interventions by the Equality and
      Human Rights Commission   4.40

G. Other Means of Enforcement by the Equality and
   Human Rights Commission   4.43
   1. The duties of the Commission   4.44
   2. Legal assistance   4.47
   3. Legal policy   4.48
   4. Inquiries, investigations, and assessments   4.49

H. Remedies   4.53
   1. Damages   4.53
   2. Section 4—declarations of incompatibility   4.71
   3. Section 10—'fast-track' procedure   4.92

I. Key Convention Concepts in the Domestic Courts   4.100
   1. Territoriality   4.101
   2. Positive obligations   4.104
   3. Legality   4.108
   4. Proportionality   4.111

J. Enforcement of the Human Rights Act in Summary   4.131

A. INTRODUCTION

4.01   The Human Rights Act was intended to 'bring rights home', so that any remedy which can be secured in Strasbourg is available in national courts and tribunals. This chapter deals with the practicalities of how the Human Rights Act seeks to achieve this objective and addresses the domestic application of the European Convention for the Protection of Human Rights and Fundamental Freedoms (Convention) concepts discussed in Chapter 2.

4.02   In recognition of the espoused aim of the Act, section 7 is constructed so that litigants can raise Convention arguments in existing causes of action, claims, and proceedings; or, if no such domestic law causes of action are available, to bring standalone proceedings to allege breach of a Convention right against a public authority as a statutory tort.

4.03   Section 7 provides that a person who claims that a 'public authority'[1] has acted, or proposes to act, in a way that is incompatible with Convention rights[2] can either bring proceedings against the authority in an appropriate court or tribunal or can raise the Convention arguments concerned in any legal proceedings, but only if he or she can show he or she is, or would be, a 'victim' of the unlawful act.[3]

4.04   The creation of new causes of action against public authorities has brought with it new procedural issues, many of which remain unresolved almost a decade after the Act came into force. One such issue is the way in which limitation periods for bringing proceedings directly under section 7(1)(a)[4] interact with other relevant limitation periods. The questions of standing and third party interventions are important, in particular to the evolution of 'public interest' litigation, because section 7(7) requires English courts to *apply* Strasbourg case law on who is a victim, not simply to 'have regard' to it. This means that the limitations which the European Court of Human Rights (ECtHR) cases impose could restrict the circumstances in which important public interest questions are raised. There are also jurisdictional questions as to where proceedings involving section 6(1) should be brought.

4.05   To 'bring rights home' effectively, the Human Rights Act was drafted to ensure that victims of violations of Convention rights could seek remedies in domestic courts which would afford them 'just satisfaction' for any breaches of Convention rights they had suffered. Reflecting this intention, the Act creates both a cause of action, including a right to damages, under section 8, *and* gives higher courts the power to grant 'declarations of incompatibility' under section 4. The courts also retain existing remedies that fall within the jurisdiction of the relevant court, so other remedies which can be and are awarded under section 8(1) are familiar, such as (in a civil law context): damages; declarations; injunctions; and a mandatory quashing or prohibiting order in judicial review proceedings governed by Part 54 of the Civil Procedure Rules (CPR). In criminal proceedings, the remedies available to a defendant who establishes a violation of his or her Convention rights include: an order withdrawing the issue of a summons; a motion to quash an indictment; a stay of the criminal proceedings as abuse of process; the dismissal of the

---

[1] The definition of this term is discussed in ch 3.
[2] Section 6(1).
[3] Section 7(1).
[4] Section 7(5).

prosecution; the exclusion of evidence (or an order requiring the inclusion of evidence); or even (to reflect the breach) a reduction in sentence. The Court of Appeal has the power to quash a conviction where there has been a breach of Article 6 in the course of the trial.

However, the case law on damages for violations of the Act is still relatively under-developed, and despite the broad phrasing of section 8 permitting courts to grant any relief or remedy within their powers as they consider 'just and appropriate', imaginative remedies remain relatively rare. 4.06

B. THE APPROPRIATE FORUM FOR AN ARGUMENT UNDER THE HUMAN RIGHTS ACT

The Human Rights Act was designed to ensure that the Convention becomes an intrinsic part of all aspects of the UK legal system and that all courts and tribunals are able to consider arguments brought under the Convention. It does not provide any sort of reference procedure whereby an argument about a Convention point must be sent to a special court for adjudication. Convention arguments are available in every public forum in which legal rights are determined, from the magistrates' court to the Supreme Court (even though only the higher courts have the power to make a declaration of incompatibility and the power to award damages is restricted—see Chapter 3). Section 7 refers to bringing proceedings against a public authority 'in the appropriate court or tribunal'[5] and to relying on Convention rights 'in any legal proceedings',[6] including as a defence. 4.07

The ambit of the phrase 'legal proceedings' is not clear, and there may be litigation in future about what constitutes a 'legal proceeding'. For example, is a complaint to a statutory ombudsman a legal proceeding? In most cases, the debate is not important because the body conducting the proceeding is itself a public authority and so under a duty to interpret the law in line with the Convention. But questions may arise in relation to non-statutory self-regulatory organizations, especially those apparently subject to contract rather than judicial review, such as the insurance ombudsman or the Jockey Club.[7] 4.08

The 'appropriate court or tribunal' is determined by rules issued under the Human Rights Act[8] but, broadly, claims go to the court or tribunal most accustomed to dealing with claims analogous to the subject matter in question. For example, the Civil Procedure (Amendment No 4) Rules 2000[9] set out the procedure to be adopted in the Administrative Court; and the Family Proceedings (Amendment) Rules 2000[10] give details of the treatment of human rights issues in the family courts. Practice Direction 9 of the Supreme Court Rules 2009[11] makes provision for the treatment of human rights points in the Supreme Court. 4.09

---

[5] Section 7(1)(a).
[6] Section 7(1)(b).
[7] See *R v Disciplinary Committee of the Jockey Club, ex p Aga Khan* [1993] 1 WLR 909.
[8] Section 7(2) and (9).
[9] SI 2000/2092.
[10] SI 2000/2267.
[11] SI 2009/1603.

4.10   Some illustrative examples of an appropriate forum are as follows. In a false imprisonment claim, a person who wishes to claim damages for breach of Article 3 (freedom from
torture or inhuman or degrading treatment) or Article 5 (the right to liberty and security
of the person) could bring a claim for breach of statutory duty under section 6(1) of the
Human Rights Act in the High Court. Alternatively, the breach could be the basis for a
habeas corpus or judicial review application. A demonstrator who is prosecuted for
obstruction of the highway or obstruction of a police officer may be able to invoke the
right to peaceful assembly in Article 11 as a defence in the Crown Court or magistrates'
court. Article 5 arguments can also be used, for example, to argue for the release of a
person before the Mental Health Review Tribunal. A taxpayer who wishes to contend
that a tax demand based on the withdrawal of an extra-statutory concession is insufficiently precise and hence contrary to Protocol 1, Article 1, might be heard before the
Special Commissioners of the Inland Revenue.

4.11   It should be remembered, however, that the lower courts and tribunals do not have
the power under section 4(5) of the Human Rights Act to issue a declaration of incompatibility. Where proceedings are brought in the county court and a question of making
a declaration of incompatibility has arisen, Part 30 of the CPR requires the court to
consider transferring the proceedings to the High Court. However, it is not necessary to
transfer the proceedings to the High Court merely because a breach of a Convention
right is alleged.[12]

4.12   This cumbersome (and potentially time-consuming) solution to the problem of jurisdiction might have been avoided if the Government had adopted a 'residual reference'
procedure akin to a reference to the Court of Justice of the European Union, for cases
where an inferior court or tribunal dealing with a Human Rights Act point considered
that there might be a case for a declaration of incompatibility that would be beyond its
jurisdiction to award. Under such a procedure the declaration could have been made by
the High Court but as part of the main proceedings.

4.13   In civil proceedings generally, where a party is seeking to rely on any provision of, or
right arising under, the Human Rights Act, or seeks a remedy available under the Act, he
or she must, in the statement of case:

(a) give precise details of the Convention right which it is alleged has been infringed
    and details of the alleged infringement;

(b) specify the relief sought;

(c) state whether the relief sought includes a declaration of incompatibility pursuant
    to section 4 of the Human Rights Act and, if so, give precise details of the legisla-
    tive provision which is alleged to be incompatible and details of the alleged
    incompatibility;

(d) state whether the relief sought includes damages in respect of a judicial act (to which
    section 9(3) applies) and, if so, the judicial act complained of and the court or tribunal
    which is alleged to have made it; and

(e) give details of any finding of unlawfulness by another court or tribunal upon which
    the claim is based.[13]

---

[12] See *V (a child) (care proceedings: human rights claims)* [2004] EWCA Civ 54 at [8].
[13] CPR Practice Direction 16, para 15.

Where a declaration of incompatibility is sought, the Court may at any time   4.14
consider whether notice should be given to the Crown so that it can be joined as a
party to the proceedings.[14] Unless the Crown has been given 21 days' formal notice
(or other such period as the court directs) the court may not make a declaration of
incompatibility.[15]

This is a complex area and reference to the detailed procedures to be followed should   4.15
be sought out from comprehensive practitioner works such as the *White Book*[16] and
Archbold.[17]

C. STANDING: WHO MAY BRING PROCEEDINGS UNDER THE HUMAN RIGHTS ACT?

Any private, natural, or legal person can use the Human Rights Act. This includes com-   4.16
panies, since to restrict the benefit of the Act to natural persons would probably infringe
the provisions of Articles 6 and 14 (right to a fair trial in respect of civil rights and obligations, and right not to be discriminated against in application of the Convention
rights).[18] By virtue of section 7(1) and (3), however, the Act cannot be used to bring
proceedings only by a person who is not, or would not be, a 'victim' of the violation
(under Article 34 of the Convention), even if he or she would otherwise have standing
to be a party to judicial review proceedings on the broader test of 'standing' employed
under Part 54 of the CPR.

The 'victim' provision means that it is necessary to determine whether a particular liti-   4.17
gant is a 'victim' in order to decide whether the litigant can use the Human Rights Act;
and if the litigant is *not* a victim, but still has standing, the court has to decide on
the extent to which the litigant can nevertheless raise Convention arguments under the
pre-Act conditions.

Prior to the Human Rights Act coming into force it was widely anticipated that the   4.18
'victim' test would severely hamper its impact and development. However, from
the early days of the Human Rights Act this anticipated problem was mitigated by the
relaxed rule on third party interventions and '*amicus*' briefs which had already evolved
before the Act came into force.[19] The powers of the new Equality and Human Rights
Commission (discussed below) also go some way to addressing this problem.

1. Victims

The concept of a victim in section 7(7) of the Human Rights Act is taken from Article   4.19
34 of the Convention as amended by Protocol 11.[20] This provides that the Court

---

[14] See CPR Pt 19 and the accompanying Practice Direction.
[15] CPR 19.4A(1).
[16] (London: Sweet & Maxwell, 2011).
[17] (London: Sweet & Maxwell, 2011).
[18] For the position of public bodies, see para 4.22 below.
[19] See, eg *R v Bow Street Magistrate, ex p Pinochet (No 2)* [2000] 1 AC 119, in which Amnesty International
was granted leave to intervene; and *R v Department of Health, ex p Source Informatics* [2000] 2 WLR 940, in
which there were four interveners raising human rights arguments.
[20] Before the amendment the provision was in Art 25, to which the earlier case law refers.

'may receive applications from any person, non-governmental organization or group of individuals claiming to be the victim of a violation'. Pursuant to section 7(7), only an applicant who would have standing as a victim to bring proceedings in the ECtHR is a victim for the purposes of section 7. According to the ECtHR, a person has standing as a victim only if directly affected by the act or the omission that is the subject of the complaint. However, in *JM v UK* the Court held that an applicant is not required to show that he or she has suffered (financial) prejudice: that is relevant only in the context of just satisfaction.[21] There is, however, no role for individual 'public defenders' of human rights to be recognized.[22]

4.20   However, in Strasbourg case law it is not necessary for standing that the applicant has actually suffered the consequences of the alleged breach, provided there is a risk of the applicant being directly affected by it in the future.[23] For example, a gay man living in Northern Ireland was allowed to complain (successfully) about the criminalization of all homosexual conduct in private between consenting males, even though he had not yet been prosecuted under the law.[24] The risk of being affected must be a real threat, not a theoretical possibility.[25] Examples include cases in which challenges were made to legislation discriminating against children born out of wedlock, who were held to be victims of that legislation,[26] and a case where a litigant successfully persuaded the Court that she was a victim of the ban on divorce in Ireland because of the consequences for certain family relationships.[27] The ECtHR approach has been reflected in English decisions such as *R (Hooper) v Secretary of State for Work and Pensions* where the House of Lords considered that the applicants were 'victims' for the purposes of the Article 34 test because they could establish that they would have claimed the benefits alleged to have breached Article 14 had it been open to them to do so.[28] Further, at least in Article 2 cases, close family members of the deceased are entitled to be treated as 'victims'.[29]

4.21   A very liberal interpretation of 'victim' by the ECtHR was seen in *Open Door and Dublin Well Woman v Ireland* where it was held that two abortion advice centres and two counsellors who *offered* abortion advice, and women of childbearing age wishing to *receive* it, all had standing to challenge an injunction which was held to breach Article 10.[30] In contrast, in *Ahmed v United Kingdom* four local government officers and their trade union (UNISON) complained about the effect of statutory regulations which restricted the political activities of civil servants.[31] The European Commission on Human Rights (ECmHR) declared the application admissible in relation to the four

---

[21] App No 37060/06, 28 September 2010, para 27.

[22] See *Klass v Germany* (1978) 2 EHRR 214. See, similarly, *JR1, Re Judicial Review* [2011] NIQB 5 (finding that an eight-year-old child did not have standing to challenge on Art 2 grounds the decision by police to introduce tasers in Northern Ireland).

[23] *Klass v Germany*, ibid; and *Marckx v Belgium* (1979) 2 EHRR 330.

[24] *Dudgeon v United Kingdom* (1981) 4 EHRR 149; and *Norris v Ireland* (1988) 13 EHRR 186.

[25] *Campbell and Cosans v United Kingdom* (1982) 4 EHRR 293. See also *R (Burke) v The General Medical Council* [2005] EWCA Civ 1003, [2005] 3 WLR 1132 for a discussion of this issue in a domestic context.

[26] *Marckx v Belgium* (1979) 2 EHRR 330.

[27] *Johnston v Ireland* (1986) 9 EHRR 203.

[28] [2005] UKHL 29, [2005] 1 WLR 1681 at [59] per Lord Hoffmann *obiter*.

[29] *Rabone v Penine Care NHS Trust* [2010] EWCA Civ 698 at [92]. See also *R v Secretary of State for the Home Department, ex p Holub* [2001] 1 WLR 1359 in which the Court of Appeal at [14] considered *obiter* that the parents of a minor whose Convention rights have been breached have standing to complain under s 7.

[30] (1992) 15 EHRR 244.

[31] (1995) 20 EHRR CD 72, 77–8.

individuals, but inadmissible in relation to UNISON, as it was not directly affected by restrictions on free speech. Similarly, in *Re Medicaments and Related Classes of Goods (No 4)* the Court of Appeal held that a trade association was not a victim as its rights were not directly affected.[32]

Applying the Article 34 test of who is a 'victim',[33] the House of Lords in *Aston Cantlow and Wilmcote with Billesley Parochial Church Council v Wallbank* confirmed that local authorities are not able to use the Human Rights Act.[34] In *R (Westminster City Council) v Mayor of London* the High Court held that a local authority could also not be considered a 'non-governmental organization' for the purposes of Article 34 and so could not bring proceedings under the Act.[35]

2. Standing of public interest groups

While the victim requirement will not generally pose a problem to a potential litigant, in the context of judicial review proceedings it could shut out public interest groups, which have traditionally been permitted to bring judicial review proceedings in appropriate cases, from initiating proceedings on the basis that they do not 'suffer' from the unlawful action.

However, as the Human Rights Act is not intended to remove existing rights, Administrative Court judges have not generally used the section 7(3) definition of 'victim' to draw back from the liberal approach they have adopted to standing in general.[36]

The stringency of the 'victim' test in the context of judicial review is mitigated in two ways:

(a) In exceptional cases, the courts will permit a declaration to be sought that a proposed course of conduct is unlawful if it is incompatible with Convention rights. These cases can be brought on the basis of 'sufficient interest' alone rather than the applicant having to establish victim status under the strict provisions of the Human Rights Act. This opens up the possibility of the court making use of the interpretative power in section 3, as well as making a declaration of incompatibility under section 4.[37] In *Rusbridger and Toynbee v Attorney-General*[38] the House of Lords warned that the courts will exercise this jurisdiction rarely and that it should not be used to 'spring-clean' the statute book by application of section 3 in cases where there is no practical question of a breach of Convention rights occurring.[39]

(b) Since the coming into force of the Equality Act 2006 and the creation of the Equality and Human Rights Commission (the Commission) there is another potential way

---

[32] [2001] EWCA Civ 1217, [2002] 1 WLR 269.

[33] *Austria Municipalities v Austria* (1974) 17 YB 338.

[34] [2003] UKHL 37, [2004] 1 AC 546. See in particular Lord Hope at [43]–[47].

[35] [2002] EWHC (Admin) 2440. See also Davis, 'Public authorities as "victims" under the Human Rights Act' (2005) 64(2) CLJ 315.

[36] A rare example of a restrictive approach is found in *Re Medicaments and Related Classes of Goods (No 4)* [2001] EWCA Civ 1217, [2002] 1 WLR 269 (distinguishing between the positions of two different trade associations).

[37] See also *Taylor v Lancashire County Council* [2005] EWCA Civ 284 where it was held *obiter* that it would not be appropriate to grant a s 4 declaration where the applicant had not been and could not be personally affected by the legislation at issue.

[38] [2003] UKHL 38, [2004] 1 AC 357.

[39] Ibid at [36] per Lord Hutton and [61] per Lord Walker. See also the Court of Appeal's comments in *R (Burke) v The General Medical Council*, n 25 above.

4. Enforcing the Human Rights Act

for this gap to be filled. The Commission may not only intervene in existing proceedings, but may also take 'own name' proceedings, including judicial review, to prevent breaches of the Human Rights Act.[40]

3. Standing of the Equality and Human Rights Commission

4.26   The issue of the Commission's standing is dealt with in the Equality Act 2006. The Commission may either institute or intervene in litigation 'if it appears to the Commission that the proceedings are relevant to a matter in connection with which the Commission has a function'.[41] To facilitate this power section 30(3) provides:

> The Commission may, in the course of legal proceedings for judicial review which it institutes (or in which it intervenes), rely on section 7(1)(b) of the Human Rights Act 1998 (breach of Convention rights); and for that purpose—
> (a) the Commission need not be a victim or potential victim of the unlawful act to which the proceedings relate,
> (b) the Commission may act only if there is or would be one or more victims of the unlawful act,
> (c) section 7(3) and (4) of that Act shall not apply . . .

Section 30(2) is of similar effect in relation to Scottish proceedings.

4.27   This gives the Commission the power to take 'test and illustrative cases'[42] directly, and intervene in cases brought by others (interventions are dealt with separately below at para 4.35). The Commission has repeatedly stated its commitment to using strategic litigation to achieve improvements to legal protection of human rights and against discrimination, and to bolster its policy initiatives and monitoring duties.

4.28   In practice, the Commission's exercise of its litigation powers in relation to the Human Rights Act to date has largely been through interventions; the first use of the Commission's power to bring a claim for judicial review in relation to human rights concerns the lawfulness of the guidance given to the security services on interviewing overseas detainees and the use of intelligence obtained as a result.[43]

D. LIMITATION PERIODS: ARE THERE TIME LIMITS FOR BRINGING A CLAIM UNDER THE HUMAN RIGHTS ACT?

4.29   Section 7(5) of the Human Rights Act creates a primary limitation period of one year for cases against public bodies alleging a breach of a Convention right, beginning with the date on which the act complained of took place. This can be extended where the court

---

[40] Equality Act 2006 s 30.
[41] Section 30(1).
[42] See *EHRC Legal Strategy 2008/09*, available at <http://www.equalityhumanrights.com>.
[43] CO/10455/2010 *R (Equality and Human Rights Commission) v the Prime Minister and others* (listed for hearing at the end of June 2011). The Commission has also occasionally exercised its power to bring proceedings in relation to equality matters: see, eg *R (EHRC) v Secretary of State for Justice* [2010] EWHC 147 (Admin) and *Commission for Equality and Human Rights v Griffin and ors* [2010] EWHC 3343 (Admin) (the latter proceedings brought in relation to discriminatory provisions in the British National Party's constitution).

72

considers it 'equitable having regard to all the circumstances'. Although in some cases the High Court has listed the factors to be taken into account under section 7(5),[44] it is clear that such a 'prescriptive approach' is not appropriate, and it is for the court to examine in the circumstances of each individual case all the relevant factors, 'look at the matter broadly and attach such weight as is appropriate'.[45]

Under section 7(5)(b) the usual one-year limitation period is also subject to any more   4.30
restrictive rule which imposes a stricter time limit in relation to the proceeding in question (for example, the three-month time limit for bringing proceedings by way of judicial review contained in Part 54 of the CPR). The one-year time limit applies only to claims that directly allege breach of the Convention by a public authority, that is, only where there is a cause of action created by section 7(1)(a). There is no time limit to the interpretative obligation in section 7(1)(b).

Since the Human Rights Act came into force, the time limits imposed on personal   4.31
injury claims have been challenged unsuccessfully by claimants who argued that the Limitation Act 1980 should be interpreted in line with Convention rights and asked the courts to apply section 3 of the Human Rights Act retrospectively.[46] In *Dunn v Parole Board* the claimant prisoner had been recalled to prison while on licence four years before instituting proceedings.[47] He argued unsuccessfully that an extension of time should be granted as he had brought his claim within one year of the House of Lords' decision in *R (Smith) v Parole Board*, which established that Article 5(4) was engaged when a prisoner was recalled.[48] The Court of Appeal rejected this argument, but importantly noted that, on the evidence, the decision in *Smith* had played no part in the prisoner's delay; if it could have been shown that he had been waiting for this decision, the court's exercise of discretion may have differed.

A critical issue that remains to be decided concerns when time begins to run in the   4.32
case of a continuing act such as unlawful segregation or detention. Section 7(5)(a) of the Human Rights Act refers to 'the date on which the act complained of took place'; the question in such cases is whether time runs from the date the act ceased, or when it began. To a potential claimant this makes all the difference. If time runs from the beginning of the act, it would not be open to a person who was subjected to a continuing unlawful act or failure to act to take proceedings to bring it to an end while it was still continuing after the expiry of one year after its commencement, without appealing to the discretion of the court to extend this period. There are also practical ramifications regarding the remedies available, as the court would have to consider whether to award 'just satisfaction' for the entirety of the period, or only for a one-year period prior to the date on which proceedings were issued. In cases involving unlawful detention the quantum differential could be very large depending on the answer to this question. In *A v Essex*

---

[44] *Weir v Secretary of State for Transport* [2004] EWHC 2772 (Ch), [2005] UKHRR 154; *Cameron v Network Rail* [2006] EWHC 1133 (QB), [2007] 1 WLR 163; *Dobson v Thames Utilities* [2007] EWHC (QB) 2021.

[45] *Dunn v Parole Board* [2008] EWCA Civ 374, [2009] 1 WLR 728.

[46] *Rowe v Kingston upon Hull City Council* [2003] EWCA Civ 1281 on whether a dyslexic's claim for negligence against his former school was within the time limit for bringing a personal injury claim under s 14 of the Limitation Act; and *A v Hoare* [2008] UKHL 6, [2008] 1 AC 844 in which a victim of an intentional sexual assault argued that the cut-off imposed by s 2 of the Limitation Act should be extended in light of the Human Rights Act.

[47] [2008] EWCA Civ 374, [2009] 1 WLR 728.

[48] [2005] UKHL 1, [2005] 1 WLR 350.

County Council Baroness Hale expressed the view (obiter) that time begins to run from the date the breach ended.[49] Given the importance of this issue, it is likely to arise for formal determination sooner rather than later.

E. RETROSPECTIVITY

4.33   Following some initial, rather confusing decisions it is now clear that, apart from the exception created by section 22(4) case law, the Human Rights Act does not apply retrospectively to the acts of courts, tribunals, or public authorities which took place prior to 2 October 2000. This encompasses criminal proceedings and appeals[50] and civil law cases.[51] The House of Lords has held that the interpretative obligation in section 3 does not, in general, apply to acts, agreements, or transactions made before the Human Rights Act came into force,[52] but their Lordships have left open the possibility that in some circumstances the presumption against the retrospective application of section 3 might be rebutted where this would not give rise to unfairness.[53] As time goes on, the retrospectivity provisions become of diminishing practical importance.

4.34   Section 6(1) created new positive causes of action for acts or omissions that took place on or after 2 October 2000, when the Human Rights Act came into force. However, it can provide a defence to proceedings brought by the public authority whenever the act or omission complained of took place—whether before or after the Act was in force. For example, a prosecution that relies on evidence gathered in violation of Article 8 in 1999 could be challenged by a defendant on that basis at a trial taking place now (after 2 October 2000—although in practice this is of course now unlikely). But a decision taken on 1 October 2000 by a public authority cannot be challenged by way of judicial review, or on the basis that it was a breach of statutory duty under section 6(1). The reason for this curious feature is that section 22(4) of the Human Rights Act (which came into force before 2 October 2000) provides that section 7(1)(b) (reliance on the Convention in legal proceedings) applies to proceedings *brought by or at the instigation of a public authority* whenever the act in question took place, but otherwise only to acts taking place after the coming into force of that section.

F. INTERVENTIONS IN HUMAN RIGHTS ACT CASES

4.35   The Commission's power to directly litigate has the potential to mitigate the restrictive provisions of section 7 of the Human Rights Act. To date, the tight terms in section 7

---

[49] [2010] UKSC 33, [2011] 1 AC 280 at [113], referring to *Somerville v Scottish Ministers* [2007] UKHL 44, [2007] 1 WLR 2734.
[50] *R v Lambert* [2001] UKHL 37, [2002] 2 AC 545; although cf *R v Kansal (No 2)* [2001] 3 WLR 1562; see also *R v Lyons* [2002] UKHL 44, [2002] 3 WLR 1562.
[51] See, most recently, *In re McCaughey* [2011] UKSC 20 at [58] per Lord Phillips. In that case, the Supreme Court held that an inquest into a death resulting from acts of agents of the state which took place before the entry into force of the Act had to comply with the procedural obligations imposed by Art 2 of the Convention. In so holding, the court reversed its previous decision in *In re McKerr* [2004] UKHL 12, [2004] 1 WLR 807, which was unsustainable in the light of the intervening judgment of the ECtHR in *Šilih v Slovenia* (2009) 49 EHRR 996.
[52] See, eg *Wilson v First County Trust* [2003] UKHL 40, [2004] 1 AC 816.
[53] Ibid at [21] per Lord Nicholls and at [101]–[102] per Lord Hope.

have been offset by public interest groups supporting individuals who can establish their claim to be victims, and also by such groups acting as third party interveners in relevant cases; the Commission itself frequently intervenes in proceedings commenced by others.

1. Interventions by public interest groups

The Human Rights Act does not give an express right to intervene, except to the Crown, and, as detailed below (para. 4.37), the Commission also has a statutory power to intervene. However, the Supreme Court and the Court of Appeal have shown themselves increasingly willing to allow third party interventions under the normal rules of court.[54] In 2000, there were five petitions for leave to intervene in House of Lords' cases (with one granted leave to make full written and oral submissions, and four written submissions alone), rising to 14 petitions only two years later in 2002 (with eight being granted full oral and written submissions, and four written submissions alone).[55] The increase has been exponential since then; indeed, in public law cases raising human rights issues in the House of Lords, interveners are now the norm rather than the exception.

The reason for this rapid growth of interventions is clear: they can provide considerable benefits to courts and litigants, particularly in the context of the Human Rights Act where experience from other countries and details of other international human rights standards may be of great use. They can draw to the court's attention the wider significance of a point in a way that an individual litigant may be unable to do. They may provide supporting statistical or other evidence. They can help the court to determine whether an interference with a Convention right is 'necessary in a democratic society' or 'proportionate' by drawing to the court's attention the wider social significance or effects of a particular outcome.[56] For example, in *YL v Birmingham City Council* detailed witness statements and submissions were presented to the courts by the British Institute of Human Rights, Help the Aged, and the National Council on Ageing, adding important contextual evidence as to the practical ramifications of the narrow definition of 'public authority' under section 6.[57] And in *R (GC & C) v Commissioner of Police of the Metropolis*, Liberty and the Commission intervened to make submissions on implementing the *S and Marper* decision of the ECtHR.[58]

The courts are also increasingly willing to allow multiple interventions, and 'joint' interventions are also becoming more commonplace. For example, in *A and ors v Secretary of State for the Home Department*[59] a consortium of 14 international human rights organizations (including Human Rights Watch and Amnesty International) intervened in the House of Lords' case, which held that evidence obtained under torture from third parties by foreign state agents is not admissible in UK domestic courts. In *Re E*[60] the

4.36

4.37

4.38

---

[54] See CPR Pt 54; Practice Direction 37 of the House of Lords' *Practice Directions Applicable to Civil Appeals*, 2007–2008 edn; and Practice Direction 34 of the House of Lords' *Practice Directions Applicable to Criminal Appeals*, 2007–2008 edn.

[55] See Hannett, 'Third Party Intervention: In the Public Interest?' [2003] PL 128.

[56] See Arshi and O'Cinneide, 'Third-party Interventions: The Public Interest Reaffirmed' [2004] PL 69.

[57] [2007] UKHL 27, [2008] 1 AC 95. The case is analysed in ch 3.

[58] *R (GC & C) v Commissioner of Police of the Metropolis* [2011] UKSC 21, [2011] 1 WLR 1230; *S and Marper* (2008) 48 EHRR 1169.

[59] [2005] UKHL 71, [2006] 2 AC 221.

[60] [2008] UKHL 66, [2008] 3 WLR 1208 at [2], [6], and [69].

House of Lords recognized the specialist expertise that statutory bodies and NGOs can and have offered in public interest cases, Lord Hoffmann noting that:

> In recent years the House has frequently been assisted by the submissions of statutory bodies and non-governmental organisations on questions of general public importance. Leave is given to such bodies to intervene and make submissions, usually in writing but sometimes orally from the bar, in the expectation that their fund of knowledge or particular point of view will enable them to provide the House with a more rounded picture than it would otherwise obtain. The House is grateful to such bodies for their help.[61]

4.39   However, judges have on occasion expressed irritation at the increased workload caused by intervening parties; it is clear that any intervention must add value and not merely repeat points made by one of the main parties to the proceedings.[62]

2. Interventions by the Equality and Human Rights Commission

4.40   The Commission, with the permission of the court, can intervene in cases, including judicial review, where the Commission is not a party.[63] The Commission made 29 interventions in its first year of existence, including one in the Grand Chamber of the European Court of Human Rights[64] and 18 in 2010. It is understood that, to date, no court or tribunal has refused an application by the Commission to intervene.

4.41   The Commission's role in an intervention is not to support one side or the other; it is to provide independent arguments to the court to promote the objectives set out for it in the Equality Act 2006 (discussed more fully below at para 4.94).[65]

4.42   The Commission has intervened in a number of cases concerning human rights, and at a range of levels. Examples include:

- *R (GC & C) v The Commissioner of Police of the Metropolitan Police*: implementation of the *S and Marper* decision of the ECtHR regarding DNA retention in the UK;[66]
- *R (Smith) v Secretary of State for Defence*: jurisdictional application of human rights protection for British military personnel; right to an Article 2 investigation;[67]
- *R (JL) v Secretary of State for the Home Department* (House of Lords): the Article 2 investigative duty arising from near-death incidents in custody;[68]
- *R (RJM) v Secretary of State for Work and Pensions* (House of Lords): the scope of Article 14 and whether 'other status' includes homelessness;[69]
- *R (G) v The Governors of X School* (Supreme Court): extent to which legal representation is required under Article 6 in employment tribunal proceedings (where the consequences go beyond the employment context);[70]

---

61 Ibid at [2].
62 Ibid at [2]–[3] per Lord Hoffmann and [69] per Lord Brown.
63 Equality Act 2006, s 30.
64 *RP v United Kingdom* App No 38245/08.
65 See Equality Act 2006, ss 3, 8–11.
66 [2011] UKSC 21.
67 [2010] UKSC 29, [2011] 1 AC 1.
68 [2008] UKHL 68, [2009] 1 AC 588.
69 [2008] UKHL 63, [2009] 1 AC 311.
70 [2011] UKSC 30, [2011] 3 WLR 237.

- *JM v United Kingdom* (ECtHR): whether same-sex couples are a 'family' for the purposes of Article 8.[71]

G. OTHER MEANS OF ENFORCEMENT BY THE EQUALITY AND HUMAN RIGHTS COMMISSION[72]

The Equality and Human Rights Commission has extensive legal powers, including the power to take judicial review proceedings in its own name to prevent breaches of the Human Rights Act, and the power to intervene in proceedings taken by others which raise human rights issues.[73] The Commission also has a range of other enforcement tools at its disposal, including the power to conduct formal inquiries and to fund organizations providing legal assistance in human rights. This allows the Commission to enforce the Human Rights Act without necessarily engaging in litigation. The Commission also undertakes legal policy work, including briefing ministers and parliamentarians on human rights issues in draft legislation, and contributing to international treaty monitoring bodies. These non-litigation legal powers are dealt with below. The Commission also has wide-ranging research, communication, and education functions which are not dealt with in this text, but which also allow it to promote human rights and ensure compliance with the Human Rights Act. It should be noted that at the time of writing the Commission's powers are under review, but the Government's consultation document proposes that its substantive human rights powers and duties remain as they are.[74]

4.43

1. The duties of the Commission

The Equality Act 2006 sets out the Commission's legal duties. Section 3 contains a general duty:

4.44

The Commission shall exercise its functions under this Part with a view to encouraging and supporting the development of a society in which—
(a) people's ability to achieve their potential is not limited by prejudice or discrimination,
(b) there is respect for and protection of each individual's human rights,
(c) there is respect for the dignity and worth of each individual,
(d) each individual has an equal opportunity to participate in society, and
(e) there is mutual respect between groups based on understanding and valuing of diversity and on shared respect for equality and human rights.

At the time of writing, this general power is also under review. Section 8 of the 2006 Act sets out the Commission's specific legal duties in relation to equality and diversity, including the duties to promote understanding and encourage good practice in relation

---

[71] Application No 37060/06, 28 September 2010.
[72] See, generally, O'Cinneide, 'The Commission For Equality And Human Rights: A New Institution For New And Uncertain Times' (2007) 36(2) Industrial Law Journal 141.
[73] See para 4.40 above.
[74] See <http://www.equalityhumanrights.com/about-us/vision-and-mission/government-consultation-on-our-future>.

to equality and diversity, and to 'work towards the elimination of unlawful discrimination'. Section 10 requires the Commission to promote understanding of the importance of good relations and encourage good practice in relations between members of different groups and others.

4.45   The Commission's specific legal duties concerning human rights are set out in section 9. 'Human rights' in this context includes the Convention rights, but also 'other human rights' not set out in the Convention.[75] Section 9(1) provides that:

The Commission shall, by exercising the powers conferred by this Part—
    (a) promote understanding of the importance of human rights,
    (b) encourage good practice in relation to human rights,
    (c) promote awareness, understanding and protection of human rights, and
    (d) encourage public authorities to comply with section 6 of the Human Rights Act 1998
(compliance with Convention rights).

In fulfilling a duty under section 8 or 10 the Commission must also take account of any relevant human rights.

4.46   Section 11(1) requires the Commission to 'monitor the effectiveness of the equality and human rights enactments' and provides that it may advise central government on its findings, make recommendations to it regarding whether to amend, repeal, or consolidate any of the equality and human rights enactments, and advise central or devolved government (in Scotland, Wales, or Northern Ireland) about the effect of an enactment, or the likely effect of a proposed change of law.[76] This 'pre-emptive' role—preventing breaches of the Human Rights Act before they occur—is not unfamiliar: the Parliamentary Joint Committee on Human Rights (JCHR) scrutinizes all government Bills and picks out those with significant human rights implications for further examination.

2. Legal assistance

4.47   The Commission's powers in relation to human rights issues with no equality dimension are limited. Unless there is an equality dimension to the case, the Commission does not have the power to give legal assistance to individuals on human rights grounds alone.

3. Legal policy

4.48   In addition to monitoring the effectiveness of equality and human rights laws, the Commission seeks through its legal work to influence the development of future legislation and policies likely to have an impact on equality and human rights. This includes: cooperating with the Scottish Commission for Human Rights, the Northern Ireland Human Rights Commission, and the Equality Commission for Northern Ireland;

---

[75] Equality Act 2006, s 9(2)(b). The Commission must, however, have particular regard to the importance of exercising its powers in relation to the Convention rights: s 9(3).

[76] Ibid, s 11(2). Recently, the Commission has published briefings (available on its website) on the following Bills, among others: Terrorism Prevention and Investigation Measures Bill; Health and Social Care Bill; Protection of Freedoms Bill; Localism Bill; Public Bodies Bill; Terrorist Asset-Freezing etc Bill; Identity Documents Bill—Commons Second Reading; Borders, Citizenship and Immigration Bill; Coroners and Justice Bill; Crime, Security, Policing and Counter-Terrorism Bill.

making submissions to international treaty monitoring bodies; and drafting statutory and non-statutory guidance.

4. Inquiries, investigations, and assessments

The Commission has a range of investigation and assessment powers. It may conduct an inquiry, or undertake an investigation or assessment (sections 16, 20, and 31). It has power to require any person to provide written or oral evidence or relevant documents, which gives teeth to its inquiry powers.   4.49

(a) *Inquiries*

The Commission may conduct 'an inquiry into a matter' relating to any of its duties under sections 8 (equality), 9 (human rights), or 10 (groups).[77] Schedule 2 to the Equality Act deals with the logistics of such inquiries: terms of reference, representations, evidence, reports, recommendations, and the effects of reports. Inquiries can be general or specific; they could be thematic (for example, related to one particular Convention right), sectoral (looking at, for example, the treatment of children in custodial establishments that are managed by private companies), or relate to one or more named parties.   4.50

In October 2008, the Commission launched an inquiry into *Recruitment and employment in the meat and poultry processing sector*. The inquiry examined how the people working in this sector are recruited, and how they are treated once they are at work. In March 2010 the Commission issued a report summarizing its findings and making recommendations which it believes will bring about change.[78] And in June 2009 the Commission published its *Human Rights Inquiry* which assessed progress towards the effectiveness and enjoyment of a culture of respect for human rights in Britain and made a number of recommendations as to how the current human rights framework might be better integrated into public service provision and explained to the public.[79]   4.51

(b) *Investigations and assessments*

An investigation is a tool that enables the Commission to investigate whether or not a particular person (natural or legal) has committed an unlawful act, or failed to comply with a notice given to that person by the Commission, or an agreement that person has made with the Commission following an earlier finding that the person has behaved unlawfully.[80] The Commission may also conduct an assessment of a public authority's compliance with the public sector duties regarding gender, race, and disability. The power to initiate investigations and assessments is restricted to the Commission's equality remit.   4.52

---

[77] Equality Act 2006, s 16(1).

[78] See <http://www.equalityhumanrights.com/uploaded_files/Inquiries/meat_inquiry_report.pdf>.

[79] See <http://www.equalityhumanrights.com/human-rights/our-human-rights-inquiry/inquiry-report/>. Three further inquiries with a human rights angle are ongoing at the time of writing: *Inquiry into home care of older people*; *Inquiry into human trafficking in Scotland*; and *Inquiry into disability-related harassment*.

[80] Equality Act 2006, s 20(1).

H. REMEDIES

1. Damages

(a) *Jurisdiction and procedure*

4.53 Section 8(1) of the Human Rights Act authorizes a court which has found that an act or proposed act of a public authority is unlawful, to grant 'such relief or remedy, or make such order, within its powers as it considers just and appropriate'. This can be used to found a claim for relief, including damages, against a public authority. Courts and tribunals of limited jurisdiction cannot award a remedy if it is outside their statutory power to do so. For example, an employment tribunal is not able to order an injunction to prevent a discriminatory dismissal going ahead (because it has no statutory power to do so), even if it were to consider this necessary to afford just satisfaction of a Convention right.

4.54 Section 8(2) permits a court to make an award of damages under the Act where it has the power to award compensation (even if it is not otherwise called 'damages'). This, in principle, includes statutory tribunals such as employment tribunals. Criminal courts cannot award damages under section 8(2).[81]

4.55 The Court of Appeal laid down procedural guidelines for courts considering claims for damages in respect of maladministration leading to a breach of Convention rights in *Anufrijeva v Southwark London Borough Council*.[82] The guidelines, which are of general importance, included the following:

(a) A claim for damages alone cannot be brought by judicial review but it should still be brought in the Administrative Court by an ordinary claim. Courts should look critically at any attempt to recover damages under the Human Rights Act for maladministration by any procedure other than judicial review.

(b) Claimants should first exhaust (or explain why it would not be more appropriate to use) any available internal complaint procedure, or proceed by making a claim to the parliamentary or local government ombudsman.

(c) If there is a legitimate claim for other relief, permission should, if appropriate, be limited to that relief, and consideration given to deferring permission for the damages claim, adjourning or staying that claim until use has been made of alternative dispute-resolution procedures.

(d) In determining quantum of damages, citations should in general be limited to three authorities, and, except in exceptional circumstances, the hearing should be limited to half a day.

(b) *Principles of assessment*

4.56 There is no automatic entitlement to damages under the Human Rights Act—courts may exercise their power to award damages to victims whose Convention rights have

---

[81] *R v Galfetti* [2002] EWCA Civ 1916, [2002] MHLR 418.

[82] [2003] EWCA Civ 1406, [2004] QB 1124. For a more detailed discussion of the practical ramifications of the guidelines laid down in *Anufrijeva*, see Clayton, 'Damage Limitation: The Courts and the Human Rights Act Damages' [2005] PL 429; and for analysis as to when the guidelines apply, see Whitfield/Public Law Project, 'Between a Rock and a Hard Place: ADR after Anufrijeva' (Winter 2003/4), available at <http://www.publiclawproject.org.uk>.

been breached but they are not bound to do so in all cases. Section 8(3) provides that damages are to be awarded only where they are necessary to afford 'just satisfaction' to the victim. When courts are deciding whether a monetary award is necessary they will take account of all the circumstances of the case, including any other remedy granted by the court or any other court, and the consequences of any decision (of that or any other court) in respect of the breach.[83]

Section 8(4) provides that a court or tribunal deciding whether to award damages and how much to award must take into account the principles applied by the ECtHR in relation to the award of compensation under Article 41 of the Convention. As Silber J pointed out in *R (N) v Secretary of State for the Home Department*,[84] section 8(4) requires the court to take into account the *principles*, whereas section 2(1) requires it to take into account the *decisions*, suggesting that it is open to the court, having identified any relevant principles from the Strasbourg case law, to then seek assistance on quantum from other sources.[85] However, it is difficult to identify a concrete set of principles from the ECtHR case law on Article 41 to which domestic courts can refer when considering awarding damages under the Human Rights Act. As the Law Commission put it, the 'most striking feature' of the Strasbourg case law on damages is 'the lack of clear principles as to when damages should be awarded and how they should be measured'.[86] Despite this practical problem, it is possible to identify the following broad themes that have been used by the ECtHR:[87]

4.57

(a) Compensation is discretionary and will be awarded only if 'necessary', bearing in mind the circumstances of the case as a whole. It is not uncommon for the Strasbourg Court to decline to award compensation on the basis that a declaration of unlawful conduct is sufficient remedy for an applicant. Equally, the ECtHR refuses to award just satisfaction to applicants, such as terrorist suspects, that it considers 'undeserving'.[88]

(b) There must be a 'causal link' between the breach of the applicant's Convention rights, any alleged resulting harm, and the compensation sought.

(c) The principle of compensation is '*restitutio in integrum*', that is, that the applicant is, so far as possible, put back into the situation in which he or she would have been but for the violation of his or her Convention rights.[89] Exemplary or punitive damages are not recoverable. The ECtHR does not expressly award aggravated damages, but the conduct of both the applicant and/or the respondent state and the gravity of the violation may either lessen or enhance the amount of damages awarded.[90]

---

[83] See, eg *Dobson v Thames Water Utilities* [2009] EWCA Civ 28 (where damages were available in nuisance against a sewerage undertaker, such damages themselves constituted just satisfaction and no further damages were awarded).

[84] [2003] EWHC 207 (Admin) at [180].

[85] See Clayton, 'Damages under the Human Rights Act', paper presented to the Human Rights Lawyers' Association, 1 December 2003; available at <http://www.hrla.org.uk>.

[86] Law Commission, *Damages under the Human Rights Act* (Law Com No 266, 2000) (Cm 4853) para 3.4.

[87] Ibid, s III. See also the analysis of Lord Woolf in *Anufrijeva v Southwark London Borough Council* [2003] EWCA Civ 1406, [2004] QB 1124.

[88] See *McCann v United Kingdom* (1995) 21 EHRR 97.

[89] *Kingsley v United Kingdom* (2002) 35 EHRR 10.

[90] For further analysis of the ECtHR's approach to exemplary, punitive, and aggravated damages, see Shelton, *Remedies in International Human Rights Law* (Oxford: Oxford University Press, 2005) 360.

4.58   The ECtHR measures 'just satisfaction' under three heads: pecuniary loss, non-pecuniary loss, and costs and expenses:

(a) *Pecuniary loss*   Where applicants have claimed for things such as loss of earnings and career prospects under Article 6(1), the ECtHR has rarely held that a procedural failing has caused pecuniary loss and refuses to speculate on what the outcome of proceedings would have been had the violation not occurred.[91] However, in *Barberà v Spain* the ECtHR held that there had been a loss of opportunity (to prove innocence) as a result of a procedural failing.[92]

(b) *Non-pecuniary loss*   The ECtHR has awarded non-pecuniary damages in respect of pain, suffering, and physical or psychological injury,[93] including distress and anxiety.[94]

(c) *Costs and expenses*   The test applied by the ECtHR is whether the costs were actually and necessarily incurred in order to prevent, or obtain redress for, the breach of the Convention, and were reasonable as to quantum.

4.59   Although the case law is limited, the approach of the English courts to damages under the Human Rights Act to date has reflected, and attempted to develop, the broad themes discernible in the ECtHR jurisprudence.[95] The principle of *restitutio in integrum* has been applied to deny successful claimants damages;[96] in relation to quantum the courts have often referred to the Strasbourg jurisprudence, although other judges have looked for inspiration from domestic comparators.[97]

(c) Quantum

4.60 The quantum of awards granted by the Strasbourg Court is generally cautious, particularly for 'non-pecuniary' damage such as in cases of unlawful detention. For example, in *Johnson v United Kingdom* the Strasbourg Court awarded damages of £10,000 for a wrongful detention in a maximum security psychiatric hospital lasting three-and-a-half years.[98]

4.61   Finally, it should be noted that the level of awards under section 8 of the Human Rights Act should not affect the proper level of damages an applicant is entitled to receive for breach of any other tort, such as false imprisonment. Section 11 of the Act provides that a person may rely on a Convention right without prejudice to any other right or freedom conferred on him or her by or under any (other) law having effect in the United Kingdom.

4.62   At the time the Human Rights Act came into force there was considerable debate over the nature of the remedy contained in the statute and the impact this would then have

---

[91] *Saunders v United Kingdom* (1997) 23 EHRR 313.
[92] (1988) 11 EHRR 360.
[93] See, eg *Aydin v Turkey* (1998) 25 EHRR 251.
[94] *Doustaly v France*, 70 Rep Judg & Dec 1998 II 850.
[95] See *Anufrijeva v Southwark London Borough Council* [2003] EWCA Civ 1406, [2004] QB 1124; and *R (Greenfield) v Secretary of State for the Home Department* [2005] UKHL 14, [2005] 1 WLR 673.
[96] See, eg *R (SL) v Commissioner of Police for the Metropolis* [2008] EWHC 1442 (Admin).
[97] See the approach adopted in *R (Bernard) v London Borough of Enfield* [2002] EWHC 2282 (Admin), (2003) UKHRR 148.
[98] (1999) 27 EHRR 296.

on the assessment of quantum.[99] The most authoritative examination of the topic was contained in the report by the Law Commission, *Damages under the Human Rights Act*,[100] which described sections 6 and 7 as 'creat[ing] a new cause of action, which is in effect a form of action for breach of statutory duty, but with the difference that the remedy is discretionary rather than of right'.

The Law Commission also expressed the view that damages for tort were the most relevant domestic analogy to damages under section 8 of the Human Rights Act, and suggested that courts could treat the quantum rules in tort as the prima facie measure to be applied—unless the results were inconsistent with Strasbourg case law under Article 41.[101]   4.63

However, in *R (Greenfield) v Secretary of State for the Home Department*,[102] Lord Bingham rejected the submissions that damages under the Human Rights Act should not be on the low side compared to tortious awards; that English courts should be free to depart from the scale of damages awarded by the ECtHR; and that English awards (whether tortious or public law remedies) should provide the appropriate comparator. He pointed out that: the objectives of the Human Rights Act were different and broader than those of a tort statute; a finding of a violation is an important part of a claimant's remedy and an important vindication of the right asserted; and the purpose of incorporating the Convention was to give claimants the same remedies they would recover in Strasbourg. He also pointed out that section 8(4) requires the courts to take into account the principles of the ECtHR in determining the amount of damages. He suggested that the courts under the Human Rights Act 'should not aim to be significantly more or less generous than the ECtHR might be expected to be, in a case where it was willing to make an award at all'.   4.64

The approach taken by the English courts to date has been disappointing, and the general principles formulated by the House of Lords in *Greenfield* are more restrictive than the terms of the Human Rights Act itself would mandate. The effect of their Lordships' approach has been that damages for breaches of Convention rights are considered and awarded rarely, with successful claimants often receiving no damages.[103] Even where they are available, they are generally much lower than the comparable awards for race or sex discrimination. There is a powerful argument that this approach not only has the effect of downgrading human rights but also frustrates the intention of the Human Rights Act, which envisaged domestic courts being able to provide an effective remedy for breaches of Convention rights. This restrictive approach also causes difficulty in obtaining public funding for cases because of the relatively low monetary value   4.65

---

[99] Lester and Pannick, 'Law Com No 266 (2000): The Impact of the Human Rights Act on Private Law: The Knight's Move' (2000) 116 LQR 380 (referring to the creation of a 'constitutional tort' of infringing Convention rights); Clayton and Tomlinson, *The Law of Human Rights* (Oxford: Oxford University Press, 2000) para 21.21 (referring to the creation of a public law remedy).

[100] Law Commission, *Damages under the Human Rights Act* (Law Com No 266, 2000) (Cm 4853) para 4.20.

[101] See *R (Bernard) v London Borough of Enfield* [2001] EWCA Civ 1831, [2002] HLR 860 in support of this approach; likewise *Anufrijeva v Southwark London Borough Council* [2003] EWCA Civ 1406, [2004] QB 1124.

[102] [2005] UKHL 14, [2005] 1 WLR 673 at [19].

[103] See, eg *R (SL) v Commissioner of Police for the Metropolis* [2008] EWHC 1442 (Admin).

assigned to human rights cases—although many should still pass the criteria for funding under the 'public interest' test.[104]

4.66   That said, the courts have made sizeable damages awards in a few recent cases, albeit without engaging in detailed reasoning in support of the amounts arrived at. For example, in *R (B) v Director of Public Prosecutions*[105] the Divisional Court found that the Director of Public Prosecutions (DPP) had breached the claimant's Article 3 rights in deciding to terminate a prosecution on the eve of the trial on the irrational basis that the victim could be put before the jury as a credible witness because he suffered from mental illness. It awarded damages in the amount of £8,000. Whilst it could not be assumed that a trial would necessarily have resulted in a conviction, the court held that '[the claimant] is to be compensated for being deprived of the opportunity of the proceedings running their proper course and the damage to his self respect from being made to feel that he was beyond the effective protection of the law'. In *OOO v Commissioner of Police of the Metropolis*[106] the court made awards of £5,000 to each claimant for breaches of the police's positive obligation to investigate (well-founded) allegations of inhuman and degrading treatment.

4.67   It should be borne in mind that, in judicial review proceedings in particular, where separate damages hearings are ordered after the substantive hearing, settlement on quantum will often be reached. This means that the reported case law does not necessarily reflect the reality of Human Rights Act awards.

(d) *Claims against judicial bodies and Parliament*

4.68   In general, it is not possible to make a claim for damages against a court which has breached the Convention, even though it is a public authority. Where a first instance court acts unlawfully, section 9 of the Human Rights Act requires proceedings in respect of its decision to be brought on appeal from the decision, by way of judicial review or in such other forum as may be prescribed by rules. However, there is provision in section 9(3) and (4) for awards of damages against the Crown where any judicial body has been guilty of a breach of Article 5 in, for example, cases of false imprisonment following a bail application. To claim this remedy, the 'appropriate person', if not already a party to the proceedings, must be joined.[107] The appropriate person (defined in section 9(5)) is the minister responsible for the court concerned, or a person or government department nominated by him or her. In *R (KB) v Mental Health Review Tribunal* the claimants were awarded 'modest' damages after they had established breaches of Article 5(4) rights arising from the failure of the MHRT to deal speedily with their applications for a review of their detention.[108]

4.69   There is *no* right in damages where the breach of the Convention is caused by an Act of Parliament. It is still not clear how the Human Rights Act intends 'just satisfaction' to be afforded in cases where the breach of the Convention is a consequence of a statutory provision, and where a court has made a declaration of incompatibility under section 4,

---

[104] This is a particular problem in Art 5 'false imprisonment' cases taken in the county courts.
[105] [2009] EWHC 106 (Admin).
[106] [2011] EWHC 1246 (QB).
[107] See also CPR 19.4A.
[108] [2003] EWHC 193 (Admin), [2004] QB 936.

given the failure to incorporate Article 13. It is possible that *ex gratia* payments of compensation under section 10 are intended to be the appropriate remedy.[109]

This is an area of law which changes rapidly, and reference should be made to up-to-date discussions and analysis in practitioner texts, such as the *White Book*, the European Human Rights Law Review, and the UK Human Rights Reports (see Chapter 10 for further details).   4.70

2. Section 4—declarations of incompatibility

One of the remedies provided by the Human Rights Act that has been used relatively regularly is the 'declaration of incompatibility'. Under section 4(2), higher courts have the option of declaring that primary legislation is incompatible with the Convention if it is impossible for them to interpret the legislation in such a way as to render it compatible. However, the making of a declaration of incompatibility does not result in the proceedings being resolved in favour of the litigant whose rights were violated. As the courts must give primacy to the statute, this declaration does not affect the validity, continuing operation, or enforcement of the legislation, and 'is not binding on the parties to the proceedings in which it is made'.[110]   4.71

Section 4 is a central part of the carefully crafted mechanism in the Human Rights Act which allows for a balance between the constitutional principles of parliamentary sovereignty and judicial protection of human rights (see Chapter 1). A declaration of incompatibility does not 'strike down' legislation but brings any tension between Convention rights and a particular statutory scheme to the attention of Parliament. It also triggers the power to take remedial action in response under section 10, which provides a 'fast-track' procedure for the amendment of legislation to bring it into line with human rights principles. However, unlike for judgments of the ECtHR, there is no legal obligation on the Government to take remedial action following a declaration of incompatibility, nor upon Parliament to accept any remedial measures the Government may propose.   4.72

A declaration of incompatibility is intended to be 'a measure of last resort . . . [which] . . . must be avoided unless it is plainly impossible to do so'.[111] The courts try to avoid making such declarations by striving to find meanings for statutory provisions that conform with the Convention under the strong interpretative obligation in section 3 of the Human Rights Act, which allows the courts to construe legislation compatibly with Convention rights.   4.73

The Supreme Court recently declined to make a declaration of incompatibility where it was possible for guidance to be disapplied and legislation interpreted in a Convention-compatible manner.[112]   4.74

---

[109] See, eg *R (H) v Mental Health Review Tribunal* [2001] EWCA Civ 415, [2001] 3 WLR 512 and the payment scheme established by the Government following a declaration of incompatibility.

[110] Section 4(6)(b). It is understood that this provision is designed to allow the Government to take a different position from that of the court should the case be argued in the ECtHR.

[111] See Lord Steyn in *R v A (No 2)* [2001] UKHL 25, [2002] 1 AC 45 at [44].

[112] *R (GC and C) v Commissioner of Police of the Metropolis* [2011] UKSC 21, [2011] 1 WLR 1230.

4.75 Even where it is not possible to interpret a provision compatibly with Convention rights, courts retain their discretion whether to grant a declaration (which is exercised according to the normal principles governing the grant of declarations). The circumstances in which a declaration might be made were set out in *Wilson v First County Trust Ltd (No 2)*.[113]

4.76 Finally, where a complaint relates to the absence of legislation it is important to note that any lacuna in a statutory scheme cannot result in a declaration of incompatibility under the Human Rights Act.[114]

(a) *Jurisdiction, procedure, and notice provisions*

4.77 The power to make declarations of incompatibility is available only in the higher courts. These include the High Court, the Court of Appeal, and the House of Lords, but not the various tribunals that sit in place of the High Court and from which appeals lie to the Court of Appeal (for example, the Employment Appeal Tribunal and the Immigration Appeal Tribunal).[115]

4.78 There is no strict requirement that a person who seeks a declaration of incompatibility is a 'victim' within the definition of section 7, provided he or she has sufficient interest and standing.[116] However, the court will normally only grant a declaration of incompatibility to a person who is a victim of an actual or proposed breach of a Convention right, and in any event a person cannot apply for a declaration of incompatibility on the basis of a hypothetical argument, or if he are she is not adversely affected by the measure in question.[117] But a declaration of incompatibility may serve a useful purpose even if the Government has already indicated an intention to change the law.[118]

(b) *Examples of declarations of incompatibility in specific cases*

4.79 Although there have been many challenges to legislation since the Human Rights Act came into force, declarations of incompatibility have been made and upheld by the courts in a relatively small number of cases. Since the Human Rights Act came into force 27 declarations of incompatibility have been made.[119] Of these:

- 19 have become final (in whole or in part) and are not subject to further appeal; and
- eight were overturned on appeal, of which one was reinstated following further appeal.[120]

---

[113] [2001] EWCA Civ 633, [2002] QB 74 at [46]; overruled on other grounds by the House of Lords at [2003] UKHL 40, [2003] 3 WLR 568.

[114] See *Re S (minors) (care order: implementation of care plan)* [2002] 2 UKHL 10, [2002] 2 AC 291.

[115] See ch 3 for further detail as to the duties of the lower courts when confronted with compatibility arguments.

[116] *R (Rusbridger) v Attorney General* [2003] UKHL 38, [2003] 3 WLR 232 at [21] per Lord Steyn.

[117] *Taylor v Lancashire County Council and Secretary of State for the Environment, Food and Rural Affairs* [2005] EWCA Civ 284, [2005] HRLR 17.

[118] *Bellinger v Bellinger* [2003] UKHL 21, [2003] 2 AC 467.

[119] This figure is correct as of 1 June 2011. A table of the 27 cases can be found at <http://www.publications.parliament.uk/pa/cm201011/cmhansrd/cm110426/text/110426w0005.htm#11042749003984>.

[120] *R (Wright and ors) v Secretary of State for Health and Secretary of State for Education and Skills* [2009] UKHL 3, [2009] 2 WLR 267.

In most instances the Government has responded to the declarations issued by the   4.80
courts by amending, repealing, or introducing new legislation. Examples include the
following:

(a) *R v Secretary of State for the Home Department, ex p Anderson* involved a challenge to
the Home Secretary's power under the Crime (Sentences) Act 1997 to set the minimum period that must be served by a mandatory life sentence prisoner before he was
considered for release on licence.[121] Following the Strasbourg ruling in *Stafford v
United Kingdom*[122] the House of Lords found that the involvement of the Home
Secretary, as a member of the executive, in fixing the tariff term of imprisonment for
those convicted of murder was incompatible with Article 6(1). The impugned law
was repealed by the Criminal Justice Act 2003 and new sentencing provisions were
introduced in Chapter 7 of, and Schedules 21 and 22 to, that Act.

(b) In *Blood and Tarbuck v Secretary of State for Health* section 28(6)(b) of the Human
Fertilisation and Embryology Act 1990 was declared incompatible with Article 8,
and/or Article 14 taken together with Article 8, to the extent that it did not allow a
deceased father's name to be given on the birth certificate of his child.[123] The law was
amended by the Human Fertilisation and Embryology (Deceased Fathers) Act 2003.

(c) In *Bellinger v Bellinger* a post-operative male-to-female transsexual appealed against a
decision that she was not validly married to her husband because the law still regarded
her as a man.[124] The House of Lords held that section 11(c) of the Matrimonial
Causes Act 1973 was incompatible with Articles 8 and 12 of the Convention as it
denied a post-operative transsexual wishing to have her marriage legally recognized
her right to respect for family and private life. The declaration of incompatibility was
made following the Strasbourg Court's decision in *Goodwin v United Kingdom*[125] and
Parliament enacted the Gender Recognition Act 2004 to remedy the breach.

(d) *R (Morris) v Westminster City Council and First Secretary of State*[126] concerned an
application for local authority accommodation by a single mother (a British citizen)
whose child was subject to immigration control. It was held that section 185(4) of
the Housing Act 1996 was incompatible with Article 14 to the extent that it required
a dependent child who was not a British citizen to be disregarded when determining
whether the parent (who is a British citizen) has priority need for housing. A similar
declaration was granted in *R (Gabaj) v First Secretary of State*,[127] except that in this
case it was the claimant's pregnant wife (rather than the claimant's child) who was
subject to immigration control. The law was amended by Schedule 15 to the
Housing and Regeneration Act 2008 (not yet in force), although the JCHR has
doubted whether these provisions are sufficient to address the incompatibility.[128]

---

[121] [2002] UKHL 46, [2003] 1 AC 837.
[122] (2002) 35 EHRR 32.
[123] Sullivan J, 28 February 2003.
[124] [2003] UKHL 21, [2003] 2 AC 467.
[125] (2002) 35 EHRR 18.
[126] [2005] EWCA Civ 1184, [2006] 1 WLR 505.
[127] CO/7458/2005, 28 March 2006.
[128] JCHR, *Monitoring the Government's Response to Human Rights Judgments: Annual Report 2008*, 31st
Report (2007–2008), HL 173, HC 1078, para 95.

(e) *R (Clift) v Secretary of State for the Home Department; Secretary of State for the Home Department v Hindawi*[129] was a conjoined appeal in which the appellants were all former or serving prisoners. The issue on appeal was whether the early release provisions, to which each of the appellants was subject, were discriminatory. Sections 46(1) and 50(2) of the Criminal Justice Act 1991 were declared incompatible with Article 14 taken together with Article 5 on the grounds that they discriminated on grounds of national origin. The provisions had already been repealed and replaced by the Criminal Justice Act 2003, but continued to apply on a transitional basis to offences committed before 4 April 2005. Section 27 of the Criminal Justice and Immigration Act 2008 therefore amended the Criminal Justice Act 1991 to remove the incompatibility in the transitional cases.

(f) In *R (Wright and ors) v Secretary of State for Health* the House of Lords found the 'provisional blacklisting' provisions for care workers in the Care Standards Act 2000 incompatible with Articles 6 and 8.[130] By the date of the House of Lords' judgment, the transition to a new scheme under the Safeguarding Vulnerable Groups Act 2006 was already underway. The new scheme did not include the feature of provisional listing which was the subject of challenge in the *Wright* case.

(g) *R (F) v Secretary of State for the Home Department* concerned the indefinite requirements imposed on those convicted of sexual offences to notify the authorities of their travel plans by virtue of the Sexual Offences Act 2003. The Supreme Court held that these requirements were incompatible with Article 8 of the Convention; a declaration of incompatibility was therefore made.[131] In June 2011 the Government published the draft Sexual Offences Act 2003 (Remedial) Order 2011 in response to the judgment.[132]

(c) *Difficulties with the declaration of incompatibility procedure*

4.81 Unfortunately the declaration of incompatibility procedure does not tend to have speedy results. For example, the amendments to the Criminal Justice Act 1991 made as a result of *Clift* (above) only came into force in July 2008, although the judgment was handed down in December 2006—and this has been one of the speediest responses.[133] In one case, the High Court made a declaration of incompatibility in November 2006,[134] the Court of Appeal overturned it in October 2007,[135] and the House of Lords then reinstated the declaration on 21 January 2009.[136] The legislation was repealed with effect from 12 October 2009.

---

[129] [2006] UKHL 54, [2007] 1 AC 484.

[130] [2009] UKHL 3, [2009] 2 WLR 267.

[131] [2010] UKSC 17, [2010] 2 WLR 992. For details of other cases, see *R (H) v Mental Health Review Tribunal* [2001] EWCA Civ 415, [2001] 3 WLR 512; *R (Wilkinson) v Inland Revenue Commissioners* [2003] EWCA Civ 814, [2003] 1 WLR 2683; and *International Transport Roth GmbH v Secretary of State for the Home Department* [2002] EWCA Civ 158, [2002] 3 WLR 344.

[132] See <http://www.homeoffice.gov.uk/publications/about-us/legislation/sexual-offences-remedial-order>.

[133] See JCHR, *Monitoring the Government's Response to Human Rights Judgments: Annual Report 2008*, 31st Report (2007–2008), HL 173, HC 1078, para 107.

[134] *R (Wright and ors) v Secretary of State for Health and Secretary of State for Education and Skills* [2006] EWHC 2886 (Admin) .

[135] [2007] EWCA Civ 999, [2008] 2 WLR 536.

[136] [2009] UKHL 3, [2009] 2 WLR 267.

Even when attempts are made to rectify the incompatibility identified in a declaration, they may not succeed in doing so. For example, it has been doubted whether the measures introduced in the Housing and Regeneration Act 2008, intended to respond to the declarations in the *Morris* and *Gabaj* cases[137] (concerning discrimination in access to social housing), remove the risk that Strasbourg or the domestic courts will find a further violation of Articles 8 and/or 14.[138]   4.82

In the anti-terrorism context, the Government has struggled to find a human rights compatible means of detaining suspected terrorists. As set out in Chapter 6, Article 3 (the right not to be subject to torture, inhuman, or degrading treatment or punishment) prevents the return of foreign nationals to countries where they would face a real risk of torture regardless of whether those nationals present a national security threat to the United Kingdom.[139] The Government first attempted to deal with this problem in 2001 by derogating from Article 5 (the right to liberty)[140] and introducing a form of detention without trial for foreign terror suspects.[141] In a landmark judgment in *A and ors v Secretary of State for the Home Department* ('the *Belmarsh* case')[142] the House of Lords held the derogation order to be in breach of the Convention, and the detention provisions to be incompatible with Articles 5 and 14 of the Convention, as the order was disproportionate and permitted detention in a way that discriminated on the grounds of nationality or immigration status. In response, the Government withdrew the derogation and repealed the provisions relating to detention without trial, instead putting in place a new regime of 'control orders' (a form of house arrest) under the Prevention of Terrorism Act 2005. Control orders have now been tested in the House of Lords and also found, in certain circumstances, to infringe the right to liberty.[143]   4.83

In response to criticism from the JCHR of its failure to speedily and effectively respond to declarations of incompatibility, the Government's rather feeble response has simply been that: 4.84

The Government has to date never refused to present remedial measures to Parliament following a final declaration of incompatibility.[144]

In our view, while the Government may never have refused to respond as such, periods of years (or even months when dealing with urgent issues or vulnerable groups) throughout which it claims to be 'considering how to remedy the incompatibility' are unacceptable, and undermine the Government's claim that the regime is compliant with Article 13 (the right to an effective remedy). It might be noted that the ECtHR has held that the declaration of incompatibility is not (yet) an effective remedy for breach of a Convention right, given the various other restrictions on its availability (the facts that it does not assist the individual litigant, that it is not binding, and that ministers can exercise the power to amend under section 10 only where there are 'compelling reasons' for doing   4.85

---

[137] See para 4.80(d) above.

[138] See JCHR, *Monitoring the Government's Response to Human Rights Judgments: Annual Report 2008*, 31st Report (2007–2008), HL 173, HC 1078, para 95.

[139] *Chahal v UK* (1997) 23 EHRR 413.

[140] Human Rights Act (Designated Derogation) Order 2001, SI 2001/3644.

[141] Anti-Terrorism, Crime and Security Act 2001, s 23.

[142] [2004] UKHL 56, [2005] 2 AC 68.

[143] *Secretary of State for the Home Department v JJ* [2007] UKHL 45, [2008] 1 AC 385.

[144] Ministry of Justice, *Responding to Human Rights Judgments: Government Response to the Joint Committee on Human Rights' Thirty-first Report of Session 2008* (Cm 7524), 5.

so—see below),[145] although it has indicated that, in time, the United Kingdom could potentially persuade the Court otherwise:

It is possible that at some future date evidence of a long-standing and established practice of ministers giving effect to the courts' declarations of incompatibility might be sufficient to persuade the Court of the effectiveness of the procedure.[146]

Regrettably, the Government appears to have taken this judgment as 'an endorsement of its current approach',[147] rather than a heavy hint from Strasbourg to adopt a clear and consistent policy. As matters stand, the declaration of incompatibility is not an effective remedy for Convention purposes, which means that a litigant need not, at present, pursue such a remedy before going to Strasbourg if it is the only one realistically available in order to exhaust domestic remedies.

4.86   A further worrying lacuna in the Act relates to the position where the Government ignores a judgment of the ECtHR condemning the United Kingdom for violating Convention rights. The domestic courts have thus far taken the general view that once a declaration of incompatibility has been made, no further relief will be granted. This issue has been particularly acute following the refusal of successive Governments to implement the judgment of the ECtHR in *Hirst v UK (No 2)*[148] in relation to the prohibition on serving prisoners being able to vote.[149]

4.87   Given the continued existence of legislation which cannot be read compatibly with Convention rights, there can be no question of a statutory tort being committed under section 6 of the Human Rights Act. Consequently, there is no right to damages under section 8 of the Act or any other remedy for the ongoing violation of Convention rights. One can therefore readily appreciate why the ECtHR has held that the declaration of incompatibility mechanism does not amount to an effective remedy for the purposes of Article 13 of the Convention.

4.88   The number of declarations will undoubtedly continue to grow as the courts grapple with the issues raised by the Convention and the Human Rights Act. To keep up to date, students and practitioners should refer to Chapter 8 for details of sources of current information.

(d) *Costs*

4.89   One serious issue is the question of how costs are awarded in cases where declarations of incompatibility are sought. In previous editions of this book, we argued that where a declaration of incompatibility is made by the court, costs should not be awarded against the unsuccessful litigant. During the passage of the Human Rights Bill, at committee stage in the House of Lords, an amendment to ensure that the Crown at least bore its own expenses was debated. The Government rejected the proposal, preferring to allow the courts to use their current discretion as to how costs are dealt with. It was suggested that factors for the court to consider included whether the case put forward by the

---

[145] Second Monitoring Report, paras 110–121. See *Burden and Burden v UK* (2008) 24 BHRC 709.

[146] *Burden and Burden v UK* (2008) 24 BHRC 709.

[147] Ministry of Justice, *Responding to Human Rights Judgments: Government Response to the Joint Committee on Human Rights' Thirty-first Report of Session 2008* (Cm 7524), 39.

[148] (2006) 42 EHRR 41.

[149] See *Traynor and anor* [2007] ScotCS CSOH 78 (Scottish Court of Session) and *R (Chester) v Secretary of State for Justice and Wakefield Metropolitan Borough Council* [2009] EWHC 2923 (Admin) (English High Court).

person seeking the declaration had merit and whether there was any wider public interest in the matter. Also relevant were the means of the parties and, of course, the outcome
of the application for a declaration.

The Privy Council has recognized that an award of costs against an unsuccessful 4.90
applicant may not always be appropriate in litigation involving important questions of
fundamental rights as '*bona fide* resort to rights under the constitution ought not to be
discouraged'.[150]

In fact, the evidence suggests that where a claimant obtains a declaration of incompat- 4.91
ibility, the courts are likely to regard him or her as having 'won' and award costs against
the relevant Secretary of State. However, this unresolved issue has a potentially 'chilling'
effect on the protection of Convention rights, as litigants may be reluctant to take test
cases under the Human Rights Act if they may obtain a declaration of incompatibility
but still face a substantial adverse costs order.[151]

3. Section 10—'fast-track' procedure

A declaration of incompatibility under section 4 should prompt legislative change— 4.92
either directly by amendment of primary legislation, or under the Human Rights Act's
fast-track procedure. Indeed, in practice declarations of incompatibility do usually
prompt such change, although this change may be slow to come about. As of 1 June
2011 19 declarations of incompatibility have become final. Of these:

- 11 have been remedied by later primary legislation;
- two have been remedied by a remedial order under section 10 of the Human Rights Act;
- three relate to provisions that had already been remedied by primary legislation at the
  time of the declaration;
- three have not yet been remedied.

As these statistics show, such changes are usually made through amendments to primary
legislation or the introduction of new legislation, and the fast-track procedure is very
rarely used. The JCHR, which has been highly critical of the Government's failure to
speedily and effectively respond to both declarations of incompatibility in the domestic
courts and adverse judgments from Strasbourg, has recommended that greater use
should be made of remedial orders.[152]

The fast-track procedure is contained in section 10 of, and Schedule 2 to, the Human 4.93
Rights Act. It is a power to take remedial action (in respect of both declarations of
incompatibility and ECtHR judgments) through the making of a remedial order in
certain circumstances. Under section 10 this power can be triggered:

(a) following a declaration of incompatibility made under section 4 where all parties have
    exercised or abandoned any rights of appeal or the time limit for appealing has expired;

---

[150] *Abnee v DPP* [1999] 2 AC 294; and *New Zealand Maori Council v Attorney General of New Zealand*
[1994] 1 AC 466.

[151] See Public Law Project Action Research Study (2001), available at <http://www.publiclawproject.org.uk>.
See also Liberty, *Litigating the Public Interest: Report of the Working Group on Facilitating Public Interest Litigation*
(July 2006), available at <http://www.liberty-human-rights.org.uk/policy/reports/litigating-the-public-interest-
july-2006.pdf >.

[152] JCHR, *Monitoring the Government's Response to Human Rights Judgments: Annual Report 2008*, 31st
Report (2007–2008), HL 173, HC 1078, para 6.

(b) where the Government decides, following a decision of the ECtHR, that a provision of legislation is incompatible with a Convention right. It is not necessary that the judgment of the Court is in favour of the applicant; or

(c) in relation to incompatible subordinate legislation, where a minister considers that it is necessary to amend the parent legislation.

4.94   If there are 'compelling reasons' for doing so, section 10 empowers a minister to make a 'remedial order' embodied in a statutory instrument that amends legislation so far as necessary to remove its incompatibility with the Convention. The Human Rights Act provides two procedures for making a remedial order: a standard procedure in Schedule 2, paragraph 2(a), and an emergency procedure in Schedule 2, paragraph 2(b).

4.95   A remedial order can be fairly wide in scope, have retrospective effect, and can 'make different provision for different cases'. This retrospective effect is limited by Schedule 2, paragraph 1(3), which states that, 'no person is to be guilty of an offence solely as a result of the retrospective effect of a remedial order'. The power to change the law retrospectively could be used to backdate a change to the date of the domestic court's decision on incompatibility or the judgment of the ECtHR.

4.96   The standard procedure[153] is a 'positive resolution procedure'. The minister must first[154] lay before Parliament a document containing a draft of the proposed order together with what is called the 'required information', which is:

(a) an explanation of the incompatibility that the proposed order seeks to remove, including particulars of the court declaration, finding, or order that caused the minister to propose a remedial order; and

(b) a statement of the reasons for proceeding under section 10 and for making an order in the terms proposed.[155]

4.97   This document must be before Parliament for at least 60 days, during which time representations about the draft order may be made to the minister, either by Parliament in the form of a report or resolution, or by any other person. The minister can amend the draft in the light of these representations. Whether or not the draft is amended it must be laid before Parliament again, this time accompanied by a summary of any representations that have been made and details of any changes made as a result. The order does not come into effect unless it is approved by a resolution of each House within 60 days after it is laid for the second time.

4.98   Under the emergency procedure[156] the minister may make the order before laying it before Parliament, but must state in the order that it appears to him or her that, because of the urgency of the matter, it is necessary to make it without prior parliamentary approval. However, after making an order under this emergency procedure the minister must[157] lay the order before Parliament, with the required information, for 60 days, during which time representations may be made, as under the standard procedure. The minister can amend the order in the light of the representations, but, whether or not it

---

153 Schedule 2, para 2(a).
154 Schedule 2, para 3.
155 Schedule 2, para 5.
156 Schedule 2, para 2(b).
157 Schedule 2, para 4.

is amended, the order must be laid before Parliament again, with a summary of representations and details of amendments, and it will cease to have effect 120 days after it was made unless it is approved by a resolution of each House. In the only example to date of the fast-track procedure being used, this was the method adopted. Following the Court of Appeal's decision in *R (H) v Mental Health Review Tribunal*[158] the Secretary of State introduced the Mental Health Act 1983 (Remedial) Order 2001[159] using this urgent procedure. This route was probably used because the problem involved fundamental rights to personal liberty and, if not rectified quickly, would have created confusion as the tribunal system would have been unsure what burden of proof it should be applying.

The power given by section 10 to amend legislation applies to both primary and secondary legislation. This provision allows campaigners, lobbyists, and lawyers to make representations to government to amend primary legislation following any case in the ECtHR that raises questions about legislation. The Government is not, of course, bound to act by way of either primary or secondary legislation, even following a declaration of incompatibility. However, if it does not do so, it would be a virtual certainty that the victim could then seek just satisfaction in the ECtHR. This would then impose an obligation on the Government as a matter of international law to remedy its violation. However, the Strasbourg Court has held on a number of occasions that the discretionary nature of the power under section 10, and the statutory limitations on the circumstances in which it can be used, prevent it from constituting an 'effective remedy' in Convention terms.

4.99

I. KEY CONVENTION CONCEPTS IN THE DOMESTIC COURTS

As discussed in Chapter 2, there are particular interpretative concepts that the ECtHR has developed in order to give meaning and effect to the Convention. The domestic courts have adopted these concepts when interpreting Convention rights under the Human Rights Act. As revealed by the number of successful applications to Strasbourg made after the Human Rights Act came into force, the domestic courts do not always apply Convention principles in the same manner as the ECtHR. The following discussion of some of the key concepts highlights points of similarity and divergence.

4.100

1. Territoriality[160]

In Chapter 2 we discussed the extraterritoriality of the Convention, and the restrictive approach adopted by the ECtHR in the case of *Bankovic v Belgium*.[161] That case involved an air strike by NATO forces in Yugoslavia, and the Court ruled that an act—which would engage the Convention if committed on the territory of a contracting state—does not ipso facto engage the Convention if carried out by that contracting state on the

4.101

---

[158] [2001] EWCA Civ 415, [2001] 3 WLR 512.
[159] SI 2001/3712.
[160] See ch 2, para 2.23.
[161] (2001) 11 BHRC 435, summarized in ch 2, para 2.23.

territory of another state outside the Council of Europe. The UK courts have also adopted a restrictive approach to the 'subtle'[162] and 'slippery'[163] concept of territoriality of the Human Rights Act.

4.102   The UK courts have considered whether the Human Rights Act has extraterritorial effect in a series of cases relating to British military action in Iraq. This question has come before the courts several times: in *R (Al-Skeini) v Secretary of State for Defence*[164] and *R (Gentle) v Prime Minister*;[165] and the Court of Appeal considered it in *R (Al-Saadoon) v Secretary of State for Defence*[166] and *R (Smith) v Oxfordshire Assistant Deputy Coroner*.[167] These cases are discussed in Chapter 6.[168]

4.103   According to the leading domestic case, *Al-Skeini*, the circumstances in which the Act will apply outside the United Kingdom are narrow. The House of Lords considered six test cases brought by families of Iraqi civilians killed by British armed forces near Basra, Iraq. They claimed that the Secretary of State for Defence had violated Article 2 (right to life) and Article 3 (prohibition of torture), both substantively and by failing to satisfy the investigative duty inherent in these articles. The first five cases involved actions by British soldiers where the victims were not placed under arrest and were not in detention; the victims died during the course of street patrols, a house search, at a military checkpoint, and in cross-fire between British troops and other gunmen. In the sixth case the victim, Mr Mousa, was arrested and died in custody in a British military detention centre. Their Lordships held that under Article 1 the essential and primary nature of the Convention's jurisdiction and scope was territorial. The 'Cyprus' line of cases[169] formed a limited exception to the principle of territoriality where a state party had effective control of an area, lawful or unlawful; however, this only applied where the controlled state was also a member of the Convention and therefore the act had taken place in the 'espace juridique' of the Convention. *Bankovic* (above) established, their Lordships held, that the exercise of authority by state agents outside their home jurisdiction was not a broad doctrine of personal jurisdiction but a limited exception to a primary doctrine of territorial jurisdiction. In the first five cases the Human Rights Act did not apply. In the case of Mr Mousa the Secretary of State had conceded that his death occurred within his jurisdiction, and a majority of their Lordships (Lord Bingham dissenting) agreed that a British military prison, operating in Iraq with the consent of the Iraqi sovereign authorities, and containing arrested suspects, fell within the narrowly limited exception exemplified by embassies, consulates, vessels, and aircraft.[170] This judgment must, however, be read in the light of the recent judgment of the Grand Chamber of the European Court of Human Rights in *Al-Skeini v UK*.[171] Contrary to the decision of their Lordships, the Court held that the Convention was engaged in relation to the killing of each of the applicants.

---

[162] *R (Al-Skeini) v Secretary of State for Defence* [2007] UKHL 26, [2008] 1 AC 153 at [44] per Lord Rodger.
[163] *R (Quark Fishing Ltd) v Secretary of State for Foreign and Commonwealth Affairs* [2005] UKHL 57, [2006] 1 AC 529 at [32] per Lord Nicholls.
[164] [2007] UKHL 26, [2008] 1 AC 153.
[165] [2008] UKHL 20, [2001] 1 AC 1356.
[166] [2009] EWCA Civ 7, [2010] 1 QB 486.
[167] [2010] UKSC 29, [2011] 1 AC 1.
[168] See paras 6.04–6.08.
[169] See, eg *Loizidou v Turkey* (1997) 23 EHRR 513.
[170] *Hess v UK* (1975) 2 D & R 72.
[171] App No 55721/07, 7 July 2011.

In *Smith*[172] the majority of the Supreme Court held, applying *Al-Skeini*, that a soldier who died whilst serving in Iraq was not within the jurisdiction of the United Kingdom when he was outside his army base. The correctness of that decision must also now be open to question, although *Smith*, like their Lordships' decision in *Al-Skeini*, remains binding on domestic courts until the Supreme Court or Parliament changes the law to reflect the Strasbourg jurisprudence.

2. Positive obligations

As discussed in Chapter 2,[173] positive obligations provide a critical interpretative tool for the ECtHR to expand the protection of the Convention beyond the bare minimum authorized by the text of the articles. Domestic courts have proved cautious in imposing positive obligations on public authorities, aware that political and economic considerations are often at stake. The nature of positive obligations was considered by the House of Lords in *R (Pretty) v DPP*, a case questioning whether the applicant, who suffered from terminal motor neurone disease, could claim a right to die under Articles 2 and 8 of the Convention.[174] Following Strasbourg authority, Lord Bingham emphasized that the question of whether a positive obligation exists depends on striking a fair balance between the general interests of the community and the interests of the individual. Diane Pretty's application was not upheld by either the House of Lords or the Strasbourg Court.[175]   4.104

Domestic cases on the scope of positive obligations have largely concerned Article 2, Article 3, and Article 8.[176] The first two sets of cases have met with the most success in domestic courts. In a trio of cases—*Amin*,[177] *Middleton*,[178] and *JL*[179]—the House of Lords found violations of the positive obligation under Article 2 to conduct an investigation into deaths or near-deaths in custody. In *Savage v South Essex Partnership NHS Foundation Trust* the House of Lords found that the obligation to protect life extends to providing a proper system for the supervision of mental patients.[180] In *R (B) v Director of Public Prosecutions*[181] and *OOO v Commissioner of Police of the Metropolis*,[182] discussed at para 4.66 above, the High Court found breaches of the state's positive obligations under Article 3.   4.105

Positive obligations under Article 8 are harder to establish. In *Re S (a care plan)* the House of Lords rejected the Court of Appeal's development of a positive obligation to secure a child in care with 'a family for life'.[183] In *Department of Work and Pensions v M* the House of Lords said that Strasbourg was 'well aware' of the dangers of any 'unrestrained and unprincipled' extension of Article 8, and stated that many social welfare   4.106

---

172 [2009] UKSC 29, [2010] 3 WLR 223.
173 See ch 2, paras 2.32–2.39.
174 [2001] UKHL 61, [2002] 1 AC 800.
175 (2002) 35 EHRR 1.
176 For further detail, see ch 7.
177 *R (Amin) v Secretary of State for the Home Department* [2003] UKHL 51, [2004] 1 AC 653.
178 *R v Coroner for Western District of Somerset, ex p Middleton* [2004] UKHL 10, [2004] 2 AC 182.
179 *R (JL) v Secretary of State for Justice* [2008] UKHL 68, [2008] 3 WLR 1325.
180 [2008] UKHL 74, [2009] 2 AC 115.
181 [2009] EWHC 106 (Admin).
182 [2011] EWHC 1246 (QB).
183 See *W and B (children: care plan)* [2001] EWCA Civ 757, [2001] 2 FLR 582.

measures with only an indirect effect on private or family life were not even within the ambit of the duty to respect it.[184] That said, the courts have begun to recognize the potential role for positive obligations in this area: in *Bryant and ors v Commissioner of Police for the Metropolis* the High Court recently held that it is arguable that the police are under a positive obligation to inform citizens of information that indicates that respect for their private life is potentially threatened.[185]

4.107   Where an omission by a public authority can be said to amount to inhuman or degrading treatment, the court may be more willing to impose a positive obligation. In *R (Limbuela) v Secretary of State for the Home Department*, for example, the House of Lords held that Article 3 required basic subsistence to be given to asylum-seekers.[186]

3. Legality

4.108   As discussed in Chapter 2,[187] the requirement of legality is a critical first step to determining whether any limitation on rights can be justified. It has been considered in the domestic context on a number of occasions since the Human Rights Act came into force. The House of Lords adopted the approach of the ECtHR in *R v Shayler*.[188] Lord Hope explained that the court had to address itself to three questions: whether there was a legal basis in domestic law for the restriction; whether the law was sufficiently accessible and precise; and, finally, whether the law had been arbitrarily applied.[189]

4.109   The Lords strayed from this strict approach in *R (Gillan) v Commissioner of Police for the Metropolis*, a case concerning the use by the Metropolitan Police of random stop-and-search powers under the Terrorism Act 2000.[190] The basis on which the police decided to stop and search individuals had never been published; nor had members of the public been informed that random stop-and-search powers were being deployed in the London area. However, their Lordships found that the bare fact that the Act authorized the powers was sufficient guarantee of legality. Lord Bingham accepted that powers were broadly drawn, but stated that 'a measure of vagueness was inevitable if excessive rigidity was to be avoided' and, in any event, there were 'strong reasons' for not publishing details of the authorizations and confirmations.[191] This approach was not in keeping with the Strasbourg jurisprudence, as the ECtHR subsequently found.[192]

4.110   Recent domestic decisions have more satisfactorily upheld the principle of legality. In *R (Laporte) v Chief Constable of Gloucestershire* the House of Lords found that action taken to prevent demonstrators from reaching a demonstration was not prescribed by domestic law as there had been no imminent breach of the peace to justify intercepting the demonstrators.[193] Likewise, in the recent case of *R (Moos and McClure) v Commissioner*

---

[184] [2006] UKHL 11, [2006] 2 WLR 637.
[185] [2011] EWHC 1314 (Admin) at [54].
[186] [2005] UKHL 66, [2006] 1 AC 396.
[187] See ch 2, paras 2.42–2.49.
[188] [2002] UKHL 11, [2003] 1 AC 247.
[189] Ibid at [56].
[190] [2006] UKHL 12, [2006] 2 WLR 537.
[191] Ibid at [33].
[192] *Gillan and Quinton v UK* Application 4158/05, 12 January 2010.
[193] [2006] UKHL 55, [2007] 2 AC 105.

of Police of the Metropolis[194] the Divisional Court held that there had been no imminent breach of the peace such as to justify 'kettling' on the facts of the case.

4. Proportionality

(a) *Introduction and overview*

As discussed in Chapter 2,[195] proportionality is the standard of review applied by the   4.111
ECtHR in its assessment of justifications for infringing limited and qualified Convention rights. This is the standard now adopted under the Human Rights Act, which has heralded a far closer level of scrutiny of public decision-making than was previously the case in ordinary domestic judicial review proceedings. In relation to all qualified rights, the question is whether any intrusion into the right is lawful, in the sense of having a lawful basis, being intended to meet a legitimate aim, and being a means of achieving that aim which is 'necessary in a democratic society'. The standard of scrutiny, in most judicial review proceedings, is therefore now that of 'proportionality' rather than the previous standard, which permitted judicial interference only in cases of 'irrationality'. However, the precise parameters of the concept of proportionality have not yet been fully defined. Moreover, the debate has sometimes turned on whether, why, and to what extent, courts ought to 'defer' to the decisions reached by other arms of government or expert decision-makers. This section considers the current law on the test for determining whether there is a departure from or exception to a Convention principle. The next section addresses the concepts of deference and the 'discretionary area of judgment'.

(b) *The development and application of the proportionality principle in domestic law*

Before the Human Rights Act came into force, the test for challenging the actions of   4.112
public authorities by way of judicial review was that they must be unlawful or 'irrational'; in Lord Diplock's oft-quoted explanation of *Wednesbury*[196] unreasonableness, 'a decision which is so outrageous in its defiance of logic or accepted moral standards that no sensible person who had applied his mind to the question to be decided could have arrived at it'.[197] It was very hard to challenge a decision on this basis; and although in later cases, where fundamental rights were at stake, the test was redefined so that the greater the interference with fundamental rights, the greater the level of scrutiny required,[198] the ECtHR held that even this reformulated level of scrutiny was insufficient to meet the requirements of Article 13 of the Convention.[199]

Despite judicial reluctance to adopt the proportionality standard in administrative   4.113
law, the concept was not alien to the English judiciary.[200] Before the Human Rights Act came into force, judges in English courts commonly encountered it in the context of EU law.[201] The language used in Convention case law differs from the more formal EU test,

---

[194] [2011] EWHC 957 (Admin).
[195] See ch 2, paras 2.61–2.66.
[196] *Associated Provincial Picture Houses Ltd v Wednesbury Corp* [1948] 1 KB 223.
[197] *Council of Civil Service Unions v Minister for the Civil Service* [1985] AC 375, 410.
[198] See the formulation in *R v Ministry of Defence, ex p Smith* [1996] QB 517.
[199] See *Smith and Grady v UK* (1999) 29 EHRR 493; *Hatton v UK* (2003) 37 EHRR 611.
[200] See Olley, 'Proportionality at Common Law' [2004] JR 197; Walker, 'Unreasonableness and Proportionality', in Supperstone, Goudie, and Walker (eds), *Judicial Review*, 3rd edn (London: Butterworths, 2005).
[201] See, eg *R v Secretary of State for Employment, ex p Equal Opportunities Commission* [1995] 1 AC 1.

but the concept of proportionality—and the Continental legal traditions from which it has derived—are very similar in both systems,[202] and in practice, proportionality principles derived from Convention case law are applied equally in cases governed by EU law (and vice versa).[203]

4.114   The classic domestic formulation of proportionality was made by the Privy Council in *De Freitas v Permanent Secretary of Ministry of Agriculture, Fisheries, Lands and Housing*.[204] Drawing on Canadian and South African jurisprudence, Lord Clyde set out a three-stage test, asking whether: the policy in question pursues a sufficiently important objective; the rule or decision under review is rationally connected with that objective; and the means adopted are no more than necessary to achieve that objective.

4.115   That approach to proportionality was expressly endorsed, in the context of the Human Rights Act, by the House of Lords in *R (Daly) v Secretary of State for the Home Department* in which Lord Steyn underlined the 'material difference' between the Convention principle of proportionality and *Wednesbury* unreasonableness.[205] He said that proportionality was a more sophisticated test than mere reasonableness or rationality as it permitted the court to assess the balance struck by the decision-maker. He emphasized, however, that proportionality did not mean a shift to a merits review, and that the intensity of the review would depend on the subject matter in hand, even in cases involving Convention rights.

4.116   Following the further decision of the House of Lords in *Huang v Secretary of State for the Home Department*,[206] a fourth limb must be added to the *De Freitas* test for assessing whether a measure constitutes a proportionate means of achieving a legitimate aim, namely whether the measure achieves a fair balance between the interests of the individuals affected and the wider community. The *Huang* test has since been widely used.[207] Properly applied, it offers a structured and rigorous approach. So, for example, in *R (Laporte) v Chief Constable of Gloucestershire*, the House of Lords rejected an argument that it should be deferential to 'on the spot' police decisions.[208] The police had failed to discharge the burden of establishing that all the actions they took were proportionate and constituted the least restriction necessary to the rights of freedom of speech and freedom of peaceful assembly. Similarly, in *Huang* itself the House of Lords held that an immigration adjudicator had to decide for him or herself whether an impugned decision to remove an asylum seeker was proportionate, and, if not, reverse it. The adjudicator must not simply check the rationality of the primary decision-maker's decision; he or she must decide proportionality on the merits.[209] And in *Manchester City Council v Pinnock*, the Supreme Court held that a court which was asked by a local authority to make an

---

[202] See *R (Countryside Alliance and ors) v Attorney General* [2007] UKHL 52, [2008] 1 AC 719.
[203] See *Secretary of State for Defence v Elias* [2006] EWCA Civ 1293, [2006] IRLR 934.
[204] [1999] 1 AC 69.
[205] [2001] 2 WLR 1622.
[206] [2007] UKHL 11, [2007] 2 AC 167. For a different set of questions to be asked, at least in an Art 8 context, see *R (F) v Secretary of State for Justice* [2010] UKSC 17, [2010] 2 WLR 992 at [41] per Lord Phillips: '(i) What is the extent of the interference with article 8 rights? (ii) How valuable are the notification requirements [regarding a sex offender's foreign travel plans] in achieving the legitimate aims [of the legislation in question]? and (iii) to what extent would that value be eroded if the notification requirements were made subject to review?'
[207] See, eg *Re E* [2008] UKHL 66, [2008] 3 WLR 1208.
[208] [2006] UKHL 55, [2007] 2 AC 105.
[209] [2007] UKHL 11, [2007] 1 AC 167.

order for possession of a person's home had to have, when assessing the proportionality of making the order, the power to resolve any relevant dispute of fact; limitation of the court's power to one based on traditional judicial review principles was inadequate.[210]

However, in many cases, the vexed notions of deference, 'discretionary area of judgment', justiciability, and proportionality have been intermingled. This confusion was evident in *R (Countryside Alliance and ors) v Attorney General*, a case concerning hunting bans.[211] The House of Lords afforded a wide 'margin of discretionary judgment' to the legislature in this matter of social policy and found that any interference with the claimants' proprietary rights under Article 1 of Protocol 1 was justifiable. However, the approaches adopted by their Lordships to the questions of proportionality and deference sharply differed. Lord Bingham suggested that a 'degree of respect' should be accorded to the decision of a majority of the country's democratically elected representatives, and stated: 4.117

The democratic process is liable to be subverted if, on a question of moral and political judgment, opponents of the Act achieve through the courts what they could not achieve in Parliament.[212]

Lord Brown disagreed:

The democratic process is a necessary but not a sufficient condition for the protection and vindication of human rights. Sometimes the majority misuses its powers. Not least this may occur when what are perceived as moral issues are involved . . . I simply cannot regard the ethical objection of the majority as a sufficient basis for holding the ban to be 'necessary'. . . . How then can the ban be reconciled with the values of 'pluralism, tolerance and broadmindedness', these 'hallmarks of a democratic society'? Most would regard adultery (assuredly a pursuit engaging article 8) as unethical (and often causing suffering too). But could an intolerant majority therefore ban it and then argue that this was 'necessary in a democratic society'? Surely not.[213]

As this disagreement indicates, and as commentators have noted,[214] despite the fact that the proper ambit of the proportionality test has reached the higher courts on a number of occasions, there has not yet emerged a principled approach to its application. 4.118

(c) *Deference and the 'discretionary area of judgment'*

The role of courts, in the Convention system of rights protections, is to scrutinize the 'necessity' of infringements to human rights. However, the ECtHR is conscious of the limits of the social judgments it can make as a supranational court, lacking sensitivity to nuances of the particular societies of the Council of Europe states. Thus, as explained in Chapter 2,[215] the European Court frequently invokes what it calls the 'margin of appreciation' to afford Member States a reasonable sphere within which it will not interfere with their power to evaluate their public policy decisions, though they are subject to review. 4.119

This doctrine is an international one, based on the limitations of the international court. It has no place in domestic arrangements for protecting human rights and should not be used when the Convention is applied by national courts. It was created to allow 4.120

---

[210] [2010] UKSC 45, [2010] 3 WLR 1441, especially at [45] and [74].
[211] [2007] UKHL 52, [2008] 1 AC 719.
[212] Ibid at [45].
[213] Ibid at [157]–[159].
[214] See, eg Hickman, 'The Substance and Structure of Proportionality' [2008] PL 694.
[215] See ch 2, paras 2.77–2.84.

national judicial bodies a degree of flexibility; to enable an international judicial review system to give due weight to local political and cultural traditions; and to take into account the geographical, cultural, philosophical, historical, and intellectual distance between the judges in Strasbourg and local institutions. The domestic courts do not need the doctrine because this gap does not exist. As the Grand Chamber stated in *A v UK*:

> The doctrine of the margin of appreciation has always been meant as a tool to define relations between the domestic authorities and the Court. It cannot have the same application to the relations between the organs of State at the domestic level . . . the question of proportionality is ultimately a judicial decision . . .[216]

4.121   In the first case on the Human Rights Act to reach the House of Lords, *R (Kebilene) v DPP*, this position was confirmed.[217] Lord Hope stated that the doctrine of margin of appreciation:

> . . . is an integral part of the supervisory jurisdiction which is exercised over state conduct by the international court. By conceding a margin of appreciation to each national system, the court has recognised that the Convention, as a living system, does not need to be applied uniformly by all states but may vary in its application according to local needs and conditions. This technique is not available to the national courts when they are considering Convention issues arising within their own countries. But in the hands of the national courts also the Convention should be seen as an expression of fundamental principles rather than as a set of mere rules. The questions which the courts will have to decide in the application of these principles will involve questions of balance between competing interests and issues of proportionality.[218]

4.122   However, in early Human Rights Act jurisprudence, a concept of 'deference' to the legislature was often (although not always) applied, which, in essence, involved the domestic courts attempting to translate the international law concept of 'margin of appreciation' into domestic law. In *International Transport Roth GmbH v Secretary of State for the Home Department*, for example, Laws LJ made plain that, for him, deference was one of the ways of resolving what he viewed as a tension between parliamentary sovereignty and fundamental rights, given the Human Right Act's halfway house between legislative supremacy and constitutional supremacy. He went so far as to say that, in some contexts, 'the deference is nearly absolute'.[219]

4.123   Commentators were highly critical of this approach, as it resulted in the scope of section 3 being inappropriately constrained, and determined by the courts' construction of the boundaries of deference.[220] Klug argued that it was fundamentally misguided, and misunderstood the scheme of the Human Rights Act:

> Concluding that there cannot be 'no-go' areas for judges under the HRA does not, however, necessarily require them to intrude on the rightful role of elected and accountable politicians. The Act was specifically structured to allow the courts to uphold rights while also retaining parliamentary authority. Behind the construction of ss 3 and 4 was a carefully thought-out constitutional arrangement that sought to inject principles of parliamentary accountability and transparency

---

[216] (2009) 26 BHRC 1.
[217] [2000] 2 AC 326.
[218] Ibid, 380.
[219] [2002] EWCA Civ 158, [2003] QB 78 at [75].
[220] Klug, 'Judicial Deference under the Human Rights Act 1998' (2003) 2 EHRLR 125.

into judicial proceedings without removing whole policy areas to judicial determination. In other words it sought to create a new dynamic between the two branches of the State.[221]

As the courts looked to the concept of deference to shape their interpretative func-   4.124
tion, they began to list factors that determined how and when the courts should 'defer'. They included vague, nebulous concepts such as 'the culture and conditions of the British State',[222] but also concrete issues, such as whether the right in question in the case was absolute or qualified, and the subject matter of the case. The concept of 'deference' is not one that appears on the face of the Human Rights Act. However, two possible theoretical bases have been advanced by commentators: (i) constitutional legitimacy, and (ii) institutional competence.

(i) *Constitutional legitimacy*   This is the suggestion that, as a matter of constitutional   4.125
law and constitutional principle, the courts are less democratically accountable, and therefore less legitimate, than the elected branches of government, in particular when dealing with issues of acute social sensitivity, such as terrorism.[223]

This approach was powerfully advanced by Lord Hoffmann in *R (Prolife Alliance) v*   4.126
BBC.[224] He held that social judgments as to the 'offensiveness' or otherwise of material contained in a proposed party election broadcast was one which Parliament had decided was apt to be reached by the broadcasters themselves, and that it would be contrary to the principle of the separation of powers for the courts to abrogate that role.

(ii) *Institutional competence*   Another, more nuanced argument for a form of deference   4.127
is based on 'institutional competence'—the idea that the courts and the legislature have differing expertise, and also differing access to the relevant information.

This approach has been proposed by, among others, Lord Steyn. He wrote an influ-   4.128
ential article in Public Law which was highly critical of Lord Hoffmann's approach in the *ProLife Alliance* case, instead commending the 'balanced approach' to deference based on institutional competence. 'At the risk of over-simplification', he said:

The rule of law requires that courts do not surrender their responsibilities. So far as the courts desist from making decisions in a particular case it should not be on grounds of separation of powers, or other constitutional principle. Deference may lead the courts not to make their own decisions on an issue. The degree of deference which the courts should show will, of course, depend on and vary with the context. The true justification for a court exceptionally declining to decide an issue, which is within its jurisdiction, is the relative institutional competence or capacity of the branches of government.[225]

This approach to deference, based on relative institutional competence, has been   4.129
applied in a number of cases, the courts indicating that there is an area of judgment

---

[221] Ibid. See also Feldman, 'Article 14 ECHR and Deference', paper delivered to the Administrative Law Bar Association, 6 December 2005 (arguing that the suggestion that certain questions are *incapable of decision* by a court, because they raise no questions of legality, in turn suggests that in certain cases there is no authority in the United Kingdom capable of authoritatively saying that a decision is unlawful and granting a remedy).

[222] *International Transport Roth GmbH and ors v Secretary of State for the Home Department* [2002] EWCA Civ 158, [2003] QB 78 at [81] per Laws LJ.

[223] See, eg *(RB) Algeria v Secretary of State for the Home Department* [2009] UKHL 10, [2009] 2 WLR 512.

[224] [2003] UKHL 23, [2004] 1 AC 185.

[225] Steyn, 'Deference: A Tangled Story' [2005] PL 346, 352.

within which the judiciary will defer, on democratic grounds, to the considered opinion of the legislature or the executive. The Lord Chancellor summarized this approach in 2006:

Whether and to what extent the courts will recognise a 'discretionary area of judgment' depends upon the subject matter of the decision being challenged, but policy decisions made by Parliament on matters of national security, criminal justice and economic policy are accorded particular respect.[226]

4.130   A third approach is to say that the language of deference is inappropriate and unhelpful, within a structured approach to proportionality analysis. Given the requirement for courts to 'give effect' to human rights principles, under section 6(1) and (3) of the Human Rights Act, the mechanism for avoiding courts overstepping the mark and becoming legislators is for Parliament to pass legislation which cannot be interpreted compatibly with the Convention (and so which renders it impossible for courts to act compatibility with the Convention, under section 6(2)). The domestic courts must themselves apply the doctrine of proportionality, and consider the limits of their 'institutional competence' only in order to determine what is proportionate in particular circumstances, having regard to the subject matter of the issue in play, and the subject matter of the particular complaint before them.[227]

J. ENFORCEMENT OF THE HUMAN RIGHTS ACT IN SUMMARY

4.131   Regardless of the rhetoric as to the constitutional significance of the Human Rights Act, its key purpose was to give citizens a practical right to use the Convention in our national courts—to 'bring rights home'. The Human Rights Act seeks to achieve this through the various mechanisms described in this chapter, bolstered by the Equality and Human Rights Commission's powers to bring cases in its own right and to inquire into human rights issues. Human rights arguments can now be made and relied upon in any court or tribunal in the United Kingdom. There remain, however, a number of logistical and conceptual difficulties with the Human Rights Act which undermine its ability to ensure that rights are 'practical and effective' rather than 'theoretical and illusory'. In particular, the courts' restrictive approach to Human Rights Act remedies has been disappointing, especially given the broad statutory leeway in section 8; and the repeated and lengthy delays by government in responding to declarations of incompatibility from the courts frustrate the Act's central purpose.

4.132   Pre-emptive measures to protect and promote human rights are, of course, preferable to 'after-the-fact' remedies. Ideally, there should be less litigation under the Human Rights Act, not because of restrictions on access to justice, but because fewer statutes, rules, or practices that violate human rights remain in force. The importance of pre-emptive measures has long been recognized by many jurisdictions throughout Europe, which

---

[226] *Review of the Implementation of the Human Rights Act*, Executive Summary (25 July 2006), 4, available at <http://www.justice.gov.uk>.

[227] See, in particular, the speech of Lord Nicholls in *Ghaidan v Godin-Mendoza* [2004] UKHL 30, [2004] 2 AC 557 at [19].

have processes of 'abstract review' whereby the judiciary is able to evaluate the general compliance of Bills or recently enacted statutes for their compatibility with Convention rights.[228] While no such process exists under the Human Rights Act (apart from the limited and exceptional approach adopted in *R (Rusbridger) v Attorney General*),[229] there are now a number of forms of pre-legislative scrutiny, including the Commission's power to advise government on the likely effect of a proposed change of law or existing enactment.[230] The Joint Committee on Human Rights also plays a crucial role, highlighting concerns at an early stage. Indeed, this is recognized by the Cabinet Office guidance to Ministers, which reminds them that, in preparing a compatibility statement for a Bill pursuant to section19 of the Human Rights Act, they should bear in mind that the Joint Committee 'will report on the ECHR issues raised by a Bill and is likely to examine closely the arguments put forward by the department justifying interference with a Convention right'.[231]

---

[228] See also the discussion of the Select Committee on the Constitution on 'advisory declarations' (in which the courts would be called upon to give guidance to the Government on Convention rights): Sixth Report (2006–2007), HL 151, para 11.

[229] [2003] UKHL 38, [2004] 1 AC 357.

[230] Equality Act 2006, s 11(2).

[231] Cabinet Office, *Guide to Making Legislation: ECHR*, 6 May 2009, available at <http://www.cabinetoffice.gov.uk>.

5

THE INTERACTION BETWEEN CONVENTION PRINCIPLES AND EUROPEAN UNION LAW

A. Introduction	5.01
B. The Developing Doctrine of Fundamental Rights in EU Law	5.03
C. The EU Charter of Fundamental Rights	5.11
D. Accession to the Convention	5.17
E. The Interaction of EU Law and Convention Principles in UK Courts	5.18
F. Conclusion	5.27

A. INTRODUCTION

This chapter concerns the ways in which Convention arguments are considered in cases within the scope of European Union (EU) law.[1] This is not the place for a wide discussion of the history or present state of development of human rights in the law of the EU. Sources of more detailed analysis of these subjects are given in Chapter 10. However, no lawyer dealing with an argument of EU law (or of application of the law of the EU by UK authorities) can afford to ignore Convention arguments. This is because: 5.01

(a) EU law is informed by Convention principles;

(b) EU law is part of the law of the United Kingdom. In the EU's fields of competence, Article 4(3) TEU requires Member States to give effect to EU law, and section 2 of the European Communities Act 1972 requires UK courts to give EU law rights effect in the United Kingdom. The doctrines of supremacy and direct effect, together with the interpretative *Marleasing*[2] principle, are relevant in this regard;

(c) sections 3 and 6 of the Human Rights Act require UK courts to give effect to Convention principles wherever possible, and this includes cases where they are relevant to interpreting questions of EU law;

---

[1] Pursuant to the Lisbon Treaty, discussed in more detail below, the distinction between the European Community and the European Union (EU) was abolished; henceforth there was to be just one body, the EU, which would have its own legal personality: see Arts 1 and 47 of the Treaty on European Union (TEU).

[2] Case C–106/89 *Marleasing SA v La Comercial Internacional de Alimentacion* [1990] ECR I–4135.

(d) the European Court of Human Rights (ECtHR) has been prepared to consider the compatibility with the Convention of actions of Member States which have been taken in order to comply with obligations under EU law;

(e) there may be circumstances in which there are tactical or procedural advantages in using the Convention through EU law, or in using Convention arguments in determining the scope of EU obligations.

5.02   This chapter outlines the developing doctrine of fundamental rights in EU case law, and then examines how EU and Convention principles will overlap in practice.

B. THE DEVELOPING DOCTRINE OF FUNDAMENTAL RIGHTS IN EU LAW

5.03   Pursuant to Article 6(2) TEU, the EU 'shall accede' to the European Convention for the Protection of Human Rights and Fundamental Freedoms (Convention). This development is considered below (see para 5.17); for present purposes it should be noted that the EU has not, at the time of writing, acceded to the Convention. However, that does not mean that the EU courts have not recognized the importance of fundamental rights protection as a matter of EU law and the 'special significance' of the Convention, to which all Member States are party, as a source of such protection.[3] The European Court of Justice (ECJ) has undoubtedly developed a doctrine of 'fundamental rights' in EU law, which the other institutions have reinforced through documents such as the Charter of Fundamental Rights. Article 2 TEU reinforces the importance of such rights in the EU legal order. It reads:

The Union is founded on the principles of human dignity, freedom, democracy, equality, the rule of law and respect for human rights, including the rights of persons belonging to minorities. These values are common to the Member States in a society in which pluralism, non-discrimination, tolerance, justice, solidarity and equality between men and women prevail.

Echoing almost word-for-word the ECJ's jurisprudence, Article 6(3) TEU provides:

Fundamental rights, as guaranteed by [the Convention] and as they result from the constitutional traditions common to the Member States, shall constitute general principles of Union law.

5.04   The growing importance of that fundamental rights jurisprudence is explained both by the expanding scope of EU competence and by increased awareness of the importance of human and other fundamental rights across the EU.

5.05   The EU—then known as the European Economic Community—began its life as a largely economic body, but its competence has gradually expanded over many areas—for example, free movement of persons, asylum, extradition, and certain aspects of foreign and security policy—which raise human rights issues that are particularly sensitive. Talk of human rights within the EU was amplified by the adoption in 1997 at the Treaty of Amsterdam of what is now Article 19 of the Treaty on the Functioning of the European

---

[3] *Opinion 2/94 on Accession by the Community to the ECHR* [1996] ECR I–1759 at [33]. The 'Copenhagen criteria' for accession require candidate countries to protect human and minority rights, which in practice means ratification of the Convention prior to accession to the Union.

Union (TFEU) and the measures which have used it as a legislative base,[4] and by the adoption in December 2000 of the Charter of Fundamental Rights (see paras 5.11–5.16 below).

The protection of fundamental rights was, however, not found in the Treaty but was 'discovered' by the ECJ as a 'general principle' of EU law. By common consent this development occurred as a reaction to the concern expressed by the German Constitutional Court in the 1970s about the ECJ's similar 'discovery' of the principles of supremacy and direct effect of EU law, which the German court saw as a potential threat to rights protected by the German Constitution.[5] There is now a considerable body of ECJ case law, much of which has stressed the importance of the Convention as a source for the EU's law of fundamental rights. In Advisory Opinion 2/94,[6] the ECJ held that the EU did not, then, have competence to accede to the Convention. However, the ECJ was at pains to assert (para 33) that: 5.06

> . . . it is well settled that fundamental rights form an integral part of the general principles of law whose observance the Court ensures. For that purpose, the Court draws inspiration from the constitutional traditions common to the Member States and from the guidelines supplied by international treaties for the protection of human rights on which the Member States have collaborated or of which they are signatories.[7]

The ECJ has applied its fundamental rights jurisprudence to Member States when they apply EU law as well as to the EU's own institutions. It has held that Member States implementing, or derogating from, EU rules must do so in a way that is compatible with fundamental rights that derive in particular from the Convention.[8] For example, in *Elliniki Radiophonia Tileorassi AE (ERT) v Dimotiki Etairia Pliroforissis (DEP)*,[9] restrictions on television licences (which constituted a derogation from free movement rights) were considered by reference to Article 10 of the Convention. In his opinion in *Konstantinidis v Stadt Altensteig-Standesamt*,[10] Advocate-General Jacobs said that an EU national could 'oppose any violation of his fundamental rights' when exercising EU free movement rights in another Member State. This was reflected by the judgment of the ECJ in *Carpenter v Secretary of State for the Home Department*.[11] In the *Carpenter* case it was held that the decision to deport the applicant interfered with her husband's free movement rights and that the United Kingdom could invoke reasons of public interest to justify the national measure which did this only if it was compatible with fundamental rights. Having regard to the case law of the ECtHR, the decision to deport   5.07

---

[4] Directive (EC) 2000/43 implementing the principle of equal treatment between persons irrespective of racial or ethnic origins [2000] OJ L180/22; and Directive (EC) 2000/78 [2000] OJ L303/16 ('the Framework Employment Directive').

[5] See, generally, Craig and De Burca, *EU Law: Text, Cases and Materials*, 4th edn (Oxford: Oxford University Press, 2008) ch 11.

[6] [1996] ECR I–1759.

[7] This is a doctrine which has frequently been reiterated in the case law of the ECJ: see, inter alia, Case C–20/00 *Booker Acquaculture Ltd (t/a Marine Harvest McConnell) v Scottish Ministers* [2003] ECR I–7411 and Case C–105/03 *Criminal Proceedings Against Pupino* [2005] ECR I-5285, paras 58–60. The ECJ has gone further, and recognized the 'special significance' of the Convention as a source of principles of EU law: see, eg Case 36/75 *Rutili v Ministre de l'Interieur* [1975] ECR 1219 and Case C–112/00 *Schmidberger v Austria* [2003] ECR I–5659, para 71.

[8] See, eg Case C–20/00 *Booker Acquaculture v Secretary of State for Scotland* [2003] ECR I–7411.

[9] Case C–260/89 [1991] ECR I–2925, paras 41–45.

[10] Case C–168/91 [1993] ECR I–1191.

[11] Case C–60/00 [2002] ECR I–6279.

the applicant did not strike a fair balance between the right of Mr Carpenter to respect for his family life and the maintenance of public order.

5.08   That does not mean that the ECJ and ECtHR always interpret Convention rights harmoniously. For example, the two courts have interpreted the principle of protection against self-incrimination in divergent ways.[12] In addition, there is sometimes a direct conflict between Convention rights and a freedom considered by EU law to be 'fundamental', such as the free movement of goods. It may be that the ECJ weighs the competing interests differently from the ECtHR.[13] Nonetheless, divergences have in practice been rare.

5.09   It has been unclear how far the ECJ regards the standards in the Convention as a minimum below which the EU may not fall, or merely as 'inspiration' or 'guidelines',[14] although it frequently refers to the jurisprudence of the ECtHR, particularly in cases where there is a directly engaged Convention right, such as Article 6 or 8.[15] That is particularly so where the right in question is also one found in the Charter of Fundamental Rights. In other cases where human rights arguments are relevant, again, the ECJ makes extensive reference to the ECtHR's decisions, and this is a developing trend.[16] However, whatever the theoretical principles, there have been some cases in which the ECJ has decided issues that plainly do engage matters within the ambit of Convention rights in a way that appears to differ from the ECtHR's decisions, without making reference to them. This arises particularly where the issue in the case is the content of a Convention right and its application to the EU legal order and its prerogatives. In *Emesa Sugar (Free Zone) NV v Aruba*,[17] for example, the ECJ reviewed its own procedures by reference to Article 6 of the Convention, distinguished the case law of the ECtHR in ways which have surprised some commentators, and held that there was no violation of the right to a fair trial.

5.10   In sum, although Convention standards are not, formally speaking, part of EU law, they are undoubtedly the most important source for establishing the 'common traditions' of the EU Member States. Whether or not the ECJ always applies Convention principles correctly, it is clear that it affords special significance to the decisions of the ECtHR, and considers them at least as persuasive as the UK courts do when considering them under section 2 of the Human Rights Act.[18] The ECJ appears to consider them, in effect, binding on the Union institutions and Member States when acting within the scope of EU law. In effect, the ECJ applies the Convention directly, by requiring EU secondary law, acts of the institutions, and rules of national law within the scope of EU law to be reviewed for conformity with Convention principles. This suggests that the

---

[12] Compare Case 374/87 *Orkem v Commission* [1989] ECR 3283 with *Funke v France* (1993) EHRR 297.

[13] For an example of such conflict, namely a conflict between freedom of expression and assembly, in the form of an environmental demonstration, and the free movement of goods, see Case C–112/00 *Schmidberger v Austria* [2003] ECR I–5659, paras 71–77.

[14] Case 136/79 *National Panasonic (UK) Ltd v Commission* [1980] ECR 2033; Case C–427/85 *Commission v Germany* [1989] ECR I–1263; Case C–299/95 *Kremzow v Austria* [1997] ECR I–2629; Case C–85/96 *Martinez Sala v Freistaat Bayern* [1998] ECR I–2691; Case C–274/96 *Criminal Proceedings Against Bickel* [1998] ECR I–7637; Case C–105/03 *Criminal Proceedings against Pupino* [2005] ECR I–5285; Case T–315/01 *Kadi v Council and Commission* (Case T-315/01) [2005] ECR II-3649.

[15] See, eg Case C-450/06 *Varec SA v Belgium* [2008] ECR I–581 (on Art 8).

[16] See, eg *Ocalan on behalf of the PKK v Council of the European Union* [2007] ECR I–439, paras 71, 81.

[17] Case C–17/98 [2000] ECR I–665.

[18] See Case C–465/07 *Elgafaji v Saatssecretaris an Justitie* [2009] WLR (D) 59, para 28.

Convention standards are (already) regarded as a requisite minimum standard of human rights protection in the EU.

C. THE EU CHARTER OF FUNDAMENTAL RIGHTS

The Charter is an EU instrument—it is wholly distinct from the Convention, though clearly informed by it. The Charter is addressed to the EU and its institutions, and Member States when they are implementing Union law, and requires states to promote the rights contained in it. Originally 'solemnly proclaimed' in 2000, it was seen by some as simply an attempt to 'codify' the fundamental rights which were protected under EU law and by others as a highly symbolic 'constitutional' moment in the EU's history. Whilst originally not legally binding,[19] that changed with the adoption of the Lisbon Treaty: now, by virtue of Article 6(1) TEU, it has the same legal status as the TEU and TFEU; in other words, it is part of EU primary law. 5.11

The preamble to the Charter refers to the values set out in Article 2 TEU and 'reaffirms' the Convention, the Social Charters adopted by the EU and the Council of Europe, and the case law of both the ECJ and ECtHR. The substance of the Charter is divided into six chapters: I Dignity; II Freedoms; III Equality; IV Solidarity; V Citizens' Rights; and VI Justice. The final chapter, VII, contains general clauses which relate to the interpretation and scope of application of the Charter, including the bodies to which it is addressed. 5.12

It will immediately be seen that the rights and principles set out in the Charter go beyond the rights found in the Convention and include various specific equality rights,[20] a host of socio-economic rights,[21] and various political rights.[22] That said, a distinction should be drawn between 'rights' and 'principles' set out in the Charter: according to Article 51(1) thereof, the rights must be 'respected'; the principles merely 'observed'.[23] The extent to which the ECJ will recognize the significance of this distinction is one of the various interesting issues which will doubtless arise for consideration. 5.13

Articles 51 to 54 of the Charter set out general provisions on its interpretation and scope of application. Article 51 provides, importantly, that the Charter applies to the EU institutions and to the Member States only when they are implementing EU law. Whilst this may have been an attempt to restrict the Charter's scope of application, it has not stopped the ECJ from applying it to acts of Member States in situations where they were not implementing EU law.[24] 5.14

---

[19] This did not stop the ECJ and even the ECtHR from regarding it as a reference point for fundamental rights protection: see, respectively, Case C–540/03 *European Parliament v Council* [2006] ECR I–5769, para 38 and *Goodwin v UK* (2002) 35 EHRR 18, para 100.

[20] See, eg Arts 24 and 25 on the rights of the child and the elderly respectively.

[21] See, eg Art 35 on the right of access to preventive healthcare and to benefit from medical treatment.

[22] See, eg Art 39 on the right to vote and to stand as a candidate at elections to the European Parliament.

[23] See also Art 52(5) of the Charter: '[t]he provisions of this Charter which contain principles may be implemented by legislative and executive acts taken by institutions, bodies, offices and agencies of the Union, and by acts of Member States when they are implementing Union law, in the exercise of their respective powers. They shall be judicially cognisable only in the interpretation of such acts and in the ruling on their legality.' See also the Explanations Relating to the Charter of Fundamental Rights [2007] OJ C303/17 (the relevance of which is explained by Art 52(7) of the Charter) on this point.

[24] See, eg Joined Cases C–570 and 571/07 *Perez and Gomez* [2010] ECR I–nyr, 1 June 2010 and Case C–34/09 *Zambrano* [2011] ECR I–nyr, 8 March 2011. See also Case C–555/07 *Kücükdeveci v Swedex GmbH*

5.15   The relationship between the Charter and the Convention is set out in Article 52(3), which provides:

> Insofar as this Charter contains rights which correspond to rights guaranteed by the Convention for the Protection of Human Rights and Fundamental Freedoms, the meaning and scope of those rights shall be the same as those laid down by the said Convention.

This provision shall not prevent Union law providing more extensive protection. In other words, Convention rights represent a minimum standard for EU law.[25] Article 53 provides that the Charter does not restrict or adversely affect fundamental rights as recognized more generally by EU law, by general international law, by international agreements to which the EU or all its Member States are party, or by the Member States' constitutions. Finally, Article 54 prohibits the abuse of the rights safeguarded by the Charter.

5.16   In *Zagorski v Secretary of State for Business, Innovation and Skills* the High Court held that the jurisdictional reach of the Charter was no wider than that of the Convention. Whilst there was no provision in the Charter akin to Article 1 of the Convention, Article 52(3) of the Charter had a 'vital bearing' on the issue: in the Court's view, not only the material but also the personal scope of the Charter was to be the same as that of the Convention.[26]

D. ACCESSION TO THE CONVENTION

5.17   The ECtHR is not, at present, prepared to consider the conformity of the actions of EU bodies themselves with Convention standards, even if creatively addressed as an application against all EU Member States.[27] As already explained, however, the TEU mandates the EU to accede to the Convention, and so the position will soon change. Protocol 8 to the Lisbon Treaty on the EU's accession to the Convention provides than any such agreement shall make provision for preserving the specific characteristics of the Union and Union law. Thus, there will be many matters that require resolution. One such matter is whether responsibility for complying with the Convention rests with the Member States, collectively or individually, or with the Union institutions. Another concerns the relationship between the ECJ and ECtHR: it is clear that the ECJ wishes to ensure that it is always in a position to assess the validity of EU acts for Convention compliance before the ECtHR itself does so (upon application by an aggrieved party), and so a mechanism will need to be devised to ensure that this will be possible. The particular scenario in which, absent a specific mechanism, there would be a risk of the ECJ not having such a review function is where a claimant indirectly challenges an EU act on Convention grounds by attacking an implementing measure of the competent national authority. If the national court considers there to be no serious grounds on which to impugn the EU

[2010] ECR I–nyr, 19 January 2010 (allowing for the Charter to be given horizontal direct effect, ie to be relied upon in proceedings between private parties).

[25] For a recent example of a case in which the ECJ has gone further than the ECtHR in terms of fundamental rights protection, see Case C–465/07 *Elgafaji v Staatssecretaris van Justitie* [2009] ECR I–921 (requirements for refugee status under Art 3 of the Convention).

[26] [2010] EWHC 3110 (Admin) at [73].

[27] See *Guérin Automobiles v 15 Members of the EU* App No 5157/99, which was declared inadmissible on 4 July 2000; and *Segi and ors v 15 Members of the EU* App No 6422/02.

act and therefore dismisses the claim, and assuming appellate courts dismiss any appeals, the claimant will have exhausted domestic remedies and so will be entitled to apply to the ECtHR.[28] The relationship between the ECtHR, the ECJ, and national constitutional courts will clearly remain under development for some time.

E. THE INTERACTION OF EU LAW AND CONVENTION PRINCIPLES IN UK COURTS

The obligation of UK courts to apply EU law on fundamental rights applies only in areas of EU competence,[29] whereas the Human Rights Act can be used directly to challenge *any* government action that has an impact on Convention rights. It might be thought, therefore, that EU law has nothing to add to Convention principles in giving effect to fundamental rights in UK courts, and (conversely) that Convention principles add nothing to questions of EU law. However, such an approach would be misconceived.   5.18

First, many cases that involve EU law rights concern the balance to be struck between a right contained in EU law and the state's power to protect a competing public interest (for example, public order or public safety). In such cases, a public authority might argue that the public interest exception to the underlying EU law right is engaged. Whether this is in fact the case involves a decision as to whether the proposed restriction on the underlying right can be justified in the public interest. The scope of the state's power to restrict the underlying EU law right may be limited by having regard to case law of the ECtHR. For example, in the *Carpenter* case described at para 5.07 above, the scope of the exception to free movement rights contained in Article 56 TFEU was limited by the ECJ 'in the light of the fundamental right to respect for family life' as it had been interpreted by the ECtHR.   5.19

Secondly, the ECtHR has been clear that the fact that a Member State may be acting so as to give effect to an obligation imposed upon it by EU law will not justify a breach of the Convention, if one exists. So, in *Cantoni v France*,[30] the ECtHR held that a national legislative provision based on a Community directive did not remove the provision from the scope of the Convention or the Member State from its responsibility to ensure that offences imposed by implementing measures complied with Article 7 of the Convention. And in *Matthews v UK*,[31] the applicant, a resident of Gibraltar, successfully challenged the failure to afford her a vote in EU elections, even though she did not reside in a territory which was defined as part of the United Kingdom for the purposes of European parliamentary elections. The ECtHR nonetheless found a breach of Article 3 of Protocol 1 by the United Kingdom. It should, however, be stressed that   5.20

---

[28] In January 2011 the Presidents of the ECJ and ECtHR issued a joint communication in which they called for the creation of a procedure which would allow for an 'internal' review, possibly under an accelerated procedure, prior to the ECtHR conducting its 'external review': see <http://www.echr.coe.int/NR/rdonlyres/02164A4C-0B63-44C3-80C7-FC594EE16297/0/2011Communication_CEDHCJUE_EN.pdf>.

[29] The UK's judges do not always agree as to what this means, as can be seen by comparing the judgments in *R v Ministry of Agriculture, Fisheries and Food, ex p Hamble Fisheries (Offshore) Ltd* [1995] 1 CMLR 553 and *R v Ministry of Agriculture, Fisheries and Food, ex p First City Trading Ltd* [1997] 1 CMLR 250, though ultimately the scope of EU competence is a matter for the ECJ itself: see, eg Case C–260/89 *Elliniki Radiophonia Tileorassi AE (ERT) v Dimotiki Etairia Pliroforissis (DEP)* [1991] ECR I–2925.

[30] Reports of Judgments and Decisions 1996-V, 1614.

[31] (1999) 28 EHRR 36.

this scenario is likely to arise only rarely, particularly now that the EU Charter of Fundamental Rights is legally binding.[32]

5.21   Thirdly, we have seen that the Charter is broader, in terms of the rights enumerated, than the Convention and that the ECJ is prepared to give it a liberal interpretation in terms of its scope of application. Where EU law is in play, therefore, it may go further than the Convention.

5.22   Fourthly, even after the incorporation of the Convention into domestic law, there may be cases in areas covered by EU law rights in which the Convention will be more effective if it is used in conjunction with EU law than on its own through the Human Rights Act. The most obvious is where the provision complained of is contained in a statute that falls within the sphere of EU competence. Pursuant to section 2 of the European Communities Act 1972 and the case law of the ECJ, EU law has supremacy over conflicting provisions of domestic law—it can override even Acts of Parliament where it is directly effective—and domestic law must be interpreted, so far as possible, in light of any relevant EU law, whether directly effective or not (the so-called *Marleasing* principle[33]). This means that EU law can be used to 'strike down' inconsistent domestic legislation.[34] This makes EU law in some respects more powerful than the Human Rights Act, which explicitly prevents the courts from using the Convention to 'strike down' incompatible primary legislation.[35]

5.23   In spheres of EU competence, it may therefore be more beneficial to use the Convention through EU law rather than through the Human Rights Act alone where the challenge is to primary legislation. Whereas the Act alone would permit the court only to declare the domestic legislation incompatible with the Convention (see section 4), if primary domestic legislation contravenes directly effective EU legislation, the national court is required to disapply the primary domestic legislation. Therefore, if a court or tribunal could be persuaded that a provision of EU law must be interpreted in accordance with the Convention, and where EU law is directly effective, the Convention standard will become part of domestic law even to the extent of overriding inconsistent domestic provisions.[36]

5.24   Fifthly, if an argument falls within both Convention and EU law, more beneficial remedies might be available under EU law than could be obtained under the Human Rights Act alone. The Human Rights Act expressly excludes the possibility of obtaining damages

---

[32] Note *Bosphorus Hava Yollari Turizm Ve Ticaret AS v Ireland* (2006) 42 EHRR 1, in which the Grand Chamber of the ECtHR said that there was a rebuttable presumption that a state would not depart from Convention standards in acting so as to comply with its obligations as a member of another international organization (such as the EU). But this presumption held only *if* the relevant international organization offered protection of fundamental rights which was *at least equivalent* to that provided by the Convention. The ECtHR found that the EU did offer such protection; however, if in any individual case the Court considered that the protection of Convention rights within the structure of the international organization was 'manifestly deficient', then the presumption could be rebutted.

[33] Case C–106/89 *Marleasing SA v La Comercial Internacional de Alimentacion* [1990] ECR I–4137. The *Marleasing* principle is that when a national court interprets domestic law in a field governed by a directive, or other non-directly effective provision of EU law, it must do so in the light of the wording and purpose of EU legislation. See also Case C–92/92 *Collins v Imtrat Handelsgesellschaft mbH* [1993] ECR I–5145.

[34] See Case 152/84 *Marshall v Southampton and South West Hampshire Area Health Authority (Teaching)* [1986] QB 401 and Case C–213/89 *Factortame* [1990] ECR I–2433.

[35] See s 3(2)(b) and (c).

[36] For example Case C–271/91 *Marshall v Southampton and South West Hampshire Area Health Authority (Teaching) (No 2)* [1993] ICR 893.

against the state for a failure to legislate (see Chapter 3, para 3.18). However, under EU law damages must in principle be available if the state has committed a 'sufficiently serious' breach of EU law (including where the Government has failed to transpose a directive into domestic law on time), as a result of which loss is suffered.[37] It appears that certain concepts such as that of proportionality are not identical under Convention and EU law.[38]

Finally, there are other tactical areas in which the interaction of EU and Convention law may be considered. For example, section 7 of the Human Rights Act gives only 'victims' of acts standing to sue. The English courts have arguably adopted a more generous attitude to representative standing in some cases involving EU law.[39] Therefore, in cases engaging EU law, it is arguable that this restrictive approach to standing would not apply, and so a 'representative' applicant may be able to argue Convention points that would not be available under the Human Rights Act alone.   5.25

Another example is that there may be a difference between an 'emanation of the state' as defined in EU law and a 'public authority' for Convention purposes. It is not yet completely settled whether there is a distinction between: 5.26

(a) the test used in judicial review proceedings,[40] in which questions as to the *sources* of power as well as the functions are potentially relevant;

(b) the test used in EU law, in which a body is held to be an emanation of the state, regardless of its legal form, if it has been made responsible pursuant to a measure adopted by the state for providing a public service, or where it has been given special powers,[41] and the definition of 'public authority' in the Human Rights Act, section 6 (see Chapter 3, paras 3.57 to 3.71).

F. CONCLUSION

It will be appreciated from this brief overview of the protection of fundamental rights under EU law that EU law, the Convention, and domestic law cannot be 'compartmentalized': the interaction between them, and the tactical benefits of pleading rights under one rather than (or in addition to) the other, must be considered carefully in any relevant case.   5.27

---

[37] See Case C–6/90 *Francovich v Italy* [1991] ECR I–5357 and Joined Cases C–46 and 48/93 *Brasserie du Pêcheur SA v Germany* [1996] ECR I–1029.
[38] See *Bank Mellat v HM Treasury* [2011] EWCA Civ 1; cf *R (Countryside Alliance) v Attorney General* [2007] UKHL 52, [2008] 1 AC 719 at [132] and [162]–[166].
[39] See, eg *R v Secretary of State for the Environment, ex p Friends of the Earth* [1996] Env LR 198, although this approach may no longer reflect the approach of the ECJ; see Case C–229/05 *Ocalan v Council of the European Union* [2007] ECR I–439, para 80.
[40] See, eg *R v Panel on Take-overs and Mergers, ex p Datafin plc* [1987] QB 815.
[41] See Case C–188/89 *Foster v British Gas plc* [1990] ECR I–3313.

6

THE CONVENTION RIGHTS:
ABSOLUTE RIGHTS

A. Introduction   6.01

B. Article 1: Jurisdiction   6.04

C. Article 2: Right to Life   6.09
   1. 'Everyone'   6.11
   2. Obligation to protect the right to life   6.19
   3. Prohibition on taking life   6.29
   4. Procedural obligation   6.33
   5. Use of force   6.48
   6. Standing   6.53

D. Article 3: Prohibition of Torture   6.55
   1. Scope of Article 3   6.58
   2. State responsibility   6.72
   3. Negative obligation   6.73
   4. Positive obligations   6.89
   5. 'Warning' decisions   6.114

E. Article 4: Prohibition of Slavery and Forced Labour   6.115
   1. Slavery and servitude   6.117
   2. Forced or compulsory labour   6.120
   3. Positive obligations   6.125

A. INTRODUCTION

This chapter summarizes the content of Articles 1–4 of the European Convention for **6.01** the Protection of Human Rights and Fundamental Freedoms (Convention). These rights are generally considered absolute, in the sense that no restriction may be placed upon them and no derogation from them may be made under Article 15. Further discussion of the nature of absolute rights can be found in Chapter 2.[1]

For each article, an overview is given of the jurisprudence of the European Court of **6.02** Human Rights (ECtHR) and any remaining important cases from the European Commission on Human Rights (ECmHR). Where the domestic courts have considered

---

[1] See ch 2, paras 2.26–2.27.

an article in claims brought under the Human Rights Act, their approach is discussed alongside the European case law, and any divergences are noted.

6.03   When inviting a court to consider Convention jurisprudence under section 2 of the Human Rights Act it is important to be aware that the decisions are context-specific and often fact-sensitive. The Strasbourg organs confine themselves to an examination of the particular case before them. They are not required to review an entire system or practice, but only to determine whether the manner in which this system or practice was applied to or affected the individual applicants gave rise to any violations of the Convention. Nevertheless, the Court often sets out new principles in cases (more often in Grand Chamber cases), and those principles will then be regularly repeated in all subsequent judgments.

B. ARTICLE 1: JURISDICTION

6.04   Article 1 binds contracting parties to the Convention to secure the other Convention rights to everyone, regardless of their nationality, 'within their jurisdiction'. This effectively establishes a jurisdictional limitation on the application of the Convention. Contracting parties are responsible under the Convention for their actions within their own territory even if the effects of their actions are felt abroad, as in cases of deportation to countries where there is a real risk of torture.[2]

6.05   It is less clear when 'jurisdiction' covers extraterritorial acts. The ECtHR set out its interpretation of extraterritorial jurisdiction in *Bankovic v UK and ors*, which concerned the question of whether the bombing of Serbia, which was not party to the Convention, by contracting parties entailed responsibility under the Convention.[3] The Court took a restrictive view of jurisdiction under Article 1, finding that the jurisdictional competence of a state was primarily territorial but recognized some limited exceptions to this principle including where a state party was in 'effective control' of a foreign territory through military occupation, invitation, or acquiescence. In those circumstances, the territory in question could fall within the jurisdiction of the contracting party.

6.06   The European Court modified its approach to extraterritoriality in the recent decision of *Al-Skeini v UK*.[4] In the domestic decision, *R (Al-Skeini and ors) v Secretary of State for Defence*, the House of Lords had followed the ECtHR's reasoning in *Bankovic*, and found that the claims under Article 2 resulting from the death of five Iraqi citizens who had been killed during the course of military operations conducted by British forces did not fall within the jurisdiction of the Convention.[5] The Grand Chamber disagreed. Conflating the categories of exceptional extraterritorial jurisdiction in *Bankovic* it held:

. . . following the removal from power of the Ba'ath regime and until the accession of the Interim Government, the United Kingdom . . . assumed in Iraq the exercise of some of the public powers normally to be exercised by a sovereign government. In particular, the United Kingdom assumed authority and responsibility for the maintenance of security in South East Iraq. In these exceptional circumstances, the Court considers that the United Kingdom, through its soldiers engaged in security operations in Basrah during the period in question, exercised authority and control

---

[2] See, eg *Chahal v UK* (1996) 23 EHRR 413.
[3] (2001) 11 BHRC 435.
[4] App No 55721/07, 7 July 2011.
[5] [2007] UKHL 26, [2008] 1 AC 153.

over individuals killed in the course of such security operations, so as to establish a jurisdictional link between the deceased and the United Kingdom for the purposes of Article 1 . . .[6]

In his concurring opinion, Judge Bonello commented that 'A considerable number of different approaches to extra-territorial jurisdiction have so far been experimented with by the Court on a case-by-case basis'.[7] It remains to be seen whether *Al-Skeini* is another experiment or the last word on jurisdiction.

Since the House of Lords' decision in *Al-Skeini*, jurisdictional issues arose in cases before the Court of Appeal in relation to the presence of UK forces in Iraq. In *R (Al-Saadoon and anr) v Secretary of State for Defence* the Court of Appeal addressed the plight of two Iraqi nationals who were in UK custody in Iraq, having been accused of the murder of two British servicemen.[8] They were about to be handed over to the Iraqi High Tribunal prior to the expiration of the United Nations Mandate for the presence of UK forces in Iraq in order to face war crimes charges, the sentence for which was death by hanging. In a remarkable narrowing of the principle of jurisdiction, the Court of Appeal held that in order for jurisdiction to be established under Article 1 the appellants had to show that the United Kingdom had the 'legal power to fulfill substantial governmental functions as a sovereign state'. The European Court rejected the Court of Appeal's reasoning. It found that respecting the applicants' Convention rights did not involve any breach of Iraqi sovereignty and the applicants' transfer violated Article 3.[9] 6.07

In *R (Smith) v Secretary of State for Defence*, a nine-Justice decision of the Supreme Court, the question arose whether Article 2 applied to British soldiers on military service in Iraq.[10] The Government argued that deaths off-base were outside the jurisdiction. By a majority of six to three, the Supreme Court agreed. The majority's conclusion is questionable in light of the decision in *Al-Skeini v UK*, and *Smith* is unlikely to be the last word on the issue. 6.08

C. ARTICLE 2: RIGHT TO LIFE

Article 2 has, not surprisingly, been described by the ECtHR as 'one of the most fundamental provisions in the Convention'.[11] With very limited exceptions, it cannot be subject to derogation under Article 15, and those exceptions are now irrelevant given the ratification and incorporation by the United Kingdom of Protocol 13. Article 2 is comprehensive, imposing a substantive obligation to protect the right to life, a substantive prohibition on the taking of life, and a procedural obligation to investigate the taking of life. The ECtHR and the domestic courts must, when called upon to make their assessment in an Article 2 case, apply 'most anxious' or 'particularly thorough' scrutiny.[12] 6.09

Although Article 2 does not prohibit the use of a death penalty that has been properly authorized, this sentence is now 'redundant' in light of Protocols 6 (which abolishes the 6.10

---

[6] *Al-Skeini v UK* (n 4 above) at para 149.
[7] Concurring opinion of Judge Bonello, at para 7.
[8] [2009] EWCA Civ 7.
[9] *Al-Saadoon and Mufdhi v UK* App No 61498/08, 2 March 2010. See also ch 9, para 9.14.
[10] [2010] UKSC 29, [2011] AC 1.
[11] *McCann v UK* (1995) 21 EHRR 97, para 197.
[12] *Sergey Shevchenko v Ukraine* App No 32478/02, 4 April 2006, para 42; *Aktaş v Turkey* [2003] ECHR 24351/94, para 271; *McCann v UK* (1995) 21 EHRR 97, para 150.

death penalty in peacetime) and 13 (which extends the abolition to wartime).[13] The ECtHR confirmed in *Al-Saadoon and Mufdhi v UK* that the Convention had been amended so as to prohibit the death penalty in all circumstances and that its use also violated Article 3.[14]

1. 'Everyone'

6.11 The precise starting point of the right to life under Article 2 is controversial. Early case law suggested it applied post-natally only.[15] However, more recent ECtHR cases have indicated that this is not a hard-and-fast line. In *Boso v Italy* the ECtHR accepted, without deciding the issue, that a foetus could potentially be a 'victim' under Article 34.[16] In *Vo v France* the Grand Chamber specifically noted that:

> The Court has yet to determine the issue of the 'beginning' of 'everyone's right to life' within the meaning of this provision and whether the unborn child has such a right.[17]

6.12 In the United Kingdom, the courts have held that, prior to birth, a foetus has no legal rights or interests.[18]

6.13 In *Evans v UK* the Grand Chamber of the ECtHR stated that in the absence of any European consensus on the scientific and legal definition of the beginning of life, 'the issue of when the right to life begins comes within the margin of appreciation which the Court generally considers that States should enjoy in this sphere'.[19]

6.14 In *Vo v France* (above) the Grand Chamber sidestepped the issue of whether Article 2 applies to the foetus, taking a 'decision not to decide', which has been criticized.[20] The applicant suffered a miscarriage after she was mistakenly given a procedure for removal of a coil while five months pregnant, and brought a criminal complaint of unintentional homicide against the doctor. The French courts held that the foetus was not a human person for the purposes of the French Criminal Code.[21]

6.15 The Grand Chamber did not decide whether Article 2 applied to the foetus, instead holding that, even if it did apply, France had not violated its provisions because its administrative remedies were sufficient. The majority considered it 'neither desirable, nor even possible . . . to answer in the abstract' the question of whether a foetus is a person.[22]

6.16 However, a minority of three judges did examine the word 'everyone' and considered that Article 2 was applicable in light of scientific advances that enable a foetus to reach

[13] Per Hammarberg, Commissioner for Human Rights, *Viewpoint* (Strasbourg: Office of the Commissioner for Human Rights, 21 August 2006). At the time of writing, all 47 members of the Council of Europe have signed Protocol 6, but Russia has yet to ratify it. Forty-five members have signed Protocol 13 and 40 have ratified it.
[14] App No 61498/08, 2 March 2010.
[15] *Paton v UK* (1980) 19 DR 244.
[16] App No 50490/99, 5 September 2002. The case was held inadmissible on other grounds.
[17] [2004] 2 FCR 577, para 82.
[18] *Evans v Amicus Healthcare Ltd* [2004] EWCA Civ 727, [2005] Fam 93.
[19] (2007) 22 BHRC 190, para 46.
[20] See also Goldberg, 'Vo v France and Fetal Rights: The Decision Not to Decide' [2005] 18 Harvard Human Rights Journal.
[21] [2004] 2 FCR 577, para19.
[22] Ibid, para 85.

viability earlier.[23] In their view, this would not necessarily render abortion illegal under the Convention; a non-absolute right to life for the foetus could be recognized, thus balancing the interests of the foetus and the mother.[24]

In *Tysiac v Poland* the ECtHR did not engage directly with the question of foetal rights under Article 2 in the case of a woman denied a therapeutic abortion despite significant risks to her eyesight as a consequence of her pregnancy.[25] Determining the case under Article 8, the ECtHR held that the failure of the Polish authorities to provide effective mechanisms for determining whether she met the conditions for obtaining a lawful abortion violated her right to a private life. In an emotive dissent, Judge Borrego Borrego held that the majority favoured 'abortion on demand' and their reasoning implied that the child's 'right to be born' contradicted the Convention.[26]   6.17

In *A, B and C v Ireland* the Court again refused to determine whether the foetus had a right to life under Article 2, reiterating that the question of when the right to life begins falls within the state's margin of appreciation.[27] The Court's reluctance to determine this issue is understandable in light of the divergence of European opinion on abortion but it is legally unsatisfactory. To apply a margin of appreciation to the scope of a concept, rather than the extent of obligation to protect a particular right, sits oddly with the 'autonomous concepts' doctrine used elsewhere in the Convention.   6.18

2. Obligation to protect the right to life

The first sentence of Article 2 imposes a positive obligation on states to protect the right to life. This obliges states to 'take appropriate steps to safeguard the lives of those within [their] jurisdiction'.[28] The principal specific duty arising from this positive obligation is to provide effective criminal legislation supported by law enforcement machinery.[29]   6.19

However, the ECtHR has affirmed that, in certain circumstances, the state will be obliged 'to take preventive operational measures to protect an individual whose life is at risk from the criminal acts of another individual'[30] or from suicide.[31] This obligation is enhanced in respect of individuals who are in state custody, given their particularly vulnerable position.[32]   6.20

One situation in which this positive obligation arises concerns the duty of the police to protect members of the public. In the famous case of *Osman v UK*, the applicant argued that the police had violated Article 2 by failing to protect him and his father from a schoolteacher known to have been obsessed with the applicant. The teacher shot and wounded the applicant and killed his father. The ECtHR held that in order for the positive obligation to be engaged, the state authorities must have known or ought to have known that there was a real and immediate risk to life yet failed to take measures within   6.21

---

[23] Ibid, concurring opinion of Judge Costa; see also the dissenting opinion of Judges Rees and Mularoni.
[24] Ibid, annex (b), para 12.
[25] (2007) 22 BHRC 155.
[26] Ibid, paras 13–15, dissent of Judge Borrego Borrego.
[27] App No 25579/05, para 237.
[28] *Osman v UK* (2000) 29 EHRR 245, para 115.
[29] *Keenan v UK* (2001) 3 EHRR 913, para 88.
[30] *Osman v UK* (2000) 29 EHRR 245.
[31] *Keenan v UK* (2001) 3 EHRR 913.
[32] Ibid, para 90; *Edwards v UK* (2002) 12 BHRC 190; *R (JL) v Secretary of State for Justice* [2008] UKHL 68, [2008] 3 WLR 1325 at [38].

the scope of their power which, judged reasonably, might have been expected to avoid that risk.[33] The police in *Osman* had done all they reasonably could and there was therefore no violation of Article 2. Likewise, in *Re Officer L*, the House of Lords focused on whether there was a real and immediate risk in determining the existence and extent of a positive obligation to take steps to protect life.[34]

6.22   The broad scope of the Article 2 positive obligation is demonstrated by the case of *Öneryildiz v Turkey*.[35] The Grand Chamber unanimously held that the state had violated Article 2 by failing to take appropriate steps to prevent the accidental death of the applicant's relatives, slum dwellers at a rubbish tip, due to a landslide there, either by implementing appropriate measures for waste storage or providing information to people living on slum land regarding the dangers they faced. The ECtHR has extended the *Öneryildiz* principle to natural disasters. In *Budayeva and ors v Russia* the ECtHR ruled that the Russian authorities had not taken all possible steps to mitigate the impact of mudslides on the applicants' lives.[36]

6.23   The ECtHR has also extended the scope of the positive obligation to encompass failure by the state to take action to prevent domestic violence. In *Opuz v Turkey* the state failed to prosecute a husband who had repeatedly attacked his wife and daughter, eventually killing his wife.[37] The ECtHR held that prosecutions should have been pursued despite the withdrawal of the victim's complaints.

6.24   Although Article 2 has the potential to touch a broad range of state activities, it is rare that it is found that the authorities ought to have known that there was a real and immediate risk to life.[38] In *Van Colle v Chief Constable of Hertfordshire Police*, a man intending to give evidence in a Crown Court trial for theft was murdered by the defendant.[39] The House of Lords held that the high threshold for state liability imposed by the *Osman* test had not been met. The fact that the victim had been an intended witness for the prosecution (the state) did not increase the nature of the duty on the police. It is understood that an application to the Strasbourg Court is now pending. Similarly, in *Mitchell v Glasgow City Council* the defendant did not violate Article 2 by its failure to protect a council tenant from a neighbour the defendant knew to have been abusive.[40]

6.25   The protective obligation also means that states must provide appropriate medical treatment to those detained.[41] However, it has never been extended to cover cases of medical negligence in public hospitals outside the context of detention by the state.[42]

6.26   In *Savage v South Essex Partnership NHS Foundation Trust*, the House of Lords considered the case of woman who escaped from detention in a mental hospital and committed suicide.[43] Their Lordships held that Article 2 could be engaged in such circumstances.

---

[33] (2000) 29 EHRR 245, para 116.

[34] [2007] UKHL 36, [2007] 1 WLR 312 at [22] *et seq.*

[35] (2004) 18 BHRC 145.

[36] App Nos 15339/02, 21166/02, 20058/02, 11673/02 and 15343/02, 20 March 2008.

[37] (2009) BHRC 159.

[38] See, eg *Younger v UK* (2003) 33 EHRR CD 252; *Mastromatteo v Italy* [2002] ECHR 37703/97.

[39] [2008] UKHL 50, [2008] All ER 977.

[40] [2009] UKHL 11, [2009] AC 874.

[41] *Tarariyeva v Russia* App No 4353/03, 13 December 2006; *Renolde v France* App No 5608/05, 16 October 2008.

[42] *Powell v UK* (2000) 30 EHRR CD 362; *Dodov v Bulgaria* App No 59548/00, 17 January 2008; *Savage v South Essex Partnership NHS Foundation Trust* [2008] UKHL 74, [2009] 2 WLR 115; *R (Humberstone) v Legal Services Commission* [2010] EWCA 1479, (2010) 118 BMLR 79.

[43] [2008] UKHL 74, [2009] 2 WLR 115.

The proper test to be applied was that set out by the ECtHR in *Keenan v UK*,[44] namely that where there is an immediate risk of a detained patient committing suicide the medical authorities must do all that can be reasonably expected of them to prevent it.

Assisted suicide was considered by the House of Lords in *R (Pretty) v Director of Public Prosecutions*[45] and the ECtHR in *Pretty v UK*.[46] It was argued that Article 2 extends beyond the right to life and protects the more comprehensive right to self-determination in relation to issues of life and death. However, both the House of Lords and the ECtHR rejected this, holding that Article 2 does not confer a right to die.[47] Despite this approach to assisted suicide, Article 2 does not impose a continuing obligation to provide treatment to patients in a permanent vegetative state.[48]   6.27

In the context of armed conflict, the House of Lords has held in *R (Gentle) v Prime Minister* that Article 2 does not apply to the process of deciding on the legality of sending British troops into combat overseas.[49] In that case, the mothers of two British soldiers who died in the Iraq conflict argued that the failure to take proper steps to ascertain whether the participation in the invasion of Iraq would comply with international law violated Article 2. The Lords held unanimously that it was impossible to infer a duty to comply with international law from the Government's positive obligation to protect life within its jurisdiction. In *R (Smith) v Secretary of State for Defence* it was accepted by the Government that the failure to protect a soldier from heatstroke could violate Article 2 where the soldier died within the jurisdiction of the Convention.[50] The Justices expressed differing views of the applicability of Article 2 in combat situations and the question whether poor equipment or training may violate Article 2 remains live.[51]   6.28

3. Prohibition on taking life

In addition to the protective obligation, Article 2 expressly prohibits the state from intentionally taking life. Unintentional taking of life is implicitly prohibited in a situation where the use of force is permitted under Article 2(2), but the force used is more than absolutely necessary and results in death.[52]   6.29

It has been held by the domestic courts that an operation to separate conjoined twins, which would inevitably result in the death of one of them, would not violate the prohibition on intentional killing since the intention of the doctors performing the operation was to save the life of one twin rather than take the life of the other.[53]   6.30

---

[44] (2001) 33 EHRR 913.

[45] [2001] UKHL 61, [2002] 1 AC 800. See also *R (Purdy) v Director of Public Prosecutions* [2009] UKHL 45, [2010] 1 AC 345.

[46] (2002) 35 EHRR 1.

[47] Cf *Savage v South Essex Partnership NHS Foundation Trust* [2008] UKHL 74, [2009] 2 WLR 115 at [11] per Lord Scott.

[48] *NHS Trust v M* [2001] Fam 348. Cf *R (Burke) v General Medical Council* [2005] EWCA Civ 1003, [2006] QB 273.

[49] [2008] UKHL 20, [2008] 1 AC 1356.

[50] [2010] UKSC 29, [2011] AC 1.

[51] Ibid at [127] per Lord Rodger and at [195] per Lord Mance.

[52] *McShane v UK* (2002) 35 EHRR 23, para 93.

[53] *Re A (children) (conjoined twins: surgical separation)* [2001] Fam 147.

6.31   Killing arising through state negligence may amount to a violation of Article 2, for example if a warning shot kills someone.[54]

6.32   Intentional killing and unintentional killing through the use of force which exceeds the Article 2(2) exceptions must be subject to criminal sanctions.[55]

4. Procedural obligation

6.33   The protection of the substantive rights under Article 2 requires that there should be an effective official investigation into deaths resulting from the use of force.[56] This investigative obligation is known as the 'procedural aspect' of Article 2. The case law under Article 2 is equally applicable to the investigative obligation under Article 3.[57]

6.34   As the ECtHR has held, the rationale for inferring an obligation to investigate is based on the positive obligation to protect life: the state is required to maintain a system of law that values and protects life.[58] The obligation is engaged both where death has resulted from state use of force, and where death has resulted from a state's failure to protect the right to life.[59] It is not necessary that a state agent is directly involved in the death.[60] In *Opuz v Turkey* the ECtHR considered that a case of prolonged domestic abuse of a mother and daughter, which had led to the mother's death, engaged the procedural obligation under Article 2.[61]

6.35   The procedural obligation can arise in respect of deaths which have occurred prior to the date of the state's ratification of the Convention where steps in the investigation have occurred post-ratification. In *Silih v Solvenia* the Court stated:

> The procedural obligation to carry out an effective investigation under Article 2 has evolved into a separate and autonomous duty [which] . . . can be considered to be a detachable obligation arising out of Article 2 capable of binding the state even when the death took place before the critical date.[62]

6.36   The Supreme Court applied *Silih* in *Re McCaughey*.[63] Overruling the earlier House of Lords' decision in *Re McKerr*,[64] the court was at pains to stress that there was no continuing obligation to investigate deaths that occurred before the introduction of the Human Rights Act, but where the state had decided to hold an inquest into such a death it had to be Article 2 compliant.

---

[54] *Ogur v Turkey* (2001) 31 EHRR 40, para 83. See also *McShane v UK* (2002) 35 EHRR 23, para 102.

[55] *Osman v UK* (2000) 29 EHRR 245 (intentional killing); *McShane v UK* (2002) 35 EHRR 23, para 93 (unintentional killing resulting from the use of force).

[56] *McCann v UK* (1995) 21 EHRR 97, para 161; *R v Coroner for Western District of Somerset, ex p Middleton* [2004] UKHL 10, [2004] 2 AC 182.

[57] See, eg *Opuz v Turkey* (2009) 27 BHRC 159, para 168.

[58] See, eg *Gül v Turkey* (2002) 34 EHRR 28, para 88; *Brecknell v UK* (2008) 46 EHRR 957, para 65. See also *R (Sacker) v West Yorkshire Coroner* [2004] UKHL 11, [2004] 1 WLR 796 at [11].

[59] See, eg *Edwards v UK* (2002) 12 BHRC 190.

[60] *Menson v UK* [2003] ECHR 47916/00; *R (JL) v Secretary of State for Justice* [2008] UKHL 68, [2008] 3 WLR 1325 at [26].

[61] (2009) 27 BHRC 159.

[62] [2009] ECHR 571, para 69.

[63] [2011] UKSC 20.

[64] [2004] UKHL 12, [2004] 2 All ER 409.

The precise form of the Article 2 investigation is flexible, but in all cases, the authori-   6.37
ties must engage the investigative mechanism on their own initiative.[65] In order to guarantee its effectiveness, the investigation must be independent,[66] prompt,[67] and open to
an element of public scrutiny.[68]

In *McShane v UK*, the applicant's husband was killed when a security forces' vehicle   6.38
struck a hoarding under which he had fallen during a disturbance in Belfast.[69] The applicant complained that there was no effective investigation into her husband's death.
Although there was a police investigation and inquest proceedings were scheduled to
commence, the ECtHR held that a number of deficiencies rendered both inconsistent
with the investigative obligation. In particular, the involvement of police officers indirectly connected with the security operation in the police investigation was held to cast
doubts on its independence. A series of delays in both the investigation and inquest proceedings, including a delay of over five months in questioning the driver of the vehicle,
demonstrated a lack of the requisite promptness.

Although the degree of public scrutiny may vary from case to case, it is necessary in all   6.39
cases for the victim's next of kin to be involved to the extent required to safeguard their
legitimate interests.[70] However, in *Hackett v UK*, concerning a sectarian murder in
Northern Ireland, the ECtHR said that in the early stages of an investigation, particularly
when there is an indeterminate possibility of other persons being criminally charged,
Article 2 may require fairly minimal family involvement.[71] As the investigation progresses,
the public and family should be informed of its findings and recommendations. The
family does not have an automatic right to be given access to police reports or investigative
materials.[72]

In *Ramsahai v Netherlands*, the Grand Chamber emphasized that the primary charac-   6.40
teristic of an effective investigation is that it is 'adequate', and adequacy may be compromised by the possibility of collusion between police officers involved in the incident.[73]
Adequacy requires that the investigation is capable of leading to the identification and
punishment of those responsible. Accordingly, civil proceedings will not constitute an
effective investigation.[74]

The domestic courts have hewed close to the ECtHR's approach to the procedural   6.41
duty under Article 2. In the cases of *R (Amin) v Secretary of State for the Home
Department*,[75] *R v Coroner for Western District of Somerset, ex p Middleton*,[76] and *R (JL)*

---

[65] *Nachova and ors v Bulgaria* [2005] ECHR 43577/98, para 111.
[66] *Brecknell v UK* (2008) 46 EHRR 957.
[67] See, eg *Angelova v Bulgaria* (2007) 23 BHRC 61; *Brecknell v UK* (2008) 46 EHRR 957.
[68] *Edwards v UK* (2002) 12 BHRC 190, paras 69–73; *Ramsahai and ors v Netherlands* [2007] ECHR
52391/99, para 353. See also *R (D) v Secretary of State for the Home Department* [2006] EWCA Civ 143,
[2006] 3 All ER 946.
[69] [2002] ECHR 43290/98.
[70] *Edwards v UK* (2002) 12 BHRC 190, para 73.
[71] (2005) 5 EHRLR 543.
[72] *R (Green) v Police Complaints Authority* [2004] UKHL 6, [2004] 1 WLR 725.
[73] [2007] ECHR 52391/99. See also *R (Saunders) v Independent Police Complaints Commission* [2008]
EWHC 2372 (Admin).
[74] *McShane v UK* [2002] ECHR 43290/98, para 125. See generally Thomas, Straw, and Friedmann,
Inquests: A Practitioner's Guide (London: LAG, 2008).
[75] [2003] UKHL 51, [2004] 1 AC 653.
[76] [2004] UKHL 10, [2004] 2 AC 182.

v Secretary of State for Justice,[77] the House of Lords found violations of the investigative obligation in the context of deaths or near-deaths in custody. *Amin* concerned a death in a young offenders' institution. The deceased, an Asian man, was battered to death with a wooden table leg by his white cellmate who had a history of violent and racist behaviour. A number of investigations were commenced, but the Secretary of State refused the family's request for a public inquiry into the death on the grounds that such an inquiry would add nothing of substance and would not be in the public interest.

6.42   The House of Lords held that the investigations conducted were neither singly nor cumulatively adequate for the purposes of Article 2. While the ECtHR had not prescribed a particular model of investigation suitable for all cases, it had laid down minimum standards that had to be adhered to whatever the form of the investigation. A properly conducted inquest could have discharged the state's obligation under Article 2 but, in its absence, it was necessary for the death to be publicly investigated before an independent judicial tribunal with an opportunity for the relatives to participate.

6.43   In *Middleton* an inquest had taken place in relation to a prisoner who hanged himself in his prison cell. The coroner directed the jury by reference to section 11(5) of the Coroners Act 1988, and the Coroners Rules, that their findings were confined to the identity of the deceased and to 'how', when, and where he came by his death, and that they could express no opinion on any other matter. 'How' was narrowly interpreted in section 11(5) and the Rules to connote 'by what means', and they could not return a verdict of neglect, since this might appear to determine criminal or civil liability.

6.44   The House of Lords, however, held that the inquest was the means by which the state sought to discharge the obligation under Article 2 to investigate the accountability of state agents for deaths which occurred when the deceased was their responsibility, and it should culminate in 'an expression of the jury's conclusion on the central, factual issues in the case'.[78] The narrow interpretation of 'how' the deceased came by his death, coupled with the jury's inability to refer to neglect previously accepted by the domestic courts, meant that in many cases the central issue could not be determined and, accordingly, the current coronial regime did not meet the requirements of Article 2.[79] The court held that the word 'how' in section 11(5) should be interpreted to connote 'by what means and in what circumstances'. The *Middleton* case led to those inquests that were held to discharge the state's Article 2 obligations becoming known as *Middleton* inquests.

6.45   The scope of the investigative duty was clarified again in *R (JL) v Secretary of State for Justice* in which the House of Lords considered the requirements of Article 2 in the context of near-suicides in prison.[80] Lord Phillips stated that 'death requires a spectrum of different types of investigation, depending upon the circumstances of the particular case'.[81] In some cases where death has resulted, a coroner's inquest will satisfy Article 2, while in others it may be necessary to hold a full-blown public inquiry (referred to as a 'D-type' inquiry).[82] In the case of a near-suicide in custody that leaves the prisoner with the possibility of a serious long-term injury, it would automatically be necessary to hold

---

[77] [2008] UKHL 68, [2008] 3 WLR 1325.
[78] [2004] UKHL 10, [2004] 2 AC 182 at [13], [16]–[20].
[79] Ibid at [30]–[32].
[80] See n 77 above.
[81] Ibid at [31].
[82] See *R (D) v Secretary of State for the Home Department* [2006] EWCA Civ 143, [2006] 3 All ER 946.

an 'enhanced investigation', which could presumably be conducted by the Independent Police Complaints Commission.[83] Their Lordships considered that a D-type inquiry might be required in a variety of circumstances that it was not appropriate to prescribe.[84] The Coroners and Justice Act 2009 now makes provision for suspending an inquest where the death is likely to be adequately investigated by an inquiry under the Inquiries Act 2005.[85]

Despite the wealth of authority that has developed in this area, there remains some uncertainty about the application of Article 2 to inquests in certain contexts. In medical negligence cases, for example, there has been confusion about the proper form of an inquest.[86] The position appears to have been clarified by the decision in *R (Humberstone) v Legal Services Commission* in which the Court of Appeal stated that a *Middleton* inquest would be necessary only in limited circumstances which did not include allegations of ordinary medical negligence where the person was not in state custody.[87] The court accepted, however, that there might be a fine line between ordinary negligence and systemic failings. In *R (Smith) v Secretary of State for Defence*, the Supreme Court examined the necessity for a *Middleton* inquest into the deaths of soldiers on active service. The majority of the court rejected the argument that all military deaths on active service required a *Middleton* inquest on the grounds that death of a soldier did not raise any presumption of a breach of the substantive obligation under Article 2. **6.46**

Compliance with the procedural obligation is closely related to the Article 13 right to an effective remedy. The very purpose of an investigation is to secure the effective implementation of domestic laws which protect the right to life and, in those cases involving state agents or bodies, to ensure their accountability for deaths occurring under their responsibility. However, violation of Article 2 stemming from non-compliance with the procedural obligation will not necessarily constitute a violation of Article 13.[88] **6.47**

5. Use of force

Article 2(2) details the circumstances in which it is permissible to use lethal force. All these situations involve curbing violence or the control of prisoners or criminals— generally, maintaining law and order. The crucial test for these exceptions is that 'no more force than is absolutely necessary' is used. The ECmHR examined this phrase in *Stewart v UK*, and held that force is 'absolutely necessary' if, having regard to the nature of the aim pursued, the dangers and risks inherent in the situation, and all relevant circumstances, it is 'strictly proportionate to the achievement of the permitted purpose'.[89] In this way, it is a stricter test than that found under paragraphs 2 of Articles 8–11. The ECmHR found that the exceptions included in Article 2(2) indicate that this provision extends to, but is not concerned exclusively with, intentional killing. **6.48**

---

[83] See *R (Reynolds) v IPCC* [2008] EWCA Civ 1160.
[84] Cf Lord Brown at [104].
[85] Coroners and Justice Act 2009, Sch 1.
[86] See *R (Goodson) v HM Coroner for Bedfordshire and Luton* [2004] EWHC 2931 (Admin); *Takoushis v HM Coroner for Inner London* [2005] EWCA Civ 1440; *Moss v HM Coroner for North and South Districts of Durham and Darlington* [2008] EWHC 2940 (Admin). See, further, Millar, 'Human Rights Considerations for the Clinical Negligence Practitioner' (2005) 11(6) AvMA Medical and Legal Journal 243.
[87] [2010] EWCA Civ 1479, (2010) 118 BMLR 79.
[88] *McShane v UK* [2002] ECHR 43290/98.
[89] (1984) 38 DR 162.

6.49   The leading case on the use of lethal force is still *McCann v UK*, in which three Provisional IRA members were shot and killed by British soldiers in Gibraltar in 1988. The ECtHR held, by a slim 10–9 vote, that there had been a violation of Article 2.[90] In making its decision, the ECtHR took into consideration 'not only the actions of the organs of the state who actually administer the force but also the surrounding circumstances including such matters as the planning and control of the actions under examination'. The concept of 'planning and control' is critical. The ECtHR held that the state must give appropriate training, instructions, and briefing to its agents who are faced with a situation where the use of lethal force is possible.[91] The state must also exercise 'strict control' over any operations that may involve use of lethal force.

6.50   Since the decision in *McCann*, the ECtHR has sometimes appeared to take a more lenient line on absolute necessity. In *Andronicou v Cyprus*, for example, police shot a gunman and his hostage, mistakenly believing that the gunman had more ammunition and weapons than he actually possessed.[92] The ECtHR held that the police actions were adequately designed and controlled to minimize the risk to the lives of the gunman and his hostage. Even though the police were mistaken about the gunman's weapons, they had good reason to believe as they did, and were pursuing the legitimate aims of Article 2(2).

6.51   Similarly, in *Bubbins v UK* the ECtHR found no violation of Article 2 where an individual was mistakenly shot dead by a police officer after he pulled a replica gun which the officer believed to be real.[93] The ECtHR held that it could not substitute its own assessment for that of the officer in the situation and that his actions were proportionate.

6.52   However, the Grand Chamber echoed *McCann* in *Nachova v Bulgaria*, reiterating both the strictness of the applicable test and the importance of operational planning.[94] The ECtHR condemned the 'deplorable disregard for the preeminence of the right to life' displayed by the manner in which the operation was planned and controlled.[95] According to the ECtHR, Article 2 requires an appropriate administrative and legal framework to be put in place to clarify when officers can use arms and force in line with international standards, and with regard to the fundamental value of life.[96]

6. Standing

6.53   Relatives of the deceased are considered 'victims' of breaches of Article 2, within the meaning of Article 34.[97] The ECtHR has also held that an individual whose life is put at serious risk may be a victim for Article 2 purposes.[98] In *Savage v South Essex Partnership NHS Foundation Trust* Lord Scott suggested (the point was not in fact in issue in the case) that complaints concerning breaches of the substantive obligations under Article 2 could not be brought by victims' relatives on the grounds that private causes of action

---

[90] (1995) 21 EHRR 97.
[91] See also *Gül v Turkey* (2002) 34 EHRR 28.
[92] (1997) 25 EHRR 491.
[93] App No 50916/99, 17 March 2005.
[94] [2005] ECHR 43577/98.
[95] Ibid, para 105.
[96] Ibid, para 97.
[97] *Brecknell v UK* App No 32457/04, 27 November 2007; *Yasa v Turkey* (1999) 28 EHRR 408; *McShane v UK* (2002) 35 EHRR 23, para 93.
[98] *Osman v UK* (2000) 29 EHRR 245.

were open to the relatives to pursue.[99] This is inconsistent with the case law of the ECtHR, which domestic courts are obliged to apply under section 2 of the Human Rights Act.[100]

It is not necessary for a person to have died in order for a claim under Article 2 to be brought. A living applicant may bring a claim for state conduct that put his or her life at grave risk.[101]   6.54

D. ARTICLE 3: PROHIBITION OF TORTURE

Article 3 concerns freedom from torture and inhuman and degrading treatment. Like Article 2, it is one of the most fundamental provisions of the Convention.[102] Its importance is reflected in its absolute and non-derogable status.[103]   6.55

It places a negative duty on the state not to inflict the proscribed suffering on human beings, as well as a positive duty to ensure that these forms of suffering are not endured. In common with Article 2, it also includes a procedural obligation to conduct an effective investigation in certain circumstances.[104]   6.56

Article 3 applies irrespective of the conduct of an applicant.[105]   6.57

1. Scope of Article 3

In *Ireland v UK* the ECtHR considered the types of treatment that are prohibited by Article 3.[106] It characterized the prohibited activities as follows: 6.58

(a) *torture*: deliberate inhuman treatment that causes very serious and cruel suffering;

(b) *inhuman treatment*: treatment that causes intense physical and mental suffering; and

(c) *degrading treatment*: treatment that arouses in the victim a feeling of fear, anguish, and inferiority capable of humiliating and debasing the victim and possibly breaking his or her physical or moral resistance.

As a threshold standard, treatment must attain 'a minimum level of severity' to fall within Article 3.[107] In *Ireland v UK* the ECtHR described the determination of this minimum level as 'relative' and set out some criteria, such as the duration of the treatment, its physical or mental effects, and, in some circumstances, the sex, age, and state of health of the victim.[108] These factors are relevant in two contexts: when determining   6.59

---

[99] [2008] UKHL 74, [2009] 2 WLR 115 at [2]–[3].

[100] See ch 4.

[101] See, eg *Acar v Turkey* [2005] ECHR 36088/97, para 79; *R (JL) v Secretary of State for Justice* [2008] UKHL 68, [2008] 3 WLR 1325.

[102] *Pretty v UK* (2002) 35 EHRR 1.

[103] *Saadi v UK* (2008) 24 BHRC 123.

[104] *Assenov v Bulgaria* (1998) 28 EHRR 652; *Šečić v Croatia* (2007) 23 BHRC 24; *R (Green) v Police Complaints Authority* [2004] UKHL 6, [2004] 1 WLR 725.

[105] *Chahal v UK* (1996) 23 EHRR 413; *Gäfgen v Germany* App No 22978/05, 3 June 2010; *Hassan-Daniel v HMRC* [2010] EWCA Civ 443.

[106] (1978) 2 EHRR 25.

[107] Ibid.

[108] Ibid, para 162.

whether the suffering caused is sufficient to amount to inhuman or degrading treatment or punishment; and when distinguishing between these lesser kinds of ill-treatment and torture.

6.60   As the Convention is a living instrument, acts that have previously been classed as inhuman treatment, for example, could well be classed differently in the future.[109] In keeping with the Strasbourg approach, the domestic courts accept that the concept of 'torture' is not immutable and may shift over time. Lord Bingham indicated in *A and ors v Secretary of State for the Home Department (No 2)* that the conduct complained of in *Ireland v UK* may well be considered to now fall within the definition of 'torture'.[110]

6.61   Further, treatment which does not violate Article 3 may nevertheless violate the right to autonomy and dignity now recognized under the rubric of Article 8.[111] Conversely, treatment may constitute such a gross breach of another article of the Convention as to amount to inhuman or degrading treatment under Article 3.[112]

(a) *Torture*

6.62   Torture is an aggravated form of inhuman or degrading treatment or punishment. Classification of treatment as torture implies suffering of a particular intensity and cruelty.[113] Such treatment will usually have a purpose such as obtaining information or a confession, or inflicting punishment.[114] The ECtHR has found that the distinction between 'torture' and 'inhuman or degrading treatment' was intended to 'attach a special stigma to deliberate inhuman treatment causing very serious and cruel suffering'.[115] The Court attaches significant importance to drawing the distinction between the different forms of ill-treatment, and will do so even where the state has accepted that its conduct broadly violated Article 3.[116]

6.63   In *Aydin v Turkey* the complainant had been raped, blindfolded, beaten, stripped, and sprayed with high-pressure water while in the custody of the Turkish security forces. This treatment was held to amount to torture. The ECtHR commented that a finding of torture would have been made even in the absence of rape.[117] The accumulation of similarly violent and humiliating treatment was classified as torture in *Selmouni v France*, where the complainant had been urinated on, threatened with a blowtorch, and severely beaten by the police.[118]

6.64   Mental anguish alone may constitute torture if it reaches a certain level of severity.[119] The ECtHR has found that the threat of torture can violate the prohibition on inhuman and degrading treatment provided it is sufficiently real and immediate.[120]

---

[109] *Selmouni v France* (2000) 29 EHRR 403.
[110] [2005] UKHL 71, [2006] 2 AC 221 at [53].
[111] *Wainwright v UK* [2006] ECHR 807.
[112] See, eg *East African Asians v UK* (1981) 3 EHRR 76.
[113] *Ireland v UK* (1978) 2 EHRR 25.
[114] *The Greek Case* (1969) 11 YB 501.
[115] See, eg *Ciorap v Moldova* [2007] ECHR 12066/02, para 62.
[116] *Gäfgen v Germany* App No 22978/05, 3 June 2010.
[117] (1997) 25 EHRR 251.
[118] (2000) 29 EHRR 403.
[119] *Denmark v Greece* (1969) 12 YB 1.
[120] *Campbell and Cosans v UK* (1982) 4 EHRR 293, para 26; *Gäfgen v Germany* App No 22978/05, 3 June 2010.

The Strasbourg Court has developed a strong principle that a state may not extradite 6.65
an individual to a country where there are substantial grounds for believing that there is
a real risk that he or she would be subjected to torture or ill-treatment.[121] This principle
has been the subject of extensive case law before both the ECtHR and domestic
courts.[122]

The House of Lords considered its duties relating to the prohibition of torture under 6.66
international law in *Jones v Saudi Arabia*.[123] The House upheld the principle of sovereign state immunity and unanimously denied jurisdiction in a claim brought by four
UK citizens to seek redress against acts of torture committed against them by a foreign
state and its officials. Although not of direct relevance to Article 3, the decision is indicative of a cautious approach to torture-related issues in the absence of a settled consensus
at international level.[124]

(b) *Inhuman and degrading treatment or punishment*
The terms 'inhuman' and 'degrading' bear different meanings under the Convention, 6.67
though one is rarely found to exist without the other.

Treatment or punishment is considered 'inhuman' where it is premeditated, applied 6.68
over a period of hours at a stretch, and causes either actual bodily injury or intense physical or mental suffering.[125] Whether treatment or punishment is degrading depends on
all the circumstances: the nature and context of the treatment or punishment and the
method and manner of its execution.[126] As judicial punishment inevitably entails a
degree of humiliation, degrading punishment must involve a degree of humiliation or
debasement that exceeds that which is usual in punishment.[127] Unlike torture, it is not
necessary that there be any specific intention or purpose such as intent to debase,
although an aim to humiliate or debase will be highly relevant.[128]

In *Ireland v UK* the ECtHR examined five techniques used by the British Government 6.69
to interrogate prisoners allegedly involved in terrorism, which included forcing them to
stand against a wall in an uncomfortable position, hooding, subjecting them to loud,
continuous noise, and depriving them of food, drink, and sleep. Although not rising to
the level of torture, the ECtHR determined that these practices constituted degrading
treatment and, therefore, violated Article 3.[129]

Race discrimination may constitute degrading treatment. In *East African Asians v UK* 6.70
the applicants were British passport holders but had been refused permission to take up
residence in the United Kingdom. The ECmHR considered that the discriminatory
immigration legislation constituted an interference with their human dignity which
amounted to degrading treatment in the sense of Article 3 of the Convention.[130]

---

[121] *Soering v UK* (1989) 11 EHRR 439.
[122] See paras 6.99–6.108 below.
[123] [2006] UKHL 26, [2007] 1 AC 270.
[124] See also the decision of the Special Immigration Appeals Commission (SIAC) in *Y v Secretary of State for the Home Department*, 24 August 2006 (SC/36/2005).
[125] See, eg *Kudla v Poland* (2002) 35 EHRR 11, para 92.
[126] *Tyrer v UK* (1978) 2 EHRR 1.
[127] Ibid.
[128] *Peers v Greece* (2001) 33 EHRR 51.
[129] (1978) 2 EHRR 25.
[130] (1981) 3 EHRR 76.

6.71   In *Soering v UK* the European Court concluded that 'death row phenomenon' experienced by many prisoners awaiting execution in the United States constituted inhuman and degrading treatment.[131] States cannot extradite suspected criminals to countries where there is a real risk of exposure to such treatment.

2. State responsibility

6.72   The state is responsible for the actions of its agents under Article 3. In *Cyprus v Turkey* the ECmHR found the state responsible for rapes committed by its soldiers as satisfactory action had not been taken to prevent these attacks and disciplinary measures after the conduct were insufficient.[132] The ECtHR held in *Ireland v UK* that the higher authorities of a state are 'under a duty to impose their will on subordinates and cannot shelter behind their inability to ensure that it is respected'.[133]

3. Negative obligation

6.73   Article 3 is generally characterized as containing both a negative obligation to refrain from inflicting harm and a positive obligation to protect people from a real and immediate risk of harm. The utility of this analysis has been questioned by Lord Brown, who suggested that 'the real issue in all these cases is whether the state is properly to be regarded as responsible for the harm inflicted (or threatened) upon the victim'.[134] The ECtHR has itself blurred the boundaries between the positive and negative duties on occasion.[135] Nevertheless, there is a critical distinction to be drawn between the two: the obligation not to do harm is absolute, while the positive obligation requires the state to do all that it reasonably can to prevent harm from occurring.[136]

(a) Counter-terrorism

6.74   The House of Lords considered the negative obligation in the leading counter-terrorism decision *A v Secretary of State for the Home Department (No 2)*,[137] the second key case concerning the Government's legislative response to the terrorist attacks in the United States on 11 September 2001. The applicants were detained under Part IV of the Anti-Terrorism, Crime and Security Act 2001 on the Home Secretary's suspicion of involvement in or links to international terrorism. They appealed against their detention to the Special Immigration Appeals Commission (SIAC). The SIAC was entitled to receive evidence that would not be admissible in court. At issue before the House of Lords was whether evidence which may have been obtained through torture abroad could be admissible in UK proceedings.

6.75   Their Lordships held unanimously that evidence of a suspect or witness which had been obtained through torture had long been regarded as inherently unreliable, unfair, offensive to ordinary standards of humanity and decency, and incompatible with the

---

[131] (1989) 11 EHRR 439; *Al-Saadoon v Mufdhi* App No 61498/08, 2 March 2010.
[132] (1976) 4 EHRR 482.
[133] (1978) 2 EHRR 25, para 159.
[134] *R (Limbuela) v Secretary of State for the Home Department* [2005] UKHL 66, [2006] 1 AC 396 at [92].
[135] *Mubilanzila Mayeka v Belgium* [2006] 3 FCR 637.
[136] See *Re E* [2008] UKHL 66, [2008] 3 WLR 1208 at [10] per Baroness Hale.
[137] [2005] UKHL 71, [2006] 2 AC 221.

principles on which courts should administer justice. The opinions drew not only on Article 3 jurisprudence and international law, but also on the common law, Lord Bingham referring to the unacceptability of torture as a 'constitutional principle',[138] Lord Nicholls as 'a bedrock moral principle in this country'.[139]

Although unanimous on the central issue, the House divided in relation to the application of the exclusionary rule. A majority determined that the SIAC should admit evidence unless it was established on the balance of probabilities that it had been obtained by torture.   6.76

In *Ahmed and anor v R* the Court of Appeal applied *A (No 2)* in considering whether a prosecution should be stayed because the defendant claimed that UK authorities had been complicit in his torture in Pakistan after he was alleged to have committed the offences.[140] The Court of Appeal dismissed the appeal on the basis that the torture must have had an impact on the trial, which in this case it had not.   6.77

In joined cases *RB (Algeria) v Secretary of State for the Home Department* the House of Lords adopted a different approach to the admission of torture evidence in a foreign trial.[141] RB and OO were terrorist suspects whom the Government wished to deport to states with a reputation for ill-treatment. They claimed that if they were deported, they would face trials at which evidence obtained by torture would be admitted. The House of Lords held that the use of evidence obtained by torture in a foreign trial would not necessarily amount to a 'flagrant denial of justice' sufficient to prevent the deportation of the suspect.[142]   6.78

(b) *Sentencing*

Criminal sentences have been an active field of Article 3 complaints. In *Kafkaris v Cyprus* the applicant was found guilty of premeditated murder which carried a mandatory sentence of life imprisonment without any possibility for a judicial body to consider the applicant's detention thereafter.[143] The majority of the Grand Chamber suggested that a sentence of life imprisonment, if irreducible, might raise an issue under Article 3. However, the provisions of the Cypriot Constitution which conferred on the President a discretion to remit, suspend, or commute a life sentence were sufficient to render the sentence reducible despite the fact that they had been exercised very infrequently.   6.79

Whole life sentences have also occupied the domestic courts. In *R v Offen* the Court of Appeal accepted that the imposition of an automatic life sentence, in circumstances where the defendant posed no significant risk to the public, could constitute inhuman and degrading treatment.[144] However, in *R v Lichniak and Pyrah* the House of Lords rejected the argument that the existence of the mandatory life sentence was per se incompatible with Article 3.[145] This decision has been applied in the context of indefinite   6.80

---

[138] Ibid at [51].
[139] Ibid at [64].
[140] [2011] EWCA Crim 184.
[141] [2009] UKHL 10, [2009] 2 WLR 512.
[142] See ch 7, para 7.80.
[143] [2008] ECHR 21906/04, para 98. See also the separate opinion of Sir Nicholas Bratza who considered that whole life sentences were intrinsically inhuman. See also *De Boucherville v Mauritius* [2008] UKPC 37, (2008) 25 BHRC 433, at [8].
[144] [2001] 1 WLR 253 at [95]. See also *R (Wellington) v Secretary of State for the Home Department* [2008] UKHL 72, [2009] 2 WLR 48, discussed below at para 6.103.
[145] [2002] UKHL 47, [2003] 1 AC 903. See also *R v Bieber* [2008] EWCA Crim 1601.

sentences of imprisonment for public protection (known as 'IPP' sentences), which the Court of Appeal found 'wholly compatible' with Article 3.[146]

(c) Detention

6.81   Prison conditions have been held to constitute degrading treatment.[147] For example, in *Price v UK* the ECtHR held that the detention of a severely disabled person in conditions where she was dangerously cold, risked developing sores because her bed was too hard, and was unable to go to the toilet or keep clean without the greatest of difficulty, constituted degrading treatment contrary to Article 3, despite the absence of any intention to subject her to degrading treatment.[148]

6.82   In a separate concurring opinion in *Price*, Judges Bratza and Costa suggested that Article 3 may be breached through a lack of adequate sentence planning, a view which could have wider ramifications in relation to systemic failings by the state to provide adequate mental health or palliative care in prison.

6.83   In a recent spate of decisions concerning prisoners, the European Court has held that detaining a minor in an adult prison violated Article 3 and that multiple transfers of a remand prisoner over a seven-year period constituted inhuman treatment.[149]

6.84   There have so far been relatively few challenges to domestic prison conditions on the basis of Article 3. In *Napier v Scottish Ministers* compensation was awarded to a prisoner who had had to endure the practice of slopping-out common in Scottish prisons at the time.[150] The ECtHR has ruled in a number of cases that overcrowding can violate Article 3[151] and in light of the ever-increasing UK prison population, it is likely that the issue will eventually be raised before the domestic courts.[152]

6.85   Detention for the purposes of immigration control may also violate Article 3. In *Riad and Idiab v Belgium* the two Lebanese applicants were detained in the transit zone of Brussels National Airport in violation of Article 3.[153] The ECtHR found that the transit zone was not an appropriate place for detaining the applicants as it aroused feelings of solitude, and had no external area for walking or taking physical exercise, no internal catering facilities, and no radio or television to ensure contact with the outside world. The conditions caused the applicants considerable mental suffering and undermined their human dignity.

6.86   Detention in the mental health context could give rise to a breach of Article 3. In *R (Munjaz) v Mersey Care NHS Trust* the House of Lords found by a majority that a hospital's policy on seclusion of mentally ill patients contained sufficient safeguards to prevent ill-treatment.[154] The case is pending before the European Court.

6.87   In *R (Bary) v Secretary of State for Justice* two immigrants with pre-existing mental health conditions who were detained indefinitely in a secure unit Category A prison

---

[146] *R v Pedley and ors* [2009] EWCA Crim 840, [2009] 1 WLR 2517.
[147] See, eg *Kalashnikov v Russia* (2002) 36 EHRR 34; *Peers v Greece* (2001) 33 EHRR 51; *Napier v Scottish Ministers* [2002] UKHR 308; *R v Governor of Frankland Prison, ex p Russell* [2000] 1 WLR 2027.
[148] (2002) 34 EHRR 53.
[149] *Güveç v Turkey* App No 70337/01, 20 January 2009; *Khider v France* App No 39364/05, 9 July 2009.
[150] [2002] UKHR 308.
[151] See, eg *Kalashnikov v Russia* (2002) 36 EHRR 34.
[152] See Livingstone, Owen, and McDonald, *Prison Law*, 4th edn (Oxford: Oxford University Press, 2008) 255.
[153] App Nos 29787/03 and 29810/03, 24 January 2008; *SD v Greece* App No 53541/07, 11 June 2009.
[154] [2005] UKHL 58, [2006] 2 AC 148.

separated from the general prison population challenged the conditions in which they were detained.[155] The High Court found that they had not satisfied the high threshold imposed by Article 3: the intention of the restrictive prison regime was not to debase the men, their mental conditions were closely monitored, and other factors were responsible for the limited deterioration in their mental health.

(d) *Mental health*
In the context of compulsory treatment for mental health disorders, the ECtHR has held that 'as a general rule, a measure which is a therapeutic necessity cannot be regarded as inhuman or degrading'.[156] The court must satisfy itself that the medical necessity has convincingly been shown to exist.[157]   6.88

4. Positive obligations

(a) *Investigative duty*
The ECtHR has held that the combined effect of Articles 1 and 3 is to require an effec-   6.89
tive official investigation into credible allegations of serious ill-treatment, whether by state agents or private actors.[158] The investigation, as with that under Article 2, should be capable of leading to the identification and punishment of those responsible for the violation. In *Boiceno v Moldova* the ECtHR emphasized that the investigation must be thorough:

> That means that the authorities must always make a serious attempt to find out what happened and should not rely on hasty or ill-founded conclusions to close their investigation or as the basis of their decisions.[159]

In *R (AM) v Secretary of State for the Home Department* a majority of the Court   6.90
of Appeal held that the Government had failed to satisfy its obligation to investigate ill-treatment during a disturbance at an immigration detention centre where detainees were kept confined while water leaked into their cells and then ordered into the exercise yard while still wet.[160] The Court of Appeal rejected the proposition that because the victim in an Article 3 claim was still alive and therefore had recourse to law, the investigation was not governed by the same principles as those under Article 2. The court held that the primary question was whether the victim could secure adequate investigation without an ad hoc inquiry instituted by the state. The purpose of the investigation was, as under Article 2, to maximize future compliance with Article 3.[161] The case law on the obligation under Article 2 should therefore be considered equally applicable to Article 3.

---

[155] [2010] EWHC 587 (Admin). See also *R (Reetha Suppiah and ors) v Secretary of State for the Home Department* [2011] EWHC 2 (Admin).
[156] *Herczegfalvy v Austria* (1992) 15 EHRR 437, para 82.
[157] Ibid. See *R (B) v Ashworth Hospital Authority* [2005] UKHL 20, [2005] 2 AC 278.
[158] *Assenov v Bulgaria* (1998) 28 EHRR 652; *Šečić v Croatia* (2007) 23 BHRC 24; *Opuz v Turkey* (2009) 27 BHRC 159.
[159] [2006] ECHR 41088/05, para 123.
[160] [2009] EWCA Civ 219.
[161] Ibid at [57].

6.91　As a result of allegations of ill-treatment of Iraqi detainees by UK forces, the Government has been forced to establish two public inquiries. The Baha Mousa Inquiry into the death of Baha Mousa in 2003 will report its findings in mid-2011. The Al Sweady Inquiry into the abuse and unlawful killing of Iraqi detainees at a British military camp in 2004 is due to begin hearings in 2011. The High Court recently rejected a challenge to the Government's refusal to hold another inquiry into allegations of abuse of Iraqi detainees on the basis that the Ministry of Defence had now established the Iraq Historic Allegations Team that would investigate claims independently.[162]

6.92　In June 2010, the Prime Minister announced that an inquiry, known as the Detainee Inquiry, would be established into claims that UK agents were complicit in torture of terrorist suspects abroad.[163] Concerns have been expressed that the inquiry will not meet the state's obligations under Article 3, in particular whether it will be able to compel disclosure of evidence and the testimony of witnesses. At the time of writing, the final decision on the extent of the Inquiry's powers has not been announced.

(b) *Prevention*

6.93　As well as refraining from inflicting treatment violating Article 3, states also have a positive obligation to prevent it. This obligation means that states must take certain steps to ensure that individuals within their jurisdiction are not subjected to torture or other forms of ill-treatment, including that administered by private individuals.[164] Furthermore, the positive obligation to prevent harm must be interpreted in a way which is not incompatible with other Convention rights. For example, social workers cannot take such extreme steps to protect a child from the potential risk of harm in a family that they disproportionately infringe the child's right to respect for his family life under Article 8.[165]

6.94　In *A v UK* the child applicant had been hit by his stepfather with a stick.[166] The stepfather was charged with assault occasioning actual bodily harm. The stepfather contended that the assault amounted to reasonable punishment, which was a defence to a charge of assault of a child by a parent, and he was acquitted. The ECtHR decided that there was a violation of Article 3 because the law failed adequately to protect the child by insufficiently defining what constituted 'reasonable punishment'.[167]

6.95　As a result of the decision, Parliament introduced section 58 of the Children Act 2004 to remove the defence of reasonable punishment to charges of assault occasioning actual bodily harm. However, it is still possible to raise the defence in cases of common assault. It remains to be seen whether section 58 will satisfy the ECtHR.[168]

---

[162] *R (Ali Zaki Mousa) v Secretary of State for Defence* [2010] EWHC 3304 (Admin).

[163] See *R (Binyam Mohamed) v Secretary of State for Foreign and Commonwealth Affairs* [2010] EWCA Civ 65, [2010] 3 WLR 554.

[164] *Mahmut Kaya v Turkey* (1999) 28 EHRR 1; *Z and ors v UK* (2002) 34 EHRR 3.

[165] *Re B* [2008] UKHL 35, [2009] 1 AC 11.

[166] (1998) 5 BHRC 137.

[167] (1999) 27 EHRR 611. See also *Tyrer v UK* (1978) 2 EHRR 1; *Campbell v UK* (1982) 4 EHRR 293; and *Costello-Roberts v UK* (1993) 19 EHRR 112.

[168] In *Northern Ireland Commissioner for Children and Young Peoples' Application* [2007] NIQB 115, the Northern Ireland High Court considered that the law satisfied Art 3. The Court of Appeal held that the Commissioner was not a victim under the Human Rights Act and did not consider the substantive issue: [2009] NICA 10. See also Hamilton, 'Smacking children: has the Government implemented the judgment of the European Court of Human Rights in *A v UK*?' (2007) 238 *Childright* 10–13.

In both *Z v UK*[169] and *E v UK*[170] the ECtHR found that the United Kingdom had   **6.96**
breached Article 3 in failing to protect children from prolonged abuse and neglect which
the authorities knew about. In *E*, they had failed to monitor the family after a stepfather
had been convicted of sexual abuse. The ECtHR held that 'a failure to take reasonably
available measures which could have had a real prospect of altering the outcome or miti-
gating the harm is sufficient to engage the responsibility of the state'.[171] The European
Court is due to consider the case of *X, Y and Z v UK* which challenges the failure by
a local authority to protect vulnerable adults known to social services from abuse by a
group of violent teenagers.[172]

The House of Lords considered the extent of the obligation to prevent harm in   **6.97**
Re E.[173] Catholic schoolgirls on their way to school in Northern Ireland were subjected
to a barrage of abuse over a number of months by protestors lining their route to school.
The House was in no doubt that the children had been subjected to inhuman and
degrading treatment, but found that the police had done all they reasonably could to
protect the children from harm.[174]

As the ECtHR made clear in the case of *Pretty v UK*, the positive obligation to prevent   **6.98**
ill-treatment does not extend to the provision of a lawful opportunity for assisted suicide
in circumstances of significant physical and mental suffering.[175]

(c) *Deportation and removal*

The positive obligation also manifests itself in the principle established in the *Soering*   **6.99**
case that a state may not extradite an individual to a country where there are substantial
grounds for believing that there is a real risk that he or she would be subjected to torture
or ill-treatment.[176]

In *Chahal v UK* the ECtHR made it plain that the question of whether Article 3   **6.100**
prevented deportation was not influenced by the fact that the individual under threat of
deportation posed a threat to national security.[177]

This issue was revisited in *Saadi v Italy*, in which the United Kingdom intervened to   **6.101**
argue that the *Chahal* principle should be modified to allow a degree of risk of torture to
be balanced against the threat posed to the public or the state.[178] The Grand Chamber
unanimously rejected these arguments and robustly reasserted the absolute character of
Article 3. It was not possible to distinguish between torture by a Convention state and
torture by another state to which the Convention state has removed the victim.[179]

Domestic courts have grappled with the implications of these decisions on a number   **6.102**
of occasions. *R (Bagdanavicius) v Secretary of State for the Home Department* concerned a
Lithuanian family who claimed that they were at risk, due to their Roma origins, of

---

[169] (2002) 34 EHRR 97.
[170] (2003) 36 EHRR 519.
[171] Ibid, para 99.
[172] App No 32666/10. The application was communicated by the Court in October 2010.
[173] [2008] UKHL 66, [2008] 3 WLR 1208.
[174] The claim failed in the ECtHR, see *PF and EF v UK* App No 28326/09, 23 November 2010.
[175] (2002) 35 EHRR 1.
[176] *Soering v UK* (1989) 11 EHRR 439.
[177] (1996) 23 EHRR 413.
[178] (2008) 24 BHRC 123.
[179] Ibid, para 138.

inhuman or degrading treatment from non-state actors if returned to Lithuania.[180] The House of Lords held that on any claim against removal on Article 3 grounds the court had to make an assessment of conditions in the receiving country so that it could determine whether there was a real risk of ill-treatment when returned, which would violate Article 3. As any harm inflicted by non-state agents would not violate Article 3 unless the state had failed to provide reasonable protection, to avoid expulsion on Article 3 grounds an individual must establish, first, a real risk of suffering serious harm from non-state agents, and secondly, that the receiving country did not provide a reasonable level of protection against such harm for those within its territory. The test was not satisfied in this case.

6.103   In *R (Wellington) v Secretary of State for the Home Department* the House of Lords considered the application of Article 3 to the extradition of a murder suspect to Missouri.[181] If found guilty, the appellant would automatically receive a sentence of life imprisonment without parole. The sentence could only be reduced by the governor, who had almost never exercised his right to commute such sentences. Relying on a passage in the ECtHR's decision in *Soering*, Lord Hoffmann held that 'the desirability of extradition is a factor to be taken into account in deciding whether the punishment likely to be imposed in the receiving state attains the "minimum level of severity" which would make it inhuman and degrading'.[182] As he accepted, this creates a 'relativist' approach to the scope of inhuman and degrading treatment.[183] Applying this reasoning, the majority of the House held that an irreducible sentence might breach Article 3 domestically, but if imposed by a foreign country it would only contravene Article 3 if it were disproportionate to the crime committed.[184] Given the ECtHR's repeated insistence on the absolute nature of Article 3, it seems unlikely that it would approve of this approach.

6.104   The House of Lords again adopted a restrictive interpretation of the *Soering* principle in *RB (Algeria) v Secretary of State for the Home Department*.[185] Their Lordships held that the two terrorist suspects could be deported because the Government could properly rely on the assurances made by Algeria and Jordan that they would not be mistreated. This was so despite the fact that the assurances did not entirely eliminate the risk of mistreatment.[186]

6.105   In *R (Klimas) v Prosecutors General Office of Lithuania* the High Court found that extradition to a Convention state in which prison conditions were said to be inhuman could not breach Article 3 because the requesting state was itself subject to human rights obligations under the Convention and the individual could challenge his conditions on arrival.[187] The decision is at odds with ECtHR case law which has held that the fact a person is removed to a contracting state does not relieve the state of its obligations under Article 3.[188]

---

[180] [2005] UKHL 38, [2005] 2 AC 668.
[181] [2008] UKHL 72, [2009] 2 WLR 48.
[182] Ibid at [24].
[183] Ibid at [27].
[184] Baroness Hale and Lord Carswell agreed with Lord Hoffmann. Lord Brown and Lord Scott preferred to interpret Art 3 as imposing absolute standards.
[185] [2009] UKHL 10, [2009] 2 WLR 512, applied in *Inzunza v USA* [2011] EWHC 920 (Admin).
[186] [2009] UKHL 10, [2009] 2 WLR 1512 at [114] per Lord Phillips.
[187] [2010] EWHC 2076 (Admin).
[188] *KRS v UK* App No 32733/08, 2 December 2008.

In a dramatic extension of the *Soering* principle, the ECtHR held in *D v UK* that   6.106
deportation of the applicant who suffered from HIV/AIDS to his home country where
he would not receive adequate medical treatment would violate Article 3.[189] The applicant was near death and the ECtHR referred to the 'very exceptional circumstances' of
the case and the 'compelling humanitarian considerations at stake'.[190]

However, in *N v Secretary of State for the Home Department* the House of Lords unani-   6.107
mously held that returning a seriously ill, HIV-positive woman to Uganda would not
constitute inhuman or degrading treatment.[191] It was accepted that her condition had
stabilized after lengthy medical treatment in the United Kingdom, and that she would
remain well for 'decades' if this continued; in Uganda, this treatment would not be
accessible to her and the inevitable outcome of this would be an early death 'after a
period of acute physical and mental suffering'.[192] Their Lordships distinguished *D v UK*
as N's present medical condition was not critical and she remained fit to travel.

N confirms that the domestic courts consider the *D* case to be wholly exceptional, and   6.108
that the obligation not to remove on health grounds will be triggered only in very
extreme factual circumstances. The ECtHR has affirmed the correctness of the House
of Lords' approach, emphasizing that expulsion of an alien who is suffering from a serious mental or physical illness to a country where the facilities for the treatment of that
illness are inferior to those available in the deporting state will only raise an issue under
Article 3 in a very exceptional case.[193]

(d) *State support*

The application of Article 3 to welfare provision has not frequently been considered by   6.109
the ECtHR. In *O'Rourke v UK* the applicant was evicted from temporary accommodation provided for him when he came out of prison.[194] He lived on the streets, to the
detriment of his various medical conditions. In an admissibility decision, the Strasbourg
Court held that this experience did not attain the requisite level of severity to engage
Article 3.

The Court of Appeal and House of Lords have found that denying state support to   6.110
individuals lacking other means of subsistence or shelter may amount to inhuman or
degrading treatment.[195] Distinguishing the decision in *O'Rourke*, the House of Lords
held in *R (Limbuela) v Secretary of State for the Home Department* that a decision to with-
draw support to an asylum-seeker under section 55 of the Nationality, Immigration and
Asylum Act 2002 violated Article 3.[196] In determining whether treatment in a particular
case had reached the minimum level of severity required by Article 3, the court was not
to apply a more exacting test where the treatment or punishment which would otherwise
be found to be inhuman or degrading was the result of legitimate government policy.
The correct test was for the court to look at the context and facts of the particular case,

---

[189] (1997) 24 EHRR 423. Cf *Bensaid v UK* (2001) 33 EHRR 205.
[190] (1997) 24 EHRR 423, para 54.
[191] [2005] UKHL 31, [2005] 2 AC 296.
[192] Ibid at [20] per Lord Hope.
[193] *Nnyanzi v UK* App No 21878/06, 8 April 2008. See also *KH (Afghanistan) v Secretary of State for the Home Department* [2009] EWCA Civ 1354.
[194] App No 39022/97, 26 June 2001.
[195] *R (Limbuela) v Secretary of State for the Home Department* [2005] UKHL 66, [2006] 1 AC 396. See also *R (Q and ors) v Secretary of State for the Home Department* [2003] EWCA Civ 364, [2004] QB 36.
[196] [2005] UKHL 66, [2006] 1 AC 396.

including factors such as the age, sex, and health of the claimant, and the length of time spent or likely to be spent without the required means of support, and ask whether the 'entire package' of work restrictions and deprivations that surrounded the claimant was so severe that it could properly be described as inhuman or degrading treatment. The threshold of severity will be crossed where a person deprived of support under section 55 is obliged to sleep in the street, or is seriously hungry or unable to satisfy the most basic requirements of hygiene. This approach arguably goes further than the ECtHR has yet and offers a rare example of domestic courts interpreting rights more generously than Strasbourg.[197]

(e) *Self-inflicted conditions*

6.111　In cases concerning political prisoners the ECtHR has been faced with the question of whether the fact that harm is self-inflicted negates or dilutes a state's positive obligation under Article 3.[198] Following periods on hunger strike a number of Turkish prisoners suffered physical and mental effects of malnutrition, which in some cases took an extreme form (irreversible brain damage). The ECtHR held that, while the Convention could not be interpreted as laying down a 'general obligation' to release a detainee on health grounds, the prisoner's clinical picture was now one of the factors which a state must take into account under Article 3 in assessing a person's fitness for detention.

6.112　The ECtHR found that their imprisonment violated Article 3, and that the self-inflicted nature of their conditions did not release Turkey from its Article 3 obligations.[199]

6.113　In *Hassan-Daniel v HMRC* the Court of Appeal, considering the state's obligations to a drug smuggler who died from ingestion of drugs while in detention, found that the criminality defence, which holds that it is offensive to public notions of fairness to compensate someone for their own criminal conduct in civil claims, did not apply to claims brought under the Human Rights Act 1998.[200]

5. 'Warning' decisions

6.114　The ECtHR will on occasion specifically indicate to a state that a particular course of conduct could violate Article 3, effectively sending a warning to the state about its future conduct.[201]

E. ARTICLE 4: PROHIBITION OF SLAVERY AND FORCED LABOUR

6.115　Article 4 concerns the twin issues of slavery or servitude (Article 4(1)) and forced or compulsory labour (Article 4(2)). Article 4(1) is another of the rights from which no

---

[197] Cf *R (EW) v Secretary of State for the Home Department* [2009] EWHC 2957 (Admin). See Leigh and Masterman, *Making Rights Real: The Human Rights Act in its First Decade* (London: Hart Publishing, 2009) 79–80.

[198] See, eg *Tekin Yildiz v Turkey* App No 22913/04, 10 November 2005.

[199] Ibid.

[200] [2010] EWCA Civ 1443.

[201] See, eg *Gürbüz v Turkey* App No 26050/04; *Kuruçay v Turkey* App No 24040/04; *Uyan v Turkey* App No 7454/04 (all 10 November 2005); *Balyemez v Turkey* App No 32495/03, 12 December 2005.

derogation is allowed under Article 15. However, the Article 4(2) prohibition is both derogable under Article 15 and subject to the exceptions listed in Article 4(3).

Relatively few Article 4 complaints have been heard by the ECtHR or ECmHR, and only one has been upheld.[202] There have been only a handful of domestic cases raising Article 4 issues.

6.116

1. Slavery and servitude

'Slavery' was eventually defined by the ECtHR in 2005. In *Siliadin v France* the ECtHR drew on historical notions, citing the Slavery Convention of 1926: 'slavery is the status or condition of a person over whom any or all of the powers attaching to the right of owner-ship are exercised'.[203] For four years the applicant, a minor at the time, whose passport was confiscated and who had no immigration status, worked for private individuals against her will and without pay, although no physical force was used. The ECtHR held that this constituted servitude and forced labour, but not slavery.

6.117

'Servitude' differs from slavery in that no ownership of the person is claimed. The ECmHR has suggested that:

6.118

In addition to the obligation to provide another with certain services the concept of servitude includes the obligation on the part of the 'serf' to live on another's property and the impossibility of changing his condition.[204]

The ECtHR's judgment in *Van Droogenbroeck v Belgium* provides further guidance as to the meaning of servitude. A sentence of two years in prison followed by ten years 'at the Government's disposal' did not amount to 'that particularly serious form of depriva-tion of liberty' that constitutes servitude; nor did it 'go beyond what is "ordinary" in this context since it was calculated to assist him in reintegrating himself into society'.[205]

6.119

2. Forced or compulsory labour

The Strasbourg approach to the concept of 'labour' is a generous one. It is not limited to physical labour and encompasses all forms of work.[206]

6.120

In order for labour to be forced or compulsory, the work or service must be 'extracted from the person under the menace of any penalty' and performed involuntarily.[207] There is clear scope for overlap between the concepts of forced labour and servitude.

6.121

The complaints deemed admissible under Article 4(2) have usually fallen into two categories: treatment of prisoners, and professionals compelled to provide their services free to the community. In *Van der Mussele v Belgium* a barrister tried to extend the boundaries of Article 4 when he claimed that being made to do *pro bono* legal work for indigent defendants violated the prohibition on forced labour.[208] The ECtHR asked

6.122

---

[202] *Siliadin v France* (2005) 20 BHRC 654.
[203] Ibid, para 122.
[204] *Van Droogenbroeck v Belgium*, Case B44 (1980) Com Rep, para 79.
[205] (1982) 4 EHRR 443, paras 58–60.
[206] *Van der Mussele v Belgium* (1983) 6 EHRR 163.
[207] *Siliadin v France* (2005) 20 BHRC 654, clarifying earlier case law of the ECmHR; *X v Germany* (1974) 17 YB 148, drawing on the International Labour Organization Convention of 1930.
[208] (1983) 6 EHRR 163. See also *Steindel v Germany* App No 29878/07, 14 September 2010.

whether the labour imposed 'a burden which was so excessive or disproportionate to the advantages attached to the future exercise of the profession that the service could not be treated as having been voluntarily accepted'.[209] Ruling against the barrister, the ECtHR relied on the fact that he had entered the profession of his own will, knowing that *pro bono* work was expected of him.[210]

6.123   Article 4 has rarely been raised in the domestic courts.[211] The House of Lords in *Sepet v Secretary of State for the Home Department* rejected an argument that Article 4 recognized a fundamental right to refuse to undertake military service on grounds of conscience.[212]

6.124   In *R (Ullah) v Special Adjudicator* the House of Lords held that a claim under Article 4, if strong enough, would succeed under Article 3, but it would be inconsistent with the humanitarian principles underpinning the Convention to accept that, if the facts were strong enough, a claim would be rejected even if it were based on Article 4 alone.[213]

3. Positive obligations

6.125   The ECtHR established in *Siliadin v France* that Article 4 entailed a specific positive obligation on Member States to penalize and prosecute effectively any act aimed at maintaining a person in a situation of slavery, servitude, or forced or compulsory labour.[214] In order to comply with this obligation the Court held that states are required to put in place a legislative and administrative framework, capable of realistic enforcement, to prohibit and punish individuals who violate Article 4. The scope of the obligation is identical to that under Article 3.[215]

6.126   Until the Coroners and Justice Act was passed in 2009, there was no offence in English law of subjecting another to servitude.[216] That failure is currently the subject of an application to the ECtHR in *N v UK*.[217]

6.127   In *Rantsev v Cyprus and Russia* the Court reiterated the positive obligations on states to prevent trafficking in human beings, which included a procedural obligation akin to that under Articles 2 and 3 to investigate trafficking once it had come to the state's attention.[218] *Rantsev* was applied in *OOO and ors v Commissioner of the Police for the Metropolis* in which a number of young Nigerian women alleged that the police had failed to investigate their complaints that they had been trafficked to the United Kingdom and held in slavery or servitude.[219] The High Court found that the police were under a duty to investigate a violation of Article 4 once a credible account of an alleged

---

[209] (1983) 6 EHRR 163, para 37.

[210] Cf *Zarb Adami v Malta* (2006) 20 BHRC 703.

[211] In addition to the two House of Lords' decisions discussed here, Art 4 was raised in the planning context in *MacLeod v Secretary of State for Communities and Local Government* [2008] EWHC 384 (Admin). The challenge was rejected as plainly unarguable.

[212] [2003] UKHL 15, [2003] 3 All ER 304.

[213] [2004] UKHL 26, [2004] 2 AC 323.

[214] (2005) 20 BHRC 654.

[215] Ibid, at para 89.

[216] Section 71. See general discussion in Joint Committee on Human Rights, Twenty Sixth Report, October 2006.

[217] App No 4239/08.

[218] (2010) 51 EHRR 1.

[219] [2011] EWHC 1246 (QB).

infringement had been brought to their attention. The trigger for the duty would not depend upon an actual complaint from a victim or near relative of a victim. The investigation, once triggered, would have to be undertaken promptly. The police had taken no steps to investigate the women's situation and had thus violated Article 4. The High Court awarded the women damages for distress and frustration.[220]

---

[220] See Ch 4, para 4.53.

THE CONVENTION RIGHTS: LIMITED AND QUALIFIED RIGHTS

A. Introduction	7.01
B. Article 5: Right to Liberty and Security	7.03
1. Deprivation of liberty	7.10
2. Exceptions to the right to liberty	7.20
3. Procedural safeguards	7.48
4. Positive obligations	7.70
5. Right to compensation	7.73
C. Article 6: Right to a Fair Trial	7.74
1. Scope of Article 6	7.79
2. Rights protected by Article 6(1)	7.104
3. Article 6(2): presumption of innocence	7.150
4. Article 6(3): specific rights in criminal cases	7.156
5. Protocol 7	7.171
D. Article 7: No Punishment Without Lawful Authority	7.172
1. 'Criminal'	7.177
2. Article 7(1): retrospective offences	7.180
3. Article 7(1): heavier penalties	7.194
4. Article 7(2): general principles of law of civilized nations	7.213
E. Article 8: Right to Respect for Private and Family Life	7.217
1. Positive obligations	7.221
2. Article 8(2)	7.226
3. Private life	7.229
4. Family life	7.266
5. Home	7.288
6. Correspondence	7.296
F. Article 9: Freedom of Thought, Conscience, and Religion	7.299
1. 'Everyone'	7.303
2. Freedom of thought, conscience, and religion	7.305
3. Manifestation of one's religion or beliefs	7.315
4. Interference with manifestation of religion or beliefs	7.322
5. Limitations under Article 9(2)	7.333
6. Section 13 of the Human Rights Act	7.345
G. Article 10: Freedom of Expression	7.349
1. 'Everyone'	7.353
2. Scope of the right	7.355

3. Positive obligations	7.367
4. Interferences with the right to freedom of expression	7.370
5. Exceptions to the right to freedom of expression	7.373
6. Margin of appreciation	7.400
7. Section 12 of the Human Rights Act	7.405
H. Article 11: Freedom of Assembly and Association	7.408
1. Overlap between Article 11 and other rights	7.411
2. Limitations: the operation of Article 11(2)	7.413
3. Freedom of peaceful assembly	7.415
4. Freedom of association	7.438
5. Article 11 and positive obligations	7.457
I. Article 12: Right to Marry and Found a Family	7.459
1. The right to marry	7.463
2. Right to found a family	7.477
3. Proportionality and Article 12	7.485
4. Positive obligations	7.487
J. Article 13: Right to an Effective Remedy	7.490
1. Effective remedy	7.492
2. National authority	7.501
3. Human Rights Act implications	7.502
K. Article 14: Prohibition on Discrimination	7.504
1. The importance of Article 14	7.504
2. Scope of Article 14	7.507
3. Discrimination	7.516
4. Justification	7.530
L. Article 15: Exceptions in Time of War	7.547
1. Non-derogable rights	7.550
2. Time of war or public emergency	7.552
3. Strictly required by the exigencies of the situation	7.556
4. International law obligations	7.561
5. Procedural requirements	7.562
6. Derogations and the Human Rights Act	7.563
M. Article 16: Restrictions on Political Activity of Aliens	7.579
N. Article 17: Prohibition of Abuse of Rights	7.587
O. Article 18: Limitation on Use of Restrictions on Rights	7.591

A. INTRODUCTION

7.01 This chapter summarizes the content of the limited and qualified rights under Articles 5–14 of the European Convention for the Protection of Human Rights and Fundamental Freedoms (Convention) and the general restrictions on rights found in Articles 15–18. Discussion of the nature of limited and qualified rights can be found in Chapter 2.[1]

---

[1] See ch 2, paras 2.28–2.31.

As in Chapter 6, an overview is given of the jurisprudence of the European Court of 7.02
Human Rights (ECtHR) and any remaining important cases from the European
Commission on Human Rights (ECmHR). Where the domestic courts have considered
an article in claims brought under the Human Rights Act, their approach is discussed
alongside the European case law and any divergences are noted.

B. ARTICLE 5: RIGHT TO LIBERTY AND SECURITY

Article 5 protects the 'right to liberty and security of person'. This is a combined right, 7.03
so the phrase 'right to liberty and security of person' should be read as a whole and not
as two distinct, watertight rights. 'Security of the person' must be read in the context of
personal liberty, not personal safety.[2] Article 5 ensures protection from deprivations of
liberty and not from other interferences with the physical liberty of the person, such as
the prevention of attack or the adequacy of welfare benefits.[3]

The specific concern of the right is to ensure that no one is deprived of liberty in an 7.04
'arbitrary fashion'.[4] In *Saadi v UK* the Grand Chamber of the ECtHR reiterated the
primacy of the notion of arbitrariness under Article 5.[5] The Court emphasized that
compliance with national law is not sufficient to render a detention lawful; it may still
be arbitrary under the Convention. The standard of arbitrariness will vary to an extent
depending on the type of detention involved, but the ECtHR indicated that where there
has been an element of bad faith or deception the standard is likely to be met.

Article 5 does not specifically apply to the conditions in which a person is detained.[6] 7.05
However, if the place and conditions of detention do not 'genuinely conform', or rationally
link, with the reason for it advanced by the state under Article 5(1)(a)–(f), Article 5 will
be violated.[7]

In addition to protecting the basic right to liberty, Article 5 provides persons who are 7.06
deprived of their liberty with a number of procedural rights, detailed in paragraphs (2)–(5).

Article 5 also applies to deprivations of liberty by a contracting state acting outside its 7.07
territory.[8] In *R (Al-Jedda) v Secretary of State for Defence* the House of Lords considered
the plight of an individual detained in Iraq for over three years without charge by UK
forces acting under United Nations authority.[9] A majority of the Lords concluded that
the United Kingdom might lawfully, where it was necessary for imperative reasons of
security, exercise the power to detain individuals as authorized by the Security Council,
but it had to ensure that the detainee's rights under Article 5 were not infringed to any
greater extent than was inherent in such detention.

---

[2] *East African Asians v UK* (1973) 3 EHRR 76.
[3] *Bozano v France* (1986) 9 EHRR 297.
[4] *Engel v Netherlands* (1976) 1 EHRR 647; *Brogan v UK* (1988) 11 EHRR 117; *Kurt v Turkey* (1998) 27 EHRR 373.
[5] (2008) 24 BHRC 123, paras 67–69.
[6] *Ashingdane v UK* (1985) 7 EHRR 528; *S v Airedale NHS Trust* [2003] EWCA Civ 1036, [2004] QB 395.
[7] *Mayeka v Belgium* App No 13178/03, para 102; *R (Suppiah) v Secretary of State for the Home Department* [2011] EWHC 2 (Admin).
[8] *Cyprus v Turkey* (First and Second Application) (1976) 4 EHRR 482; *Freda v Italy* (1980) 21 DR 250.
[9] [2007] UKHL 58, [2008] 1 AC 332.

7.08   Article 5 rights are not absolute and can be derogated from under Article 15. However, as these guarantees are of such fundamental importance in a democratic society and 'executive detention is the antithesis of the right to liberty and security of person',[10] any UK Government attempt to derogate from Article 5 will be scrutinized by the courts.[11]

7.09   The United Kingdom lodged a derogation from Article 5(1)(f) with the Council of Europe following the terrorist attacks in the United States on 11 September 2001, the purpose of which was to enable the detention without trial of foreign nationals suspected of links to international terrorism under the provisions of the Anti-Terrorism, Crime and Security Act 2001. In the famous case of *A and ors*, the House of Lords held that the derogation was incompatible with Articles 5 and 14 of the Convention and therefore unlawful.[12] The Grand Chamber upheld the reasoning of the House of Lords.[13]

1. Deprivation of liberty

7.10   Article 5 is concerned with actual deprivation of liberty rather than with mere restrictions on liberty or movement.[14] As the ECtHR noted in *HM v Switzerland*, restrictions on freedom of movement are the concern of Article 2 of Protocol 4 (which is not a Convention right for the purposes of the Human Rights Act).[15]

7.11   However, it will not always be easy to distinguish between a 'deprivation of' and a 'restriction on' liberty, since the difference is one of degree rather than nature or substance.[16] Furthermore, the case law is fact-specific and many of the leading cases are now very dated.[17] In *Guzzardi v Italy* the ECtHR made clear that in determining whether there has been a deprivation:

the starting point must be the concrete situation of the individual concerned and account must be taken of a whole range of factors arising in a particular case such as the type, duration, effects and manner of implementation of the measure in question.[18]

This guidance has been repeatedly cited by the ECtHR in later cases.[19]

7.12   Examples of circumstances which the Strasbourg organs have held to amount to deprivations of liberty include long-term measures such as house arrest;[20] short-term measures such as detention in order to carry out a compulsory blood test;[21] detention of foreign nationals for an hour prior to their being put on a chartered aircraft in order to be expelled from the country;[22] and detention of a five-year-old in an immigration

---

[10] *A and ors v Secretary of State for the Home Department* [2004] UKHL 56, [2005] 2 AC 68 at [222] per Baroness Hale.

[11] See, eg *A and ors*, ibid.

[12] Ibid.

[13] (2009) 26 BHRC 1.

[14] *Engel v Netherlands* (1976) 1 EHRR 647, para 58.

[15] [2002] ECHR 39187/98. See also *Austin v Commissioner of Police for the Metropolis* [2009] UKHL 5, [2009] 2 WLR 372 at [42].

[16] *Ashingdane v UK* (1985) 7 EHRR 528, para 41.

[17] See, eg *Guzzardi v Italy* (1980) 3 EHRR 333; *X v Germany* (1981) 24 DR 158.

[18] (1980) 3 EHRR 333, para 92.

[19] See, eg *HL v UK* (2004) 40 EHRR 761, para 89.

[20] *Greek Case* (1969) 12 YB 186.

[21] *X v Austria* (1979) 18 DR 154.

[22] *X and Y v Sweden* (1977–1978) 7 DR 123.

detention centre without her parents.[23] An 'informal' patient in a mental hospital has also been held to be deprived of liberty.[24] However, the ECtHR has held that a change in a prisoner's security categorization does not engage Article 5, even though it has an effect on his likely release date,[25] and some curfews may not constitute deprivations of liberty.[26]

In domestic law, the notion of a deprivation of liberty has been restrictively interpreted. The House of Lords has considered its meaning in relation to the Government's anti-terrorism measures on a number of occasions. In the case of *R (Gillan) v Commissioner of Police for the Metropolis* concerning random stop-and-search powers under the Terrorism Act 2000 (TA 2000) the House of Lords adopted a narrow approach to the issue of 'deprivation', holding that Article 5(1) did not bite.[27] This was despite the fact that an individual who has been stopped has no choice but to comply with the search as there is a statutory power to detain, reasonable force may be used to enforce compliance, and non-compliance is criminally punishable.   7.13

The court sounded a warning note concerning Strasbourg and comparative precedent on this issue as the jurisprudence 'is closely focused on the facts of particular cases, and this makes it perilous to transpose the outcome of one case to another where the facts are different'.[28] In *Gillan v UK* the ECtHR did not determine the application of Article 5, but noted that the coercive element of stop-and-search procedures were indicative of a deprivation of liberty.[29] The judgment suggests that the House of Lords may have adopted too limited an approach.   7.14

The fact-sensitive approach to Article 5 is also illustrated by the House of Lords' determination of three cases concerning the lawfulness of 'control orders' under the Prevention of Terrorism Act 2005. Control orders were imposed on suspected terrorists in place of indefinite detention, which the House of Lords had ruled unlawful in *A and ors* (above). In *Secretary of State for the Home Department v JJ* the House of Lords considered the terms of a control order which confined the suspected terrorist to a one-bedroom flat for 18 hours every day, required visitors to be approved in advance and prevented him from leaving a defined urban area.[30] By a majority of three to two it was held that the control orders constituted a deprivation of liberty. The majority emphasized that the factual scenarios in such cases may differ and it was therefore inappropriate to specify a formula by which the legality of a control order could be tested. In dissent, Lord Hoffmann argued that: 7.15

In order to preserve the key distinction between the unqualified right to liberty and the qualified rights of freedom of movement, communication, association and so forth, it is essential not to give an over-expansive interpretation to the concept of deprivation of liberty.[31]

---

[23] *Mubilanzila Mayeka v Belgium* [2006] 3 FCR 637.
[24] *HL v UK (Bournewood)* (2004) 40 EHRR 761.
[25] *Ashingdane v UK* (1985) 7 EHRR 528.
[26] *Cyprus v Turkey* (1976) 4 EHRR 484, para 235; *Raimondo v Italy* (1994) 18 EHRR 237, para 39.
[27] [2006] UKHL 12, [2006] 2 AC 307.
[28] Ibid at [23].
[29] (2010) 28 BHRC 420.
[30] [2007] UKHL 45, [2008] 1 AC 385.
[31] Ibid at [44].

7.16   In the cases of *E* and *MB*, the House of Lords unanimously held that various lesser restrictions did not amount to deprivations of liberty.[32] The control order cases are considered further in relation to Article 6 below.[33] The Terrorism Prevention and Investigation Measures Bill currently before Parliament will impose lesser residence requirements on terrorist suspects that are unlikely to offend Article 5.

7.17   In *Austin v Metropolitan Police Commissioner* the House of Lords continued to adopt a restrictive approach to Article 5, finding that the detention of thousands of protestors for several hours inside a police cordon in central London did not constitute a deprivation of liberty.[34] Noting that detention for public safety or public order was not a permissible ground for detention under Article 5(1), the Lords held that a pragmatic approach to the substance of the right needed to be adopted which took account of the purpose of the detention. Where, as here, the police had a legitimate purpose and had not acted disproportionately in their pursuit of it the court would not consider that a deprivation of liberty had occurred. It might be thought that this effectively sanctions preventive detention, which the ECtHR has explicitly ruled unlawful under Article 5(1)(c).[35] This approach to deprivation of liberty mirrors that adopted in relation to Article 3.[36] Faced with absolute rights, the courts apply a proportionality analysis normally reserved for justifying a breach of a qualified right to determine the scope and content of the article. The correctness of this approach is open to question and *Austin* is to be heard by the ECtHR.[37]

7.18   The Court of Appeal adopted a more nuanced and careful analysis of the meaning of deprivation of liberty in *P and Q v Surrey County Council*.[38] The court was asked to determine whether arrangements made for the care of two sisters with serious learning difficulties constituted a deprivation of liberty. In finding that they had not been deprived of their liberty, it considered issues such as the relevance of a person's objections to their confinement, the purpose of the arrangements, and the effect on the person's normal living arrangements. The High Court held that there was a breach of Article 5 where a parent and children were detained unlawfully pending deportation.[39]

7.19   These cases, as well as others in the mental health and immigration detention contexts, illustrate the fact-sensitive approach necessary under Article 5(1).[40]

2. Exceptions to the right to liberty

7.20   Article 5(1) sets out an exhaustive list of exceptions to the prohibition on deprivation of liberty in paragraphs (a)–(f). This list is to be given a narrow interpretation, and the

---

[32] *Secretary of State for the Home Department v E and anor* [2007] UKHL 47, [2008] 1 AC 499; *Secretary of State for the Home Department v MB* [2007] UKHL 46, [2008] 1 AC 440. See also *Secretary of State for the Home Department v AH* [2008] EWHC 1018 (Admin).

[33] See para 7.102 below.

[34] [2009] UKHL 5, [2009] 2 WLR 372.

[35] *Lawless v Ireland* (1961) 1 EHRR 15. See para 7.30 below.

[36] See *R (Wellington) v Secretary of State for the Home Department* [2008] UKHL 72, [2009] 2 WLR 48, discussed in ch 6, para 6.103.

[37] *Austin v UK* App Nos 39692/09, 40713/09, 41008/09, to be heard in September 2011.

[38] [2011] EWCA Civ 190.

[39] *R (Suppiah) v Secretary of State for the Home Department* [2011] EWHC 2 (Admin).

[40] See, eg *Re A and C* [2010] EWHC 978 (Fam), [2010] 2 FLR 1363.

excepted forms of detention must be both lawful and in accordance with a procedure prescribed by law.[41]

The United Kingdom fell foul of these principles in *HL v UK*. The ECtHR found   7.21
that the system for detaining mental patients without capacity breached Article 5 because there were no fixed procedural rules governing the admission and continued detention of the patients.[42]

(a) *Article 5(1)(a)*

Article 5(1)(a) permits 'the lawful detention of a person after conviction by a competent   7.22
court'. A competent court under this article is one with jurisdiction to try the case.[43] It is not necessary that the proceedings before the court have fully complied with all the requirements of Article 6. Only if a conviction occurs as a result of proceedings which were a 'flagrant denial of justice' will Article 5(1)(a) be violated by the failure to conform with Article 6 standards.[44]

In order for a detention to be 'lawful' there must be a court judgment that justifies the   7.23
confinement, as well as lawful procedures followed to effect the detention. Strasbourg has held that Article 5(1)(a) does not permit the ECtHR to review convictions or sentences imposed by a domestic court, though any such decision would have to comply with Articles 3 and 6.[45]

Strasbourg considered the relationship between detention and conviction under   7.24
Article 5(1)(a) in *Weeks v UK*.[46] A prisoner who had received an indeterminate life sentence was recalled to prison after his release. The ECtHR held that it was necessary for there to be a causal connection between the original conviction and detention. In this case the causal connection had not been broken because the prisoner remained a danger to the public. The Court reached a different conclusion in *Stafford v UK*.[47] The continued detention of a prisoner after he had served a prison sentence for forgery on the basis of an earlier mandatory life sentence from which he had been released on licence was not sufficiently causally connected to his original conviction to satisfy the requirements of Article 5(1)(a).

The House of Lords addressed the application of Article 5(1)(a) in *Secretary of State*   7.25
for Justice v James.[48] The claimant was convicted of a violent offence and sentenced to an indeterminate sentence for public protection. His only hope for release was to prove to the Parole Board that he no longer proved a threat to the public. However, the Secretary of State had failed to provide sufficient places on the behaviour programmes that the claimant needed to undertake to prove to the Parole Board that he no longer proved a threat. As a result, the Parole Board was unable to recommend his release. The court found that the failure to provide behaviour programmes did not itself breach Article 5(1)(a). It was only when a matter of years had passed without the Parole Board being able to

---

[41] *Winterwerp v Netherlands* (1979) 2 EHRR 387; *Amuur v France* (1996) 22 EHRR 533; *A and ors* (2009) 26 BHRC 1; *Medvedyev v France* App No 3394/03, 29 March 2010.
[42] (2004) 40 EHRR 761. See discussion in *G v E* [2010] EWCA Civ 822, [2011] 1 FLR 239.
[43] *X v Austria* (1987) 11 EHRR 112.
[44] *Stoichkov v Bulgaria* (2007) 44 EHRR 14.
[45] *Krzycki v Germany* (1978) 13 DR 57; *Weeks v UK* (1987) 10 EHRR 293.
[46] (1987) 10 EHRR 293. See also *Van Droogenbroeck v Belgium* (1983) 4 EHRR 443, para 40.
[47] (2002) 35 EHRR 32. Cf *Waite v UK* (2003) 36 EHRR 54; *R (Hirst) v Secretary of State for the Home Department* [2006] EWCA Civ 945, [2006] 1 WLR 3083.
[48] [2009] UKHL 22, [2010] 1 AC 553.

conduct an effective review of the case that the causal connection between the conviction and detention could arguably be broken.

(b) Article 5(1)(b)

7.26   Article 5(1)(b) sanctions the detention of a person who has failed to observe a court order or fulfil a legal obligation. The court orders can include failure to pay a court fine,[49] submit to a court-ordered medical examination,[50] and breach of a bind-over to keep the peace.[51] Legal obligations found to justify detention have included the obligation to undertake military service[52] and keep an identity card.[53] In domestic law, failure by a bankrupt to cooperate with a trustee in bankruptcy has also been found to fall within Article 5(1)(b).[54]

7.27   The ECtHR has held that the order or obligation must be clear, the person detained must usually be given an opportunity to comply, and detention must be the only reasonable way to secure the fulfilment of the order or obligation. This test was applied in *Beet v UK*, the ECtHR finding that the magistrates acted outside their jurisdiction in jailing a pensioner who had not paid her council tax.[55] In *Gatt v Malta* the ECtHR examined for the first time the system of detention for non-compliance with the lawful order of a court that occurs commonly across Europe.[56] The Court emphasized the importance of the proportionality of the measure, stating that the authorities must take account of circumstances such as the purpose of the order, the practical possibility of complying with it, and the length of the detention.

(c) Article 5(1)(c)

7.28   Article 5(1)(c) concerns the arrest or detention of suspects in the course of the administration of criminal justice. In essence, it contemplates arrest and detention on remand. Arrest or detention is lawful only if it is based on a reasonable suspicion that a person has committed a crime, or when it is reasonably considered necessary to prevent a person from committing a crime or from fleeing after committing one. Detention must be a proportionate measure in the circumstances.[57]

7.29   The test of reasonable suspicion is an objective one; an honestly held suspicion is insufficient. The applicants in *Fox v UK* had been arrested under the Northern Ireland (Emergency Provisions) Act 1978, which required only that the arresting official 'genuinely and honestly' suspected the person arrested to be a terrorist.[58] The ECtHR found a violation of Article 5(1)(c) on the basis that this was a lower standard than reasonable suspicion, as 'reasonable suspicion supposes the existence of facts or information which would satisfy an objective observer that the person concerned may have committed the offence'.[59]

---

[49] *Airey v Ireland* (1977) 8 DR 42 (ECommHR).
[50] *X v Germany* (1975) 3 DR 92.
[51] *Steel v UK* (1998) 28 EHRR 603.
[52] *Johansen v Norway* (1985) 44 DR 155.
[53] *Freda v Italy* (1980) 21 DR 250.
[54] *Hickling v Baker* [2007] EWCA 287, [2007] 1 WLR 2386.
[55] [2006] RA 384. Cf *Benham v UK* (1996) 22 EHRR 293.
[56] App No 28221/08, 27 July 2010.
[57] *Ladent v Poland* App No 11036/03, 18 March 2008.
[58] (1990) 13 EHRR 157.
[59] Ibid, para 32. Cf *Murray v UK* (1994) 19 EHRR 193; *O'Hara v UK* (2002) 34 EHRR 32.

Article 5(1)(c) does not create a power of preventive detention. In *Lawless v Ireland*   7.30
(No 3) the state argued that the second limb of Article 5(1)(c), permitting detention
where it is reasonably necessary to prevent a crime, allowed preventive detention of terrorist suspects.[60] The ECtHR held that this would 'lead to conclusions repugnant to the
fundamental principles of the Convention'.[61] An arrest is lawful under Article 5(1)(c)
only if the purpose is to bring the detainee before a competent legal authority, though
the fact that the suspect may not ultimately be brought before a court or charged with
a crime does not undermine the arrest since 'the existence of such a purpose must be
considered independently of its achievement'.[62]

In *R (Laporte) v Chief Constable of Gloucestershire* the House of Lords considered the   7.31
detention of a group of anti-war protestors who had been detained on their coach on the
way to a demonstration.[63] The police believed that some protesters were likely to cause
a breach of peace, and so the coaches were prevented from proceeding to the demonstration and forcibly returned. The Court of Appeal had held that whether a breach of the
peace was sufficiently imminent to justify taking action was dependent on all the circumstances. Article 5-compliant action required to prevent an apprehended breach of
the peace might, in certain situations, involve action affecting a wholly innocent individual. This approach was clearly out of step with Strasbourg jurisprudence and was
rejected by the House of Lords. Though the case was determined under Articles 10 and
11, their Lordships held, in line with ECtHR jurisprudence, that no power or duty arose
to take any preventive action whatsoever unless and until the police reasonably believed
that an actual breach of the peace was imminent.

(d) *Article 5(1)(d)*
Article 5(1)(d) covers the detention of minors. The accepted European classification of   7.32
a 'minor' is a person under the age of 18. This exception is designed primarily to cover
education and the detention of children for purposes such as placement in care or secure
accommodation.

(e) *Article 5(1)(e)*
Article 5(1)(e) is drafted in language which now appears very dated. It permits the deten-   7.33
tion of those with infectious diseases, persons of unsound mind, alcoholics, drug addicts,
and vagrants. According to early Strasbourg authorities, these people are specified
because 'they have to be considered as occasionally dangerous for public safety' and 'their
own interests may necessitate their detention'.[64]

The ECtHR has emphasized that in applying Article 5(1)(e), it is essential that there   7.34
be legal certainty and an absence of arbitrariness. The detention must be 'necessary' in
the circumstances and in accordance with the principle of proportionality.[65] In our view,
an extremely high standard of justification would be necessary to render such detention
proportionate. The mere fact of being, for example, a drug addict will be unlikely to

---

[60] (1961) 1 EHRR 15.
[61] Ibid, para 14. See also *M v Germany* (2009) 28 BHRC 521.
[62] *Brogan v UK* (1988) 11 EHRR 117.
[63] [2006] UKHL 55, [2007] 2 AC 105.
[64] *Guzzardi v Italy* (1980) 3 EHRR 333.
[65] *Enhorn v Sweden* App No 56529/00, 25 January 2005, para 36.

justify detention under Article 5(1)(e) without some other factor (such as an objective reason to believe that the person in question would harm himself or herself or others).

7.35   The combination of the requirement of 'lawfulness' under Article 5(1)(e) and the obligation on the state to allow judicial review of detention under Article 5(4) has led to a number of decisions against measures in states, including the United Kingdom, relating to the detention of psychiatric patients and residential care for those who lack capacity. There have been very few cases relating to the other categories of person covered by Article 5(1)(e).

7.36   The ECtHR has held that three elements will be necessary to justify the detention of persons of unsound mind:

(a) the individual must be reliably shown to be of unsound mind;

(b) the mental disorder must be of a kind or degree warranting compulsory confinement;

(c) the mental disorder must be persisting.[66]

7.37   Subsequent cases have confirmed that the burden of proof in establishing these criteria when both detaining and continuing to detain mental patients falls on the authorities.[67]

7.38   Article 5(1)(e) imposes no requirement that the mental condition be amenable to treatment.[68] In *Reid v UK* the ECtHR held, agreeing with the decision of the Privy Council, that:

confinement may be necessary not only where a person needs therapy, medication or other clinical treatment to cure or alleviate his condition, but also where the person needs control and supervision to prevent him, for example, causing harm to himself or other persons.[69]

7.39   Article 5(1)(e) is frequently addressed by domestic courts dealing with mental health claims.[70] The important decision of the European Court in *HL v United Kingdom* identified what became known as the 'Bournewood gap'.[71] The Court held, contrary to the House of Lords, that the use by HL's doctors of the common law doctrine of necessity did not meet the requirement in Article 5 of the European Convention that such a detention must be carried out 'in accordance with a procedure prescribed by law'. There was therefore a gap in the protection afforded to mental health patients who had been admitted to hospital or residential care without due process. In response to *HL*, a complex procedure for authorizing a deprivation of liberty for individuals who lack capacity was introduced under the Mental Capacity Act 2005. It was recently found by the Court of Appeal to 'plug the Bournewood gap'.[72]

7.40   In another mental health case now being considered by the European Court, *R (H) v Secretary of State for the Home Department*, the House of Lords held that deferral of the

---

[66] *Winterwerp v Netherlands* (1979) 2 EHRR 387; *Johnson v UK* (1997) 27 EHRR 296.

[67] See, eg *Reid v UK* [2003] ECHR 94, paras 69–74.

[68] Ibid.

[69] Ibid, para 52.

[70] See, eg *R (Munjaz) v Mersey NHS Trust* [2005] UKHL 58, [2006] 2 AC 148; *R (H) v Secretary of State for Health* [2005] UKHL 60, [2006] 1 AC 441; *R (B) v Ashworth Hospital Authority* [2005] UKHL 20, [2005] 2 AC 278; *R v Grant* [2001] EWCA Crim 2611, [2002] QB 1030.

[71] (2004) 40 EHRR 761.

[72] *G v E* [2010] EWCA Civ 822, [2011] 1 FLR 239.

implementation of conditional discharge from hospital did not breach Article 5 except in so far as there had been a failure to reconsider the case (Article 5(4)).[73]

In *Enhorn v Sweden*, one of the rare cases to address the other grounds for detention 7.41 under Article 5(1)(e), the ECtHR emphasized the 'last resort' nature of the power to detain in order to prevent the spreading of infectious diseases.[74] In assessing the lawfulness of such detention the 'essential criteria' which the ECtHR requires are that the spreading would be dangerous for public health and safety; detention of the person is necessary in order to prevent spreading; and less severe measures have been considered and found to be insufficient to safeguard the public interest. The ECtHR took a stricter view in relation to delay in release than that in *Johnson*, stating simply, 'when these criteria are no longer fulfilled, the basis for the deprivation of liberty will cease to exist'.[75]

(f) *Article 5(1)(f)*

Article 5(1)(f) provides wide grounds for deprivation of liberty. In *Zamir v UK* it was 7.42 held that, in a deportation context, the lawfulness of the detention depends only on whether the intention behind the detention was the deportation of the detainee; detention can only be justified if the intended deportation was the genuine reason for the detention.[76] The ECtHR will not examine the proportionality of the decision to deport.[77] The scope of its review is limited to examining whether there is a legal basis for the detention and whether the decision of the courts on the question of lawfulness could be described as arbitrary in light of the facts of the case. As the domestic courts have put it, Article 5(1)(f) requires that 'the power to detain be exercised reasonably and for the prescribed purpose of facilitating deportation'.[78]

The ECmHR expanded the scope of Strasbourg review in *Lynas v Switzerland*, hold- 7.43 ing that detention can cease to be lawful if the extradition or deportation proceedings are not carried out diligently or amount to an abuse of power.[79]

The case of *Chahal v UK* introduced a further limit on state power under Article 5(1)(f) 7.44 by finding that detention is justified only if actual deportation proceedings are in progress.[80] While proceedings must be brought with requisite diligence, the majority of the ECtHR did not consider that the applicant's detention for over four years while proceedings were conducted violated Article 5(1)(f). The Grand Chamber reiterated the requirement that deportation proceedings be in progress in *A and ors v UK*.[81]

In a controversial judgment on the application of Article 5(1)(f) to asylum seekers 7.45 who had surrendered to immigration authorities and then been detained by the United

---

[73] [2003] UKHL 59, [2004] 2 AC 253; *MH v UK* App No 11577/06.
[74] (2005) 41 EHRR 633.
[75] Ibid, para 44.
[76] (1983) 40 DR 42. See also *R (Vovk) v Secretary of State for the Home Department* [2006] EWHC 3386 (Admin).
[77] *Saadi v UK* (2008) 47 EHRR 427; *SK (Zimbabwe) v Secretary of State for the Home Department* [2011] UKSC 23 at [76].
[78] *R (Lumba and Mighty) v Secretary of State for the Home Department* [2011] UKSC 12, [2011] 2 WLR 671 at [30].
[79] (1976) 6 DR 141.
[80] (1996) 23 EHRR 413, para 113.
[81] (2009) 26 BHRC 1.

Kingdom in 'reception centres', a majority of the Grand Chamber in *Saadi v UK* agreed with the domestic courts[82] and found that:

> until a state has 'authorised' entry to the country, any entry is 'unauthorised' and the detention of a person who wishes to effect entry and who needs but does not yet have authorisation to do so, can be, without any distortion of language, to 'prevent his effecting an unauthorised entry'.[83]

A minority of six judges held that Article 5(1)(f) did not justify the detention of those who had not sought to evade the authorities.

7.46   By contrast, in *R (Nadarajah) v Secretary of State for the Home Department* the Court of Appeal found that the appellants' confinement in an immigration detention centre violated Article 5(1)(f).[84] The policy under which they were held was not accessible and therefore their detention failed to meet the standard of lawfulness imposed by the Convention. Domestic decisions on the lawfulness of immigration detention are based on principles enshrined in English law prior to the Human Rights Act 1998, known as the *Hardial Singh* principles, which guarantee the same, if not greater, protection as Article 5(1)(f).[85]

7.47   The UK derogation from Article 5(1)(f) and its consideration in the case of *A and ors* is discussed in detail under Article 15 below.[86]

3. Procedural safeguards

(a) *Article 5(2)*

7.48   Under Article 5(2), everyone arrested has the right to be informed promptly in a language he or she understands of the reasons for the arrest and of any charge. The ECtHR has held that the purpose of this obligation is to enable the arrested person to challenge the lawfulness of the detention.[87]

7.49   The European Court has held that the terms 'arrest' and 'charge' under Article 5(2) are not intended to limit the duty to give reasons to the criminal context.[88] The duty applies equally to all detention, including that of mental health patients. Reasons need not be in writing, and formal notification may not be necessary if the reasons are made clear during the arrest. It will generally be insufficient only to make reference to the relevant statutory provisions authorizing the arrest.[89]

7.50   In *Saadi v UK* the ECtHR found that the Government had violated Article 5(2).[90] The applicant was arrested and detained in an immigration reception centre without explanation until his representative was informed of the basis for his detention some

---

[82] See *R (Saadi and ors) v Secretary of State for the Home Department* [2002] UKHL 41, [2002] 1 WLR 3131.

[83] *Saadi v UK* (2008) 24 BHRC 123, para 65. Cf *Riad and Idiab v Belgium* App Nos 29787/03 and 29810/03, 24 January 2008.

[84] [2003] EWCA Civ 1768. See also *R (Lumba and Mighty) v Secretary of State for the Home Department* [2011] UKSC 12, [2011] 2 WLR 671.

[85] *R v Governor of Durham Prison, ex p Hardial Singh* [1984] 1 WLR 704; *SK (Zimbabwe) v Secretary of State for the Home Department* [2011] UKSC 23 at [12].

[86] See para. 7.555.

[87] *X v UK* (1982) 4 EHRR 188.

[88] *Van der Leer v Netherlands* (1990) 12 EHRR 567, para 27.

[89] *Ireland v UK* (1978) 2 EHRR 25.

[90] (2008) 24 BHRC 123.

76 hours after his arrest. The Grand Chamber held that reasons had not been supplied promptly.

(b) *Article 5(3)*

There are two limbs to Article 5(3). First, it requires that anyone arrested shall be brought promptly before a judge or other officer authorized by law to exercise judicial power. The aim of this requirement is to impose a limit on the length of detention authorized by Article 5(1)(c) and thereby ensure that provisional detention is not unreasonably prolonged.[91] Secondly, the trial should occur within a reasonable time and bail should be granted unless there are sufficient reasons not to release the detainee. Article 5(3) applies solely to criminal offences.[92] The Grand Chamber has held that these two requirements are not 'logically or temporally linked'.[93]   7.51

The reasonableness of a period of detention under the first limb of Article 5(3) (being brought promptly before a judge) is a matter of fact and degree.[94] In *Wemhoff v Germany* the ECtHR developed a two-part test: are the reasons advanced for the detention relevant and sufficient, that is, does the public interest outweigh the right to liberty in an individual case; and if so, have the proceedings been unduly prolonged by avoidable delay?[95] Periods of detention that have been held to contravene Article 5(3) include detention without charge for four days and six hours,[96] and detention in police custody for 14 days.[97] Furthermore, the ECtHR has repeatedly highlighted that the official reviewing detention must be independent in order to satisfy Article 5(3).[98]   7.52

In response to the terrorist threat posed by Al-Qaeda, the UK Government repeatedly extended the pre-charge detention period permitted for individuals suspected of terrorist offences from the standard 36 hours allowed under the Police and Criminal Evidence Act 1984. Under the Terrorism Act 2000 the maximum period of detention without charge in such cases was seven days. This was amended to extend detention to 14 days by the Criminal Justice Act 2003, and to 28 days by the Terrorism Act 2006. The 28-day period was subject to yearly renewal by affirmative order, and the Coalition Government recently allowed the period to revert to 14 days. The issue remains the subject of debate, and draft legislation enabling short-term extensions of detention has recently been published.[99]   7.53

In relation to the second limb of Article 5(3) the presumption is that bail should be granted, and denial of bail must be justified by relevant and sufficient reasons. In *Gault v UK* the ECtHR held that the fact that the applicant's third retrial would be held promptly was not sufficient reason for denial of bail.[100] As the Court emphasized, Article 5(3) does not permit a choice for the authorities between a speedy trial and granting bail.   7.54

---

[91] *Wemhoff v Germany* (1968) 1 EHRR 25; *Neumeister v Austria* (1968) 1 EHRR 91.
[92] *De Wilde, Ooms and Versyp v Netherlands* (1971) 1 EHRR 373.
[93] *McKay v UK* (2006) 24 BHRC 471.
[94] *Punzelt v Czech Republic* (2000) 33 EHRR 1159.
[95] (1968) 1 EHRR 25.
[96] *Brogan v UK* (1988) 11 EHRR 117.
[97] *Aksoy v Turkey* (1996) 23 EHRR 553. See also, *Sakik and ors v Turkey* (1998) 26 EHRR 662; *Öcalan v Turkey* (2003) 37 EHRR 10.
[98] See, eg *Klamecki v Poland* (2003) 39 EHRR 7.
[99] Draft Detention of Terrorist Suspects (Temporary Extension) Bills.
[100] (2008) 46 EHRR 1202; *Allen v UK* [2011] Crim LR 147.

It is legitimate for the courts to adjust the amount required by way of bail to reflect the gravity of the offence or the extent of financial liability.[101]

7.55   Reasons for refusing bail that are justified include:

(a) a risk that the accused will fail to appear at the trial;[102]

(b) a risk that the accused may interfere with the course of justice;[103]

(c) a risk of further offences;[104] and

(d) the preservation of public order.[105]

In any of these situations, the reason advanced must be justified by the facts in the particular case. In *Caballero v UK* the automatic denial of bail under section 25 of the Criminal Justice and Public Order Act 1994 was held to be a breach of Article 5(3).[106] Parliament amended this section in order to comply with the judgment.

7.56   The House of Lords considered the amended section 25 in *R (O) v Crown Court at Harrow*.[107] The appellant, accused of various sexual offences, remained in detention after the judge refused to extend the limit as the prosecution had not acted with due diligence in bringing the case to trial. The Lords held that there was no breach of Article 5(3) in such circumstances so long as the refusal of bail remained justified under section 25.

(c) *Article 5(4)*

7.57   Under Article 5(4), any detainee must be able to challenge the lawfulness of his detention. Review must be by a court and must be speedy. The 'court' does not necessarily have to be a classic court of law, which is formally part of the state's judicial machinery. However, the body must 'exhibit the necessary judicial procedures and safeguards appropriate to the kind of deprivation of liberty in question, including most importantly independence of the executive and of the parties'.[108] In addition, the body must have the ability to decide the lawfulness of the detention and to order release if detention is found to be unlawful.[109]

7.58   In *Weeks v UK* the ECtHR found that the Parole Board could be considered a court for the purposes of Article 5(4) but for the inadequate procedures for involving the detainee in the review of his detention.[110] These deficiencies were corrected and the Parole Board now fulfils the function of a court under Article 5(4).

7.59   The ECtHR has deliberately refrained from stating timeframes that will or will not be considered speedy; this issue cannot be assessed in the abstract. It has explicitly noted that Article 5(4)'s expedition requirement is more exacting than that of Article 6(1): 'while one year per instance may be a rough rule of thumb in Article 6(1) cases, Article 5(4), concerning issues of liberty, requires particular expedition'.[111]

---

[101] *Mangouras v Spain* App No 12050/04, 28 September 2010.
[102] *Stögmüller v Austria* (1969) 1 EHRR 155.
[103] *Wemhoff v Germany* (1968) 1 EHRR 25.
[104] *Toth v Austria* (1991) 14 EHRR 551.
[105] *Letellier v France* (1991) 14 EHRR 83.
[106] (2000) 30 EHRR 643.
[107] [2006] UKHL 42, [2007] 1 AC 249.
[108] *Benjamin and Wilson v UK* (2003) 36 EHRR 1, para 33. See also *Chahal v UK* (1996) 23 EHRR 413.
[109] *Benjamin and Wilson v UK*, ibid.
[110] (1987) 10 EHRR 293.
[111] *Reid v UK* [2003] ECHR 94, para 79.

Accordingly, the approach of the ECtHR is to examine the particular facts of the case   7.60
before it and to consider whether, in those specific circumstances, there was a failure to
proceed with reasonable speed. Domestic law will not be determinative of this issue.[112]

However, in *Zamir v UK* the ECmHR held that seven weeks between applying for   7.61
habeas corpus and the actual hearing violated Article 5(4).[113]

In cases of prolonged detention, this right has ongoing effect and the article requires   7.62
the availability of a process to enable the lawfulness of the detention to be reviewed at
reasonable intervals.[114]

There has been a series of key cases where the ECtHR has held that Article 5(4)   7.63
requires a regular review of the lawfulness of continuing detention, particularly where
the circumstances of the detention change over time affecting justification for detention.
Thus, there have been successful challenges to the lawfulness of detention: in psychiatric
hospitals;[115] during post-tariff mandatory life imprisonment, where the Home Secretary
has a veto power over Parole Board decisions;[116] during the discretionary period of discretionary life sentences;[117] and of young people convicted of murder and detained.[118]

In the decision of *Winterwerp v Netherlands* the ECtHR held that the judicial pro-   7.64
ceedings referred to in Article 5(4) need not always be attended by the same guarantees
as those required by Article 6(1) for civil or criminal litigation.[119] In *Reinprecht v Austria*
the Court found that a public hearing, which is a specific right under Article 6, does not
extend to proceedings concerning the review of the lawfulness of detention.[120] Noting
the differing purposes of the guarantees of Articles 5 and 6, the Court held that this 'difference of aims explains why Article 5(4) contains more flexible procedural requirements
than Article 6 while being much more stringent as regards speediness'.[121] However,
certain guarantees will apply equally to Article 5. Adversarial proceedings, the exchange
of evidence, and equality of arms, for instance, are essential features of the protections in
Article 5(4).[122] In *Allen v UK* the European Court held that Article 5(4) guaranteed the
right for those charged with criminal offences to appear at the prosecution's appeal
against bail.[123]

In *A and ors v UK*, concerning the indefinite detention of foreign terrorist suspects   7.65
under the Anti-Terrorism Crime and Security Act 2001, the Grand Chamber considered
the extent of disclosure required by the guarantee of procedural fairness in Article 5(4).[124]
In the proceedings before the Special Immigration Appeals Commission, the applicants
had been denied access to 'closed material', deemed too sensitive to reveal on the grounds
of national security. The 'special advocate' procedure designed by the Government was
intended to remedy any unfairness in the lack of disclosure by permitting the special

---

[112] See, eg *Yaman v Turkey* App No 32446/96, 2 November 2004.
[113] (1983) 40 DR 42.
[114] *Bezicheri v Italy* (1989) 12 EHRR 210.
[115] *X v UK* (1980) Series B 41.
[116] *Stafford v UK* (2002) 35 EHRR 32.
[117] *Weeks v UK* (1987) 10 EHRR 293; *Thynne v UK* (1990) 13 EHRR 666.
[118] *Hussain v UK* (1996) 22 EHRR 1; *T and V v UK* (1999) 30 EHRR 121.
[119] (1979) 2 EHRR 387.
[120] [2005] ECHR 67175/01.
[121] Ibid, para 40.
[122] *Sanchez-Reisse v Switzerland* (1986) 9 EHRR 71; *Weeks v UK* (1987) 10 EHRR 293; *Klamecki v Poland*
(2003) 39 EHRR 7.
[123] App No 18837/06, 30 March 2010.
[124] (2009) 26 BHRC 1.

advocate to see the closed material and make submissions on the detainee's behalf. The Grand Chamber concluded that there was no difficulty in principle with such a procedure so long as the allegations in the open material were 'sufficiently specific' for the detainee to provide information to his representatives with which to refute them. This was the case in respect of five of the applicants. In two cases, however, the open material consisted of general assertions that the detainee would have been unable to refute. In these cases Article 5(4) was breached.[125]

7.66   Appellants before the domestic courts have frequently raised arguments founded on Article 5(4). In the mental health context, the High Court has stated that:

> regular reviews by the court are not merely desirable, not merely a matter of good practice; they go, as both the Strasbourg jurisprudence and the domestic case-law make clear, to the very legality of what is being done.[126]

The most common Article 5(4) challenges arise in the context of Parole Board proceedings.[127] Article 5(4) deeply divided their Lordships in the case of *Roberts v Parole Board*.[128] At issue was the creation of a special advocate procedure in order to prevent Roberts from discovering the source of information concerning him. The majority held that the procedure was either covered by an express authorization stemming from the Parole Board Rules, or could be implied from the duty of the Board to conduct hearings which reconciled the interests of the prisoner, the public, and the informant. Such a procedure, they held, may or may not comply with Article 5(4), but this can only be judged after the case by determining whether the process as a whole has resulted in a procedure and decision which involves 'significant injustice to the prisoner'.[129] The minority disagreed, finding that the lack of specific authorization for the procedure rendered it unlawful.

7.67   As in many of the cases before the ECtHR, a central focus of the domestic courts has been on the period of detention after a prisoner has served the determinate part of the sentence (known as the tariff period in life sentences) when he remains detained on the grounds of continuing dangerousness. The courts have established that once a prisoner has been lawfully detained within the meaning of Article 5(1)(a), the review required by Article 5(4) is incorporated within the sentence of the original court and the prisoner is entitled to no further review beyond the normal appeal process.[130] However, the position becomes more complex after the determinate or tariff element of the sentence has been served.

7.68   In *R (Noorkoiv) v Home Secretary and Parole Board*, the Court of Appeal considered the delay between the expiry of the tariff period of the appellant's automatic life sentence and the decision of the Parole Board to release him.[131] The court held that the delay of two months was incompatible with Article 5(4). The fact that the delay occurred as a

---

[125] The effect of this was felt in relation to Art 6 in *Secretary of State for the Home Department v AF (No 3)* [2009] UKHL 28. See also *R (Rex Cart and ors) v Upper Tribunal and anor* [2009] EWHC 3052 (Admin).

[126] *Re BJ (Incapacitated Adult)* [2009] EWHC 3310 (Fam), [2010] 1 FLR 1373 at [10].

[127] For a full discussion, see Livingstone, Owen, and Macdonald, *Prison Law*, 4th edn (Oxford: Oxford University Press, 2008).

[128] [2005] UKHL 45, [2005] 2 AC 738.

[129] Ibid at [83] per Lord Woolf.

[130] *R (Giles) v Parole Board* [2003] UKHL 42, [2004] 1 AC 1.

[131] [2002] HRLR 36.

result of resource constraints was no justification in light of the 'imperative need to release from prison any post-tariff prisoner who no longer remains a danger'.[132]

The House of Lords considered the application of Article 5(4) to prisoners serving determinate sentences who had reached a point in their sentence when legislation governing early release meant that they could be considered for release by the executive.[133] In contrast with prisoners serving indeterminate sentences, who were entitled to speedy review by a court after the expiry of their tariff, those entitled to consideration for early release under the legislative scheme did not enjoy a right to review by a court. A similarly narrow attitude to Article 5(4) was adopted in *Secretary of State for Justice v James*.[134] The House of Lords held that in a case where the Parole Board had been repeatedly denied the reports necessary to complete its review 'it will only be if the [parole] system . . . breaks down entirely' that Article 5(4) would be violated.[135] The Court of Appeal recently adopted a more generous approach, finding that 'routine delays' in referring prisoners' cases to the Parole Board may breach Article 5(4).[136]

7.69

4. Positive obligations

The positive obligations recognized under Article 5 have been relatively limited. It has been accepted that Article 5 imposes an obligation to protect vulnerable individuals from deprivation of liberty by private actors. In *Storck v Germany* the applicant alleged a violation of Article 5 because of her forced confinement in a private psychiatric institution.[137] The ECtHR held that the authorities were obliged to 'to take measures providing effective protection of vulnerable persons, including reasonable steps to prevent a deprivation of liberty of which the authorities have or ought to have knowledge'.[138]

7.70

In *Re A and C* the High Court considered the extent of local authority obligations where the authority is aware of restrictions on the liberty of vulnerable individuals.[139] The Court set out in detail the measures that should be taken in such circumstances, including investigation, monitoring, and taking reasonable steps to bring the situation to an end.[140]

7.71

The ECtHR and domestic courts have held that Article 5(4) is not concerned with detention conditions or the treatment of those detained.[141]

7.72

5. Right to compensation

Article 5(5) guarantees a right to compensation if a person has been detained in violation of Article 5. This provision requires a binding award of compensation that can be

7.73

---

132 Ibid, para 58.
133 *R (Black) v Secretary of State for Justice* [2009] UKHL 1, [2009] 2 WLR 282.
134 [2009] UKHL 22, [2010] 1 AC 553.
135 Ibid at [21].
136 *R (Faulkner) v Secretary of State for Justice and anor* [2010] EWCA Civ 1434.
137 (2006) 43 EHRR 6.
138 Ibid, para 102.
139 *Re A and C* [2010] EWHC 978 (Fam), [2010] 2 FLR 1363.
140 Ibid, paras 80–96.
141 *Ashingdane v UK* (1985) 7 EHRR 528, paras 44, 52; *R (Cawser) v Secretary of State for the Home Department* [2003] EWCA Civ 1522; though see *Mayeka v Belgium* [2006] 3 FCR 637.

enforced by the courts.[142] It is reflected in section 9(3)–(5) of the Human Rights Act for detentions after the Act is in force.[143] Only compensatory—not exemplary—damages can be awarded.[144] In determining damages under Article 5, regard must be had to the limits of damages under section 8 of the Human Right Act and to the fact that a finding of breach may be sufficient compensation.[145]

C. ARTICLE 6: RIGHT TO A FAIR TRIAL

7.74 The right to a fair trial is a paradigm human right. It is central to the existence of the rule of law, because the guarantee of all other rights depends upon the proper administration of justice.[146] As the House of Lords held in *Secretary of State for the Home Department v AF (No 3)* the right to a genuinely fair trial is a 'core principle' which cannot give way to competing concerns.[147] It has 'a position of pre-eminence in the Convention'[148] and is explicitly referred to in the Preamble. Given the importance of the rule of law to a democratic society, the courts have repeatedly emphasized that Article 6 should be given a broad and purposive interpretation, and its exceptions narrowly construed. In *Delcourt v Belgium*, for example, the ECtHR stated that:

> In a democratic society within the meaning of the Convention, the right to a fair administration of justice holds such a prominent place that a restrictive interpretation of Article 6(1) would not correspond to the aim and the purpose of that provision.[149]

7.75 In keeping with this broad interpretive approach, Article 6 offers protection which goes beyond the trial itself, extending to any part of the criminal or civil process which may impact on the outcome of a case. For example, considering whether or not a trial is fair can include making sure that proper procedures have been followed by the police at the investigation and charging stages.

7.76 Article 6 does not apply to all proceedings which one might consider to be 'legal', and the nature of proceedings must therefore be carefully considered together with a number of other significant limitations set out in Article 6. Article 6(1) applies to determinative legal proceedings generally, whether criminal or civil. Although the specific guarantees in Article 6(2) and (3) relate to criminal cases only, the overarching requirements of Article 6(1) may under certain circumstances require similar guarantees even in civil proceedings.

---

[142] See, eg *Brogan v UK* (1988) 11 EHRR 117; *Fox v UK* (1990) 13 EHRR 157; *Caballero v UK* (2000) 30 EHRR 643; *Curley v UK* (2001) 31 EHRR 14.

[143] *R (Wright) v Secretary of State for the Home Department* [2006] EWCA Civ 67.

[144] Human Rights Act, s 9; *R (KB) v Mental Health Review Tribunal (Damages)* [2003] EWHC 193 (Admin), [2004] QB 936.

[145] *R (Degainis) v Secretary of State for Justice* [2010] EWHC 137 (Admin).

[146] *Golder v UK* (1975) 1 EHRR 524, para 35; Jayawickrama, *The Judicial Application of Human Rights Law* (Cambridge: Cambridge University Press, 2002) 480.

[147] [2009] UKHL 28, [2009] 3 WLR 74.

[148] Harris, O'Boyle, Bates, and Buckley, *Harris, O'Boyle and Warbrick: Law of the European Convention on Human Rights*, 2nd edn (Oxford: Oxford University Press, 2009) 202.

[149] (1970) 1 EHRR 335, para 25. See also *Moreira de Azevedo v Portugal* (1990) 13 EHRR 721, para 66; *R (Morgan Grenfell and Co Ltd) v Special Commissioner of Income Tax* [2002] UKHL 21, [2003] 1 AC 563; *Multiplex v Croatia* App No 58112/00, 10 July 2003, para 44.

Criminal practitioners should also bear in mind that the Article 6(1) case law may be of relevance to them, even when it concerns civil matters.

The courts have repeatedly held that the right to a fair trial protected by Article 6(1) is absolute in the sense that a conviction obtained in breach of it cannot stand, but the constituent elements of Article 6 are not unlimited. 'The only balancing permitted is in respect of what the concept of a fair trial entails.'[150] The central consideration in any limitation of the constituent rights is whether the essence of the overarching right to a fair hearing is preserved.[151] In determining whether this is the case, the ECtHR will have regard to the proceedings as a whole, including appellate proceedings, and may consider whether or not the appellate proceedings have rectified any defect which arose at the first instance hearing.[152] In *Gafgen v Germany*, an important recent case on Article 3, the ECtHR held that in the context of the use of evidence obtained by torture, the fairness of a criminal trial was only compromised where breach had been shown to have had a bearing on the outcome of the proceedings against the defendant.[153] The judgment of fairness is fact-sensitive and dependent on the issues of the particular case.[154] It must also be noted that fairness is a constantly evolving concept so procedures once deemed to be fair may occasionally merit reassessment.[155]

Although derogation from Article 6 is permitted in theory, any such derogation would be extremely difficult to justify. 7.78

1. Scope of Article 6

The ECtHR has repeatedly confirmed that the definitions of the core elements of 7.79 Article 6(1)—'determination', 'civil rights and obligations', and 'criminal charge'—are to be given an *autonomous* (or independent) Convention meaning. This ensures that the application of the fair trial guarantee is consistently and fairly applied, and is not dependent on the varying meanings of such terms in the national laws of Member States.[156] The ECtHR concerns itself with what fairness demands in particular circumstances.[157] Thus, although an examination of the claimant's rights as a matter of domestic law is the proper starting point, it is also necessary to look behind appearances and investigate the realities of the procedure.[158]

As with Articles 2 or 3, a Member State may be responsible for violation of Article 6 7.80 by exposing an individual within its jurisdiction to an unfair trial by deporting or extraditing him or her to a third country.[159] However, there is no breach of Article 6 unless

---

[150] See, eg *Heaney and McGuinness v Ireland* (2001) 33 EHRR 12; *R v A (No 2)* [2001] UKHL 25 at [38] per Lord Steyn who confirmed *Brown v Stott* [2001] 2 WLR 817.

[151] See, eg *Heaney and McGuinness v Ireland* (2001) 33 EHRR 12; *R v Sellick (Santino)* [2005] EWCA Crim 651, [2005] 1 WLR 3257.

[152] *Edwards v UK* (1993) 15 EHRR 417.

[153] (2011) 52 EHRR 1. See Greer, 'Should police threats to torture suspects always be severely punished? Reflections on the Gafgen case', (2011) 11(1) HRLR 67–89.

[154] *R v S* [2010] EWCA Crim 1579.

[155] *R v H* [2004] UKHL 3, 2 AC 134.

[156] *Engel and ors v Netherlands* (1979–80) 1 EHRR 647; *Adolf v Austria* (1982) 4 EHRR 313.

[157] *Konig v Federal Republic of Germany* (1978) 2 EHRR 170.

[158] *Crosbie v Secretary of State for Defence* [2011] EWHC 879 (Admin) at [80].

[159] *Soering v United Kingdom* (1989) 11 EHRR 439.

there is a real risk of a 'flagrant violation' of fundamental rights.[160] This very high threshold was applied by the House of Lords in *RB (Algeria) v Secretary of State for the Home Department* to allow the return of suspected terrorists to states known to violate fundamental rights.[161] By contrast, the High Court found that the *Ullah* threshold was met in the case of four men whose extradition had been requested by the Rwandan Government.[162]

(a) *Determination*

7.81 Article 6 applies only to the 'determination' of civil rights or obligations, or criminal charges. 'Determination' essentially requires that there be a dispute or 'contestation',[163] and a resolution procedure. It encompasses all proceedings (including those between private parties), the result of which is 'decisive' for civil rights and obligations[164] or which involves the individual being 'substantially affected' in relation to a criminal charge.[165] Article 6, therefore, requires the following criteria to be met:

(i) there must be a genuine and serious dispute ('contestation') of a legal nature which is related to a recognized right or to the scope or the manner in which it is exercised;[166]

(ii) the outcome of the proceedings is directly decisive for these rights and obligations (this requires something more than a 'tenuous connection or remote consequences');[167] and

(iii) these rights are 'civil' in the autonomous sense of the Convention.

7.82 The Strasbourg and domestic case law contain many examples of quasi-legal proceedings that were held to fall outside the scope of Article 6 because there was no 'determination'—most notably, inquiries or investigations. For example, in *Fayed v UK* the ECtHR held that Article 6 was not engaged in relation to a Department of Trade and Industry inspectors' highly critical report on a takeover by the applicant that was essentially investigative, and did not itself determine any dispute.[168]

7.83 Although the courts usually consider only final decisions to be 'determinations', in certain circumstances pre-trial proceedings and interim decisions will also fall within the term's remit. For example, the House of Lords in *R (Wright and ors) v Secretary of State for Health and Secretary of State for Education and Skills* held that the interim 'listing' of care workers, which prevented them working with vulnerable adults, had so great an effect on the rights of the persons affected as to amount to a determination, even though in theory the measures were only provisional.[169] The precise ambit of the concept of

---

[160] *R (Ullah) v Secretary of State for the Home Department* [2004] UKHL 26.
[161] [2009] UKHL 10 [2009] 2 WLR 512.
[162] *Brown v Rwanda* [2009] EWHC 770 (Admin). See also *Orobator v Governor of HMP Holloway* [2010] EWHC 58 (Admin).
[163] See, eg *König v Germany* (1978) 2 EHRR 170, para 87.
[164] *Ringeisen v Austria* (1971) 1 EHRR 466, para 94.
[165] *De Weer v Belgium* (1980) 2 EHRR 439, para 46; *Heaney and McGuinness v Ireland* (2001) 33 EHRR 12; *Quinn v Ireland* [2000] ECHR 36887/97.
[166] *Pudas v Sweden* (1988) 10 EHRR 380.
[167] See *Le Compte, Van Leuven and De Meyere v Belgium* (1982) 4 EHRR, para 47.
[168] (1994) 18 EHRR 393.
[169] [2009] UKHL 3, [2009] 2 WLR 267 at [21] per Baroness Hale.

'determination' will be the subject of a decision by the Supreme Court in *R(G) v Governing Body of X School*.[170]

Costs proceedings have usually been regarded as part of a 'determination' of civil rights and obligations.[171]   7.84

(b) Civil rights and obligations

The autonomous Convention meaning of 'civil rights and obligations'[172] requires the existence of a right characterised as being a civil right by national law'.[173] This term does not include mere expectations or hopes.[174] As the ECtHR explained in *König v Germany*:   7.85

> Whether or not a right is to be regarded as civil within the meaning of this expression in the Convention must be determined by reference to the substantive content and effects of the right—and not its legal classification—under the domestic law of the state concerned . . . Only the character of the right (at issue) is relevant.[175]

The mere fact that the right or obligation is governed by administrative law does not prevent it from also having a civil, or private law character; but rights which exist purely in administrative law are not regarded as civil rights.

As an example, in *Pudas v Sweden* the ECtHR held that grant of a taxi licence entailed certain consequential rights and the civil right under Swedish law to continue the business under the licence.[176]   7.86

In many respects, 'civil rights and obligations' is a wide phrase. It has been held to cover areas as diverse as property rights,[177] family rights,[178] the right to engage in commercial activities, the right to compensation, the right to practice a profession,[179] and certain welfare benefits. The House of Lords indicated (obiter) that a 'without notice' local authority application to close a care home on health and safety grounds would constitute a determination of civil rights and obligations),[180] and so would anti-social behaviour orders,[181] control orders,[182] and confiscation proceedings following conviction.[183]   7.87

---

[170] On appeal from [2010] EWCA Civ 1 (UKSC judgment forthcoming at time of writing).

[171] See, eg *Robins v UK* (1998) 26 EHRR 527; *Ziegler v Switzerland* [2002] ECHR 33499/96.

[172] See, eg *Benthem v Netherlands* (1986) 8 EHRR 1, para 34; *Ferrazzini v Italy* (2002) 34 EHRR 1068. See, generally, Dutertre, *Key Case-Law Extracts: European Court of Human Rights* (Strasbourg: Council of Europe, 2004) 171–9.

[173] *Roche v United Kingdom* (2006) 42 EHRR 30; See also *Acquaviva v France* App No 19248/91, 21 November 1995, para 46; *Le Compte and ors v Belgium* (1983) 5 EHRR 533, para 47; *Powell & Rayner v United Kingdom* (1990) 12 EHRR 355.

[174] Ibid.

[175] (1978) 2 EHRR 170, paras 89, 90.

[176] (1988) 10 EHRR 380.

[177] *Sporrong & Lonnroth v Sweden* (1983) 5 EHRR 35.

[178] See, eg *W v United Kingdom* (1987) 10 EHRR 29.

[179] See, eg *König v Germany* (1978) 2 EHRR 170; *Wickramsinghe v UK* App No 31503/96, 9 December 1997 (ECmHR), analysed in [1998] EHRLR 338. Cf *R (Puri) v Bradford Teaching Hospitals NHS Foundation Trust* [2011] EWHC 970 (Admin).

[180] *Jain v Trent Strategic Health Authority* [2009] UKHL 4, [2009] 2 WLR 248.

[181] *R (McCann) v Crown Court at Manchester* [2002] UKHL 39, [2003] 1 AC 787.

[182] *Secretary of State v F (No 3)* [2009] UKHL 28; cf *R v Twomey and ors (No 2)* [2011] EWCA Crim 8.

[183] *R v Briggs-Price* [2009] UKHL 19; see also *Serious Organised Crime Agency v Gale* [2010] EWCA Civ 759, [2010] 1 WLR 2881.

7.88   However, matters of pure administrative discretion are not covered. These include decisions as to tax obligations,[184] categorization of prisoners,[185] 'age assessments' of individuals claiming to be children (although disputed decisions are determined by an independent and impartial tribunal thus engaging Article 6),[186] the right to stand for public office,[187] refusal to issue a passport, decisions on the listing of persons for asset freezing,[188] the right to freedom of movement within the EU,[189] and immigration decisions.

7.89   The distinction between 'civil' or 'private' rights, and 'pure public rights' is also an autonomous concept which does not exactly chime with the distinction between these concepts in domestic law. In *Ringeisen v Austria* the ECtHR noted that Article 6 may be triggered in situations where the public law decisions of public authorities have clear consequences for the private law rights of individuals, but is not engaged unless the intrinsic nature of the right or obligation determined is 'private'.[190] The ECtHR considers the substance of the right and balancing the public law features against the private law features. If private law features are predominant, Article 6 will apply.[191]

7.90   In *R (Alconbury Developments Ltd) v Secretary of State for Environment, Transport and the Regions* Lord Hoffmann appeared to draw a similar distinction, stating:

> Apart from authority, I would have said that a decision as to what the public interest requires is not a 'determination' of civil rights and obligations. It may affect civil rights and obligations but it is not, and ought not to be, a judicial act such as article 6 has in contemplation.[192]

Thus, planning determinations were held to involve civil rights within the meaning of Article 6, although these determinations might traditionally be considered by English lawyers to involve 'public law rights' only.[193]

7.91   However, as a result of the ECtHR's dynamic interpretation of the Convention the phrase has continued to expand.[194] The concept of 'pure public rights' has been significantly reduced in recent years, with the ECtHR increasingly willing to find a 'civil right' within, or alongside, a public law right. So, for example, in *Stec v UK* the Grand Chamber held that an emergency assistance benefit with contributory elements was property within the scope of Protocol 1, Article 1, and therefore was a 'civil right' for the purposes of considering a breach of Article 14.[195]

---

[184] *Ferrazzini v Italy* (2002) 34 EHRR 1068 in relation to direct taxation; see also *King v United Kingdom* [2004] STC 911.

[185] *Brady v UK* (1979) 3 EHRR 297.

[186] *R (A) v Croydon London Borough Council; R (M) v Lambeth London Borough Council* [2008] EWCA Civ 1445. This was overturned on appeal: [2009] UKSC 8.

[187] *Pierre-Bloch v France* (1998) 26 EHRR 202.

[188] *Secretary of State for the Foreign Office and Commonwealth Affairs v Maftah* [2011] EWCA Civ 350.

[189] *Adams and Benn v UK* (1997) 23 EHRR CD 160.

[190] See, eg *Pudas v Sweden* (1988) 10 EHRR 380.

[191] *Feldbrugge v Netherlands* (1986) 8 EHRR 425; *Deumeland v Germany* (1986) 8 EHRR 448 (Series A-100); *Ali v Birmingham City Council* [2010] UKSC 8.

[192] [2001] UKHL 23, [2003] 2 AC 295 at [74] per Lord Hoffmann. See also *Secretary of State for the Foreign Office and Commonwealth Affairs v Maftah* [2011] EWCA Civ 350.

[193] *R (Alconbury Developments Ltd) v Secretary of State for Environment, Transport and the Regions* [2001] UKHL 23, [2003] 2 AC 295.

[194] *Salesi v Italy* (1998) 26 EHRR 187.

[195] See the decision on admissibility in (2005) 41 EHRR SE18 and decision on facts in (2006) 43 EHRR 1017.

The application of this approach in domestic law, however, is unclear. Whereas in   7.92
R (Husain) v Asylum Support Adjudicator the right to asylum support (which was provided in the form of accommodation and vouchers to meet an individual's other
essential living needs) was found to be a civil right for the purposes of Article 6(1),[196] in
R (Kehoe) v Secretary of State for Work and Pensions (which pre-dated *Stec*),[197] the House
of Lords held that the legislature had not created a civil right in relation to the recovery
of child maintenance. In *Kehoe* the applicant applied to the Child Support Agency under
the Child Support Act 1991 for a maintenance assessment in respect of her four children
to be made against her former husband. The House of Lords held that Article 6 was
concerned only with safeguarding rights accorded by national law rather than requiring
that particular substantive rights should be accorded, and enforcement of the obligation
to pay child support maintenance under the Child Support Act 1991 (CSA) was at the
discretion of the Secretary of State and not the person applying for its enforcement. This
position has been criticized for overlooking the fact that the applicant had a pre-existing
right to recover child benefit which the CSA added to but did not take away.[198]

Recent case law has followed this restrictive jurisprudence: for example, on school   7.93
exclusions;[199] and 'age assessments' of asylum seekers, regarding whether or not they are
'children' and so are protected under the Children Act 1989.[200] In the latter case, the
court was reluctant to accept, in the absence of clear authority from Strasbourg, that
Article 6 required the judicialization of claims to welfare services of the kind in the applicants' case. In *R (Begum) v Tower Hamlets* the House of Lords was prepared to assume
that a decision by a local authority as to housing for a homeless person under the Housing
Act 1996 did involve a 'civil right'.[201] However, in *Ali v Birmingham City Council* the
Supreme Court held that it did not.[202] Lord Hope stated:

. . . cases where the award of services or benefits in kind is not an individual right of which the
applicant can consider himself the holder, but is dependent upon a series of evaluative judgments
by the provider as to whether the statutory criteria are satisfied and how the need for it ought to
be met, do not engage article 6(1). In my opinion they do not give rise to 'civil rights' within the
autonomous meaning that is given to that expression for the purposes of that article.[203]

See, too, *Secretary of State for the Foreign Office and Commonwealth Affairs v Maftah* in
which Sedley LJ held that a challenge to the existence of an asset freezing order did not
engage Article 6, because:

. . . it is the nature and purpose of the administrative action which determines whether its impact
on private law rights is such that a legal challenge to it involves a determination of civil rights.[204]

---

[196] [2001] EWHC Admin 852; see also *Begum v Tower Hamlets LBC* [2002] EWCA Civ 239.
[197] [2005] UKHL 48, [2006] 1 AC 42.
[198] See Burrows, 'In Practice: Enforcement of Child Maintenance: Kehoe' [2009] Fam Law 1086.
[199] See *R (B) v Head Teacher and Governing Body of Alperton Community School* [2001] EWHC Admin 299, [2001] ELR 359.
[200] *R (A) v Croydon London Borough Council; R (M) v Lambeth London Borough Council* [2008] EWCA Civ 1445.
[201] [2003] UKHL 5, [2003] 2 AC 430.
[202] [2010] UKSC 8, [2010] 2 AC 39.
[203] Ibid, para 49.
[204] [2011] EWCA Civ 350 at [24] per Lord Justice Sedley.

By contrast, determinations of the Regulation of Investigatory Powers Tribunal (which usually concern the substantive right to privacy) are classified as determinations of 'civil rights'.[205]

7.94   One area where the distinction between public and 'civil rights' has caused particular difficulties is in relation to employment issues. The traditional view was that matters concerning public employment did not concern 'civil rights' as defined by Strasbourg.[206] However, in *Pellegrin v France* the Grand Chamber held that only decisions concerning those with functions relating to the 'specific activities' of the public service and direct or indirect participation in the powers conferred by public law would be outside the protection provided by Article 6.[207] In *Eskelinen v Finland*[208] the Grand Chamber repeated that Article 6 was not excluded from determinations of employment disputes on the basis of the special relationship between the civil servant and the state. It was presumed to apply, unless the dispute in issue clearly related to the exercise of state power.[209] This issue was considered yet again by the Grand Chamber in two cases, *Sabeh el Leil v France*[210] and *Cudak v Lithuania*,[211] both concerning state immunity in employment proceedings taken by embassy employees. In both cases jurisdiction was relinquished to the Grand Chamber. Judgment is still pending in *Sabeh el Leil v France* but in *Cudak* the ECtHR found that where a claim for sexual harassment concerning conduct in an embassy was dismissed on grounds of state immunity, there was a violation of Article 6(1).

(c) Criminal charge

7.95   Article 6 protects an individual who is 'charged with a criminal offence' when he or she is subject to a procedure for the 'determination' of that criminal charge. The term 'charge' should be given a substantive rather than a formal meaning, in the sense that the court should consider the scope of what is at stake and not the mere classification in domestic law.[212]

7.96   (i) *What is 'criminal'?* When deciding whether proceedings are 'criminal' for the purposes of the Convention, the courts are not bound by the label given by the state. In *Engel v Netherlands*.[213] the Court held that a determination that an individual faced a criminal charge rested on three criteria:

(a) the classification of the offence under the domestic legal system which should be the initial starting point;

(b) the nature of the offence; and/or

(c) the nature and degree of severity of the penalty 'liable to be imposed'.

---

[205] App Nos IPT/01/62 and IPT/01/77, 23 January 2003.
[206] See, eg *Kosieck v Germany* (1987) 9 EHRR 328; *Neigel v France* (2000) 30 EHRR 310; *Balfour v UK* (1997) EHRLR 665; *Huber v France* (1998) 26 EHRR 457.
[207] (2001) 31 EHRR 651, para 66.
[208] (2007) 45 EHRR 43.
[209] Ibid, para 62. *Eskelinen* was also applied in *R (MK (Iran)) v Secretary of State for the Home Department* [2009] EWHC 3452 (Admin).
[210] App No 34869/05 which has been relinquished to the Grand Chamber.
[211] App No 15869/02.
[212] *Deweer v Belgium* (1979–80) 2 EHRR 439, paras 42, 44, and 46.
[213] (1976) 1 EHRR 647.

In practice the last two criteria have carried the greatest significance The *Engel* criteria have been regularly applied by the Strasbourg and domestic courts.[214] The courts have emphasized that the first criterion, the domestic classification, must be seen as 'no more than a starting point'.[215] One important consideration is whether the intention of a provision is punitive or preventative: preventative measures are generally not considered to be 'criminal'.[216]

The second and third of the *Engel* criteria are usually considered as alternatives.[217] For the criminal protections of Article 6 to apply it is enough either that the offence in question is of a 'criminal' nature, or that the offence makes the person liable to what amounts to a 'criminal' sanction given its nature or degree of severity.[218] However, a cumulative approach may be adopted where separate analysis of each individual criterion does not make it possible to reach a clear conclusion as to the existence of a criminal charge.[219]   7.97

In relation to the second criterion, the criminal limb of Article 6 may be engaged by the nature of the matter determined, notwithstanding its relatively minor nature. For example, tax and surcharge proceedings have been held to constitute criminal charges where they have a deterrent and punitive purpose despite having a relatively light penalty;[220] and committal proceedings for contempt are also considered criminal given that liberty is at stake and that the acts in question must be proved to the criminal standard of proof.[221]   7.98

The third *Engel* criterion is often the key issue. The Court held in *Engel* that 'in a society subscribing to the rule of law, there belong to the "criminal" sphere deprivation of liberty liable to be imposed as a punishment, except those which by their nature, duration or manner of execution cannot be appreciably detrimental' so the courts must take into account 'the seriousness of what is at stake, the traditions of the Contracting States and the importance attached by the Convention to respect for the physical liberty of the person'.[222] It is the nature and severity of the penalty 'liable to be imposed' which   7.99

---

[214] See, eg *Campbell and Fell v UK* (1985) 7 EHRR 165; *Ezeh and Connors v UK* (2004) 39 EHRR 1 (Grand Chamber); see, eg *Tangney v Governor of Elmley Prison and Secretary of State for the Home Department* [2005] EWCA Civ 1009; *MB v Secretary of State for the Home Department* [2007] UKHL 46, [2008] 1 AC 440; *R (G) v Governing Body of X School* [2010] EWCA Civ 1.

[215] *Engel v Netherlands* (1976) 1 EHRR 647, para 82; *R (LG) Board of Governors of Tom Hood School* [2010] EWCA Civ 142 (Admin), [2009] EWHC 369.

[216] *MB v Secretary of State for the Home Department* [2007] UKHL 46, [2008] 1 AC 440; *R (McCann) v Crown Court at Manchester* [2002] UKHL 39, [2003] 1 AC 787; *R (G) v Governing Body of X School* [2010] EWCA Civ 1 (this issue was not subject to appeal to Supreme Court).

[217] *Özturk v Germany* (1984) 6 EHRR 409; *Lutz v Germany* (1988) 10 EHRR 182; [1987] ECHR 9912/82.

[218] See, eg *Öztürk v Germany* (1984) 6 EHRR 409, para 54; *Lutz v Germany* (1988) 10 EHRR 182, para 55.

[219] See, eg *Bendenoun v France* (1994) 18 EHRR 54, para 47; *Benham v UK* (1996) 22 EHRR 293, para 56; *Garyfallou AEBE v Greece* (1999) 28 EHRR 344, para 33; *Lauko v Slovakia* (2001) 33 EHRR 40, para 57; *Ezeh and Connors v UK* (2004) 39 EHRR 1 (Grand Chamber), para 86; *Tangney v Governor of Elmley Prison and Secretary of State for the Home Department* [2005] EWCA Civ 1009 at [24].

[220] See, eg *Jussila v Finland* (2007) 45 EHRR 39 (Grand Chamber).

[221] *Daltel Europe Ltd (in liquidation) and 5 ors v Hassan Ali Makki and ors* [2006] EWCA Civ 94; *Raja v Van Hoogstraten* [2004] EWCA Civ 968, [2004] 4 All ER 793; *Hammerton v Hammerton* [2007] EWCA Civ 248, [2007] 2 FLR 1133.

[222] *Engel v Netherlands* (1976) 1 EHRR 647, para 82.

is determinative, rather than the penalty actually incurred.[223] The ECtHR has also held that 'where deprivation of liberty is at stake, the interests of justice in principle call for legal representation'.[224]

7.100   Thus, although classification of prisoners, for example, falls outside the criminal sphere,[225] prison discipline does engage the criminal limb of Article 6,[226] even in respect of proceedings which are not classified as 'criminal' in domestic law.[227]

7.101   However, since a prisoner serving a life sentence is not vulnerable to a punishment imposing additional days of imprisonment, the Court of Appeal has held that internal disciplinary charges against such a prisoner do not amount to 'criminal charges'.[228] Parole Board decisions are not criminal because the decisions to release depend upon assessment of risk to the public rather than punishment.[229]

7.102   The domestic courts have adopted a narrow definition of 'criminal charge' in the context of suspected terrorists, focusing on the intention of the measures rather than their effects. For example, the House of Lords has found that non-derogating control orders are not 'criminal' since they are preventive in purpose, even though they impose very severe restrictions on the controlee's private life and freedom of movement.[230] However, the civil limb of Article 6(1) applied and entitled those subject to such orders to 'such measure of procedural protection as was commensurate with the gravity of the potential consequences'.[231] The domestic courts have also held that registration on the Sex Offenders' Register is not criminal determination as, inter alia, it does not involve a punishment and is not a public announcement of guilt.[232] Nor does exclusion from school involve the determination of a criminal charge.[233]

7.103   (ii) *What is a charge?*   In addition to satisfying the 'criminal' criteria, the allegation must also constitute a 'charge'. These two features are often considered coterminously but the ECtHR has confirmed that for a person to be charged, his or her situation must be 'substantially affected'.[234] This may take place at arrest, charge, or when the person becomes aware that 'immediate consideration' is being given to a possible prosecution, depending on the facts of the case.[235] However, car owners being required to identify the driver of a speeding vehicle at the time it was caught on a speed camera or radar-trap are not 'substantially affected' so as to be 'charged' within the autonomous meaning of

---

[223] See *Campbell and Fell v UK* (1985) 7 EHRR 165, para 72; *Weber v Switzerland* (1990) 12 EHRR 508, para 34; *Demicoli v Malta* Series A No 210, 27 August 1991, para 34; *Benham v UK* (1996) 22 EHRR 296, para 56; *Garyfallou AEBE v Greece* (1999) 28 EHRR 344, paras 33–34; *Ezeh and Connors v UK* (2004) 39 EHRR 1 (Grand Chamber), para 120.

[224] *Benham v UK*, (1996) 22 EHRR 296, para 61.

[225] *R (Sunder) v Secretary of State for the Home Department* [2001] EWHC Admin 252, [2001] All ER (D) 55 (Apr).

[226] *Campbell and Fell v UK* (1985) 7 EHRR 165, para 69.

[227] *Ezeh and Connors v UK* (2004) 39 EHRR 1 (Grand Chamber); *Jussila v Finland* (2007) 45 EHRR 39.

[228] *Tangney v Governor of Elmley Prison* [2005] EWCA Civ 1009.

[229] *R (Smith) v Parole Board* [2005] UKHL 1.

[230] *MB v Secretary of State for the Home Department* [2007] UKHL 46, [2008] 1 AC 440.

[231] Ibid at [24].

[232] *R (R) v Durham Constabulary* [2005] UKHL 21, [2005] 2 All ER 369. See also *R (G) v Governing Body of X School* [2010] EWCA Civ 1 (proceedings rendering a person liable to being placed on the Independent Safeguarding Authority lists).

[233] *R (V) v Independent Appeal Panel for Tom Hood School* [2010] EWCA Civ 142.

[234] *DeWeer v Belgium* (1980) 2 EHRR 439, para 46.

[235] *X v UK* (1978) 14 DR 26 (1998) 25 EHRR CD88.

Article 6(1).[236] The courts have confirmed that giving warnings or cautions to offenders does not amount to the determination of a criminal 'charge',[237] but there has been a suggestion that this position may change in light of the scheme of 'conditional cautions' under the Police and Justice Act 2006, as they include a power for prosecutors to attach punitive measures as conditions of cautions.[238] This has not yet been tested in the courts.

2. Rights protected by Article 6(1)

Article 6(1) sets the overall standard of what a fair trial requires, whether the context is civil or criminal. The more extensive detailed provisions in Article 6(2) and (3) apply only to criminal charges, though equivalent guarantees may be required in particular civil circumstances. Courts have frequently held that common law and Article 6(1) standards of fairness march 'hand in hand', and that the result ought to be the same whichever is applied.[239]   7.104

The court will imply into Article 6(1) such safeguards as are necessary to guarantee a 'real and effective' fair trial. For example, Article 6 implicitly guarantees the right of access to a court.[240] This may necessitate that the grant of legal aid even in civil cases will be required if the case is particularly complex and the principle of 'equality of arms' requires.[241] The provision of legal aid will depend on the facts and circumstances of each case.[242] Article 6(1) does not compel states to provide appeal courts, but, where they exist, they must comply with Article 6 and effective access must therefore be ensured.[243]   7.105

Although the elements of the right to a fair trial under Article 6(1) which apply to both civil and criminal proceedings may be limited in the public interest, this does not mean that they are qualified rights. It is essential that any attempt to limit the constituent elements of Article 6 is seen as a different exercise to the approach taken to qualify rights guaranteed under Articles 8, 9, 10, and 11. Article 6 limitations are subject to a particularly strict test of necessity and proportionality.[244] In no case may they restrict or reduce the access left to the individual in such a way or to such an extent that the very essence of the right is impaired.[245]   7.106

---

[236] *Rieg v Austria* App No 63207/00, [2005] ECHR 184, para 54; *O'Halloran and Francis v UK* (2008) 46 EHRR 21.

[237] *R v UK* (2007) 44 EHRR SE17; *R (R) v Durham Constabulary* [2005] UKHL 21, [2005] 2 All ER 369.

[238] Discussed by Brownlee, 'Conditional cautions and fair trial rights in England and Wales: form versus substance in the diversionary agenda?' (2007) Crim LR 129.

[239] *R v Parole Board, ex p West* [2005] UKHL 1 [2005] 1 All ER 755; *Kulkarni v Milton Keynes NHS Hospital Trust* [2009] EWCA Civ 789, [2009] IRLR 829; *Secretary of State for the Home Department v AF (No 3)* [2009] UKHL 28 at [96] per Lord Scott, [2010] 2 AC 269.

[240] *Golder v UK* (1975) 1 EHRR 524; *Moldovan and ors v Romania* (2007) 44 EHRR 16.

[241] *Airey v Ireland* (1979) 2 EHRR 305.

[242] *Steel and Morris v UK* (2005) 41 EHRR 22.

[243] *Sommerfeld v Germany* (2003) 36 EHRR 33, although this was not considered further in the Grand Chamber's decision: *Sommerfeld v Germany* (2004) 38 EHRR 35.

[244] *Van Mechelen v Netherlands* (1998) 25 EHRR 647.

[245] See *Golder v UK* (1975) 1 EHRR 524; *Belgian Linguistic Case No 2* (1968) 1 EHRR 252; and *Secretary of State for the Home Department v AF (No 3)* [2009] UKHL 28 at [106] per Baroness Hale, [2010] 2 AC 269.

(a) *General entitlements in criminal and civil proceedings under Article 6(1)*

7.107   A litigant, or potential litigant, has the following rights to:

(i)   real and effective access to a court. Under certain circumstances a lack of state legal assistance can interfere with the right of access to court depending upon the nature and complexity of the case;[246]

(ii) a hearing before an independent and impartial tribunal established by law;

(iii) a hearing in public;

(iv) a hearing within a reasonable time;

(v)   a real opportunity to present their case. This is premised on the concept of the need for 'equality of arms' between the parties and may include the provision of legal assistance or an oral hearing if the circumstances require this; and

(vi) a reasoned decision.

7.108   (i) *Access to a court*   The right of access to a court is one of the checks on the danger of arbitrary power.[247] Although the right of access to a court is not explicitly set out under Article 6(1), in the early decision of *Golder v UK* the ECtHR recognized the right as a prerequisite of the exercise of the right to have a claim heard at all.[248] Thus, in that case, a prisoner's lack of access to a lawyer was held to violate his right of (effective) access to a court. A right of access to a court may be violated by, for example, a substantive provision,[249] a procedural rule (such as an immunity),[250] or an administrative practice.[251] When deciding whether the right of access is barred by a practice or provision, the domestic courts have said that the 'crucial question' is whether, as a matter of substance rather than procedure, the relevant provision of national law has the effect of preventing an issue that ought to be decided by a court from being so decided.[252]

7.109   The nature of the right of access to the court calls for regulation by the state and may vary in time and place according to the needs and resources of the community and of individuals.[253] However, these restrictions must not be such as to limit the effectiveness of the right; restrictions imposed must be legally certain,[254] pursue a legitimate aim,[255] and be proportionate to the aim pursued.[256]

7.110   A number of categories of restriction on the access right have emerged. They include restrictions linked to types of actions (eg immunities, limitation periods, strike-out provisions), or to classes of litigant (minors, vexatious litigants, bankrupts, and prisoners).[257] 'Special advocate' procedures will not necessarily violate Article 6, provided the essence of the right to a fair trial is not impaired. A procedural bar, such as requiring a mental

---

[246] *Airey v Ireland* (1979) 2 EHRR 305.
[247] *Wilson v First County Trust Ltd (No 2)* [2003] UKHL 40, [2004] 1 AC 816 at [35].
[248] (1975) 1 EHRR 524.
[249] *Ashingdane v UK* (1985) 7 EHRR 528, para 57.
[250] *Osman v UK* (2000) 29 EHRR 245.
[251] *Golder v UK* (1975) 1 EHRR 524.
[252] *Wilson v First County Trust Ltd (No 2)* [2003] UKHL 40, [2004] 1 AC 816 at [35].
[253] *Golder v UK* (1975) 1 EHRR 524.
[254] *Société Levage Prestations v France* (1996) 24 EHRR 351, paras 40–50.
[255] *Ashingdane v UK* (1985) 7 EHRR 528.
[256] *Canea Catholic Church v Greece* (1999) 27 EHRR 521, paras 34–42.
[257] *M v United Kingdom* (1987) 52 DR 269.

patient to obtain leave of the court before issuing a claim, or a restriction of the types of claims which can be brought (eg on the basis of state immunity) must be properly scrutinized for compatibility with Article 6. However, they will not necessarily violate the right of access to a court.[258] Similarly, to deny access to a court or on grounds of an immunity will only be compatible with Article 6(1) if it satisfies the tests of necessity and proportionality.[259]

The ECtHR has sometimes rejected the UK's approach to immunities. For example, in *Osman v UK* it held that a blanket ban on bringing a negligence action against the police for failure to prevent a crime against a foreseeable target, on public policy grounds, violated the claimant's right of access to a court under Article 6(1). It prevented a court considering the competing public interests in a case before it, and so constituted a disproportionate interference with a person's right to a determination on the merits. This decision was criticized, academically[260] and judicially.[261] The House of Lords in *Barrett v Enfield LBC* stated that there was no 'blanket immunity' and the test had been misunderstood by Strasbourg.[262] Rather, the test was whether the imposition of a duty of care was 'fair, just and reasonable' in all the circumstances. **7.111**

The ECtHR in *Z and ors v UK* (an Article 3 case) accepted the House of Lords' clarification in *Barrett*.[263] *Z v UK* retained the principle that any automatic exclusionary rule based on public policy will still violate Article 6, but endorsed a more flexible 'fair, just and reasonable approach'. The House of Lords has since affirmed that there is no automatic 'knock-out' immunity from suit for the police, and instead a flexible, context-specific, test applies.[264] **7.112**

(ii) *A hearing before an independent and impartial tribunal established by law*   Article 6(1) requires an 'independent and impartial tribunal established by law'. The courts have held that it is 'of fundamental importance in a democratic society that the courts should inspire confidence in the public and above all, as far as criminal proceedings were concerned, in the accused'.[265] If a defendant raises the issue of impartiality, it must be investigated unless it is 'manifestly devoid of merit'.[266] **7.113**

When deciding whether a tribunal is independent, the following factors are to be considered: **7.114**

(i) the way its members are appointed;

(ii) their term of office;

---

[258] See, eg *Seal v Chief Constable of South Wales* [2007] UKHL 31, [2007] 1 WLR 1910 (case pending before the ECtHR); *Seal v UK* (2010) ECHR 1976; *Markcovic v Italy* (2007) 44 EHRR 52 (Grand Chamber); *Jones v Kingdom of Saudi Arabia* [2006] UKHL 26, [2007] 1 AC 270; following *Al-Adsani v UK* (2001) 34 EHRR 273. See also *Matthews v Ministry of Defence* [2003] UKHL 4, [2003] 1 AC 1163 (Art 6(1) not engaged by legislation preventing an ex-serviceman from bringing a personal injury claim against the Ministry of Defence); *Fogarty v UK* (2002) 34 EHRR 302; cf *Cudak v Lithuania* (2010) 51 EHRR 15.

[259] *Tinnelly & Sons Ltd and ors and Mcelduff and ors v UK* (1999) 27 EHRR 249.

[260] See, eg Gearty, '*Osman* Unravels' (2002) 65 MLR 87, (1998) 29 EHRR 245.

[261] *Barrett v Enfield London Borough Council* [2001] 2 AC 550.

[262] Ibid.

[263] (2002) 34 EHRR 97. See also *Al-Adsani v UK* (2001) 34 EHRR 273; *McElhinney v Ireland* (2002) 34 EHRR 13; *Fogarty v UK* (2002) 34 EHRR 302.

[264] *Brooks v Commissioner for Police for the Metropolis* [2005] UKHL 2, [2005] 2 AC 176.

[265] *Padovani v Italy* App No 13396/87, 26 February 1993, para 27.

[266] *Remli v France* (1996) 22 EHRR 253.

(iii) the existence of safeguards against outside pressures; and

(iv) whether the body appears independent.[267]

This final point is important as the courts are not only concerned with actual impartiality, but also require the appearance of impartiality. The ECtHR has ruled that any doubts entertained by an accused as to lack of impartiality of a court have to be both subjectively and objectively justified.[268]

7.115   The ECtHR found a breach of Article 6(1) in *McGonnell v UK* where the bailiff, who presided over the Royal Court of Guernsey in legal proceedings concerning the applicant's planning appeal, had also been sitting as the deputy bailiff over the States of Deliberation when the earlier, detailed development plan had been adopted.[269] However, there is no absolute requirement for complete separation of powers. For example, in *Kleyn v Netherlands* it was held that a body that both advised on the drafting of legislation and then determined appeals against planning decisions did not violate Article 6.[270] In *Jorgic v Germany* the ECtHR examined the concept of a tribunal 'established by law', and found that a prosecution for genocide in a German court did not breach the principle of legality, as genocide was a *jus cogens* and domestic law reasonably permitted extraterritorial jurisdiction in such cases.[271]

7.116   The ECtHR has found a number of violations in respect of military tribunals.[272] The Court has ruled that some court martials have violated the impartiality requirement.[273] The Court has also ruled that the trial of a civilian by military court martial, in the absence of special circumstances, will always be contrary to Article 6.[274]

7.117   The United Kingdom amended its procedures, introducing the Armed Forces Act 1996, but the ECtHR found in *Morris v UK* that, while these changes went 'a long way' to addressing the problems identified in the earlier decisions, the court martial procedure still did not comply with Article 6(1).[275] The House of Lords subsequently distinguished the ECtHR's conclusion, finding in *R v Spear* that the 'European Court did not receive all the help that was needed to form a conclusion' as it did not have all the relevant information about safeguards against impartiality or lack of independence.[276]

7.118   In *Re Twaite* the Court of Appeal held that majority verdicts given by a board of lay members in a court martial did not inherently contravene Article 6.[277]

---

[267] *Ringeisen v Austria* (1979–80) 1 EHRR 455; *Campbell and Fell v the United Kingdom* (1985) 7 EHRR 165; *Le Compte, Van Leuven and De Meyere v Belgium* (1983) 5 EHRR 183; *Belilos v Switzerland* (1988) 10 EHRR 466.

[268] *Remli v France* (1996) 22 EHRR 253; *Findlay v United Kingdom* (1997) 24 EHRR 221; *Incal v Turkey* (2000) 29 EHRR 449; and *Grieves v United Kingdom* (2004) 39 EHRR 2.

[269] (2000) 30 EHRR 289. See also *Langborger v Sweden* (1989) 12 EHRR 416; *Pabla Ky v Finland* (2006) 42 EHRR 34; *Olujic v Croatia* (2011) 52 EHRR 26; *R (Barclay) v Secretary of State for Justice* [2008] EWCA Civ 1319.

[270] (2004) 38 EHRR.

[271] (2008) 47 EHRR 207. See also *Lavents v Latvia* App No 58442/00, 28 November 2002; *Zand v Austria* [1981] ECC 50.

[272] See, eg *Incal v Turkey* (2000) 29 EHRR 449.

[273] See, eg *Findlay v UK* (1997) 24 EHRR 221; *Hood v UK* (2000) 29 EHRR 365.

[274] *Martin v United Kingdom* (2007) 44 EHRR 31.

[275] (2002) 34 EHRR 52. See also *Grieves v UK* (2004) 39 EHRR 2.

[276] [2002] UKHL 31, [2003] 1 AC 734 at [12] per Lord Bingham.

[277] [2010] EWCA Crim 2973, [2011] 1 Cr App R 249.

The majority of UK cases relating to impartiality under this head involve criminal 7.119
proceedings and, more particularly, allegations of jury bias. The specific facts of the cases
are important in determining whether evidence of possible bias or preference on the part
of a juror will undermine the presumption of impartiality. In a surprising decision, the
Court of Appeal in *R v Alexander* held that there was no reason to rebut the presumption
that the jury was impartial despite the fact that the foreman of the jury had subsequently
written, following the verdict, to proposition prosecuting counsel, referring to his performance in the trial and the achievement of convictions in a congratulatory fashion.[278]
The court held that the test was whether a fair-minded and informed observer would
not have concluded that there was a real possibility, or real danger, that the jury was
biased. A crucial issue is whether the allegation of bias is investigated. In *Farhri v France*,
there was an allegation of improper communication between the prosecutor and members of the jury which was not investigated and this was found to violate the complainant's right to a hearing by an independent and impartial tribunal.[279]

The ECtHR has also considered the question of possible juror bias in a number of 7.120
cases. In *Pullar v UK*, the ECtHR found no violation of Article 6 when the applicant was
convicted by a jury that included an employee of a key prosecution witness.[280] By contrast, a violation was found in *Sander v UK*.[281] During the applicant's trial, a letter was
received by the judge from a jury member complaining that two fellow jurors were
making racist remarks and jokes. The ECtHR held that the judge, having been informed
of a serious allegation and in possession of a partial admission, should have discharged
the jury. Redirection of the jury to stress the importance of avoiding racial prejudice was
inadequate.[282] However, it should be noted that a judge is under no obligation to discharge jurors simply because there is an allegation by a defendant of a juror making a
racist comment. In *R v Bajwa*, the alleged racist comment had not been admitted
and the judge had applied himself with 'great care and sensitivity' in investigating the
issue.[283] It should be noted that the House of Lords has ruled that evidence emerging
after the verdict has been delivered of things said by jurors is inadmissible and cannot be
used as evidence of an article violation.[284] The importance of jury deliberations remaining secret has been acknowledged by the ECtHR as a legitimate feature of English trial
law.[285]

In principle, a jury trial may be rendered unfair by adverse media publicity particu- 7.121
larly when 'publicity is unremitting and sensational'.[286] However, the ECtHR has held
that the fact that high profile criminal cases will inevitably attract comment by the media
does not mean that any media comment will inevitably prejudice a defendant's right to
a fair trial. Cogent evidence of concerns about jurors' impartiality will be required to
convince the court that the trial was unfair.[287]

---

[278] [2004] EWCA Crim 2341.
[279] (2009) 48 EHRR 34; *Gregory v United Kingdom* (1998) 25 EHRR 577.
[280] (1996) 22 EHRR 391. In similar vein, see *R v Thoron (Francois Pierre)* [2001] EWCA Crim 1797.
[281] (2001) 31 EHRR 44.
[282] Cf the domestic consideration of *Sander* in *R v Qureshi* [2001] EWCA Crim 1807, [2002] 1 WLR
518.
[283] [2007] EWCA Crim 1618. Cf. *R v OKZ* [2010] EWCA Crim 2272.
[284] *R v Mirza (Shabbir Ali)* [2004] UKHL 2.
[285] *Gregory v United Kingdom* (1998) 25 EHRR 577.
[286] *Abu-Hamza No 1 v UK* App No 31411/07, 18 January 2011, para 39.
[287] Ibid.

7.122   (iii) *Public hearing*   A public hearing is an essential feature of the right to a fair trial.[288] Article 6(1) explicitly provides a right to a public hearing, in order to protect litigants 'from the administration of justice in secret with no public scrutiny'[289] and to maintain public confidence in the judicial system.[290] This right applies to traditional courts as well as to any other hearings that come under Article 6, including disciplinary hearings of professionals.[291] This usually, but not universally, requires an oral hearing attended by the parties (in criminal cases the prosecutor and the accused, and in civil cases by the civil parties) which is open to the public.[292] An oral hearing is not necessarily required at appellate level.[293] If a public hearing is not held in a lower court, the defect may be cured by a public hearing at a higher level but only if the appeal court is able to consider the merits of the case and is competent to deal with the entirety of the matter.[294]

7.123   It is possible for an individual to voluntarily waive the right to a public hearing, for example where the claimant has entered into a contractual agreement providing for arbitration.[295] A waiver must be made in an unequivocal manner and must not run counter to any important public interest.[296] In the criminal context, the Court of Appeal Criminal Division has held that the right to a public hearing under Article 6 will not be violated where national security concerns or the need to protect witnesses lead to a criminal trial being held wholly or partly in private.[297] Any restriction imposed must be 'strictly required' in the particular factual circumstances of the case.[298]

7.124   On occasion the ECtHR will accept general presumptions in favour of private hearings, for example as in *B v UK* concerning the presumption of privacy in hearings under the Children Act 1989.[299] However, where a case concerned the transfer of custody of a child to a public institution rather than a dispute between parents over a child's residence, then the reasons for excluding a case from public scrutiny had to be subjected to careful examination.[300]

7.125   The requirement for a public hearing includes an obligation that judgment is also to be pronounced publicly. Unlike the limitations that apply to a public trial, the right to public pronouncement of the judgment is unqualified. This does not necessarily require that the judgment be read in open court, provided the outcome is publicly available.[301]

7.126   (iv) *Reasonable time*   Article 6(1) calls for the hearing to be held within a 'reasonable time'. Unlike Article 5(3), which applies only to individuals under arrest, this provision applies to civil and criminal cases and whether an accused is being held or is on bail.

---

[288] *Axen v Germany* (1984) 6 EHRR 195.
[289] *Pretto v Italy* (1984) 6 EHRR 182, para 21.
[290] *Diennet v France* (1996) 21 EHRR 554, para 33.
[291] Ibid.
[292] *Fischer v Austria* (1995) 20 EHRR 349.
[293] *Axen v Germany* (1984) 6 EHRR 195; *Monnell and Morris v UK* (1988) 10 EHRR 205.
[294] *Diennet v France* (1996) 21 EHRR 554.
[295] *Stretford v Football Association* [2007] EWCA Civ 238, [2007] All ER (Comm) 1.
[296] *Håkansson and Sturesson v Sweden* (1991) 13 EHRR 1; cf *Deweer v Belgium* (1979–80) 2 EHRR 439.
[297] *R v Yam* [2008] EWCA Crim 269.
[298] Ibid at [34].
[299] (2002) 34 EHRR 19.
[300] *Moser v Austria* [2007] 1 FLR 702.
[301] *Pretto v Italy* (1984) 6 EHRR 182.

The guarantee 'underlines the importance of rendering justice without delays which might jeopardise its effectiveness and credibility'.[302] This issue accounts for more judgments at the ECtHR than any other and frequently reflects systemic problems with patterns of systemic violations in some countries.[303]

The 'time' that must be 'reasonable' is the period between the laying of the 'charge' and the imposition of the sentence or final determination in civil matters. What constitutes a reasonable time will depend on the circumstances. However, particularly relevant factors include the complexity of the case, the applicant's conduct and that of the competent authorities, and the importance of what was at stake for the applicant.[304] The advanced age of the applicant may also be relevant.[305] Complexity concerns questions of fact as well as law.[306] Another key factor is the length of time since the events occurred, before the institution of proceedings.[307]   7.127

Delay by an applicant weakens a complaint that a dispute has not been resolved within a reasonable time, but a litigant must not be penalized for making use of all available procedures to pursue their defence, nor can they be expected to expedite proceedings against them.[308] In relation to the conduct of the authorities, the state is under a duty to ensure those who play a role in proceedings avoid unnecessary delay and only delays that are attributable to the state are relevant.[309] A more rigorous standard applies if the accused is in custody and a delay in proceedings may cause pre-trial detention to be unlawful under Article 5(3).[310] Certain types of civil cases will need to be dealt with more expeditiously than others, such as those concerning children or a life-threatening illness.[311] The ECtHR will include all the time taken to resolve the matter, including appeals and the resolution of who pays the costs in the proceedings.[312]   7.128

The House of Lords took a robust approach to the right to a hearing within a 'reasonable time' in *Magill v Porter*. It was held that this right is an independent element of Article 6(1), which should not be subsumed by general considerations of the right to a fair trial and which does not require the complainant to show himself prejudiced by the delay.[313] Furthermore, breach of the right is not dependent upon evidence of prejudice having been caused by the delay.[314] However, in *Bangs v Connex South Eastern* a more   7.129

---

[302] *Stögmüller v Austria* (1979–80) 1 EHRR 155.

[303] See Greer, *The European Convention on Human Rights: Achievements, Problems and Prospects* (Cambridge: Cambridge University Press, 2006).

[304] *Gast and Popp v Germany* (2001) 33 EHRR 37; *Pélissier and Sassi v France* (2000) 30 EHRR 715; *Georgiev v Bulgaria* App No 4551/05, 24 February 2011.

[305] *GOC v Poland* App No 48001/99, 23 October 2001.

[306] *Triggiani v Italy* [1991] ECHR 20.

[307] *Korbely v Hungary* (2008) 25 BHRC 382. Cf *McFarlane v Ireland* [2010] ECHR 1272.

[308] *Eckle v Federal Republic of Germany* (1983) 5 EHRR 1.

[309] *Zimmerman and Steiner v Switzerland* (1984) 6 EHRR 17; *Boddaert v Belgium* (1993) 16 EHRR 242; *Ewing v UK* (1988) 10 EHRR 141.

[310] *Jablonski v Poland* (2003) 36 EHRR 27.

[311] *Hokkanen v Finland* [1996] 1 FLR 289; *Damnjanovic v Serbia* [2009] 1 FLR 339; *H v France* (1990) 12 EHRR 74.

[312] See, eg *Somjee v UK* (2003) 36 EHRR 16; *Darnell v UK* (1993) 18 EHRR 205; *Darnell v UK* (1993) 18 EHRR 205.

[313] [2001] UKHL 67, [2002] 2 AC 357. See also *Attorney General's Reference (No 2 of 2001)* [2001] 1 WLR 1869; *R v HM Advocate* [2002] UKPC D3, [2004] 1 AC 462.

[314] [2001] UKHL 67, [2002] 2 AC 357. See also *Attorney General's Reference (No 2 of 2001)* [2001] 1 WLR 1869; *R v HM Advocate* [2002] UKPC D3, [2004] 1 AC 462.

restrictive view was adopted, the Court of Appeal appearing to require 'a real risk' that the substance of the right to a fair trial has been undermined by the delay.[315]

7.130   The implications of a breach of the 'reasonable time' requirement in the criminal context are not clear. Although this usually leads to a quashing of the conviction, in the case of *Spiers v Ruddy and HM Advocate General* the Privy Council held that a breach of reasonable time requirement did not mean that proceedings must be automatically discontinued, so long as the breach was acknowledged and addressed through, for example, expedition, a reduction in sentence, or compensation.[316] The Privy Council held that it would not be incompatible with the defendant's Article 6(1) right for the Lord Advocate to continue to prosecute him unless there could no longer be a fair trial or it was otherwise unfair to try the defendant. In civil matters, the Court of Appeal held in *Bangs v Connex South Eastern* that unreasonable delay by the tribunal in promulgating its decision can be properly treated as a serious procedural error or material irregularity giving rise to a question of law in the 'proceedings before' the tribunal where the delay means that there is a real risk that a litigant has been deprived of the substance of his or her right to a fair trial under Article 6(1).[317]

7.131   (v) *The opportunity to present one's case*   To be real and effective, this aspect of Article 6(1) must include the principle of equality of arms, which means that a fair balance must be struck between the parties. What that means varies with the circumstances. What is required is 'a reasonable opportunity' to present one's case and evidence 'under conditions that do not place [one] at a substantial disadvantage vis-à-vis [one's] opponent'.[318] This will sometimes, but not always, require disclosure of evidence relied on by the other party[319] and an entitlement to be present at the hearing. This requirement can be breached merely by procedural inequality, without the need for quantifiable unfairness.[320]

7.132   The extent to which Article 6(1) requires disclosure is a fact-sensitive issue. The ECtHR has held that generally all evidence must be produced in the presence of the accused at a public hearing with a view to adversarial argument.[321] But, Article 6 does not automatically mean 'an absolute or unqualified right to see every document'.[322] There may be competing interests, such as protecting witnesses or keeping secret police methods of investigation of crime. However, measures that restrict defence rights have to be strictly necessary to be permissible under Article 6, and must leave the essence of the right unimpaired.[323]

7.133   In *AF (No 3)* the House of Lords applied the decision of the Grand Chamber in *A and ors v UK*[324] and held that non-disclosure could not go so far as to deny a party knowledge of the essence of the case against him.[325] If the open material used against a

---

[315] [2005] EWCA Civ 14, [2005] 2 All ER 316.
[316] [2007] UKPC D2, [2008] AC 873. See also *Attorney General's Reference (No 2 of 2001)* [2001] 1 WLR 1869; *R v HM Advocate* [2002] UKPC D3, [2004] 1 AC 462.
[317] [2005] EWCA Civ 14, [2005] 2 All ER 316.
[318] Ibid.
[319] See *Ruiz-Mateos v Spain* (1993) 16 EHRR 505; *Ruiz Torija v Spain* (1995) 19 EHRR 55.
[320] *Bulut v Austria* (1997) 24 EHRR 84; *Fischer v Austria* [2002] ECHR 3382/96.
[321] See, eg *Edwards v UK* (1992) 15 EHRR 417; *Lamy v Belgium* (1989) 11 EHRR 529.
[322] *Roberts v Nottinghamshire Healthcare NHS Trust* [2008] EWHC 1934 (QB) at [25].
[323] *Rowe and Davis v UK* (2000) 30 EHRR 1.
[324] (2009) 26 BHRC 1.
[325] *Secretary of State for the Home Department v AF (No 3)* [2009] UKHL 28, [2010] 2 AC 269.

controlee consisted purely of general assertions, and the case against him was based solely or to a decisive degree on closed materials, the requirements of a fair trial would not be satisfied, regardless of how cogent the case based on the closed materials might be. Where the interests of national security were concerned in the context of combating terrorism, however, it might be acceptable not to disclose the source of evidence that founded the grounds of suspecting that a person had been involved in terrorism-related activities.

The domestic courts have considered whether Article 6(1) guarantees a right to legal representation in disciplinary proceedings which may be determinative of a person's civil right to practice his or her profession. In *R (G) v Governors of X School* the Court of Appeal held that the level of procedural protection afforded by Article 6 will depend on what is at stake for the individual in question, but legal representation was required to give effect to Article 6(1) in the circumstances of the case.[326]   7.134

(vi) *A reasoned decision*   Article 6(1) requires a court to give reasons for its judgment.   7.135
The extent of this duty varies according to the nature of the decision and the circumstances of the case.[327] 'Sparse' reasoning will not violate Article 6(1) per se, and a detailed answer is not required to every argument,[328] but the court must address the essential issues submitted to its jurisdiction.[329] This right is particularly important in cases where the applicant wishes to exercise a right of appeal.[330] In relation to lay juries, the court has upheld the validity of their use, provided there are safeguards in the proceedings for the applicant to be able to understand why he or she had been found guilty.[331] This case was applied, domestically, in *R v Lawless*.[332]

The common law duty to give reasons has been held to be sufficient to satisfy Article 6   7.136
requirements.[333]

(b) *Specific safeguards in respect of determination of criminal charges*
The overarching protection offered by Article 6(1) is further supplemented by the spe-   7.137
cific guarantees in Article 6(2) and (3). The courts have, under Article 6(1) alone or in association with the specific protections of Article 6(2) and (3), considered matters as diverse as evidence from anonymous witnesses;[334] entrapment;[335] witnesses giving evidence behind screens;[336] accomplices;[337] undercover agents;[338] undercover police

[326] [2010] EWCA Civ 1, [2010] IRLR 222; Supreme Court judgment awaited at time of writing. See also *Kulkarni v Milton Keynes Hospital NHS Trust* [2009] EWCA Civ 789, [2009] IRLR 829.
[327] See, eg *McGinley and Egan v UK* (1999) 27 EHRR 1.
[328] *Van de Hurk v Netherlands* (1994) 18 EHRR 481.
[329] *Helle v Finland* (1997) 26 EHRR 159, paras 55–60; *Hiro Balani v Spain* (1995) 19 EHRR 566.
[330] *Hadjianastassiou v Greece* (1993) 16 EHRR 219.
[331] *Taxquet v Belgium* App No 926/05, 16 November 2010. See Roberts, 'Does Article 6 of the European Convention on Human Rights Require Reasoned Verdicts in Criminal Trials?' (2011) 11 HRLR 2.
[332] [2011] EWCA Crim 59.
[333] *English v Emery Reimbold & Strick* [2002] EWCA Civ 605.
[334] *Kostovski v Netherlands* (1989) 12 EHRR 434; *Windisch v Austria* (1990) 13 EHRR 281; *Doorson v Netherlands* (1996) 22 EHRR 330; *Van Mechelen v Netherlands* (1997) 25 EHRR 647.
[335] *Teixeira de Castro v Portugal* (1999) 28 EHRR 101.
[336] *X v UK* (1992) 15 EHRR CD 113.
[337] *X v UK* (1976) 74 DR 115.
[338] *X v Germany* (1989) 11 EHRR 84.

officers; and pleas of guilt from co-defendants.[339] Article 6(1) also affords criminal defendants specific protections which are implied into its text. They include:

(i) a limited right to silence;

(ii) the right to effective participation in their trials;

(iii) the right to equality of arms.

7.138   (i) *Right to silence*   The right to silence and the privilege against self-incrimination are core, albeit implicit, elements of the right to a fair trial.[340] They are regarded by the ECtHR as 'generally recognised international standards which lie at the heart of the notion of a fair procedure under article 6'.[341] They support the presumption of innocence and protect against 'improper compulsion' by the police and judicial authorities.[342] They mean that an accused may not be compelled to answer questions during the investigation or to testify in court.[343] Thus, the use of improperly obtained evidence would violate Article 6(1).[344]

7.139   However, these notions are not absolute.[345] The ECtHR has confirmed that it may be permissible for a trial judge to leave a jury with the option of drawing an adverse inference from an accused's silence as occurs under the Criminal Justice and Public Order Act 1994. The jury must be properly directed as to a defendant's silence.[346] However, in *Adetoro v UK* the ECtHR found that a judge's failure to direct a jury properly in relation to the defendant's silence in a police interview did not violate Article 6(1) because he had not been convicted on the strength of his silence alone and there had been no unfairness in the trial as a whole.[347] Thus, adverse inferences cannot be the primary ground for conviction and a violation of Article 6 is to be determined in the light of all the circumstances of the case, having particular regard to the situations where inferences may be drawn, the weight to be attached to them, and the degree of compulsion inherent in the situation.[348]

7.140   A test of general fairness alone is not a sufficient safeguard to ensure that a person's Convention rights are protected. Some actions will violate Article 6 protection in principle irrespective of the fairness of later proceedings. In *Salduz v Turkey* the ECtHR held that the absence of a lawyer while in police custody had irretrievably affected a defendant's rights and this could not be remedied by his opportunity to challenge the evidence against him at trial or subsequently on appeal.[349] This was a violation of Article 6(3)(c) in conjunction with Article 6(1).[350] This was applied domestically by the Supreme

---

[339] *MH v UK* [1997] EHRLR 279.
[340] *Murray v United Kingdom* (1994) 18 EHRR CD1; *Funke v France* [1993] 1 CMLR 897.
[341] Ibid.
[342] *Saunders v UK* (1997) 23 EHRR 313; *Saunders v UK* (1997) 23 EHRR 313.
[343] *R v Kearns* [2002] EWCA Crim 748, [2002] 1 WLR 2815.
[344] *Jalloh v Germany* (2007) 44 EHRR 32. See also *G v UK* (1983) 35 DR 75; *Gafgen v Germany* (2011) 52 EHRR 1; Greer, 'Should police threats to torture suspects always be severely punished? Reflections on the Gafgen case' (2011) 11(1) HRLR 67 .
[345] *Condron v UK* (2001) 31 EHRR 1.
[346] Ibid. See also *Beckles v UK* (2003) 36 EHRR 13; *Heaney and McGuinness v Ireland* (2001) 33 EHRR 12.
[347] [2010] All ER (D) 109 (Apr).
[348] *John Murray v UK* (1994) 18 EHRR CD1. Cf *Heaney and McGuinness v Ireland* (2001) 33 EHRR 12.
[349] (2009) 49 EHRR 19 at [54].
[350] Ibid.

Court in *Cadder v HM Advocate*.[351] 'Admirable' as they were, later safeguards to the right to a fair trial could not rectify the unfairness which arose from a detained person having answered questions in the absence of a lawyer in his first interview.[352]

The privilege against self-incrimination does not apply to the production of blood, hair, or other physical or objective specimens used in forensic analysis, or voice samples.[353] Car owners can be required to disclose the driver of a vehicle in relation to a speeding offence as this was part and parcel of a regulatory regime relating to the use of motor cars and did not limit the privilege against self-incrimination sufficiently to constitute a breach of Article 6(1).[354]   7.141

(ii) *Right to effective participation*   One of the 'essential requirements' of Article 6(1) read with Article 6(3)(d) is that a person 'charged with a criminal offence' is entitled to take part in the hearing and to be present when tried,[355] subject only to very tightly defined exceptions.[356] This is because a defendant has to be given a proper opportunity to question witnesses giving evidence against him or her.[357] Thus, the entitlement is not only to be physically present, but to be present in a meaningful sense: to be able to hear, follow, and understand proceedings, and to effectively participate through giving evidence and through a lawyer. For example, if the defendant is a child, the proceedings should take account of his or her age, level of maturity, and intellectual and emotional capabilities. This may involve special treatment.[358] Effective participation requires that the defendant has a broad understanding of the nature of the trial process and of what is at stake, including the significance of any possible penalty.[359]   7.142

(iii) *Equality of arms*   The comments made in the preceding section on equality of arms also relate to criminal cases. In criminal cases, equality of arms means that a defendant and prosecution should enjoy a relatively level playing field at trial. This protection under Article 6(1) overlaps with some of the specific guarantees of Article 6(3) and the requirement for adversarial proceedings.[360] In practice, the requirement of equality of arms includes each party being afforded the opportunity to cross-examine the other's evidence and findings.[361] This can include, when read with Article 6(3), an obligation on the prosecution to disclose any material in their possession, or to which they could gain access, which may assist the accused in exonerating him or herself or in obtaining a reduction in sentence.[362] It also means that defence and prosecution witnesses should be examined under the same conditions.[363] Both parties should certainly have the right to   7.143

---

[351] [2010] UKSC 43 (SC) at [70] per Lord Rodgers.
[352] Ibid.
[353] *PG and JH v UK* [2001] ECHR 44787/98.
[354] *O'Halloran and Francis v UK* (2008) 46 EHRR 21.
[355] *Hulki Gunes v Turkey* (2006) 43 EHRR 15.
[356] *Hermi v Italy* (2008) 46 EHRR 46. Cf *Ekbatani v Sweden* (1991) 13 EHRR 504.
[357] *Hermi v Italy* (2008) 46 EHRR 46.
[358] *SC v UK* (2004) 40 EHRR 226.
[359] Ibid. Applied domestically in *R (C) v Sevenoaks Youth Court* [2009] EWHC 3088 (Admin).
[360] *Ruiz-Mateos v Spain* (1993) 16 EHRR 505; *Krcmar v Czech Republic* (2001) 31 EHRR 41.
[361] *X v Austria* (1972) 42 CD 145.
[362] *Jespers v Belgium* (1983) 5 EHRR CD305; *Foucher v France* (1998) 25 EHRR 234. Cf *Mckeown v UK* App No 6684/05, 11 January 2011; *Allison v Her Majesty's Advocate* [2010] UKSC 6; *McInnes v Her Majesty's Advocate* [2010] UKSC 7.
[363] *Bönisch v Austria* (1987) 9 EHRR 191.

be represented by counsel, as well as the right to appear in person. In some cases equality of arms will require one party to be legally aided.[364]

7.144   In *Secretary of State for the Home Department v MB* Lord Bingham said the ability of an individual to meet the case against him or her is integral to the notion of equality of arms which in turn is inherent in the concept of a fair trial.[365] However, mechanisms such as special advocates[366] and public interest immunity (PII) certificates,[367] which prevent the defendant directly knowing the evidence against him or her, will not necessarily violate Article 6(1) provided they do not undermine the very essence of the right (see above). The ECtHR jurisprudence, however, illustrates that evidence may only be withheld from the defendant if strictly necessary, a standard substantially higher than ordinary proportionality, and that evidence *must* be disclosed where it is necessary for an accused person to meet the case against him or her.[368]

7.145   The equality of arms guarantee is frequently read with Article 5(4) of the Convention, which allows the defendant to see the case against him or her so that he or she may challenge detention.

(c) *Composite approach*

7.146   The court assesses the fairness of a trial by reference to the process as a whole. It is the overall process which must reach the required standard.

7.147   A first instance decision determinative of civil rights and obligations need not necessarily meet Article 6(1) standards on its own, provided it is subject to supervision on an appeal or susceptible to judicial review, which is compliant.[369] However, the converse is not true: it cannot be said that there can never be an Article 6 breach if there is a fair appeal. Some breaches cannot be cured by appeal.[370]

7.148   In the case of *Tsfayo v UK* the ECtHR held that a housing benefit review board staffed by councillors was not 'independent' because the members of the board were members of the local authority which stood to gain from the decision, and it was not one where the decision-maker 'required a measure of professional knowledge of experience'; the issue was simply one of fact. Judicial review could not adequately correct errors of fact because the Administrative Court 'did not have jurisdiction to rehear the evidence or substitute its own views as to the applicant's credibility'.[371] However, in *Ali v Birmingham*

---

[364] *Steel and Morris v UK* (2005) 41 EHRR 22.

[365] *Secretary of State for the Home Department v MB; Secretary of State for the Home Department v AF* [2007] UKHL 46, [2008] 1 AC 440.

[366] *A and ors v UK* (2009) 26 BHRC 1; *Al-Rawi v Security Service* [2010] EWCA Civ 482 (Supreme Court decision pending); *Tariq v Home Office* [2010] EWCA Civ 462 (Supreme Court decision pending); *Secretary of State for the Home Department v MB; Secretary of State for the Home Department v AF* [2007] UKHL 46, [2008] 1 AC 440. See also *Secretary of State for the Home Department v AF (No 3)* [2009] UKHL 28, [2010] 2 AC 269.

[367] *Rowe and Davis v UK* (2000) 30 EHRR 1.

[368] See, eg *Fitt v UK* (2000) 30 EHRR 480; *Garcia Alva v Germany* (2001) 37 EHRR 335; *R v H* [2004] UKHL 3, [2004] 2 AC 134; *Secretary of State for the Home Department v MB; Secretary of State for the Home Department v AF* [2007] UKHL 46, [2008] 1 AC 440.

[369] See, eg *Edwards v UK* (1992) 15 EHRR 417, paras 51–54.

[370] *Findlay v UK* (1997) 24 EHRR 221; *Rowe and Davies v UK* (2000) 30 EHRR 1; *Condron and Condron v UK* (2000) 31 EHRR 1; *De Cubber v Belgium* (1985) 7 EHRR 236; and *R (G) v Governing Body of X School* [2011] UKSC (judgment awaited).

[371] (2009) 48 EHRR 18, para 47. See also *Begum v Tower Hamlets LBC* [2003] UKHL 5, [2003] 2 AC 430; *R (Wright) v Secretary of State for Health* [2009] UKHL 3, [2009] 1 AC 739.

City Council the Supreme Court local authority decisions on the award of accommodation to homeless people under the Housing Act 1996 did not engage Article 6 because such decisions were based on evaluative judgments that meant the individual housing entitlement did not amount to a 'civil right'.[372]

In the event of unfairness, the ECtHR does not necessarily require a 'full judicial rehearing' of all matters of fact and discretion when dealing with administrative decision-making in specialized areas. Where the decision-maker has examined the facts, a review of the lawfulness of the decision may suffice.[373] Guidance on when a full merits review would be required was given in a Northern Irish case, *Re Brown's Application*.[374] The Court suggested that the 'bare judicial review' approach might be appropriate where the fact-finding process undertaken by the administrative body is tangential or incidental—the implication being that a more robust form of judicial review could be required when the fact-finding is central. 7.149

3. Article 6(2): Presumption of innocence

Article 6(2) provides that everyone charged with a criminal offence shall be presumed innocent until proven guilty according to law. However, an equivalent protection is implied into certain civil cases which the Convention regards as 'criminal', such as professional disciplinary proceedings. This presumption is violated if a judicial decision or, in some circumstances, a statement by a public official concerning a person charged with a criminal offence, reflects an opinion that he or she is guilty before his or her guilt has been proved according to law.[375] The presumption requires, inter alia, that when carrying out their duties, the members of a court should not start with the preconceived idea that the accused has committed the offence charged; the burden of proof is on the prosecution, and any doubt should benefit the accused. For the presumption to be meaningful the prosecution will need to produce evidence of guilt in the trial[376] and the defendant has a right to be heard in his or her own defence.[377] 7.150

Article 6(2) governs criminal proceedings in their entirety 'irrespective of the outcome of the prosecution'—so an acquittal or the lack of any conviction will not negate the state's responsibility for violating the presumption of innocence by prejudging the accused's guilt.[378] However, it applies only to the offence with which the accused is charged and does not extend to the sentencing process when decisions are being made regarding the length of sentence, quantum of a fine, or the amount of property to be confiscated,[379] although the House of Lords has held that the presumption of innocence does apply to confiscation proceedings via the civil limb of Article 6(1).[380] 7.151

The ECtHR has held that the presumption of innocence may be violated in particular circumstances where, following an acquittal, a court or other authority expresses an 7.152

---

[372] [2010] 2 AC 39.
[373] *Bryan v UK* (1995) 21 EHRR 342.
[374] [2003] NIJB 168. See also *Re Brolly (Anne)* [2004] NIQB 69.
[375] *Allenet de Ribemont v France* (1995) 20 EHRR 557; *Fatullayev v Azerbaijan* (2011) 52 EHRR 2.
[376] *Barberà v Spain* (1988) 11 EHRR 360.
[377] *Minelli v Switzerland* (1983) 5 EHRR 554.
[378] See, eg *Kazmierczak v Poland* App No 4317/04, 10 March 2009, para 55.
[379] See, eg *Phillips v UK* (2001) 11 BHRC 280; *R v Rezvi* [2002] UKHL 1; *R v Benjafield* [2002] UKHL 2, [2003] 1 AC 1099.
[380] *R v Briggs-Price* [2009] UKHL 19.

opinion of continuing suspicion which amounts in substance to a determination of guilt of the person concerned.[381] In *R (Adams) v Secretary of State for Justice* the Supreme Court held that these cases did not lead Article 6(2) to have any bearing on the question whether a person should be entitled to compensation for a miscarriage of justice.[382]

(a) *Reverse onus provisions*

7.153 'Reverse onus' provisions that require the defendant to prove certain elements of his or her defence do not violate the presumption of innocence per se as long as the overall burden of establishing guilt remains with the prosecution.[383] Equally, the provision does not necessarily prevent presumptions of law or fact from being in favour of the prosecution and against the defendant. These presumptions must be 'within reasonable limits'.[384]

7.154 In *R (Kebilene) v DPP* certain members of the House of Lords indicated, in obiter comments, that reverse onus provisions may not violate Article 6(2).[385] However, the use of section 3 of the Human Rights Act to translate an apparently legal burden into an evidential burden in *R v Lambert* indicated that at least in certain circumstances, the domestic courts would hold that the placement of a legal burden on an accused contravenes Article 6(2).[386] The leading decision is now *Sheldrake v DPP*, which confirms that reverse onus provisions may on occasion breach Article 6(2).[387] However, the House of Lords rejected as 'inappropriate' the guidance set out by a five-judge Court of Appeal in that case, and did not provide clear principles for courts to apply in future cases.

(b) *Right to silence*

7.155 The right to silence and 'adverse inferences' have been considered by the ECtHR under Article 6(1) in conjunction with Article 6(2).[388] It has been held that 'there can be no doubt that the right to remain silent under police questioning and the privilege against self-incrimination are generally recognized international standards which lie at the heart of the notion of a fair procedure under Article 6'.[389] Cases in relation to the right to silence are set out at 7.138–7.139 above.

4. Article 6(3): specific rights in criminal cases

7.156 In addition to the safeguards set out in Article 6(1), an individual facing a criminal charge benefits from the additional rights set out in Article 6(3). Article 6(3) is described

---

[381] See, eg *Sekanina v Austria* (1994) 17 EHRR 221; *Orr v Norway* App No 31283/04, 15 May 2008.

[382] [2011] UKSC 18.

[383] *Lingens v Austria* (1982) 4 EHRR 373.

[384] *Salabiaku v France* (1988) 13 EHRR 379; *R v G* [2008] UKHL 37, [2009] 1 AC 92.

[385] [2000] 2 AC 326. See also *Barnfather v Islington Education Authority* [2003] EWHC 418 (Admin), [2003] 1 WLR 238.

[386] [2001] UKHL 37, [2002] 2 AC 545. See also *Lynch v DPP* [2001] EWHC Admin 882, [2003] QB 137.

[387] [2004] UKHL 43, [2005] 1 AC 264.

[388] *Murray v UK* (1996) 22 EHRR 29; *Saunders v UK* (1996) 23 EHRR 313 (violation of Art 6(1) by the use at the applicant's criminal trial of statements obtained from him by DTI Inspectors in exercise of their statutory powers under the Companies Act 1985 to compel him to answer questions and provide information). For domestic discussion of *Saunders*, see *R v Dimsey* [2001] UKHL 46, [2002] 1 AC 509.

[389] *Murray v UK* (1996) 22 EHRR 29; *Funke v France* [1993] 1 CMLR 897.

as containing 'an enumeration of specific applications of the general principle stated in paragraph 1 of the Article'.[390] It establishes five specific safeguards which constitute a non-exhaustive list of the minimum rights to be afforded a defendant.

(a) Article 6(3)(a)

Article 6(3)(a) guarantees the defendant the right 'to be informed promptly, in a lan-   7.157
guage which he understands and in detail, of the nature and cause of the accusation against him'. It relates to the information required to be given to the accused at the time of the charge or the commencement of the proceedings, and requires the prompt, intelligible notification of charges. Vague and informal knowledge is insufficient.[391] Thus, it goes further than the requirement of notification of reasons for detention under Article 5(2). The right to know the case against the accused is essential to preparing an informed defence. It also ensures that the offence of which a person is convicted is the one with which he or she was charged.[392] Article 6(3) (a) also requires that a defendant be notified in a language that he or she understands,[393] and that the charges be formulated with adequate precision.[394] However, although oral explanations of the content and import of written charges may be sufficient, if the defendant is not conversant with the court's language, he or she may be put at a disadvantage if he or she is not provided with a written translation of the indictment in a language he or she understands.[395] The protection is context-specific, so where, for example, the charge is serious and the person charged has mental problems and difficulties understanding the charge, states must do more than simply inform him or her of the bare charge.[396]

(b) Article 6(3)(b)

Article 6(3)(b) requires that the accused be given adequate time and facilities to   7.158
mount a defence. This is linked to Article 6(3)(c) and the right to legal assistance. The principle is relative and will depend on all the circumstances of the case, including the complexity and the stage of the proceedings.[397] A balance has to be achieved between allowing adequate time and ensuring proceedings are conducted within a reasonable time. However, the courts have held that sufficient time to allow proper preparation is essential.[398] The ECtHR's approach is pragmatic, but the Court has confirmed that Article 6(3)(b) recognizes 'the right of the accused to have at his disposal, for the purpose of exonerating himself or to obtain a reduction in his sentence, all relevant elements that have been or could be collected by the competent authorities'.[399] Complaints have been declared inadmissible because the defect has been cured on appeal, but this does not discharge the judge of the duty to confirm that this right is being protected in proceedings. If it is not, the judge must also consider whether the

---

[390] *Artico v Italy* (1981) 3 EHRR 1, para 32; *Edwards v UK* (1992) 15 EHRR 417.

[391] *T v Italy* [1992] ECHR 14104/88.

[392] *Pélissier and Sassi v France* (2000) 30 EHRR 715.

[393] *Brozicek v Italy* (1989) 12 EHRR 371.

[394] *Mattoccia v Italy* (2003) 36 EHRR 47.

[395] *Kamasinski v Austria* (1991) 13 EHRR 36.

[396] *Vaudelle v France* (2003) 37 EHRR 16.

[397] *Albert and Le Compte v Belgium* (1983) 5 EHRR 533.

[398] *Öcalan v Turkey* (2005) 41 EHRR 45.

[399] *Jespers v Belgium* (1983) 5 EHRR CD 305. See also *Can v Austria* (1985) 8 EHRR 121 and *Hadjinastassiou v Greece* (1992) 16 EHRR 219.

trial can proceed.[400] Any restrictions on the right must be no more than strictly necessary and must be proportionate to identified risks.[401]

7.159   The right under Article 6(3)(b) is fact-specific, and does not extend to a free-standing positive duty on those bringing disciplinary proceedings to gather exculpatory evidence in favour of those accused of misconduct. In *R (Johnson and Maggs) v Professional Conduct Committee of the Nursing and Midwifery Council* (a disciplinary case which fell to be decided as a 'criminal' case in accordance with Article 6) it was held that the professionals accused of misconduct had not been at a disadvantage in obtaining the documents themselves. Beatson J held that a two-stage test was to be applied: first, whether the challenges in the circumstances of the case provided sufficient information to enable those charged to know, with reasonable clarity, the case they had to meet, and whether they knew enough about the charges to enable them to prepare their defences; secondly, and if the first stage was not satisfied, whether the only remedy was a stay of proceedings.[402]

(c) Article 6(3)(c)
7.160   Article 6(3)(c) provides that everyone charged with a criminal offence has:

(i)   the right to defend him or herself;

(ii) the right to legal assistance of his or her choosing; and

(iii) the right to free legal assistance if the interests of justice so require and he or she lack sufficient means.

7.161   The provision aims to guarantee the right to an effective defence.[403] Thus, it is not necessary to prove that the absence of legal assistance had caused actual prejudice in order to establish a violation. These principles apply to the pre-trial stages as well as to the trial itself.[404] In *Imbrioscia v Switzerland*, the ECtHR was asked to consider whether the defendant was entitled to have a lawyer present at pre-trial questioning. It held that Article 6(3) may be relevant to the pre-trial stages if and so far as the fairness of the trial is likely to be seriously prejudiced by an initial failure to comply with its provisions.[405] The ECtHR went further in *Salduz v Turkey*, confirming that:

> . . . as a rule, access to a lawyer should be provided as from the first interrogation of a suspect by the police, unless it is demonstrated in the light of the particular circumstances of the case that there are compelling reasons to restrict this right. Even where compelling reasons may exceptionally justify denial of access to a lawyer, such restriction . . . must not unduly prejudice the rights of the accused under Article 6. The rights of the defence will in principle be irretrievably prejudiced when incriminating statements made during police interrogation without access to a lawyer are used for a conviction.[406]

---

[400] *UK Campbell and Fell v UK* (1985) 7 EHRR 165.

[401] *Kurup v Denmark* (1986) 8 EHRR CD 93; *Kröcher and Möller v Switzerland* (1984) 6 EHRR 345.

[402] [2008] EWHC 885 (Admin).

[403] See *R (G) v Governors of X School* [2009] EWHC 504 (Admin), [2009] ELR 206 where the disciplinary and disqualification process in play did not give rise to rights under Art 6(3), but did give rise to a right to legal representation under Art 6(1). UKSC judgment awaited at time of writing.

[404] *Imbrioscia v Switzerland* 1993 17 EHRR 441.

[405] (1993) 17 EHRR 441. Ibid; *Magee v UK* (2001) 31 EHRR 822.

[406] (2008) 26 BHRC 223 at [55].

Access to a lawyer has been considered by domestic courts.

The provision also gives the right for a detained person charged with a criminal   7.162
offence to communicate with his or her lawyer out of hearing of other persons. In *S v
Switzerland* the ECtHR confirmed that '[f]ree communication between a lawyer and his
detained client is a fundamental right which is essential in a democratic society, above all
in the most serious of cases'.[407] Consequently, it rejected an argument that intrusive acts
such as surveillance of a lawyer, the presence of a police officer at consultation, or the
interception of communication were necessary because of fears of collusion.

Article 6(3)(c) also covers the right to free legal assistance on the grounds of (1)   7.163
insufficient means, and (2) the interests of justice. In *Benham v UK* the ECtHR considered whether the lack of availability of full legal aid for a committal hearing in a poll
tax case constituted a violation of Article 6. In answering this question, the ECtHR
stated that regard must be had to the severity of the penalty at stake and the complexity
of the case. In general, the ECtHR held that where 'deprivation of liberty is at stake,
the interests of justice in principle call for legal representation'.[408] In the particular case
the ECtHR found a violation of Article 6(1) and (3)(c) of the Convention taken
together. Legal aid may also be required 'in the interests of justice' for an appeal against
conviction or sentence.[409] This is particularly relevant when an appellant appears for
him or herself against a QC and a junior counsel for the Crown, as occurred in *Granger
v UK*. The ECtHR in that case found a violation of Article 6(3)(c), citing the defendant's obvious lack of understanding regarding the intricacies of the law in the face of
the professional prosecution.[410] The Court of Appeal has also held that this right
extends to committal proceedings for contempt of court as, in the absence of unreasonable behaviour, a litigant in person, a person who is liable to be sent to prison, is entitled to legal representation.[411]

The right to be provided with legal representation means the right to be provided   7.164
with genuine and effective representation, not the mere presence of a lawyer.[412] Assigning
a legal representative does not in itself ensure the effectiveness of assistance afforded to
an accused.[413] Thus, failures on the part of the lawyer can effectively deprive the accused
of his right to legal assistance.[414] However, the state cannot be held responsible for every
shortcoming of the accused's lawyer.[415] The duty on the court is to 'intervene only if a
failure by legal aid counsel to provide effective representation is manifest or sufficiently
brought to their attention in some other way'.[416] It should also be noted that although
the right is formulated as a choice between acting in person or being legally represented,
the ECtHR has confirmed that the right to represent oneself in person is not an absolute
one.[417]

---

[407] (1991) 14 EHRR 670. See also *Brennan v UK* (2002) 34 EHRR 18.
[408] (1996) 22 EHRR 293. See also *Perks and others v United Kingdom* (2000) 30 EHRR 33.
[409] *Granger v UK* (1990) 12 EHRR 469. See also *Hoang v France* (1993) 16 EHRR 53.
[410] (1990) 12 EHRR 469.
[411] *Hammerton v Hammerton* [2007] EWCA Civ 248.
[412] *Artico v Italy* (1980) 3 EHRR 1.
[413] *Imbrioscia v Switzerland* (1994) 17 EHRR 441.
[414] *Czekalla v Portugal* [2002] ECHR 657.
[415] *Sannino v Italy* (2009) 48 EHRR 25.
[416] *Kamasinski v Austria* (1991) 13 EHRR 36, para 65.
[417] *Croissant v Germany* (1993) 16 EHRR 135.

(d) *Article 6(3)(d)*

7.165   Article 6(3)(d) ensures the accused's right 'to examine or have examined witnesses against him and to obtain the attendance and examination of witnesses on his behalf under the same conditions as witnesses against him'. This is in keeping with the 'equality of arms' principle outlined in Article 6(1). Although it refers to 'witnesses', it has been held to cover physical evidence. For example, the ECtHR found that the right had been violated in *Papageorgiou v Greece* where the court in a fraud trial had failed, despite repeated requests, to produce originals of cheques.[418]

7.166   This provision does not guarantee an absolute right to call witnesses or a right to force the domestic courts to hear a particular witness. The requirement imposes an overall requirement of fairness, including equality of arms, so an applicant will have to establish that the failure to hear a particular witness prejudiced his or her case.[419] The ECtHR has held that this question falls within a wide margin of appreciation on the part of judicial authorities.[420] Limitations on the right are possible, and the ECtHR has approved them on a variety of grounds, such as vulnerable witnesses giving evidence anonymously, behind screens, or via pre-recorded video interviews.[421] The ECtHR has held that a genuine fear of reprisals may justify reliance on hearsay evidence but this should be counter-balanced with procedures which preserve the rights of the defence and that these procedures may vary from case to case.[422] However the permissible justifications for anonymous witnesses are strictly limited.[423] A conviction cannot be based either solely or to a decisive extent on evidence from anonymous witnesses.[424] Finally, it must also be noted that the obligation to permit challenges to the witness in person may have to be balanced against the state's obligation to protect life under Article 2. The courts have held that to compel police or military witnesses to give evidence without anonymity may, in extreme circumstances, constitute a breach of their Article 2 right to life.[425]

7.167   The House of Lords concluded in *R v Davis* that the domestic law in this area had intruded too far upon the right. Their Lordships found that the law had developed incrementally in such a way that while no single step towards trials with anonymous witnesses was obviously wrong, the cumulative effect of these individual steps had eroded the essence of the right under Article 6(3)(d).[426] The effect of the judgment was to prevent witnesses from giving evidence anonymously if concealing their identity from the defendant and their lawyers hindered cross-examination or other challenges to their credibility. In response, Parliament rushed to legislate to overturn the ruling, and the Criminal Evidence (Witness Anonymity) Act 2008 was passed within days. This has abolished the existing common law rules on anonymity of witnesses and replaced them with a framework in which witness anonymity orders could be granted by the court on

---

[418] (2004) 38 EHRR 30.

[419] *X v Switzerland*, (1982) 28 DR 127.

[420] Ibid.

[421] See, eg *SN v Sweden* (2004) 39 EHRR 13; *PS v Germany* (2003) 36 EHRR 61; see also *R v Camberwell Green Youth Court, ex p D* [2005] UKHL 4, [2005] 1 WLR 393. Cf *PS v Germany* (2003) 36 EHRR 61.

[422] *Saïdi v France* (1994) 17 EHRR 251; *Van Mechelen and ors v Netherlands* (1998) 25 EHRR 647; *R v Davis* [2008] UKHL 36; *Al-Rawi v Security Service* [2010] EWCA Civ 482 (appeal pending); *Doorson v Netherlands* (1996) 22 EHRR 330, para 67.

[423] *Van Mechelen and ors v Netherlands* (1998) 25 EHRR 647.

[424] *Doorson v Netherlands* (1996) 22 EHRR 330; *Kostovski v Netherlands* (1990) 12 EHRR 434.

[425] *Re Officer L* [2007] UKHL 36, [2007] 1 WLR 2135.

[426] [2008] UKHL 36.

the application of the prosecutor or defendant. The Act has since been replaced by sections 86 to 97 of the Coroners and Justice Act 2009.[427]

In *Al-Khawaja v UK* the ECtHR propounded a rule whereby the introduction in   7.168
evidence of a hearsay statement which constituted the sole or decisive evidence against the defendant would breach Article 6(3)(d) and the general right to a fair trial under Article 6, unless the defendant had had an opportunity at some stage to cross-examine the maker of the statement, or unless the maker of the statement was kept from giving evidence through fear induced by the defendant.[428] This rule conflicted with the decision of the Court of Appeal in *R v Horncastle*.[429] The Court of Appeal held that provided the provisions of the Criminal Justice Act 2003 were observed, there was no breach of Article 6 and in particular Article 6(3)(d), if the conviction was based solely or to a decisive degree on hearsay evidence admitted under the Criminal Justice Act 2003. In a striking departure from normal practice, the Supreme Court declined to follow the ECtHR on the basis that it was a rare occasion 'where this court has concerns as to whether a decision of the Strasbourg Court sufficiently appreciates or accommo-dates particular aspects of our domestic process'.[430] Amongst the reasons given for this conclusion, the court found that in almost all the ECtHR cases in which violations of Article 6(3)(d) had been found it was clear that if the law of England and Wales had been applied, the relevant evidence would have been declared inadmissible, and the defendant would not have been convicted.

(e) *Article 6(3)(e)*

Article 6(3)(e) guarantees the right to the free assistance of an interpreter if the accused   7.169
cannot understand or speak the language used in court. The ECtHR has held, in *Luedicke and ors v Germany*, that the provision absolutely prohibits a defendant being ordered to pay the costs of an interpreter.[431] Further, it confirmed that this principle covered 'those documents or statements in the proceedings instituted against him which is necessary for him to understand in order to have the benefit of a fair trial'.[432] However, in *Kamasinski v Austria* the Court held that this did not necessarily mean that written translations of all documentation had to be provided. Assistance is provided so that the defendant 'should be . . . [able] to have knowledge of the case against him and to defend himself, notably by being able to put before the court his version of the events'.[433]

Once it has been established that interpretation is required, informal and unprofes-   7.170
sional assistance is unlikely to be sufficient. In *Cuscani v UK* the ECtHR found a viola-tion of Article 6(3)(e) after a judge had accepted defence counsel's suggestion that they 'make do and mend' in the absence of an interpreter and instead call on the accused's brother to assist when required. The ECtHR held that the trial judge should have guarded the defendant's interests 'with scrupulous care' and satisfied himself that the

---

[427] See Ormerod, Choo, and Easter, 'The "Witness Anonymity" and "Investigative Anonymity" Provisions' [2010] Crim LR 368. For a discussion of relevant case law, see Ormerod, 'Evidence: hearsay evidence—anonymous witness' [2011] 6 Crim LR, 475–479.
[428] (2009) 49 EHRR 1.
[429] [2009] EWCA Crim 964.
[430] [2009] UKSC 14 at [11].
[431] (1979–80) 2 EHRR 149.
[432] Ibid, paras 40, 48.
[433] (1991) 13 EHRR 36.

absence of an official interpreter did not prejudice the defendant's full involvement in his sentencing hearing.[434]

5. Protocol 7

7.171   Protocol 7 supplements and, in some cases, deals with gaps in Article 6 protection. For example, it supplements the protection afforded to criminal defendants by providing a right of appeal against conviction (Protocol 7, Article 2); and it provides procedural protection for aliens whom the state seeks to expel (Protocol 7, Article 1). Protocol 7 is analysed below in Chapter 8, paras 8.129–8.156

D. ARTICLE 7: NO PUNISHMENT WITHOUT LAWFUL AUTHORITY

7.172   Article 7 guards against the retrospective application of criminal law. It provides 'effective safeguards against arbitrary prosecution, conviction and punishment'[435] and is thus a crucial element of the rule of law, the protection of which is one of the central purposes of the Convention.[436] Article 15 permits no derogation from Article 7 in time of war or other emergency.

7.173   Article 7(1) has two limbs: it forbids finding an individual guilty of a crime which was not a crime at the time it was committed (the prohibition on 'retrospective offences'), and it forbids a heavier penalty being imposed than that which was in effect at the time of the crime (the prohibition on 'heavier penalties').

7.174   The ECtHR has made clear that three interrelated principles underpin Article 7.[437] First, 'only the law can define a crime and prescribe a penalty'. Secondly, an offence must be clearly defined in law, enabling individuals to know what acts and omissions will attract criminal liability. Thirdly, 'the criminal law must not be extensively construed to an accused's detriment, for instance by analogy'.

7.175   Article 7(1) covers both legislation and the actions of the courts, subject to the narrow exception detailed in Article 7(2).[438]

7.176   Having regard to its potentially wide application, Article 7 is relatively underused both in Strasbourg and domestically. In many cases involving criminal laws with uncertain content or scope, reliance is placed only on Articles 5 and 6, together with one of the qualified rights if they are engaged (such as Articles 10 and 11 in relation to public order offences). Many of these cases also raise issues under Article 7 but claimants tend not to argue the point.

---

[434] (2003) 36 EHRR 2.
[435] *Korbely v Hungary* (2009) 25 BHRC 382, para 69.
[436] See, eg *Jorgic v Germany* (2007) 25 BHRC 287, para 100.
[437] *Kokkinakis v Greece* (1994) 17 EHRR 397.
[438] *Kafkaris v Cyprus* (2008) 25 BHRC 591, para 139.

1. 'Criminal'

Article 7 is applicable only to criminal proceedings resulting in a conviction and/or the imposition of a criminal penalty. It does not bite if a prosecution is abandoned.[439]   7.177

Measures not covered by Article 7, since they do not result in a finding of guilt or the imposition of a criminal penalty, include changes to parole rules[440] and remission procedures,[441] extradition,[442] and procedures for adding a conviction to an individual's criminal record.[443] There are also a number of early Strasbourg authorities holding that Article 7 does not apply to preventive detention[444] or internment[445] (although such measures may, of course, violate Article 5).   7.178

Article 7 is not applicable to civil proceedings. However, as with Articles 5 and 6, 'criminal' is an autonomous concept and proceedings which are classified as civil domestically may nevertheless be considered criminal by Strasbourg.[446]   7.179

2. Article 7(1): retrospective offences

The first sentence of Article 7(1) prohibits convicting or punishing people for behaviour which was not criminal under national or international law at the time it was committed. It guards against both the development of the law to impose criminal liability on acts that were not previously considered criminal and the extension of existing offences to include acts which were not previously covered by the offence.[447]   7.180

When speaking of 'law', Article 7—as elsewhere in the Convention—is referring to a concept that incorporates qualitative requirements, notably those of accessibility and foreseeability.[448]   7.181

Most complaints made under the first sentence of Article 7(1) raise the uncertainty or lack of precision of laws already in place, rather than entirely new statutes or laws being made which apply retrospectively. The key issue is usually whether the development or application of the existing law in the case was 'reasonably foreseeable'.   7.182

A paradigmatic example of such a case was *R v R*, heard before the passing of the Human Rights Act 1998, in which the House of Lords abolished the common law immunity for husbands who raped their wives.[449] In finding that the immunity was anachronistic and offensive, their Lordships held that 'the common law is . . . capable of evolving in the light of changing social, economic and cultural developments'.[450]   7.183

---

[439] *X v UK* 3 Digest 211 (1973).
[440] *Hogben v UK* (1986) 46 DR 231.
[441] *Kafkaris v Cyprus* (2008) 25 BHRC 591.
[442] *X v Netherlands* (1976) 6 DR 184; *Marais v Governor of HMP Brixton* [2001] EWHC 1051 (Admin).
[443] *X v Germany* 3 YB 254.
[444] *De Wilde Ooms and Versyp v Belgium* (1971) 1 EHRR 373, para 87; cf *M v Germany* (2009) 28 BHRC 521.
[445] *Lawless v Ireland (No 3)* (1961) 1 EHRR 15, para 19.
[446] 'Autonomous concepts' in the Convention are explained further in ch 2, paras 2.14–2.26.
[447] *Kingston v UK* App No 27837/95, 9 April 1997.
[448] *Cantoni v France* Reports of Judgments and Decisions 1996-V, 15 November 1996, 1627, para 29; *O'Carroll v UK* App No 35557/03, 15 March 2005, 6.
[449] [1992] 1 AC 599.
[450] Ibid, 601.

7.184   The House of Lords' decision was upheld when the case reached Strasbourg.[451] The ECtHR held that with the benefit of legal advice, the applicant husband could have foreseen that his actions might attract criminal liability and therefore Article 7 was not violated. The Court of Appeal has subsequently held that, even where the marital rape occurred in 1970, a solicitor would have advised that exceptions to the 'irrevocable consent' rule were being developed and so the development in the law did not offend Article 7.[452]

7.185   *Cantoni v France*[453] and *Chauvy v France*[454] have reiterated that the reasonable foreseeability requirement may be satisfied if the individual could have regulated his or her behaviour following appropriate legal advice. The ECtHR considers the legal advice caveat to be particularly relevant to individuals engaged in professional or commercial activities which are risky, such as selling alternative medicines (*Cantoni*) or publishing (*Chauvy*).

7.186   Laws that confer a discretion are not inconsistent with the Convention provided the scope of the discretion and the manner of its exercise are indicated with sufficient clarity. In the case of *O'Carroll v UK* the applicant was convicted of knowingly evading the prohibition on the importation of indecent material, in connection with his receipt of photographs of a young naked child engaging in normal outdoor activity, such as playing on a beach.[455] He unsuccessfully argued that the law was not sufficiently precise for him to know in advance whether his behaviour was criminal. The ECtHR held that the fact that it is for a jury to decide in indecency cases whether the matter in question is indecent is not in breach of Article 7. The ECtHR will give greater leeway in areas involving imprecise concepts, such as 'indecency'.

7.187   In a series of cases, the ECtHR considered convictions based on international criminal law. In *Jorgic v Germany* it found that the conviction of a Bosnian Serb for genocide did not infringe Article 7.[456] It did not prevent the gradual clarification of the criminal law by judicial determination from case to case. Conversely, in *Kononov v Latvia* the Grand Chamber, disagreeing with the Chamber's judgment, found that the applicant could have reasonably foreseen that acts committed during the Second World War amounted to a war crime under the *jus in bello* applicable at the time. There was therefore no violation of Article 7.[457] The Grand Chamber reached a different conclusion in respect of an applicant convicted for crimes against humanity committed during the Hungarian Revolution of 1956 on the basis that it was not established by the domestic courts that his crimes were part of state policy and therefore one of the constituent elements of the crime was absent.[458]

7.188   English law has long recognized a general prohibition on retrospectivity in the criminal law.[459] In *R v Rimmington* Lord Bingham set out two common law principles

---

[451] *SW v UK* (1995) 21 EHRR 363.
[452] *R v C* [2004] EWCA Crim 292, [2004] 1 WLR 2098.
[453] App No 17862/91, 15 November 1996.
[454] [2004] ECHR 64915/01.
[455] App No 35557/03, 15 March 2005.
[456] (2008) 47 EHRR 6.
[457] (2009) 25 BHRC 317.
[458] *Korbely v Hungary* (2009) 25 BHRC 382.
[459] *R v Misra* [2004] EWCA Crim 2375, [2005] 1 Cr App R 328 at [29]–[34].

on retrospectivity that are 'entirely consistent with article 7(1) of the European Convention':460

... no one should be punished under a law unless it is sufficiently clear and certain to enable him to know what conduct is forbidden before he does it; and no one should be punished for any act which was not clearly and ascertainably punishable when the act was done.461

It is clear that in the domestic courts, as in Strasbourg, the requirement of legal certainty has been flexibly interpreted. Given the relative paucity of Article 7 cases, it is as yet unclear whether the domestic courts' approach is wholly in line with that of the ECtHR.   7.189

The leading domestic case prior to the enactment of the Human Rights Act was *C v DPP*, in which Lord Lowry set out criteria for 'judicial lawmaking' in the criminal sphere.462 These criteria are broader than those set out in the Strasbourg jurisprudence, and do not rule out a court setting aside 'fundamental legal doctrines' in an individual case (although such a course should not be taken 'lightly'). Article 7 places further limits on judicial creativity beyond those set out by Lord Lowry, and the criteria he proposes should be treated with caution.   7.190

The House of Lords has indicated that, even when dealing with a precisely drafted statute, Article 7 may allow for some interpretative leeway.463 The Northern Ireland Court of Appeal found that defendants who belonged to the 'Real Irish Republican Army' (Real IRA) belonged to a proscribed organization within the meaning of the Terrorism Act 2000, even though that Act proscribed only the IRA and not the Real IRA, a separate organization. The House of Lords stated that the Court of Appeal had been correct to reject the defendants' Article 7 submission: 'while acknowledging, on the authority of *Kokkinakis v Greece* that a criminal offence must be clearly defined in law, the court was of opinion that the offence charged against the acquitted person had been clearly defined'.464   7.191

Their Lordships reached the same conclusion in *R v Rimmington* in respect of the common law offence of public nuisance.465 Lord Rodger stated: 7.192

While a lack of coherence in defining the scope of an offence may offend modern eyes, it does not follow that there is any violation of article 7. If the individual elements of the crime are identified clearly enough and the law is applied according to its terms, potential offenders and their advisers know where they stand: they cannot complain because the law could perhaps have been formulated more elegantly.466

The Article 7 compliance of strict liability offences was considered in *R v Muhamad*.467 The appellant argued that a strict liability offence was inconsistent with the general requirement for sufficiently clear criminal provisions. The Court of Appeal rejected this, holding that only legal uncertainty, rather than factual uncertainty, contravenes Article 7.   7.193

---

460 [2005] UKHL 63, [2006] 1 AC 459 at [33].
461 Ibid at [32].
462 [1996] AC 1, 28.
463 *R v Z* [2005] UKHL 35, [2005] 2 AC 645.
464 Ibid at [15] per Lord Bingham; citing with approval [2005] NI 106 at [51]–[52].
465 [2005] UKHL 63, [2006] 1 AC 459.
466 Ibid at [45].
467 [2002] EWCA Crim 1856, [2003] QB 1031.

In *R v Budimir and Rainbird* the Court of Appeal found that Article 7 had not been breached by the fact that the legislation criminalizing the defenda offence failed to comply with a procedural requirement imposed by EU law and was therefore technically unenforceable against them.[468]

3. Article 7(1): heavier penalties

7.194 Article 7(1) also prohibits the imposition of a heavier penalty than that applicable at the time the offence was committed. Where the law changes between the time of the commission of an offence and final judgment in a defendant's case, the court must apply the law more leniently to the defendant.[469]

(a) *Penalty*

7.195 As with the term 'criminal', 'penalty' has an autonomous meaning and the classification of a measure in domestic law will not be decisive. Relevant factors include:[470]

(a) whether the measure was imposed following a conviction for a criminal offence (the ECtHR's 'starting point' in Article 7 cases);[471]

(b) its classification in domestic law;

(c) its nature and purpose;

(d) the procedures involved in its making;

(e) the procedures involved in its implementation; and

(f) its severity.

7.196 In *Adamson v UK* the ECtHR found that the retrospective imposition on the applicant, a man who had been convicted of a sex offence but had served his sentence and been released, of an obligation to register with the police was not a 'penalty' and therefore did not violate Article 7.[472] In *M v Germany* the ECtHR found that a measure which turned a limited period of detention into an unlimited period constituted an additional penalty.[473]

7.197 In *Welch v UK* the applicant was arrested on drug charges in November 1986. In January 1987 a law concerning the seizure of any proceeds gained as a result of the drug trade came into effect. The applicant argued that if this new law were applied to him, it would constitute retrospective criminal legislation in breach of Article 7. The ECtHR ruled that the retrospective application of the confiscation order was a penalty and offended Article 7. It found that Welch faced more 'far-reaching detriment' as a result of the government seizure than he would have at the time he perpetrated the crimes.[474]

---

[468] [2010] EWCA Crim 1486, [2010] 3 CMLR 1377.
[469] *Scoppola v Italy* [2009] ECHR 10249/03.
[470] *Welch v UK* (1995) 20 EHRR 247, paras 27, 28; *Adamson v UK* App No 42293/98, 26 January 1999.
[471] *Jamil v France* (1995) 21 EHRR 65.
[472] App No 42293/98, 26 January 1999. See also *Gardel v France* App No 16428/05, 17 December 2009.
[473] (2009) 28 BHRC 521.
[474] (1995) 20 EHRR 247, para 34.

In *Gurguchiani v Spain* the European Court held for the first time that deporta-   7.198
tion may constitute a penalty where it replaced a custodial sentence imposed on the
accused.[475]

There is a question mark over the domestic courts' approach to the meaning of 'pen-   7.199
alty' within Article 7. They have tended to adopt a narrow approach, treating the factors
identified by the ECtHR in *Welch v UK* as a checklist of requirements, each of which
must be satisfied in order for a measure to be considered a 'penalty'. In *Gough v Chief
Constable of Derbyshire*, for example, the Court of Appeal found that orders banning
attendance at, and travel to, football matches do not constitute penalties.[476] In *R v Field;
R v Young* the Court of Appeal held that an order disqualifying the appellants from
working with children was not a penalty, and so could be imposed in respect of offences
committed before the implementation of the statutory provisions creating the order.[477]
The domestic courts in *Gough* and *Field; Young* focused almost exclusively on the aim of
the measure and did not fully consider its severity or the behaviour to which it was
linked.

It seems that if the measure is primarily intended to be 'preventive' rather than puni-   7.200
tive the domestic courts will usually find it Article 7-compliant. In *AT (Pakistan) v
Secretary of State for the Home Department* the Court of Appeal held that automatic
deportation could not be characterized as a penalty as one reason for such a measure was
to prevent a person reoffending in the United Kingdom.[478] The court appears to have
been unaware of the decision in *Gurguchiani v Spain* and its conclusion is therefore open
to question.

(b) *Sentencing*

The rule against heavier penalties may also be violated by a failure to apply the relevant   7.201
sentencing rules, even if the distinction between the appropriate and actual sentence is
minimal.[479] This strict approach is in keeping with the importance of the rule of law
under the Convention. However, in a series of cases the ECtHR has pared back its earlier
approach under this limb of Article 7(1). It has imported the 'foreseeability' test from the
first limb of Article 7(1) and applied it in relation to whether or not a heavier penalty has
been imposed than that which the offence attracted at the time of commission. In doing
so it has given a widened margin of appreciation to states than had previously been the
case under Article 7. The reasoning in these cases gives cause for concern as it weakens
protection from retrospective penalties.

In *Taylor v UK* the ECtHR found no breach of Article 7 where a 15-year-old boy   7.202
received an 18-month custodial sentence following his conviction for theft and
assault.[480] He had just passed his fourteenth birthday at the time of the offence, but
owing to delays on the part of the Crown Prosecution Service and Stratford Youth
Court his case did not come to trial until a year later, 11 days after his 15 birthday.

---

[475] App No 16012/06, 15 December 2009.
[476] [2002] EWCA Civ 351, [2002] QB 1213.
[477] [2002] EWCA Crim 2913, [2003] 1 WLR 882.
[478] [2010] EWCA Civ 567, [2010] NLJR 806.
[479] See, eg *Gabarri Moreno v Spain* App No 68066/01, 22 July 2003. The judgment is available only in
French.
[480] App No 48864/99, 3 December 2002.

Had he been convicted of these offences when aged 14 he could not have received a custodial sentence.

7.203   The ECtHR accepted the Government's argument that the relevant statutory provisions were clear and foreseeable given legal advice, as in English law the basic rule for determining what sentencing power the court has is the defendant's age at the date of conviction, not his age at the date of commission. The ECtHR thus upheld the imposition of a penalty to which Taylor was not liable at the time he committed the offence on the basis of foreseeability.

7.204   The Grand Chamber has taken the *Taylor v UK* principle a step further. In *Achour v France* it held that the rule against heavier penalties will not be violated by a new statutory provision if the development is broadly foreseeable given previous criminal justice policies.[481] As the French courts had taken 'a clear and consistent position since the late nineteenth century' on the application of new recidivism rules, the applicant was 'manifestly capable' of regulating his conduct in light of this case law.[482]

7.205   It is also clear from *Achour v France* that the practice of taking past events into consideration should be distinguished from the notion of retrospective application of the criminal law. In that case the applicant had been found guilty of drug trafficking in 1984, and served time in prison until 1986. In 1994 new provisions came into effect which changed the law on recidivism. They stipulated that where a person who had already been convicted of a serious crime or offence punishable by ten years' imprisonment committed, within ten years of the expiry of the previous sentence, a further offence, the maximum sentence and fine imposable for any further offence should be doubled. The applicant was sentenced in 1997 for a further drug offence and had his sentence doubled on the basis of the 1997 laws. The Grand Chamber (overturning an earlier Chamber decision) found no violation of Article 7. He was not being punished for the earlier offence; rather, the new rules had been applicable when he committed the second offence in 1997, as he had been a recidivist in legal terms at that time.[483]

7.206   In the case of *Kafkaris v Cyprus* the Grand Chamber considered Article 7 in relation to a prisoner sentenced to life imprisonment for pre-meditated murder.[484] At the time of his sentence, the provisions of the Cypriot Criminal Code provided for a mandatory full-life sentence but the executive and authorities worked on the assumption that the Prison Regulations, which provided for remission of life sentences, imposed a maximum sentence of 20 years. A change to the Prison Regulations then abolished remission of life sentences and the applicant was expected to serve a full-life term.

7.207   The Grand Chamber found that there was no question of the retrospective imposition of a heavier penalty because the change in the law was not a part of the 'penalty' imposed upon him but rather related solely to the 'execution of the sentence'. Nonetheless, a majority of the Grand Chamber held that there had been a breach of Article 7. Recognizing for the first time a free-standing notion of 'quality of law' in Article 7, akin to the 'prescribed by law' criterion in relation to the qualified rights, the majority concluded that Cypriot law was not sufficiently clear for the applicant to discern the scope of the penalty of life imprisonment and therefore Article 7 had been breached. As the dissenting judges noted,[485] the majority's

---

[481] (2007) 45 EHRR 2.
[482] Ibid, para 52.
[483] (2007) 45 EHRR 2.
[484] (2008) 25 BHRC 591.
[485] See the joint partly dissenting opinion of Judge Loucaides and Judge Jociene.

reasoning is obscure. If the nature of the sentence was unforeseeable at the time of its imposition, then a later extension in that same sentence ought logically to constitute a heavier penalty. It remains to be seen whether the ECtHR will apply the notion of the 'quality of law' in future judgments on Article 7.[486]

In line with the Strasbourg jurisprudence on sentencing, the domestic courts have held that an increase in sentencing guidelines is not inconsistent with Article 7, provided the sentence does not exceed the maximum applicable at the time of commission of the offence.[487]   7.208

In *R v Offen* the Court of Appeal rejected the argument that the imposition of an automatic life sentence after the commission of a second serious offence constituted a heavier penalty for the first offence.[488] The correctness of this approach has been confirmed by the Grand Chamber's decision in *Achour v France*.[489]   7.209

There has been a stream of cases concerning the application of Article 7 to 'extended' sentences.[490] These sentences comprise both a custodial and a licence period, and may be imposed upon individuals convicted of certain serious offences. The domestic courts have followed the approach in *Achour v France*. In *R v Uttley* the House of Lords held that the imposition of the licence period for sentences prior to coming into effect of the relevant statute would not breach Article 7.[491] The defendant in *Uttley* had his complaint against the UK Government declared inadmissible by the ECtHR, indicating that the position adopted by the House of Lords is Convention-compliant.[492]   7.210

In *R v Bamber* the Court of Appeal upheld a whole life tariff for murder imposed after a review of the sentence in accordance with the Criminal Justice Act 2003 on the basis that the law against retrospectivity ensured that the sentence could not be increased or extended following review.[493]   7.211

In a rare finding of a violation of Article 7, the Court of Appeal held that the enforcement of a confiscation order made against an individual under the Drug Trafficking Act 1994 would offend the prohibition on heavier penalties as the order would have been discharged under the Act in force at the time of the offence.[494] However, the appellant had not sought an appropriate remedy—a declaration of incompatibility—and thus the court could not itself discharge the order.   7.212

4. Article 7(2): general principles of law of civilized nations

Article 7(2) sets out a narrow exception to the general principles embodied in Article 7(1). It permits retrospectivity in relation to behaviour which was 'criminal according to the general principles of law recognized by civilized nations'. The original purpose   7.213

---

[486] See *Ismoilov and ors v Russia* [2008] ECHR 2947/06 for an example of the concept applied in relation to Art 5.

[487] *R v Alden and Wright* [2001] EWCA Crim 296, [2001] 2 Cr App R 275; *R v Bao* [2007] EWCA Crim 2871.

[488] [2001] 1 WLR 253.

[489] (2007) 45 EHRR 2.

[490] *JT* [2003] EWCA Crim 111; *R v R (B)* [2003] EWCA Crim 2199, [2004] 1 WLR 490; *R (Uttley) v Secretary of State for the Home Department* [2004] UKHL 38, [2004] 1 WLR 2278.

[491] Ibid.

[492] App No 36946/03, 29 November 2005.

[493] [2009] EWCA Crim 962.

[494] *Togher v Revenue and Customs Prosecution Office* [2007] EWCA Civ 686, [2008] QB 476.

behind it was to ensure that the rule against retrospectivity did not affect the laws passed in the aftermath of the Second World War in order to punish war crimes, treason, and collaboration.[495]

7.214   As Article 7(1) already provides that it will not be violated if the conduct in question was illegal under international law at the time of commission, Article 7(2) is rarely relied upon in European Court decisions. The Court has repeatedly held that where it makes a finding under Article 7(1) it will not consider Article 7(2).[496]

7.215   The scope of the conduct covered by Article 7(2) is unclear. It could cover, for example, behaviour condemned by the international community, but not yet having achieved the status of an international 'crime', such as (arguably) 'aggression'.[497]

7.216   Domestic courts have relied not only on the ECtHR's flexibility principle under Article 7(1); they have also pointed to the Article 7(2) exception. In the marital rape cases, for example, the courts have noted that Article 7(2) provides ample justification for a man's trial for the rape of his wife, according to the general principles recognized by civilized nations.[498]

E. ARTICLE 8: RIGHT TO RESPECT FOR PRIVATE AND FAMILY LIFE

7.217   The overarching concern of Article 8 is to protect 'rights of central importance to the individual's identity, self-determination, physical and moral integrity, maintenance of relationships with others and a settled and secure place in the community'.[499] These rights apply to 'everyone', which includes legal persons in some circumstances.[500]

7.218   Article 8 formally comprises four elements: private life; family life; home; and correspondence; but it is a sprawling article that encompasses a growing number of diverse rights, including the right to privacy. In some cases an interference will affect more than one of the elements of Article 8, and in rare cases all four elements will be violated.[501] Given their scope, Article 8 rights are often closely connected to other rights protected under various other Convention articles, in particular Articles 9, 10, 11, and Protocol 1, Article 1.

7.219   Article 8 has provided extremely fertile ground for domestic litigation. It has been raised in a vast number of contexts and has proved influential in many areas. The impact of Article 8 on domestic law has been more marked than that of some other articles. This is in part because of the absence of any established free-standing right to privacy in UK law prior to the Human Rights Act 1998.[502]

---

[495] *Papon v France* App No 54210/00, 15 November 2001, ECHR 2001-XII.

[496] See, eg *Streletz, Kessler and Krenz v Germany* (2001) 33 EHRR 751, para 108.

[497] See, further, *R v Jones and Ayliffe* [2006] UKHL 16, [2007] 1 AC 136.

[498] See, eg *R v C* [2004] EWCA Crim 292, [2004] 1 WLR 2098.

[499] *Connors v UK* (2005) 40 EHRR 9, para 82.

[500] *Wieser and Bicos Beteiligungen v Austria* (2008) 46 EHRR 54.

[501] See *Ayder and ors v Turkey* [2004] ECHR 23656/94, para 119; *Selçuk and Asker v Turkey* (1998) 26 EHRR 477, para 86; *Menteş and ors v Turkey* [1998] ECHR 23186/94, para 73.

[502] See *Wainwright v Home Office* [2003] UKHL 53, [2004] 2 AC 406; *Wainwright v UK* (2006) 42 EHRR 41. See also *Malone v Commissioner of Police* [1979] Ch 344; *Kaye v Robertson* [1991] FSR 62.

Since the introduction of the Human Rights Act 1998 domestic judgments concern- 7.220
ing Article 8 have generally been in step with Strasbourg, sometimes even going further
than the ECtHR.[503] Like the ECtHR, the domestic courts' threshold for engaging
Article 8(1) is generally low, as Lord Bingham acknowledged in *London Borough of
Harrow v Qazi*.[504] However, there have been a number of cases in which domestic courts
and Strasbourg markedly diverge.[505] In common with their approach under other articles of the Convention, the domestic courts have on occasion adopted a narrow view of
the rights protected under Article 8 and a relaxed approach to proportionality under
Article 8(2).

1. Positive obligations

The notion of 'respect' under Article 8 encompasses both a positive and a negative 7.221
aspect. As the ECtHR explained in early cases:

[It] does not merely compel the state to abstain from interference: in addition to this, there may
be positive obligations inherent in an effective respect for private and family life even in the sphere
of the relations of individuals between themselves.[506]

This dual aspect has given the article much of its breadth in both European and domestic law. Since the early decisions under Article 8, which recognized positive obligations
only where there was a serious impact on core rights, the positive aspect of Article 8 now
accounts for a very significant part of the ECtHR's jurisprudence.[507]

The principles applicable to the positive and negative obligations will be similar.[508] In 7.222
imposing either such obligation, regard must be had to the fair balance that has to be
struck between the competing interests of the individual and of the community as a
whole.[509] As the ECtHR has held, the concept of 'respect' is 'not precisely defined' and
therefore the state enjoys a certain margin of appreciation in how it discharges its positive
or negative obligations.[510]

Many of the positive obligations recognized under Article 8 have been procedural. It 7.223
is well-established, for example, that there is an obligation on the state to allow parents
sufficient involvement in decisions taken by public authorities in relation to fostering
and access arrangements and taking children into care.[511] In domestic law, the High
Court has recently held that it is arguable that the police may be under a positive obligation to inform citizens of information that indicates that respect for their private life is

---

[503] In particular, in relation to non-traditional relationships, see *Ghaidan v Godin-Mendoza* [2004] UKHL
30, [2004] 2 AC 557; *Fitzpatrick v Sterling Housing* [2001] 1 AC 27.
[504] [2003] UKHL 43, [2004] 1 AC 983 at [8]–[10]. See also *R (Wood) v Commissioner of Police of the
Metropolis* [2009] EWCA Civ 414 at [28].
[505] See, eg *S and Marper v UK* (2008) 48 EHRR 1169; *Kay v UK* App No 37341/06, 21 September
2010.
[506] *Marckx v Belgium* (1979) 2 EHRR 330, para, 31; *Airey v Ireland* (1979) 2 EHRR 305, para 32; *M v
Secretary of State for Work and Pensions* [2006] UKHL 11, [2006] 2 AC 91 at [62].
[507] See Mowbray, *The Development of Positive Obligations under the European Convention on Human Rights
by the European Court of Human Rights* (London: Hart Publishing, 2004).
[508] See, eg *Evans v UK* (2008) 46 EHRR 34, para 75.
[509] See, eg *Von Hannover v Germany* (2006) 43 EHRR 7, para 57; *Botta v Italy* (1998) 4 BHRC 81, para 33;
Keegan v Ireland (1994) 18 EHRR 342, para 49.
[510] *Ucar v Turkey* [2006] ECHR 52392/99, para 135.
[511] *W v UK* (1987) 10 EHRR 29; *R v UK* (1988) 10 EHRR 74; *T and KM v UK* (2002) 34 EHRR 2.

potentially threatened.[512] The House of Lords has held that barring individuals suspected of misconduct from work without the right to make representations violates Article 8.[513]

7.224 Article 8 may also impose substantive positive obligations on the state. The ECtHR has accepted that in some circumstances it may be necessary to provide social housing in order to fulfil Article 8 obligations.[514] In *Anufrijeva v Southwark LBC* the Court of Appeal held that Article 8 was capable of imposing a positive obligation on the state to provide an individual with welfare support in order to ensure respect for his or her private and family life, although it was unlikely that it would require an individual to be provided with welfare support when his or her predicament was not sufficiently severe to engage Article 3.[515]

7.225 The imposition of positive obligations is not unbounded, however. Controversially, the ECtHR has refrained from recognizing obligations in relation to provisions for the disabled. In *Botta v Italy*, for example, it was held that respect for private life did not extend to giving a disabled person a right of access to the beach.[516] The ECtHR and the domestic courts have repeatedly held that Article 8 does not guarantee a right to medical treatment or particular level of social care.[517] It is notable, too, that both Strasbourg and the domestic courts often take a 'light touch' approach to justification in cases raising positive obligations, emphasizing the resource implications of imposing a positive obligation.[518]

2. Article 8(2)

7.226 Article 8 is a qualified right. In order to be justified, however, an interference by the state with a person's Article 8 rights must fall within one of the exceptions detailed in Article 8(2) and must meet the general requirements of justification (it must be in accordance with law and necessary in a democratic society).

7.227 Concerns about whether or not a measure is in accordance with the law arise relatively rarely under Article 8. However, in the case of *Liberty v UK*, for example, the ECtHR considered the system of mass interception of telephone calls between the United Kingdom and Ireland, finding that the law did not 'indicate with reasonable clarity the scope and manner of exercise of the relevant discretion conferred on the public authorities'.[519] In a recent decision in *Gillan v UK* the ECtHR, in disagreement with the

---

[512] *Bryant and ors v Commissioner of Police for the Metropolis* [2011] EWHC 1314 (Admin) at [54].
[513] *R (Wright) v Secretary of State for Health and anor* [2009] UKHL 3, [2009] 2 WLR 267; see also *R (Royal College of Nursing and ors) v Secretary of State for the Home Department* [2010] EWHC 2761 (Admin).
[514] *Marzari v Italy* (1999) 28 EHRR CD 175; *O'Rourke v UK* App No 39022/97, 26 June 2001; cf *Chapman v UK* (2001) 10 BHRC 48.
[515] [2003] EWCA Civ 1406, [2004] QB 1124.
[516] (1998) 26 EHRR 241; *R (D) v Haringey LBC* [2005] EWHC 2235 (Admin).
[517] *Sentges v Netherlands* [2003] ECHR 715; *Pentiacova v Moldova* (2005) 40 EHRR SE23; *R (T and ors) v London Borough of Haringey* [2005] EWHC 2235 (Admin); *R (AC) v Berkshire West Primary Care Trust* [2011] EWCA Civ 247; *R (Condliff) v North Staffordshire PCT* [2011] EWHC 872 (Admin); *R (Macdonald) v Royal Borough of Kensington and Chelsea* [2010] EWCA Civ 1109.
[518] *Abdulaziz, Cabales and Balkandali v UK* (1985) 7 EHRR 471, para 67; *Pentiacova v Moldova* App No 14462/03, 4 January 2005; *R (W) v Lambeth LBC* [2002] EWCA Civ 613, [2002] 2 FLR 327; *Ekinci v London Borough of Hackney* [2001] EWCA Civ 776, [2002] HLR 2.
[519] (2009) 48 EHRR 1, para 69.

House of Lords, held that the powers of stop and search under the Terrorism Act 2000 were overbroad and did not contain adequate safeguards against abuse.[520] The decision highlights that the requirement that an interference must be 'in accordance with the law' imposes a substantive as well as a formal burden on the state to ensure that the quality of the law accords with Convention safeguards against arbitrariness.

The bulk of cases turn on questions of proportionality under Article 8(2). A different   7.228
degree of scrutiny applies depending on the nature of the right at stake. Thus, in cases concerning the 'most intimate aspects of private life' the Court adopts a tough standard of review.[521] The cases considered under the four elements of Article 8 below illustrate the fact-sensitive application of the proportionality standard.

3. Private life

The ECtHR takes a broad approach to the notion of 'private life'. In *Niemietz v Germany*   7.229
the Court held that the concept could not be restricted to an 'inner circle' in which an individual chooses to live his or her life, but also encompassed the right to develop one's personality through relationships with others.[522] More recently, the ECtHR has referred to a 'zone of interaction of a person with others' in public or private that falls within private life.[523] In *Gillan v UK* the ECtHR affirmed this approach and found that a search of a person and his belongings conducted by a police officer in a public place constituted a 'clear interference' with Article 8.[524]

Increasingly, the ECtHR emphasizes the importance of the principle of personal   7.230
autonomy manifested in the ability to conduct one's life as one chooses.[525] As it stated in *Pretty v UK*:

Though no previous case has established as such any right to self-determination as being contained in Article 8 of the Convention, the Court considers that the notion of personal autonomy is an important principle underlying the interpretation of its guarantees.[526]

The Court found that there could be an interference with Article 8 where an individual was prevented by law from exercising his or her choice about how and when to die, but such an interference was justified by Article 8(2).[527]

'Physical and mental integrity' are also aspects of private life that the state is obliged   7.231
to protect.[528] This has led to findings of violations for failure to obtain consent for medical treatment[529] and failure to protect women from domestic violence.[530] In *Tysiac v Poland* the ECtHR found that the failure to permit the applicant to have a therapeutic abortion in order to protect her sight from deterioration violated her right to a private

---

[520] (2010) 28 BHRC 420.
[521] See, eg *Dudgeon v UK* (1981) 4 EHRR 149.
[522] (1992) 16 EHRR 97, para 29.
[523] *PG v UK* [2001] ECHR 44787/98, para 56; *Peck v UK* (2003) 36 EHRR 41, para 57.
[524] (2010) 28 BHRC 420.
[525] Marshall, 'A right to personal autonomy at the European Court of Human Rights' (2008) EHRLR 337.
[526] (1998) 26 EHRR 241, para 32.
[527] See also *R (Purdy) v DPP* [2009] UKHL 45, [2010] 1 AC 345.
[528] See, eg *Bensaid v UK* (2001) 33 EHRR 205, para 47.
[529] *MAK and RK v UK* App Nos 45901/05 and 40146/06, 23 March 2010.
[530] See, eg *A v Croatia* App No 55164/08, 14 October 2010.

life.[531] In *Tysiac* the Court preferred to analyse the case on the basis of physical integrity rather than personal autonomy, but it is now clear from the decision in *A, B and C v Ireland* that the right to personal autonomy will also be engaged in the abortion context.[532] In many cases the line between physical integrity and personal autonomy may not always need to be clearly drawn.

7.232   The domestic courts have spoken in similar terms of the notion of private life. Lord Bingham held in *R (Razgar) v Secretary of State for the Home Department* that it extended 'to those features which are integral to a person's identity or ability to function socially as a person'.[533] In *R Purdy v DPP* the House of Lords accepted, that Article 8 encompassed a right to choose how to die.[534] Baroness Hale said: 'If we are serious about protecting autonomy we have to accept that autonomous individuals have different views about what makes their lives worth living.'[535]

7.233   In *R (Countryside Alliance) v Attorney General*, the House of Lords found that Article 8(1) was not engaged by the ban on hunting with dogs under the Hunting Act 2004.[536] A majority of their Lordships considered that the public nature of fox hunting distinguished it from cases such as *Pretty* that had involved 'very personal and private concerns'.[537] Only Lord Brown lamented that Article 8(1) did not cover 'wider concepts of self-fulfilment'. In fact, the Strasbourg approach to private life is likely to encompass hunting activities. As the ECtHR has stated, Article 8 protects the 'totality of social ties' between an individual and his community.[538]

7.234   As the cases discussed above illustrate, it is impossible to identify precisely the boundaries of private life, but the following examples illustrate some of the areas in which Strasbourg and the domestic courts have found that it exists for the purposes of Article 8(1).

(a) *Sexuality and transsexuality*

7.235   It is clear that sexuality is not only an element of private life for the purposes of Article 8, but 'a most intimate aspect' of the individual's private life.[539] Homosexual activity falls within the sphere of private life.[540] The ECtHR held in *Smith and Grady v UK* that investigations conducted by the Ministry of Defence into the sexual orientation of members of the services, together with their consequent discharge from the armed forces, constituted 'especially grave' interferences with their private lives. The ECtHR rejected the Government's argument that such a policy was justified to preserve the morale of the fighting forces, saying that the Ministry of Defence could not ignore widespread and developing views in other contracting states in favour of the admission of homosexuals into the armed forces of those states.[541] Similarly, in *EB v France* the Court found a violation of Article 14 in conjunction with Article 8 in circumstances where the

---

[531] (2007) 22 BHRC 155.
[532] App No 25579/05, 16 December 2010.
[533] [2004] UKHL 27, [2004] 2 AC 368.
[534] [2009] UKHL 45, [2010] 1 AC 345.
[535] Ibid at [66].
[536] [2007] UKHL 52, [2008] 1 AC 719.
[537] Ibid at [15].
[538] *Üner v Netherlands* (2007) 45 EHRR 14, para 59.
[539] *Dudgeon v UK* (1981) 4 EHRR 149.
[540] *ADT v UK* (2001) 31 EHRR 33.
[541] (2000) 29 EHRR 548.

homosexual applicant, who was in a stable long-term relationship, was refused approval for adoption having regard, among other things, to her 'conditions of life'.[542]

Article 8 has been held to protect the right of a transsexual to have his or her new gender respected by the state, though it does not impose any obligation to provide gender reassignment surgery.[543] In *B v France* the ECtHR held that the French Government violated Article 8 when it refused to allow a change to the applicant's birth certificate.[544] Though the ECtHR took a different view in a number of cases from the United Kingdom in the 1980s and 1990s,[545] in the landmark case of *Goodwin v UK* it was held that the United Kingdom had failed to comply with a positive obligation to ensure the right of the applicant, a post-operative male-to-female transsexual, to respect for her private life, in particular through the lack of legal recognition given to her gender reassignment.[546] The Court found that there was no longer a margin of appreciation on such issues as society could 'reasonably be expected to tolerate a certain inconvenience to enable individuals to live in dignity and worth in accordance with the sexual identity chosen by them at great personal cost'.[547]

7.236

Following the *Goodwin* case, the House of Lords issued a declaration of incompatibility in relation to legislation that failed to recognize the validity of a purported marriage in 1981 between a man and a male-to-female transperson.[548] The law was subsequently changed by the Gender Recognition Act 2004.[549]

7.237

In *R (AB) v Secretary of State for Justice* the High Court considered that a decision to keep a post-operative male-to-female transsexual in a women's prison violated Article 8.[550]

7.238

(b) *Parenthood*

The ECtHR has consistently held that the right to start a family is not protected by respect for family life, which depends on existing family relations.[551] However, decisions about whether or not to become a parent may fall within the scope of private life. In *Evans v UK*[552] the Grand Chamber of the ECtHR upheld the Court of Appeal's decision that the legal obligation to obtain the male partner's consent to the storage and implantation of embryos created prior to the breakdown of his relationship with the applicant did not violate Article 8.[553] The Court accepted that 'private life' encompassed the right to respect for the decision to become a parent, but that right had to be balanced with the male partner's right under Article 8 to choose not to become a parent. The domestic law struck a fair balance between the two rights.

7.239

---

[542] (2008) 47 EHRR 21.

[543] *R (AC) v Berkshire West Primary Care Trust* [2011] EWCA Civ 247.

[544] (1992) 16 EHRR 1.

[545] *Rees v UK* (1986) 9 EHRR 56; *Cossey v UK* (1990) 13 EHRR 622; *Sheffield v UK* (1999) 27 EHRR 163.

[546] (2002) 35 EHRR 447.

[547] Ibid, para 91.

[548] *Bellinger v Bellinger* [2003] UKHL 21, [2003] 2 AC 467.

[549] See also *Grant v UK* (2007) 44 EHRR 1 considering the delay in implementing the legislation.

[550] [2009] EWHC 2220 (Admin).

[551] See paras 7.226–7.227 above.

[552] *Evans v UK* (2008) 46 EHRR 34.

[553] (2007) 22 BHRC 190. Cf *L v Human Fertilisation and Embryology Authority* [2008] EWHC 2149 (Fam), [2008] 2 FLR 1999.

7.240   In contrast to *Evans*, in *Dickson v UK* the ECtHR took the view that there had been a violation of Article 8 on account of the refusal to allow a request for artificial insemination treatment by a prisoner whose wife was at liberty, since a fair balance had not been struck between the conflicting public and private interests.[554] In a recent decision concerning IVF (in-vitro fertilization) the ECtHR found that there was no obligation on the state to provide IVF but if it made such provision it had to do so in a non-discriminatory manner.[555]

7.241   The ECtHR has recently held that Article 8 protects the right to choose where to give birth. In *Ternovszky v Hungary* the Court found that the liability of midwives to prosecution for assisting at home births violated Article 8.[556]

(c) *Private information*

7.242   The right to a private life under Article 8 also includes the right in certain circumstances not to have private information retained by the state or disclosed to third parties. This includes, for example, the retention of private information by the police,[557] the unnecessary disclosure of confidential medical data in legal proceedings,[558] and the unauthorized passing on of medical information from a hospital to authorities in the process of verifying a claim for social insurance and disability benefit.[559] Article 8 also imposes a positive obligation on the state to provide copies of personal information it stores unless there are compelling reasons for refusing to do so.[560]

7.243   In *R (S) v Chief Constable of South Yorkshire* the House of Lords considered the long-term retention of DNA taken in the course of criminal investigations as authorized by section 64 of the Police and Criminal Evidence Act 1984.[561] A majority of their Lordships found that while the taking and use of such information could constitute an interference under Article 8(1), the retention of the samples could not.

7.244   In a striking decision, the Grand Chamber in *S and Marper v UK* held that the majority of the House of Lords had adopted too narrow a view; DNA retention was an interference with the right to privacy.[562] Moreover, 'the blanket and indiscriminate nature of the powers of retention of the fingerprints, cellular samples and DNA profiles of persons suspected but not convicted of offences' failed to strike a fair balance between the interests of the state and individual.[563] In response to the decision the Coalition Government put forward proposals in the Protection of Freedoms Bill for reforming the DNA database to bring it into line with the Scottish system under which arrangements are made for limited retention or deletion depending on individual circumstances. The Bill was in its early stages when the Supreme Court decided the appeal in *R (GC) v Metropolitan Police Commissioner*,[564] a rerun of *S and Marper*. It was common ground that the existing

---

[554] (2007) 24 BHRC 19.
[555] *ISH and ors v Austria* App No 57813/00, 1 April 2010.
[556] App No 67545/09, 14 December 2010.
[557] *S and Marper v UK* (2008) 48 EHRR 1169; *R (Wood) v Metropolitan Police Commissioner* [2009] EWCA Civ 414, [2009] 4 All ER 951.
[558] *Z v Finland* (1998) 25 EHRR 371.
[559] *MS v Sweden* (1999) 28 EHRR 313.
[560] *KH v Slovakia* App No 32881/04, 28 April 2009.
[561] [2004] UKHL 39, [2004] 4 All ER 193.
[562] App Nos 30562/04 and 30566/04, 4 December 2008.
[563] Ibid, para 125.
[564] [2011] UKSC 21.

system violated Article 8. The Supreme Court read down section 64 so that it imposed a wide discretion on the police to issue guidelines on the management of the database that ensured respect for Article 8 rights.

The Supreme Court has also considered the compatibility of lifelong registration of 7.245 sex offenders with Article 8. In *R (F) v Secretary of State for the Home Department* the Court held that the absence of a mechanism by which a sex offender could review his or her lifelong inclusion on the register was a disproportionate interference with his or her private life.[565]

The ECtHR has on occasion found that private life encompasses the right to protect 7.246 one's reputation.[566] However, the ECtHR recently appeared to retreat from this position. In *Karakó v Hungary* it distinguished personal integrity, which is protected by Article 8, from mere reputation, which is explicitly referred to as a restriction on the exercise of free speech under Article 10(2).[567] The judgment did not explicitly overrule earlier decisions of the Court and it is therefore unclear whether harm to reputation which does not have an impact on personal integrity is protected by Article 8. The Supreme Court considered this case law in *Re Guardian News Media* finding that reputation was an aspect of private life and that the ECtHR had not intended to remove it from the scope of Article 8.[568] Further clarification from Strasbourg is likely.

(d) *Surveillance*

In general, most forms of surveillance by the state will constitute an interference with the 7.247 right to private life and may also interfere with the right to respect for correspondence.[569] However, in *Peck v UK* the ECtHR held that real-time CCTV footage did not infringe Article 8(1) where the images were not recorded.[570]

In *PG v UK* the ECtHR found that the recording of a suspect in his police cell inter- 7.248 fered with his right to respect for private life.[571] In *R (Wood) v Metropolitan Police Commissioner* the Court of Appeal found that the retention by police of photographs of a protestor in the street for the purposes of gathering evidence about possible civil disorder violated Article 8.[572] However, Article 8 was not engaged by the mere taking of a photograph in the absence of aggravating circumstances.

(e) *Environmental damage*

The ECtHR has accepted that environmental damage, such as the amount of air traffic over 7.249 an applicant's home, may interfere with an individual's private life even if the intrusions are 'unavoidable consequences of measures not directed against private individuals'.[573] In *Lopez Ostra v Spain* it was held that permitting a waste treatment plant to operate in breach of a licence condition may affect the right of enjoyment of people's homes and so affect their

---

565 [2010] UKSC 17.
566 See, eg *Pfeifer v Austria* (2007) 24 BHRC 167.
567 App No 39311/05, 28 July 2009.
568 [2010] UKSC 1. See also *Spiller and anor v Joseph and ors* [2010] UKSC 53, [2011] AC 852, at [75].
569 See, eg *Halford v UK* (1997) 24 EHRR 523 (interception of telephone calls); *Khan v UK* (2001) 31 EHRR 45 (listening device in home).
570 (2003) 36 EHRR 41.
571 [2001] ECHR 44787/98.
572 [2009] EWCA Civ 414, [2009] 4 All ER 951.
573 *Rayner v UK* (1986) 47 DR 5. See also *Hatton v UK* (2002) 34 EHRR 1. In both cases it was held that the intrusions were justified under Art 8(2).

right to private and family life even if it did not adversely affect their health.⁵⁷⁴ The Court has also consistently held that the failure of the authorities to deal with noise pollution by private individuals may violate Article 8.⁵⁷⁵

7.250   While the state enjoys a margin of appreciation in relation to environmental decisions, the ECtHR will carefully scrutinize the decision-making process undertaken by the state in imposing particular environmental burdens on groups of its citizens.⁵⁷⁶ In *Fadeyeva v Russia* the ECtHR held:

> ... it is certainly within the Court's jurisdiction to assess whether the Government approached the problem with due diligence and gave consideration to all competing interests. In this respect, the Court reiterates that the onus is on the State to justify, using detailed and rigorous data, a situation in which certain individuals bear a heavy burden on behalf of the rest of the community.⁵⁷⁷

Where the state fails to show how its analysis led to a particular policy decision, the ECtHR will draw an adverse inference that insufficient weight has been given to the interests of communities that are particularly badly affected. In certain circumstances, therefore, failure to conduct an environmental impact assessment (EIA) will violate the right to respect for private life, family life, and home under Article 8.⁵⁷⁸

7.251   The domestic courts have applied this line of Strasbourg jurisprudence in a number of cases.⁵⁷⁹

(f) Public space

7.252   In earlier jurisprudence, the Strasbourg Court appeared to suggest that the concept of private life did not apply to public spaces. However, it is now clear that the key concept is not whether an activity takes place 'in private' or in public, but whether there is adequate respect for a 'reasonable expectation of privacy'.⁵⁸⁰

(g) Private life and the media

7.253   Article 8 protects individuals from unjustified press intrusion into their private lives. Justification is generally based on the right to freedom of expression, and the case law on the right to privacy is therefore intimately connected to that under Article 10.

7.254   The ECtHR has often been willing to find that Article 8 outweighs the rights of the media.⁵⁸¹ In *Lindon, Otchakovsky-Laurens and July v France* the Grand Chamber considered the publication of a novel that attacked Jean-Marie Le Pen, the leader of the French National Front.⁵⁸² It concluded that the applicants' convictions for defamation did not violate Article 10. While it was correct that the applicants were permitted to make immoderate statements, particularly with regard to extremist politicians, the claim that Le Pen was 'chief

⁵⁷⁴ (1995) 20 EHRR 27. See also *Taskin v Turkey* (2006) 42 EHRR 50.
⁵⁷⁵ See, eg *DEES v Hungary* App No 2345/06, 9 November 2010.
⁵⁷⁶ *Hatton v UK* (2002) 34 EHRR 1.
⁵⁷⁷ [2005] ECHR 55723/00, para 128.
⁵⁷⁸ *Piera Giacomelli v Italy* [2006] ECHR 59909/00.
⁵⁷⁹ See, eg *Dennis v Ministry of Defence* [2003] EWHC 793 (QB), [2003] Env LR 34; *Andrews v Reading Borough Council* [2005] EWHC 256 (QB). Cf *Marcic v Thames Water Utilities* [2003] UKHL 66, [2004] 2 AC 42.
⁵⁸⁰ *Peck v UK* (2003) 36 EHRR 41.
⁵⁸¹ See, eg *Von Hannover v Germany* (2005) 40 EHRR 1; *Pfeifer v Austria* (2009) 48 EHRR 8. See also discussion of Art 10 at paras 7.397–7.399 below.
⁵⁸² (2008) 46 EHRR 35.

of a gang of killers' and a 'vampire who thrives on the bitterness of his electorate' overstepped permissible limits.[583]

The leading ECtHR case on the right to privacy is *Von Hannover v Germany* (the **7.255** *Princess Caroline* case), in which the ECtHR considered whether the publication of paparazzi photographs of the Princess in various public places, including at restaurants, shops, and a beach club, violated her right to privacy.[584] The Court held that although the Princess was in a public place she had a 'reasonable expectation of privacy' and Article 8 was therefore engaged. In reaching this conclusion, the Court emphasized that the Princess was not performing any public functions. It reiterated that justification under Article 10 will depend on the importance of the contribution made by photos or articles to a debate of general interest.[585]

The ECtHR recently revisited its privacy jurisprudence in *Mosley v UK*.[586] The *News* **7.256** *of the World* published details about the unconventional sexual practices of Max Mosley, the grandson of Oswald Mosley and the president of Formula One's ruling body. The High Court awarded Mosley substantial damages, noting that the fact that his behaviour might be viewed by some with disapproval did not deprive him of the right to privacy.[587] In his complaint to the ECtHR Mosley argued that Article 8 imposed a pre-notification requirement on newspapers intending to publish details of a person's private life. While the ECtHR accepted that the *News of World* had 'flagrantly' violated Mosley's private life, it found that a pre-notification requirement risked creating a chilling effect on freedom of speech. Whether or not such a requirement was necessary fell within the state's margin of appreciation. The Court did not retreat from its position that reports must contribute to a debate of general public interest and emphasized that a 'narrow interpretation' of Article 10 would be adopted where sensational and titillating reporting was involved.

Prior to the coming into force of the Human Rights Act, domestic law did not recog- **7.257** nize a right to privacy in the terms developed by the ECtHR. The tortious actions of breach of confidence and intentional infliction of emotional suffering failed to provide any form of redress to an individual whose privacy had been intruded upon by the media. Article 8 has significantly altered the legal landscape and given rise to some of the most controversial decisions under the Human Rights Act.

In one of the first 'privacy' cases, *Douglas and ors v Hello! (No 3)*, the Court of Appeal **7.258** held that as a result of the Strasbourg decision in *Von Hannover* the courts were required to develop the existing cause of action for breach of confidence in such a way as to give effect to the competing rights of privacy and freedom of expression conferred by Articles 8 and 10 of the Convention.[588] There would be no new cause of action for breach of privacy.

---

[583] Ibid.
[584] (2006) 43 EHRR 7.
[585] See also *Tammer v Estonia* (2001) 10 BHRC 543; *News Verlags GmbH and Co KG v Austria* (2000) 9 BHRC 625; *Krone Verlag GmbH and Co KG v Austria* [2002] ECHR 34315/96; *Eerikainen and ors v Finland* [2009] ECHR 3514/02. Cf *Editions Plon v France* [2004] ECHR 58148/00.
[586] App No 48009/08, 10 May 2011.
[587] *Mosley v News Group Newspapers* [2008] EWHC 1777 (QB), [2008] NLJR 1112.
[588] [2005] EWCA Civ 595, [2006] QB 125 at [53].

7.259   The House of Lords considered these issues in *Campbell v MGN*, in which Naomi
          Campbell sought damages for the publication of various details and photographs relating
          to her treatment for drug addiction.[589] Lord Hoffmann stated:

> . . . the new approach takes a different view of the underlying value which the law protects. Instead
> of the cause of action being based upon the duty of good faith applicable to confidential personal
> information and trade secrets alike, it focuses upon the protection of human autonomy and
> dignity—the right to control the dissemination of information about one's private life and the
> right to the esteem and respect of other people.[590]

Similarly, Lord Nicholls explained that respect for privacy was the 'underlying value' of
the tort of breach of confidence, which was now 'better encapsulated as misuse of private
information'.[591]

7.260   Following Strasbourg authority, their Lordships held that the critical question to be
          asked in such cases was whether a reasonable person of ordinary sensibilities, if placed in
          the same situation as the subject of the disclosure, rather than the recipient, would find
          the disclosure offensive. Noting that photographs are in general a particularly intrusive
          means of invading privacy, a majority of their Lordships found that Naomi Campbell
          had a reasonable expectation of privacy in relation to the details of her treatment. The
          publication could not be justified under Article 8(2) or by reference to freedom of
          expression.[592]

7.261   In *Re S (a child) (identification: restrictions on publication)*, a case concerning the iden-
          tification of children in legal proceedings, the House of Lords gave valuable guidance on
          the balance to be struck between Articles 8 and 10 where they are in conflict:

> First, neither article [8 or 10] has *as such* precedence over the other. Secondly, where the values
> under the two articles are in conflict, an intense focus on the comparative importance of the
> specific rights being claimed in the individual case is necessary. Thirdly, the justifications for inter-
> fering with or restricting each right must be taken into account. Finally, the proportionality test
> must be applied to each.[593]

7.262   On an application of those principles, their Lordships held that the interference with
          the child's Article 8 rights, albeit distressing, was indirect and not of the same order
          when compared with cases of juveniles directly involved in criminal trials. By contrast,
          the Article 10 rights at issue concerned the freedom of the press, subject to statutory
          restrictions, to report proceedings at criminal trials, which was a valuable check on the
          criminal process and promoted public confidence in the administration of justice. The
          consequence of granting the relief sought would be the inhibiting of the press to report
          criminal trials, at the expense of informed debate about criminal justice.

7.263   The Supreme Court considered the balance between Articles 8 and 10 in *Re Guardian
          News and Media* in which the press applied to the court to lift the anonymity orders in
          proceedings concerning the freezing of suspected terrorists assets.[594] In a detailed factual

---

[589] [2004] UKHL 22, [2004] 2 AC 457. The Lords' decision on this point was upheld in *MGN v UK*
App No 39401/04, 18 January 2011.
[590] Ibid at [51].
[591] Ibid at [14]. See also *McKennitt v Ash* [2006] EWCA Civ 1714, [2007] 3 WLR 194.
[592] See also *Murray v Express Newspapers plc* [2008] EWCA Civ 446, [2008] 3 WLR 1360.
[593] [2004] UKHL 47, [2005] 1 AC 593 at [17]. See also *A v B* [2002] EWCA Civ 237, [2003] QB 195;
In re BBC [2009] UKHL 34, [2009] 3 WLR 142.
[594] [2010] UKSC 1, [2010] 2 AC 697. See also *In re BBC* [2009] UKHL 34, [2010] 1 AC 145.

analysis of the balance between Article 8 and 10 in that case, the court found that Article 10 held sway. By anonymizing the parties, the court accepted that it would be harder for the press to interest readers in reports of the court proceedings. The fact that the individuals might be subject to negative publicity as a result of their lifting of anonymity could not be sufficient reason for curtailing freedom of the press.

The balancing act performed by judges in privacy cases became the subject of fierce media criticism in 2011 when it emerged that on a number of occasions the High Court had granted 'super-injunctions' preventing both the publication of private material and the very existence of the injunction itself.[595] As a result, Lord Neuberger was commissioned to write a report into the procedure relating to prior restraint in privacy cases. His report revealed that such injunctions were rarely granted and generally lasted for a very short period.[596] He recommended that in accordance with section 12 of the Human Rights Act 1998[597] the media be made aware when such an injunction had been applied for.   7.264

There are signs in recent cases that the courts may be willing to take a more relaxed approach to the 'general public interest'. In *ETK v News Group Newspapers* the Court of Appeal acknowledged the need for the press to be able to shame the famous, stating: 'To restrict publication simply to save the blushes of the famous . . . could have the wholly undesirable chilling effect on the necessary ability of publishers to sell their newspapers.'[598] Nonetheless, the court granted an injunction to prohibit disclosure of the claimant's extra-marital affair in order to protect the interests of his children.   7.265

4. Family life

Article 8 jurisprudence has undergone an evolution, and the definition of 'family life' now firmly encompasses more non-traditional relationships. As Lord Bingham explained in *EM (Lebanon) v Secretary of State for the Home Department*, 'there is no pre-determined model of family or family life to which article 8 must be applied'.[599]   7.266

In assessing whether or not family life exists, it is the substance, not the form of the individual's circumstances that matters. The key question is whether there is 'real existence in practice of close family ties'[600] which is essentially a question of fact.[601] In *M v Secretary of State for Work and Pensions* the House of Lords referred to 'the love, trust, confidence, mutual dependence and unconstrained social intercourse which are the essence of family life', in contrast with 'personal and sexual autonomy' at the heart of private life.[602] It was not prepared to hold that a same-sex relationship was 'family life' for the purposes of Article 8, but the relationship between that couple and its children   7.267

---

[595] See, eg *John Terry v Persons Unknown* [2010] EWHC 119 (QB); *Donald v Ntuli* [2010] EWCA Civ 1276, [2011] 1 WLR 294.
[596] Report of the Committee on Super-Injunctions; available at <http://www.judiciary.gov.uk/media/media-releases/2011/committee-reports-findings-super-injunctions-20052011>.
[597] See para 7.405 below.
[598] [2001] EWCA Civ 439 at [13].
[599] [2008] UKHL 64, [2009] 1 All ER 559 at [37].
[600] *K v UK* (1986) 50 DR 199; *Lebbink v Netherlands* [2004] 3 FCR 59.
[601] *Singh v Entry Clearance Officer* [2004] EWCA Civ 1075, [2005] QB 608 at [20]; *EM (Lebanon) v Secretary of State for the Home Department* [2008] UKHL 64, [2009] 1 All ER 559 at [37].
[602] [2006] UKHL 11, [2006] 2 AC 91 at [5] per Lord Bingham.

was; and the ECtHR held in *JM v UK* that in 2010 a same-sex couple would be regarded as a family.[603]

7.268   The boundaries between Article 8 and Article 12, which protects the right to marry and found a family, are not always distinct. It is clear, however, that Article 8 does not itself protect the right to found a family; it is only applicable once family life is established, although the ambit of Article 8 will be wider for the purposes of Article 14.[604]

(a) *Couples*

7.269   Formal unions, such as a valid marriage between husband and wife, clearly fall within family life.[605] Engagements may also give rise to family life, if supported by evidence of the parties' intention to marry.[606]

7.270   The ECtHR has accepted that 'de facto family ties' may exist in the absence of such a formalized relationship. In *Kroon v Netherlands* the ECtHR determined that factors such as cohabitation and the stability of the relationship may serve to demonstrate that a relationship has sufficient constancy to amount to family life.[607] Polygamous unions may also constitute family life.[608]

(b) *Homosexual and transsexual unions*

7.271   The ECtHR's approach to homosexual unions has evolved. In early ECtHR case law homosexual relationships were not protected as family life, although they were protected under the right to private life.[609] The ECtHR finally recognized that a stable relationship between cohabiting same-sex individuals was rightly classified as family life in *Schalk and Kopf v Austria*.[610] However, the ECtHR held that Article 8 read with Article 14 did not guarantee homosexuals the right to marry.[611]

7.272   A similar evolution has occurred in relation to transsexual relationships. In *Goodwin v UK*, in a departure from its earlier case law,[612] the ECtHR has held that the failure to recognize the acquired gender of a post-operative transsexual in order for that person to marry violated the right to private life and the right to marry under Article 12.[613] In *X, Y and Z v UK* the ECtHR found de facto family ties between X, a transsexual, Y, his female partner, and Z, Y 's child by artificial insemination.[614] In light of these judgments and the new approach to homosexual unions, it is likely that if an appropriate case reached Strasbourg, the Court would recognize that transsexual unions also fall within the meaning of family life.[615]

---

[603] (2010) 30 BHRC 60.

[604] See, eg *EB v France* (2008) 47 EHRR 21.

[605] See *Benes v Austria* (1992) 72 DR 271.

[606] *Wakefield v UK* (1990) 66 DR 251.

[607] (1994) 19 EHRR 263.

[608] *A and A v Netherlands* (1992) 72 DR 118.

[609] *Secretary of State for Work and Pensions v M* [2006] UKHL 11, [2006] 2 AC 91 at [30], though the ECtHR indicated in *JM v UK* (2010) 30 BHRC 60 that a same-sex couple would nowadays be regarded as a family.

[610] App No 30141/04, 24 June 2010.

[611] See Art 14 at paras 7.507–7.515 below.

[612] See, eg *Rees v UK* (1987) 9 EHRR 56; *Cossey v UK* (1991) 13 EHRR 622.

[613] *Goodwin v UK* (2002) 35 EHRR 447.

[614] (1997) 24 EHRR 143.

[615] *H v Finland* App No 37359/09, concerning the automatic conversion of a transsexual's marriage into a civil partnership, may prove to be such a case. It was communicated to the Government in April 2010. See also the evolutive approach in *JM v UK* (2010) 30 BHRC 60.

In this area, the domestic approach has proved more flexible than that of the ECtHR. 7.273
The narrow approach to 'family life' taken by the ECtHR in *S v UK*[616] was not followed
in *Ghaidan v Godin-Mendoza*[617] or *Fitzpatrick v Sterling Housing Association Ltd*,[618] the
House of Lords holding that the terms 'spouse' and 'family' respectively under the Rent
Act 1977 could apply to a homosexual partner.

However, in *Secretary of State for Work and Pensions v M* the House of Lords adopted 7.274
a narrow view, holding that on the present state of Strasbourg jurisprudence homosexual
relationships did not fall within the scope of the right to respect for family life. While
their Lordships anticipated the shift in the ECtHR's case law that has now occurred, it
'was not for the courts of this country to pre-empt that decision'.[619] At the time of writing, the ECtHR decision in *Schalk and Kopf* has not yet been considered by the domestic courts, but in light of the progressive domestic decisions in this area it is likely to be
welcomed.[620]

Many of the issues relating to recognition of same-sex couples should no longer arise 7.275
in domestic law as the Civil Partnership Act 2004 permits the legal union of same-sex
couples in a manner analogous to marriage.

(c) *Parents and children*
The biological parent/child relationship is well-recognized in Article 8 case law.[621] 7.276
The ECtHR has held that 'the mutual enjoyment by parent and child of each other's
company constitutes a fundamental element of family life'.[622] In *Boughanemi v France*
the Court held that the tie between parent and child, regardless of whether the child is
legitimate, could only be broken in 'exceptional circumstances'.[623]

Biological ties give rise to a strong presumption of family life,[624] but it is not conclusive. 7.277
In *X v UK* the ECmHR held that no sufficient nexus existed between the biological father
and an unborn foetus,[625] and a similar result was reached in *G v Netherlands* concerning
a sperm donor.[626]

The ECtHR has accepted that family life subsists between estranged parent and child 7.278
(following a relationship break-up or period of separation) provided a genuine and close
tie continues to exist.[627]

The right of a child to identify his or her parents is encompassed by family life.[628] 7.279
However, such cases may raise others' Article 8 rights that conflict with the applicant's
right to family life. In *Odievre v France*, for example, the Grand Chamber held that there

---

[616] (1986) 47 DR 274.
[617] [2004] UKHL 30, [2004] 2 AC 557.
[618] [2001] 1 AC 27.
[619] [2006] UKHL 11, [2006] 2 AC 91 at [30] per Lord Nicholls. The ECtHR found a violation of Art 14
taken with Art 1 of Protocol 1: *JM v UK* (2010) 30 BHRC 60.
[620] See *HC (Malaysia) Secretary of State for the Home Department* [2010] EWCA Civ 1014.
[621] *Ahmut v Netherlands* (1996) 24 EHRR 62.
[622] *B v UK* (1988) 10 EHRR 87. See also *EM (Lebanon) v Secretary of State for the Home Department* [2008]
UKHL 64, [2009] 1 All ER 559 at [6].
[623] (1996) 22 EHRR 228, para 35.
[624] *Keegan v Ireland* (1994) 18 EHRR 342.
[625] (1980) 19 DR 244.
[626] (1993) 16 EHRR CD 38.
[627] *Berrehab v Netherlands* (1988) 11 EHRR 322.
[628] *Mikuli v Croatia* [2002] 1 FCR 720; *Jevremovic v Serbia* [2007] 2 FCR 671; *S v London Borough of
Lambeth* [2007] 1 FLR 152.

was no violation of Article 8 or 14 in circumstances where the applicant was unable to obtain information about her natural family owing to French rules governing 'anonymous births' that protected the mother's interest in anonymity.[629]

7.280　　Other familial relationships, such as that between grandparents and grandchildren[630] and siblings,[631] may also constitute family life, as may adoption[632] and foster relationships,[633] depending always on the facts. The courts will examine factors such as contact, length of the relationship, dependency, and emotional ties.

7.281　　Family life also encompasses proceedings aimed at dissolving legal family ties. In *Mizzi v Malta*, for example, the ECtHR accepted that a legal presumption of the husband's paternity of a child born during the period of the marriage, combined with the absence of any domestic remedy by which he could have challenged it, violated his right to respect for both private and family life. The ECtHR found a violation of Article 8, as this was 'a situation in which a legal presumption is allowed to prevail over biological reality'.[634]

7.282　　The ECtHR has held on a number of occasions that the right to family life does not encompass a right to adoption.[635] Refusal to permit adoption may, however, fall within the ambit of private life for the purposes of Article 14.[636]

(d) Immigration

7.283　　The right for an 'alien' to enter or to reside in a particular country is not guaranteed by respect for family life,[637] but the ECtHR has held that the refusal of entry or the removal of a person from a country where close members of his family are living may amount to an infringement of the right to respect for family life.[638] If the family can go elsewhere to re-establish itself the ECtHR will hold that the immigration procedures do not violate that right.[639] Similarly, there may be no violation if the disruption is of the applicant's own making because he or she has breached immigration controls.[640] In many cases, however, an interference with Article 8(1) will easily be established and the state will be required to justify its interference under Article 8(2).[641]

7.284　　In *Uner v Netherlands*, the leading case on immigration and the right to family life, the ECtHR considered the withdrawal of a residence permit and deportation of a Turkish immigrant who had founded a family in the Netherlands and then committed a series of criminal offences.[642] The court accepted that the state was pursuing the legitimate aims under Article 8(2) of protecting public safety and preventing crime, and set out a variety

---

[629] (2003) 14 BHRC 526.

[630] *GHB v UK* [2000] EHRLR 545.

[631] *Mustafa and Armag an Akın v Turkey* App No 4694/03, 6 April 2010; *Senthuran v Secretary of State for the Home Department* [2004] EWCA Civ 950, [2004] 4 All ER 365.

[632] *Pini and ors v Romania* App Nos 78028/01 and 78030/01, 22 June 2004.

[633] *Gaskin v UK* (1989) 12 EHRR 36.

[634] [2006] 1 FCR 256 at [113]. See also *Kroon* (1994) 19 EHRR 263, para 40.

[635] See, eg *Fretté v France* [2003] 2 FCR 39.

[636] *EB v France* (2008) 47 EHRR 21.

[637] *Abdulaziz, Cabales and Balkandali v UK* (1985) 7 EHRR 471.

[638] *Moustaquim v Belgium* (1991) 13 EHRR 802.

[639] *Gul v Switzerland* (1996) 22 EHRR 93.

[640] *X v UK* (1987) 11 EHRR 48.

[641] See, eg *Omoregie v Norway* App No 265/07, 31 July 2008.

[642] (2007) 45 EHRR 14. In the domestic context see, eg *HM (Iraq) v Secretary of State for the Home Department* [2010] EWCA Civ 1322.

of factors that had to be taken into account in the proportionality analysis, including the seriousness and nature of the offence, the length of the applicant's stay in the country from which he or she was to be expelled, the nationalities of the various persons concerned, whether there were children of the marriage, and the seriousness of the difficulties the spouse was likely to encounter in the applicant's country of origin. The Court also made it explicit that the best interests of the children were a relevant consideration in the analysis. Weighing up all these factors, the Court found that the state had struck a fair balance between state interests and respect for the applicant's family life, and noted that if his children followed him to Turkey they would still be able to return to the Netherlands to visit other family members by virtue of their Dutch citizenship.

A significant proportion of domestic decisions on family life under Article 8 concerns   7.285
the removal of immigrants and asylum seekers from the United Kingdom. In general, it is accepted that Article 8(1) will be engaged by interference with family ties existing in the United Kingdom, but immigration control will almost always constitute a legitimate aim for removal under Article 8(2).[643] The critical issue will therefore be the proportionality of the interference. In a rare single judgment of the Appellate Committee in *Huang v Secretary of State for the Home Department*, their Lordships held:

In an article 8 case where [the proportionality] question is reached, the ultimate question for the appellate immigration authority is whether the refusal of leave to enter or remain, in circumstances where the life of the family cannot reasonably be expected to be enjoyed elsewhere, taking full account of all considerations weighing in favour of the refusal, prejudices the family life of the applicant in a manner sufficiently serious to amount to a breach of the fundamental right protected by article 8.[644]

According to their Lordships, it was not necessary that a claim pass a further test of 'exceptionality',[645] but it would be a 'small minority' of cases that would succeed under Article 8.[646]

Since the decision in *Huang*, the House of Lords has accepted that Strasbourg author-   7.286
ity suggests that 'it will rarely be proportionate' to order removal of a spouse to a country where the other spouse cannot reasonably be expected to reside or to sever 'a genuine and subsisting relationship between parent and child'.[647] In *ZH (Tanzania) v Secretary of State for the Home Department* the Supreme Court held that when the deportation of a parent also entailed the removal of a child, the best interests of the child were a primary consideration.[648] Lord Kerr stated: 'Where the best interests of the child clearly favour a certain course, that course should be followed unless countervailing reasons of considerable force displace them.'[649] This approach arguably goes further than the ECtHR has done, but it is undoubtedly warranted by the provisions of the United Nations Convention on the Rights of the Child (UNCRC).[650]

---

[643] See, eg *LK (Serbia) v Secretary of State for the Home Department* [2007] EWCA Civ 1554 at [8].

[644] [2007] UKHL 11, [2007] 2 AC 167 at [20].

[645] Correcting a misinterpretation of the House of Lords' decision in *R (Razgar) v Secretary of State for the Home Department* [2004] UKHL 27, [2004] 2 AC 368.

[646] *Huang v Secretary of State for the Home Department* [2007] UKHL 11, [2007] 2 AC 167 at [20].

[647] *EB (Kosovo) v Secretary of State for the Home Department* [2008] UKHL 41, [2008] 3 WLR 178 at [12]. See also *Chikwamba v Secretary of State for the Home Department* [2008] UKHL 40, [2008] 1 WLR 1420.

[648] [2011] UKSC 4.

[649] Ibid at [46].

[650] The UK lifted its reservation to the UNCRC concerning immigration matters in 2008.

7.287   In cases where an appellant's right to a family life may be breached in the country to which he or she is removed, the domestic courts have held that removal will only be unlawful if it would 'so flagrantly violate [the appellant's] Article 8 rights as to completely deny or nullify those rights'.[651] In *EM (Lebanon) v Secretary of State for the Home Department*, the House of Lords found that the return of a mother and child to Lebanon where the child would be taken into the father's custody constituted such a flagrant denial.[652]

5. Home

7.288   In *Buckley v UK* the ECtHR highlighted that whether a habitation is a 'home' is highly fact-specific, and depends on 'the existence of sufficient and continuous links'.[653] The House of Lords has suggested that 'home' constitutes the place where a person 'lives and to which he returns and which forms the centre of his existence'.[654]

7.289   'Home' has been held to include a long-term hospital stay,[655] second homes,[656] and offices[657] in certain circumstances.

7.290   *Gillow v UK* makes clear that the notion of 'home' may extend to the place where one intends to live.[658] The applicants were absent from their house in Guernsey for 18 years because the husband's job caused him to travel. The Government refused the couple a new residence permit when they finally returned, arguing that this was not their home. The ECmHR and ECtHR held that, in this case, there was a right to 're-establish home life'.

7.291   So far, however, the Court has never found a violation of the notion of respect for home by a failure to provide a particular home, although it has accepted that a positive obligation to provide a home may arise in some circumstances.[659] This right may also be covered by the developing jurisprudence on legitimate expectations under Protocol 1, Article 1.[660]

7.292   The question of the compatibility of possession orders with the right to respect for the home has vexed Strasbourg and the domestic courts. The Commission rejected as inadmissible complaints against possession orders. In *Ure v UK* the applicant's tenancy came to an end on expiry of a notice to quit given by his wife, formerly a joint tenant with him, and possession was ordered.[661] The ECmHR held that his complaint under Article 8 was manifestly ill-founded because the alleged interference with his rights under the article was justified under Article 8(2).

---

[651] *R (Ullah) v Special Adjudicator* [2004] UKHL 26, [2004] 2 AC 323; approving *Devaseelan v Secretary of State for the Home Department* [2002] UKIAT 702.
[652] [2008] UKHL 64, [2008] 2 FLR 2067 at [37].
[653] (1996) 23 EHRR 101.
[654] *London Borough of Harrow v Qazi* [2003] UKHL 43, [2004] 1 AC 983 at [8] per Lord Bingham.
[655] *Collins v UK* App No 11909/02, 15 October 2002; *R v North and East Devon District Health Authority, ex p Coughlan* [2001] QB 213.
[656] *Demades v Turkey* [2003] ECHR 16219/90.
[657] *Niemietz v Germany* (1992) 16 EHRR 97; *Peev v Bulgaria* [2007] ECHR 64209/01.
[658] (1986) 11 EHRR 335.
[659] See ch 6, para 6.109 above.
[660] See ch 8, para 8.02.
[661] App No 28027/95, 27 November 1996. See also *Wood v UK* (1997) 24 EHRR CD 69.

Subsequently, the ECtHR has found that possession and eviction proceedings must   7.293
be attended by procedural safeguards.[662] In *McCann v UK*, the Court held that as regards
those safeguards, whenever a person risked losing his or her home there must be a possibility of having the proportionality of the eviction measure determined by an independent tribunal.[663] A similar result was reached in *R v North and East Devon District Health
Authority, ex p Coughlan* in which the Court of Appeal found that respect for the home
obliged the health authority to act fairly in removing a disabled resident from a care
home after it had promised her that she could remain there for life.[664]

The House of Lords considered the applicability of Article 8 to repossession proceed-   7.294
ings in a series of cases. After adopting too narrow a view of Article 8(1) in *London
Borough of Harrow v Qazi*,[665] a majority of the seven-member board of the House of
Lords concluded in *Kay v Lambeth London Borough Council* that a possession order
would infringe Article 8(1), but that the county courts could work on the assumption
that domestic law satisfied the requirements of Article 8(2) and would not generally
need to apply the proportionality test.[666] Article 8(2) would be relevant only in cases
where the legislation itself could be impugned. A majority of the Lords reached the same
conclusion in *Doherty v Birmingham City Council*.[667]

In *Kay v UK* the ECtHR favoured the minority approach in *Doherty* finding that an   7.295
individual resisting possession should in principle be able to have the proportionality of
the measure determined by an independent tribunal in the light of the relevant principles under Article 8, notwithstanding that, under domestic law, the right of occupation
had come to an end.[668] The Supreme Court very swiftly adopted the approach of the
ECtHR in three housing cases heard soon after the ECtHR decision. The court emphasized that it would be rare for proportionality to be seriously arguable.[669]

6. Correspondence

The right to respect for one's correspondence is a right to uninterrupted and uncensored   7.296
communication with others. In a telephone-tapping case, *Malone v UK*, the ECtHR
found that the British Government violated Article 8 when it intercepted the phone calls
of the applicant, an antique dealer convicted of receiving stolen goods.[670] This decision
has been applied to the monitoring of office correspondence including emails.[671]

The majority of cases concerning correspondence relate to interception of prisoners'   7.297
phone calls and letters. The ECtHR has taken a consistently strict approach to such
interference, finding that while some measure of control over prisoners' correspondence

---

[662] *Connors v UK* (2005) 40 EHRR 9.
[663] [2008] LGR 474.
[664] [2001] QB 213. Cf *Collins v UK* App No 11909/02, 15 October 2002.
[665] [2003] UKHL 43, [2004] 1 AC 983.
[666] (2006) 20 BHRC 33.
[667] [2008] UKHL 57.
[668] App No 37341/06, 21 September 2010.
[669] *Manchester City Council v Pinnock* [2010] UKSC 45; *London Borough of Hounslow v Powell; Leeds City
Council and Hall* [2011] UKSC 8.
[670] (1984) 7 EHRR 14.
[671] See, eg *Halford v UK* (1997) 24 EHRR 523; *Copland v UK* (2007) 25 BHRC 216.

may be justified, 'indiscriminate, routine checking' will violate Article 8.[672] In *Szuluk v UK* the ECtHR considered that the monitoring of a prisoner's correspondence with a doctor by a prison medical officer violated Article 8.[673]

7.298   One of the leading domestic cases on the standard of review under the Human Rights Act, *R (Daly) v Secretary of State for the Home Department*, concerned inspection of a prisoner's privileged legal correspondence.[674] The House of Lords held that the prison's policy interfered with the prisoner's rights to a significantly greater extent than could be justified.

F. ARTICLE 9: FREEDOM OF THOUGHT, CONSCIENCE, AND RELIGION

7.299   Article 9 protects the rights to hold religious and non-religious beliefs, to change those beliefs, and to manifest them in 'worship, teaching, practice and observance', whether alone or with others, in public or in private. In emphasizing the importance of freedom of thought, conscience, and religion, the ECtHR has stated that:

> Freedom of thought, conscience and religion is one of the foundations of a 'democratic society' within the meaning of the Convention. It is, in its religious dimension, one of the most vital elements that go to make up the identity of believers and their conception of life, but it is also a precious asset for atheists, agnostics, sceptics and the unconcerned. The pluralism indissociable from a democratic society, which has been dearly won over the centuries, depends on it.[675]

7.300   The right to hold and change beliefs is often said to be absolute, while the right to manifest one's religion or beliefs can be limited under Article 9(2).[676] However, there is often no clear distinction between 'holding' and 'manifesting' beliefs, as many religions have an inherent requirement that their followers proselytize. The need to 'bear witness in word and deed' is bound up with the very existence of the conviction itself.[677] Indeed, without a right to proselytize the 'freedom to change one's religion or belief, enshrined in Article 9, would be likely to remain a dead letter'.[678] Nonetheless, the distinction between holding and manifesting a belief remains critical to the application of Article 9.

7.301   It is apparent that Article 9 will often overlap with other Convention protections, most notably Articles 10, 11, and 14, and Protocol 1, Article 2. In cases raising issues under both Articles 9 and 10 an applicant's complaints are often considered solely under Article 10 if possible (perhaps because the reach of Article 10(1) is clearer than that of 9(1)).[679]

---

[672] See, eg *Jankauskas v Lithuania* [2005] ECHR 59304/00; *AB v Netherlands* (2003) 37 EHRR 48; *Wasilewski v Poland* (2004) 38 EHRR 10; *Petrov v Bulgaria* App No 15197/02, 22 May 2008.

[673] [2009] ECHR 845.

[674] [2001] UKHL 26, [2001] 2 AC 532.

[675] *Kokkinakis v Greece* (1994) 17 EHRR 397, para 31.

[676] See, eg *Darby v Sweden* Series A No 187, 9 May 1989, para 44; ECtHR judgment: (1991) 13 EHRR 774.

[677] *Kokkinakis v Greece* (1994) 17 EHRR 397, para 31.

[678] Ibid.

[679] See, eg *Paturel v France* App No 54968/00, 22 December 2005; *R (Singh) v Chief Constable of West Midlands Police* [2006] EWCA Civ 1118, [2007] 2 All ER 297.

Article 9 has not had equivalent impact to some of the other qualified rights, notably   7.302
Article 10, in Strasbourg or the domestic courts.[680] Claims fail either on the grounds
that there has been no interference with a 'manifestation' of belief[681] or, increasingly, on
the basis that such an interference is justified.[682]

1. 'Everyone'

The rights protected by Article 9 are guaranteed to 'everyone' (including 'aliens', regard-   7.303
less of whether they are yet resident in the state concerned).[683]

While this primarily refers to individuals, it also encompasses churches and associa-   7.304
tions with religious or philosophical aims, both in their own capacity and as representative of their members.[684] The Grand Chamber has held that Article 9 must be interpreted
in light of Article 11, and that, consequently, the organization of religious communities
must be protected by Article 9, as 'the believers' right to freedom of religion encompasses
the expectation that the community will be allowed to function peacefully, free from
arbitrary state intervention'.[685]

2. Freedom of thought, conscience, and religion

(a) *Scope of the freedom*

Article 9 protects a very broad range of beliefs, including both religious and non-religious.   7.305
Belief systems based on personal morality, such as pacifism[686] and veganism,[687] are protected by the Convention. The ECtHR has not yet considered whether political convictions, such as republicanism, are within the ambit of Article 9.[688]

In order to attract the protection of Article 9, the thoughts or beliefs must attain a   7.306
'certain level of cogency, seriousness, cohesion and importance'.[689] In *Campbell and Cosans
v UK* the ECtHR distinguished between 'beliefs' (protected by Article 9) and 'convictions'
(protected by Protocol 1, Article 2) on the one hand, and 'opinions' and 'ideas' (protected
by Article 10) on the other, though in particular cases these categories may overlap.[690]
Whether the applicant can show that he or she holds a belief rather than a lesser conviction, opinion, or idea is sometimes difficult to predict and will turn on the facts of the
particular case.

---

[680] See Hopkins and Yeginsu, 'Religious Liberty in British Courts: A Critique and Some Guidance' (2008)
49 Harv Int LJ; available at <http://www.harvardilj.org/online/134>.

[681] See, eg *Ahmad v UK* (1981) 4 EHRR 126; *Copsey v Devon Clays Ltd* [2005] EWCA Civ 932, [2005]
IRLR 811; *R (SB) v Governors of Denbigh High School* [2006] UKHL 15, [2007] 1 AC 100.

[682] *Leyla Sahin v Turkey* (2007) 44 EHRR 5; *Surayanda v Welsh Ministers* [2007] EWCA Civ 893.

[683] *Darby v Sweden* Series A No 187, 9 May 1989. See, further, Jayawickrama, *The Judicial Application of
Human Rights Law* (Cambridge: Cambridge University Press, 2002) 641, n 8.

[684] See, eg *X and Church of Scientology v Sweden* (1979) 16 DR 68. Such churches or associations may be
considered 'victims' within the meaning of Art 34 if they are non-governmental organizations: *Holy Monasteries
v Greece* (1997) 23 EHRR 387, para 47.

[685] *Hasan and Chaush v Bulgaria* (2002) 34 EHRR 55. See also *Kimlya and ors v Russia* [2009] ECHR
76836/01.

[686] *Arrowsmith v UK* (1978) 3 EHRR 218.

[687] *H v UK* (1992) 16 EHRR CD 44, 45; *Jakóbski v Poland* (2010) 30 BHRC 417.

[688] The point was not argued in *McGuinness v UK* App No 39511/98, 8 June 1999.

[689] *Campbell and Cosans v UK* (1982) 4 EHRR 293, para 36.

[690] Ibid.

7.307   The judgment of the House of Lords in *R (Williamson) v Secretary of State for Education and Skills* provides guidance for domestic courts determining whether a particular belief falls within Article 9.[691] Lord Nicholls reiterated that Article 9 protects non-religious and non-theistic views:

> The atheist, the agnostic and the sceptic are as much entitled to freedom to hold and manifest their beliefs as the theist. These beliefs are placed on an equal footing for the purpose of this guaranteed freedom. Thus, if its manifestation is to attract protection under Article 9 a non-religious belief, as much as a religious belief, must satisfy the modest threshold requirements implicit in this article. In particular, for its manifestation to be protected by article 9 a non-religious belief must relate to an aspect of human life or behaviour of comparable importance to that normally found with religious beliefs.[692]

7.308   However, the domestic courts have also taken the view that not all opinions or convictions, however sincerely or deeply held, constitute beliefs in the sense protected by Article 9 does not protect pro-hunting views, despite the hunters' view that 'hunting is at the very core of mankind's psyche'.[693] Nor does it protect beliefs that are not founded on religious or philosophical viewpoints, such as a belief that children should not be raised by a same-sex couple.[694]

7.309   Freedom of religion has been held to include a negative aspect not to be required to disclose one's religion. In the case of *Sinan Isik v Turkey* the Strasbourg Court ruled that it violated Article 9 to require a citizen to indicate his or her religion in his or her application for an ID card or formally ask for the religion box to be left empty.[695] The judgment has potentially broad ramifications for all official documents or registers.

(b) *State activities*

7.310   The existence of a state church does not, in itself, infringe Article 9, provided the system includes specific safeguards for the individual's freedom of religion. An individual may not be forced to be directly involved in religious activities against his will (unless he has voluntarily joined as a minister of that religion),[696] nor can the state compel an individual to pay taxes to a church.[697] However, in *C v UK* the ECmHR found no violation of Article 9 where there is a duty to pay general taxes that are not earmarked for a specific religious purpose, even if the state uses some of the money to support religious communities or religious activities.[698]

7.311   Article 9 does not guarantee a right to refuse to perform military service on the grounds of belief. In *Bayatyan v Armenia* the ECtHR refused to find that the applicant's two-year prison sentence for failure to perform military service violated Article 9 on the basis that Article 4(3)(b) left it open to states to choose whether to recognize conscientious objectors

---

[691] [2005] UKHL 15, [2005] 2 AC 246.

[692] Ibid at [24].

[693] *R (Countryside Alliance) v Attorney General* [2006] EWCA Civ 817 at [177] [2007] QB 305; citing *Chassagnou and ors v France* (1999) 29 EHRR 615. Confirmed by the House of Lords at [2007] UKHL 52, [2008] 1 AC 719.

[694] *McClintock v Department of Constitutional Affairs* [2008] IRLR 29.

[695] App No 21924/05, 2 February 2010.

[696] *X v Denmark* (1976) 5 DR 157.

[697] *Darby v Sweden* (1990) 13 EHRR 774.

[698] (1983) 37 DR 142.

in their arrangements for military service.[699] The case has recently been heard by the Grand Chamber.

The House of Lords considered the taxation of religious establishments in *Church of*   7.312
Jesus Christ of Latter Day Saints v Gallagher.[700] In a narrow interpretation of the ambit of Article 9, it found no interference with freedom of religion taken with Article 14 where the Mormon church was unable to claim an exemption on local government rates because the church was not open to the public. Lord Scott dissented, arguing that levying taxation on a place of religious worship would be capable of breaching Article 9, and therefore withholding relief from the rates fell within its ambit for the purposes of Article 14.

The ECtHR has frequently emphasized the state's role as 'the neutral and impartial   7.313
organizer of the exercise of various religions, faiths and beliefs', and held that this duty of neutrality and impartiality is incompatible with any power on the state's part to assess the legitimacy of religious beliefs or the way in which those beliefs are expressed.[701] Accordingly, the state's role is to ensure mutual tolerance between opposing groups and, in case of conflict, 'not to remove the cause of the tension by eliminating pluralism, but to ensure that the competing groups tolerate each other'.[702] Any regulatory functions carried out by the state in relation to religious organizations must therefore be undertaken with complete neutrality.[703]

The domestic courts have similarly emphasized that the role of the state and the   7.314
courts is a neutral one. In a dispute between a local authority and prospective Christian foster parents who opposed same-sex relationships on religious grounds, Munby LJ set out the position of the common law, which mirrors the Convention approach:

> The starting point of the common law is thus respect for an individual's religious principles coupled with an essentially neutral view of religious beliefs and benevolent tolerance of cultural and religious diversity. A secular judge must be wary of straying across the well-recognized divide between church and state. It is not for a judge to weigh one religion against another. The court recognises no religious distinctions and generally speaking passes no judgment on religious beliefs or on the tenets, doctrines or rules of any particular section of society. All are entitled to equal respect.[704]

3. Manifestation of one's religion or beliefs

The right to manifest one's religion or beliefs complements the primary right of freedom of   7.315
thought, conscience, and religion. In deciding whether an applicant's conduct constitutes

---

[699] [2009] ECHR 23459/03.

[700] [2008] UKHL 56, [2008] 1 WLR 1852.

[701] *Manoussakis and ors v Greece* Reports of Judgments and Decisions 1996-IV, 26 September 1996, 1365; *Hasan and Chaush v Bulgaria* (2002) 34 EHRR 55, para 78; *Moscow Branch of the Salvation Army v Russia* (2006) 44 EHRR 912, para 58.

[702] *Serif v Greece* App No 38178/97, ECHR 1999-IX, para 53; *Supreme Holy Council of the Muslim Community v Bulgaria* [2004] ECHR 39023/97. Cf *Mirolubovs and ors v Latvia* App No 798/05, 15 September 2009.

[703] *Metropolitan Church of Bessarabia v Moldova* [2001] ECHR 45701/99. Cf the ECtHR's approach to manifestation of belief in *Leyla Sahin v Turkey* (2007) 44 EHRR 5 discussed at para 7.328 below.

[704] *R (Johns) v Derby City Council* [2011] EWHC 375 (Admin) at [41]. See also *Ladele v London Borough of Islington* [2009] EWCA Civ 1357, [2010] IRLR 211; *Catholic Care v Charity Commission* [2010] EWHC 520 (Ch), [2010] 4 All ER 1041; *R (E) v The Governing Body of JFS and ors* [2009] UKSC 15, [2010] 1 All ER 319 at [157]; *Macfarlane v Relate* [2010] EWCA Civ 771, [2010] IRLR 872 at [23]–[25].

a manifestation, the ECtHR first identifies the nature and scope of the belief. If the belief takes the form of a perceived obligation to act in a specific way, then, in principle, doing that act pursuant to that belief is itself a manifestation of that belief in practice. In such cases the act is 'intimately linked' to the belief.[705]

7.316   The Strasbourg organs have generally taken a very narrow approach to manifestation, finding that there must be a direct connection between the belief and manifestation. For example, where a pacifist distributed leaflets to soldiers urging them to decline service in Northern Ireland, this was not an expression of her 'pacifist ideas' as it had a broader aim—to contest British policy in Northern Ireland;[706] and the refusal by a church minister to perform administrative duties in protest at amendments to national abortion legislation was not an expression of his anti-abortion beliefs.[707]

7.317   As these cases illustrate, manifestation of belief is generally afforded close legal protection only where it is in the private sphere of the practice of a religion, and not where the manifestation of faith has an effect on the practices and behaviour of others in the secular world. For example, in *Pichon v France*, the ECtHR refused to find a violation of Article 9 when pharmacists were convicted for refusing to prescribe contraceptive pills, on grounds of conscience.[708]

7.318   The ECtHR has recently showed some signs of relaxing this strict approach. In *Jakobski v Poland* the Court accepted that the refusal of a Buddhist prisoner's request for vegetarian food fell within the protection of Article 9 even though vegetarianism was not a mandatory requirement of Buddhism.[709] The Court stated that where the applicant's decision 'can be regarded as motivated or inspired by a religion and was not unreasonable' Article 9 would be engaged.[710] It did not explicitly distinguish its earlier case law and it remains to be seen whether this approach will be adopted in the future.

7.319   The domestic courts have considered what constitutes a manifestation of a religion or belief on a number of occasions. In general, they have taken as restrictive a view as the European Court. In a rare example of a broad interpretation of manifestation, the House of Lords in *R (Williamson) v Secretary of State for Education and Skills* found that parents of children in a private Christian school who wished teachers to impose corporal punishment upon the pupils were manifesting a religion or belief.[711] Their Lordships held that the statutory ban on corporal punishment in schools interfered with the parents' rights under Article 9(1) (although the ban was justified under Article 9(2)), because the essence of the parents' belief was that it was part of proper upbringing that children should, where necessary, be disciplined in a particular way at home and at school, and so, when they placed their children in a school that practised corporal punishment, the parents were manifesting that belief.

7.320   Like the ECtHR, the domestic courts require a causal link between the belief and the manifestation. For example, in *Campbell v South Northamptonshire District Council*, an

---

[705] *Application 10295/82 v UK* (1983) 6 EHRR 558; *R (Williamson) v Secretary of State for Education and Employment* [2005] UKHL 15, [2005] 2 AC 246; *R (Watkins-Singh) v Governing Body of Aberdare Girls' School* [2008] EWHC 1865 (Admin), [2008] ELR 561.

[706] *Arrowsmith v UK* (1978) 3 EHRR 218.

[707] *Knudsen v Norway* App No 11045/84, 42 DR 247.

[708] App No 49853/99, 2 October 2001.

[709] App No 18429/06, 7 December 2010. See also *R (Imran Bashir) v The Independent Adjudicator and anor* [2011] EWHC 1108 (Admin).

[710] App No 18429/06, 7 December 2010, para 45.

[711] [2005] UKHL 15, [2005] 2 AC 246.

appeal against the refusal of housing benefit, the Court of Appeal found no violation of Article 9 or 14 as there was no link between the refusal of housing benefit for members of a religious housing cooperative living on church property and the manifestation of their beliefs.[712] They could have elected to have entered into a commercial relationship with the church, or have lived communally in property let from a housing association—neither would have required any alteration or diminution of their communal living practices.

In *Ghai v Newcastle City Council* the High Court found that a desire to be cremated on an open-air funeral pyre was a manifestation of Hindu belief because it was 'sufficiently close to the core of one strand of orthodox Hinduism'.[713] The court distinguished the position of Sikhs, for whom open-air cremation was simply a matter of tradition rather than of belief. 7.321

4. Interference with manifestation of religion or beliefs

The threshold for establishing an interference with a manifestation of belief is generally a high one. Where an individual is left with a choice whether or not to comply with his or her religious obligations, Strasbourg has traditionally found that no interference will arise. Thus, in *Karaduman v Turkey*, in which a Muslim woman challenged a refusal to let her graduate from university unless she was photographed without her headscarf, the Commission found that the fact that the applicant had chosen to pursue higher education in a secular university meant that she had submitted to its rules and no interference was established.[714] 7.322

The ECtHR made the same point in the context of restrictions on kosher slaughterhouses in *Jewish Liturgical Association Cha'are Shalom Ve Tesedek v France* stating: 7.323

. . . there would be interference with the freedom to manifest one's religion only if the illegality of performing ritual slaughter made it impossible for ultra-orthodox Jews to eat meat from animals slaughtered in accordance with the religious prescriptions they considered applicable.[715]

In the employment field the ECmHR, in *Ahmad v UK*, dismissed a complaint in which a teacher demanded that his employers accommodate his obligation to attend religious worship on a Friday. The Commission, finding that he remained free to resign if and when he found that his teaching obligations conflicted with his religious duties, dismissed his claim as manifestly ill-founded.[716] Similarly, in *Stedman v UK* the ECmHR rejected the complaint of a Christian applicant who had been dismissed for refusing to work on Sundays on the basis that the employee could resign.[717] 7.324

These cases are in stark contrast to the Court's approach to dismissal on the basis of religious belief per se. In *Ivanova v Bulgaria*, the Court found a 'flagrant violation' of the right to hold religious beliefs where a member of an evangelical community was dismissed from her teaching post because of her religious beliefs and affiliation with 7.325

---

[712] [2004] EWCA Civ 409, [2004] 3 All ER 387.
[713] [2009] EWHC 978 (Admin), [2009] NLJR 713 at [101]. The Court of Appeal ([2010] EWCA Civ 59, [2010] 3 All ER 380) allowed the appeal on a different point.
[714] (1993) 74 DR 93.
[715] (2000) 9 BHRC 27, para 80.
[716] (1981) 4 EHRR 126.
[717] (1997) 23 EHRR 168.

the community in question.[718] The distinction between dismissal for manifesting a belief and dismissal for holding such a belief seems too fine to support such contrary conclusions.

7.326　　Where manifestation of a belief is made impossible, an interference may be estab-lished. Prisoners, for example, are subject to the coercive power of the state and have no choice but to abide by its rules. Failure to permit them to take part in weekly worship[719] or restricting their access to a priest[720] violates their Article 9 rights. In *R (Imran Bashir) v The Independent Adjudicator and anor* the High Court recently held that disciplining a Muslim prisoner for failing to provide a urine sample while he was fasting interfered with Article 9.[721]

7.327　　The ECtHR has appeared willing to accept that an interference can arise where restric-tions make it practically difficult, if not impossible, to manifest a belief. In the admissi-bility decision, *Dahlab v Switzerland*, the ECtHR found that a prohibition on a female teacher wearing a headscarf while teaching in a primary school interfered with the man-ifestation of her religious beliefs despite the fact that she could in theory have taught at a private school where she could have worn the headscarf.[722] However, the Court found that the wearing of a headscarf might have a proselytizing effect on young children that outweighed the teacher's right to manifest her beliefs. Therefore, the interference was justified under Article 9(2) and the application was manifestly ill-founded.

7.328　　In the controversial decision in *Leyla Sahin v Turkey* (the 'Sahin' case) the Grand Chamber found that a ban on students wearing headscarves at the University of Istanbul interfered with the applicant's right to manifest her beliefs.[723] This was so despite the fact that the applicant had been able to wear the headscarf at her former university and chose to continue her studies abroad. However, the Grand Chamber held that the ban was a proportionate response to the need to promote secularism in Turkey. The Court took a different approach in *Ahmet Arslan and ors v Turkey* in which members of a reli-gious group toured the streets of Ankara in distinctive religious dress.[724] The Court found that their criminal convictions for wearing religious garb in public were unjusti-fied on the basis that dressing as they did in a public place did not pose the same threat to secularism as it did in public institutions.

7.329　　The leading House of Lords' decision on manifestation under Article 9 remains *R (SB) v Governors of Denbigh High School* (the 'Shabina Begum' case).[725] The claimant, a Muslim schoolgirl, attended a mixed-sex, multi-community school outside her family's catchment area. Female pupils were offered three options for the school uniform, which had been adopted in consultation with local mosques, and included a loose-fitting shal-war kameeze and headscarf. Contrary to school policy, the claimant wished to wear a 'jilbab', a long coat-like garment that was considered to represent stricter adherence to the tenets of the Muslim faith. She argued that the uniform policy interfered with her right to manifest her religion under Article 9(1).

---

[718] (2007) 23 BHRC 208.
[719] *Kuznetsov v Ukraine* [2003] ECHR 39042/97.
[720] *Poltoratskiy v Ukraine* [2003] ECHR 38812/97.
[721] [2011] EWHC 1108 (Admin).
[722] [2001] ECHR 42393/98.
[723] (2005) 41 EHRR 8.
[724] App No 41135/98, 23 February 2010. Judgment available in French only.
[725] [2006] UKHL 15, [2007] 1 AC 100.

A majority of their Lordships accepted that Article 9(1) was 'engaged', as wearing the   7.330
jilbab was a sincere manifestation of her religious belief, but found that the refusal to
allow the claimant to attend school wearing a jilbab did not amount to an interference
with her right to manifest her religious beliefs. The case was determined shortly after the
decision of the Grand Chamber in the *Sahin* case, in which a ban on wearing a headscarf
at university was deemed to constitute an interference. Lord Hoffmann distinguished
Sahin on the basis that there were other schools that Shabina Begum might have attended
where she could wear the jilbab, while all the universities in Turkey imposed a similar
ban on headscarves. Notably, this choice-based rationale did not feature as part of the
ECtHR's reasoning in *Sahin*, despite the fact that the applicant had been able to wear
her headscarf at another university in Turkey and had chosen to continue her studies
abroad. The dissenting judges did not eschew this choice-based analysis. The House of
Lords is thus wedded to the unsatisfactory notion that if a claimant could have chosen
to avoid the dispute over the manifestation of his or her belief, there can have been no
interference for the purposes of Article 9.

The High Court has since applied the approach in *Shabina Begum* to challenges to   7.331
school uniform policy based on Article 9.[726] However, it reached a very different conclusion in *R (Watkins-Singh) v Governing Body of Aberdare Girls' High School*.[727] The claimant schoolgirl brought a complaint under the Race Relations Act 1976 alleging that the
school had discriminated against her in refusing to allow her to wear the Sikh 'kara' (a
thin silver bangle). Distinguishing the cases on justification under Article 9(2), the court
found that there was no justification for the indirect race discrimination suffered by the
claimant. In a passage fundamentally at odds with the approach of the European Court
in cases such as *Dahlab* and *Sahin*, the judge stated:

. . . there is a very important obligation imposed on the school [by the Race Relations Act 1976]
to ensure that its pupils are first tolerant as to the religious rites and beliefs of other races and other
religions and second to respect other people's religious wishes. Without those principles being
adopted in a school, it is difficult to see how a cohesive and tolerant multi-cultural society can be
built in this country.[728]

The judgment illustrates the unsatisfactory legal position whereby the statutory dis-   7.332
crimination regimes relating to race, religion, and belief may provide greater protection
for religious freedom to those who are caught by them than the protection accorded to
everyone by Article 9.[729]

5. Limitations under Article 9(2)

Article 9 is a qualified right, and the right to manifest one's beliefs and convictions may   7.333
therefore be subject to the limitations set out in Article 9(2). It is notable that Article 9
is the only qualified right in the Convention that does not permit the state to interfere
with it on the basis of 'national security'.

---

[726] *R (Playfoot) v Governing Body of Millais School* [2007] EWHC 1698 (Admin), [2007] ELR 484; *R (X) v The Headteacher of Y School* [2007] EWHC 298 (Admin), [2007] ELR 278.
[727] [2008] EWHC 1865 (Admin), [2008] ELR 561.
[728] Ibid at [84].
[729] See discussion under Art 14 at para 7.529 below.

7.334   Any such limitation must meet the threefold test set out in *Sunday Times v UK*:[730] it must be (i) prescribed by law; (ii) in pursuit of a 'legitimate aim' set out in Article 9(2); and (iii) 'necessary in a democratic society', which includes a requirement of proportionality.

7.335   As under the other qualified rights, the first two limbs of the test are generally satisfied without much difficulty,[731] and the central dispute concerns the application of the proportionality standard. On occasion, the European Court has adopted a rigorous approach to proportionality under Article 9(2). Where, for example, an applicant complains of a criminal or civil penalty arising as a result of the manifestation of his or her beliefs, the Court will scrutinize the state's justification carefully.

7.336   In *Kokkinakis v Greece* a criminal conviction of two Jehovah's Witnesses who engaged in door-to-door evangelism was held to have a legitimate aim, but to be a disproportionate response, because no consideration had been given to whether the couple had used improper means to evangelize; hence, there was a violation of Article 9.[732] Similarly, in the important case of *Thlimmenos v Greece* the Grand Chamber recognized that the exclusion of the applicant from the profession of chartered accountancy on account of a criminal conviction for religious objection to military service was disproportionate and in breach of Article 14 taken in conjunction with Article 9.[733]

7.337   A less-exacting approach is taken to complaints concerning failure to accommodate beliefs.[734] The ECtHR has consistently emphasized that in societies where several religions coexist it may be necessary to limit the right in order to reconcile the interests of the various groups and to ensure that all beliefs are respected.[735] For example, in *Dahlab v Switzerland*, the prohibition on a teacher wearing a headscarf at work was held not to have violated her right to freedom of religion, because it was designed to ensure the religious neutrality of the public education service in a society with diverse religious views and was therefore considered within the state's margin of appreciation.[736]

7.338   A majority of the Grand Chamber adopted the same approach in the *Sahin* case, upholding the prohibition on wearing headscarves in university on the basis that the principles of secularism and equality was fundamental to Turkish society.[737] Citing the words of the ECtHR in *Dahlab*, the majority found that the ban pursued a legitimate aim because the headscarf constituted a 'powerful external symbol . . . imposed on women by a religious precept' that infringed gender equality and posed a danger to the secular foundation of the Turkish state.[738] In a judgment notable for its deference to the arguments of the national authorities and courts, the Grand Chamber conducted only the briefest proportionality analysis, finding that the ban was within the margin of appreciation. In a strong dissent, Judge Tulkens stated that 'In a democratic society, I believe that it is necessary to seek to harmonise the principles of secularism, equality and liberty, not to weigh one against the other'.[739]

---

[730] (1979) 2 EHRR 245.

[731] For an example of cases in which the ECtHR found an interference not 'in accordance with law', see *Poltoratskiy v Ukraine* [2003] ECHR 38812/97; *Perry v Latvia* [2007] ECHR 30273/03.

[732] (1994) 17 EHRR 397.

[733] (2000) 31 EHRR 411. See also discussion at para 7.521 below.

[734] See, eg *McGuinness v UK* App No 39511/98, 8 June 1999.

[735] *Kokkinakis v Greece* (1994) 17 EHRR 397, para 33.

[736] [2001] ECHR 42393/98.

[737] (2007) 44 EHRR 5.

[738] Ibid, para 111.

[739] Ibid, para 4.

The Grand Chamber invoked the margin of appreciation to reach a different result in **7.339**
a highly controversial decision concerning the display of the crucifix in Italian public
schools. The Court found that the crucifix was a 'passive symbol' that did not have
an influence on pupils and held that the decision whether to display the crucifix was
one which fell within the state's margin of appreciation. The case was determined under
the right to education in Article 2 of Protocol 1 and Article 9 was not considered in any
detail. The Grand Chamber received more state party interventions in this case than in
any other before and the decision may be informed in part by a desire by the Court to
avoid inflaming tensions about its role.

Article 9(2) has been the subject of consideration in a number of domestic cases. The **7.340**
statutory ban on corporal punishment of children in schools was held to be proportionate given the importance of protecting children.[740] Limiting Article 9(1) rights through
nuisance and harassment prohibitions was justified in the interests of public order.[741]
The criminalization of cannabis interfered with a Rastafarian's right to manifest his religion, but it was a justifiable limitation under Article 9(2).[742] A ban in Northern Irish
prisons on Catholic prisoners wearing Easter lilies to commemorate the Irish 1916
Rising was held to be proportionate and the 'minimum interference' possible in the
circumstances.[743] The slaughter of a sacred bullock belonging to a Hindu temple and
suffering from bovine tuberculosis was proportionate to meet the needs of public
health.[744]

The House of Lords in the *Shabina Begum* case found no interference with the claim- **7.341**
ant's rights under Article 9(1), but nevertheless went on to hold that, had there been an
interference, it would have been justified under Article 9(2).[745] The refusal to permit the
claimant to wear the jilbab was a proportionate response to the legitimate aim of protecting the rights and freedoms of others. The critical factor that appears to have influenced
this conclusion was the care with which the school had designed a uniform policy that
responded to the range of religious identities in the school community and permitted a
wide variety of dress.[746]

Article 9 informed the application of the Employment Equality (Religion or Belief) **7.342**
Regulations 2003[747] in a number of cases concerning the conflict between an employee's
religious belief and providing services to same-sex couples. In *London Borough of Islington
v Ladele* the Court of Appeal considered the case of a registrar and committed Christian
who was dismissed by the council because she refused to perform civil partnerships on the
grounds that same-sex unions were a sin.[748] In accepting that Article 9 was relevant to the
application of the Regulations, the court noted the restrictive Strasbourg case law on
Article 9 and found that the registrar's religious views 'should not be permitted to override'
the council's need to ensure equal respect for the homosexual community.

[740] *R (Williamson) v Secretary of State for Education and Employment* [2005] UKHL 15, [2005] 2 AC 246.
[741] *Church of Jesus Christ of Latter Day Saints v Price* [2004] EWHC 3245 (Admin).
[742] *R v Taylor* [2001] EWCA Crim 2263, [2002] 1 Cr App R 519.
[743] *R v Byers* [2004] NIQB 23.
[744] *Surayanda v Welsh Ministers* [2007] EWCA Civ 893. See also *R (Ghai) v Newcastle upon Tyne City Council* [2009] EWHC 978 (Admin).
[745] [2006] UKHL 15, [2007] 1 AC 100.
[746] Ibid at [33] per Lord Bingham, and at [98] per Baroness Hale.
[747] SI 1160/2003 Religion and belief are now protected characteristics under s 4 of the Equality Act 2010.
[748] [2009] EWCA Civ 1357, [2010] IRLR 211.

7.343   In *Macfarlane v Relate Avon Ltd*, a case concerning a counsellor who had been dismissed for refusing to counsel same-sex couples, the Employment Appeal Tribunal concluded that there was no interference with Article 9(1) 'where a person has voluntarily accepted an employment or role which does not accommodate that practice or observance and there are other means open to the person to observe his or her religion without undue hardship or inconvenience'.[749] On appeal, the Court of Appeal refused the request of the appellant to conduct a full proportionality analysis under Article 9, stating that there was 'no room' for such an analysis.[750] The manifestation of discriminatory religious beliefs thus fall foul of the Convention, whether analysed in terms of an interference with Article 9(1) or proportionality under Article 9(2). *Ladele* and *Macfarlane* will be heard by the ECtHR.[751]

7.344   Further litigation in this area may arise as a result of the intended repeal of the provision of the Civil Partnership Act 2004 which prevents civil partnerships from taking place in religious premises.[752]

6. Section 13 of the Human Rights Act

7.345 During the parliamentary debates on the Human Rights Bill, members of certain churches became concerned that the effect of Article 9 would be to prevent them from selecting employees in a manner consistent with the ethos and beliefs of their organization.[753]

7.346   The solution adopted by the Government is contained in section 13 of the Act. It provides that:

> If the court's determination of any question under the Act might affect the exercise by a religious organization (itself or its members collectively) of the Convention right to freedom of thought, conscience, and religion, it must have particular regard to the importance of that right.[754]

7.347   Lord Nicholls in *R (Williamson) v Secretary of State for Education and Employment* noted that section 13 emphasizes the importance of the Article 9 right, as 'it is one of two Convention rights singled out for special mention, the other being freedom of expression'.[755]

7.348   Section 13 is really no more than an exhortation to apply the balance inherent in Article 9 properly and it has not featured prominently in the domestic cases concerning Article 9. It was not referred to in the judgments in *Ladele* or *Macfarlane*. As Richards J has put it, 'whilst there is a need to have specific regard to the rights protected by Article 9, s 13 of the 1998 Act does not give greater weight to those rights than they would otherwise enjoy under the Convention'.[756]

---

[749] [2010] EWCA Civ 880, [2010] IRLR 872.
[750] See also *R (Johns) v Derby City Council* [2011] EWHC 375 (Admin); *Catholic Care v Charity Commission for England and Wales* [2010] EWHC 520 (Ch), [2010] 4 All ER 1041.
[751] App Nos 51671/10 and 36516/10, communicated to the Government on 21 April 2011.
[752] Section 6(1)(b). The Coalition Government has stated that it intends to bring into force s 202 of the Equality Act 2010 repealing s 6(1)(b). See Government Equality Office, 'Civil partnerships on religious premises: a consultation' (February 2011).
[753] For details see *Hansard*, HL, cols 747–801 (5 February 1998).
[754] For further discussion of s 13, see ch 3, para 3.81.
[755] [2005] UKHL 15, [2005] 2 AC 246 at [19].
[756] *R (Amicus-MSF and ors) v Secretary of State for Trade and Industry* [2004] EWHC 860 (Admin), [2004] ELR 311 at [41].

G. ARTICLE 10: FREEDOM OF EXPRESSION

Freedom of expression has been described as 'the lifeblood of democracy'.[757] In *Handyside*   7.349
v UK the ECtHR described it as 'one of the essential foundations of . . . a [democratic]
society, one of the basic conditions for its progress and for the development of every
man'.[758] Other theoretical justifications advanced for protecting freedom of expression
are the advancement of truth in a 'market place of ideas',[759] and self-expression.[760] In
McCartan Turkington Breen, Lord Bingham observed that:

> In a modern developed society, it is only a small minority of citizens who can participate directly
> in the discussions and decisions which shape the public life of that society. The majority can par-
> ticipate only indirectly, by exercising their rights as citizens to vote, express their opinions, make
> representations to the authorities, form pressure groups and so on. But the majority cannot par-
> ticipate in the public life of their society in these ways if they are not alerted to and informed about
> matters which call or may call for consideration and action. It is very largely through the media,
> including of course the press, that they will be so alerted and informed. The proper functioning of
> a modern participatory democracy requires that the media be free, active, professional and inquir-
> ing. For this reason, the courts, here and elsewhere, have recognized the cardinal importance of
> press freedom.[761]

The philosophical underpinning of Article 10 is thus rooted firmly in a notion of individual self-fulfilment experienced through participation in democratic debate.[762]

Article 10 commonly overlaps with other rights, such as the right to manifest one's   7.350
beliefs (Article 9),[763] the right to protest (Article 11),[764] and the right to vote and stand
for office (Protocol 1, Article 3).[765] Despite the close relationship between Article 10
and other democratic rights, it can on occasion clash with values considered to be vital
to democracy. This conflict causes Strasbourg and domestic courts difficulty. On occasion, they have struggled to strike a balance between the importance of the right to
freedom of expression to a democratic system and competing social interests protected
under Article 10(2) or by other Convention rights, such as the right to a fair trial,[766] the
right of access to a court,[767] the protection of the democratic process,[768] others'

---

[757] *R v Secretary of State for the Home Department, ex p Simms* [2000] 2 AC 115, 126 per Lord Steyn. See
also *Handyside v UK* (1976) 1 EHRR 737, para 49; *McCartan Turkington Breen v Times Newspapers Ltd* [2001]
2 AC 277, 297.
[758] (1976) 1 EHRR 737, para 49.
[759] See, eg *Abrams v US* 250 US 616 (1919), 630 per Justice Holmes.
[760] See, eg *Procunier v Martinez* 416 US 396 (1974) per Justice Marshall.
[761] *McCartan Turkington Breen v Times Newspapers Ltd* [2001] 2 AC 277, 290G–291A.
[762] See also *R v Secretary of State for the Home Department, ex p Simms* [2000] 2 AC 115; *R (Animal
Defenders International) v Secretary of State for Culture, Media and Sport* [2008] UKHL 15, [2008] 1 AC 1312
at [28] per Lord Bingham.
[763] *Leyla Sahin v Turkey* (2005) 41 EHRR 8.
[764] See, eg *Hashman and Harrup v UK* (2000) 30 EHRR 241; *Rekvenyi v Hungary* (2000) 30 EHRR 519;
R (Laporte) v Chief Constable of Gloucestershire Constabulary [2006] UKHL 55, [2007] 2 AC 105.
[765] See, eg *Hirst v UK (No 2)* (2006) 42 EHRR 41; *Kudeshkina v Russia* App No 29492/05, 26 February
2009.
[766] See, eg *Sunday Times v UK* (1979) 2 EHRR 245.
[767] *MGN v UK* App No 39401/04, 18 January 2011.
[768] See, eg *Bowman v UK* (1998) 26 EHRR 1.

privacy,[769] and the right to respect for freedom of thought, conscience, and religion.[770] Thus, in the Grand Chamber's controversial decision upholding an absolute ban on a major Turkish political party, freedom of expression had to be sacrificed to the pre-eminent need to protect the democratic and secular foundations of the state.[771]

7.351   The domestic courts have recognized the right to freedom of expression at common law for many years.[772] As Laws LJ has evocatively put it, 'freedom of expression is as much a sinew of the common law as it is of the European Convention'.[773] The House of Lords has held on a number of occasions that the common law recognition of freedom of speech is consistent with Article 10.[774] Against this background, the courts have declared that the central impact of the Human Rights Act in this area is to 'strengthen' protection of freedom of expression in the United Kingdom rather than alter it entirely.[775] Nonetheless, Article 10 has had an impact across a wide variety of areas, in particular in the field of media law,[776] but also in relation to advertising,[777] defamation,[778] contempt of court,[779] criminal law,[780] copyright,[781] prisoners,[782] public inquiries,[783] and public protest.[784]

7.352   Despite judicial assertions that freedom of expression receives the same level of protection at common law as under the Convention, it is clear from adverse results for the UK Government in Strasbourg in Article 10 cases that a gap may exist between the standards applied by Strasbourg and the domestic courts.[785] In particular, there are

---

[769] See, eg *Lingens v Austria* (1986) 8 EHRR 103; *Mosley v UK* App No 48009/08, 10 May 2011; *Campbell v MGN Ltd* [2004] UKHL 22, [2004] 2 AC 457.

[770] See, eg *Otto-Preminger Institute v Austria* (1994) 19 EHRR 34.

[771] *Refah Partisi v Turkey* (2003) 14 BHRC 1.

[772] See, eg *Cassell and Co Ltd v Broome* [1972] AC 1027; *McCartan Turkington Breen v Times Newspapers* [2001] 2 AC 277; *R v Shayler* [2002] UKHL 11, [2003] 1 AC 247.

[773] *R v Advertising Standards Authority Ltd, ex p Vernons Organization Ltd* [1992] 1 WLR 1289, 1293A.

[774] *Derbyshire County Council v Times Newspapers Ltd* [1993] AC 534, 551; *R (ProLife Alliance) v BBC* [2003] UKHL 23, [2004] 1 AC 185. See also *Spiller and anor v Joseph and ors* [2010] UKSC 53, [2011] AC 852 All ER 947, at [79].

[775] *Reynolds v Times Newspapers Ltd and ors* [1999] 4 All ER 609, 621.

[776] See, eg *Douglas v Hello! Ltd* [2001] QB 96; *Campbell v MGN* [2004] UKHL 22, [2004] 2 AC 457; *R (Pro-Life Alliance) v BBC* [2003] UKHL 23, [2004] 1 AC 185.

[777] *Hertel v Switzerland* (1998) 28 EHRR 534; *Markt Intern Verlag v Germany* (1989) 12 EHRR 161; *R (British American Tobacco) v Secretary of State for Health* [2004] EWHC 2493 (Admin), [2005] ACD 27; *R (Animal Defenders International) v Secretary of State for Culture, Media and Sport* [2008] UKHL 15, [2008] 2 WLR 781.

[778] See, eg *Loutchansky v Times Newspapers Ltd* [2001] EWCA Civ 1805, [2002] QB 783; *O'Shea v MGN* [2001] EMLR 40.

[779] See, eg *Attorney General v Scotcher* [2005] UKHL 36, [2005] 1 WLR 1867.

[780] See, eg *R v Perrin* [2002] EWCA Crim 747; *R (Laporte) v Chief Constable of Gloucestershire Constabulary* [2006] UKHL 55, [2007] 2 AC 105; *Dehal v DPP* [2005] EWHC 2154 (Admin), (2005) 169 JP 581.

[781] See, eg *Ashdown v Telegraph Group* [2001] EWCA Civ 1142, [2002] 1 Ch 149.

[782] See, eg *R v Secretary of State for the Home Department, ex p Simms* [2000] 2 AC 115; *R (Hirst) v Secretary of State for the Home Department* [2002] EWHC 602 (Admin), [2002] UKHRR 758; *R (Nielsen) v Secretary of State for the Home Department* [2004] EWCA Civ 1540, [2005] 1 WLR 1028.

[783] See, eg *Persey and ors v Secretary of State for Environment, Food and Rural Affairs* [2002] EWHC 371 (Admin), [2003] QB 794; *R v Secretary of State for Health, ex p Wagstaff and Associated Newspapers* [2001] 1 WLR 292.

[784] *R (Laporte) v Chief Constable of Gloucestershire Constabulary* [2006] UKHL 55, [2007] 2 AC 105.

[785] See, eg *Steel and Morris v UK* (2005) 41 EHRR 22; *Bowman v UK* (1998) 26 EHRR 1; *MGN v UK* App No 39401/04, 18 January 2011.

circumstances in which the domestic courts have not given the rigorous scrutiny to alleged justifications for restrictions on freedom of expression that one finds in some of the Strasbourg case law.[786]

1. 'Everyone'

Article 10 states that 'everyone has the right to freedom of expression'. This includes both natural and legal persons, such as the media and non-governmental organizations,[787] as well as a company whose activities are commercial.[788]   7.353

The Strasbourg organs recognize that freedom of expression is enjoyed by state employees, including civil servants,[789] doctors,[790] army officers,[791] police,[792] and the judiciary,[793] although the applicant's status may affect the ECtHR's view on the proportionality of an interference.[794] Potential recipients of information can be 'victims' for the purposes of Article 34.[795] However, trade unions cannot claim victim status on behalf of their members whose right to freedom of expression may have been violated.[796]   7.354

2. Scope of the right

Article 10 encompasses the freedom to hold ideas and incorporates the right to receive opinions and information, as well as the right to express them.[797]   7.355

Article 10(1) encompasses the right to communicate or to express oneself in any medium.[798] Words, pictures, images, and actions intended to express an idea or to present information (such as public protest, demonstration, film, or symbolic acts such as flag-burning) can constitute expression.[799] Expressive activities as diverse as graffiti,[800] dress,[801] and street performance[802] have been found to fall within Article 10(1).   7.356

---

[786] See, eg *R (Farrakhan) v Secretary of State for the Home Department* [2002] EWCA Civ 606, [2002] QB 1391.

[787] *Tarsasag a Szabadsagjogokert v Hungary* [2009] ECHR 37374/05.

[788] See, eg *Autotronic AG v Switzerland* (1990) 12 EHRR 485; *Sunday Times v UK* (1979) 2 EHRR 245; *Groppera Radio AG v Switzerland* (1990) 12 EHRR 321.

[789] *Vogt v Germany* (1995) 21 EHRR 205; *Ahmed v UK* (2000) 29 EHRR 1; *Guja v Moldova* App No 14277/04, 12 February 2008.

[790] *Frankowicz v Poland* App No 53025/99, 16 December 2008.

[791] *Grigoriades v Greece* (1997) 27 EHRR 464.

[792] *Rekvenyi v Hungary* (2000) 30 EHRR 519.

[793] *Wille v Lichtenstein* (1999) 30 EHRR 558.

[794] See, eg *Rekvenyi v Hungary* (2000) 30 EHRR 519; *Kudeshkina v Russia* App No 29492/05, 26 February 2009.

[795] *Open Door Counselling & Dublin Well Woman v Ireland* (1992) 15 EHRR 244.

[796] *Powell v Ireland* App No 15404/89, 16 April 1991; *Hodgson and Woolf v UK* (1987) 51 DR 136.

[797] *Sunday Times v UK (No 1)* (1979) 2 EHRR 245; *Groppera Radio AG v Switzerland* (1990) 12 EHRR 321; *Open Door Counselling & Dublin Well Woman v Ireland* (1992) 15 EHRR 244.

[798] *Oberschlick v Austria* (1997) 25 EHRR 357, para 57.

[799] *Stevens v UK* (1986) 46 DR 245.

[800] *N v Switzerland* (1983) 34 DR 208.

[801] *Vajnai v Hungary* App No 33629/06, 8 July 2008.

[802] *H & K v UK* (1983) 34 DR 218.

7.357   Three broad types of expression have been held to attract the protection of Article 10:

(a) political expression;[803]

(b) artistic expression;[804] and

(c) commercial expression.[805]

As the ECtHR has emphasized, Article 10(1) does not apply solely to certain types of information or ideas, or forms of expression, and thus the categories of protected expression are not closed.[806]

7.358   Political expression is broadly defined to include comment on a matter of general public interest.[807] The House of Lords has held that it would be wrong in principle to distinguish between political discussion and 'other matters of serious public concern';[808] both will be equally protected by Article 10. Public interest includes legitimate, robust comment on public figures.[809] Political expression generally receives greater protection than the other forms, though there is no express theoretical basis for this distinction.[810] While the ECtHR has never gone so far as the US Supreme Court in *New York Times v Sullivan*,[811] which requires proof of malice in defamation cases brought by public figures, it affords considerable protection to those who criticize politicians and other public figures, such as judges, whether or not the views they express are facts or based on opinion, and whether or not they are politely or elegantly expressed, unless they are 'gratuitous personal attacks'.[812]

7.359   Artistic expression contributes 'to the exchange of ideas and opinions which is essential for a democratic society'.[813] In a majority opinion in the case of *Vereinigung Bildender Künstler v Austria* the ECtHR held that an injunction prohibiting the display of photographs of the heads of various well-known figures, including Mother Teresa, on bodies engaging in sexual activities was disproportionate.[814] By contrast, in *Lindon v Austria* the Court held that the conviction for defamation of a novelist who 'impugned the honour' of National Front leader, Jean Marie Le-Pen, did not violate Article 10.[815]

7.360   Commercial expression also attracts the protection of Article 10(1). In particular, commercial speech sometimes also raises matters of legitimate public debate and concern.[816] However, statements made for purely commercial reasons are frequently considered not to contribute to a debate on the public interest and fall 'outside the basic nucleus

---

[803] See, eg *Lingens v Austria* (1986) 8 EHRR 103; *Bowman v UK* (1998) 26 EHRR 1; *R (Animal Defenders International) v Secretary of State for Culture, Media and Sport* [2008] UKHL 15, [2008] 1 AC 1312.

[804] See, eg *Müller v Switzerland* (1988) 13 EHRR 212; *Wingrove v UK* (1996) 24 EHRR 1; *Vereinigung Bildender Künstler v Austria* (2008) 47 EHRR 5.

[805] See, eg *Barthold v Germany* (1985) 7 EHRR 383; *Colman v UK* (1993) 18 EHRR 119.

[806] *Thorgeirson v Iceland* (1992) 14 EHRR 843, para 64.

[807] Ibid; *Hertel v Switzerland* (1999) 28 EHRR 534.

[808] *Reynolds v Times Newspapers Ltd* [2001] 2 AC 127, 204 per Lord Nicholls.

[809] *Lingens v Austria* (1986) 8 EHRR 407; *Janovwskiv v Poland* (1999) 29 EHRR 705; *Yankov v Bulgaria* (2005) 41 EHRR 854; *Reynolds v Times Newspapers Ltd* [2001] 2 AC 127.

[810] *Thorgeirson v Iceland* (1992) 14 EHRR 843, para 64.

[811] (1964) 376 US 254.

[812] *Oberschlick v Austria* (1997) 25 EHRR 357; *De Haes v Belgium* (1997) 25 EHRR 1.

[813] *Vereinigung Bildender Künstler v Austria* (2008) 47 EHRR 5, para 26.

[814] Ibid.

[815] (2008) 46 EHRR 35.

[816] *Hertel v Switzerland* (1998) 28 EHRR 534.

protected by the freedom of expression'.[817] Consequently, the ECtHR often applies a wide margin of appreciation to any restriction upon purely commercial speech. Similarly, the domestic courts have emphasized that commercial expression has less significance than political or artistic expression.[818] In *R (British American Tobacco Ltd) v Secretary of State for Health*, for example, the High Court found that while the right to advertise tobacco fell within the protection of Article 10, the ban imposed by the Government was easily justified by the overwhelming health and economic costs of smoking.[819]

In order to protect an environment in which free expression and debate is possible, Article 10 also affords strong protection to the elements of a free press, such as working practices and principles that facilitate the gathering of information as well as the actual expression of views. In *Roemen and Schmit v Luxembourg* a journalist successfully claimed that his right not to reveal his sources had been violated by searches of his home and property following the publication of an article he had written accusing a politician of tax fraud, which was supported by legal documents.[820] The ECtHR held that 'the protection of journalistic sources is one of the cornerstones of freedom of the press'.[821] The House of Lords accepted this principle in *Ashworth Hospital Authority v MGN* but held that in exceptional circumstances an order to disclose sources may be justifiable.[822]   7.361

Expression does not generally fall outside the protection of Article 10(1) on the basis of its content. Both popular and unpopular expression is protected, including speech that might 'offend, shock or disturb'[823] or insult another person.[824] In *Jersild v Denmark* the ECtHR found that the conviction of a journalist for aiding and abetting racist insults made in a television show violated his right to freedom of expression.[825] In *R (Farrakhan) v Secretary of State for the Home Department*, the Court of Appeal accepted that Louis Farrakhan's right to freedom of expression was engaged in circumstances where he intended to propagate anti-Semitic views.[826] There are, however, limits to the extent to which offensive expression must be tolerated. The ECtHR has traditionally been cautious in the extent of the protection it gives to artistic expression that is likely to offend, for example.[827] However, offensive images produced for a serious artistic purpose are likely to receive stronger protection under Article 10 than obscene publications in other contexts that lack artistic merit.[828]   7.362

---

[817] *Markt Intern Verlag v Germany* (1989) 12 EHRR 161, para 32.

[818] *Miss Behavin' Ltd v Belfast City Council* [2007] UKHL 19, [2007] NI 89, at 16.

[819] [2004] EWHC 2493 (Admin), [2005] ACD 27. Cf *R (North Cyprus Tourism Centre Ltd) v Transport for London* [2005] EWHC 1698 (Admin).

[820] [2003] ECHR 102. See also *Saygili v Turkey* App No 19353/03, 8 January 2008.

[821] [2003] ECHR 102, para 46. See also *Sanoma Uitgevers BV v Netherlands* [2010] ECHR 38224/03.

[822] [2002] UKHL 29, [2002] 1 WLR 2033.

[823] *Handyside v UK* (1976) 1 EHRR 737, para 49; *Jersild v Denmark* (1994) 19 EHRR 1; *R (ProLife Alliance) v BBC* [2003] UKHL 23, [2004] 1 AC 185; *Grobbelaar v News Group Newspapers Ltd* [2002] UKHL 40, [2002] 1 WLR 3024.

[824] *De Haes and Gijsels v Belgium* (1997) 25 EHRR 1; *Livingstone v Adjudication Panel for England* [2006] EWHC 2533 (Admin), [2006] LGR 799 at [36], [39].

[825] (1994) 19 EHRR 1.

[826] [2002] EWCA Civ 606, [2002] QB 1391. See also *DPP v Collins* [2006] UKHL 40, [2006] 1 WLR 2223; *Connolly v DPP* [2007] EWHC 237 (Admin), [2008] 1 WLR 276; *R (Naik) v Secretary of State for the Home Department and anor* [2010] EWHC 2825 (Admin).

[827] *Muller v Switzerland* (1988) 13 EHRR 212; *Handyside v UK* (1976) 1 EHRR 737; *Otto Preminger Institut v Austria* (1994) 19 EHRR 34.

[828] *Vereiningun blidender Kunstler v Austria* (2008) 47 EHRR 5; *Miss Behavin' Ltd v Belfast City Council* [2007] UKHL 19, [2007] NI 89 at [16]; *Connolly v DPP* [2007] EWHC 237 (Admin); *Interfact v Liverpool City Council* [2005] EWHC 995 (Admin), [2005] 1 LR 3118.

7.363   The ECtHR and domestic courts may also accept restrictions on such speech under Article 10(2) or Article 17, to protect others from hate speech.[829] Expression is generally not protected if it is inimical to the concept of a society based on tolerance, pluralism, and broadmindedness. Thus, the Court will not permit Article 10 to protect Holocaust denial or expression of extremist anti-democratic ideas.[830] And the law may be used to avoid the potential expression of violent anti-Semitic opinion, as the Court of Appeal did in *Farrakhan*.[831] But the representation of extreme racist views may be protected by Article if the intention is to expose and explain, rather than to promote, those views.[832] In *Gaunt v OFCOM* the High Court held that a 'rant' by a radio presenter did not attract the protection of Article 10.[833] The Court stated: 'An inhibition from broadcasting shouted abuse which expresses no content does not inhibit, and should not deter, heated and even offensive dialogue which retains a degree of relevant content.'[834]

7.364   Until recently, Article 10 did not guarantee a right of access to information and applicants had to rely on the protection of other articles to obtain access to personal material.[835] As Lord Rodger explained in *In Re Guardian News and Media* in which media organizations applied to the Supreme Court to have anonymity orders discharged, the press do not have a right 'to be supplied with information which would otherwise not be available to them'.[836] However, the Supreme Court did not consider the recent ECtHR judgment in *Tarsasag a Szasbadsagjogokert v Hungary*.[837] In that case the Hungarian Civil Liberties Union was denied access to legal documents relating to the government's drugs policy. The Court tentatively suggested that it had advanced towards recognizing a general right of access to information under Article 10. Nonetheless, the Court decided the case on the limited basis that the state had interfered with the right of the press to access official documents in their role as a 'social watchdog'.

7.365   *Tarsasag* was applied in *Independent News and Media Limited and ors v A*.[838] The Court of Appeal upheld a decision to allow media representatives to attend Court of Protection proceedings that were normally held in private on the basis that *Tarsasag* established a broad right of access to court proceedings. The High court has subsequently sought to restrict the impact of the *Tarsasag* judgment in *R (Guardian News and Media) v City of Westminster Magistrates' Court and anor*.[839] The court distinguished *A* on the basis that it concerned attendance at court proceedings and held that the press did not have 'an unfettered right of access' to official documents. The *Guardian* was not entitled to see documents in extradition proceedings that had been referred to in open court.

7.366   While *Tarsasag* may not have embraced a fully fledged right of access to information, the High Court's interpretation was arguably too narrow. It is very likely that there will

---

[829] See, eg *Le Pen v France* App No 18788/09, 20 April 2010; *Féret v Belgium* App No 15615/07, 16 July 2009. Judgments available in French only.

[830] *Glimmerveen and Hagenbeek v Netherlands* App Nos 8348/78 and 8406/78 (1979) 18 DR 187.

[831] See para 7.362 above.

[832] *Jersild v Denmark* (1994) 19 EHRR 1.

[833] [2010] EWHC 1756 (QB), [2010] NLJR 1045.

[834] Ibid at [50].

[835] See, eg *Gaskin v UK* (1989) 12 EHRR 36; *KH v Slovakia* App No 32881/04, 28 April 2009.

[836] [2010] UKSC 1, [2010] 2 AC 697. Cf *R (Binyam Mohamed) v Secretary of State for Foreign and Commonwealth Affairs* [2010] EWCA Civ 65, [2010] 3 WLR 554 at [175].

[837] [2009] ECHR 37374/05.

[838] [2010] 3 All ER 32. See also *Sugar v BBC* [2010] EWCA Civ 715, [2011] 1 All ER 101.

[839] [2010] EWHC 3376 (Admin).

be further development of the law in this area in both Strasbourg and the domestic courts.

3. Positive obligations

The duty to protect the right to freedom of expression also imposes certain obligations upon states to help facilitate the exercise of that freedom. In common with Article 8, the Court has recognized strong procedural obligations under Article 10. In *Fuentes Bobo v Spain* the ECtHR held that Spain was in breach of Article 10 by having failed to provide a legal framework which provided an adequate remedy to protect a journalist who was dismissed by a state broadcaster for criticism of its management.[840] In *Özgür Gündem v Turkey* the ECtHR found that Turkey had a positive obligation to take investigative and protective measures following a violent and threatening campaign against a pro-PKK newspaper.[841]   7.367

In an important recent decision of the Grand Chamber in *Sanoma Uitgevers BV v Netherlands* the Court held that the right to protect journalistic sources should be safeguarded by sufficient procedural guarantees, including the guarantee of review by a judge or other independent and impartial decision-making body, before the police or the public prosecutor have access to information capable of revealing such sources.[842]   7.368

The ECtHR has generally been cautious about imposing substantive obligations on the state.[843] However, in *Manole and ors v Moldova* the ECtHR developed a strikingly broad obligation to ensure that the public had access to a balanced, informative, and pluralistic broadcasting service.[844] If the state decided to set up or maintain a public broadcasting service, it was essential for it to be structurally independent and impartial and to provide a forum for public debate.   7.369

4. Interferences with the right to freedom of expression

In general, it will not be difficult to establish an interference with the right to freedom of expression.[845] An interference can take any form. The ECtHR has held for example that confiscation of materials found on the applicant during a search including cassettes, paperback books, a diary, and a map interfered with her right to freedom of expression.[846]   7.370

Interferences with freedom of expression most commonly concern either 'prior restraint' on publication or post-expression sanctions. Prior restraints, such as injunctions, are not inherently incompatible with Article 10 but they require careful scrutiny and will only be justified in exceptional circumstances.[847] News has a very short shelf-life, and the courts have taken this into account in regularly rejecting pre-publication   7.371

---

[840] (2000) 31 EHRR 1115.

[841] (2001) 31 EHRR 49.

[842] [2010] ECHR 38224/03.

[843] See, eg *Appleby v UK* (2003) 37 EHRR 38.

[844] [2009] ECHR 13936/02.

[845] Cf *R (Rusbridger) v Attorney General* [2003] UKHL 38, [2004] 1 AC 357, an exceptional case in which Art 10(1) did not apply.

[846] *Foka v Turkey* App No 28940/95, 24 June 2008.

[847] *The Observer and The Guardian v UK* (1991) 14 EHRR 153; *Sunday Times v UK (No 2)* (1991) 14 EHRR 229; *Cumpana and Mazare v Romania* App No 33348/96, 17 December 2004. See also s 12(3) of the Human Rights Act 1998, discussed in ch 3, para 3.78.

delays or restrictions. In *Sunday Times v UK (No 1)* the ECtHR recognized that delaying the publication of news may amount in practice to it never being published, as news quickly becomes stale and delay would rob it of its interest and value.[848]

7.372   Post-expression sanctions can take the form of civil, criminal, or disciplinary penalties for publication, such as an award of damages for defamation or a sentence of imprisonment under hate speech legislation. As the ECtHR and domestic courts have held, the danger of such retrospective sanctions is that they have a chilling effect on freedom of speech that deters future public discussion of the subject.[849] Thus, in *Tolstoy Miloslavsky v UK* the ECtHR examined an award of libel damages finding that at £1.5million, it was so high as to stifle freedom of speech.[850]

5. Exceptions to the right to freedom of expression

7.373   As a result of the relative ease of establishing an interference with Article 10(1), the majority of cases are determined in relation to the very substantial internal limits on the right to freedom of expression. Article 10(1) provides that it does not prevent states from requiring the licensing of broadcasting, television, or cinema enterprises. The list of exceptions under Article 10(2) is more extensive and specific than in relation to other articles. Further, Article 10(2) specifically states that the exercise of the freedoms in Article 10(1) 'carries with it duties and responsibilities',[851] a phrase that does not appear in the other qualified rights. Article 10(1) can also be balanced against other rights in the Convention that may override the protection afforded to freedom of expression.

(a) *Licensing exception*

7.374   When the right to freedom of expression is limited pursuant to the licensing exception in Article 10(1), it is not necessary that any of the objectives in Article 10(2) be pursued. However, the interference must still be compatible with the broad requirements of the second paragraph.[852]

7.375   The ECtHR has recognized that restrictions should be minimal and there is a presumption in favour of free access to transmissions. For example, in *Groppera Radio AG v Switzerland* the ECtHR stated that rejections of licence applications should not be manifestly arbitrary or discriminatory, and the necessity for any restriction must be 'convincingly established'.[853]

7.376   The domestic courts have, in general, adopted a light-touch approach to the review of licensing and broadcast decisions. In the leading case, *R (Prolife Alliance) v BBC*, the House of Lords considered a decision by the BBC pursuant to its statutory broadcasting code to refuse to broadcast a party election broadcast that showed an abortion in graphic detail on the ground that it contained offensive material.[854] The Court of Appeal had held that it was only in very rare circumstances that a party election broadcast could

---

[848] (1979) 2 EHRR 245.
[849] See, eg *Jersild v Denmark* (1994) 19 EHRR 1, para 44; *Jameel and ors v Wall Street Journal Europe* [2006] UKHL 44, [2007] 1 AC 359 at [154].
[850] (1995) 20 EHRR 442.
[851] See *Lindon, Otchakovsky-Laurens and July v France* (2008) 46 EHRR 35, para 67.
[852] *Informationsverein Lentia v Austria* (1994) 17 EHRR 93.
[853] (1990) 12 EHRR 485, para 61.
[854] [2003] UKHL 23, [2004] 1 AC 185.

properly be rejected by broadcasters on the grounds of taste and decency, and the broadcasters had failed to give sufficient weight to the pressing imperative of free political expression. By a majority (Lord Scott dissenting), the House of Lords disagreed, finding that the broadcasters had followed the statutory guidance without error and the court should not disturb their decision.

In *R (Animal Defenders International) v Secretary of State for Culture, Media and Sport*   7.377
the House of Lords held that the total prohibition on political advertising on television was proportionate to the need to ensure a level playing field for the expression of all lawful political opinions.[855] No such prohibition applied to other forms of media, including radio and cinema, but their Lordships concluded that the 'immediacy of television' explained why there was a pressing social need for such a prohibition.[856] Distinguishing the decision of the European Court in a very similar case,[857] Lord Bingham held that great weight should be accorded to the legislative decision because politicians were 'peculiarly sensitive to the measures necessary to safeguard the integrity of our democracy'.[858] The logic of this decision is questionable in light of the phenomenal power of the internet to disseminate information that rivals, if not exceeds, the 'immediacy of television'.

(b) *General limitations under Article 10(2)*

Despite the apparently wide restrictions under Article 10(2), it is evident from the case   7.378
law that the ECtHR will require a strong justification for interfering with the right to freedom of expression. It has developed a rigorous three-stage approach, first set out in the *Sunday Times* case, when examining a claimed justification under Article 10(2).[859] In order to be justified the interference must be: (i) in accordance with law; (ii) in pursuance of a legitimate aim; and (iii) 'necessary in a democratic society'. The Grand Chamber restated these principles in *Lindon, Otchakovsky-Laurens and July v France*, emphasizing that exceptions must be 'strictly construed' and the need for them must be 'established convincingly'.[860] With some notable exceptions,[861] the European Court has adopted a reasonably robust approach to protecting freedom of speech.

In applying the three-stage test, the ECtHR generally resists the notion of 'balancing'   7.379
freedom of expression under Article 10(1) against the purported legitimate aim under Article 10(2). As the ECtHR put it in the *Sunday Times* case, it 'is faced not with a choice between two conflicting principles, but with a principle of freedom of expression that is subject to a number of exceptions which must be narrowly interpreted'.[862] Thus, the two paragraphs are not equal; the right protected by Article 10(1) has presumptive weight.

(i) *In accordance with law*   In common with the other qualified rights, any restriction   7.380
on freedom of expression must have a legal basis and be adequately accessible and sufficiently foreseeable. The ECtHR has generally found that this requirement has been

---

[855] [2008] UKHL 15, [2008] 1 AC 1312.
[856] Ibid at [30].
[857] *VGT Vereingegen Tierfabriken v Switzerland* (2001) 10 BHRC 473.
[858] [2008] UKHL 15, [2008] 1 AC 1312 at [33].
[859] *Sunday Times v UK (No 1)* (1979) 2 EHRR 245.
[860] (2008) 46 EHRR 35, para 45.
[861] See, eg *Refah Partisi v Turkey* (2003) 14 BHRC 1.
[862] *Sunday Times v UK (No 1)* (1979) 2 EHRR 245, para 65.

fulfilled.863 However, in *Sanoma Uitgevers BV v Netherlands* the Grand Chamber found that the procedure for protecting journalist's sources was inadequate and not 'in accordance with the law'.864 *Sanoma* provides an example of the principle of 'quality of law' that imposes substantive legal requirements into the notion of accordance with the law.865

7.381   The common law will not in principle fail to satisfy the requirement that an interference is prescribed by law.866 However, in *Hashman and Harrup v UK* the ECtHR concluded that ordering the applicants to be bound over to keep the peace on the basis that their conduct was wrong in the judgment of fellow citizens was not sufficiently precise to satisfy Article 10(2).867

7.382   (ii) *Legitimate aim*   The only legitimate restrictions on freedom of expression are those outlined under Article 10(2), namely:

(a) national security,868 territorial integrity,869 or public safety;870

(b) prevention of disorder871 or crime;872

(c) protection of health873 or morals;874

(d) protection of the reputation875 or rights of others;876

(e) prevention of the disclosure of information received in confidence;877

(f) maintaining the authority and impartiality of the judiciary.878

It is usually accepted that an interference with freedom of expression pursues a legitimate aim, often because the state relies on the broad notion of the 'rights of others'. The nature of the aim pursued will affect the enquiry into necessity and the application of the margin of appreciation.

7.383   (iii) *'Necessary in a democratic society'*   This is usually the critical question in Article 10 cases.879 A variety of factors will be relevant in the proportionality enquiry, including the

---

863 See, eg ibid. Cf *Gaweda v Poland* (2004) 39 EHRR 4.

864 [2010] ECHR 38224/03.

865 See ch 2, para 2.44.

866 *Sunday Times v UK (No 1)* (1979) 2 EHRR 245; *Tolstoy Miloslavsky v UK* (1995) 20 EHRR 442; *Steel v UK* (1998) 26 EHRR 603.

867 (2000) 30 EHRR 241.

868 See, eg *Observer v UK* (1991) 14 EHRR 153; *Sunday Times v UK (No 2)* (1991) 14 EHRR 229; *Brind and McLaughlin v UK* (1994) 77 ADR 42; *R v Shayler* [2002] UKHL 11, [2003] 1 AC 247.

869 See, eg *Piermont v France* (1995) 20 EHRR 301; *Üstün v Turkey* [2007] ECHR 37685/02.

870 See, eg *Ceylan v Turkey* (2000) 30 EHRR 73.

871 See, eg *Engel v Netherlands* (1979–80) 1 EHRR 647; *Steel v UK* (1998) 28 EHRR 603; *Dehal v DPP* [2005] EWHC 2154 (Admin), (2005) 169 JP 581.

872 See, eg *Marlow v UK* App No 42015/98, 5 December 2000.

873 See, eg *R (British and American Tobacco) v Secretary of State for Health* [2004] EWHC 2493 (Admin), [2005] ACD 27.

874 See, eg *Open Door and Dublin Well Woman v Ireland* (1992) 15 EHRR 244; *Akdaş v Turkey* App No 41056/04, 16 February 2010; *Miss Behavin' Ltd v Belfast City Council* [2007] UKHL 19, [2007] NI 89.

875 See, eg *Lindon, Otchakovsky-Laurens and July v France* (2008) 46 EHRR 35; *Mosley v News Group Newspapers Ltd* [2008] EWHC 1777 (Admin), [2008] NLJR 1112.

876 See, eg *Otto-Preminger-Institute v Austria* (1994) 19 EHRR 34; *Norwood v DPP* [2003] EWHC 1564 (Admin), (2005) 169 JP 581.

877 See, eg *Guja v Moldova* [2008] ECHR 14277/04.

878 See, eg *Sunday Times v UK (No 1)* (1979) 2 EHRR 245.

879 See the discussion of proportionality in general in ch 2, paras 2.61–2.66.

extent of the limitation on expression, or 'chilling effect', the value of the particular form of expression, the objective of the expression, the medium employed by the speaker, the importance of the counter-balancing interest that the limitation on the expression in question intends to protect, and whether less-restrictive means of protecting that interest are available.

For example, amendments to the Public Order Act 1986 introduced by the Crime and Justice Act 2008 created new offences of acts intended or likely to incite hatred against a group of persons defined by religious belief or lack of it, or on grounds of sexual orientation. But the concerns of free-speech campaigners meant that these provisions were all explicitly limited so that discussion, criticism, or expressions of antipathy, dislike, ridicule, insult, or abuse of particular religious groups or the practices of their adherents, or sexual minorities and practices of their adherents were not offences. Moreover, prosecutions can only be brought with the consent of the Director of Public Prosecutions.[880]   7.384

Consistent with the theoretical basis for protecting freedom of expression, the ECtHR has repeatedly made clear that there is very limited scope under Article 10(2) for restrictions on debates concerning questions of public interest regardless of whether they are polemical, aggressive, provocative, or even exaggerated.[881]   7.385

In *Steel and Morris v UK* the European Court considered the case of two Greenpeace protestors who had distributed leaflets critical of the fast-food chain McDonald's.[882] The ECtHR held that although the leaflets contained untrue and damaging statements, there was no reasonable relationship of proportionality between the injury to McDonald's reputation and the interference with the applicants' rights to freedom of expression. In particular, it was noted that the damages awarded were very substantial when compared to the applicants' limited resources and that McDonald's was a 'large and powerful corporate' entity.[883]   7.386

The objective of the expression will be critical to determining whether any restriction upon it is proportionate. For example, it will be harder to justify restrictions on racist speech that is intended to inform rather than offend.[884] The ECtHR will also take into account the medium of the publication when assessing whether an interference is proportionate. Television will have greater immediacy and impact than other forms of media, for example.[885]   7.387

The ECtHR has repeatedly required particularly convincing justification for penal sanctions.[886] For example, in *Scharsach v Austria* it was held that by imposing criminal sanctions on a journalist and publisher who commented that a right-wing politician was a 'closet Nazi' the Austrian state had acted disproportionately.[887] Two recent cases suggest a shift in this approach. In *Hoffer and Annen v Germany* the Court found no   7.388

---

[880] See Public Order Act 2008, ss 29J and 29JA, and Part 3A.
[881] *Prager and Oberschlick v Austria* (1995) 21 EHRR 1; *Thoma v Luxembourg* (2001) 36 EHRR 359.
[882] (2005) 41 EHRR 22.
[883] Ibid, para 96.
[884] See *Jersild v Denmark* (1994) 19 EHRR 1, para 33. See also *Lehideux v France* (1998) 5 BHRC 540, para 53.
[885] See, eg *Gunduz v Turkey* App No 35071/97, 4 December 2003; *Murphy v Ireland* (2003) 38 EHRR 212; *R (Animal Defenders International) v Secretary of State for Culture, Media and Sport* [2008] UKHL 15, [2008] 1 AC 1312.
[886] *Kyprianou v Cyprus* (2007) 44 EHRR 27.
[887] (2005) 40 EHRR 22. Cf *Prager and Oberschlick v Austria* (1995) 21 EHRR 1.

violation of pro-life activists' convictions for distributing defamatory material about a doctor who performed abortions on the basis that the relatively modest fines imposed were a proportionate response to the inflammatory statements.[888] Similarly, in *Monteiro da Costa Noqueira v Portugal* a majority of the Court accepted that Article 10 was not violated by criminal sanctions imposed on a doctor and politician for making defamatory allegations about criminal activity of public figures.[889]

7.389 The ECtHR considered the impact of the internet in libel claims in *Times Newspapers Ltd v UK (Nos 1 and 2)*.[890] In domestic law, the publication of a daily newspaper's archives on its website expose it indefinitely to libel actions. Although the Court found that there had been no violation in that case, it nevertheless held that libel proceedings brought after a significant lapse of time might well, in the absence of exceptional circumstances, give rise to a disproportionate interference under Article 10.

7.390 In common with the European case law, domestic determinations of proportionality will turn on the precise factual context. Contrast *Hammond v DPP*[891] and *Dehal v DPP*,[892] for example. In *Hammond* the prosecution of an evangelical Christian who bore anti-gay signs around a town centre was held to meet the pressing social need to show tolerance to all members of society, and held to be proportionate because Hammond was provoking violence.

7.391 The High Court reached the opposite conclusion in *Dehal*. The appellant had been convicted for a public order offence after he put up a poster on a notice board at a Sikh temple describing the temple's President in abusive and insulting language. In a model application of the three-stage *Sunday Times* test, Moses J held that the mere fact that the words were irritating, contentious, unwelcome, or provocative was not enough to justify a criminal penalty unless they were intended to provoke violence. The appellant's right to freedom of expression had been breached.

7.392 The High Court reached a similar conclusion in relation to a disciplinary sanction imposed on former London Mayor Ken Livingstone after he told a journalist that he was 'just like a concentration camp guard'. The Court held that disciplinary action was not 'shown to be necessary in a democratic society even though the higher level of protection appropriate for the expression of political opinion was not engaged'.[893] By contrast in *Munim Abdul and ors v Director of Public Prosecutions* the prosecution of protestors who shouted defamatory and inflammatory abuse at a parade of British soldiers who had served in Afghanistan and Iraq was proportionate on the grounds that their behaviour posed a clear threat to public order.[894]

7.393 Although domestic case law generally follows the three-stage test set out in *Sunday Times v UK* for assessing whether an interference with Article 10 rights is justified, in some cases this test as applied to the facts of domestic cases is at odds with the Strasbourg approach. In *R (Farrakhan) v Secretary of State for the Home Department*, for example, the Court of Appeal was prepared to accept that the radical preacher's presence in the United

---

[888] (2011) 29 BHRC 654.
[889] App No 4035/08, 11 January 2011. Judgment available in French only.
[890] [2009] ECHR 3002/03.
[891] [2004] EWHC 69 (Admin), (2004) 168 JP 601. See also *Norwood v DPP* [2003] EWHC 1564 (Admin), (2005) 169 JP 581.
[892] [2005] EWHC 2154 (Admin), (2005) 169 JP 581.
[893] *Livingstone v Adjudication Panel for England* [2006] EWHC 2533 (Admin), [2006] LGR 799 at [39].
[894] [2011] EWHC 247 (Admin).

Kingdom 'might provide a catalyst for disorder' that justified the Home Secretary's refusal to allow him to enter the country, despite the absence of any evidence of the potential for disorder.[895]

The House of Lords considered the role of Article 10(2) in *R v Shayler*, in which a 7.394 former member of the security services disclosed confidential material contrary to the Official Secrets Act 1989.[896] He argued that disclosure had been in the national interest, and prosecution under the Act would infringe his right to freedom of expression. Accepting that the legislation interfered with Article 10(1), the House of Lords held that any restriction on freedom of expression should be subject to very close scrutiny. However, in concluding that the restrictions imposed by the Act were proportionate and pursued the legitimate aim of protecting national security, their Lordships did not engage in a thorough proportionality analysis, accepting that existing procedures for disclosure of concerns were adequate.

The Court of Appeal has adopted a firmer approach to necessity. In *R (Tabernacle) v* 7.395 *Secretary of State for Defence* the court considered the rights under Articles 10 and 11 of a long-standing group of protesters that staged regular anti-nuclear protests on land owned by the Ministry of Defence, which wished to prevent the protesters from camping there.[897] The court held that in order for the Secretary of State to justify measures prohibiting the protest, he had to demonstrate 'a substantial objective justification . . . amounting to an undoubted pressing social need'.[898] This he had failed to do: the objections to the encampment merely concerned 'nuisance points', such as problems with traffic and lavatories. Moreover, the Secretary of State had not previously complained about the encampment in the 23 years it had existed on the site. The court's approach reveals an encouraging willingness to conduct a genuine and informed balancing exercise in which government assertions are not accepted at face value.

(c) *Conflicts with other Convention rights*

In cases where Article 10 conflicts with another Convention right, the ECtHR will assess 7.396 whether a 'fair balance' has been struck between the competing rights and interests. In such cases the ECtHR cannot give presumptive weight to either right, and must instead attempt to 'balance' the competing interests within the particular factual parameters of the case before it.

The most common conflict arises between freedom of information, and the right to 7.397 privacy under Article 8. The case law in this area is discussed above under Article 8.[899] On occasion, rights under Article 10 can also conflict with other rights.[900]

The ECtHR recently considered the relationship between Article 10 and the Article 6 7.398 right of access to a court for civil litigants bringing defamation proceedings. In *Campbell v MGN (Costs)* the House of Lords held that conditional fee agreements (CFAs), under

---

[895] [2002] EWCA Civ 606, [2002] QB 1391 at [58]. See also *R (Naik) v Secretary of State for the Home Department and anor* [2010] EWHC 2825.
[896] [2002] UKHL 11, [2003] 1 AC 247.
[897] [2009] EWCA Civ 23.
[898] Ibid at [39].
[899] See paras 7.253–7.265 above.
[900] See *R (Woolas) v Election Court* [2010] EWHC 3168 (Admin), [2010] NLJR 1756 in which a three-judge Divisional Court considered the balance between Art 10 and the rights of electors not to be misled under Art 3 of Protocol 1.

which an award of costs is increased by a success fee payable to legal representatives, did not breach Article 10 so long as the amount was proportionate.[901] The European Court disagreed.[902] The Court relied on the findings of the Jackson Review into Civil Litigation Costs, which recommended that success fees should not be recoverable from defendants. The ECtHR held that success fees at the rate of 100 per cent interfered with Article 10 by having a chilling effect on the press. The domestic costs regime did not strike a fair balance between Article 8 and Article 10. In response to the decision, the Government has stated that it intends to introduce primary legislation to reform the CFA regime along the lines proposed in the Jackson Review.[903]

7.399   In some cases the conflict between Article 10 and other rights under the Convention may be so profound that Article 17 applies. Denial of the Holocaust, for example, is deemed so offensive and contrary to established historical fact that it is removed from the protection of Article 10 by Article 17.[904] In *Norwood v UK* the ECtHR held that the display of a poster stating 'Islam Out of Britain—Protect the British People', with a photo of the Twin Towers in flames, was such a vehement attack against Muslims that it was incompatible with Convention values.[905]

6. Margin of appreciation

7.400   The ECtHR has claimed that in all cases, it exercises strict supervision of the margin of appreciation because of the crucial importance of the Article 10 right.[906] However, given the cultural sensitivity of much expression, the ECtHR in fact has frequent recourse to this concept in order to defer to the courts of individual Member States, which are closer to the interests to be balanced in any individual Member State. In particular, in cases involving public morals[907] or commercial speech[908] the breadth of the margin is wider than that pertaining in cases involving an issue that affects the general interest, even where a criminal penalty is at issue.[909]

7.401   The ECtHR set out its reasons for applying a margin of appreciation in relation to cases raising questions of morality in the early case of *Handyside v UK*. The Court stated:

. . . it is not possible to find in the domestic law of the various Contracting States a uniform European conception of morals. The view taken by their respective laws of the requirements of morals varies from time to time and from place to place, especially in our era which is characterised by a rapid and far-reaching evolution of opinions on the subject. By reason of their direct and continuous contact with the vital forces of their countries, State authorities are in principle in a

---

901 [2005] UKHL 61, [2005] 1 WLR 3394.
902 *MGN v UK* App No 39401/04, 18 January 2011.
903 Ministry of Justice, 'Reforming Civil Litigation Funding and Costs in England and Wales—Implementation of Lord Justice Jackson's Recommendations: The Government Response' (March 2011).
904 See, eg *Chauvy v France* (2005) 41 EHRR 29; *Garaudy v France* App No 65831/01, 24 June 2003.
905 (2005) 40 EHRR SE11. In *Woolas* [2010] EWHC 3168 (Admin), [2010] NLJR 1756 also, it was held that deliberate falsehoods calculated to incite racial hatred did not attract the protection of Art 10.
906 *United Christian Broadcasters Ltd v UK* App No 44802/98, 7 November 2000.
907 See, eg *Handyside v UK* (1976) 1 EHRR 737.
908 See, eg *VGT Verein Gegen Tierfabriken v Switzerland* (2002) 34 EHRR 4.
909 *Hertel v Switzerland* (1999) 26 EHRR 534.

better position than the international judge to give an opinion on the exact content of these requirements as well as on the 'necessity' of a 'restriction' or 'penalty' intended to meet them.[910]

This approach has subsequently been applied in a variety of contexts. In *Otto-* 7.402 *Preminger Institute v Austria* the ECtHR decided that it was within the state's margin of appreciation to decide to seize a film that satirized God, Jesus, and Mary where the predominantly Catholic population might be offended by the film.[911] A similar conclusion was reached in *Wingrove v UK*, in which the British Board of Film Classification refused a certificate for a video called *Visions of Ecstasy*.[912]

The same approach has been taken in relation to religious advertising. In *Murphy v* 7.403 *Ireland* the ECtHR held that it was within the state's margin of appreciation to impose a total ban on religious adverts in light of the population's particular religious sensitivities.[913] By contrast in *Akdaş v Turkey* the ECtHR considered that the Turkish applicant's conviction for publishing a French erotic novel that had first been published in France in 1907 did not fall within the state's margin of appreciation because the book formed part of a 'European literary heritage' which all Europeans were entitled to access.[914]

Some commentators have criticized the application of the doctrine for reducing the 7.404 scope of the protection of Article 10. In *Mosley v UK* the Court found that whether or not a pre-notification requirement should be imposed on the press to protect a person's privacy fell within the state's margin of appreciation. The case did not concern an inherently sensitive issue such as public morals and the ECtHR may have invoked the margin of appreciation in order to avoid a political storm.[915]

7. Section 12 of the Human Rights Act

Section 12(1) of the Human Rights Act requires courts considering the potential grant 7.405 of injunctive relief to afford 'particular regard' to the importance of freedom of expression. Section 12(2) and (3) enjoin courts not to grant ex parte orders restraining freedom of expression, or prior restraints, without strong justification for doing so. The provision is a 'comfort clause'; it was introduced during the passage of the Human Rights Act to address the media's concerns about potential conflicts between privacy and freedom of expression, and in support of the principle that news is a time-sensitive commodity.

The addition of section 12 has not had a significant impact on domestic jurispru- 7.406 dence.[916] The House of Lords has confirmed that section 12(3) has altered the applicable test for the grant of an injunction preventing publication. Their Lordships indicated that the general approach is that the courts should be very slow to grant an injunction where the applicant has not satisfied the court that he or she is more likely than not to succeed

---

[910] (1976) 1 EHRR 737, para 48.
[911] (1994) 19 EHRR 34.
[912] (1996) 24 EHRR 1.
[913] (2003) 38 EHRR 212.
[914] App No 41056/04, 16 February 2010. Judgment available in French only.
[915] [2011] ECHR 48009/08. See Clayton and Tomlinson, *The Law of Human Rights*, 2nd edn (Oxford: Oxford University Press, 2009) 1454.
[916] See ch 3, para 3.79.

at trial.[917] However, it has not altered the courts' approach to the balancing of factors inherent in a proper analysis of conflicts between Article 10 and other articles.

7.407   Lord Neuberger's recent report on 'super-injunctions' considered the procedure adopted in applications for injunctions preventing publication of private material.[918] The media was concerned that applications for injunctions were too often made without notice. The report emphasized that section 12(2) requires advance notification of an application for an injunction and stated that only exceptional circumstances would justify departure from this rule.

H. ARTICLE 11: FREEDOM OF ASSEMBLY AND ASSOCIATION

7.408   Article 11 protects the twin rights of freedom of peaceful assembly and freedom of association. Most international human rights instruments treat these as distinct rights—only the Convention and the Universal Declaration of Human Rights (UDHR) combine them in a single article. Both rights are of a political nature and both have a collective dimension, as they both protect 'people power'—individuals uniting and gathering to express or protect their common interests. Together with the right to freedom of expression, these rights are essential to the proper functioning of a democratic and pluralistic society.

7.409   Article 11 includes an express right to form and join trade unions. This was omitted from the original draft, but added at a later stage. The *travaux préparatoires* show that this is intended (as with the UDHR[919]) to be 'a right distinct from the right of association in general'.[920]

7.410   The majority of the domestic cases concerning Article 11 have been concerned with freedom of assembly or the right to protest, whereas the bulk of the Strasbourg jurisprudence concerns the 'association' limb of Article 11.

1. Overlap between Article 11 and other rights

7.411   Article 11 rights often overlap with Articles 9 (freedom of thought, conscience, and religion)[921] and 10 (freedom of expression).[922] This is because the protection of opinions and beliefs and the freedom to express them is one of the objectives of the freedom of assembly and association enshrined in Article 11.[923] The importance of the interrelationship of Articles 10 and 11 in particular has repeatedly been emphasized by the ECtHR, and this line of authority was unanimously endorsed by the House of Lords in *R (Laporte) v Chief Constable of Gloucestershire*.[924] Article 11 rights may also interlink with Article 8,

---

[917] *Cream Holdings v Banerjee* [2004] UKHL 44, [2005] 1 AC 253; *Scottish National Party v BBC* [2010] SC 495 (Court of Session).

[918] Report of the Committee on Super-Injunctions (20 May 2011); available at <http://www.judiciary.gov.uk/media/media-releases/2011/committee-reports-findings-super-injunctions-20052011>.

[919] UDHR, Art 20 (freedom of association) and Art 23(4) (right to form and join trade unions).

[920] *Travaux Préparatoires: Article 11*, Council of Europe, DH (56) 16 Or Fr, 9–11 (16 August 1956).

[921] See, eg *Chassagnou and ors v France* (1999) 29 EHRR 615; *R (Parminder Singh) v Chief Constable of West Midlands Police* [2006] EWCA Civ 1118, [2006] 1 WLR 3374.

[922] See, eg *Hashman and Harrup v UK* (2000) 30 EHRR 241; *Rekvenyi v Hungary* (2000) 30 EHRR 519; *Christian Democratic People's Party v Moldova* App No 28793/02, 14 February 2006; *R (Laporte) v Chief Constable of Gloucestershire* [2006] UKHL 55, [2007] 2 AC 105.

[923] *Christian Democratic People's Party v Moldova* App No 28793/02, 14 February 2006, para 62.

[924] [2006] UKHL 55, [2007] 2 AC 105.

for example where the authorities collate or retain information on an individual's political opinions or activities,[925] or when police photograph or film protestors or would-be protestors.[926] Article 5 may also play a part, for example, where 'crowd control' measures such as cordons or 'kettling' are adopted at marches or demonstrations.[927]

The ECtHR has a very structured approach when dealing with cases raising issues under both Article 11 and another article. If the case concerns the right to peaceful assembly, the ECtHR will examine the interference under Article 11, using it as the *lex specialis* (specialist law), but then refer to the other articles in assessing the effect of the interference and the question of proportionality.[928] In contrast, the domestic courts often sideline Article 11, for example focusing on Article 10 rather than 11 even though the 'expression' in question involves a protest or demonstration. However, in *R (Laporte) v Chief Constable of Gloucestershire* both Lord Rodger and Lord Carswell expressly approved the Strasbourg approach of treating Article 11 as the *lex specialis* and Article 10 as the *lex generalis* in protest cases.[929] In cases involving the association limb of Article 11 both the ECtHR and the domestic courts may primarily focus on Article 9, 10, or 11, depending on the context and facts.   7.412

2. Limitations: the operation of Article 11(2)

As with Articles 8, 9, and 10, an interference with the freedoms of assembly or association will breach Article 11 unless it satisfies the three-part *Sunday Times* test: the limitation is 'prescribed by law', directed towards one or more of the legitimate aims set out in Article 11(2), and 'necessary in a democratic society' for the achievement of that aim.[930] This three-part test is explained in more detail in Chapter 2. During the drafting of Article 11 the legitimate aims set out in Article 11(2) were expanded to include certain restrictions on the full freedom of association of members of the police, armed forces, and administration of the state, at the insistence of the United Kingdom.[931]   7.413

Courts will often be required to 'balance' competing Convention rights to determine whether limitations on Article 11(1) rights are justified 'for the protection of the rights and freedoms of others'. However, the ECtHR will only conduct a balancing exercise where the competing right or freedom is also set out in the Convention. A different, more rigorous test applies where the Government relies on the 'rights and freedoms of others' in a more general sense. The ECtHR has said: 7.414

It is a different matter where restrictions are imposed on a right or freedom guaranteed by the Convention in order to protect 'rights and freedoms' not, as such, enunciated therein. In such a case only indisputable imperatives can justify interference with enjoyment of a Convention right.[932]

---

[925] *Segerstedt-Wiberg and ors v Sweden* (2007) 44 EHRR 2.
[926] *R (Wood) v Commissioner of Police for the Metropolis* [2008] EWHC 1105 (Admin), (2008) HRLR 34; analysed by Harris, 'Photo Opportunity' (2009) 153(13) SJ 6.
[927] See, eg *Austin v Commissioner of Police of the Metropolis* [2009] UKHL 5, [2009] 2 WLR 372; analysed by Mackie, 'The lady doth protest' (2009) 153(16) SJ 32; *R (Laporte) v Chief Constable of Gloucestershire* [2006] UKHL 55, [2007] 2 AC 105.
[928] *Ezelin v France* (1991) 14 EHRR 362.
[929] [2006] UKHL 55, [2007] 2 AC 105 at [85] per Lord Rodger and at [93] per Lord Carswell.
[930] *Sunday Times v UK (No 1)* (1979) 2 EHRR 245.
[931] *Travaux Préparatoires: Article 11*, n 920 above, 5–6.
[932] *Chassagnou v France* (1999) 29 EHRR 615, para 113.

3. Freedom of peaceful assembly

7.415   The internationally recognized right to hold demonstrations has English origins, beginning with the ancient right to petition the English crown. Since the eighteenth century
peaceful protests gradually replaced riots as a means of public expression in the United
Kingdom.[933] Yet, despite this 'long history',[934] peaceful protests had little protection in
the English law prior to the Human Rights Act.[935]

7.416   In recent years a number of high-profile incidents has sparked public debate on the
importance of and limitations on the right to protest, such as repeated police and
Government attempts to remove the long-term protests established opposite the Houses
of Parliament, climate change protests, anti-capitalist demonstrations, abusive protests
from bystanders during soldiers' marches on return from Iraq, and student protests over
tuition fees. These issues have often reached the courts and relevant cases are considered
below.

7.417   It should be noted that, unusually, this is an area in which the Northern Irish and
Scottish courts have arguably more experience than that of their English and Welsh
counterparts. They have considered and applied Article 11 in a large number of appeals
against authorities' decisions to prohibit or place conditions upon processions, particularly those organized by the Orange Order and Orange Lodges.

(a) *Scope of the right to peaceful assembly*

7.418   The right to freedom of peaceful assembly is one of the foundations of a democratic
society. Given its importance, it must not be restrictively interpreted. It has been held
to apply to marches and processions,[936] private and public meetings,[937] press confer-
ences, static protests, 'sit-ins' or occupations of buildings or land,[938] and counter-
demonstrations.[939] This right may be exercised by individuals, associations, and
corporate groups.[940] Because freedom of assembly protects 'the abstract possibility of
holding an undisturbed peaceful assembly', its organizers may claim to be directly
concerned by 'any negative decision of the authorities'.[941] Parties (other than the organizers) who intend to, but are prevented from, participating in a protest will also have
standing in Strasbourg and under section of the Human Rights Act, but where no
protest took place the courts may require evidence that the applicant did intend to take
part before accepting that he or she is a 'victim'.[942]

7.419   The ECtHR has held that, if the state stores personal information on individuals
related to their political opinions, affiliations, and activities, in violation of Article 8, this
will *ipso facto* constitute an interference with the right to freedom of peaceful assembly

---

[933] Harris, *The Right to Demonstrate* (Hong Kong: Rights Press, 2007).

[934] See, eg JCHR, *Demonstrating Respect for Rights? A Human Rights Approach to Policing Protest*, Seventh
Report (2008–2009), HL 47-I, HC 320-I (3 March 2009).

[935] See *R (Laporte) v Chief Constable of Gloucestershire* [2006] UKHL 55, [2007] 2 AC 105 at [34].

[936] See, eg *Christians Against Racism and Facism v UK* (1983) 21 DR 138.

[937] See, eg *Rassemblement Jurassien and Unité Jurassienne v Switzerland* (1979) 17 DR 93.

[938] See, eg *G v Germany* (1989) 60 DR 256; *R (Tabernacle) v Secretary of State for Defence* [2009] EWCA
Civ 23.

[939] See Mead, 'The Right to Peaceful Protest under the European Convention on Human Rights' (2007)
4 EHRLR 345.

[940] See, eg *Hyde Park and ors v Moldova (No 4)* App No 18491/07, 7 April 2009, paras 34–36.

[941] *Bączkowski and ors v Poland* App No 1543/06, 3 May 2007.

[942] *Patyi and ors v Hungary* App No 5529/05, 7 October 2008, paras 26–28.

and association. There is no requirement to advance evidence indicating that the storage of such information has hindered the individuals' Article 11 rights in practice.[943]

Article 11 applies only to peaceful gatherings; it does not encompass 'a demonstration where the organisers and participants have violent intentions which result in public disorder'.[944] Violent assemblies are thus completely excluded from its scope.[945] However, if the intention is to hold a peaceful assembly, the possibility or even likelihood of a violent counter-demonstration or disruption of the assembly by unwelcome violent participants cannot remove the assembly from the scope of Article 11(1).[946] In such a case, issues regarding the risks of violence would instead fall to be determined under Article 11(2).[947]   7.420

An Article 11 claim may still be successful even if the demonstration was not halted by the authorities' actions. For example, in *Bączkowski and ors v Poland* the organizers of an anti-discrimination march succeeded in persuading the ECtHR that Article 11 had been breached by the Warsaw authorities' various attempts to thwart what the mayor had described as 'propaganda about homosexuality', despite the fact that ultimately the march had gone ahead on the planned days. The Court accepted that the applicants had taken a risk given the official ban in force at the time, and that this *could* have discouraged the applicants and others from participation.[948]   7.421

Surprisingly, given that the ECtHR has made it clear that the right to peaceful assembly must not be restrictively interpreted, a number of domestic judgments regarding protest have concluded that Article 11 is not even engaged. For example, the House of Lords in *R (Gillan) v Commissioner of Police of the Metropolis* found that the application of random 'stop and search' powers[949] to peaceful protestors did not constitute a prima facie interference with Article 11.[950] Similarly in *R (Wood) v Metropolitan Police Commissioner* the Court of Appeal found that taking photographs of a protester in the street did not engage his Article 11 rights.[951]   7.422

Article 8 and 11 issues were intertwined in *Gillan*, and heavy reliance was placed on the conclusion in *R (S and Marper) v Chief Constable of South Yorkshire Police* that retention of DNA samples of acquitted and unconvicted individuals did not interfere with Article 8.[952] Following the Strasbourg judgment in *S and Marper v UK* rejecting the Lords' narrow approach to Article 8, the Lords' restrictive conclusion on Article 11 is also open to question.[953] The issue was not addressed in *Gillan v UK* as the ECtHR concluded that the statutory provisions were not provided by law under Article 8(2).[954]   7.423

---

[943] *Segerstedt-Wiberg and ors v Sweden* (2007) 44 EHRR 2, para 107.
[944] *G v Germany* (1989) 60 DR 256.
[945] See also paras 7.587 below concerning Art 17 of the Convention.
[946] See *Christians against Racism and Facism v UK* App No 8440/78, 16 July 1980 (admissibility decision) (ECmHR); *Anderson v UK* App No 33689/96, 27 October 1997 (admissibility decision) (ECmHR); analysed in (1998) EHRLR 218 and McLean, *Property and the Constitution* (Oxford: Hart Publishing, 1999) 24–26.
[947] See, eg *R (Parminder Singh) v Chief Constable of West Midlands Police* [2006] EWCA Civ 1118, [2006] 1 WLR 3374.
[948] App No 1543/06, 3 May 2007.
[949] Terrorism Act 2000, s 44.
[950] [2006] UKHL 12, [2006] 2 AC 307.
[951] [2009] EWCA Civ 414, [2009] 4 All ER 951.
[952] [2004] UKHL 39, [2004] 1 WLR 2196.
[953] *S and Marper v UK* (2008) 48 EHRR 1169.
[954] (2010) 28 BHRC 420.

(b) *Limitations*

7.424 Most assembly cases turn on the question of the necessity and proportionality of the interference. In making this assessment the courts are alert to the need to protect protests that annoy or give offence:

> If every probability of tension and heated exchange between opposing groups during a demonstration was to warrant its prohibition, society would be faced with being deprived of the opportunity of hearing differing views.[955]

Similarly, in the case of *R (Tabernacle) v Secretary of State for Defence* (regarding the compatibility of byelaws prohibiting camping in the vicinity of atomic weapons establishments with Articles 10 and 11) the Court of Appeal stated that:

> Rights worth having are unruly things. Demonstrations and protests are liable to be a nuisance. They are liable to be inconvenient and tiresome, or at least perceived as such by others who are out of sympathy with them.[956]

7.425 As with Article 10, the courts will require particularly convincing reasons to justify an interference with an assembly involving political speech or debate on questions of public interest.[957] And, given the importance of tolerance in a democratic society, in any case involving peaceful protest, a 'high threshold' will need to be overcome before it can be established that the protest will unreasonably infringe the rights and freedoms of others.[958]

7.426 This was affirmed by the House of Lords in *R (Laporte) v Chief Constable of Gloucestershire*.[959] The police stopped coaches of protesters on their way to a protest demonstration at Fairford air base. The House of Lords held that, since there had been no indication of any imminent breach of the peace when the coaches were intercepted and searched, and since the defendant had not considered that such a breach was then likely to occur, the action taken in preventing the claimant from continuing to the demonstration had been an interference with her right to demonstrate at a lawful assembly, which was not prescribed by domestic law; further, that in any event the police action had been premature and indiscriminate and represented a disproportionate restriction on her rights under Articles 10 and 11. *Laporte* was applied by the High Court in *R (Moos and anor) v Commissioner of the Police of the Metropolis*.[960] The court held that the 'kettling' of climate change protesters during the G20 Summit in London was disproportionate on the basis that the protestors did not pose an imminent threat of breach of the peace.

7.427 (i) *Blanket measures* In early cases the Strasbourg organs occasionally upheld blanket bans on assemblies. For example, in *Christians Against Racism and Fascism* the ECmHR upheld a two-month ban on any demonstrations in London, finding it to be justified

---

[955] *Öllinger v Austria* App No 76900/01, 29 June 2006, para 36; *Stankov and the United Macedonian Organisation Illinden v Bulgaria* App Nos 29221/95 and 29225/95, ECHR 2001-IX, para 87.

[956] [2009] EWCA Civ 23 at [43].

[957] *Öllinger v Austria* App No 76900/01, 29 June 2006, para 38; *R (Laporte) v Chief Constable of Gloucestershire* [2006] UKHL 55, [2007] 2 AC 105.

[958] OSCE/ODIHR, *Guidelines on Freedom of Peaceful Assembly*, 29 March 2007, paras 70–71.

[959] [2006] UKHL 55, [2007] 2 AC 105.

[960] [2011] EWHC 957 (Admin).

given the tense atmosphere at that time caused by National Front demonstrations,[961] and in *Pendragon v UK* the ECmHR upheld a four-day prohibition on all large assemblies within a radius of four miles from Stonehenge, based on past disorder caused there by Druid followers.[962]

However, in recent cases the ECtHR has been highly critical of 'sweeping measures of a preventative nature' based on vague exhortations of the need to protect national security or public order, finding that such blanket measures do 'a disservice to democracy and often endanger it'.[963] It will scrutinize such bans especially closely. Similarly, in the carefully reasoned case of *Aberdeen Bon-Accord Loyal Orange Lodge 701 v Aberdeen City Council* the sheriff's court in Scotland held that the council's reasons for an outright ban on a procession were not made out and that, in any event, such a draconian measure as a 'complete prohibition' was disproportionate to the 'concern that the procession might promote religious intolerance and might interfere with the rights of other citizens to go about their business freely and lawfully'. The court emphasized that 'tolerance is what is required in a democratic society and that includes toleration of views or sentiments which may not coincide with one's own'.[964]   7.428

(ii) *Regulation of assemblies*   Requiring authorization for an assembly will not necessarily constitute an interference under Article 11. As the ECtHR put it in *Aldemir v Turkey*:   7.429

> Any demonstration in a public place may cause a certain level of disruption to ordinary life and encounter hostility. This being so, it is important that associations and others organising demonstrations, as actors in the democratic process, respect the rules governing that process by complying with the regulations in force.[965]

The Court of Appeal has also noted that some protests 'betray a kind of arrogance . . . which assumes that spreading the word is always more important than the mess which, often literally, the exercise leaves behind'. In such a case, 'firm but balanced regulation may well be justified'.[966] An authorization procedure may even be required as part of the state's positive obligation under Article 11 to ensure that a protest is peaceful and that participants are not deterred from expressing their views by a fear of violence.[967]

However, regulation should not represent a hidden obstacle to freedom of assembly.[968] The ECtHR has emphasized that, even when there is a notification requirement and it has not been complied with, 'to disband the ensuing, peaceful assembly solely because of the absence of the requisite prior notice, without any illegal conduct by the participants, amounts to a disproportionate restriction on freedom of assembly'.[969]   7.430

Despite this clear statement of the law from Strasbourg, the domestic approach to the question of prior authorization is questionable. Of particular note is the ban on spontaneous or 'without notice' protest around the Houses of Parliament in Westminster   7.431

---

[961] App No 8440/78, 16 July 1980.

[962] App No 3146/96, 19 October 1998.

[963] See, eg *Stankov v Bulgaria* App Nos 29221/95 and 29225/95, ECHR 2001-IX, para 97.

[964] 2002 SLT (Sh Ct) 52; discussed in Sir John Orr's *Review of Marches and Parades in Scotland* (Edinburgh: Scottish Executive, 2005), para 5.15.

[965] App No 32124/02, 18 December 2007, para 43.

[966] *R (Tabernacle) v Secretary of State for Defence* [2009] EWCA Civ 23 at [43].

[967] *Rassemblement Jurassien and Unité Jurassienne v Switzerland* (1979) 17 DR 93, 119 (ECmHR).

[968] *Aldemir v Turkey* App No 32124/02, 18 December 2007, para 43.

[969] *Bukta v Hungary* App No 25691/04, 17 July 2007, para 36.

contained in the Serious Organised Crime and Police Act 2005 (SOCPA). SOCPA introduced a number of new criminal offences applicable to the 'designated area' in the vicinity of Parliament, including organizing a demonstration in a public place there without prior authorization, which effectively ruled out spontaneous protests.[970] There have been a number of controversial SOCPA prosecutions involving 'peaceful, low-key protestors' who did not provide advance notification to the police of their activities.[971] The future of statutory regulation of protests around Parliament Square in currently being considered by Parliament in the Police Reform and Social Responsibility Bill which repeals the relevant provisions of SOCPA. The Bill criminalizes encampments and the use of sound equipment around Parliament.

7.432   SOCPA was introduced in part to deal with Brian Haw's 'permanent peace protest' in Parliament Square that has been joined by various other permanent protesters. There have been repeated attempts to remove these protests. In *Hall and ors v Mayor of London* the Mayor of London brought proceedings against the various protesters claiming that they were trespassing on Parliament Sqaure Gardens and breaking certain byelaws.[972] The Court of Appeal found that the appellants were trespassers but that it was necessary to assess whether the Convention rights provided a defence to the claim. The court held that the removal of the protesters was proportionate with regard to the fact that there was no absolute prohibition on the protest and the rights of others who had been prevented from using the square.[973] The protesters moved their campsite to the pavement and Westminster City Council is currently pursuing proceedings to evict them.

7.433   In examining whether a refusal to authorize an assembly or the imposition of restrictive conditions are proportionate, the domestic courts and the ECtHR will pay particular attention to any possible 'less restrictive means' the state could have taken to protect the legitimate aim in question without unduly impairing the right to assemble. For example, in *Öllinger v Austria* the ECtHR accepted that an assembly to commemorate Salzburg Jews killed by the SS during the Second World War could interfere with other cemetery-goers' rights to manifest their religion and mourn their dead, yet nevertheless found that prohibiting the assembly violated Article 11. In the circumstances, having a police presence on hand in case of disruption was a 'viable alternative' that would preserve the applicants' freedom of assembly while respecting mourners' sensitivities.[974]

7.434   (iii) *Counter-demonstrations*   Freedom of peaceful assembly includes both the freedom to demonstrate and to counter-demonstrate. In *Plattform 'Ärzte für das Leben' v Austria* the applicant anti-abortion protestors complained that the state had failed to prevent the disruption of their protest by pro-abortion counter-protestors. Both the ECmHR and ECtHR held that there was a positive duty on the state to protect demonstrators from counter-demonstrators, but there was no violation of Article 11 in the particular factual circumstances.[975]

7.435   (iv) *Penalties*   Given the severity of criminal sanctions the courts must examine the proportionality of such measures closely in each individual case. Criminal penalties imposed

---

[970] Section 132(1)(a).
[971] See, eg *Blum v Director of Public Prosecutions* [2006] EWHC 3209 (Admin).
[972] [2010] EWCA Civ 817.
[973] See also *The Mayor of London v Brian Haw and ors* [2011] EWHC 585 (QB).
[974] App No 76900/01, 29 June 2006.
[975] (1988) 13 EHRR 204.

on protestors who have been involved in violence, public disorder, or disruption of the highway have been upheld as Convention-compliant in a number of cases, but where such penalties are imposed on individuals without evidence that they *personally* behaved in a violent or disruptive manner they are highly likely to be disproportionate.[976] For example, in *Ezelin v France* subjecting a lawyer who had taken part in a demonstration that had become violent to a disciplinary reprimand, even though his personal actions were lawful, was held to be a disproportionate infringement of his Article 11 rights to make his beliefs known in a peaceful way.[977] The United Kingdom has a number of strict liability offences that have on their face no scope for exceptions where the defendant was acting peacefully and non-violently at all times.[978] The compatibility of such offences with Article 11 has not yet been tested in Strasbourg.

(v) *Assemblies on private property*   The question of whether the state's positive obliga-   7.436
tion to protect the right to peaceful assembly requires it to permit access onto privately owned property to protest has been considered in Strasbourg on a number of occasions. In the leading case of *Appleby and ors v UK* the ECtHR found no violation of Article 10 or 11 where the applicants had been prevented from campaigning in a private shopping centre.[979] It held that there is no 'freedom of forum'[980] inherent in Article 10 and no requirement of automatic access to private property in order to exercise Article 10 or 11 rights. It noted that the applicants had alternative ways of making their views known to the public, such as gathering elsewhere and canvassing door-to-door. However, the ECtHR did note that a positive obligation could arise in other circumstances, for example in a corporate town.

Another exception to the *Appleby* principle might arise where the privately owned   7.437
venue itself is directly connected to the very point of the protest. As in *Öllinger*, the choice of venue would then be an essential part of the point the demonstrators wished to make. However, such an argument did not succeed in *R (Brehony) v Chief Constable of Greater Manchester*.[981] Restrictions imposed on a protest against Marks & Spencer's involvement in Israel were considered proportionate, even though the protest was moved some distance away from the store, thus defeating the object of urging customers not to shop there.

4. Freedom of association

(a) *Scope of the right*

Although recognized in all major international and regional human rights instruments,   7.438
the nature and scope of freedom of association is controversial. Some courts and commentators have endorsed a narrow definition of freedom of association, concluding that collective bargaining and strike activity are not protected by freedom of association. Others have adopted broader definitions, holding that freedom of association includes

---

[976] See *Steel v UK* Reports of Judgments and Decisions 1998-VII, No 91, 23 September 1998 (Art 10, but reasoning readily applicable in Art 11 cases).
[977] (1991) 14 EHRR 362.
[978] Such as the SOCPA offences discussed above, para 7.432.
[979] App No 44306/98, 6 May 2003.
[980] Ibid, para 47.
[981] (2005) EWHC 640 (Admin), *The Times*, 15 April 2005.

the freedom to pursue common purposes and to engage in collective activities, and is not merely the freedom to form and join associations. The ECtHR and domestic case law reflects this tension. The ECtHR has held that the elements of the right of association are not finite, but 'subject to evolution depending on particular developments in labour relations'.[982]

7.439   The contrast in approaches to freedom of association is evident in the only two association cases yet to have reached the House of Lords, both concerning hunting bans: *R (Countryside Alliance) v Attorney General*[983] and *Whaley v Lord Advocate*.[984] Their Lordships divided on the question of whether Article 11 was engaged. Lord Brown and Lord Rodger thought that it was not, because the hunt members were still free to meet; they were simply banned from doing certain things when they got together. Lord Bingham, Lord Hope, and Baroness Hale had more difficulty, on the basis that 'there can be no point in protecting the right to meet without protecting at least some of the things you might want to do together'.[985] As Article 11 refers expressly to the activities of trade unions, Lord Bingham was not prepared to rule it out. Lord Hope and Baroness Hale took the view that it should be read in the context of Articles 9 and 10, as 'Article 9 says that you can believe what you like and manifest those beliefs, and Article 10 says that you can say what you like. And Article 11 says that you can get together with others to do all of this'.[986] In *Whaley* Baroness Hale thus concluded:

These articles, then, are designed to protect the freedom to share and express opinions, and to try and persuade others to one's point of view, which are essential political freedoms in any democracy. On this view, the right of the hunt and its followers to gather together publicly to demonstrate in favour of their sport and against the ban, perhaps even by riding over the countryside to demonstrate what they do, is protected by Article 11. But the right to chase and kill the fox or the stag or the mink or the hare is not.[987]

7.440   (i) *Right to form and join associations*   The right to freedom of association protects the right to join or form 'associations', including political parties and trade unions. But Article 11 does not create a right to membership of a particular association in all circumstances. In *Cheall v UK* the ECmHR decided that generally an individual has no right to belong to a particular trade union. The decision to expel Mr Cheall was analysed as the decision of a private body exercising its rights under Article 11 not to associate with him. However, the ECmHR made the point that the right of the trade union to choose its members is not absolute:

For the right to join a union to be effective the state must protect the individual against any abuse of a dominant position by trade unions . . . Such abuse might occur, for example, where exclusion or expulsion was not in accordance with union rules or where the rules were wholly unreasonable or arbitrary or where the consequences of exclusion or expulsion resulted in exceptional hardship such as job loss because of a closed shop.[988]

---

[982] *Demir v Turkey* [2009] 1 RLR 766 at para 146.
[983] [2007] UKHL 52, [2008] 1 AC 719.
[984] [2007] UKHL 53, [2007] SLT 1209.
[985] Lady Hale, 'Hunting in the House of Lords', Eldon Lecture 2008 (delivered at Northumbria University, 28 February 2008) 13.
[986] Ibid, 14.
[987] [2007] UKHL 53, [2007] SLT 1209 at [118].
[988] (1985) 42 DR 178.

An example of an exclusionary policy being upheld by the courts can be found in   7.441
RSPCA v Attorney General and ors, where the RSPCA sought guidance as to whether it
could adopt a membership policy that excluded individuals who wished to change its
policy on hunting. The court found that the freedom of association of the RSPCA itself
'embraces the freedom to exclude from the association those whose membership it honestly believes to be damaging the interests of the Society'. The exclusionary policy would
not therefore violate Article 11.[989]

The ECtHR has accepted that a refusal to register or give legal status to an association   7.442
may constitute an interference under Article 11(1), where this has the effect of preventing collective action in a field of mutual interest.[990] But a refusal to register will not
always constitute an interference. In *Gorzelik v Poland*, for example, the Grand Chamber
upheld a refusal to register an association as a 'national minority' rather than an 'ethnic
regional group'. It found that the disputed restriction was essentially concerned with 'the
label which the association could use in law' rather than its ability to act collectively in a
field of mutual interest. As such, it did not go to the core or essence of freedom of association, and the restriction was not disproportionate. This finding was despite the fact
that the 'label' of national minority carried with it improved election privileges.[991]

(ii) *Right to non-association*   Although not expressly mentioned, Article 11 also pro-   7.443
tects the right to refuse to join an association. The ECtHR first recognized this in *Young,
James and Webster v UK*, holding that 'the negative aspect of freedom of association
is necessarily complementary to, and a correlative of and inseparable from its positive
aspect'.[992]

The 'closed shop' is not always a violation of Article 11. In *Young*, it was, because the   7.444
refusal to join a union led to 'a threat of dismissal involving loss of livelihood' which was
'a most serious form of compulsion' and, as such, struck 'at the very substance of the
freedom guaranteed by Article 11'.[993] In contrast, in the unusual circumstances of *Sibson
v UK* an employer exercised his contractual right to transfer an employee to a different
depot after he resigned from one union to join another and others refused to work with
him. The ECtHR held that Mr Sibson's treatment did not 'strike at the very substance
of the freedom of association guaranteed by Article 11' because there was no question of
his losing his job.[994] In *Sørenson and Rasmussen v Denmark* the ECtHR emphasized that
the Convention is a living instrument, and account must be taken of changing percep-
tions of the relevance of closed shop agreements for securing the effective enjoyment of
trade union freedoms.[995] The Grand Chamber rejected the distinction between pre-
entry and post-entry closed shops, and held the interference with the applicants' rights
to be disproportionate as the Government had failed to demonstrate that closed shops
are 'an indispensable tool' for protecting trade union freedoms.

---

[989] [2002] 1 WLR 448.
[990] *Sidiropolous and ors v Greece*, 10 July 1998, Reports of Judgments and Decisions 1998-IV, para 40;
Tsonev v Bulgaria App No 45963/99, 13 July 2006; *United Macedonian Organization Ilinden and ors v Bulgaria*
(1998) 26 EHRR CD 103.
[991] App No 44158/98, 17 February 2004, paras 105–106.
[992] (1982) 4 EHRR 38, para 59; *Vörður Ólafsson v Iceland* App No 20161/06, 27 April 2010.
[993] (1982) 4 EHRR 38, 59.
[994] (1993) 17 EHRR 193. On unwanted transfers, see also *Ademyilmaz and ors v Turkey* App Nos 41496/98,
41499/98, 41501/98, 41502/98, 41959/98, 41602/98, 43606/98, 21 March 2006.
[995] App No 52562/99, 11 January 2006, para 58.

7.445   (iii) *Public and professional bodies*   Professional regulatory bodies set up by a state to regulate a profession, with compulsory membership within a profession, do not fall within this definition of an 'association'.[996] A bar association, architects' association, and medical practitioners' association have been held to be outside the definition; but a taxi drivers' association has been held to fall within it.[997]

7.446   Bodies that are a necessary and inevitable part of membership in a democratic community are also excluded from the scope of Article 11. An objection to being associated with government and its policies through the payment of taxes, for example, could not be made out under Article 11. In the words of a former judge of the US Supreme Court, the state 'is one club to which we all belong'.[998]

7.447   (iv) *Trade union activities*   As with other Convention rights, freedom of association must be practical and effective. The ECtHR has thus held that the state must 'both permit and make possible' freedom for individual trade unionists to protect their interests by trade union action.[999] In *Sanchez Navajas v Spain* the ECtHR considered that it could infer from Article 11, read in the light of Article 28 of the European Social Charter, that workers' representatives should have access to appropriate facilities to enable them to perform their trade union functions rapidly and effectively.[1000]

7.448   However, despite their commitment to 'real and effective' Article 11 rights, the ECtHR and domestic courts have traditionally been reluctant to recognize that collective bargaining,[1001] strike action,[1002] and a right to be consulted[1003] are closely connected to freedom of association. The Convention remains markedly more restrained in this area than other international instruments such as the European Social Charter.[1004] The law is developing, however. In *Demir and anor v Turkey* the ECtHR recently recognized that Article 11 protects the right to collective bargaining as an essential element of the right to form and join a trade union. As the ECtHR held, it is 'one of the principal means—even the foremost of such means—for trade unionists to protect their interests'.[1005] In *Enerji v Turkey* the Court acknowledged that Article 11 enshrined a right to strike.[1006] However, the right could be made subject to certain conditions and restrictions as provided by national law.

7.449   Domestic law generally adopts a conservative approach towards collective rights. While recent decisions suggest greater willingness on the part of the courts to interpret legislative provisions governing strike action in light of Article 6 of the European Social

---

[996] *Le Compte v Belgium* (1981) 4 EHRR 1.

[997] *Sigurdur A Sigurjónsson v Iceland* (1993) 16 EHRR 462.

[998] Per Justice Holmes; cited by Justice Brandeis in *Duplex Printing Press Co v Deering* 254 US 443 (1921), 448.

[999] *National Union of Belgian Police v Belgium* (1975) 1 EHRR 578, para 39.

[1000] App No 57442/00, 21 June 2001.

[1001] *Schmidt and Dahlstrom v Sweden* (1976) 1 EHRR 632; *Swedish Engine Drivers' Union v Sweden* (1979) 1 EHRR 617; *Gustafsson v Sweden* (1996) 22 EHRR 409; *R (National Union of Journalists) v Central Arbitration Committee* [2005] EWCA Civ 1309. Cf *Wilson and Palmer v UK* (2002) 35 EHRR 20.

[1002] *Schmidt and Dahlstrom* (1976) 1 EHRR 632, para 36.

[1003] *National Union of Belgian Police v Belgium* (1975) 1 EHRR 578.

[1004] See Art 6 of the Council of Europe's Social Charter 1961 and the Industrial Labour Organisation Conventions.

[1005] [2009] IRLR 766 at [129].

[1006] App No 68959/01, 21 April 2009. Judgment available only in French.

Charter and Article 11, the statutory limitations on the right to strike are unlikely to be deemed non-compliant with Article 11.[1007]

(b) *Limitations*

As with freedom of assembly, most association cases turn on the question of whether an interference is 'necessary in a democratic society'.[1008] The ECtHR has emphasized that the Article 11(2) exceptions are to be construed strictly: only 'convincing and compelling reasons'[1009] can justify restrictions on freedom of association, and 'all such restrictions are subject to a rigorous supervision by the Court'.[1010] This strict approach is due to the 'direct relationship between democracy, pluralism and the freedom of association'.[1011] The ECtHR's jurisprudence on Article 11(2) attaches particular importance to pluralism, tolerance, and broadmindedness. In that context, the ECtHR has held that although individual interests must on occasion be subordinated to those of a group, democracy does not simply mean that the views of the majority must always prevail: a balance must be achieved that ensures the fair and proper treatment of minorities and avoids any abuse of a dominant position.[1012]

The ECtHR has recognized the importance of certain types of associations in ensuring pluralism and democracy. It has often noted the 'essential role' played by political parties in this regard, but has also stated that:

Associations formed for other purposes, including those protecting cultural or spiritual heritage, pursuing various socio-economic aims, proclaiming or teaching religion, seeking an ethnic identity or asserting a minority consciousness are also important to the proper functioning of democracy.[1013]

Dissolution or banning of associations that pursue objectives contrary to the state will rarely be justified under Article 11. Two examples stand out. In *Refah Partisi v Turkey* the Grand Chamber unanimously upheld the ECtHR's majority finding that the ban was justified as a state is entitled to prevent implementation of a political programme that is inconsistent with Convention norms and which, if given effect, might jeopardize civil peace and a country's democratic regime.[1014] In *Herri Batasuna and Batasuna v Spain* a political party linked to the terrorist organization, ETA, was dissolved.[1015] The Court endorsed the position of the domestic courts in finding that a refusal to condemn violence amounted to an attitude of tacit support for terrorism, in the context of long-term threat from Basque terrorism.

7.450

7.451

7.452

[1007] See, eg *British Airways Plc v Unite the Union* [2010] EWCA Civ 669, [2010] IRLR 423; *RMT v Serco Ltd* [2011] EWCA Civ 226, [2011] IRLR 399.

[1008] For a rare example of a violation on the basis that an interference was not 'in accordance with law', see *Maestri v Italy* App No 39748/98, 17 February 2004.

[1009] *Tüm Haber Sen and Çinar v Turkey* App No 28602/95, 21 February 2006, para 35.

[1010] See, eg *United Communist Party of Turkey and ors v Turkey* Reports of Judgments and Decisions 1998-I, 30 January 1998, para 42; *Socialist Party and ors v Turkey* Reports of Judgments and Decisions 1998-III, 25 May 1998, para 41; *Refah Partisi (The Welfare Party) and ors v Turkey* (2003) 14 BHRC 1, para 86.

[1011] *Gorzelik and ors* (2005) 40 EHRR 4, para 88.

[1012] See *Young, James and Webster v UK* (1982) 4 EHRR 38, para 63; *Chassagnou and ors v France* (1999) 29 EHRR 615, para 112.

[1013] *Gorzelik and ors* (2005) 40 EHRR 4, para 92.

[1014] (2003) 14 BHRC 1.

[1015] App Nos 25803/04 and 25817/04, 30 June 2009.

7.453   However, the ECtHR has stated that the power set out in *Refah Partisi* 'must be used sparingly'.[1016] In a series of cases against Turkey[1017] and Bulgaria[1018] the ECtHR has found that the mere fact that an association expresses separatist views and demands territorial changes in speeches, demonstrations, or manifestos does not per se amount to a threat to a country's territorial integrity. Views or words which may appear 'shocking and unacceptable' to the authorities and the majority of the population should not be suppressed on this basis.

7.454   Further, in assessing whether an organization truly propagates violence the ECtHR will take into account that an association's declarations may include 'an element of exaggeration' and harsh, acerbic language in order to attract attention.[1019]

7.455   Article 11(2) permits states to place limitations on the exercise of the Article 11(1) rights by members of the armed forces, police, or members of the administration of the state, although this clause appears to be of diminishing importance in the light of the case of *Tüm Haber Sen and Cinar v Turkey* (analysed below).[1020] In *Council of Civil Service Unions v UK* (the 'GCHQ' case) the ECmHR took the view that staff at GCHQ were 'members of the administration of the State' and that therefore there was no breach of the Convention in the decision of the UK Government to prohibit them from trade union membership.[1021] By contrast, in *Vogt v Germany* the ECmHR found that German schoolteachers were not 'members of the administration of the State', and the ECtHR held that this part of Article 11(2) 'should be interpreted narrowly in the light of the post held by the official concerned'.[1022]

7.456   The case of *Tüm Haber Sen and Çinar v Turkey*, concerning the dissolution of a civil servants' trade union, indicates that even when an individual does fall within this part of Article 11(2), a strict approach to the question of justification is nevertheless required.[1023] The ECtHR held that, to justify interfering with the freedom of association of members of the armed forces, the police, or the administration of the state, 'only convincing and compelling reasons' would suffice.[1024]

5. Article 11 and positive obligations

7.457   In addition to imposing a negative obligation on the authorities not to interfere unjustifiably with the protected rights, Article 11 contains a positive obligation on states to secure the effective enjoyment of those rights.[1025] For example, in *Plattform 'Ärtze für*

[1016] *Gorzelik and ors* (2005) 40 EHRR 4, para 95.

[1017] *Freedom and Democracy Party (ÖZDEP) v Turkey* App No 23885/94 ECHR 1999-VIII, para 41; *Yazar and ors v Turkey* App Nos 22723/93, 22724/93 and 22725/93 ECHR 2002-II, paras 57, 58.

[1018] *Stankov and United Macedonian Association Ilinden v Bulgaria* App Nos 29221/95 and 29225/95, ECHR 2001-IX, para 97; *United Macedonian Association Ilinden v Bulgaria* (1998) 26 EHRR CD 103, para 76.

[1019] *United Macedonian Association Ilinden v Bulgaria* (1998) 26 EHRR CD 103, para 77.

[1020] App No 28602/95, 21 February 2006.

[1021] (1987) 50 DR 228.

[1022] (1995) 21 EHRR 205.

[1023] App No 28602/95, 21 February 2006.

[1024] Ibid, para 35. The Court relied on provisions of the International Labour Organization (ILO) and Art 5 of the European Social Charter in reaching this conclusion (see para 39).

[1025] *Wilson and Palmer v UK* (2002) 35 EHRR 20.

das leben' v Austria (a freedom of assembly case), the ECtHR ruled that the state had a duty to protect the participants in a peaceful demonstration from disruption by a violent counter-demonstration:

Genuine, effective freedom of peaceful assembly cannot . . . be reduced to a mere duty on the part of the state not to interfere: a purely negative conception would not be compatible with the object and purpose of Article 11 . . . Article 11 sometimes requires positive measures to be taken, even in the sphere of relations between individuals, if need be.[1026]

The ECtHR has also held on a number of occasions that a state's failure to act to protect association violated Article 11. For example, Article 11 was breached where domestic law did not prohibit employers offering financial disincentives to trade union membership.[1027] In *Danilenkov and ors v Russia*, the Court ruled that the state had a positive obligation to establish a judicial system that provided effective and clear protection against any discrimination based on membership of a trade union.[1028]   7.458

I. ARTICLE 12: RIGHT TO MARRY AND FOUND A FAMILY

Article 12 has two constituent rights—the right to marry and the right to found a family. The state is expressly given considerable discretion to regulate the exercise of these rights.   7.459

While it has obvious links to the right to respect for family life in Article 8, Article 12 is a distinct provision (*lex specialis*) and is of much narrower scope, focusing on the right to marry and found a family rather than incidents flowing from it. The ECtHR affirmed the distinction between Articles 8 and 12 in *P, C and S v UK*, holding that complaints regarding interference with family life between a parent and child engage Article 8, but cannot be raised under Article 12.[1029] In general, the Strasbourg organs have taken a much narrower approach to the scope of Article 12 than that of Article 8.   7.460

In cases raising issues under both Article 8 and Article 12, the ECtHR has held that an interference with family life that is justified under Article 8(2) cannot at the same time constitute a violation of Article 12.[1030]   7.461

The rights under Article 12 apply not only to citizens, but also to aliens and stateless persons.[1031]   7.462

1. The right to marry

(a) *Regulation and formalities*

The right to marry is a right that can only be exercised in accordance with national law and it is therefore for the state to decide how it wishes to regulate marriage. Both formal   7.463

[1026] (1988) 13 EHRR 204, para 32.
[1027] *Wilson and Palmer v UK* (2002) 35 EHRR 20. See also *Young, James and Webster v UK* (1981) 4 EHRR 38, para 49; *Gustafsson v Sweden* Reports of Judgments and Decisions 1996-II, 25 April 1996, para 45; *Sørensen and Rasmussen v Denmark* App Nos 52562/99 and 52620/99, 11 January 2006, para 57.
[1028] App No 67336/01, 30 July 2009.
[1029] (2002) 35 EHRR 31.
[1030] *Boso v Italy* App No 50490/99, ECHR 2002-VII.
[1031] *Sanders v France* (1996) 87 B-DR 160, 163.

rules (for example, concerning matters such as notice, publicity, and witnesses) and substantive rules (such as requirements relating to consent, capacity, prohibited degrees of consanguinity, or the prevention of bigamy) governing marriage are generally a matter for the state. The Convention leaves it to states to determine marriageable age. National laws imposing a minimum age of consent for lawful marriage do not amount to a breach of the right to marry under Article 12, even if they conflict with differing religious laws as to marriageable age.[1032]

7.464   The rules governing marriage must not be arbitrary or interfere with the essence of the right. For example, the imposition by the state of any substantial period of delay may injure the very essence of the right, whereas a shorter period will not.[1033]

7.465   In *Hamer v UK*[1034] and *Draper v UK*[1035] the ECmHR ruled that prohibiting prisoners from marrying was an arbitrary interference with their Article 12 rights because it served no legitimate state objective.

7.466   In *B v UK* a father-in-law and daughter-in-law challenged the provisions of the Marriage Act 1949 which prevented them from marrying, subject to obtaining a waiver through a private act of Parliament.[1036] The ECtHR found that the inconsistency between the Government's stated objectives and the waiver 'undermined the rationality and logic of the measure' and rendered it arbitrary.

7.467   Regulations must also be compatible with the exercise of other Convention rights, in particular Article 9, though this does not impose a positive obligation to match civil and religious marriage laws, nor preclude a requirement that a religious marriage ceremony may also need to be affirmed or registered under civil law.[1037]

(b) *Non-nationals*

7.468   The ECtHR has consistently held that conditions may be attached to the marriage of non-nationals in Member States for the purposes of ascertaining whether the marriage is genuine or one of convenience.[1038]

7.469   In *R (Baiai and ors) v Secretary of State for the Home Department* the House of Lords considered measures put in place by the Home Office to prevent 'sham marriages' among persons subject to immigration control.[1039] With some limited exceptions, all such persons were required to seek a certificate from the Home Secretary regardless of the status of their partner. In practice, almost all such applications were refused without regard to the applicants' individual circumstances. Their Lordships held that while the Government could legitimately take measures to prevent 'sham' marriages, the scheme

---

[1032] *Khan v UK* (1986) 48 DR 253.

[1033] *Hamer v UK* (1979) 24 DR 5; *F v Switzerland* (1987) 10 EHRR 411; cf *Shara and Rinia v Netherlands* (1985) 8 EHRR 307.

[1034] (1979) 24 DR 5.

[1035] (1980) 24 DR 72.

[1036] (2004) 39 EHRR 30.

[1037] *X v Germany* (1974) 1 DR 64; *Adams and Khan v UK* (1967) 10 YB 478. See, further, *Selim v Cyprus: Friendly Settlement* App No 47293/99, 16 July 2002.

[1038] *Sanders v France* (1996) 87 B-DR 160, 163; *Klip and Krüger v Netherlands* (1997) 91 A-DR 66, 71; *R (Baiai and ors) v Secretary of State for the Home Department* [2008] UKHL 53, [2008] 3 All ER 1094 at [29].

[1039] [2008] UKHL 53, [2008] 3 All ER 1094.

disproportionately infringed the rights of non-nationals. Invoking Nazi race laws, Baroness Hale stated:

Denying to members of minority groups the right to establish formal, legal relationships with the partners of their choice is one way of setting them apart from society, denying that they are 'free and equal in dignity and rights'.[1040]

The Government amended the scheme in response to the judgment in *Baiai*. The amended scheme was challenged in *O'Donoghue and ors v UK*.[1041] The ECtHR found that the scheme did not comply with Article 12 on the basis that whether or not to grant a certificate of approval was not based solely on the genuineness of the proposed marriage; it imposed a blanket prohibition on the exercise of the right to marry on all persons in a specified category; and the system of refunding fees to needy applicants was not an effective means of removing any breach of Article 12 as the very requirement to pay a fee acted as a powerful disincentive to marriage.   7.470

(c) *Gender and the right to marry*

Until recently, Article 12 provided only a right to marry a person who was biologically of the opposite sex.[1042] According to Strasbourg, the adoption of biological criteria to determine sex for the purposes of marriage was 'a matter encompassed within the power of Contracting States to regulate by national law the exercise of the right to marry'.[1043]   7.471

However, in the striking decision of *Goodwin v UK* the ECtHR held that: 7.472

While it is for the Contracting State to determine *inter alia* the conditions under which a person claiming legal recognition as a transsexual establishes that gender reassignment has been properly effected or under which past marriages cease to be valid and the formalities applicable to future marriages . . . the Court finds no justification for barring the transsexual from enjoying the right to marry under any circumstances.[1044]

Domestic law is now in line with Strasbourg's position. In *Bellinger v Bellinger* their Lordships issued a declaration of incompatibility, holding that section 11(c) of the Matrimonial Causes Act 1973 could not be construed so as to give effect to the decision of the ECtHR in *Goodwin*.[1045] Parliament then passed the Gender Recognition Act 2004, which provides that the marriage of a person who has obtained a 'full gender recognition certificate' to a person of the same biological sex as their original sex will not be rendered void on the basis that the parties are not respectively male and female.   7.473

[1040] Ibid at [44].
[1041] App No 34848/07, 14 December 2010.
[1042] *Rees v UK* (1986) 9 EHRR 56; *Cossey v UK* (1990) 13 EHRR 622; *Sheffield and Horsham v UK* (1998) 27 EHRR 163.
[1043] *Cossey v UK* (1990) 13 EHRR 622.
[1044] (2002) 35 EHRR 447, para 103.
[1045] [2003] UKHL 21, [2003] 2 AC 467.

(d) Same-sex marriage

7.474 The European Court does not recognize the rights of same-sex couples to marry.[1046] In *Schalk and Kopf v Austria* the Court held that the absence of European consensus on the rights of same-sex couples meant that the Convention could not yet be interpreted to create such a right.[1047] Interestingly, the Court considered the Charter of Fundamental Rights of the European Union, which includes in Article 9 a right to marry without a reference to men or women, thus leaving the decision to the states whether or not to recognize same-sex marriages. On the basis of this, the ECtHR concluded that it:

> . . . would no longer consider that the right to marry enshrined in Article 12 must in all circumstances be limited to marriage between two persons of the opposite sex. Consequently, it cannot be said that Article 12 is inapplicable to the applicants' complaint. However, as matters stand, the question whether or not to allow same-sex marriage is left to regulation by the national law of the Contracting State.[1048]

Until same-sex couples are afforded more consistent protection across Europe Article 12 will not expand to include them within its scope.

7.475 Domestic law is compatible with this approach. In *Wilkinson v Kitzinger* the High Court was asked to declare that the recognition of a Canadian marriage between two women domiciled in England, valid as a matter of the law of British Columbia, was valid as a marriage in the United Kingdom.[1049] Alternatively, that its recognition as a civil partnership under the Civil Partnership Act 2004, rather than a marriage, rendered English law incompatible with Articles 8, 12, and 14 of the Convention. The judge held that there was no such incompatibility: to afford legal recognition to same-sex relationships as civil partnerships rather than as 'marriages' met a legitimate aim of social policy and was proportionate.

(e) Dissolution of marriage

7.476 The right to marry does not include its corollary—the right to dissolve or formally end a marriage.[1050] The *travaux préparatoires* to the Convention indicate that the omission of 'dissolution' from the text of Article 12 was a deliberate departure from the wording of Article 16 of the Universal Declaration on Human Rights.[1051]

2. Right to found a family

7.477 Article 12 also protects the right to 'found a family', again subject to 'national laws governing the exercise of this right'. This right has so far only been considered in the context of marriage; Article 12 does not create a free-standing right to found a family in the absence of a marital relationship.[1052]

[1046] *Rees v UK* (1986) 9 EHRR 56; *Cossey v UK* (1990) 13 EHRR 622. See also the decision of the ECJ in *Grant v South-West Trains* [1998] ICR 449.

[1047] App No 30141/04, 24 June 2010.

[1048] Ibid, para 61.

[1049] [2006] EWHC 2022 (Fam), [2007] 1 FLR 295.

[1050] *Johnston and ors v Ireland* (1986) 9 EHRR 203.

[1051] Collected Edition of the Travaux Préparatoires, vol 1, 268.

[1052] *Marckx v Belgium* (1979) 2 EHRR 330.

(a) *Adoption*

A family can be founded by the adoption of children.[1053] However, the Strasbourg   7.478
organs have affirmed the early decision in *X and Y v UK*[1054] that Article 12 does not
create a right to adopt.[1055] It might, however, form part of the right to personal development under Article 8.[1056]

The Court of Appeal in *Briody v St Helen's and Knowsley Health Authority* ruled that   7.479
Article 12 does not require that a woman rendered infertile by the negligence of an NHS
hospital be entitled to damages that would enable her to proceed with a surrogacy
arrangement, nor does it include a right to be supplied with a child.[1057]

(b) *Artificial insemination*

The scope of Article 12 as a basis for challenges to restrictions and regulations on arti-   7.480
ficial insemination or other reproductive technologies has yet to be fully tested in
Strasbourg. Cases raising these issues are more frequently brought under Article 8.[1058]

The ECmHR admitted complaints under Articles 8 and/or 12 about the refusal by the   7.481
state to allow artificial insemination by donor treatment of prisoners' wives in 1987[1059]
and 1991,[1060] and the Grand Chamber considered the issue in *Dickson v UK*.[1061]

Dickson concerned a challenge to the Secretary of State's refusal to give a husband   7.482
access to artificial insemination facilities in order for his wife to conceive. By the time of
his release, his wife would be too old to conceive and the refusal therefore extinguished
their right to have a child together. By four to three, the ECtHR held that there was no
violation of Article 8 or 12 on the grounds that the United Kingdom did not impose a
blanket restriction on such activity and took relevant factors, such as the gravity of the
offence and the welfare of the child, into account in striking a fair balance between
the competing interests.[1062] The Grand Chamber disagreed. Deciding the case under
the right to family life in Article 8, it held that the policy of permitting artificial insemination only in 'exceptional circumstances' did not accord due weight to the prisoner's
rights and breached Article 8.

There is now a gap between the approach in domestic law and the Strasbourg juris-   7.483
prudence. Prior to *Dickson* the Court of Appeal held that Article 12 would not be
breached in such circumstances.[1063] This decision will need to be revisited in light of the
Grand Chamber's decision.

Whether Article 12 includes a right to avail oneself of advances in reproduction tech-   7.484
nology and, if so, whether a positive obligation arises upon the state to facilitate access
to such technology, or even to provide it, are future questions that are likely to arise
under Article 12.

[1053] *Van Oosterwijck v Belgium* (1979) 3 EHRR 581.
[1054] (1977) 12 DR 32.
[1055] *Fretté v France* (2004) 38 EHRR 21, para 32; *EB v France* (2008) 47 EHRR 21, para 41.
[1056] *EB v France* (2008) 47 EHRR 21, paras 42–46.
[1057] [2001] EWCA Civ 1010, [2002] QB 856.
[1058] See, eg *Evans v UK* (2008) 46 EHRR 34, discussed under Art 8 at para 7.239 above.
[1059] *PG v UK*, App No 10822/84, 7 June 1987.
[1060] *GS and RS v UK* App No 17142/90, 10 July 1991.
[1061] (2007) 24 BHRC 19.
[1062] (2006) 46 EHRR 419.
[1063] *R v Secretary of State for the Home Department, ex p Mellor* [2001] EWCA Civ 472, [2002] QB 13.

3. Proportionality and Article 12

7.485   Article 12 is not explicitly qualified in the same way as Articles 8–11 and there has been some confusion over whether the right is in fact qualified by the same criterion as specified in those articles.[1064] In general, the ECtHR permits limitations as specified by national laws as long as they do not infringe 'the very essence of the right', but it does not normally apply the three-part proportionality analysis adopted under Articles 8–11.[1065]

7.486   Whatever the formal approach to proportionality under Article 12, recent cases suggest that the standard of review applied by the ECtHR and the domestic courts will be a rigorous one.[1066]

4. Positive obligations

7.487   Article 12 has not thus far been interpreted to impose extensive positive obligations on the state. The ECtHR has held that there is no obligation to ensure that a married couple can cohabit or consummate their marriage.[1067] Nor is there a duty to provide living accommodation or subsistence to maintain a family.[1068] Obligations such as these are more likely to arise as a consequence of respect for private and family life under Article 8.[1069]

7.488   In line with this approach, the Northern Ireland Court of Appeal held in *Re Connor's Application for Judicial Review* that Article 12 does not confer an absolute right to cohabitation on spouses, and that such a right may be interfered with where necessary and proportionate.[1070]

7.489   Positive obligations under Article 12 have also been considered by the European Court of Justice (ECJ). In *KB v NHS Pensions Agency*, the ECJ followed the ECtHR's decision in *Goodwin* in finding a violation of Article 12, but held that it was for the national courts to decide whether a transsexual could rely on the EC Treaty to gain benefits for his or her partner.[1071]

J. ARTICLE 13: RIGHT TO AN EFFECTIVE REMEDY

7.490   Article 13 does not provide a free-standing right to an effective remedy. A claim under Article 13 must be brought in conjunction with an alleged breach of another Convention right. That breach need not be established in order for the ECtHR to find a violation of Article 13, but it must be 'arguable'.[1072] Article 13 will not apply where the applicant

---

[1064] See *R (Baiai and ors) v Secretary of State for the Home Department* [2008] UKHL 53, [2008] 3 All ER 1094 at [46] per Baroness Hale.

[1065] See, eg *Goodwin v UK* (2002) 35 EHRR 447. Cf *F v Switzerland* (1987) 10 EHRR 411 where the ECtHR came closer to applying the standard proportionality analysis.

[1066] See, eg *Dickson v UK* (2007) 24 BHRC 19; *R (Baiai and ors) v Secretary of State for the Home Department* [2008] UKHL 53, [2008] 3 All ER 1094.

[1067] *Hamer v UK* (1979) 24 DR 5; *Draper v UK* (1980) 24 DR 72.

[1068] *Andersson and Kullman v Sweden* (1986) 46 DR 251.

[1069] See, eg *Dickson v UK* (2007) 24 BHRC 19. See also the discussion under Art 8 at para 7.221 above.

[1070] [2004] NICA 45.

[1071] (Case C-117/01) [2004] ECR I-541.

[1072] *Boyle and Rice v UK* (1988) 10 EHRR 425.

can obtain a remedy under another article that proscribes specific remedies, such as the right to review of detention under Article 5(4) or fair trial rights under Article 6(1).[1073]

Article 13 is not incorporated into UK law under the Human Rights Act. This omis- 7.491 sion is discussed further below and in Chapter 3.[1074]

1. Effective remedy

The right to an effective remedy means that there must be both domestic procedures for 7.492 dealing with the substance of an 'arguable complaint' and for granting appropriate relief in cases of actual breach of the Convention.[1075] Accordingly, as the ECtHR stated in *Klass v Germany*, the available remedy must 'involve the determination of the claim as well as the possibility of redress'.[1076]

The scope of the Article 13 obligation varies depending on the nature of the com- 7.493 plaint. For example, in the case of a violation of Article 2, Article 13 will require, in addition to the payment of compensation where appropriate, an effective investigation capable of leading to the identification and punishment of those responsible for the deprivation of life, including effective access for the complainant to the investigation procedure.[1077] By contrast, compensation alone may be a sufficient remedy for breaches of other articles. In all cases the requisite remedy must be 'effective' in both practice and law.[1078] The requirement of practical efficacy means that exercise of the remedy must not be unjustifiably hindered by the acts or omissions of state authorities.[1079]

The question will often be whether all the procedures, in the lower tribunals and the 7.494 courts, taken together, amount to an 'effective remedy'. For example, *Silver v UK* con-cerned a complaint by a prisoner that his correspondence had been interfered with con-trary to Article 8 and that no effective remedy was available in respect of that breach. The ECtHR took the view that neither the prison board of visitors, the Parliamentary Commissioner for Administration, the Home Secretary, nor subsequent judicial review of the Home Secretary's decisions provided sufficiently effective remedies to comply with Article 13.[1080]

The United Kingdom came under Article 13 scrutiny in relation to allegations of 7.495 child abuse, triggering Article 3. In both *Z v UK*[1081] and *DP and JC v UK*[1082] the lack of any appropriate means of obtaining a determination of allegations that the local authority had failed to protect the applicants from ill-treatment during childhood was found to breach Article 13. More recently, the ECtHR has found a violation of Article 13 where parents of a child mistakenly taken into care before the Human Rights Act came into force could only bring a claim in negligence or judicially review the authori-ties' decisions.[1083]

[1073] *Hakansson and Sturesson v Sweden* (1990) 13 EHRR 1.
[1074] See ch 3, para 3.76.
[1075] *Aksoy v Turkey* (1996) 23 EHRR 553.
[1076] (1978) 2 EHRR 214.
[1077] *Keenan v UK* (2001) 3 EHRR 913; *Edwards v UK* (2002) 35 EHRR 487.
[1078] *Aksoy v Turkey* (1996) 23 EHRR 553.
[1079] Ibid.
[1080] (1983) 5 EHRR 347.
[1081] (2002) 34 EHRR 3.
[1082] (2003) 36 EHRR 14.
[1083] *RK and AK v UK* [2009] 1 FLR 274. See also *MAK and RK v UK* [2010] 2 FLR 451.

7.496   The ECtHR has been critical of formal remedies that prevent examination of the merits of a claim. Thus, much of the Strasbourg case law concerning the United Kingdom addresses the extent to which *Wednesbury*-based judicial review (the standard before the implementation of the Human Rights Act), in which issues of fact can rarely be considered, can be treated as an effective remedy.[1084]

7.497   Whether the ECtHR has regarded judicial review as an adequate remedy appears to depend on the context, and, in particular, whether the ECtHR was satisfied that the domestic courts can afford a sufficient degree of review properly to examine the legality of the executive's actions in the particular circumstances. In the pre-Human Rights Act cases, the ECtHR's approach varied. In *Soering v UK* the applicant was threatened with extradition to the United States to face a charge of murder, to a state in which he risked being placed on death row (contrary to Article 3). The fact that a UK court had jurisdiction to set aside a decision to extradite for this reason convinced the ECtHR that judicial review was an effective remedy for the purposes of Article 13.[1085] Thus, in *Vilvarajah v UK*, the ECtHR held that it had already decided that judicial review was an adequate remedy in the context of extradition, even though, in that case, the applicant had already left the United Kingdom.[1086]

7.498   However, in *Chahal v UK* the ECtHR held that there was no effective remedy for violation of Article 3, and hence a violation of Article 13, where a suspected terrorist was detained in custody for deportation purposes in response to the Home Secretary's determination that he was a threat to national security. The ECtHR found that Article 13 required independent scrutiny of the Article claim, which did not take into consideration the national security threat.[1087] The Special Immigration Appeals Commission was set up in response to this judgment.

7.499   In *Smith and Grady v UK* the domestic courts could only review whether the policy of excluding homosexuals from the armed forces was irrational, not whether it met a pressing social need or was a proportionate infringement of Article 8. Even the heightened 'anxious scrutiny' standard was held inadequate to comply with Article 13.[1088] In *Hatton v UK* the Grand Chamber of the ECtHR held that Article 13 had been violated because judicial review did not allow for consideration of whether an increase in night flights was a justifiable limitation on the right to respect for the private and family lives of those who lived near Heathrow airport.[1089] The standard of review is an issue which, theoretically at least, should have fallen into abeyance after the implementation of the Human Rights Act, though it remains possible that it could yet form the ground of a complaint in an appropriate case.

7.500   In a number of cases brought after the implementation of the Human Rights Act, the European Court has found that declarations of incompatibility issued under section 4 are not an effective remedy for a breach of a Convention right. The primary failing of the section 4 mechanism is that it places no binding legal obligation on the executive or legislature to amend the law following a declaration of incompatibility,

---

[1084] See, eg *Peck v UK* (2003) 36 EHRR 41; *Hatton v UK* (2003) 37 EHRR 28.
[1085] (1989) 11 EHRR 439. See also *Bensaid v UK* (2001) 33 EHRR 10.
[1086] (1991) 14 EHRR 248.
[1087] (1996) 23 EHRR 413.
[1088] (2000) 29 EHRR 548. See also *Peck v UK* (2003) 36 EHRR 719. Cf *D v UK* (1997) 24 EHRR 423.
[1089] (2003) 37 EHRR 611.

nor can it form the basis of a monetary award of compensation.[1090] In *Burden and Burden v UK* the Grand Chamber held that as a result of these inadequacies a failure to seek a declaration did not mean that the applicant had not exhausted his domestic remedies.[1091] However, the Grand Chamber suggested that there might come a time when the ministerial practice of amending the law in response to a declaration was so certain that a declaration might in fact give rise to a binding obligation. If that point were reached it would be necessary to seek a declaration before making an application to the ECtHR.

2. National authority

The authority with the ability to provide the remedy must be independent of the body alleged to have breached the Convention obligation.[1092] If a body is sufficiently independent for Article 6 purposes it will also satisfy this requirement under Article 13.   7.501

3. Human Rights Act implications[1093]

Article 13 was omitted from the rights incorporated by the Human Rights Act because it was believed that the provisions of the Act itself provided an effective remedy as contemplated under Article 13.[1094] As the European case law on declarations of incompatibility shows, this has not proved to be the case.[1095]   7.502

Despite the fact that Article 13 is not incorporated, the English courts have had regard to the right since, by virtue of section 2 of the Act, Strasbourg case law must be taken into account when a UK court is considering a case 'in connection with' an incorporated right. In *R (Al-Skeini) v Secretary of State for Defence*, for example, Lord Brown held that Article 13 would be violated if the domestic courts were unable to consider extraterritorial complaints in line with the Strasbourg case law on the reach of Article 1.[1096] In *RB (Algeria) v Secretary of State for the Home Department* the House of Lords applied *Chahal v UK*[1097] in reaching its conclusion that the Special Immigration Appeals Commission procedure determined whether deportation would violate Article 3 to the extent required by Article 13.[1098]   7.503

[1090] See *Dodds v UK* App No 59314/00, 8 April 2003; *Walker v UK* App No 37212/02, 16 March 2004; *Pearson v UK* App No 8374/03, 27 April 2004; *B and L v UK* App No 36536/02, 29 June 2004.

[1091] (2008) 24 BHRC 709.

[1092] *Govell v UK* App No 27237/95, 14 January 1998; *Khan v UK* (2000) 31 EHRR 45; *Taylor-Sabori v UK* (2003) 36 EHRR 17.

[1093] See also ch 3.

[1094] *Brown v Stott* [2001] 1 WLR 817, 847; *In Re S (FC) and ors* [2002] UKHL 10, [2002] 2 AC 291 at [61]. See also Clayton and Tomlinson, *The Law of Human Rights*, 2nd edn (Oxford: Oxford University Press, 2009) paras 21.02–21.03.

[1095] See para 7.500 above.

[1096] [2007] UKHL 26, [2008] 1 AC 153 at [147]–[149].

[1097] (1996) 23 EHRR 413.

[1098] [2009] UKHL 10, [2009] 2 WLR 512.

K. ARTICLE 14: PROHIBITION ON DISCRIMINATION

1. The importance of Article 14

7.504   Affording equality of respect to all persons, treating like cases alike, and treating unlike cases differently, are axioms of rational behaviour in a society which treats each individual as having fundamentally equal worth. Equality of treatment is 'one of the building blocks of democracy'.[1099] The non-discrimination guarantee contained in Article 14 is therefore a key provision of the Convention. As Lord Nicholls explained in *Ghaidan v Godin Mendoza*:

> Discriminatory law undermines the rule of law because it is the antithesis of fairness. It brings the law into disrepute. It breeds resentment. It fosters an inequality of outlook which is demeaning alike to those unfairly benefited and those unfairly prejudiced.[1100]

Recent decisions of the ECtHR have also explained the importance and value of a realistic application of the equal treatment guarantee in protecting and preserving a democratic society.[1101]

7.505   Until recently, the case law of the ECtHR on Article 14 was relatively undeveloped. However, it has become more sophisticated, with recent important decisions such as those of the Grand Chamber in *Stec v UK* and *DH v Czech Republic*[1102].

7.506   In earlier cases, the ECtHR declined to consider discrimination law arguments where there was also a breach of a substantive right.[1103] In *Buckley v UK* Judge Pettiti regretted that the ECtHR had missed 'an opportunity to produce . . . a critique of national law and practice with regard to Gypsies and travellers in the UK that would have been transposable to the rest of Europe, and thereby partly compensate for the injustices they suffer'.[1104] However, later cases indicate an evolving interest in protecting minority rights and a more imaginative and substantive approach to the applicability of equality concepts to legal protection of minority groups.[1105]

2. Scope of Article 14

7.507   Article 14 guarantees that everyone shall enjoy Convention rights and freedoms without 'discrimination' on a broad variety of grounds. The listed grounds of prohibited discrimination are non-exhaustive examples only ('any grounds *such as* . . .'), and 'other status' has been broadly defined. However, although Article 14 is 'deceptively simple',[1106]

[1099] Per Lord Hoffmann in *Matadeen v Pointu* [1999] AC 98 (Privy Council).

[1100] [2004] UKHL 30, [2004] 2 AC 557 at [9]. See also other speeches in *Gaidan*, and the decision of the House of Lords in *A v Secretary of State for the Home Department* [2004] UKHL 56, [2005] 2 AC 68.

[1101] *DH v Czech Republic* (2007) 23 BHRC 526.

[1102] *Stec v UK* (2005) 41 EHRR SE295; *DH v Czech Republic* (2007) 23 BHRC 526.

[1103] Eg *Airey v Ireland* (1979) 2 EHRR 305; *Dudgeon v UK* (1981) 4 EHRR 149, para 69; *Smith and Grady v UK* (2000) 29 EHRR 548; *Buckley v UK* [1996] ECHR 20348/92.

[1104] [1996] ECHR 20348/92, dissenting opinion of Judge Pettiti.

[1105] (2001) 33 EHRR 399; *Aziz v Cyprus* App No 69949/01; *JM v UK* (2010) 30 BHRC 60; *Opuz v Turkey* App 33401/02, 9 September 2009, 200–202.

[1106] *AL (Serbia) v Secretary of State for the Home Department* [2008] UKHL 42, [2008] 4 All ER 1127 at [20] per Baroness Hale.

its application is not straightforward. It guarantees only *equal application* of the law of the Convention, and not a free-standing guarantee of equal treatment.

The protection afforded by Article 14 is therefore narrower than that found in other, more open-ended guarantees of equal treatment, such as that contained in Article 26 of the International Covenant on Civil and Political Rights 1966, or Protocol 12 to the Convention itself (which the United Kingdom has declined to ratify). Article 14 requires only that the enjoyment of other Convention rights be secured without discrimination. This means that it can operate only within the 'ambit' or scope of another Convention right: 7.508

. . . Article 14 complements the other substantive provisions of the Convention and the Protocols. It has no independent existence since it has effect solely in relation to 'the enjoyment of the rights and freedoms' safeguarded by those provisions. Although the application of article 14 does not necessarily presuppose a breach of those provisions—and to this extent it is autonomous—there can be no room for its application unless the facts at issue fall within the ambit of one or more of the latter.[1107]

In *National Union of Belgian Police v Belgium* the ECtHR said, 'it is as though Article 14 formed an integral part of each of the articles laying down rights and freedoms whatever their nature'.[1108]   7.509

The application of Article 14 does not require a *breach* of another article but merely that the facts of the case come within the ambit of another article.[1109] However, whether alleged discrimination 'falls within the ambit' of another Convention right is not always a straightforward issue.[1110] In broad terms, Article 14 will come into play whenever the subject matter of the disadvantage 'constitutes one of the modalities' of the exercise of a right guaranteed or whenever the measures complained of are 'linked' to the exercise of a right guaranteed.[1111]   7.510

It is enough for a claimant to establish that the disadvantage relates to the subject matter of another substantive Convention right, even if the state has chosen to make provision which is not itself required by the Convention.[1112] For example, in *Schmidt v Germany*, where only men were obliged to serve in a voluntary fire brigade or to pay a financial contribution in lieu, the ECtHR found that the requirements for work did not amount to 'forced or compulsory labour' in Article 4 but nevertheless came within the ambit of Article 4 and thus engaged Article 14.[1113]   7.511

[1107] *Abudulaziz, Cabales and Balakandi v UK* (1985) 7 EHRR 471, para 71.

[1108] (1975) 1 EHRR 578.

[1109] *Abdulaziz, Cabales and Balkandali v UK* (1985) 7 EHRR 471; *Botta v Italy* (1998) 26 EHRR 241, para 39.

[1110] See the different views reached by the House of Lords and the European Court of Human Rights on whether criteria for assessing child support obligations which differentiated between those with same-sex and opposite partners fell within the ambit of 'family life': *M v Secretary of State for Work and Pensions* [2006] UKHL 11, [2006] 2 AC 91 at [13]–[16] per Lord Nicholls; but held to breach Art 14 by the ECtHR in *JM v UK* (2010) 30 BHRC 60.

[1111] *Petrovic v Austria* (2001) 33 EHRR 307, paras 22, 28.

[1112] See *Ghaidan v Godin-Mendoza* [2004] UKHL 30, [2004] 2 AC 557 at [6] per Lord Nicholls.

[1113] (1994) 18 EHRR 513. See also *Van der Mussele v Belgium* (1984) 6 EHRR 162; *Zarb Adami v Malta* (2007) 44 EHRR 33, para 46; *Belgian Linguistics (No 2)* (1968) 1 EHRR 252, para 9; *Petrovic v Austria* (2001) 33 EHRR 307; *Inze v Austria* (1987) 10 EHRR 394; *Abdulaziz, Cabales and Balkandali v UK* (1985) 7 EHRR 471, paras 65, 71, 72.

7.512   This approach was confirmed by the Grand Chamber in *Stec v UK*, which held that the prohibition of discrimination extends to 'those additional rights, falling within the scope of any Convention article, for which the State has voluntarily decided to provide'. Therefore, although Article 1 of Protocol 1 does not create a right to acquire property, and places no restriction on a state's freedom to decide whether or not to have in place a social security scheme, 'if a State does decide to create a benefits scheme it must do so in a manner compatible with Article 14'.[1114]

7.513   However, it goes too far to claim that even a tenuous link with another Convention provision will suffice for Article 14 to come into play.[1115] And in other cases the courts have limited the scope of Article 14 by taking a restricted view of what falls within the ambit of another right. In the widely criticized decision of *Botta v Italy*, it was held that the complaint that a disabled person could not obtain access to a public beach was not within the ambit of Article 8, and so could not even found the basis of a complaint under Article 14.[1116]

(a) *'Protected grounds' or 'status'*

7.514   The grounds upon which discrimination is prohibited by Article 14 are very wide. The particular grounds of prohibited discrimination specified are only examples ('without discrimination on any ground *such as . . .*'). The non-exhaustive examples given in Article 14 conclude with the open-ended phrase 'or other status' ('*toute autre distinction*' in the French text).

7.515   In *Kjeldsen, Busk Madsen and Pedersen v Denmark* the ECtHR equated 'other status' with 'personal characteristic'.[1117] This has been broadly interpreted by the Strasbourg bodies, which have held that marital status,[1118] ownership of a particular breed of dog,[1119] trade union membership, military status,[1120] conscientious objection,[1121] residence,[1122] and imprisonment are prohibited grounds of discrimination. In *S and Marper v UK*[1123] the ECtHR rejected the approach of the House of Lords in *R (S and Marper) v Chief Constable of South Yorkshire Police*.[1124] The ECtHR held that a rule that those who had been charged or investigated by the police could have fingerprints or DNA samples held indefinitely amounted to discrimination on the basis of that status (ie having been charged or investigated, though not convicted). This reflected the Court's previous finding in *Sidabras v Lithuania* that historic facts that affect status

---

[1114] (2006) 43 EHRR 1017, paras 40, 55. Affirmed as a matter of domestic law in *RJM v Secretary of State for Work and Pensions* [2008] UKHL 63, [2008] 3 WLR 1023; and by the Grand Chamber in *Carson v UK* App No 42184/05, 16 March 2010, para 64–65.

[1115] See per Lord Hoffmann in *R (Carson) v Secretary of State for Work and Pensions* [2005] UKHL 37, [2006] AC 173; and the House of Lords in *Secretary of State for Work and Pensions v M* [2006] UKHL 11, [2006] 2 AC 91 at [60].

[1116] (1998) 4 BHRC 81.

[1117] (1979–80) 1 EHRR 711.

[1118] *Sahin v Germany* (2003) 36 EHRR 43.

[1119] *Bullock v UK* (1996) 21 EHRR CD 85.

[1120] *Engel v Netherlands* (1979–80) 1 EHRR 647.

[1121] *Thlimmenos v Greece* (2000) 31 EHRR 411.

[1122] *Darby v Sweden* (1990) 13 EHRR 774; *Carson v UK* App No 42184/05, 16 March 2010, 70–71.

[1123] App Nos 30562/04 and 30566/04, 4 December 2008.

[1124] [2004] UKHL 39, [2004] 1 WLR 2196 at [51].

(in that case, former membership of the KGB) are included within the protection of Article 14.[1125]

3. Discrimination

(a) *The concept*

Not all forms of differentiation amount to discrimination in Convention terms. Otherwise, Article 14 would have 'absurd results'.[1126] Discrimination occurs when: 7.516

(i) there is discriminatory treatment of individuals in 'relevantly similar'[1127] or analogous[1128] situations; and

(ii) there is no 'objective or reasonable justification' for the distinction in treatment.[1129]

The ECtHR has recognized that the 'right not to be discriminated against in the enjoyment of the rights guaranteed under the Convention is also violated when States without an objective and reasonable justification fail to treat differently persons whose situations are significantly different'.[1130] It has also recognized the concept of indirect discrimination,[1131] and is beginning to develop the concept of a positive obligation to ensure equal protection of the laws.[1132] 7.517

(b) *Persons in an analogous situation*

Article 14 only affords the right to equal treatment to those who can show that their situation is genuinely 'analogous' or comparable with that of the other with whom equality is sought. The burden lies on the applicant to establish that there has been different treatment afforded to him or her and to another in a similar or analogous situation. Without evidence of differential treatment on a prohibited ground the claim will fail.[1133] 7.518

The ECtHR has often decided cases alleging discriminatory treatment by determining that no Article 14 question is raised because the comparison is not truly with a person in an analogous situation. For example, in *Van der Mussele v Belgium* the ECtHR held that trainee barristers could not legitimately be compared with trainees in other professions because the differences between their situations were too great.[1134] In *Stubbings v UK* the ECtHR rejected as 'artificial' the applicants' submission that as victims of child sexual abuse they were in an analogous position to victims of injuries inflicted negligently, as opposed to intentionally.[1135] In *Carson v UK*[1136] the Grand Chamber held that pensioners who retired abroad to countries with which the United Kingdom had not entered bilateral agreements were not in an analogous or comparable 7.519

[1125] (2006) 42 EHRR 6.
[1126] *Belgian Linguistics (No 2)* (1968) 1 EHRR 252, para 10.
[1127] *National and Provincial Building Society v UK* (1997) 25 EHRR 127, para 88.
[1128] *Lithgow v UK* (1986) 8 EHRR 329.
[1129] *Fredin v Sweden* (1991) 13 EHRR 784.
[1130] *Thlimmenos v Greece* (2000) 31 EHRR 411, para 44.
[1131] *DH v Czech Republic* (2008) 47 EHRR 3.
[1132] *Opuz v Turkey* App No 33401/02, 9 June 2009.
[1133] See, eg *Kaya v Turkey* (1998) 28 EHRR 1, para 113.
[1134] (1983) 6 EHRR 163.
[1135] (1996) 23 EHRR 213, para 71.
[1136] App No 42184/05, 16 March 2010.

situation to those who had retired within the United Kingdom or to countries with which the United Kingdom did have such an agreement. Differences in entitlement to pension uprating therefore did not even require justification.

7.520   This approach has the potential to weaken the protection offered by Article 14 since examination of the core complaint may be precluded by technical points concerning the inappropriateness of comparators precisely because they are in a more favourable position. In more recent domestic cases on the concept of Article 14, courts have begun to stress that the selection of a comparator is only part of a 'framework' of useful analysis. It is not a barrier to asking the overarching question, namely whether two cases are sufficiently similar to require a court to ask itself whether the difference in treatment is nonetheless justified.[1137]

(c) *Failure to treat like cases differently*

7.521   It is important to understand that Article 14 does not prohibit, and may indeed require, different treatment of groups in order to correct 'factual inequalities' between them.[1138] In the leading case of *Thlimmenos v Greece*, the ECtHR considered the ban imposed by a professional regulatory body on anyone with a criminal record. The applicant had such a record because he had objected, on religious and conscientious grounds, to performing military service. Though the blanket ban on those with any criminal record was not intended to discriminate against those who had refused military service for reasons of conscience, it nonetheless had a particular adverse effect on persons with the applicant's belief, which was disproportionate and could not be justified, and was therefore held to be discriminatory on grounds of religion, contrary to Articles 9 and 14.[1139]

(d) *Indirect discrimination*

7.522   The idea that unlike cases may, in some circumstances, require different treatment overlaps with, but is not identical to, the developing concept of indirect discrimination.[1140]

7.523   Indirect discrimination, also known as 'disparate effect' or 'adverse effect' discrimination, may arise when apparently neutral policies or laws have a disproportionate impact upon a particular individual or group. The *Belgian Linguistics* decision (above) implied that the Convention is capable of covering both direct and indirect discrimination since the ECtHR suggested that justification of a measure would be required where the 'aims *and effects*' were prima facie discriminatory. For a long time, the Strasbourg case law on this topic remained relatively undeveloped. For example, in *Abdulaziz v UK*[1141] the ECtHR declined to treat as indirectly discriminatory Immigration Rules that disqualified those who had not met their partners from entering the country for marriage, even though the 'practical effect' of the rule was race discrimination against South Asian

---

[1137] See *R (Carson) v Secretary of State for Work and Pensions* [2005] UKHL 37, [2006] AC 173 at [3] per Lord Nicholls; *AL (Serbia) v Secretary of State for the Home Department* [2008] UKHL 42, [2008] 4 All ER 1127 at [24]–[28] per Baroness Hale.

[1138] *Stec v UK* (2006) 43 EHRR 1017, para 51; *Belgian Lingusitics (No 2)* (1968) 1 EHRR 252, para 10: *Thlimmenos v Greece* (2000) 31 EHRR 411, para 44.

[1139] (2000) 31 EHRR 411.

[1140] The conceptual distinction was analysed by Elias LJ (with whom Maurice Kay LJ and Mummery LJ agreed) in *AM (Somalia) v Entry Clearance Officer* [2009] EWCA Civ 634.

[1141] (1985) 7 EHRR 471.

groups with a tradition of arranged marriage. The ECtHR did not analyse the issue of indirect discrimination as an independent question, preferring to run it together with the question of justification.

However, the *Thlimennos* case (above) acknowledged that it was the effects of a par-   7.524
ticular policy or rule which fell to be justified, and the ECtHR clearly endorsed this approach to indirect discrimination in *McShane v UK*.[1142]

Thlimennos addressed the question of whether it was justified to apply a generally   7.525
acceptable rule without exceptions to allow for those particularly affected by it. The concept of indirect discrimination is a challenge to the justifiability of the very existence of such a rule, at least in its undifferentiated form. The ECtHR developed the concept of indirect discrimination only slowly. In *Nachova and ors v Bulgaria* the Grand Chamber indicated that the burden of proof in such cases lies on the applicants, and the standard of proof is 'beyond reasonable doubt'—a high threshold that will limit the number of successful claims.[1143]

However, statistics did suffice as the basis for a finding of sex discrimination in the   7.526
recent case of *Zarb Adami v Malta*.[1144] The applicant was called for jury service and fined when he failed to appear. He submitted that both the practice of excusal from jury service and the sanction were discriminatory on the basis of sex. In support of this con-tention he produced statistics demonstrating a large discrepancy in the number of women and men enrolled as jurors. As both men and women were in theory equally liable to serve as jurors and to be exempted, the 'only explanation' for the discrepancy could be that there had been a discriminatory administrative practice.

A more realistic approach to establishing indirect discrimination has now been firmly   7.527
established by the landmark decision of the Grand Chamber in *DH v Czech Republic*.[1145] In that case, overturning an earlier Chamber judgment, the Grand Chamber took the major step of recognizing that de facto discrimination could be proved by analysis of the effects of a policy on a particular group, which therefore fell to be justified. The case concerned the significantly disproportionate placing of Roma children in 'special schools' with a reduced curriculum. The statistics for the over-representation of Roma children in such schools were such that the Court was prepared to find indirect discrimination that fell to be justified without analysing the precise facts of the individual cases before it. This represents a substantial broadening of the Court's protection against discrimina-tory policies or practices that have a disparate adverse effect on particular groups without any overt discriminatory intention.

This decision brings the law of the Convention close in line with discrimination law   7.528
in other jurisdictions, such as Canada, Australia, and South Africa, which have long recognized the objectionable nature of indirect discrimination. They have noted that not only does indirect discrimination lead to the social exclusion, political marginalization, and personal humiliation of minorities, it may lead to systemic discrimination. For example, factors (such as discrimination against part-time working) may have the effect of causing the marginalized group more profoundly affected by them to 'internalize' the

---

[1142] (2002) 35 EHRR 23, para 135. See also *Hugh Jordan v UK* (2003) 37 EHRR 2; *Nachova and ors v Bulgaria* [2005] ECHR 43577/98.
[1143] Ibid.
[1144] (2007) 44 EHRR 33, paras 74–75, 80–84.
[1145] App No 57325/00, [2007] ECHR 922.

barriers as being in some way natural and necessary, and fail to see them as discriminatory. The Canadian Supreme Court has said that:

Discrimination is then reinforced by the very exclusion of the disadvantaged group because the exclusion fosters the belief . . . that the exclusion is the result of 'natural' forces, for example, that women 'just can't do the job'.[1146]

7.529   Domestic courts have not had the same difficulty as the Strasbourg Court in recognizing that Article 14 encompasses both direct and indirect discrimination.[1147] In *R (Watkins-Singh) v Governing Body of Aberdare Girls' School*[1148] the Administrative Court held—basing itself on the important judgment of the ECtHR in *DH v Czech Republic*[1149]—that the existence of an unexamined school uniform rule prohibiting all jewellery (with no exception for a Sikh *kara*) was unjustified indirect discrimination, the failure to recognize and respect the needs and rights of members of minority groups was a serious matter, not only because it was of detriment to members of those groups, but because it was damaging to the development of a democratic society based on the values of tolerance, pluralism, and broadmindedness.

4. Justification

7.530   Where it is established that people in factually similar or analogous circumstances are treated dissimilarly, or people in relevantly different situations are treated similarly, a case of prima facie discrimination arises. This will breach Article 14 unless the differences (or failures to differentiate) have an objective and reasonable justification. This means more than a rational explanation. In *Belgian Linguistics* the ECtHR said:

The existence of such a justification must be assessed in relation to the aims and effects of the measure under consideration, regard being had to the principles which normally prevail in democratic societies. A difference of treatment in the exercise of a right laid down in the Convention must not only pursue a legitimate aim: Article 14 is likewise violated when it is clearly established that there is no reasonable relationship of proportionality between the means employed and the aim sought to be realised.[1150]

7.531   The burden of proof is on the respondent state to justify the differential treatment with reference to these twin criteria (legitimate aim and proportionality). It is central to the protection afforded by Article 14 to understand that what falls to be justified is the discriminatory application or effect of the measure, and not the measure itself.[1151]

7.532   Early Strasbourg jurisprudence on justification was often unclear, with the Strasbourg bodies blurring the separate questions of whether there had been different treatment of people in analogous situations, and whether this differential treatment was justified.

[1146] *CNR v Canada (Human Rights Commission)* [1987] 1 SCR 1114, para 34. See also *Waters v Public Transport Corporation* (1991) 173 CLR 349, para 36.

[1147] *R (L and ors) v Manchester City Council* [2001] EWHC 707 (Admin) at [91].

[1148] [2008] EWHC 1865 (Admin), [2008] ELR 561.

[1149] (2007) 23 BHRC 526.

[1150] (1968) 1 EHRR 252, para 10.

[1151] *A and ors v Secretary of State for the Home Department* [2004] UKHL 56, [2005] 2 AC 68 at [68] per Lord Bingham.

(a) *Legitimate aim*

It is for the respondent state to advance a 'legitimate aim' in order to justify a prima facie   7.533
discriminatory measure, and states' defences have occasionally fallen at the first hurdle.[1152]

However, this is a relatively easy condition for states to fulfil. Article 14, unlike   7.534
Articles 8–11, has no inbuilt list of legitimate aims. The ECtHR has accepted, for example, that supporting and encouraging the traditional family unit[1153] and 'promoting
linguistic unity'[1154] constitute legitimate aims for Article 14 purposes.

(b) *Proportionality*

If the respondent state establishes that its differential treatment pursues a legitimate aim,   7.535
it must also establish that there is a 'reasonable relationship of proportionality' between
the aim and the means chosen to pursue it.

The ECtHR has rejected purported justifications by respondent states based on gen-   7.536
eralizations rather than objective evidence. For example, in *Marckx v Belgium* the ECtHR
rejected the state's unsubstantiated assertion that mothers of illegitimate children were
more likely to abandon them.[1155] However, where a difference in treatment is based on
evidence of real differences in situation or need, then difference of treatment may be
justified.[1156]

(c) *Margin of appreciation*

In assessing justification under Article 14 the ECtHR affords states 'a certain margin of   7.537
appreciation in assessing whether or not and to what extent differences in otherwise
similar situations justify a different treatment'.[1157] The margin's breadth depends on 'the
circumstances, the subject matter and its background',[1158] but the final decision as to
observance of the Convention's requirements rests with the Court.[1159]

Greater leeway is afforded in cases involving an absence of a common standard among   7.538
the contracting states.[1160] However, the ECtHR is increasingly willing to operate the
'living instrument' doctrine to develop protection—for example in relation to discrimination against transsexuals. It has explicitly stated that it will have regard to the changing
conditions in contracting states and respond, for example, to any emerging consensus as
to the standards to be achieved.[1161]

Discrimination based exclusively on certain 'suspect' grounds, such as sex, will not   7.539
usually be accepted by the ECtHR. 'Very weighty reasons' or 'particularly serious

---

[1152] See, eg *Canea Catholic Church v Greece* (1999) 27 EHRR 521, para 47.
[1153] *Marckx v Belgium* (1979) 2 EHRR 330, para 32.
[1154] *Belgian Linguistics (No 2)* (1968) 1 EHRR 252, para 9.
[1155] (1979) 2 EHRR 330, para 32.
[1156] *R (Hooper) v Secretary of State for Work and Pensions* [2005] UKHL 29, [2005] 1 WLR 1681.
[1157] *Barrow v UK* [2006] ECHR 42735/02, para 34. See also *Gillow v UK* (1986) 11 EHRR 335; *Inze v
Austria* (1987) 10 EHRR 394.
[1158] *Rasmussen v Denmark* (1984) 7 EHRR 371, para 40; *Zarb Adami v Malta* (2007) 44 EHRR 33, para 74.
[1159] *Zarb Adami v Malta* (2007) 44 EHRR 33, para 74.
[1160] *Petrovic v Austria* (2001) 33 EHRR 307, paras 36–43.
[1161] *Zarb Adami v Malta* (2007) 44 EHRR 33, para 74; citing *Unal Tekeli* [2004] ECHR 29865/96,
para 54; and *Stafford v UK* (2002) 35 EHRR 32, para 68. See also the development of the concept of
suspect grounds of discrimination, to include sexual orientation: *EB v France* (2008) 47 EHRR 21; and
the recent development of the concept of 'family life' to include same-sex relationships: *JM v UK* (2010)
30 BHRC 60.

reasons' would have to be put forward before the ECtHR could regard a difference of treatment based on such a ground as compatible with the Convention.[1162] However, the 'very weighty reasons' approach has not been applied to provisions which have only an indirectly discriminatory effect on 'suspect grounds' by the domestic courts: see *AM (Somalia) v Entry Clearance Officer*.[1163]

7.540 Over the years the ECtHR has gradually expanded the grounds that will require particularly weighty or serious reasons if discrimination is to be justified,[1164] using the 'living instrument' doctrine, and these now include nationality, religion, sexual orientation,[1165] race,[1166] marital status, and birth.[1167]

7.541 This approach of applying heightened scrutiny to certain categories of discrimination ('suspect classes') is well developed in US Supreme Court jurisprudence. It received a subtle analysis by the House of Lords in *R (RJM) v Secretary of State for Work and Pensions*.[1168]

7.542 In a series of recent cases concerning the UK's uneven pension provisions for men and women and the resulting inequality of various linked benefits, the ECtHR grappled with the tension between the rationale underpinning the margin of appreciation doctrine and the 'suspect grounds' principle.

7.543 In *Stec v UK* various applicants (both female and male) complained of aspects of a system of invalidity benefits, which had previously existed without discrimination, but were then 'cut off' at state retirement age (60 for women, 65 for men), resulting in new sex discrimination in the reduced earnings allowance (REA) scheme. The Grand Chamber noted that 'as a general rule, very weighty reasons would have to be put forward before the Court could regard a difference in treatment based exclusively on the ground of sex as compatible with the Convention'. On the facts of the case, however, it held that the differences in treatment were within the state's margin of appreciation. The need to 'cut off' entitlement to REA at presumed date of retirement was based on economic and social judgments made by the UK Government; the gradual equalization of pension ages across the Council of Europe was permissible, and the discrimination caused by the link between state retirement age and receipt of REA had been held by the ECJ to be within that permitted by EC law.[1169]

7.544 Though the continued existence of unequal pension ages per se was not the issue in *Stec*, the Court went on to consider whether they were themselves justified. It held that, in the light of the original justification for the measure as correcting financial inequality between the sexes, the slowly evolving nature of the change in women's working lives, and

---

[1162] *Van Raalte v Netherlands* (1997) 24 EHRR 503, para 39; *Schuler-Zgraggen v Switzerland*, Series A No 263, 24 June 1993, para 67; *Schmidt v Germany* (1994) 18 EHRR 513, para 24; *Karner v Austria* App No 40016/98, 24 July 2003; *BB v UK* App No 53760/00, 10 February 2004; *Abdulaziz, Cabales and Blakandali v UK* (1985) 7 EHRR 471, para 78; *DH v Czech Republic* (2007) 23 BHRC 526, para 196.

[1163] [2009] EWCA Civ 634 at [16] though note that in *R (E) v Governing Body of JFS* [2009] UKSC 15, [2010] 1 All ER 319, the Supreme Court adopted the strongly structured *Huang* test to the justification for indirect race discrimination, albeit under the Race Relations Act 1976.

[1164] For a discussion of the development of the concept, see Van Dijk and Van Hoof, *Theory and Practice of the European Convention on Human Rights* (Kluwer: The Hague, 1998) 728.

[1165] *L and V v Austria* (2003) 36 EHRR 55; *EB v France* (2008) 47 EHRR 21, para 91.

[1166] *East Africans v UK* (1981) 3 EHRR 76, para 207.

[1167] *Inze v Austria* (1987) 10 EHRR 394, para 41; *Pla v Andorra* (2004) 42 EHR 522, para 61.

[1168] [2008] UKHL 63, [2008] 3 WLR 1023 per Lord Walker.

[1169] *Stec v UK* (2006) 43 EHRR 1017, para 51.

the absence of a common standard among the contracting states, these matters fell within the state's margin of appreciation.[1170] *Stec* has been followed in *Barrow v UK*.[1171]

The House of Lords has rejected an over-technical approach to the concept of justification,[1172] recommending a 'simple and non-technical approach' to asking whether or not there is 'enough of a relevant difference between X and Y to justify different treatment'.[1173] This non-technical approach has much to recommend it, provided it does not result in thinly reasoned, impressionistic, hunch-based judgments.   7.545

(d) *Positive obligations*

Recent case law contains the germ of the idea that the state has a positive obligation to ensure that systems of legal protection—such as the criminal justice system—operate in such a way as to guarantee equal protection of the law to specific groups, such as women or racial minorities. Where the evidence suggests inadequate domestic remedies, and a system which betrays an overall unresponsiveness to gender or racially based aggression, failure to investigate in a specific case may amount to violation of Article 14, read with Articles 2 or 3.[1174]   7.546

L. ARTICLE 15: EXCEPTIONS IN TIME OF WAR

Article 15 allows a government to derogate from certain of its Convention obligations during 'war or other public emergency threatening the life of the nation'. Such derogation is only permitted to the extent strictly required by the exigencies of the situation. Further, a state cannot under any circumstances use Article 15 to derogate from certain fundamental Convention provisions.   7.547

The central object of Article 15 is to enable the derogating state to return to normality and respect all human rights as soon as possible, premised on the notion that it is sometimes necessary to limit human rights in order to protect them. This rationale is not without its critics, and it has been stated that the question of derogations is an issue 'of the integrity of the Convention system of protection as a whole'.[1175]   7.548

There are five requirements for a valid derogation under Article 15:   7.549

(a) it must relate to a right that is derogable;

(b) there must be a 'war or public emergency threatening the life of the nation';

(c) the measures taken must be 'strictly required by the exigencies of the situation';

(d) the measures must comply with the state's international law obligations; and

(e) the procedural requirements must be satisfied.

[1170] Ibid, paras 64–65.

[1171] [2006] ECHR 42735/02, para 35.

[1172] Inviting courts to treat with caution the suggested approach of the Court of Appeal in *Michalak v Wandsworth LBC* [2002] EWCA Civ 271, [2003] 1 WLR 617.

[1173] *R (Carson) v Secretary of State for Work and Pensions* [2005] UKHL 37, [2006] AC 173 at [2] per Lord Nicholls, and at [31] per Lord Hoffmann.

[1174] See *Petropoulou-Tsakisi v Greece* [2007] ECHR 44803/04; *Opuz v Turkey* App No 33401/02, 9 June 2009 at paras 199–202.

[1175] *Brannigan and McBride v UK* (1993) 17 EHRR 297 per Judge Makarczyk (dissenting).

1. Non-derogable rights

7.550 Article 15(2) specifies the Convention provisions from which no derogation is permitted: Article 2 (right to life—other than deaths resulting from lawful acts of war); Article 3 (prohibition on torture and inhuman or degrading treatment or punishment); Article 4(1) (prohibition on slavery and servitude); and Article 7 (prohibition on retrospective application of the criminal law).

7.551 It is possible that in the future the ECtHR may extend the list of non-derogable rights by accepting the notion of consequential non-derogability. For example, in *Aksoy v Turkey* the ECtHR observed that prompt judicial intervention (Article 5(3)) can lead to detection of ill-treatment, which is a non-derogable prohibition (Article 3).[1176]

2. Time of war or public emergency

7.552 The precondition to any derogation under Article 15 is the existence of war or a 'public emergency threatening the life of the nation'. No derogation concerning the former has yet been made. The ECtHR has defined the latter as 'an exceptional situation of crisis or emergency that affects the whole population and constitutes a threat to the organised life of the community of which the state is composed'.[1177]

7.553 The strict nature of this threshold requirement, however, is arguably considerably qualified by the fact that the ECtHR affords states 'a wide margin of appreciation' in determining whether or not they are facing such a public emergency. The ECtHR considers that national authorities are in a better position than national judges to assess the situation.[1178] Unsurprisingly, given this margin, the claimed existence of a state of emergency has not yet been rejected by the ECtHR.

7.554 However, the ECmHR has rejected such a claim. In the *Greek Case* the Greek Government failed to persuade the Commission that there had been a public emergency threatening the life of the nation such as would justify derogation.[1179] In its opinion, the ECmHR described the features of such an emergency:

(a) it must be actual or imminent;

(b) its effects must involve the whole nation;

(c) the continuance of the organized life of the community must be threatened; and

(d) the crisis or danger must be exceptional, in that the normal measures or restrictions, permitted by the Convention for the maintenance of public safety, health, and order, are plainly inadequate.

7.555 In *A and ors v UK* the Grand Chamber considered the UK's derogation from Article 5(1) under the Anti-Terrorism, Crime and Security Act 2001 on the grounds that the terrorist threat posed by Al-Qaeda was a 'public emergency threatening the life of the nation'.[1180] The Grand Chamber noted that the Court's case law had never incorporated

---

[1176] (1996) 23 EHRR 553.

[1177] *Lawless v Ireland* (1961) 1 EHRR 1.

[1178] Ibid, para 28; *A and ors v UK* (2009) 26 BHRC 1.

[1179] (1969) 12 YB 1, para 153. See also Cavanaugh, 'Policing the Margins' (2006) 4 EHRLR 422, 436–437.

[1180] (2009) 26 BHRC 1.

any requirement that the emergency be temporary and thus the derogation could not be invalidated on the ground that the threat posed by Al-Qaeda and the consequent derogation were likely to be ongoing. Nor did the Grand Chamber accept the reasoning of Lord Hoffmann who, in a minority in the House of Lords, had rejected the existence of an emergency, stating that the threat had to imperil 'our institutions of government or our existence as a civil community'.[1181] In the Grand Chamber's view that was too high a standard and a 'much broader' range of factors could legitimately be taken into account in determining the threat.[1182] The Grand Chamber applied a wide margin of appreciation to the Government's assessment of the threat and held that the Government was entitled to conclude that such an emergency existed.

3. Strictly required by the exigencies of the situation

As stated in Article 15(1) and above, derogation is permitted only 'to the extent strictly required by the exigencies of the situation'. The ECmHR in *Ireland v UK* stated: 7.556

There must be a link between the facts of the emergency on the one hand and the measures chosen to deal with it on the other. Moreover, the obligations under the Convention do not entirely disappear. They can only be suspended or modified 'to the extent that is strictly required' as provided in Article 15.[1183]

Again, the ECtHR will afford states a wide margin of appreciation in relation to this   7.557
condition. However, the ECtHR still retains a supervisory role.[1184] Factors that are relevant to supervision of the margin include the nature of the rights affected by the derogation, the nature and duration of the emergency, and any safeguards against arbitrary state behaviour.[1185] The Court has insisted that general references to terrorism will not be sufficient evidence that a derogation is strictly required.[1186]

In *A and ors v UK* the Grand Chamber followed the decision of the majority of the   7.558
House of Lords and held that the UK's derogation from Article 5(1) did not satisfy the requirement of strict necessity.[1187] The derogating measures were disproportionate in that they drew a distinction between national and non-nationals contrary to Article 14 of the Convention.

The ECtHR is particularly strict in assessing the territorial scope of a derogation. In   7.559
Yaman v Turkey it held that it would undermine the 'object and purpose of Article 15' if, when assessing the scope of the derogation, it extended its effects to parts of Turkey not explicitly named in the derogation notice.[1188]

A similarly strict approach was adopted in *Sakik v Turkey*. The derogation was aimed   7.560
at fighting terrorism and was stated as applying to the state of emergency region. The applicants were arrested outside that region, although as part of a general operation linked to fighting terrorism in that region. The ECtHR held that Turkey could not rely

---

[1181] [2004] UKHL 56, [2005] 2 AC 68 at [96].
[1182] (2009) 26 BHRC 1, para 179.
[1183] (1978) 2 EHRR 25, para 588.
[1184] Ibid.
[1185] *Brannigan and McBride v UK* (1993) 17 EHRR 297.
[1186] *Demir v Turkey* (2001) 33 EHRR 43.
[1187] (2009) 26 BHRC 1.
[1188] App No 32446/96, 2 November 2004.

on the derogation in relation to the arrests as they were outside the territorial scope of the derogation.[1189]

4. International law obligations

7.561　Any derogation must be consistent with the state's 'other obligations under international law' (Article 15(1)). This includes both treaty obligations and obligations arising under customary international law.

5. Procedural requirements

7.562　Article 15(3) sets out the procedural requirements when derogating from a Convention obligation. Although not expressly stated, notification to the Council of Europe must be without delay.[1190]

6. Derogations and the Human Rights Act

7.563　Section 1(2) of the Human Rights Act allows the Government to avoid the incorporation of the Convention to the extent that it has lodged a 'derogation' with the Council of Europe, as defined in section 14. Thus, as a matter of international law, the Government, by lodging a derogation in Strasbourg, can, to the extent that the derogation is lawful under Article 15, avoid a particular obligation in particular circumstances.[1191]

7.564　　Section 14 of the Act identifies 'designated derogations', which, under section 16, are permitted to continue for up to five years. Section 14(5) allows the Secretary of State to amend Schedule 3 to the Act to enable the continuation of the current derogation and to add any future derogations.

7.565　　The Act does not permit the United Kingdom to make a 'designated derogation' for the purposes of domestic law unless it reflects an actual derogation lodged with the Council of Europe.

7.566　　The effect of making a designated derogation is to exclude the article in question from being a 'Convention right' for the purposes identified in that derogation.[1192] Any derogation is likely to be specific and to refer to particular statutory powers.

7.567　　The United Kingdom currently has no derogations lodged. It has, in the past, invoked Article 15 in relation to Northern Ireland and, following the attacks of 11 September 2001, the entirety of the United Kingdom.

(a) Northern Ireland

7.568　Until February 2001 a derogation was in force that allowed the police to detain people in Northern Ireland under the Prevention of Terrorism (Temporary Provisions) Act 1989 for up to seven days. The derogation followed *Brogan v UK*, where the ECtHR had decided that periods of longer than four days' detention for interrogation without access to a judge violated the Article 5(3) requirement to bring the suspect before a judge

---

[1189] Reports of Judgments and Decisions 1997-VII, 26 November 1997.
[1190] *Lawless v Ireland* (1961) 1 EHRR 1.
[1191] See Chowdhury, *Rule of Law in a State of Emergency* (London: Pinter, 1989).
[1192] See s 1(2).

'promptly'.[1193] The lawfulness of the derogation was then subject to an unsuccessful challenge in *Brannigan and McBride v UK*.[1194] The introduction of judicial authorization for extended detentions in the Terrorism Act 2000 allowed this derogation to be withdrawn.

(b) *United Kingdom*

After the terrorist attacks in the United States on 11 September 2001, the UK Government concluded that certain non-nationals present in the United Kingdom were affiliated with Al-Qaeda and posed a national security threat. While the Immigration Act 1971 allowed for the deportation of non-UK citizens whose presence in the United Kingdom was 'not conducive to the public good' (including on grounds of national security), the Convention prevented the return of such individuals to countries where they faced a real risk of ill-treatment contrary to Article 3.   7.569

In order to address this problem, the Government introduced provisions in Part IV of the Anti-Terrorism, Crime and Security Act 2001 that gave the Home Secretary the power to detain non-nationals indefinitely based solely on whether he had a reasonable belief that the person's presence in the United Kingdom was a risk to national security and that he suspected that the person was a terrorist. The provisions were plainly contrary to the right to liberty under Article 5. The Government therefore made an order derogating from Article 5(1)(f),[1195] which permits the detention of a non-national with a view to deportation only where 'action is being taken with a view to deportation',[1196] on the grounds that the Al-Qaeda threat constituted a public emergency threatening the life of the nation within the meaning of Article 15.   7.570

The lawfulness of this derogation was successfully challenged before the House of Lords in the first of the twin *A and ors v Secretary of State for the Home Department* cases.[1197] The case was brought by nine foreign nationals who had been detained under the 2001 Act. In perhaps the most important judgment since the Human Rights Act came into force, an enlarged House of Lords allowed the appeal by a majority of eight to one, quashing the derogation order and declaring that the statutory provisions were incompatible with Articles 5 and 14.   7.571

A majority did, however, accept that the threshold requirement that there be a 'public emergency threatening the life of the nation' was satisfied, despite the absence of a specific threat of an immediate attack. Given the nature of the large-scale terrorist attacks that had occurred, the executive and Parliament had not erred in assessing that there was a risk of terrorist attack at some unspecified time.   7.572

In so finding, they noted that 'great weight' was to be accorded to the judgments of the Home Secretary, the executive, and Parliament in this regard as, in Lord Bingham's words: 7.573

They were called on to exercise a pre-eminently political judgment. It involved making a factual prediction of what various people around the world might or might not do, and when (if at all) they might do it, and what the consequences might be if they did. Any prediction about the future

[1193] (1988) 11 EHRR 117.
[1194] (1993) 17 EHRR 539.
[1195] Human Rights Act 1998 (Designated Derogation) Order 2001, SI 2001/3644.
[1196] *Chahal v UK* (1996) 26 EHRR 413, para 112.
[1197] [2004] UKHL 56, [2005] 2 AC 68.

behaviour of human beings (as opposed to the phases of the moon or high water at London Bridge) is necessarily problematical. Reasonable or informed minds may differ, and a judgment is not shown to be wrong or unreasonable because that which is thought likely to happen does not happen. It would have been irresponsible not to err, if at all, on the side of safety.[1198]

7.574   This approach to the question of whether the Government's assessment met the Article 15 criteria was rejected by Lord Hoffmann, who dissented on this point. He ruled that there was no public emergency threatening the life of the nation and that the Government therefore fell at the first hurdle:

This is a nation which has been tested in adversity, which has survived physical destruction and catastrophic loss of life. I do not underestimate the ability of fanatical groups of terrorists to kill and destroy, but they do not threaten the life of the nation. Whether we would survive Hitler hung in the balance, but there is no doubt that we shall survive Al-Qaeda . . . Terrorist violence, serious as it is, does not threaten our institutions of government or our existence as a civil community.[1199]

7.575   Despite the non-intrusive approach adopted by the majority as to the question of the existence of a state of emergency, the measures themselves were subjected to strict scrutiny. Their Lordships held that the 'exigencies of the situation' test is 'a test of strict necessity, or, in Convention terminology, proportionality',[1200] and it must be particularly closely applied if the right infringed is personal liberty—among the most fundamental of Convention rights. Baroness Hale reiterated the centrality of the Article 5 guarantee:

Neither the common law, from which so much of the European Convention is derived, nor international human rights law allows indefinite detention at the behest of the executive, however well-intentioned. It is not for the executive to decide who should be locked up for any length of time, let alone indefinitely. Only the courts can do that and, except as a preliminary step before trial, only after the grounds for detaining someone have been proved. Executive detention is the antithesis of the right to liberty and security of person.[1201]

7.576   The measures adopted were not strictly required, as they did not rationally address any threat to security, nor were they proportionate. They applied only to non-nationals, and not to British nationals who might pose the same threat. They were also capable of applying 'the severe penalty of indefinite detention' on individuals without any hostile intentions towards the United Kingdom, simply on the basis of their links to other individuals who may, in turn, be linked to Al-Qaeda. Further, this was unjustifiable discrimination on the basis of nationality or immigration status, which violated Article 14; and this approach was inconsistent with the UK's international human rights treaty obligations to afford equality before the law and to protect the human rights of all individuals within its territory.

7.577   *A and ors* demonstrates that the domestic courts are likely to afford greater leeway to the Government in its determination as to whether or not a derogation may be required. However, any measures implemented pursuant to that derogation will be subjected to

---

1198 Ibid at [29].
1199 Ibid at [96].
1200 Ibid at [30] per Lord Bingham.
1201 Ibid at [222].

close scrutiny, particularly if they impact upon rights considered fundamental under the common law, the Convention, or international law.

The Grand Chamber recently affirmed the House of Lords' reasoning in *A and ors v UK*.[1202]   7.578

M. ARTICLE 16: RESTRICTIONS ON POLITICAL ACTIVITY OF ALIENS

On its face, Article 16 allows states considerable latitude to interfere with the political rights of aliens. However, the provision has barely featured in the Strasbourg jurisprudence. Only one case has ever reached the ECtHR under Article 16, *Piermont v France*.[1203] In January 1977, the Parliamentary Assembly of the Council of Europe recommended the removal of Article 16. Although Article 16 remains in force, the Strasbourg authorities have emphasized that it should have little, if any, impact.   7.579

In *Piermont* the ECmHR expressly recognized that the provision was outdated. It observed that: 7.580

> Those who drafted it were subscribing to a concept that was then prevalent in international law, under which a general, unlimited restriction of the political activities of aliens was thought legitimate . . . The Commission reiterates, however, that the Convention is a living instrument, which must be interpreted in the light of present day conditions, and the evolution of modern society.[1204]

Consonant with this interpretative direction, the expression 'political activities' might apply only narrowly to the setting-up and operation of political parties, expressions of opinion in connection with these parties, and voting in elections.

The ECmHR and ECtHR in *Piermont* also indicated that members of the European Parliament cannot be regarded as aliens within any jurisdiction in the European Union.[1205]   7.581

The restrictive Strasbourg approach to Article 16 has been followed by the domestic courts. In *R (Farrakhan) v Secretary of State for the Home Department* the Court of Appeal described the provision as 'something of an anachronism',[1206] indicating that it is unlikely to feature prominently, if at all, in domestic decisions.   7.582

In the authors' view, three further factors indicate that any little relevance Article 16 retains is fast diminishing.   7.583

First, the notion of European citizenship created by the Maastricht Treaty and the powerful EU prohibition against discrimination on grounds of nationality means that Article 16 is likely to be trumped by Community considerations when the 'alien' is an EU national.[1207]   7.584

[1202] (2009) 26 BHRC 1.

[1203] (1995) 20 EHRR 301.

[1204] Ibid, Commission Report, paras 59–69.

[1205] (1995) 20 EHRR 301, para 64. Cf the jointly dissenting opinion of Judges Ryssdal, Matscher, and Jungwiert, and Sir John Freedland, para 4.

[1206] [2002] EWCA Civ 606.

[1207] See *Farrakhan v Secretary of State for the Home Department* [2001] EWHC Admin 781 at [19] per Turner J.

7.585   Secondly, Strasbourg and the domestic courts are increasingly protective of political activity, and both have recognized the pre-eminent importance of freedom of political expression.[1208] This trend, viewed in the context of the 'increased internationalization of politics'[1209] and the need for those 'opposed to official ideas and positions . . . to find a place in the political arena',[1210] suggests that the application of Article 16 to Articles 10 and 11 must be extremely limited.

7.586   Finally, the House of Lords in *A and ors v Secretary of State for the Home Department* cited with approval wide-ranging commentary, common law authority, and international instruments against the differential treatment of non-nationals in the exercise of Convention rights.[1211] Although *A* was not concerned with Article 16, or the articles to which it applies, their Lordships' opinions may nevertheless be seen as indicative of a move away from the 'anachronistic' motivations underpinning Article 16.

N. ARTICLE 17: PROHIBITION OF ABUSE OF RIGHTS

7.587   The aim of Article 17 is to safeguard the provisions of the Convention from abuse at the hands of those who wish to use the Convention's provisions to undermine the rights of others.[1212] The ECtHR has described its 'general purpose' as being 'to prevent individuals or groups with totalitarian aims from exploiting in their own interests the principles enunciated by the Convention'.[1213] It may be invoked by persons against a government, or be used by a government to defend its actions against persons who wish to undermine the protections and values of the Convention.

7.588   While Article 17 may be invoked by a state to restrict an individual's reliance on rights where he aims to destroy the rights of others, it may only be applied in relation to the rights that are being abused with this aim in mind. For instance, in *Lawless v Ireland* the ECtHR held that it could not be used to deny IRA members the right to liberty or a fair trial.[1214]

7.589   Much of the case law under Article 17 concerns freedom of expression and racial hatred.[1215] In the admissibility decision *Norwood v UK*, for example, the ECtHR upheld the domestic decision applying Article 17.[1216] The applicant, who worked for the British National Party (BNP), claimed that his rights under Articles 10 and 14 had been violated by police removal of a BNP poster from the window of his flat and his subsequent prosecution for a public order offence. The poster consisted of a photograph of

---

[1208] See para 7.358 above.
[1209] *Piermont v France* (1995) 20 EHRR 301, para 5 per Judges Ryssdal, Matscher, and Jugwiert, and Sir John Freedland (dissenting).
[1210] Ibid, para 76.
[1211] [2004] UKHL 56, [2005] 2 AC 68.
[1212] *Zdanoka v Latvia* (2007) 45 EHRR 17, para 99.
[1213] *Norwood v UK* (2004) 40 EHRR SE 111.
[1214] (1961) 1 EHRR 1.
[1215] See, eg *WP and ors v Poland* App No 42264/98, 2 September 2004; *Garaudy v France* App No 65831/01, 24 June 2003; *Schimanek v Austria* App No 32307/96, 1 February 2000; *Glimmerveen and Hagenbeek v Netherlands* App Nos 8348/78 and 8406/78, 11 October 1979. For a discussion of the applicability of Art 17 to hate speech, see Cooper and Marshall Williams, 'Hate speech, holocaust denial and international human rights law' (1999) 6 EHRLR 593.
[1216] [2003] Crim LR 888.

the Twin Towers of the World Trade Center in flames, the words 'Islam out of Britain—Protect the British People', and a symbol of a crescent and star in a prohibition sign. The ECtHR held that the poster constituted such a vehement attack against Muslims that Article 17 applied and the applicant could not rely on Article 10. This decision has been criticized:[1217] Article 17 is a powerful but blunt tool that should be used sparingly.

Article 17 has been raised in the domestic courts on a number of occasions. In *Douglas v Hello! Ltd* Sedley LJ noted that it would be inconsistent with Article 17 and section 3 of the Human Rights Act to read section 12 of the Act as giving the right to freedom of expression presumptive priority over other rights.[1218] The House of Lords in *DPP v Collins* also noted that Article 10 may not be invoked in a manner incompatible with Article 17.[1219] The respondent in that case had been convicted of an offence under the Communications Act 2003 following repeated calls and messages to his MP in which he referred to 'Wogs', 'Pakis', 'black bastards', and 'Niggers'. He did not argue that his conviction was inconsistent with Article 10, and Lord Bingham stated that he was 'right not to do so' as 'effect must be given . . . to Article 17 of the Convention'.[1220] In *London Borough of Islington v Ladele* the Employment Appeal Tribunal (EAT) found 'considerable force' in the argument that Article 17 applied where a registrar and committed Christian invoked Article 9 to protect her refusal to perform civil partnerships on the grounds that same-sex unions were a sin.[1221]   7.590

O. ARTICLE 18: LIMITATION ON USE OF RESTRICTIONS ON RIGHTS

Article 18 is a parasitic provision. An allegation that the state has acted for reasons other than those permitted under the qualified rights in Article 18(2) must be brought in conjunction with an allegation that another article has been breached. There may be a violation of Article 18 even if there is no violation of that article taken alone.[1222]   7.591

Article 18 is inapplicable to absolute rights, such as Article 3. It follows from the terms of Article 18 that 'a violation may only arise where the right or freedom concerned is subject to restrictions permitted under the Convention'.[1223]   7.592

Article 18 effectively requires a finding of 'bad faith' on the part of a state. It is, unsurprisingly, extremely difficult to make out a violation, and the Strasbourg organs have very rarely found a breach of Article 18.[1224] In the majority of cases the Strasbourg organs either found that it was unnecessary to examine the Article 18 complaint in light   7.593

[1217] Clayton and Tomlinson, *The Law of Human Rights*, 2nd edn (Oxford: Oxford University Press, 2009) para 15.245.

[1218] [2001] QB 967.

[1219] [2006] UKHL 40, [2006] 1 WLR 2223.

[1220] Ibid at [14].

[1221] [2009] IRLR 154 at [126]. The EAT's decision was upheld on appeal: [2009] EWCA Civ 1357, [2010] IRLR 211 without comment on this issue.

[1222] *Kamma v Netherlands* (1974) 1 DR 4.

[1223] *Gusinskiy v Russia* (2004) 16 BHRC 427, para 73; *Oates v Poland* App No 35036/97, 11 May 2000.

[1224] See, eg *De Becker v Belgium* (1958) 2 YB 214; *Bozano v France* (1984) 39 DR 119; *Gusinskiy v Russia* (2004) 16 BHRC 427.

of their adverse findings against the state under substantive articles,[1225] or they held that the Article 18 complaint was unsubstantiated on the evidence.[1226]

7.594   In *Gusinskiy v Russia* the ECtHR found that the applicant's liberty had been restricted for a legitimate purpose under the Convention ('for the purpose of bringing him before a competent legal authority on reasonable suspicion of having committed an offence') but also for a purpose outside Article 5, namely to force him to sell his media business to the state on unfavourable terms.[1227] The detention was thus applied for a purpose other than that provided in the Convention, and the state had violated Article 18.

7.595   Article 18 has been raised before the domestic courts on a number of occasions, but only as an aid to interpretation of other Convention articles. The courts have referred to Article 18 in passing, finding that phrases such as 'necessary . . . in the interests of national security' and 'lawfulness' must be read in light of the strict requirements of Article 18.[1228] We are not aware of any domestic case in which a violation of Article 18 itself has been alleged.

[1225] See, eg *Kaya and ors v Turkey* App No 33420/96, 21 November 2005.
[1226] *Nesibe Haran v Turkey* App No 28299/95, 6 October 2005.
[1227] (2004) 16 BHRC 427.
[1228] See, eg *R v Shayler* [2002] UKHL 11, [2003] 1 AC 247 at [57]; *S v Airedale NHS Trust* [2002] EWHC 1780 (Admin) at [91]; *R (Middleton) v Secretary of State for the Home Department* [2003] EWHC 315 (Admin) at [64]; *A v Scottish Ministers* 2002 SC (PC) 63 at [28].

8

THE CONVENTION PROTOCOLS

A. Introduction	8.01
B. Protocol 1, Article 1: Protection of Property	8.02
1. The three rules	8.07
2. Possessions	8.09
3. Positive obligations	8.23
4. Interference with the right to property	8.26
5. Limitations	8.36
C. Protocol 1, Article 2: Right to Education	8.60
1. Scope of the right	8.64
2. Parental right to educate children in conformity with convictions	8.75
3. General limitations	8.83
4. Discrimination	8.86
D. Protocol 1, Article 3: Right to Free Elections	8.88
1. 'Legislature'	8.92
2. 'Elections'	8.94
3. Right to vote	8.98
4. Right to stand for election	8.102
5. Electoral systems	8.108
E. Protocol 4	8.113
1. Protocol 4, Article 1	8.114
2. Protocol 4, Article 2	8.116
3. Protocol 4, Article 3	8.122
4. Protocol 4, Article 4	8.125
5. Ratification of Protocol 4 by the United Kingdom	8.126
F. Protocol 6	8.127
G. Protocol 7	8.129
1. Protocol 7, Article 1	8.133
2. Protocol 7, Article 2	8.140
3. Protocol 7, Article 3	8.146
4. Protocol 7, Article 4	8.151
5. Protocol 7, Article 5	8.156
H. Protocol 12	8.159
I. Protocol 13	8.161

A. INTRODUCTION

8.01 This chapter summarizes the content of the significant Protocols of the European Convention. As in Chapters 6 and 7, an overview is given of the jurisprudence of the European Court of Human Rights (ECtHR) and any remaining important cases from the European Commission on Human Rights (ECmHR). Where the Protocol has been incorporated under the Human Rights Act the approach of domestic courts is discussed alongside the European case law, and any divergences are noted.

B. PROTOCOL 1, ARTICLE 1: PROTECTION OF PROPERTY

8.02 The extent to which, and the way in which, property interests should be protected by human rights instruments have always been controversial questions. The right to property is recognized in the Convention and the Universal Declaration of Human Rights, but it was omitted in both the International Covenant of Civil and Political Rights (ICCPR) and the International Covenant of Economic, Social and Cultural Rights (ICESCR). The subject was debated at length when these two documents were being drafted, and all accepted that individuals had a right to own property, but it proved impossible to reach agreement on a suitable text.[1]

8.03 Attempts to draft a Convention right to property were bedevilled by similar difficulties. Some argued that property was an economic interest rather than a civil/political right, and should not be protected in a human rights Convention. Others (including the United Kingdom) were sensitive to the possibility of a court interfering with important political choices, such as the state's power to nationalize industries, to create redistributive socio-economic programmes, to tax, and to fine.

8.04 These controversies explain why the initial Convention did not contain an article protecting property interests; why the right protected is to 'peaceful enjoyment of possessions' rather than a right actually to possess;[2] and why the ECtHR continues to afford a very wide margin of appreciation to states in reaching essentially political judgments about whether it is in the public interest for property rights to be curtailed.

8.05 This picture is very gradually changing, both quantitatively and qualitatively. There has been a steady increase in the number of applications raising Protocol 1, Article 1 issues. There has also been an increase in the proportion of successful applications under this article, either taken alone or with Article 14. Many of these cases relate to the expropriation of land within new EU Member States or accession states, linked to the provision of funding for motorways and other infrastructure. Finally, the ECtHR continues to expand the meaning of 'possessions' to incorporate 'legitimate expectations' and even non-contributory statutory benefit entitlements, thus extending the scope of the right.

---

[1] See, further, Jayawickrama, *The Judicial Application of Human Rights Law: National, Regional and International Jurisprudence* (Cambridge: Cambridge University Press, 2002) 909–910.

[2] See, generally, Kingston, 'Rich people have rights too? The status of property as a fundamental right', in Heffernan (ed), *Human Rights: A European Perspective* (Dublin: Round Hall Press, 1994); Anderson, 'Compensation for Interference with Property' (1999) 6 EHRLR 543; Whale, 'Pawnbrokers and parishes: the protection of property under the Human Rights Act' (2002) EHRLR 67.

There has been fairly active domestic litigation involving Protocol 1, Article 1. It is **8.06**
broadly in line with the Strasbourg jurisprudence, but the domestic courts have too
frequently adopted the 'hands-off' approach of the ECtHR, and mistakenly appropriated
the margin of appreciation into domestic law.[3] As we emphasize elsewhere, the margin
of appreciation should never be applied by domestic courts.[4]

1. The three rules

In *Sporrong and Lönnroth v Sweden* the ECtHR analysed Protocol 1, Article 1, and inter- **8.07**
preted it as containing 'three distinct rules'.[5] This interpretation of Protocol 1, Article 1
was followed in subsequent cases.[6] In order to establish that there is a prima facie
interference with the right to property it must be shown that:

(a) the peaceful enjoyment of the applicant's possessions has been interfered with by the
    state (rule 1); or

(b) the applicant has been deprived of possessions by the state (rule 2); or

(c) the applicant's possessions have been subjected to control by the state (rule 3).

But interference, deprivation, or control will not violate Protocol 1, Article 1 if done 'in
the public interest' or 'to enforce such laws [as the state] deems necessary to control the
use of property in the public interest'.

Much of the earlier case law on the three rules is confusing, with the ECmHR and **8.08**
ECtHR often dealing with rules 2 and 3 before considering rule 1.[7] In recent cases, the
ECtHR has adopted a more general approach, preferring to focus on the general principles in Protocol 1, Article 1 rather than finding it necessary to decide which of the
three rules is applicable.[8] First, the ECtHR examines whether there has been an interference with the applicant's possessions. This interference may be direct or indirect, and
may involve an actual deprivation or control which prevents peaceful enjoyment of the
property, or any other form of interference. Secondly, the ECtHR examines whether
that interference is justified.

2. Possessions

The ECtHR has interpreted the concept of 'possessions' broadly. The term has an **8.09**
autonomous meaning and the definition in domestic law is not determinative.[9]

---

[3] See, eg *R (Countryside Alliance) v Attorney General* [2007] UKHL 52, [2008] 1 AC 719 at [126]–[127]
per Baroness Hale; *Belfast City Council v Miss Behavin'* [2007] UKHL 19, [2007] NI 89 at [16] per Lord
Hoffmann; *Sinclair Collis Ltd v Secretary of State for Health* [2010] EWHC 3112 (Admin).

[4] See ch 4, paras 4.112–4.130.

[5] (1982) 5 EHRR 35, para 61. Note that the ECtHR made clear in later judgments that the three rules are
not 'distinct' in the sense of being unconnected: *James and ors v UK* (1986) 8 EHRR 123; *Pye v UK* (2008) 46
EHRR 34.

[6] See, eg *Lithgow v UK* (1986) 8 EHRR 329, para 106.

[7] See, eg *James and ors v UK* (1986) 8 EHRR 123.

[8] See, eg *Katsaros v Greece* (2003) 36 EHRR 58; *Jokela v Finland* (2003) 37 EHRR 26; *Bulves AD v Bulgaria*
App No 3991/03, 22 January 2009. Cf *Pye v UK* (2008) 46 EHRR 34, in which the ECtHR returned to the
three-rule analysis.

[9] See, eg *Holy Monasteries v Greece* (1998) 25 EHRR 640; *Öneryildiz v Turkey* (2004) 18 BHRC 145
(Grand Chamber).

8.10   In addition to physical items and land, 'possessions' have been held to include contractual rights,[10] leases,[11] company shares,[12] crystallized debts,[13] the goodwill of a
business,[14] and liquor licences,[15] and the benefit of such statutory pecuniary entitlements as from time to time exist.[16] Intangible claims to items of pecuniary value are also
'possessions' even before the claims have been realized: a claim for compensation in
tort,[17] a right to compensation for lost land,[18] and a retired judge's claim to a social
tenancy have all been held to constitute property.[19]

8.11   Future potential possessions will only come within the scope of Protocol 1, Article 1
if they have already been earned or an enforceable, or at least arguably enforceable, claim
to them exists.[20]

8.12   Domestic cases on the scope of 'possessions' in Protocol 1, Article 1 are inconsistent.
On the one hand, the domestic courts have applied a broad definition of 'possessions' in
certain cases, accepting that legitimate expectations (even those arising from *ultra vires*
acts of public authorities)[21] and non-contributory benefits[22] may be covered. On the
other hand, a narrow approach has been evident in cases concerning a range of interests.
For example, housing benefit has been held to fall outside the right to property,[23] and in
cases of benefit overpayments the overpaid money does not constitute a 'possession'.[24]
However, the House of Lords has now affirmed the decision of the Grand Chamber in
Stec v UK,[25] finding that disability premium was a possession for the purposes of Protocol
1, Article 1 taken with Article 14.[26]

8.13   The narrow scope of the domestic approach to possessions was recently criticized by
the ECtHR in *JM v UK*.[27] The House of Lords had held in *Secretary of State for Work and
Pensions v M* that the payment of child support did not fall within the ambit of Article 1
of Protocol 1 for the purposes of Article 14 because it was primarily concerned with the
expropriation of assets for a public purpose and not with the enforcement of a personal
obligation.[28] Drawing a parallel with its jurisprudence on social security benefits, the

---

[10] *Association of General Practitioners v Denmark* (1989) 62 DR 226.
[11] *Mellacher v Austria* (1989) 12 EHRR 391.
[12] *Bramelid and Malmstrom v Sweden* (1982) 29 DR 64.
[13] *Agneesens v Belgium* (1998) 58 DR 63.
[14] *Van Marle and ors v Netherlands* (1986) 8 EHRR 483. Lord Bingham considered this area of Strasbourg
jurisprudence unclear in *R (Countryside Alliance) v Attorney General* [2007] UKHL 52, [2008] 1 AC 719 at
[21]. See also *R (New London College) v Secretary of State for the Home Department* [2011] EWHC 856 (Admin)
in which the High Court considered that a student sponsor licence was equivalent to a liquor licence.
[15] *Tre Traktörer AB v Sweden* (1989) 13 EHRR 309.
[16] *Stec v UK* (2005) 41 EHRR SE 295, para 43; affirmed by the Grand Chamber at (2006) 43 EHRR
1017.
[17] *Pressos Compañia Naviera SA v Belgium* (1995) 21 EHRR 301.
[18] *Broniowski v Poland* (2004) 15 BHRC 573.
[19] *Teteriny v Russia* [2005] ECHR 11931/03.
[20] *Wendenburg v Germany* (2003) 36 EHRR CD 154.
[21] *Rowland v Environment Agency* [2003] EWCA Civ 1885, [2005] Ch 1.
[22] *R (Carson) v Secretary of State for Work and Pensions* [2005] UKHL 37, [2006] 1 AC 173.
[23] *Campbell v South Northamptonshire DC* [2004] EWCA Civ 409, [2004] 3 All ER 387.
[24] *B v Secretary of State for Work and Pensions* [2005] EWCA Civ 929, [2005] 1 WLR 3796.
[25] (2006) 20 BHRC 348.
[26] *R (RJM) v Secretary of State for Work and Pensions* [2008] UKHL 63, [2008] 3 WLR 1023.
[27] App No 37060/06, 28 September 2010.
[28] [2006] UKHL 11.

ECtHR rejected this distinction and held that the domestic rules on payment of child support by same-sex partners were discriminatory.

(a) *Intellectual property rights*

Protocol 1, Article 1 encompasses intellectual property rights, such as patents,[29] trade marks,[30] and copyright.[31]   8.14

However, in *Anheuser-Busch v Portugal* (the '*Budweiser*' case), the ECtHR ruled that while a registered trade mark is a 'possession', a trade mark application is not.[32]   8.15

(b) *Public law rights*

(i) *State pensions and benefits*   Early ECtHR cases suggested that non-contributory   8.16
benefits gained by virtue of public law were not protected by Protocol 1, Article 1.[33] It is now clear from the decision of the Grand Chamber in *Stec v UK*[34] that, at least in so far as entitlement to statutory benefits from time to time existing, such rights are protected. In *Stec* it was held that there was no longer any valid analytical distinction between those social security entitlements derived from contributions and those non-contributory benefits funded through general taxation. While Protocol 1, Article 1 provided no right to the continuing provision of any particular social security benefit (that is, the state could remove it if it regarded it as being in the general public interest to do so), there was a defined statutory right to be paid a particular benefit in accordance with the rules of a statutory scheme for so long as it continued to exist, irrespective of whether the scheme was contributory or non-contributory. Consequently, such entitlements unequivocally fall within the ambit of Protocol 1, Article 1 for the application of Article 14.[35]

However, economic and social policy remains a matter for Member States. The fact   8.17
that a social security benefit falls with the ambit of the concept of a 'possession' does not compel the Member State to continue to provide that benefit,[36] and even in cases where the Convention guarantees benefits to persons on the basis of what they have contributed into the social insurance system, the ECtHR has held that this cannot be interpreted as conferring an entitlement to a pension of a particular amount.[37]

---

[29] *Smith Kline and French Laboratories Ltd v Netherlands* (1990) 66 DR 70; *Lenzing AG v UK* [1999] EHRLR 132.

[30] *Anheuser-Busch v Portugal* (2007) 23 BHRC 307.

[31] *France 2 v France* App No 30262/96, 15 January 1997 (recognized through the 'rights of others' clause in Art 10(2)).

[32] (2007) 23 BHRC 307. See, further, Burkhart, 'Trade marks are possessions—but applications are not (yet)' (2006) 1 Journal of Intellectual Property Law and Practice 240.

[33] The evolution can be traced through the cases of *X v Netherlands* (1971) 3 CD 9; *Muller v Austria* (1975) 3 DR 25; *Carlin v UK* App No 27537/95; *Gaygusuz v Austria* (1996) 23 EHRR 364, para 41; *Poirrez v France* (2005) 40 EHRR 2, para 817; *Willis v UK* (2002) 35 EHRR 21; *Wessels-Bergevoert v Netherlands* [2002] ECHR 34462/97.

[34] *Stec v UK* (2006) 43 EHRR 1017.

[35] The ECtHR reiterated its approach in *Stec* in *Carson v UK* (2010) 29 BHRC 22. See also *JM v UK* [2010] ECHR 1361; *R (British Gurkha Welfare Society and ors) v Ministry of Defence* [2010] EWCA Civ 1098.

[36] *Stec v UK* (2006) 43 EHRR 1017.

[37] *Muller v Austria* (1975) DR 25; *Carson v UK* (2010) 29 BHRC 22.

8.18 (ii) *Legitimate expectations*   The ECtHR has recognized that an individual may have a property right in the event of a sufficient 'legitimate expectation' of a benefit which is economic or property-like in nature.[38] The Grand Chamber in *Malhous v Czech Republic* defined 'possessions' so as to include legitimate expectations—existing possessions or assets, including claims, in respect of which an applicant can argue that he or she has a legitimate expectation of obtaining the effective enjoyment of a property right.[39]

8.19   In *Pine Valley Developments Ltd and ors v Ireland*, for example, a grant of planning permission created a legitimate expectation of benefits sufficient for it to qualify as a 'possession',[40] and a promise to provide land to displaced refugees sufficed in *Broniowski v Poland*.[41]

8.20   *Stretch v UK* demonstrates the ECtHR's expansive approach to this concept. The Court held that Mr Stretch had a legitimate expectation that a lease granted to him by the local authority would be renewed and that the failure to renew breached his rights under Protocol 1, Article 1. This was despite the fact that the original grant had been *ultra vires*.[42]

8.21   The ECtHR has made clear that there are limits to the expectations it will recognize: if the claim is insufficiently concrete it will not constitute a 'possession'. In *Nerva v UK*, for example, the ECtHR found that waiters had no legitimate expectation that their tips would not be taken into account as part of their remuneration when calculating whether they were receiving the statutory minimum wage.[43] The distinction—repeatedly drawn by the ECtHR—is between a 'mere hope' and a 'legitimate expectation'.[44]

8.22   Claims that have no grounding in the domestic legal order are also considered to be outside the ambit of Protocol 1, Article 1.[45] The criterion is not whether there is a 'genuine dispute' or an 'arguable claim', but a basis for claiming the possession in national law.

3. Positive obligations

8.23   The right to property includes a positive obligation on the state to take necessary and reasonable steps to protect it. In *Öneryildiz v Turkey* a landslide and explosion at a municipal refuse tip had destroyed the applicant's home and killed nine members of his family.[46] The Grand Chamber held that the state's failure to take steps to protect the applicant's property violated Protocol 1, Article 1. The ECtHR has adopted a similar approach to the state's obligation to protect property in the event of a natural disaster.[47]

---

[38] See, further, Allen, *Property and the Human Rights Act 1998* (London: Hart Publishing, 2005) 40–78; Sales, 'Property and Human Rights: Protection, Expansion and Disruption' [2006] JR 141, paras 15–18.

[39] [2001] ECHR 33071/96.

[40] (1992) 14 EHRR 319.

[41] (2005) 40 EHRR 21.

[42] (2004) 38 EHRR 12. See also *Beyeler v Italy* (2001) 33 EHRR 52.

[43] (2003) 36 EHRR 4.

[44] See *MA v Finland* (2003) 37 EHRR CD 210; *Caisse Regionale de Credit Agricole Mutuel v France* App No 58867/00, 19 October 2004; *Von Maltzan v Germany* (2006) 42 EHRR SE 11.

[45] *Kopecky v Slovakia* (2005) 41 EHRR 43, para 52; *Wilson v First County Trust* [2003] UKHL 40, [2004] 1 AC 84 (contract improperly executed, hence unenforceable consumer credit agreement not a possession).

[46] App No 48939/99, 30 November 2004.

[47] *Budayeva and ors v Russia* App Nos 15339/02, 21166/02, 20058/02, 11673/02, and 15343/02, 20 March 2008.

The domestic courts have also recognized that Protocol 1, Article 1 includes a positive   8.24
obligation. In *Marcic v Thames Water Utilities Ltd* the House of Lords accepted that the
failure by Thames Water to prevent regular flooding of Mr Marcic's house with sewage
was a prima facie breach of his right to property.[48]

The article also incorporates an implicit procedural obligation.[49] The state must   8.25
afford a reasonable opportunity to individuals to put their case in order to challenge
measures which interfere with their possessions. However, in *Bank Mellat v HM Treasury*
a majority of the Court of Appeal considered that the failure to allow a suspected terrorist to make representations before he was made subject to an asset freezing order did not
breach this requirement.[50]

4. Interference with the right to property

Possessions may be interfered with in many ways by the state. The most straightforward   8.26
example is when there has been a deprivation of possessions. However, the state may also
interfere with the right through excessive or arbitrary controls, or any other acts or omissions that have the effect of interfering with the use or enjoyment of the property.

(a) *Deprivation of possessions*
In assessing whether an individual has been deprived of property the ECtHR will look   8.27
at the realities of the situation, not the label.[51] In some circumstances the formal legal
title may remain with the owner of the property, but if his or her rights are rendered
useless in practice this may amount to a de facto deprivation.

The House of Lords in *Aston Cantlow v Wallbank* held that when individuals were   8.28
obliged to fulfil an obligation which they had voluntarily taken on, they were not being
deprived of their possessions for the purposes of Protocol 1, Article 1.[52]

(b) *Controls on the use of property*
The second paragraph of Protocol 1, Article 1 provides that the state is entitled to   8.29
'control' the use of property 'in accordance with the general interest or to secure the
payment of taxes or other contributions or penalties'. The ECtHR has held that this is
to be construed in light of the general principle enunciated in the opening sentence of
Protocol 1, Article 1. Controls on use of property are therefore subject to the fair balance
test in the same way as deprivations of possessions.[53]

Applicants will often argue that a measure constitutes a de facto deprivation, but the   8.30
ECtHR will instead find that it amounts only to a 'control'. In *Air Canada v UK*, for
example, the applicants argued that the seizure of their aeroplane following a drugs find

---

[48] [2003] UKHL 66, [2004] 2 AC 42.
[49] See, eg *Jokelala v Finland* [2003] EHRR 26; *Megadat.com Srl v Moldova* App No 21151/04, 8 April 2008.
[50] [2011] EWCA Civ 1, [2011] 2 All ER 802. Cf *R (New London College) v Secretary of State for the Home Department* [2011] EWHC 856 (Admin).
[51] *Sporrong and Lönnroth v Sweden* (1982) 5 EHRR 35, para 63.
[52] [2003] UKHL 37, [2004] 1 AC 546.
[53] *Pye v UK* (2008) 46 EHRR 34; *R (Countryside Alliance) v Attorney General* [2007] UKHL 52, [2008] 1 AC 719.

on board, and the requirement that they pay £50,000 to have it returned, amounted to a deprivation; the ECtHR instead held that it was 'a control on the use of property'.[54]

8.31   The ECtHR has held that planning controls,[55] inheritance laws, and taxes[56] constitute systems of controls. In *Pye v UK* the Grand Chamber, disagreeing with the Chamber, found that the UK's statutory provisions, which transferred ownership from registered landowners to squatters after 12 years of adverse possession, constituted a control on the use of land rather than a deprivation of possessions.[57]

8.32   Controls on the use of property have also included laws requiring positive action by property owners, as in *Denev v Sweden*, where environmental laws obliged a landowner to plant trees.[58]

8.33   In a number of cases the ECtHR has held that housing laws suspending or staggering the enforcement of eviction orders by residential property owners against their tenants constitute 'controls on the use of property'. The ECtHR stated in *Mellacher v Austria* that the housing field is 'a central concern of social and economic policies',[59] warranting a wide margin of appreciation both with regard to its assessment of the existence of a problem of public concern warranting measures of control, and as to the choice of the detailed rules for the implementation of such policies.

8.34   In *R (Countryside Alliance) v Attorney General* the House of Lords characterized a ban on fox hunting with dogs under the Hunting Act 2004 as a control on the use of property rather than a deprivation of possessions.[60] More recently, the High Court held that the ban on cigarette vending machines in the Health Act 2009 was a control on, rather than a deprivation of, the rights of cigarette vendors.[61]

(c) Interference with peaceful enjoyment

8.35   An interference with the right to property may occur where there is no deprivation or control, provided it impinges upon the applicant's ability to peacefully enjoy or use the possessions in question. In *Stran Greek Refineries v Greece*, for example, an arbitral award in favour of the applicant company was a possession, and there was an interference when the state passed legislation rendering the award unenforceable.[62]

5. Limitations

8.36   In determining the level of permissible interference with the right to property the ECtHR distinguishes between the types of interference. It will, in general, apply closer scrutiny to interferences involving deprivations or expropriation than to those involving control alone.

8.37   However, the test applied is broadly similar: the interference must be lawful and must achieve a 'fair balance' between the demands of the general interests of the community

---

[54] (1995) 20 EHRR 150.
[55] *Pine Valley Developments and ors v Ireland* (1992) 14 EHRR 319.
[56] *Gasus-Dosier and Fördertechnik v Netherlands* (1995) 20 EHRR 403.
[57] (2008) 46 EHRR 34.
[58] (1989) 59 DR 127.
[59] (1989) 12 EHRR 391.
[60] [2007] UKHL 52, [2008] 1 AC 719.
[61] *Sinclair Collis Ltd v Secretary of State for Health* [2010] EWHC 3112 (Admin).
[62] (1994) 19 EHRR 293.

and the protection of the fundamental rights of individuals. There must be a reasonable relationship of proportionality between the means employed and the aim pursued. The availability of an effective remedy and compensation is relevant in assessing whether a fair balance has been struck.

(a) *Conditions provided by law*

The deprivation of property must be 'subject to the conditions provided for by law'. This requirement was not satisfied in *Hentrich v France*. A law creating a right of pre-emption over land to enable the Commissioner of Revenue to collect tax was held to violate Protocol 1, Article 1 because it 'operated arbitrarily and selectively and was scarcely foreseeable, and it was not attended by the basic procedural safeguards'.[63] In common with jurisprudence under the qualified rights, the ECtHR also applies the substantive notion of 'quality of law' to Protocol 1, Article 1.[64]

8.38

(b) *The public interest*

In deciding whether a deprivation is in the public interest the ECtHR also affords the state a wide margin of appreciation in deciding what public interest demands. The characterization of an objective of deprivation as being in the public interest is a question left almost exclusively to the determination of the state. The domestic courts have seized on the ECtHR's light touch in this area and applied a gentle standard of review.

8.39

The ECtHR's approach to the public interest is evident from cases such as *James and ors v UK*[65] and *Pye v UK*.[66] In *James* the ECtHR considered the compulsory transfer of ownership of residential properties in central London to the tenants of those properties pursuant to the Leasehold Reform Act 1967, which was designed to protect long-term tenants' moral entitlement to their properties at the end of their leases. The property owners complained that the compulsory nature of, and the calculation of, the price of the transfers violated Protocol 1, Article 1.

8.40

The ECtHR was unanimous in holding that compulsory transfer from one individual to another may be a legitimate means of promoting the public interest and that the objective of eliminating social injustice by leasehold reform is within the state's margin of appreciation. It also emphasized that the public interest need not be equated with the general interest, or the interests of the majority. A deprivation of property effected in pursuance of legitimate social, economic, or other policies may be 'in the public interest' even if the community at large derives no direct benefit from that deprivation.[67] The compulsory transfer at issue was not disproportionate, nor was it unreasonable to restrict the right of enfranchisement to less valuable houses since they were perceived as cases of greatest hardship.

8.41

Similarly, in *Pye v UK* the UK's adverse possession laws which gave squatters ownership of registered land after 12 years were found to fall within the state's margin of appreciation 'unless they give rise to results which are so anomalous as to render the

8.42

---

[63] (1994) 18 EHRR 440.
[64] *Sud Fondi Srl and ors v Italy* App No 75909/01, 20 January 2009.
[65] (1986) 8 EHRR 123.
[66] (2008) 46 EHRR 34.
[67] Ibid, para 45. See also *Allard v Sweden* (2004) 39 EHRR 14, para 52.

legislation unacceptable'. In dissent, Judge Loucaides disputed the existence of a public interest in the measures, noting that in fact they encouraged the illegal use of land.

8.43   The domestic courts now follow the ECtHR's lead on adverse possession. In *Beaulane Properties v Palmer*[68] the High Court had restricted the meaning of 'adverse possession' in order not to infringe the appellant's rights under Protocol 1, Article 1, but this approach was reversed by the Court of Appeal in *Ofulue v Bossert*.[69] The Court simply applied *Pye v UK*, finding that a margin of appreciation applied to the domestic legislation. It effectively abdicated the Court's responsibility properly to scrutinize the legislator's determination of the public interest.

8.44   The notion of the 'public interest' was addressed by the House of Lords in *R (Countryside Alliance) v Attorney General*.[70] Under the Hunting Act 2004, Parliament banned fox hunting with dogs. The appellants, some of whom relied on fox hunting for their livelihood, complained that the ban interfered with their right under Protocol 1, Article 1. Their Lordships proved remarkably reluctant to scrutinize the precise nature of the public interest at stake. Lord Hope held simply that 'It was open to [the legislature] to form their own judgment as to whether [the hunting activities] caused a sufficient degree of suffering . . . for legislative action to be taken to deal with them'.[71]

(c) 'Fair balance'

8.45   The need to strike a fair balance between the public interest and the rights of individual property owners pervades the whole of Protocol 1, Article 1, including its second paragraph. Thus, in *Spadea v Italy* it was held that the applicants had been treated fairly by the laws suspending a tenant eviction order,[72] whereas the applicant in *Scollo v Italy* had not.[73] In both cases the suspensions of the eviction orders had the reasonable aim of preventing a large number of people all becoming homeless at the same time. The facts of each case meant that the application of the fair balance test produced different results.

8.46   *Sporrong v Sweden* related to town planning in Stockholm.[74] The applicants owned properties that were subject to lengthy expropriation permits and prohibitions on construction. The ECtHR held that there had been an interference with the applicants' rights of property by rendering the substance of ownership 'precarious and defeasible', which subjected them to an individual and excessive burden and did not achieve a fair balance between the protection of the individual right to property and wider public interest.

8.47   Again, in *Chassagnou v France* the ECtHR found that to compel small landowners, who were opposed to hunting, to transfer hunting rights over their land enabling others to hunt on it, did not strike a fair balance.[75] Compensation, which involved a right to hunt on others' property, did not assist in achieving a fair balance since the compensation was not valuable to the landowners, who neither hunted nor accepted hunting, and so the compulsion constituted an individual and excessive burden.

---

[68] [2005] EWHC 817 (Ch), [2006] Ch 79.
[69] [2008] EWCA Civ 7, [2008] 3 WLR 1253.
[70] [2007] UKHL 52, [2008] 1 AC 719.
[71] Ibid at [78].
[72] (1995) 21 EHRR 482.
[73] (1995) 22 EHRR 514.
[74] (1982) 5 EHRR 35.
[75] (2000) 29 EHRR 615.

Such an excessive burden may also be present when a home is destroyed and the applicant has no alternative accommodation (thus overlapping with Article 8).[76]

8.48

In a series of cases the ECtHR has accepted that bankruptcy systems pursue a legitimate aim (protection of the rights of others) but in order to be proportionate they must be limited to what is strictly necessary. This stringent test is in keeping with the severe impact of bankruptcy on the individual.[77]

8.49

The Grand Chamber recently emphasized the importance of striking a fair balance in awarding compensation for expropriation of property. In *Perdigão v Portugal* the expropriation compensation awarded to the applicant had been completely absorbed by court costs.[78] In such circumstances, the Court found that the difference in legal character between the obligation on the state to pay compensation for expropriation and the obligation on a litigant to pay court costs did not prevent an overall examination of the proportionality of the interference complained of under Protocol 1, Article 1.

8.50

The fair balance test will be more loosely applied in relation to the state's decisions concerning conferment of welfare benefits, as this involves a question of scarce resources.[79] However, Article 14 operates as a check on discriminatory schemes.[80] The ECtHR will also closely examine the circumstances of any group whose existing benefits are to be removed. For example, in *Ásmundsson v Iceland* the ECtHR found a breach of Protocol 1, Article 1 when a disability pension was removed from a small class of disabled persons, but not others. This imposed an excessive and disproportionate burden on the applicant which was not justified by community interests.[81]

8.51

Taxation schemes are subjected to little scrutiny by the ECtHR, as the ability of the state to levy tax is specifically preserved in the second paragraph of Protocol 1, Article 1. The fair balance test generally applies to tax cases only in so far as it requires procedural guarantees to establish the applicant's liability to make payments—the state can decide for itself as to levels of tax, and the means of assessment and collection. As the ECtHR stated in one case, it 'will respect the legislature's assessment in [enforcing tax obligations] unless it is devoid of reasonable foundation'.[82] This permissive approach has even extended to retrospective taxation schemes.[83]

8.52

Forfeiture laws have been regularly upheld as proportionate by the ECtHR.[84] The ECtHR has also upheld the proportionality of confiscation orders under the Drug Trafficking Act 1994. In *Phillips v UK* the ECtHR rejected the complaint that such confiscation orders were unreasonably extensive, given the important role such penalties play in efforts to combat drug trafficking.[85]

8.53

---

[76] See also *Allard v Sweden* (2004) 39 EHRR 14, para 54.

[77] See, eg *Luordo v Italy* [2003] ECHR 32190/96; *Stockholms Forsakrings-och Skadestandjuridik AB v Sweden* [2004] BPIR 218.

[78] App no 24768/06, 16 November 2010.

[79] See, eg *Carson v UK* (2010) 29 BHRC 22.

[80] Cf *Stec v UK* (2006) 43 EHRR 1017; *Barrow v UK* [2006] ECHR 42735/02; *Burden and Burden v UK* (2008) 24 BHRC 709.

[81] (2005) 41 EHRR 42.

[82] *Gasus Dosier- und Fördertechnik GmbH v Netherlands* (1995) 20 EHRR 403.

[83] *National and Provincial Building Society v UK* (1997) 25 EHRR 127.

[84] See, eg *Handyside v UK* (1976) 1 EHRR 737; *Allgemeine Gold und Silberscheideanstalt v UK* (1986) 9 EHRR 1; *Air Canada v UK* (1995) 20 EHRR 150.

[85] (2001) 11 BHRC 280.

8.54   The domestic courts apply the 'fair balance' test where they find a prima facie interference under Protocol 1, Article 1.[86] As in Strasbourg, proportionality is used as the measure for assessing a 'fair balance'. The courts have in general been prepared to accept justifications for interferences with property rights without great scrutiny.[87]

8.55   In *Marcic v Thames Water Utilities Ltd*, for example, the House of Lords adopted a hands-off approach to the fair balance test, stating that it considered the pertinent question to be whether the scheme set up by Thames Water to control the sewage system which had flooded Mr Marcic's house had 'an unreasonable impact' on Mr Marcic. As it did not, the court found the interference with his property rights to be justified.[88]

8.56   In *R (Countryside Alliance) v Attorney General* the House of Lords noted that there was no test of strict necessity under Protocol 1, Article 1, and that property rights could be 'more readily overridden' than the core rights such as Articles 8 and 9.[89]

8.57   In *Sinclair Collis v Secretary of State for Health*[90] the High Court stated that it would not interfere with a legislative judgment to ban cigarette vending machines cases unless it 'was *manifestly without foundation so as to be disproportionate*'. The court used a test formulated by the ECtHR in Article 1, Protocol 1 cases when it applies a margin of appreciation.[91] The balance struck in *Sinclair Collis* was correct, but the invocation of the margin of appreciation by the national court was inappropriate.[92] The High Court applied the proportionality test more carefully in *R (Petsafe Ltd and anor) v The Welsh Ministers* to find that the ban on electronic pet collars that gave pets an electric shock was proportionate to the aim of promoting animal welfare.[93]

(d) *Compensation*

8.58   The basic approach to compensation was set out by the ECtHR in *Holy Monasteries v Greece*:

> In this connection, the taking of property without payment of an amount reasonably related to its value will normally constitute a disproportionate interference and a total lack of compensation can be considered justifiable under Protocol 1, Article 1 only in exceptional circumstances. Article 1 does not, however, guarantee a right to full compensation in all circumstances, since legitimate objectives of 'public interest' may call for reimbursement of less than the full market value.[94]

8.59   A similar approach was taken in *Gaganus v Turkey* where the Court held that, in general, the amount of compensation in cases of expropriation in the public interest should bear a reasonable relationship to the value of the property.[95] However, the ECtHR emphasized in *Lithgow v UK* that where a state considers that objectives of public interest

---

[86] See, eg *R (Trailer and Marina Level Ltd) v Secretary of State for the Environment, Food and Rural Affairs* [2004] EWCA Civ 1580, [2005] 1 WLR 1267.
[87] See, eg *Rowland v Environment Agency* [2003] EWCA Civ 1885, [2005] Ch 1.
[88] [2003] UKHL 66, [2004] 2 AC 42.
[89] [2007] UKHL 52, [2008] 1 AC 719 at [163] per Lord Brown.
[90] [2011] EWCA Civ 437.
[91] See, eg *Jahn v Germany* (2006) 42 EHRR 49.
[92] See ch 4, paras 4.112–4.130.
[93] [2010] EWHC 2908 (Admin).
[94] (1994) 20 EHRR 1, para 71.
[95] App No 39335/98, 5 June 2001.

justify reimbursement at less than the full market value, the ECtHR will respect the national legislature's judgment unless manifestly without reasonable foundation.[96]

C. PROTOCOL 1, ARTICLE 2: RIGHT TO EDUCATION

The existence and scope of 'a right to education' is one of the more controversial **8.60** Convention questions. During the drafting of Protocol 1, many states expressed concern that the existence of such a right would impose onerous positive obligations upon governments. In an attempt to assuage these concerns, the opening sentence of Protocol 1, Article 2 was changed from its original positive form ('Every person has the right to education') to the current negative expression ('No person shall be denied the right to education').

Several states, including the United Kingdom, have entered reservations to Article 2 **8.61** of Protocol 1. The UK reservation relates to the second sentence of the article (the requirement that education be provided in conformity with parents' religious and philosophical convictions). The United Kingdom has accepted this provision only so far as it is compatible with the provision of efficient instruction and training and the avoidance of unreasonable public expenditure. The reservation is set out in Part II of Schedule 3 to the Human Rights Act.

Strasbourg and domestic jurisprudence concerning Protocol 1, Article 2 is limited. **8.62** This is often said to be due to the weak, negative phrasing of the article itself. However, Convention rights with even weaker phrasing—notably Protocol 1, Article 3, the implied right to vote—have developed despite this constraint.[97] The underdevelopment of Protocol 1, Article 2 is primarily due to the lack of cases that go to Strasbourg. The leading ECtHR decision remains *Belgian Linguistics (No 2)*,[98] decided in 1968, and only a handful of cases are heard each year.

Other rights that involve personal development, such as Article 8 and the 'audience **8.63** right' (the right to receive information) under Article 10, have developed rapidly in recent years. The principles developed in these cases may also be relevant in the context of the right to education.

1. Scope of the right

In *Belgian Linguistics (No 2)* the ECtHR held that despite the negative formulation, the **8.64** first sentence of Protocol 1, Article 2 clearly enshrines a positive right.[99] The content of that right was identified as follows:

(a) a right to an effective education;

(b) a right of access to existing educational institutions;

---

[96] (1986) 8 EHRR 329. See the House of Lords' decisions in *R v Rezvi; R v Benjafield* [2002] UKHL 1, [2003] 1 AC 1099 for consistent domestic findings on the issue of confiscation orders.
[97] See, eg *Hirst v UK (No 2)* (2005) 19 BHRC 546.
[98] (1968) 1 EHRR 252.
[99] Ibid.

(c) a right to be educated in the national language or in one of the national languages; and

(d) a right to obtain official recognition of completed studies.

8.65   The significance of the negative formulation was held to be that the article does not require states to establish at their own expense, or to subsidize, education of any particular type or at any particular level. Since all Member States at the time of signing the Protocol possessed, and continued to possess, a general and official educational system, there was no question of requiring each state to establish such a system. Rather, the article obliged states to guarantee that individuals could take advantage of the existing means of instruction.[100]

8.66   The right is that of the student, which can be exercised by the parents on his or her behalf when he or she is young and by the student personally when he or she grows older.

8.67   The state may require parents to send their children to school or to educate them adequately at home.[101] It may allow private education and schools, but is under no obligation to fund or subsidize these arrangements.

8.68   Until 2005 the extent of the article's applicability to higher education was unclear. Although the ECmHR as far back as 1965 stated that Protocol 1, Article 2 included 'entry to nursery, primary, secondary and higher education',[102] in a series of decisions over the next 30 years it observed that 'the right to education envisaged in Article 2 is concerned primarily with elementary education and not necessarily advanced studies such as technology'.[103]

8.69   The Grand Chamber in *Leyla Sahin v Turkey* finally clarified that Protocol 1, Article 2 undoubtedly does extend to higher education. Any existing institutions of higher education clearly come within its scope, 'since the right of access to such institutions is an inherent part of the right set out in that provision'.[104]

8.70   The Court applied *Leyla Sahin* in *Eren v Turkey*, in which it found a violation of the right where a university student's exam results had been arbitrarily annulled, thereby excluding the student from the whole university system.[105]

8.71   Despite the range of educational activities that Protocol 1, Article 2 touches, it has not proved a potent right for domestic litigants. The leading domestic case on the scope of the right is *Ali v Head Teacher and Governors of Lord Grey School*, in which the House of Lords considered the right in the context of a child temporarily excluded from school for alleged arson.[106] Lord Bingham, with whom the majority of their Lordships concurred, stated:

> . . . the guarantee is, in comparison with most other Convention guarantees, a weak one, and deliberately so. There is no right to education of a particular kind or quality, other than that prevailing in the state. There is no Convention guarantee of compliance with domestic law. There is no Convention guarantee of education at or by a particular institution. There is no Convention

---

[100] *Simpson v UK* (1989) 64 DR 188.
[101] *Family H v UK* (1984) 37 DR 105.
[102] *Belgian Linguistics* (1968) 1 EHRR 252, para 22.
[103] *X v UK* (1975) DR 2, para 50; *Kramelius v Sweden* App No 21062/92, 17 January 1996.
[104] (2007) 44 EHRR 5, paras 134, 141.
[105] [2006] ELR 155. See also *Timishev v Russia* [2005] ECHR 55762/00.
[106] [2006] UKHL 14, [2006] 2 AC 363.

objection to the expulsion of a pupil from an educational institution on disciplinary grounds, unless (in the ordinary way) there is no alternative source of state education open to the pupil . . . The test, as always under the Convention, is a highly pragmatic one, to be applied to the specific facts of the case: have the authorities of the state acted so as to deny to a pupil effective access to such educational facilities as the state provides for such pupils?[107]

Their Lordships held that the student had not been denied effective access to education on the basis that he had been offered a place at a pupil referral unit, which his parents had refused.

In *Re JR17's Application for Judicial Review* the Supreme Court applied *Ali* and found 8.72
that a child's suspension from school for three months in the run-up to public examinations did not constitute a denial of the Convention right to education when very limited home tutoring had been provided.[108] The court noted that the Convention guarantees access only to that education provided by the state and not to education of a particular quality or degree.

In the context of the provision of special education, the Supreme Court in *A v Essex* 8.73
County Council considered the case of an autistic child who was not provided with schooling for 19 months.[109] The court rejected the approach of the Court of Appeal,[110] which had held that the state's failings needed to have been systemic to engage the Convention. However, the fact that there had been a breach of domestic legal provisions obliging the local authority to provide education did not lead to a breach of Protocol 1, Article 2. The court found that a triable issue arose only in very narrow circumstances, namely where it could have been shown that the defendant had either failed to make inquiries during any period that it knew the child was not receiving effective education or that such investigations as it conducted were wholly inadequate. Overall, the potential for domestic claims founded on the right to education is very limited.[111]

However, the narrow domestic approach may need to be reconsidered in light of the 8.74
ECtHR's judgment in *Ali v UK*,[112] handed down after the Supreme Court's decisions in *JR17* and *A v Essex*. While the ECtHR accepted that the student's temporary exclusion had been proportionate as adequate alternative provision had been offered to him, it observed that the situation 'might well be different if a pupil of compulsory school age were to be permanently excluded from one school and were not able to subsequently secure full-time education in line with the national curriculum at another school'.[113] The ECtHR therefore appears to have accepted that the requirement imposed by domestic law that a child access the national curriculum is a relevant standard by which to judge compliance with Protocol 1, Article 2. As a result it is possible that a student could claim a breach of the Convention if the education to which he or she is legally entitled under domestic law is not provided. The conclusions of the Supreme Court in *A v Essex* are likely to be revisited.

---

[107] Ibid at [24].
[108] [2010] UKSC 27, [2010] NI 105.
[109] [2010] UKSC 33, (2010) 30 BHRC 1.
[110] [2008] EWCA Civ 364, [2008] ELR 321.
[111] See also *Holub and anor v Secretary of State for the Home Department* [2001] 1 WLR 1359. See also *R (Mdlovu) v Secretary of State for the Home Department* [2008] EWHC 2089 (Admin).
[112] (2011) 30 BHRC 44.
[113] Ibid, para 60.

2. Parental right to educate children in conformity with convictions

8.75   The second sentence of Protocol 1, Article 2 seeks to prevent the state from indoctrinating children through the education system, by providing to parents the right to have their religious and philosophical convictions respected. This applies to all educational systems, public or private, and to all functions the state exercises with respect to education, be they academic or administrative.

8.76   The provision naturally overlaps very significantly with Article 9, and complaints brought under the second sentence of Protocol 1, Article 2 will generally be coupled with a complaint under Article 9. While such cases will be influenced by Article 9, the ECtHR has emphasized that they will be determined under Protocol 1, Article 2 as it is the 'lex specialis' in the area of education.[114]

8.77   In *Campbell and Cosans v UK* two parents challenged the existence of corporal punishment in state schools, on the basis that it was contrary to their philosophical beliefs.[115] The ECtHR upheld their complaint, finding that the obligation to respect religious and philosophical convictions is not confined to the content of educational instruction but includes the organization and financing of public education, the supervision of the educational system in general, and questions of discipline.

8.78   The House of Lords considered the converse situation in *R (Williamson) v Secretary of State for Education and Employment*.[116] The claimant parents argued that the statutory ban on corporal punishment in schools was contrary to their belief in the necessity of physical punishment and thus in violation of Protocol 1, Article 2. The House of Lords accepted that a belief in corporal punishment constituted a conviction for the purposes of Article 9 and by implication for Protocol 1, Article 2, and further held that the notion of education under the second sentence was wide enough to include the manner in which discipline was maintained in school. However, the legislation pursued the legitimate aim of protecting children, and the total prohibition on corporal punishment was proportionate in the circumstances.

8.79   The extent to which the religious and philosophical convictions of parents can influence the provision of education is limited in a number of ways. First, the conviction itself must come within the limited definition set out in *Campbell v UK*. The parents must also show that the holding of the belief is the reason for their objection to what the state is doing, and that they have brought the reason for their objection to the attention of the authorities. Lastly, the state will not violate Protocol 1, Article 2 if the education system conveys religious or philosophical knowledge in an objective, critical, and pluralistic manner.

8.80   In *Kjeldsen v Denmark* parents challenged a law which made sex education a compulsory component of the curriculum of state primary schools.[117] The ECtHR held that while the state was forbidden from pursuing indoctrination, the instruction subject to challenge was a way of objectively conveying information and did not therefore offend the parents' religious and philosophical convictions to the extent forbidden by Protocol 1, Article 2.

---

114   *Folgerø v Norway* (2007) 23 BHRC 227, para 54.
115   (1982) 4 EHRR 293.
116   [2005] UKHL 15, [2005] 2 AC 246.
117   (1976) 1 EHRR 711. See also *Valsamis v Greece* (1996) 24 EHRR 294.

The ECtHR adopted a tougher approach in *Folgerø v Norway*, which concerned the **8.81** refusal to grant total exemption to pupils in primary and early secondary education from lessons in Christianity, religion, and philosophy.[118] Non-Christian parents alleged that the obligation on their children to follow these lessons had been in breach of the parents' right to ensure that their children received an education in conformity with their religious and philosophical convictions. The Grand Chamber held that the state had not taken sufficient care that information and knowledge included in the curriculum be conveyed in an objective, critical, and pluralistic manner, and the system for partially exempting students from the lessons was not an adequate mechanism to safeguard respect for the parents' convictions.

By contrast, in *Lautsi v Italy* the Grand Chamber found that the display of crucifixes **8.82** in Italian state school classrooms did not violate Protocol 1, Article 2.[119] Unlike the lessons in *Folgerø*, the crucifix was essentially a 'passive symbol'.[120] The Court held that in light of Italy's historical development, the decision to display a crucifix fell with the state's margin of appreciation.

3. General limitations

Other than the limitation set out in the second sentence of the article, there are no other **8.83** specific qualifications to the right to education. The state may supply any explanation for an interference with the right, but in order to be lawful the measures must be foreseeable and bear a reasonable relationship of proportionality between the means adopted and the alleged aim.[121]

In *Leyla Sahin v Turkey* the Grand Chamber considered the prohibition on the hijab **8.84** at universities in Turkey.[122] The applicant was a medical student who had been subjected to disciplinary proceedings after refusing to remove her hijab in classes. By a majority of 16 to 1, the ECtHR held that the purpose of the ban was to protect the secular character of educational institutions. The action taken against the applicant did not impair 'the very essence of her right to education'[123] and any restriction was a proportionate means of pursuing the legitimate aim of secularism. The case is notable for its very limited discussion of the educational consequences of the headscarf ban for students such as Ms Sahin. Like other cases involving Turkish secularism, the decision of the ECtHR can be explained in part by the extreme political sensitivity of the issues at stake.[124]

The House of Lords followed the *Leyla Sahin* case in *R (Begum) v Denbigh High School* **8.85** in which a girl was excluded from school for wearing the jilbab (a Muslim dress that covered her whole body).[125] Dealing only cursorily with the right to education, the House of Lords referred to their analysis in the *Ali* case (above), finding that the pupil's

---

[118] (2007) 23 BHRC 227.
[119] [2011] ECHR 30814/06.
[120] Ibid, para 29.
[121] *Leyla Sahin v Turkey* (2007) 44 EHRR 5; *Ali v UK* (2011) 30 BHRC 44.
[122] (2007) 44 EHRR 5.
[123] Ibid, para 161.
[124] See, eg *Refah Partisi (the Welfare Party) and ors v Turkey* (2003) 14 BHRC 1, discussed in ch 7, para 7.452.
[125] [2006] UKHL 15, [2007] 1 AC 100.

exclusion from education was a result of her unwillingness to comply with a uniform rule that pursued a legitimate aim.

4. Discrimination

8.86 In common with all articles of the Convention, Protocol 1, Article 2 is subject to the prohibition on discrimination in Article 14 of the Convention. This issue was raised in the leading case on Protocol 1, Article 2, *Belgian Linguistics (No 2)*, which concerned legislation that dictated the language of education in certain areas of Belgium.[126] A school that failed to comply with the language rules could suffer penalties, which included denial of public support and non-recognition. The ECtHR held that Article 14, read with Protocol 1, Article 2, could not be interpreted as guaranteeing children or parents a right to education in a language of their choice. The measures adopted by the Belgian Government for the legitimate purpose of achieving linguistic unity were proportionate to meet that purpose.

8.87 In a series of recent cases, the Grand Chamber of the ECtHR has addressed educational discrimination in the context of placement of Roma children in special schools. In a thorough analysis of the Czech schooling system in *DH v Czech Republic*,[127] the Court held that as a specific type of disadvantaged and vulnerable minority, the Roma required special protection, including in the sphere of education. The placement of Roma in schools for children with mental disabilities meant that they received an education that compounded their difficulties and compromised their subsequent personal development. Although the state did not intend to discriminate, it could not justify the disproportionate adverse effect on the applicants' education. The ECtHR subsequently reached the same conclusion in relation to the Croatian[128] and Greek[129] systems, reiterating the principle that separate does not mean equal.

D. PROTOCOL 1, ARTICLE 3: RIGHT TO FREE ELECTIONS

8.88 By Article 3 of Protocol 1, states that have ratified the Protocol undertake to hold free elections. Although the provision appears to impose an obligation upon the state rather than conferring a right upon an individual, it was held in *Mathieu-Mohin v Belgium* that Protocol 1, Article 3 does give rise to an individual right and can be the object of a complaint.[130]

8.89 The ECtHR in *Mathieu-Mohin* established several general principles. First, it held that Protocol 1, Article 3 extends to the subjective rights of participation—the right to vote and the right to stand for election to the legislature. However, it went on to state that the rights are not absolute. A state could impose conditions on the right to vote and to stand for election, provided that the conditions pursue a legitimate aim, are not disproportionate, and do not thwart the free expression of the opinion of the people in the choice of the legislature.

---

[126] (1968) 1 EHRR 252.
[127] (2007) 23 BHRC 526.
[128] *Oršuš and ors v Croatia* (2010) 28 BHRC 558.
[129] *Sampanis v Greece* App No 32526/05, 5 June 2008.
[130] (1987) 10 EHRR 1.

The Grand Chamber has reiterated these principles. It explained in *Zdanoka v Latvia* 8.90
that the right is akin to Articles 10 and 11, as it guarantees respect for pluralism of opinion in a democratic society.[131] However, unlike Articles 8–11, no limitations are specified in the text of the Convention. In their absence, the ECtHR has developed the
concept of 'implied limitations', which it has held is of 'major importance for the determination of the relevance of the aims pursued by the restrictions on the rights guaranteed
by the provision'.[132] States are 'always free to rely on any legitimate aim' in their justification of restrictions on the right.[133] As the right is phrased in collective terms the proportionality test will not be strictly applied and there is no test of 'necessity' or 'pressing
social need'.[134]

Historically, the ECtHR tended to afford states a very generous margin of apprecia- 8.91
tion in limiting the rights, but the decision in *Hirst v UK (No 2)* signalled a different
approach.[135] In that case, the ECtHR held that the absolute bar to prisoners voting
violated Protocol 1, Article 3. It is clear that Strasbourg will now conduct a more rigorous review of the justification advanced by states for interference with rights arising
under this article, and the older authorities that demonstrate a more 'hands-off' approach
are not a reliable guide to its application.

1. 'Legislature'

Protocol 1, Article 3 concerns only the choice of the 'legislature'. The term 'legislature' 8.92
is not confined to the national Parliament and its meaning will vary according to the
constitutional structure of the state in question. For example, Belgian regional councils
have been held to be constituent parts of the legislature,[136] yet a French regional council
has been held not to come within the article.[137]

The flexibility of the term 'legislature' is demonstrated by the finding in *Matthews v* 8.93
UK that the European Parliament had the requisite features of a 'legislature' for the residents of Gibraltar.[138] However, the ECmHR decided that other elected bodies, such as
the former metropolitan county councils in England, are not 'legislatures' for the purpose
of Protocol 1, Article 3.[139]

2. 'Elections'

While the meaning of 'legislature' may have a degree of flexibility, a tighter approach is 8.94
taken to the meaning of 'elections'. The ECmHR has ruled that referenda are not subject
to Protocol 1, Article 3.[140]

---

[131] (2007) 45 EHRR 17, para 115. See also *Yumak and Sadak v Turkey* (2009) 48 EHRR 1.
[132] *Zdanoka v Latvia* (2007) 45 EHRR 17, at para 115.
[133] *Georgian Labour Party v Georgia* [2008] ECHR 9103/04, para 124.
[134] See *Zdanoka v Latvia* (2007) 45 EHRR 17.
[135] (2006) 42 EHRR 41. See the discussion in House of Commons library briefing paper SN/PC/01764,
'Prisoner's voting rights'.
[136] *Mathieu Mohin v Belgium* (1987) 10 EHRR 1.
[137] *Malarde v France* App No 46813/99, 5 September 2000.
[138] (1999) 28 EHRR 361.
[139] *Booth-Clibborn v UK* (1985) 43 DR 236.
[140] *X v Germany* (1975) 3 DR 98; *X v UK* (1975) 3 DR 165.

8.95   The ECtHR has also held that presidential elections are not included,[141] although this will depend on the precise political structures in any given state.

8.96   In one of the few domestic cases under Protocol 1, Article 3, the Supreme Court recently considered the law governing elections in the Crown Dependency of Sark, one of the Channel Islands. In *R (Barclay) v Secretary of State for Justice and anor*[142] the claimants challenged a new law designed to reform Sark's constitutional arrangements by which the Seigneur (head of state) and the Seneschal (President of the Sark Parliament and chief judge) remained unelected. The claimants contended that this breached their rights under Protocol 1, Article 3.

8.97   The Supreme Court held that there had been no breach of the claimants' rights on the grounds that the Strasbourg cases put 'no narrow focus on one particular element of democracy'.[143] The electoral rules needed to be examined in the round and in the light of historical and political factors. Applying those principles, there was no requirement that all members of a legislature be elected. Even if there were such an obligation under Protocol 1, Article 3, the constitutional history of Sark would justify its limitation.

3. Right to vote

8.98   Protocol 1, Article 3 contains an implied right to vote. The state may set conditions on this right, such as minimum age requirements and, in some circumstances, residency.[144] As 'any departure from the principle of universal suffrage risks undermining the democratic validity of the legislature thus elected and the laws which it promulgates', such conditions must not impair the very essence of the right.[145] Exclusion of any groups or categories of the general population must be reconcilable with the article's underlying purposes and its democratic character.[146]

8.99   In *Moore v UK* the applicant argued that his right to vote was impaired as mental health patients were prevented from using a hospital as their residential address in order to register on the electoral roll. The Government reached a friendly settlement with the applicant, agreeing to amend the Representation of the People Act 1983.[147]

8.100   In *Hirst v UK (No 2)* the Grand Chamber found that the UK's automatic and indiscriminate statutory bar on convicted prisoners voting was an arbitrary and disproportionate restriction on a vitally important Convention right.[148] It fell outside any acceptable margin of appreciation, however wide, and violated Protocol 1, Article 3. The Court went further in *Frodl v Austria*, holding that an automatic and general ban on all those

---

[141] *Guliyev v Azerbaijan* App No 35584/02, 27 May 2004; *Boškoski v the Former Yugoslav Republic of Macedonia* App No 11676/04, 2 September 2004.

[142] [2009] UKSC 9, [2010] 1 AC 464 .

[143] Ibid at [64].

[144] *Hilbe v Liechtenstein* App No 31981/96, ECHR 1999-VI; *Melnychenko v Ukraine* App No 17707/02, ECHR 2004-X, para 56.

[145] *Hirst v UK (No 2)* (2006) 42 EHRR 41, para 62.

[146] *Labita v Italy* App No 26772/95, 6 April 2000. See, eg *Alajos Kiss v Hungary* App No 38832/06, 20 May 2010; *Sitaropoulos and anor v Greece* App No 42202/07, 8 July 2010.

[147] App No 37841/97, 30 May 2000; cited in Leach, *Taking a Case to the European Court of Human Rights*, 2nd edn (Oxford: Oxford University Press, 2005) 368.

[148] (2006) 42 EHRR 41, para 82. The Registration Appeal Court of Scotland issued a declaration of incompatibility in relation to this point: *Smith v Scott* [2007] CSIH 9. See also *Frodl v Austria* App No 20201/04, 8 April 2010.

serving a sentence of at least a year and whose crime was committed with intent also violated Protocol 1, Article 3 because it lacked the crucial 'discernible and sufficient link between the sanction and the *conduct and circumstances* of the individual concerned'.[149] In *Scoppola v Italy*, the Court reiterated that an automatic ban on voting by particular categories of prisoners without individual consideration was unacceptable: any decision on disenfranchisement should be taken by a court and be duly reasoned.[150]

The Government continues to prevaricate over implementing the judgment, and so there has been substantial further litigation. In *Smith v Scott*[151] the Court of Session made a declaration under section 4 of the Human Rights Act that section 3(1) of the Representation of the People Act 1983 was incompatible with Protocol 1, Article 3. In later cases, the courts have considered such a declaration pointless because one has already been made.[152] The only remedies for disenfranchised prisoners therefore lie in applications to the ECtHR. Approximately 2,500 such claims have been lodged. The House of Commons recently passed a symbolic motion calling on the Government not to repeal the current ban. In *Green and anor v UK* the ECtHR held that the ongoing violation of Protocol 1, Article 3 did not at this stage give rise to a right to compensation.[153] However, it is not clear that it will continue to take that line if no further steps are taken to implement the *Hirst* decision.   8.101

4. Right to stand for election

Protocol 1, Article 3 also includes a right to stand for election to the legislature.[154] The right has been characterized as the 'passive' aspect of Protocol 1, Article 3, as opposed to the 'active' right to vote. However, the ECtHR has emphasized that 'it is essential to take a holistic approach to the impact which restrictions on either right may have on securing [the right to free elections]'.[155]   8.102

Legislation establishing domestic residence requirements for a parliamentary candidate is not, as such, incompatible with Protocol 1, Article 3. However, the ECtHR has found that, while states have a margin of appreciation as to eligibility conditions of this kind in the abstract, the principle that rights must be effective requires that eligibility procedures themselves contain sufficient safeguards to prevent arbitrary decisions.[156]   8.103

Thus, it found a violation when an individual was denied registration as a candidate on the basis of residence where the domestic law governing proof of residency lacked the necessary certainty and precision.[157] Similarly, in *Podkolzina v Latvia* the disqualification of a candidate on the grounds of lack of competence in Latvia violated Protocol 1,   8.104

---

[149] (2011) 52 EHRR 5.

[150] App No 126/05, 18 January 2011, para 43.

[151] [2007] SLT 137,

[152] *Traynor and anor v Secretary of State for Scotland* [2007] ScotCS CSOH 78, Court of Session; *R (Chester) v Secretary of State for Justice and Wakefield Metropolitan Borough Council* [2009] EWHC 2923 (Admin).

[153] App Nos 60041/08 and 60054/08, 23 November 2010. See also *Tovey and ors v Ministry of Justice* [2011] EWHC 271 (QB).

[154] *Ganchev v Bulgaria* App No 28858/95, 25 November 1996, para 130; *Sadak and ors v Turkey* (2003) 36 EHRR 23, para 33.

[155] *Tanase v Moldova* [2008] ECHR 7/08, para 113.

[156] *Zdanoka v Latvia* (2007) 45 EHRR 17.

[157] *Melnychenko v Ukraine* (2004) 19 BHRC 523.

Article 3 because the body that determined competence did not exhibit the necessary procedural safeguards against arbitrariness.[158]

8.105   The right to stand for election includes the right to sit as a member of the legislature once elected. The ECmHR held, in a short admissibility decision, that the contingent right to take up one's seat is not violated by a requirement that elected MPs in the United Kingdom, including Northern Irish Republicans, take the oath of allegiance to the Queen.[159]

8.106   In *R (Barclay) v Secretary of State for Justice and the Lord Chancellor* the Supreme Court considered that the prohibition on aliens standing for election in Sark was justifiable in light of its constitutional history.[160]

8.107   In *R (Woolas) v The Parliamentary Election Court* the High Court upheld the decision of the Election Court, concluding that dishonest statements made by a parliamentary candidate in election campaign literature were aimed at the destruction of the right to free elections and were not protected by Article 10.[161]

5. Electoral systems

8.108   There is no obligation to introduce a specific system of voting, such as proportional representation. The state has a wide margin of appreciation in this regard. It does not have to introduce a system of voting which ensures that all votes have equal weight as regards the outcome of the election, or that all candidates have equal chances of victory.

8.109   In *Liberal Party v UK* a challenge was made to the system of 'first past the post' elections in the United Kingdom, which inevitably disadvantaged smaller political parties.[162] The ECmHR found the complaint inadmissible, stating that the UK system was a fair one overall and that it did not become unfair because of the results that flowed from it.[163]

8.110   The ECtHR in *Mathieu-Mohin* observed that any electoral system must be assessed in the light of the political evolution of the country concerned. Features that would be unacceptable in the context of one system may be justified in another, as long as the chosen system provides for conditions that will ensure the 'free expression of the opinion of the people in the choice of the legislature'.[164]

8.111   In *Bowman v UK* the ECtHR examined the relationship of Article 3 of Protocol 1 to Article 10 of the Convention (freedom of expression) in the context of electoral laws. The impugned legislation limited the amount of money spent by unauthorized persons on publications during an election period. This limit was found to be a disproportionate infringement on the right of free speech, which was not outweighed by the need to hold free elections.[165]

---

[158] [2002] ECHR 46726/99. See also *Tanase v Moldova* [2008] ECHR 7/08.
[159] *McGuinness v UK* App No 39511/98, 8 June 1999.
[160] [2009] UKSC 9, [2010] 1 AC 464.
[161] [2010] EWHC 3169 (Admin).
[162] (1980) 4 EHRR 106.
[163] The same position was taken by the ECtHR in *Gitonas v Greece* (1980) 21 DR 211.
[164] (1998) 26 EHRR 691.
[165] (1998) 26 EHRR 1.

The ECtHR has rarely been called upon to determine the validity of the result of an election. In one such case the ECtHR considered the invalidation of votes in a parliamentary election.[166] It held that the process had been arbitrarily conducted in violation of the right to free elections. 8.112

E. PROTOCOL 4

Protocol 4 was opened for signature in September 1963, and, for reasons discussed below, although it has been signed by the United Kingdom, it has not yet been ratified. 8.113

1. Protocol 4, Article 1

No one shall be deprived of his liberty merely on the ground of inability to fulfil a contractual obligation. This provision is almost identical to Article 11 of the UN's ICCPR, to which the United Kingdom is subject, and it is impossible to find an example of a UK law that would breach it. It applies only to contractual obligations, and does not affect imprisonment for breach of a court order, such as inability to pay a fine. It is limited to an 'inability to fulfil a contractual obligation', thus excluding from its application a refusal to fulfil such an obligation by someone with the means to fulfil it. 8.114

The word 'merely' excludes cases in which the defaulter acts fraudulently or maliciously. Thus, in *X v Germany* this article did not protect a person who was detained for refusing to execute an affidavit in respect of his property at the request of his creditor.[167] 8.115

2. Protocol 4, Article 2

Freedom of movement within a territory applies to 'everyone', including aliens 'lawfully' in a territory. The power of a state to control the entry of non-nationals is preserved by the inclusion of the word 'lawfully'.[168] 8.116

This right of free movement is limited by the restrictions found in Protocol 4, Article 2(3) and (4). All such restrictions are subject to the principle of proportionality, the doctrine of the margin of appreciation, and must be in accordance with law.[169] 8.117

The restrictions in Article 2(3) are familiar (national security or public safety, the maintenance of public order, the prevention of crime, for the protection of health or morals, or for the protection of the rights and freedoms of others). Any restriction is subject to the requirement that it be necessary in a democratic society. These restrictions are similar in content to those found in Articles 8–11 of the Convention. 8.118

However, Article 2(4) permits further restrictions based on a criterion not found elsewhere, that of the 'public interest'. This formulation was preferred by the Committee of Experts, a majority of whom rejected a reference to 'economic welfare' being included. 8.119

---

[166] *Kovach v Ukraine* [2008] ECHR 39424/02. See also *Kerimova v Azerbaijan* App no 20799/06, 30 September 2010.

[167] (1971) 14 YB 692.

[168] *Omwenyeke v Germany* App No 44294/04, 20 November 2007.

[169] For examples of cases concerning Protocol 4, Art 2, see *X v Belgium* (1981) 24 DR 198; *Schmid v Austria* (1985) 44 DR 195; *Raimondo v Italy* (1994) 18 EHRR 237; *Foldes v Hungary* [2006] ECHR 41463/02; *Gochev v Bulgaria*, App No 34383/03, 26 November 2009.

However, it is highly likely that their chosen term 'public interest' is broad enough to include consideration of the economic welfare of society in any event.

8.120　　The freedom to leave a state applies to nationals and aliens alike, and is subject to the same restrictions that apply to freedom of movement within a state.[170]

8.121　　Protocol 4, Article 5, which applies to the Protocol as a whole, provides that if a state that ratifies the Protocol declares that it also applies to an external territory, that external territory is to be treated as separate from the state's metropolitan territory for the purposes of Protocol 4, Articles 2 and 3.

3. Protocol 4, Article 3

8.122　　Protocol 4, Article 3 prohibits expulsion from, and protects entry to, an individual's national territory.

8.123　　An expulsion occurs when 'a person is obliged permanently to leave the territory of the state without being left the possibility of returning later'.[171] Extradition is not within this definition and is outside the scope of this article.[172]

8.124　　Protocol 4, Article 5 applies, so that a state's external territories declared subject to the article are considered separate from the metropolitan territory. This would have allowed the United Kingdom to distinguish between nationals denied entry under the British Nationality Act 1981.

4. Protocol 4, Article 4

8.125　　This article refers to expulsion by a collective measure, as opposed to an expulsion following an individual decision about a particular person.[173] In *A v Netherlands* it was held that it was not a collective expulsion where a number of asylum seekers from the same country had been expelled for similar reasons as each had received an individual, reasoned decision.[174] In such a case the issue of discriminatory treatment may, of course, arise.

5. Ratification of Protocol 4 by the United Kingdom

8.126　　Prior to the passing of the Human Rights Act 1998, the UK Government stated that although Protocol 4 protects 'important rights, and we would like to see them given formal recognition in our law', there were 'potential conflicts' with 'existing laws in relation to different categories of British nationals' which prevented ratification.[175] Concerns that Protocol 4 may confer rights on categories of British nationals who do not currently have that right have prevented ratification.[176]

---

[170] *X v Germany* (1997) 9 DR 190; *M v Germany* (1984) 37 DR 113; *Piermont v France* (1995) 20 EHRR 301.
[171] *X v Austria* (1974) 46 CD 214.
[172] *Bruckmann v Germany* (1974) 17 YB 458.
[173] On the meaning of 'expulsion', see para 8.123 below.
[174] (1988) 59 DR 274.
[175] *Rights Brought Home: The Human Rights Bill* (Cm 3782, 1997) paras 4.10–4.11.
[176] Department of Constitutional Affairs, *Report of the Outcome of an Interdepartmental Review conducted by the Department of Constitutional Affairs* (July 2004) app 6, p 40.

F. PROTOCOL 6

Protocol 6 prohibits the death penalty in times of peace and thereby overrides the exception   8.127
permitting the death penalty under Article 2. The Protocol came into force on 1 March
1985 and all Member States have ratified it except for Russia, which is a signatory and
observes a moratorium.

Protocol 6 was ratified by the United Kingdom in 1999. As originally drafted, the   8.128
Human Rights Act did not incorporate Protocol 6, but by the time it came into force, it
had been inserted into Schedule 1. Protocol 6 has now been superseded by Protocol 13,
prohibiting the death penalty in all circumstances.

G. PROTOCOL 7

Following the adoption by the General Assembly of the United Nations of the   8.129
International Covenant on Civil and Political Rights (ICCPR) in 1966, the Council of
Europe commissioned its Committee of Experts to investigate any problems that could
be caused by the coexistence of the European Convention and the ICCPR. The
Committee's report[177] on differences between the two documents led to Parliamentary
Assembly recommendations,[178] further work, and, eventually, Protocol 7.

Protocol 7 seeks to bring the Convention into line with the ICCPR. It came into   8.130
force on 1 November 1988.

The United Kingdom is the only Member State not yet to be a signatory. The previ-   8.131
ous Government explained that the United Kingdom would not be in a position to
accede to Protocol 7 until legislation to abolish or equalize three rules of matrimonial
property law had been passed. Part 15 of the Equality Act 2010 was designed to achieve
this aim. However, there do not currently seem to be any proposals to ratify this Protocol.
Nonetheless, the United Kingdom has ratified the ICCPR and it must respect the rights
under Protocol 7 as a matter of international law.

The Strasbourg jurisprudence on Protocol 7 is sparse, but the Council of Europe   8.132
has published an explanatory memorandum which, although not binding upon the
ECtHR, is an additional aid to interpretation.[179]

1. Protocol 7, Article 1

This provision affords a minimum guarantee that the procedural rights specified are com-   8.133
plied with by a state seeking to expel a lawfully resident alien. The Memorandum stresses
that such an individual already benefits from certain guarantees under the Convention and
international law, and makes clear that this is a residual article, which 'enables protection
to be granted in those cases which are not covered by other international instruments'.[180]

---

[177] Report of the Committee of Experts, Doc H (70) 7 (1969).
[178] Recommendation 683 (1972) and Recommendation 791 (1976).
[179] *Text of Protocol No 7 and Explanatory Memorandum*, CE Doc H (84) 5 (Strasbourg: Council of Europe, 1984).
[180] Ibid, paras 6–7.

8.134   It is a precondition that the person is 'lawfully resident'. The article does not therefore apply to an alien who has arrived but not yet passed through immigration control, a person in transit or admitted for a limited period for a non-residential purpose, or those awaiting a decision on a residence application.[181]

8.135   The term 'lawfully' refers to domestic law, and it is for that law to determine the conditions under which the person's presence is lawful. The provision applies to aliens who enter unlawfully but who have regularized their position, but not to those whose permits have expired or who are in breach of conditions.[182]

8.136   Expulsion means any measure compelling the departure of an alien from the territory, except extradition, and is a concept independent of any national law definition. A decision to expel must be made in 'accordance with law'.[183] The Memorandum states baldly that 'no exceptions may be made to this rule'.[184] However, in exceptional cases involving public order or national security, an alien may be expelled *before* the exercise of his or her rights. The rights to review must be available after expulsion, and the principles of proportionality should be taken into account.[185]

8.137   The sub-paragraphs to Protocol 7, Article 1 set out three specific guarantees, namely that the person concerned may submit reasons against his or her expulsion, have the case reviewed, and be represented before the relevant authority.

8.138   According to the Memorandum, the right to have the case reviewed does not require a two-stage process before different authorities—merely that the 'competent authorities' should review the case in the light of the reasons against expulsion. The alien is not entitled to an oral hearing—a written procedure will suffice. It does not need to be the authority upon whom the final decision to expel rests, but may have only power of recommendation to the body that does make the final decision.

8.139   The ECmHR has held that a decision to deport does not involve a determination of the person's civil rights or of a criminal charge within the meaning of Article 6 of the Convention.[186] Accordingly, Protocol 7, Article 1 does not affect the interpretation of Article 6. The competent authority does not have to comply with the Article 6 characteristics of a judicial body.

2. Protocol 7, Article 2

8.140   Protocol 7, Article 2 extends the general right to a fair trial provided by Article 6 of the Convention. This article recognizes the right of everyone convicted of a criminal offence to have his or her conviction or sentence reviewed by a higher tribunal. However, it does not require that in every case the individual be entitled to have both his or her conviction and sentence so reviewed. For example, if he or she has pleaded guilty the right may be restricted to a review of sentence only.[187]

---

[181] Ibid, para 9.
[182] See Baroness Royall of Blaisdon, *Hansard*, HL, col 710, 9 February 2010.
[183] *CG and ors v Bulgaria* App No 1365/07, 24 April 2008.
[184] Ibid, para 11.
[185] *Chahal v UK* (1996) 23 EHRR 413; *CG and ors v Bulgaria* App No 1365/07, 24 April 2008.
[186] *Agee v UK* (1976) 7 DR 164; see also *Explanatory Memorandum*, n 163 above, para 16.
[187] *Explanatory Memorandum*, n 179 above, para 17.

Where a person has pleaded guilty, the right to appeal may be limited to one against 8.141
sentence only, and may be satisfied by leave to appeal proceedings where leave is not
granted.

The right is restricted to offences tried by bodies that are 'tribunals' for the purpose of 8.142
Article 6 of the Convention, and so excludes cases of a disciplinary nature.

Other limits are found in Article 2(2): offences of a 'minor character' are excluded, as 8.143
are cases where the person was convicted by the highest tribunal, or following an appeal
against acquittal.

The right to appeal may be satisfied by leave to appeal proceedings where leave is not 8.144
granted.

As 'the modalities for the exercise of the right and the grounds on which it may be 8.145
exercised' are matters to be determined by domestic law, the appeal may be limited to
law, or may also include questions of fact.[188]

3. Protocol 7, Article 3

A right to compensation for miscarriages of justice is established by Protocol 7, Article 3, 8.146
subject to conditions. The person must have been convicted of a criminal offence by a
'final decision', and suffered punishment as a result. A decision is final where it is irrevocable in that no further ordinary remedies are available, the parties have exhausted such
remedies, or have allowed the time limit to expire without availing themselves of the
remedy.[189] Thus, Protocol 7, Article 3 does not apply in cases where a conviction is
overturned on an ordinary appeal, or when charges are dismissed in the trial court.

According to the Memorandum, the right to compensation arises only: 8.147

where the person's conviction has been reversed or he has been pardoned, in either case on the
grounds that a new or newly discovered fact shows conclusively that there has been a miscarriage
of justice—that is, some serious failure in the judicial process involving grave prejudice to the
convicted person.[190]

Article 2 operates on a 'clean hands' principle: there will be no right to compensation 8.148
if it is shown that the non-disclosure of the unknown fact in time was wholly or partly
attributable to the convicted person.[191]

The nature of the procedures to establish a miscarriage of justice is a matter of domes- 8.149
tic law or practice for the state (although states are obliged to make provision for compensation in all cases to which Article 3 applies).[192] Once a miscarriage of justice is
established, the intention of the article is that compensation should be paid by the state.
If it is not, a violation of this article will have occurred.

In the United Kingdom the relevant provision is section 133 of the Criminal Justice 8.150
Act 1988. The Supreme Court recently considered Protocol 7, Article 3 in relation to the
statutory scheme in *R (Adams) v Secretary of State for Justice*.[193] The court did not consider

---

[188] Ibid, para 18.
[189] Ibid, para 22.
[190] Ibid, para 32. See *Matveyev v Russia* App No 26601/02, 3 July 2008.
[191] *Explanatory Memorandum*, n 179 above, para 24.
[192] Ibid, para 25.
[193] [2011] UKSC 18. See also *R (Mullen) v Secretary of State for the Home Department* [2004] UKHL 18,
[2005] 1 AC 1.

that it assisted in determining the meaning to be given to the term 'miscarriage of justice' in domestic law.

4. Protocol 7, Article 4

8.151 Article 4 of Protocol 7 incorporates the protection against double jeopardy into the Convention. It is limited to the same national jurisdiction, so that it remains possible to be convicted of the same offence in different jurisdictions. It applies only to criminal proceedings. A 'final' conviction must have been recorded.[194]

8.152 Article 4(2) allows the reopening of a case in exceptional circumstances, where there is evidence of new or newly discovered facts, or where there has been a fundamental defect in the previous proceedings.

8.153 The Court of Appeal has considered Article 4(2) where a defendant had previously been convicted of wounding with intent and acquitted of attempted murder. The court ruled that a subsequent prosecution for murder following the death of the victim from her injuries did not breach Protocol 7 as the 'new fact' of her death had emerged since the first trial.[195]

8.154 The 'fundamental defect' exception finds effect in domestic law in the Criminal Procedure and Investigations Act 1996, sections 54–56.

8.155 The Criminal Justice Act 2003 has abolished the double jeopardy rule in some circumstances. It makes provision for the quashing of an acquittal and an order for a retrial in respect of certain serious offences where there is 'new and compelling evidence'.[196] These provisions were introduced by Parliament following the Macpherson Report on the Stephen Lawrence Inquiry[197] and a report by the Law Commission.[198] Concerns have been raised as to the Convention-compliance of these measures, although in our view the provisions in themselves appear to be compliant, but their application in an individual case may give rise to a complaint under Protocol 7, Article 4, or even Article 6.

5. Protocol 7, Article 5

8.156 This article places an obligation on the state to provide a system of laws by which spouses have equal rights and responsibilities concerning matters of private law, such as property rights and their relations with their children. It does not apply to areas of law external to the relationship of marriage, such as administrative, fiscal, criminal, social, ecclesiastical, or labour laws.[199]

8.157 It is concerned only with spouses, and specifically precludes the period before marriage. The article is not meant in any way to prevent the state from taking such measures as are necessary in the interests of children; nor is it to prevent the state taking

---

[194] This has the same meaning as under Protocol 7, Art 3.

[195] *R v Kerry Rena Young* [2005] EWCA Crim 2963.

[196] Criminal Justice Act 2003, s 78.

[197] *The Stephen Lawrence Inquiry: Report of an Inquiry by Sir William Macpherson of Cluny* (Cm 4262-I, 1999).

[198] *Double Jeopardy and Prosecution Appeals* (Law Com No 267, 2001).

[199] This article was the basis for changes made to the common law by Part 15 of the Equality Act 2010, which was drafted by Lord Lester and accepted by the previous Government on the basis that there would then be no obstacle in the way of ratifying the whole Protocol.

due account of 'all relevant factors' when reaching decisions about the distribution of property upon the dissolution of marriage.[200]

This article—as is also the case with Article 12 of the Convention—does not   8.158
include a right to divorce. The Memorandum states that the words 'in the event of its dissolution . . . do not imply any obligation on a State to provide for dissolution of marriage or to provide any special forms of dissolution'.[201]

H. PROTOCOL 12

Protocol 12 came into force on 1 April 2005. It provides a substantive right to equality of   8.159
treatment in like situations. Unlike Article 14 of the Convention, this is a free-standing equality right, which does not need to 'piggy-back' on an existing Convention right. It applies the expansive grounds of prohibited discrimination in Article 14 (including sex, race, religion, and 'other status') to the exercise of 'any right set forth by law' and to the actions (including the obligations) of public authorities.

The United Kingdom has not yet signed or ratified Protocol 12. Various concerns   8.160
have been raised about the potential breadth of its protection.[202] As the Joint Committee on Human Rights has stated, these concerns are unwarranted.[203] As a signatory to a variety of international human rights instruments concerning equality and non-discrimination, the United Kingdom has already accepted the principles enshrined in Protocol 12. The development of Protocol 12 is effectively stymied by the Government's approach: the United Kingdom will not ratify it until the ECtHR has clarified its parameters, but the ECtHR is hindered in doing so because the most populous Member States, including the United Kingdom, have decided not to ratify it.

I. PROTOCOL 13

Protocol 13 abolishes the death penalty in all circumstances. In so doing, it closes the   8.161
gap left by Protocol 6, which did not exclude the death penalty in respect of acts committed in time of war or of imminent threat of war. Protocol 13 is non-derogable and no reservations may be made in respect of it.[204]

The United Kingdom ratified Protocol 13 on 10 October 2003, and in 2004   8.162
Protocol 13, Article 1 was incorporated into the Human Rights Act in place of Protocol 6.[205]

---

[200] *Explanatory Memorandum*, n 179 above, para 38.
[201] Ibid, para 39.
[202] Department of Constitutional Affairs, *Report of the Outcome of an Interdepartmental Review conducted by the Department of Constitutional Affairs* (July 2004) app 6, p 41.
[203] Joint Committee on Human Rights, 17th Report (2005–2006), HL 99, para 33.
[204] Protocol 13, Arts 2, 3.
[205] Human Rights Act (Amendment) Order 2004, SI 2004/1574, art 2(3).

9

BEYOND THE DOMESTIC COURTS: TAKING A CASE TO STRASBOURG

A. Introduction	9.01
B. The Structure and Jurisdiction of the Court	9.08
C. Making an Application	9.10
1. Urgent cases and interim measures	9.13
2. Court's response to a letter of introduction	9.15
3. Representation	9.16
4. Application form	9.17
D. Admissibility and Merits	9.18
1. Who is a 'victim'?	9.21
2. Against whom can an application be brought?	9.22
3. Extent of jurisdiction	9.23
4. The application must concern a Convention issue	9.24
5. Exhaustion of domestic remedies	9.25
6. Six-month time limit	9.28
7. Other inadmissibility grounds	9.29
8. Decision on admissibility	9.37
9. Consideration by a Chamber and communication to the Government	9.38
10. Friendly settlements	9.41
11. Pilot judgments	9.42
12. Assessing the merits	9.43
13. Court's investigative powers	9.45
14. Third-party interventions	9.46
15. Oral hearing	9.47
16. Judgment	9.49
17. Applications to the Grand Chamber	9.50
18. Remedies	9.51
E. Funding for Cases in Strasbourg	9.55
1. Domestic Legal Services Commission funding	9.56
2. Other sources of funding	9.58
3. Strasbourg legal aid	9.59
F. Implementation of Judgments	9.62

A. INTRODUCTION

9.01 The Human Rights Act 1998 did not, and could not, end the practice of taking UK cases to the Strasbourg Court. First, this is because the Human Rights Act 1998 maintains parliamentary sovereignty, so it is likely that there will be cases in which breaches of Convention rights will still arise in primary legislation which cannot be rectified in domestic courts and where Parliament does not legislate to amend the law following a declaration of incompatibility. To date, however, the Government has responded to all such declarations of incompatibility (either by repealing or amending the offending law, or by enacting new legislation).[1] Secondly, domestic courts are more likely than an international body to succumb to local pressure from politicians and the state, and may not always be as robust in their protection of human rights as the Court in Strasbourg. Thirdly, the Strasbourg Court may differ from the domestic courts in its interpretation of particular Convention rights. For example, in *S and Marper v UK*[2] the Grand Chamber took a very different view of the collection and retention of DNA samples and data and Article 8. The Administrative Court,[3] the Court of Appeal,[4] and the House of Lords[5] all rejected the victims' cases and the House of Lords decided that Article 8 was barely engaged, whereas the 17 judges in Strasbourg were unanimous in finding a violation.[6] Fourthly, it is sensible for individuals with the stamina and real issues to test to seek redress there, including those who seek compensation where the domestic court has made a declaration of incompatibility and compensation is not available. Fifthly, since in practice the definitive interpretation of the Convention is reserved to the Strasbourg Court, practitioners are likely to want to contribute to this definitive jurisprudence.[7] Sixthly, the Coalition Government may amend the Human Rights Act, perhaps restricting the jurisdiction of the UK courts. If that happens, then, depending on what legislation replaces it, Strasbourg may be the only means of directly enforcing Convention rights.[8]

9.02 The European Court of Human Rights (ECtHR) is a court of last resort and not an appeal court: it has never been permissible to take a case there without exhausting domestic remedies first, and this requirement is more likely to be strictly imposed now that the Convention is part of domestic law. However, a declaration of incompatibility is not regarded as an effective remedy for the purposes of Article 13, although the Court has not closed the possibility of this being the case in future.[9]

---

[1] However, the Parliamentary Joint Human Rights Committee (JCHR) has expressed real concerns about delays in implementation: see JCHR, *Monitoring the Government's Response to Human Rights Judgments: Annual Report 2008* 31st Report (2007–2008), HL 173, HC 1078 (31 October 2008).

[2] [2008] ECHR 1582, App Nos 30562/04 and 30566/04, 4 December 2008.

[3] *R (S) v Chief Constable of South Yorkshire Police and the Secretary of State for the Home Department* and *R (Marper) v Chief Constable of South Yorkshire Police and the Secretary of State for the Home Department* [2002] EWHC 478 (Admin), [2002] EWCA Civ 1275 and *R (LS) v Chief Constable of South Yorkshire and R (Marper) v Chief Constable of South Yorkshire* [2004] UKHL 39.

[4] [2003] EWCA Civ 1275, [2002] 1 WLR 3223.

[5] [2004] UKHL 39, [2004] 1 WLR 2196.

[6] See also *Hirst v UK* (2006) 42 EHRR 41 where, on the right of prisoners to vote, the Court also took a much stronger pro-rights line.

[7] See Lord Bingham in *R (Anderson) v Secretary of State for the Home Department* [2002] UKHL 46, [2003] 1 AC 837 at [18].

[8] See Preface.

[9] See para 9.27 below.

Interestingly, the number of cases against the United Kingdom lodged with the ECtHR before and after the Human Rights Act came into force seems to have remained roughly the same.[10] However the number of allocated cases[11] against the United Kingdom pending in the Court on 31 December 2010 was 2,766, twice that in 2008 or 2009.[12] The Court found only 14 violations of the Convention in 2010 in relation to UK cases, making the United Kingdom in 2010 the sixteenth highest 'violator' of the 45 countries subject to the Court's jurisdiction. The number of cases 'communicated' (referred to the Government for it to make its response, the initial sifting stage) has reduced from 163 in 2000 to 68 in 2010 (although an increase from the figure of 48 in 2008).[13]

9.03

This chapter outlines the procedure for making applications to the European Court in Strasbourg. It is included to ensure that those who have exhausted the domestic remedies in the United Kingdom have information on how to proceed further. The system for dealing with applications changed in 1998. Prior to this date, the process involved two bodies: the European Commission of Human Rights (which dealt with admissibility issues and gave its view of the merits) and the ECtHR (which gave judgments).

9.04

Over the last ten to 15 years there has been a huge increase in the number of cases that have been dealt with by the Court (partly as a result of the accession of a significant number of countries from Eastern Europe). By the end of 2010 there were 139,650 allocated cases pending, with most of those cases being taken against five countries: Russia (28 per cent); Turkey (11.3 per cent); Romania (8.4 per cent); Ukraine (7.6 per cent); and Italy (7.1 percent).[14] Changes to speed up the Court's procedures and processes and to reduce the number of cases taking up its time (particularly at the admissibility stage) are urgently needed. The latest batch of proposals to deal with the problem were discussed in Interlaken in February 2010 and resulted in a number of proposals, but it was not clear at the time of writing exactly what changes might be made or when.[15] However, a further conference with another declaration containing new proposals was held in Izmir in Turkey in April.[16]

9.05

The amendments to the Convention set out in Protocol 14 were designed to make a number of changes to the system to try to solve this problem. It is the new system that is described in this chapter.[17]

9.06

For more information on the procedure in the Court, see the amended Convention itself and the new Rules of Procedure of the European Court of Human Rights, June 2010: references to 'rules' in this chapter are to these rules unless otherwise stated.[18]

9.07

---

[10] Survey of Activities of the European Court of Human Rights, Council of Europe.

[11] These are applications which are ready for decision because the file is complete and which have been allocated to a judicial function. Uncompleted applications (that is, cases not allocated) are disposed of administratively because the applicant fails to submit the properly filled in application form and/or necessary supporting documentation within the prescribed time limit.

[12] This is probably as a result of a sudden influx of cases from prisoners challenging the continued blanket ban on voting rights.

[13] The figures year by year are erratic.

[14] ECtHR, *Annual Report for 2010*.

[15] See the Interlaken Declaration, 19 February 2010.

[16] The Izmir Declaration, see the Council of Europe website for the up-to-date position.

[17] The changes made by Protocol 14 came into force on 1 June 2010. For the previous procedure, see the fifth edition of this book.

[18] See also Leach, *Taking a Case to the European Court of Human Rights*, 2nd edn (Oxford: Oxford University Press, 2005); a new edition of this publication dealing with the new rules and procedure is due to be published in 2011.

The ECtHR's very helpful website (<http://www.echr.coe.int>) gives access to the amended Convention and all the rules and to the practice directions referred to below.

B. THE STRUCTURE AND JURISDICTION OF THE COURT

9.08   The Court consists of one judge nominated by each of the countries belonging to the Council of Europe. These persons act in an individual capacity and cannot be government officials (though they can be ex-government lawyers). The vast majority of decisions in cases will be made by single judges or committees of three. In cases that lead on to substantive judgments the Court will sit in Chambers of seven judges. Reserve judges may also sit, so that the case does not need to be reheard if one judge falls ill, or cannot for some other reason deliberate. Where the Chamber considers that a case raises a serious question affecting the interpretation of the Convention, or where the resolution of a question before it might result in an inconsistency in the Court's case law, it may relinquish jurisdiction to a Grand Chamber of 17 judges, under Article 30 of the Convention. Alternatively, within three months of a decision of a Chamber, any of the parties may request that the case be referred to the Grand Chamber under Article 43. This is an exceptional procedure, and the request will be accepted only if the case raises a serious question affecting the interpretation or application of the Convention or a serious issue of general importance. The first case referred to the Grand Chamber from the United Kingdom under Article 43, *Hatton v UK*,[19] which concerned the Article 8 rights of those in the vicinity of Heathrow Airport, was decided in 2003.

9.09   The Court can hear applications of alleged violations of the Convention brought by other Member States—as occurred, for example, when the Republic of Ireland complained to the Court about the UK's interrogation practices used in Northern Ireland.[20] But this is rare.[21] In practice the majority of applications are now brought by individuals against states.

C. MAKING AN APPLICATION

9.10   Applications should be directed to:

> The Registrar of the European Court of Human Rights
> Council of Europe
> F-67075 Strasbourg-Cedex
> France
> Tel: 00 33 3 88 41 2018
> Fax: 00 33 3 41 27 30

9.11   It is sensible to make the application on and in the form provided by the Court (available from its website). The following information is required by the Court:

(a) the applicant's name, date of birth, nationality, sex, occupation, and address;

(b) the name, address, and occupation of anyone acting as the representative;

---

[19] (2003) 37 EHRR 28.
[20] *Ireland v UK* (1978) 2 EHRR 25.
[21] There are two inter-state cases pending, both by Georgia against Russia.

(c) the respondent country;

(d) a clear and concise statement of the facts, including, of course, the exact dates;

(e) a succinct statement of the alleged violation of the Convention and the relevant arguments (this should include the relevant domestic law and any relevant Convention case law);

(f) a succinct statement of compliance with the admissibility criteria, including the six months rule and the details of all remedies (including any appeal) which have been pursued within the country concerned and, where appropriate, an explanation of why any available remedies have not been pursued (see below);

(g) the object of the application (for example, the repeal or amendment of certain legislation, or the reversal of a decision and compensation); and

(h) copies of the judgments, decisions, and any other documents relating to the application.[22]

It is possible to write a short initial letter to the Court setting out the basic details of the application, and this will be sufficient to interrupt the six-month time limit provided that the letter sets out in summary form the subject matter of the application and a completed application is sent within eight weeks of this being requested by the Court.[23] The essence of the application and the Convention articles that are alleged to have been violated should be set out as succinctly as possible, in clear and simple language. Sending in a detailed and full application at the start will, however, speed up the very long process only very slightly.   9.12

1. Urgent cases and interim measures

The Court's full procedures take some time (five years or more in many cases), but it will give priority to very urgent cases (for example, where a person's life or well-being is immediately threatened, as in the case of a motor neurone disease sufferer in *Pretty v United Kingdom*[24]). The Court has now amended its rules allowing urgent and important cases to be dealt with more quickly.[25] The Court can also be asked to implement its interim measures procedure. In rule 39 the Chamber or its President may indicate to the parties interim measures which it considers should be adopted. This will often be a request to refrain from taking action that will prejudice the case—for instance by not deporting someone where the case concerns arguments about the possibility of Article 3 breaches if that person is sent out of the jurisdiction. In such cases, the Court should be contacted directly to ask it to request the Government to refrain from acting until the application has been considered. Telephone contact can be useful to alert the Registry of a request about to be made, which of course then has to be in writing (a telephone call on its own would not be enough). The Court now has a dedicated fax line for such   9.13

---

[22] Rule 47.

[23] Rule 47(5). For useful information on how to make an application, see ECtHR, Practice Direction: Institution of Proceedings, 1 November 2003, as amended on 22 September 2008 and 24 June 2009.

[24] (2002) 35 EHRR 1.

[25] See 'The Court's Priority Policy' which sets out the criteria to be considered following the amendment to r 41.

315

requests and all requests should initially be sent using this line.[26] The Court has expressed its concern about the number of cases wrongly brought under this procedure so it is sensible to get this right.[27]

9.14   The United Kingdom has, until very recently, always respected requests from the ECtHR for interim measures. However, in December 2008 the Government decided not to comply with a request from the ECtHR to refrain from handing over two people in Iraq to the Iraqi High Tribunal pending their trial for killing two British servicemen.[28] The Secretary of State for Defence stated that:

> This follows the unanimous court of appeal ruling that Mr Al-Saadoon and Mr Mufdhi do not fall within the jurisdiction of the European Convention on Human Rights. After 31 December 2008, the UK had no legal power to detain any individuals in Iraq and continued detention would be a breach of the UK's international law obligations.[29]

The Court in Strasbourg however found that:

> In conclusion, the Court does not consider that the authorities of the Contracting State took all steps which could reasonably have been taken in order to comply with the interim measure taken by the Court. The failure to comply with the interim measure and the transfer of the applicants out of the United Kingdom's jurisdiction exposed them to a serious risk of grave and irreparable harm.[30]

2. Court's response to a letter of introduction

9.15   The Court will reply by sending the standard application form. The Court will register the application and give it a case number.

3. Representation

9.16   Legal representation must be by a lawyer authorized to practice in any Convention country and resident in one of them, unless the President of the Chamber decides otherwise.[31] The Court has the power to direct that an applicant be so represented, and at any hearing representation is required unless the President of the Court decides otherwise.[32]

4. Application form

9.17   All applications must be made on the application form provided by the Registry and available on the ECtHR's website.[33]

---

[26] For more details, see Practice Direction: Requests for Interim Measures, 5 March 2003, amended 16 October 2009 and 7 July 2011.

[27] Court press release, 28 July 2011 which also gives a link to the statistics by country for interim measures accepted or refused.

[28] See the judgment of the Court of Appeal, *R (Al-Saadoon and anor) v Secretary of State for Defence* [2009] EWCA Civ 7.

[29] Reported in the *Guardian*, 1 January 2009.

[30] *Al-Saadoon and others v UK* App No 61498/08, 2 March 2010, [2010] ECHR 282, para 165.

[31] Rule 36.

[32] Rule 36(2).

[33] Rule 47.

D. ADMISSIBILITY AND MERITS

The Court's jurisdiction is limited and applications can be considered only if they meet the   9.18
admissibility criteria set out in Article 35 of the Convention, which are rigorously applied
and which are set out in turn below. More than 95 per cent of cases are dismissed as being
'inadmissible',[34] and it is therefore critically important to ensure that an application complies with the admissibility requirements, and contains all the facts and arguments of law.
To have a real chance of success, it is necessary for the application to set out the facts, the
relevant domestic law, and detailed submissions on the law of the Convention. One of
the best ways of setting out the application is to model it on a judgment of the Court.[35]

Article 34 provides that an application under the Convention can be brought by 'any   9.19
person, non-governmental organization or group of individuals claiming to be the victim
of a violation'. Neither individuals nor legal persons have to be citizens of the state concerned, nor of any Member State. They do not have to be resident or physically present
in the territory. Applications may not be brought by governmental organizations or
other 'emanations of the state'.

Although applications may be brought by groups of individuals and non-governmental   9.20
organizations (NGOs), the organization or group must itself be a victim of a violation.
Thus, trade unions and NGOs can make applications about an action by the state but
only if it was directed towards them. Finally, groups, trade unions, and NGOs can, of
course, provide their members with representation, but cannot make applications on
behalf of their members.

1. Who is a 'victim'?

An applicant must be one of three types of victim: actual, potential, and indirect. An   9.21
actual victim is someone who is personally affected by the alleged violation. It is not
necessary to show that any detriment has been suffered, although this will be relevant to
the remedy. A *potential victim* is one who is at risk of being directly affected by a law or
administrative act.[36] An *indirect victim* is one who is immediately affected by a violation
which directly affects another, such as a family member of someone imprisoned or killed.
Family members of those killed or imprisoned can also successfully include in their cases
applications about *direct violations* of their rights—for example Article 3 in disappear-
ance cases. Another example of an indirect victim is a family member of someone
deported or facing deportation.

2. Against whom can an application be brought?

Only states are parties to the Convention, and therefore only those states can commit   9.22
violations. Where there are several state organs involved, it will not be necessary for this

---

[34] Of the 7,997 cases against the UK that were 'allocated' (see n 11 above), only 348 were declared
admissible between 1998 and the end of 2008: European Court of Human Rights, *Annual Report for 2008*.

[35] See Leach, *Taking a Case to the European Court of Human Rights*, 2nd edn (Oxford: Oxford University
Press, 2005), for model applications.

[36] See, eg *Dudgeon v UK* (1981) 4 EHRR 149 or *Burden v UK* App No 13378/05, 12 December 2006,
[2006] ECHR 1064.

purpose to identify which level of the state organization is responsible. Applications cannot be brought against private persons or institutions. However, the application may be based on the state's failure to fulfil positive obligations to ensure that human rights are respected by private persons within the state's jurisdiction.[37]

3. Extent of jurisdiction

9.23   Under Article 1, signatory states are required to 'secure to everyone *within their jurisdiction*' (emphasis added) the rights and freedoms protected by the Convention. This means that states are liable for all events that take place in the territory for which they are responsible, not just those affecting their own nationals, and even if the effects of the events might be felt outside the Council of Europe area. For example, cases have been brought concerning deportation to places where torture might occur, such as in *Chahal v UK*.[38] But the jurisdiction of a state may also extend to the acts of state servants that take place beyond the physical territory of the state.[39] The crucial test for jurisdiction is whether or not the state was exercising *de facto* control over the events in question. For a general discussion of the principles, see *Bankovic v UK and ors*[40] and *Al-Skeini v UK*.[41]

4. The application must concern a Convention issue

9.24   The Court's jurisdiction extends only to applications relating to the rights and freedoms contained in the Convention and the Protocols that the Member State in question has ratified.[42]

5. Exhaustion of domestic remedies

9.25   The ECtHR has consistently held that it 'may only deal with the matter after all domestic remedies have been exhausted'.

9.26   This rule is applied strictly in practice. It applies only to the remedies that are available, sufficient, and which relate to the breaches alleged. In considering the nature of the remedy, the Court takes into account 'the principles of flexibility and avoidance of undue formalism developed in its case-law on Article 35, in particular that it is sufficient if the applicant has raised the substance of his Convention application before the domestic authorities'.[43] If a potential applicant to the Court is in doubt as to whether alternative remedies have been exhausted, it is usually sensible for the remedy to be pursued, though a 'protective' application to the ECtHR could be lodged simultaneously to avoid falling

---

[37] See ch 2.

[38] (1996) 23 EHRR 413.

[39] See, eg *Loizidou v Turkey* (1997) 23 EHRR 513 concerning the effects of Turkish-sponsored troops in Cyprus.

[40] (2007) 44 EHRR SE5. See ch 2, para 2.23.

[41] App No 55721/07 [2011] ECHR 1093.

[42] The UK has yet to ratify Protocols 4, 7, and 12 so UK claimants cannot found applications on breaches of the rights contained in those protocols.

[43] See, for instance, the case of *John Shelley v UK* (2008) 46 EHRR SE16, quoting *Cardot v France* (1991) 13 EHRR 853, para 34.

foul of the six-month time limit should the Court subsequently decide that the remedy was not effective and did not need to be pursued.

It is most unlikely that a declaration of incompatibility will be regarded as an effective remedy for the purposes of Article 13. This means that, at present, the ECtHR is unlikely to exclude a case at the admissibility stage for failure to exhaust domestic remedies if the only domestic remedy realistically available was a declaration of incompatibility. This was confirmed in *Burden and Burden v UK* where, in a lengthy discussion, the ECtHR held itself not to be satisfied that a declaration of incompatibility could be considered to be an effective judicial remedy.[44] However, the ECtHR did accept that, should evidence emerge at a 'future date' of a 'long-standing and established practice' of the Government giving effect to courts' declarations of incompatibility, this might support a different conclusion.[45] The best advice therefore for the purposes of an application to the Court would be to seek one anyway.[46]

9.27

6. Six-month time limit

Applications to the ECtHR must be made within six months of the final decision of the domestic proceedings or, where there are no effective domestic remedies, of the violation of the Convention. There is very little flexibility for cases brought outside this time limit, though lack of knowledge of the violation may make a later application possible. For example, in *Hilton v UK*[47] a journalist was refused a job within the BBC, but discovered that this was as a result of a secret vetting process only nine years later.

9.28

7. Other inadmissibility grounds

Under Article 35(2) and (3), the Court may declare an application inadmissible on further grounds, which are dealt with in turn below.

9.29

(a) *Anonymity*
Anonymous applications are inadmissible, although the complainant may request on the application form that he or she wishes his or her identity to be kept confidential (apart from disclosure to the Member State itself).[48]

9.30

(b) *Petition is 'substantially the same as' previous applications*
This restriction prevents successive applications by the same applicant in respect of the same facts, and is not interpreted by the Court to restrict applications in respect of different instances even if the issues are substantially the same. Similarly, the provision does not act to bar a second application where new facts have arisen since the first application.

9.31

---

[44] (2007) 44 EHRR 51, paras 30–40; confirmed by the Grand Chamber at (2008) 47 EHRR 38.
[45] (2007) 44 EHRR 51, paras 30–40.
[46] See *Carson v UK* App No 42184/05, 16 March 2010 [2010] ECHR 338, where the Art 8 complaint was dismissed inadmissible on the grounds of non-exhaustion.
[47] (1998) 57 DR 108.
[48] Rule 32. See Practice Direction: Requests for Anonymity, 14 January 2010.

(c) *Examination by another international body*

9.32 If the matter has already been submitted to, and dealt with by, some other international procedure and contains no new information, it will be inadmissible. This is very unlikely to be an issue, because the only comparable procedures that the United Kingdom has ratified are the petition processes under the Convention for the Elimination of All Forms of Discrimination Against Women and, more recently, the Convention on the Rights of People with Disabilities.

(d) *Incompatible with the provisions of the Convention*

9.33 This ground covers applications which do not concern the rights and freedoms protected by the Convention, as well as situations in which the applicant is not within the jurisdiction of a Member State, or where the application is not directed against the state at all.

(e) *Manifestly ill-founded*

9.34 This is the most difficult criterion to assess. Ostensibly, this term is applied to applications that, on a preliminary examination, do not disclose any possible ground on which a violation could be established. Although the test is a prima facie one used to screen out clearly unmeritorious applications, it is applied very strictly. In effect, the Court's assessment of whether an application is 'ill-founded' is a strict merits test. The Court's assertion that a case is 'manifestly ill-founded' is not the same as saying that it is unarguable. Many cases that are plainly arguable are excluded on this ground.

(f) *No significant disadvantage*

9.35 The Court can declare the case inadmissible if 'the applicant has not suffered a significant disadvantage'.[49] Even if that assessment has been made by the Court, the Court needs to consider whether or not the application should be examined to ensure respect for human rights under the Convention and that the matter has already been considered by a domestic tribunal. All three criteria have been met before a case can be declared inadmissible:

- the applicant must not have suffered a significant disadvantage;
- respect for human rights does not require an examination of the application on the merits; and
- the case has already been rejected on its merits in a domestic tribunal.

It is not clear how this new provision will be used by the Court but there is a danger that workload levels in the Court may drive the judges to use the provision to restrict access to the Court and to decide that more applications are inadmissible.

(g) *Abuse of the right of petition*

9.36 The fact that an applicant does not come to the Court with 'clean hands' or for a proper motive will not itself be a reason to reject the application. An inadmissibility ruling on this ground may arise, rather, if the application contains obviously untrue evidence, or where the applicant is demonstrably vexatious.

---

[49] Article 35(3)(b). This is a new provision introduced by Protocol 14.

8. Decision on admissibility

A decision on admissibility will take several months and can take longer. The ECtHR   9.37
will give its decision on admissibility in writing. Clearly inadmissible cases will go to
the Single Judge within a few weeks, but where the issue is less clear the decision will
be made by a Committee or the Chamber. This question may be decided without
further contact with the applicant or without communicating the case to the government concerned, or it may seek the government's observations, and even seek a hearing
before deciding the issue of admissibility (although this is very rare). In the majority of
cases the inadmissibility decision will be made only on the basis of the application and
the material provided by the applicant.[50] The Court is not required to seek any further
submissions or alert the applicant that this approach is being taken, and is unlikely to do
so. Over 95 per cent of the cases declared inadmissible exit the system at this early stage.
No specific reasons will be given for the decision and there is no appeal against decisions
on admissibility.

9. Consideration by a Chamber and communication to the Government

If the case is not declared inadmissible at the initial stage it will be referred to a Chamber   9.38
of the Court, which will decide on what further action needs to be taken in respect of
the application. Often applications are declared inadmissible by the Chamber at this
stage without the opportunity for any further evidence or submissions. Alternatively, the
Chamber may decide that further information is required from the applicant and/or
state concerned. If this occurs, the application is formally 'communicated' to the state,
which is then invited to make any observations it thinks fit relating to the application.

In such cases, the state is sent the Judge Rapporteur's report (a statement of the facts   9.39
of the case), together with a series of questions that the Court would like the parties
to answer. The applicant will be notified of this step and sent a copy. It may take well
over 12 months for the case to reach this stage and can easily be two years. For those
interested in monitoring pending cases, and for NGOs or others interested in intervening, this is the first point at which the Court discloses any details of cases in the system.
In selected cases, the report sent to the parties will be published on the Court's website.

Once the government has replied, the applicant is given a chance to respond in   9.40
writing.[51] In most cases the Court will want to decide admissibility and merits cases
together. In the past, in very rare cases, the Court has invited the parties to make oral
submissions on admissibility. In these circumstances the parties will also be asked to
make submissions on the merits at the same time (see below for the procedure).

10. Friendly settlements

Article 38(1)(b) provides that once the Court has declared an application admissible, it   9.41
shall place itself at the disposal of the parties concerned with a view to securing a friendly
settlement. This phase runs in parallel with the Court's investigation of the merits.

---

[50] Article 35 and r 49.
[51] For the form for all pleadings, see Practice Direction: Written Pleadings, 1 November 2003 and amended
22 September 2008.

Thus, after a positive admissibility decision, the Court will write to the parties, asking whether or not they wish to explore the possibility of a settlement and, if so, inviting proposals on the subject. The Court acts as a go-between if the parties do enter into negotiations.

11. Pilot judgments

9.42   The Court has developed a new procedure as a means of dealing with large groups of identical cases that derive from the same underlying problem.[52] In such circumstances the Court will select one or more for priority treatment and will use that case or cases to try to achieve a solution that will resolve the issues in all of those other identical cases. The Court will, in such cases, freeze all the other applications pending the resolution of the lead case. The first pilot-judgment case concerned the so-called Bug River cases from Poland.[53]

12. Assessing the merits

9.43   Once the Court has made a positive admissibility decision it undertakes an investigation into the merits of the application. In practice, the Court will usually deal with admissibility and merits at the same time.

9.44   The amendments provided in Protocol 14 allow a committee of three judges to decide on issues of admissibility and merits of an application where the issues in the case are already the subject of well-established case law from the Court. This provision is designed to deal with repetitive violation cases and cases that all stem from the same fault in a domestic system (for example, primary legislation which has already been held to violate the Convention).

13. Court's investigative powers

9.45   The Court is empowered to obtain any evidence that it considers capable of providing clarification of the facts of the case, either of its own motion or at the request of any party to the application (or a third party—see para 9.46 below).[54] This can even include deputing its judges, usually three or four for fact-finding hearings, to conduct an inquiry or take evidence in some other way. In practice, however, this occurs only very rarely.

14. Third-party interventions

9.46   According to Article 36 and rule 44, the President of the Court may permit any state, or any natural or legal person, to submit written observations about the application. Such applications can arise because a possible lacuna exists in areas of the argument, which neither the state nor the applicant is willing to fill. The United Kingdom has used the

---

[52] Rule 61; see The Pilot-Judgment Procedure: Information note issued by the Registrar.
[53] *Broniowski v Poland*, App No 31443/96, 28 September 2005 [2005] ECHR 647. See also the first pilot judgment against the UK at para. 9.52 below.
[54] Rule 49.

intervention process itself and unsuccessfully intervened in the case of *Saadi v Italy*.[55] This case concerned deportation and the absolute nature of the prohibition of treatment contrary to Article 3 of the Convention. The United Kingdom was concerned that the Court's jurisprudence meant that the risk of such treatment in the country to which the applicant was to be sent could not be weighed against the reasons (including the protection of national security) put forward by the respondent state to justify expulsion. NGOs often intervene to set out their view of human rights, or because the case raises an issue of particular interest to them. A third party has 12 weeks from the date the notification has been 'communicated' to the state party (see para 9.39 above).[56] The details of selected cases communicated to state parties are now published on the Court's website. Liberty has frequently intervened in cases, as, for example, it did recently in *S and Marper v UK*.[57] The Equality and Human Rights Commission can also seek to intervene in cases in the Court, and did so for the first time in February 2009 in the case of *RP v United Kingdom*,[58] and has intervened regularly in UK cases since that time. Businesses also intervene on occasion: for example, in the case of *Hatton v UK*[59] (concerning night flights from Heathrow airport and the effect on the private lives of those living under the flight path), both British Airways and an environmental pressure group, Friends of the Earth, submitted written interventions.

15. Oral hearing

Hearings, even on the merits of an application, are now extremely rare and the vast majority of cases are decided on the papers alone. If a hearing is to take place (whether for an admissibility decision or otherwise), the applicant will be notified and contacted by the Registry with a date for the hearing (it is difficult to alter the date once it has been fixed). The parties will also be invited to send their final arguments to the Court to aid the work of the interpreters. The languages of the Court are English and French. 9.47

Hearings are held in the Human Rights Building in Strasbourg, France. In practice, hearings take approximately two hours, with the parties each being allowed only 30 minutes in all to present their case (followed by a brief period in which to respond to the other party and answer any questions posed by the judges). 9.48

16. Judgment

Chamber judgments are not read in open court, although the judgment of a Grand Chamber will be read out in summary. In both cases printed copies are made available, and electronic copies can be sent to the parties and are published on the internet. The judgment of a Chamber does not become final until: 9.49

• the parties declare that they will not be requesting referral of the case to the Grand Chamber;

• three months after the date of the judgment; or

---

[55] (2008) 24 BHRC 123.
[56] See r 44(1)(b).
[57] App Nos 30562/04 and 30566/04, 4 December 2008.
[58] App No 38245/07.
[59] (2003) 37 EHRR 28.

- when a panel of five judges of the Court rejects the request for referral to the Grand Chamber.

17. Applications to the Grand Chamber

9.50 Under Article 43, either party can seek permission for a referral to the Grand Chamber.[60] In order to gain permission, either party must satisfy the vetting panel of five judges that there exists either a serious question affecting the interpretation of the Convention or the Protocols thereto, or a serious issue of general importance. This request must be made within three months of the Chamber judgment. The process involves a re-examination of the case rather than an appeal as such. It is very rare for a case to be referred to the Grand Chamber after a hearing by a Chamber.

18. Remedies

9.51 Where the Court finds that a violation of the Convention has occurred, it is required under Article 41 to consider whether the applicant is entitled to any compensation and/ or costs, under the concept of 'just satisfaction'. Any award is at the complete discretion of the Court and a specific claim must have been made by the applicant. A claim can include pecuniary loss and non-pecuniary loss.[61] The Court has also left open the issue of aggravated damages in a suitable case, but to date has declined to award any form of exemplary or punitive damages:

The purpose of the Court's award in respect of damage is to compensate the applicant for the actual harmful consequences of a violation. It is not intended to punish the Contracting State responsible. The Court has therefore, until now, considered it inappropriate to accept claims for damages with labels such as 'punitive', 'aggravated' or 'exemplary'.[62]

9.52   The Court has only rarely ordered a state to take or refrain from taking specific action, but will occasionally include specific provisions within its declaration of the law. In property cases the Court has ordered the return of property, and in unlawful detention cases the release of the detained person. In the case of *Greens v UK*,[63] which concerned the right of prisoners to vote and the failure of the Government to amend the law, and first decided by the Court in *Hirst v UK*,[64] the Court, in the first pilot judgment decision involving the United Kingdom, decided that the United Kingdom must:

(a) bring forward, within six months of the date upon which the present judgment becomes final, legislative proposals intended to amend the 1983 Act and, if appropriate, the 2002 Act in a manner which is Convention-compliant; and

(b) enact the required legislation within any such period as may be determined by the Committee of Ministers.[65]

---

[60] Rule 73.
[61] See Practice Direction: Just Satisfaction Claims, 28 March 2007, issued by the President of the Court.
[62] Ibid, para 9.
[63] App No 60041/08, 23 November 2010 [2010] ECHR 1826.
[64] (2006) 42 EHRR 41.
[65] 23 November 2010.

This approach to an apparently reluctant state appears to be very novel. The Government sought a reference to the Grand Chamber but the Court rejected this application for a referral.

It has also been suggested that in the future the Court may be willing to order that a criminal conviction obtained in breach of Article 6 should be quashed or subject to a re-trial.[66]   9.53

Costs cannot be awarded against an applicant.   9.54

E. FUNDING FOR CASES IN STRASBOURG

Funding for cases to Strasbourg is very meagre. However, it is important for potential applicants to be aware that they cannot be held liable to pay the Government's costs, and that in the statistically rare case of their application being successful, at least some of their legal costs will be met by the Government.   9.55

1. Domestic Legal Services Commission funding

The *Legal Services Commission Manual* states that 'Legal Help may be used to assist clients in making initial applications to ECtHR'.[67] However, further funding in England and Wales is unlikely to be available. The Access to Justice Act 1999 provides in section 19 that the Legal Services Commission 'may not fund as part of the Community Legal Service or Criminal Defence services relating to any law other than that of England and Wales, unless any such law is relevant for determining any issue relating to the law of England and Wales'.   9.56

The structure of the Human Rights Act does not make the Convention part of the law of England and Wales directly. It might be possible to argue that Convention law could be 'relevant for determining any issue relating to the law of England and Wales', but an applicant will generally have had to exhaust domestic remedies first, and the ECtHR, unlike the European Court of Justice, does not allow interim references to resolve the interpretation of a Convention issue.   9.57

2. Other sources of funding

Trade unions or pressure groups may fund litigation or provide legal representation themselves, or lawyers may act *pro bono* or on a conditional fee basis in important cases.   9.58

3. Strasbourg legal aid

The Court itself will provide legal aid (subject to means), but only for those cases which are communicated to the Government. As most cases fail before this stage this is a real disincentive for lawyers to take cases. However, legal costs are recoverable where an   9.59

---

[66] See Leach, *Taking a Case to the European Court of Human Rights*, 2nd edn (Oxford: Oxford University Press, 2005), 100.

[67] ID-066, para 8.2, sub-para 1.

application is successful.[68] No fees are payable to the Court and there is no liability to meet the costs of the Government in any event.

9.60   Once communication has occurred, legal aid will be available for those who would qualify on income and capital grounds for civil legal aid in the United Kingdom (even if in an assessment for UK legal aid a contribution would have been required). Legal aid is available from Strasbourg, although the means test for legal aid is carried out by the civil legal aid authorities in the United Kingdom. No contributions towards legal aid are required, however. Legal aid, once granted, will pay a lump sum to cover all the fees and expenses in the case (currently €850).[69] If the case is never communicated, no legal aid is available.

9.61   Further payments are available to assist in friendly settlement negotiations and to cover representation by one lawyer at any hearing (currently €300), and the travel and accommodation costs of the lawyer and the applicant. In certain circumstances Strasbourg legal aid will stretch to two lawyers.

F. IMPLEMENTATION OF JUDGMENTS

9.62   The Committee of Ministers of the Council of Europe is responsible for ensuring that judgments are implemented by the state concerned.[70] When supervising the implementation of judgments the Committee is concerned to ensure that any just satisfaction awarded has been paid and:

individual measures have been taken to ensure that the violation has ceased and that the injured party is put, as far as possible, in the same situation as the party enjoyed prior to the violation of the Convention; general measures have been adopted, preventing new violations similar to that or those found or putting an end to continuing violations.[71] In January 2011 the procedure used to monitor the execution of judgments was reformed and more of the documents and records of meetings are available.[72]

9.63   The Parliamentary Joint Human Rights Committee (JCHR) has also taken a keen interest in implementation and the execution of Court judgments.[73] For instance the JCHR's report of October 2008 expressed serious concerns about the Government's long-standing failure to address the question of prisoners' voting rights after the judgment in *Hirst v UK*.[74] The issue remains unresolved in Spring 2011, more than five years after the ECtHR ruled that a blanket denial of prisoners' rights violated Article 3 of Protocol 1. At the time of writing it was unclear whether or not (and if so how) the Government intended to comply with the judgment (see the Preface for more details and the wider political context).

---

[68] Rule 91.

[69] Legal aid rates applicable since 1 January 2009.

[70] Article 46 of the Convention; and the Rules of the Committee of Ministers for the Supervision of the Execution of Judgments and of the Terms of Friendly Settlements.

[71] Ibid, r 6.

[72] For more details see the website of the Committee of Ministers <http://www.coe.int/t/dghl/monitoring/execution/default_EN.asp?>.

[73] JCHR, *Monitoring the Government's Response to Human Rights Judgments: Annual Report 2008*, 31 October 2008.

[74] (2006) 42 EHRR 41.

10

RESEARCHING HUMAN RIGHTS JURISPRUDENCE

A. Introduction		10.01
B. Convention Jurisprudence		10.03
	1. Pre-Protocol 11	10.04
	2. Protocol 11	10.06
	3. Weight of authorities	10.08
	4. Referencing system	10.09
C. Finding Convention Case Law		10.10
	1. European Court judgments: official reports	10.10
	2. European Commission	10.13
	3. Websites	10.16
	4. Bibliographic resources on Convention case law	10.18
	5. *Travaux préparatoires*	10.19
D. Finding Human Rights Act Materials		10.20
	1. Law reports, journals, and books	10.21
	2. Electronic and online resources	10.24
	3. Use of *Hansard*	10.27

A. INTRODUCTION

This chapter provides details of the practicalities of conducting research into human rights law. The Strasbourg institutions have taken on an increasing caseload over the last decade: between the inception of the European Court of Human Rights (ECtHR) in 1959 and 1998 the Court delivered 837 judgments, whereas in 2010 alone 2,607 judgments were handed down.[1] Domestic judgments concerning human rights are now handed down almost daily. The information below provides some assistance in navigating this daunting jurisprudence to locate the most relevant and important cases. **10.01**

The Convention, and the Universal Declaration of Human Rights from which it grew, have been used as models for the written constitutional guarantees of human rights in many Commonwealth constitutions. Not only do UN instruments provide important legal standards that practitioners need to be aware of, but judgments from fora such as the Privy Council, the Constitutional Court of South Africa, and the Supreme **10.02**

---

[1] Registry of the Court, *European Court of Human Rights: Analysis of Statistics 2010* (January 2011).

Courts of Canada and New Zealand often contain useful and considered guidance on questions involving fundamental rights. Researching international and comparative human rights law is outside the scope of this chapter, but good guidance can be found in the American Society for International Law's *Guide to Electronic Resources for International Law* (<http://www.asil.org/erghome.cfm>), and both the international law (<http://www.un.org/law>) and the human rights (<http://www.un.org/rights>) sections of the UN website and the home page of the International Court of Justice (<http://www.icj-cij.org>).

B. CONVENTION JURISPRUDENCE

10.03 The European Convention for the Protection of Human Rights and Fundamental Freedoms (Convention) was adopted in 1950, ratified by the United Kingdom in 1951, and entered into force in 1953. To understand the Convention case law, it is necessary to understand the history of how cases were brought in the Strasbourg institutions.

1. Pre-Protocol 11

10.04 Before 1 November 1998 a two-tiered system examined applications lodged in Strasbourg. Initially, the European Commission on Human Rights (ECmHR), an entirely separately staffed body, would examine the facts of the application and deliver an admissibility decision on the case, together with a decision on the merits if the Commission declared the petition admissible. This decision, although critical for determining whether or not a case would go forward to a full hearing, was not binding on the ECtHR itself. Often the ECtHR would deliver a final judgment that was substantially different to the decision reached by the Commission.

10.05 Protocol 11 came into force in 1998 and replaced the old system of adjudication with a new, more streamlined system which abolished the ECmHR. Although the ECmHR no longer exists, its decisions detailing the admissibility or otherwise of applications and opinions on the merits of individual cases are still of relevance to the proper interpretation of the Convention. As with judgments from the ECtHR itself, this jurisprudence 'must be taken into account' under the Human Rights Act by any domestic court or tribunal determining a question involving Convention rights.

2. Protocol 11

10.06 Since 1 November 1998 the two-tier system has been replaced with a single, permanent Court. The Rules of Court of the ECtHR, adopted on 4 November 1998, set out in full the competence of, and procedure before, the new institution. Now, three judges of the ECtHR sit in Committee to determine whether an application is 'admissible'. If it is admissible, seven judges sitting as a Chamber determine the merits of the petition. However, cases involving important questions affecting the interpretation of the Convention may be dealt with by a Grand Chamber of 17 judges, either because the original Chamber cedes jurisdiction, or (rarely) where the Grand Chamber re-hears an important case on a review (Article 43). Judgments of the new Court emerge from each of the different Sections (from I through to IV), which are headed by designated

Presidents of Sections and are composed of a varying number of judges. This new system has created the possibility of different Chambers taking different views until an issue is resolved by the Grand Chamber.[2]

The Committee of Ministers plays a supervisory role under Article 46(2). This encompasses not only supervising the execution of judgments, but also ensuring that future violations do not take place with equivalent facts to the ones already dealt with. Reports and resolutions are issued to monitor compliance with judgments and the steps that have been taken to implement the ECtHR's decisions.   10.07

3. Weight of authorities

As the Convention is a 'living instrument' and is to be interpreted in the light of present-day conditions, there is no formal doctrine of precedent binding the ECtHR. However, there are a number of factors to be taken into account when considering how much weight should be given to a particular decision from Strasbourg: 10.08

(a) Court judgments are of more importance than decisions of the ECmHR or the Committee of Ministers. Decisions of the Committee of Ministers are made by politicians, not judges, without the benefit of legal argument, and are less commonly cited than ECtHR or ECmHR judgments.

(b) Judgments of the plenary Court and decisions or opinions of the plenary Commission are the most authoritative. Decisions that are unanimous or have large majorities are more likely to be followed or to be influential than those decided by a narrow majority. A decision of the Grand Chamber on review is a 'second hearing' of an important case and commands greater authority than the previous plenary Court.

(c) Recent decisions are more valuable than decisions made some time ago because the Convention is interpreted as a 'living instrument'. As such, its meaning will develop over time, and new case law will develop in an organic way without old case law being specifically overruled.

(d) Caution is needed where Strasbourg organs have relied on the 'margin of appreciation' in concluding that there was no violation of the Convention, as this doctrine has no direct application in domestic law (see ch 4, paras 4.119–4.120).

(e) Admissibility decisions rarely set out the ECtHR's own views and are less helpful than merits decisions that give an opinion on the law. While cases are often deemed inadmissible because they are 'manifestly ill-founded', this is not the same as a finding that the point of law involved is unarguable. It may depend on the facts in issue, or application of the margin of appreciation. Nevertheless, a decision that a particular case is inadmissible, on the basis that it is manifestly unfounded, may be the only indication of the view of the Strasbourg organs on the point of law in issue, as such cases never go further. Since the Human Rights Act does not impose a strict doctrine of precedent, these decisions need not prevent a well-founded case on the same point being raised in an English court.

---

[2] See, eg *Hatton v UK* (2002) 34 EHRR 1.

4. Referencing system

10.09   Once lodged, all applications to Strasbourg are given a number commencing with five digits, and then two digits representing the year of the application. Occasionally, the case before the Court involves sensitive issues and demands confidentiality, and so the applicant is referred to by a letter, for example, *W v UK*. These numbers can be found 'attached' to the names of the parties in all ECtHR documentation and are an important aid when searching for case law.

C. FINDING CONVENTION CASE LAW

1. European Court judgments: official reports

10.10   Judgments of the ECtHR before 1996 are published by the Council of Europe in 'Series A' and 'Series B'. Series A contains the full text of the ECtHR's judgments, and from 1985 also contains extracts of the ECmHR's decisions on the merits of applications. Series B contains selective extracts from the pleadings, arguments, and relevant documentation lodged at the ECtHR for individual cases. These reports are cited as 'Series A, no 152' or 'A/152' (or 'Series B, no 123', 'B/123'). Judgments from 1996 onwards are published in the Reports of Judgments and Decisions (RJD) (published by Carl Heymanns Verlag). Every judgment has numbered paragraphs to help locate specific passages. These reports are very specialist and can be difficult to find. However, if a case is reported in either Series A or the RJD, this fact is recorded in the ECtHR's own online database, HUDOC (see para 10.16 below).

10.11   A widely available domestic alternative is the *European Human Rights Reports* (EHRR) (published by Sweet & Maxwell), although it should be noted that not all judgments of the European Court are reported in this series. The first volume was published in 1979 and references to these reports take the form of year of publication, followed by volume number, and lastly a numbered reference. Prior to 2001, this final number referred to the page at which the judgment was reported, but since 2001 (and volume 34) this number refers to the case itself. For example, *Tolstoy Miloslavsky v United Kingdom* (1995) 20 EHRR 442 refers to the twentieth volume of the EHRR at page 442; whereas *Hatton v United Kingdom* (2002) 34 EHRR 1 refers to the first case printed in the thirty-fourth volume of the EHRR.

10.12   Other useful sources of judgments include *Butterworths Human Rights Cases* (BHRC) and digests in the *European Human Rights Law Review* (EHRLR).

2. European Commission

10.13   The majority of the decisions from the ECmHR are published by the Council of Europe in the Decisions and Reports series (DR). These numerical volumes contain cases from 1974 to 1995. There are several indexes (published at 15–20 volume intervals) which contain lists of names, application numbers, and, usefully, summaries of judgments by keyword and article numbers. References to these reports appear as year, volume number, and page number. For example, *Rayner v United Kingdom* (1986) 47 DR 5 refers to the forty-seventh volume of the DRs at page 5. DRs are difficult to locate and are available only in good law libraries or, for some volumes, via The Stationery Office (<http://www.tso.co.uk>).

The EHRR series contains extracts and summaries of some ECmHR decisions. In volumes 1 to 14 these are part of the ordinary text, but from volume 15 onwards (approximately 1993) they appear in a separate section at the end of the bound copies of the series. References to these Commission Decisions are abbreviated as 'EHRR CD'.   10.14

Other useful sources of judgments include the *Digest of Strasbourg Case Law* and, for early, pre-1974 decisions, the *Yearbook of the European Convention on Human Rights* (cited as 'YB'), both of which are published by the Council of Europe.   10.15

3. Websites

The ECtHR maintains a free, searchable database of most ECtHR judgments and ECmHR decisions. The HUDOC database can be accessed via <http://www.echr.coe.int> and has an online users' guide to help navigate through the search engine. General tips to remember include selecting the appropriate databases to search at the top of the screen (language, type of judgment, and so on) and, if known, using the application number and rough date of judgment to focus searches. The database is comprehensive, constantly updated, and is the best way to locate very recent judgments. It also contains press releases summarizing important judgments. Additionally, the Court publishes Annual Reports containing statistics and developments in the case law over the previous year and has recently started publishing monthly and annual analyses of court statistics. On a monthly basis the ECtHR issues 'Case Law Information Notes' which highlight and summarize important cases. The ECtHR has also started publishing useful 'Factsheets' on particular areas of human rights law addressed by the Court. This information can be found at <http://www.echr.coe.int>.   10.16

The ECHR Blog is a useful resource for commentary on ECtHR decisions and links to academic articles: <http://www.echrblog.blogspot.com>.   10.17

4. Bibliographic resources on Convention case law

Useful publications on Convention case law are as follows: 10.18

European Human Rights Law Review (EHRLR) (London: Sweet & Maxwell, 1996 to date).

Mowbray, *Cases and Materials on the European Convention on Human Rights* (Oxford: Oxford University Press, 2007).

Harris, O'Boyle, and Warbrick, *Law of the European Convention on Human Rights*, 2nd edn (Oxford: Oxford University Press, 2009).

Jacobs, White, and Ovey, *The European Convention on Human Rights*, 4th edn (Oxford: Oxford University Press, 2006).

Reid, *A Practitioners Guide to the European Convention on Human Rights*, 3rd edn (London: Sweet & Maxwell, 2008).

Simor, *Human Rights Practice* (London: Sweet & Maxwell, 2001 to date).

5. *Travaux préparatoires*

10.19 In interpreting the Convention, the ECtHR has very occasionally considered the *travaux préparatoires*, or preparatory documents, relating to the drafting of the Convention. They are published by the Council of Europe in *The Collected Edition of the Travaux Préparatoires of the European Convention on Human Rights* and are available through specialist law libraries. They are also now available online in the ECtHR's increasingly comprehensive electronic library at <http://www.echr.coe.int/Library/COLENTravauxprep.html>. The *travaux préparatoires* are used rarely by the ECtHR, and as a means of confirming its interpretation of a Convention provision only when such an interpretation leaves the meaning ambiguous or obscure, or leads to a result that is manifestly absurd.

D. FINDING HUMAN RIGHTS ACT MATERIALS

10.20 Researching domestic human rights jurisprudence should be carried out in exactly the same way as other domestic legal research. Since the Act specifically provides that 'human rights' cases are not decided by a specialist court or tribunal but can arise in any existing forum, the well-known sets of law reports (Law Reports, Weekly Law Reports, Administrative Court Digest, etc) will contain details of cases raising human rights points and are an important point of reference. However, since the implementation of the Human Rights Act, several series of specialist reports, journals, and books have been published to help lawyers understand the human rights context and locate relevant materials more easily.

1. Law reports, journals, and books

10.21 The *Human Rights Law Reports—UK Cases* (Sweet & Maxwell, 2000 to date) and the *United Kingdom Human Rights Reports* (Jordans, 2000 to date) report the most important decisions on human rights points determined by UK courts.

10.22 The *European Human Rights Law Review* (see para 10.18 above) also contains articles and commentary on domestic cases raising human rights issues. Other useful publications include the *Human Rights Alerter* (Sweet & Maxwell) and the *Human Rights Updater* (LexisNexis UK), which cover some Strasbourg decisions as well as domestic cases. *Public Law* (Sweet & Maxwell), *Criminal Law Review* (Sweet & Maxwell), *Modern Law Review* (Sweet & Maxwell), and *Judicial Review* (Hart Publishing) are journals which regularly contain articles and case digests of interest to those researching human rights points.

10.23 Books that provide a good, detailed commentary on the framework and case law of the Human Rights Act include:

> Beatson, Grosz, Hickman, Singh, and Palmer, *Human Rights: Judicial Protection in the United Kingdom* (London: Sweet & Maxwell, 2008).
>
> Lester and Pannick, *Human Rights Law and Practice*, 3rd edn (London: Butterworths, 2009).
>
> Clayton and Tomlinson, *Human Rights Law*, 2nd edn (Oxford: Oxford University Press, 2009).

2. Electronic and online resources

The main legal publishers provide subscription-based online services incorporating a mixture of different law reports and texts according to their publishing lists. For example: **10.24**

- Westlaw UK's Human Rights subscription package (<http://www.sweetandmaxwell.co.uk>) offers access to the EHRR, EHRLR, and Simor's *Human Rights Practice*.
- LexisNexis Library's online database (<http://www1.lexisnexis.co.uk/lnb/legal/legal.html>) indexes a range of human rights materials including the *Butterworths Human Rights Cases* reports and the full text of Lester and Pannick.
- Lawtel (<http://www.lawtel.com>) offers a Human Rights Service encompassing recent transcripts of judgments from domestic courts and commentary provided by experts.

However, there are a growing number of free websites that offer valuable information on human rights jurisprudence. For locating case law, the British and Irish Legal Information Institute's database (<http://www.bailii.org>) offers a good starting point. The webpage of the Parliamentary Joint Committee on Human Rights (JCHR) (<http://www.parliament.uk/parliamentary_committees/joint_committee_on_human_rights.cfm>) indexes a number of detailed reports and evidence taken in support of the JCHR's remit of scrutinizing all new legislation presented to Parliament and undertaking inquiries on human rights issues. The JCHR also monitors the Government's implementation of Strasbourg judgments and response to declarations of incompatibility made by domestic courts. The JCHR's correspondence with ministers and other officials, which can be found on the Committee's webpages, often elicits details of the Government's proposed legislative and policy responses to important human rights judgments. **10.25**

The most exciting recent development in human rights resources was the launch of the UK Human Rights Blog, which provides excellent summaries of human rights cases from the ECtHR and domestic courts and in-depth articles on current legal issues: <http://ukhumanrightsblog.com/>. The UK Supreme Court blog is also a good resource for commentary on Supreme Court cases and occasional articles on human rights issues: <http://ukscblog.com/>. **10.26**

3. Use of *Hansard*

Since the landmark decision of the House of Lords in *Pepper v Hart*,[3] parliamentary statements by ministers may, in certain circumstances, be admissible in order to interpret an Act of Parliament. The principles (set out in the speech of Lord Browne-Wilkinson) indicate that references to *Hansard* may be admissible where: **10.27**

(a) legislation is obscure or ambiguous, or leads to an absurdity;

(b) the material relied upon consists of one or more statements by a minister or other promoter of the Bill, and such other material as is necessary to understand such statements and their effect; and

(c) the statements relied upon are clear.

---

[3] [1993] AC 593.

10.28   There has rarely, if ever, been a series of parliamentary debates in which Members of
Parliament have referred quite so repeatedly and self-consciously to the *Pepper v Hart*
principle as during the passage of the Human Rights Bill. Since there are aspects of the
Act which could be ambiguous, *Hansard* statements may be admissible in court when
arguing regarding its meaning. *Hansard* is accessible online at <http://www.publications.
parliament.uk>.[4] It should be borne in mind, however, that some of the *Hansard* statements are controversial, and it is by no means clear that they should be regarded as any
more than 'persuasive' by the courts that consider them.

---

[4] For a detailed examination of the parliamentary debates leading up to the passing of the Human Rights
Act, see Cooper and Marshall-Williams, *Legislating for Human Rights: Parliamentary Debates on the Human
Rights Bill* (London: Hart Publishing/JUSTICE, 2000).

APPENDIX 1

Human Rights Act 1998

CHAPTER 42
ARRANGEMENT OF SECTIONS

Introduction

Section
1. The Convention Rights.
2. Interpretation of Convention rights.

Legislation

3. Interpretation of legislation.
4. Declaration of incompatibility.
5. Right of Crown to intervene.

Public authorities

6. Acts of public authorities.
7. Proceedings.
8. Judicial remedies.
9. Judicial acts.

Remedial action

10. Power to take remedial action.

Other rights and proceedings

11. Safeguard for existing human rights.
12. Freedom of expression.
13. Freedom of thought, conscience and religion.

Derogations and reservations

14. Derogations.
15. Reservations.
16. Period for which designated derogations have effect.
17. Periodic review of designated reservations.

Judges of the European Court of Human Rights

18. Appointment to European Court of Human Rights.

Parliamentary procedure

19. Statements of compatibility.

Supplemental

20. Orders etc. under this Act.
21. Interpretation, etc.
22. Short title, commencement, application and extent.

SCHEDULES

Schedule 1—The Articles.
        Part I—The Convention.
        Part II—The First Protocol.
        Part III—Article 1 of the Thirteenth Protocol.

Schedule 2—Remedial Orders.

Schedule 3—Derogation and Reservation.
        Part I—Derogation (repealed).
        Part II—Reservation.

Schedule 4—Judicial Pensions.

HUMAN RIGHTS ACT 1998
1998 CHAPTER 42

An Act to give further effect to rights and freedoms guaranteed under the European Convention on Human Rights; to make provision with respect to holders of certain judicial offices who become judges of the European Court of Human Rights; and for connected purposes.

[9th November 1998]

BE IT ENACTED by the Queen's most Excellent Majesty, by and with the advice and consent of the Lords Spiritual and Temporal, and Commons, in this present Parliament assembled, and by the authority of the same, as follows:—

Introduction

1. The Convention Rights[1]

(1) In this Act 'the Convention rights' means the rights and fundamental freedoms set out in—
   (a) Articles 2 to 12 and 14 of the Convention,
   (b) Articles 1 to 3 of the First Protocol, and
   (c) Article 1 of the Thirteenth Protocol,
   as read with Articles 16 to 18 of the Convention.

(2) Those Articles are to have effect for the purposes of this Act subject to any designated derogation or reservation (as to which see sections 14 and 15).

(3) The Articles are set out in Schedule 1.

(4) The [Secretary of State] may by order make such amendments to this Act as he considers appropriate to reflect the effect, in relation to the United Kingdom, of a protocol.

(5) In subsection (4) 'protocol' means a protocol to the Convention—
   (a) which the United Kingdom has ratified; or
   (b) which the United Kingdom has signed with a view to ratification.

(6) No amendment may be made by an order under subsection (4) so as to come into force before the protocol concerned is in force in relation to the United Kingdom.

2. Interpretation of Convention rights[2]

(1) A court or tribunal determining a question which has arisen in connection with a Convention right must take into account any—
   (a) judgment, decision, declaration or advisory opinion of the European Court of Human Rights,
   (b) opinion of the Commission given in a report adopted under Article 31 of the Convention,
   (c) decision of the Commission in connection with Article 26 or 27(2) of the Convention, or
   (d) decision of the Committee of Ministers taken under Article 46 of the Convention,
   whenever made or given, so far as, in the opinion of the court or tribunal, it is relevant to the proceedings in which that question has arisen.

---

[1] This section was amended by the Transfer of Functions (Miscellaneous) Order 2001, SI 2001/3500, art 8, Sch 2, pt I, para 7(a), the Secretary of State for Constitutional Affairs Order 2003, SI 2003/1887, art 9, Sch 2, para 10(1), and the Human Rights Act (Amendment) Order 2004, SI 2004/1574, art 2(1).

[2] This section was amended by the Secretary of State for Constitutional Affairs Order 2003, SI 2003/1887, art 9, Sch 2, para 10(2), and the Transfer of Functions (Lord Chancellor and Secretary of State) Order 2005, SI 2005/3429, art 8, Schedule, para 3.

(2) Evidence of any judgment, decision, declaration or opinion of which account may have to be taken under this section is to be given in proceedings before any court or tribunal in such manner as may be provided by rules.

(3) In this section 'rules' means rules of court or, in the case of proceedings before a tribunal, rules made for the purposes of this section—

    (a) by the Lord Chancellor or the Secretary of State, in relation to any proceedings outside Scotland;

    (b) by the Secretary of State, in relation to proceedings in Scotland; or

    (c) by a Northern Ireland department, in relation to proceedings before a tribunal in Northern Ireland—

        (i) which deals with transferred matters; and

        (ii) for which no rules made under paragraph (a) are in force.

Legislation

3. Interpretation of legislation

(1) So far as it is possible to do so, primary legislation and subordinate legislation must be read and given effect in a way which is compatible with the Convention rights.

(2) This section—

    (a) applies to primary legislation and subordinate legislation whenever enacted;

    (b) does not affect the validity, continuing operation or enforcement of any incompatible primary legislation; and

    (c) does not affect the validity, continuing operation or enforcement of any incompatible subordinate legislation if (disregarding any possibility of revocation) primary legislation prevents removal of the incompatibility.

4. Declaration of incompatibility

(1) Subsection (2) applies in any proceedings in which a court determines whether a provision of primary legislation is compatible with a Convention right.

(2) If the court is satisfied that the provision is incompatible with a Convention right, it may make a declaration of that incompatibility.

(3) Subsection (4) applies in any proceedings in which a court determines whether a provision of subordinate legislation, made in the exercise of a power conferred by primary legislation, is compatible with a Convention right.

(4) If the court is satisfied—

    (a) that the provision is incompatible with a Convention right, and

    (b) that (disregarding any possibility of revocation) the primary legislation concerned prevents removal of the incompatibility, it may make a declaration of that incompatibility.

(5) In this section 'court' means—

    (a) [the Supreme Court];[3]

    (b) the Judicial Committee of the Privy Council;

    (c) the [Court Martial Appeal Court];[4]

---

[3] Subsection (5)(a) was amended by the Constitutional Reform Act 2005, s 40(4), Sch 9, Pt 1, para 66(1), (2).

[4] Subsection (5)(c) was amended by the Armed Forces Act 2006, s 378(1), Sch 16, para 156.

(d) in Scotland, the High Court of Justiciary sitting otherwise than as a trial court or the Court of Session;

(e) in England and Wales or Northern Ireland, the High Court or the Court of Appeal.

(f) [the Court of Protection, in any matter being dealt with by the President of the Family Division, the Vice-Chancellor or a puisne judge of the High Court.][5]

(6) A declaration under this section ('a declaration of incompatibility')—

(a) does not affect the validity, continuing operation or enforcement of the provision in respect of which it is given; and

(b) is not binding on the parties to the proceedings in which it is made.

5. Right of Crown to intervene[6]

(1) Where a court is considering whether to make a declaration of incompatibility, the Crown is entitled to notice in accordance with rules of court.

(2) In any case to which subsection (1) applies—

(a) a Minister of the Crown (or a person nominated by him),

(b) a member of the Scottish Executive,

(c) a Northern Ireland Minister,

(d) a Northern Ireland department,

is entitled, on giving notice in accordance with rules of court, to be joined as a party to the proceedings.

(3) Notice under subsection (2) may be given at any time during the proceedings.

(4) A person who has been made a party to criminal proceedings (other than in Scotland) as the result of a notice under subsection (2) may, with leave, appeal to the [Supreme Court][7] against any declaration of incompatibility made in the proceedings.

(5) In subsection (4)—

'criminal proceedings' includes all proceedings before the [Court Martial Appeal Court];[8] and 'leave' means leave granted by the court making the declaration of incompatibility or by the [Supreme Court].[9]

Public authorities

6. Acts of public authorities

(1) It is unlawful for a public authority to act in a way which is incompatible with a Convention right.

---

[5] Subsection (5)(f) was inserted by the Mental Capacity Act 2005, s 67(1), Sch 6, Para 43.

[6] The references to the House of Lords in subsections (4) and (5) have been amended by the Constitutional Reform Act 2005, s 40(4), Sch 9, Pt 1, para 66(1), (3). The function under subs (2) is exercisable by the National Assembly for Wales concurrently with any Minister of the Crown by whom it is exercisable, in so far as it relates to any proceedings in which a court is considering whether to make a declaration of incompatibility within the meaning of s 4, in respect of subordinate legislation made, in relation to Wales, by a Minister of the Crown in the exercise of a function which is exercisable by the National Assembly: National Assembly for Wales (Transfer of Functions) (No 2) Order 2000, SI 2000/1830, art 2.

[7] Subsection (4) was amended by the Constitutional Reform Act 2005, s 40(4), Sch 9, Pt 1, para 66(1), (3).

[8] Subsection (5) amended by the Armed Forces Act 2006, s 378(1), Sch 16, para 157.

[9] Subsection (5) was amended by the Constitutional Reform Act 2005, s 40(4), Sch 9, Pt 1, para 66(1), (3).

(2) Subsection (1) does not apply to an act if—

    (a) as the result of one or more provisions of primary legislation, the authority could not have acted differently; or

    (b) in the case of one or more provisions of, or made under, primary legislation which cannot be read or given effect in a way which is compatible with the Convention rights, the authority was acting so as to give effect to or enforce those provisions.

(3) In this section 'public authority' includes—

    (a) a court or tribunal, and

    (b) any person certain of whose functions are functions of a public nature,

but does not include either House of Parliament or a person exercising functions in connection with proceedings in Parliament.

(4) [. . .][10]

(5) In relation to a particular act, a person is not a public authority by virtue only of subsection (3)(b) if the nature of the act is private.

(6) 'An act' includes a failure to act but does not include a failure to—

    (a) introduce in, or lay before, Parliament a proposal for legislation; or

    (b) make any primary legislation or remedial order.

7. Proceedings[11]

(1) A person who claims that a public authority has acted (or proposes to act) in a way which is made unlawful by section 6(1) may—

    (a) bring proceedings against the authority under this Act in the appropriate court or tribunal, or

    (b) rely on the Convention right or rights concerned in any legal proceedings, but only if he is (or would be) a victim of the unlawful act.

(2) In subsection (1)(a) 'appropriate court or tribunal' means such court or tribunal as may be determined in accordance with rules; and proceedings against an authority include a counterclaim or similar proceeding.

(3) If the proceedings are brought on an application for judicial review, the applicant is to be taken to have a sufficient interest in relation to the unlawful act only if he is, or would be, a victim of that act.

(4) If the proceedings are made by way of a petition for judicial review in Scotland, the applicant shall be taken to have title and interest to sue in relation to the unlawful act only if he is, or would be, a victim of that act.

(5) Proceedings under subsection (1)(a) must be brought before the end of

    (a) the period of one year beginning with the date on which the act complained of took place; or

    (b) such longer period as the court or tribunal considers equitable having regard to all the circumstances,

but that is subject to any rule imposing a stricter time limit in relation to the procedure in question.

---

[10] Subsection (4) was repealed by the Constitutional Reform Act 2005, ss 40(4), 146, Sch 9, Pt 1, para 66(1), (4), Sch 18, Pt 5.

[11] This section was amended by the Secretary of State for Constitutional Affairs Order 2003, SI 2003/1887, art 9, Sch 2, para 10(2) and the Transfer of Functions (Lord Chancellor and Secretary of State) Order 2005, SI 2005/3429, art 8, Schedule, para 3.

(6) In subsection (1)(b) 'legal proceedings' includes—
  (a) proceedings brought by or at the instigation of a public authority; and
  (b) an appeal against the decision of a court or tribunal.
(7) For the purposes of this section, a person is a victim of an unlawful act only if he would be a victim for the purposes of Article 34 of the Convention if proceedings were brought in the European Court of Human Rights in respect of that act.
(8) Nothing in this Act creates a criminal offence.
(9) In this section 'rules' means—
  (a) in relation to proceedings before a court or tribunal outside Scotland, rules made by [the Lord Chancellor] or the Secretary of State for the purposes of this section or rules of court,
  (b) in relation to proceedings before a court or tribunal in Scotland, rules made by the Secretary of State for those purposes,
  (c) in relation to proceedings before a tribunal in Northern Ireland—
      (i) which deals with transferred matters; and
      (ii) for which no rules made under paragraph (a) are in force,
      (iii) rules made by a Northern Ireland department for those purposes,
  and includes provision made by order under section 1 of the Courts and Legal Services Act 1990.
(10) In making rules, regard must be had to section 9.
(11) The Minister who has power to make rules in relation to a particular tribunal may, to the extent he considers it necessary to ensure that the tribunal can provide an appropriate remedy in relation to an act (or proposed act) of a public authority which is (or would be) unlawful as a result of section 6(1), by order add to—
  (a) the relief or remedies which the tribunal may grant; or
  (b) the grounds on which it may grant any of them.
(12) An order made under subsection (11) may contain such incidental, supplemental, consequential or transitional provision as the Minister making it considers appropriate.
(13) 'The Minister' includes the Northern Ireland department concerned.

8. Judicial remedies

(1) In relation to any act (or proposed act) of a public authority which the court finds is (or would be) unlawful, it may grant such relief or remedy, or make such order, within its powers as it considers just and appropriate.
(2) But damages may be awarded only by a court which has power to award damages, or to order the payment of compensation, in civil proceedings.
(3) No award of damages is to be made unless, taking account of all the circumstances of the case, including—
  (a) any other relief or remedy granted, or order made, in relation to the act in question (by that or any other court), and
  (b) the consequences of any decision (of that or any other court) in respect of that act,
  the court is satisfied that the award is necessary to afford just satisfaction to the person in whose favour it is made.
(4) In determining—
  (a) whether to award damages, or
  (b) the amount of an award,
  the court must take into account the principles applied by the European Court of Human Rights in relation to the award of compensation under Article 41 of the Convention.

(5) A public authority against which damages are awarded is to be treated—

    (a) in Scotland, for the purposes of section 3 of the Law Reform (Miscellaneous Provisions) (Scotland) Act 1940 as if the award were made in an action of damages in which the authority has been found liable in respect of loss or damage to the person to whom the award is made;

    (b) for the purposes of the Civil Liability (Contribution) Act 1978 as liable in respect of damage suffered by the person to whom the award is made.

(6) In this section—

'court' includes a tribunal;

'damages' means damages for an unlawful act of a public authority; and

'unlawful' means unlawful under section 6(1).

9. Judicial acts[12]

(1) Proceedings under section 7(1)(a) in respect of a judicial act may be brought only—

    (a) by exercising a right of appeal;

    (b) on an application (in Scotland a petition) for judicial review; or

    (c) in such other forum as may be prescribed by rules.

(2) That does not affect any rule of law which prevents a court from being the subject of judicial review.

(3) In proceedings under this Act in respect of a judicial act done in good faith, damages may not be awarded otherwise than to compensate a person to the extent required by Article 5(5) of the Convention.

(4) An award of damages permitted by subsection (3) is to be made against the Crown but no award may be made unless the appropriate person, if not a party to the proceedings, is joined.

(5) In this section—

'appropriate person' means the Minister responsible for the court concerned, or a person or government department nominated by him;

'court' includes a tribunal;

'judge' includes a member of a tribunal, a justice of the peace or, in Northern Ireland, a lay magistrate and a clerk or other officer entitled to exercise the jurisdiction of a court;

'judicial act' means a judicial act of a court and includes an act done on the instructions, or on behalf, of a judge; and

'rules' has the same meaning as in section 7(9).

Remedial action

10. Power to take remedial action

(1) This section applies if—

    (a) a provision of legislation has been declared under section 4 to be incompatible with a Convention right and, if an appeal lies;

      (i) all persons who may appeal have stated in writing that they do not intend to do so;

      (ii) the time for bringing an appeal has expired and no appeal has been brought within that time; or

      (iii) an appeal brought within that time has been determined or abandoned;

    (b) it appears to a Minister of the Crown or Her Majesty in Council that, having regard to a finding of the European Court of Human Rights made after the coming into force of this

---

[12] This section was amended by the Justice (Northern Ireland) Act 2002, s 10(6), Sch 4, para 39.

section in proceedings against the United Kingdom, a provision of legislation is incompatible with an obligation of the United Kingdom arising from the Convention.

(2) If a Minister of the Crown considers that there are compelling reasons for proceeding under this section, he may by order make such amendments to the legislation as he considers necessary to remove the incompatibility.

(3) If, in the case of subordinate legislation, a Minister of the Crown considers—

(a) that it is necessary to amend the primary legislation under which the subordinate legislation in question was made, in order to enable the incompatibility to be removed, and

(b) that there are compelling reasons for proceeding under this section,

he may by order make such amendments to the primary legislation as he considers necessary.

(4) This section also applies where the provision in question is in subordinate legislation and has been quashed, or declared invalid, by reason of incompatibility with a Convention right and the Minister proposes to proceed under paragraph 2(b) of Schedule 2.

(5) If the legislation is an Order in Council, the power conferred by subsection (2) or (3) is exercisable by Her Majesty in Council.

(6) In this section 'legislation' does not include a Measure of the Church Assembly or of the General Synod of the Church of England.

(7) Schedule 2 makes further provision about remedial orders.

Other rights and proceedings

11. Safeguard for existing human rights

A person's reliance on a Convention right does not restrict—

(a) any other right or freedom conferred on him by or under any law having effect in any part of the United Kingdom; or

(b) his right to make any claim or bring any proceedings which he could make or bring apart from sections 7 to 9.

12. Freedom of expression

(1) This section applies if a court is considering whether to grant any relief which, if granted, might affect the exercise of the Convention right to freedom of expression.

(2) If the person against whom the application for relief is made ('the respondent') is neither present nor represented, no such relief is to be granted unless the court is satisfied—

(a) that the applicant has taken all practicable steps to notify the respondent; or

(b) that there are compelling reasons why the respondent should not be notified.

(3) No such relief is to be granted so as to restrain publication before trial unless the court is satisfied that the applicant is likely to establish that publication should not be allowed.

(4) The court must have particular regard to the importance of the Convention right to freedom of expression and, where the proceedings relate to material which the respondent claims, or which appears to the court, to be journalistic, literary or artistic material (or to conduct connected with such material), to—

(a) the extent to which—

(i) the material has, or is about to, become available to the public; or

(ii) it is, or would be, in the public interest for the material to be published

(b) any relevant privacy code.

(5) In this section—

'court' includes a tribunal; and

'relief' includes any remedy or order (other than in criminal proceedings).

13. Freedom of thought, conscience and religion

(1) If a court's determination of any question arising under this Act might affect the exercise by a religious organisation (itself or its members collectively) of the Convention right to freedom of thought, conscience and religion, it must have particular regard to the importance of that right.

(2) In this section 'court' includes a tribunal.

Derogations and reservations

14. Derogations[13]

(1) In this Act 'designated derogation' means any derogation by the United Kingdom from an Article of the Convention, or of any protocol to the Convention, which is designated for the purposes of this Act in an order made by the Secretary of State.

(2) . . .

(3) If a designated derogation is amended or replaced it ceases to be a designated derogation.

(4) But subsection (3) does not prevent the Secretary of State from exercising his power under subsection (1) to make a fresh designation order in respect of the Article concerned.

(5) The Secretary of State must by order make such amendments to Schedule 3 as he considers appropriate to reflect—

(a) any designation order; or

(b) the effect of subsection (3).

(6) A designation order may be made in anticipation of the making by the United Kingdom of a proposed derogation.

15. Reservations[14]

(1) In this Act 'designated reservation' means—

(a) the United Kingdom's reservation to Article 2 of the First Protocol to the Convention; and

(b) any other reservation by the United Kingdom to an Article of the Convention, or of any protocol to the Convention, which is designated for the purposes of this Act in an order made by the Secretary of State.

(2) The text of the reservation referred to in subsection (1)(a) is set out in Part II of Schedule 3.

(3) If a designated reservation is withdrawn wholly or in part it ceases to be a designated reservation.

(4) But subsection (3) does not prevent the Secretary of State from exercising his power under subsection (1)(b) to make a fresh designation order in respect of the Article concerned.

(5) The Secretary of State must by order make such amendments to this Act as he considers appropriate to reflect—

(a) any designation order; or

(b) the effect of subsection (3).

---

[13] This section was amended by the Human Rights Act (Amendment) Order 2001, SI 2001/1216, art 2, the Transfer of Functions (Miscellaneous) Order 2001, SI 2001/3500, art 8, Sch 2, Pt I, para 7(b), and the Secretary of State for Constitutional Affairs Order 2003, SI 2003/1887, art 1.

[14] [This section was amended by the Transfer of Functions (Miscellaneous) Order 2001, SI 2001/3500, art 8, Sch 2, Pt I, para 7(c). It was further amended by the Secretary of State for Constitutional Affairs Order 2003, SI 2003/1887, art 9, Sch 2, para 10(1).]

16. Period for which designated derogations have effect[15]

(1) If it has not already been withdrawn by the United Kingdom, a designated derogation ceases to have effect for the purposes of this Act at the end of the period of five years beginning with the date on which the order designating it was made.

(2) At any time before the period—
   (a) fixed by subsection (1), or
   (b) extended by an order under this subsection,
   comes to an end, the Secretary of State may by order extend it by a further period of five years.

(3) An order under section 14(1) ceases to have effect at the end of the period for consideration, unless a resolution has been passed by each House approving the order.

(4) Subsection (3) does not affect—
   (a) anything done in reliance on the order; or
   (b) the power to make a fresh order under section 14(1).

(5) In subsection (3) 'period for consideration' means the period of forty days beginning with the day on which the order was made.

(6) In calculating the period for consideration, no account is to be taken of any time during which—
   (a) Parliament is dissolved or prorogued; or
   (b) both Houses are adjourned for more than four days.

(7) If a designated derogation is withdrawn by the United Kingdom, the Secretary of State must by order make such amendments to this Act as he considers are required to reflect that withdrawal.

17. Periodic review of designated reservations

(1) The appropriate Minister must review the designated reservation referred to in section 15(1)(a)—
   (a) before the end of the period of five years beginning with the date on which section 1(2) came into force; and
   (b) if that designation is still in force, before the end of the period of five years beginning with the date on which the last report relating to it was laid under subsection (3).

(2) The appropriate Minister must review each of the other designated reservations (if any)—
   (a) before the end of the period of five years beginning with the date on which the order designating the reservation first came into force; and
   (b) if the designation is still in force, before the end of the period of five years beginning with the date on which the last report relating to it was laid under subsection (3).

(3) The Minister conducting a review under this section must prepare a report on the result of the review and lay a copy of it before each House of Parliament.

Judges of the European Court of Human Rights

18. Appointment to European Court of Human Rights

(1) In this section 'judicial office' means the office of—
   (a) Lord Justice of Appeal, Justice of the High Court or Circuit judge, in England and Wales;
   (b) judge of the Court of Session or sheriff, in Scotland;
   (c) Lord Justice of Appeal, judge of the High Court or county court judge, in Northern Ireland.

(2) The holder of a judicial office may become a judge of the European Court of Human Rights ('the Court') without being required to relinquish his office.

(3) But he is not required to perform the duties of his judicial office while he is a judge of the Court.

---

[15] This section was amended by the Human Rights Act (Amendment) Order 2001, SI 2001/1216, art 3. It was further amended by the Secretary of State for Constitutional Affairs Order 2003, SI 2003/1887, art 9.

(4) In respect of any period during which he is a judge of the Court—

   (a) a Lord Justice of Appeal or Justice of the High Court is not to count as a judge of the relevant court for the purposes of section 2(1) or 4(1) of the [Senior Courts Act 1981][16] (maximum number of judges) nor as a judge of the [Senior Courts] for the purposes of section 12(1) to (6) of that Act (salaries etc);[17]

   (b) a judge of the Court of Session is not to count as a judge of that court for the purposes of section 1(1) of the Court of Session Act 1988 (maximum number of judges) or of section 9(1) (c) of the Administration of Justice Act 1973 ('the 1973 Act') (salaries etc.);

   (c) a Lord Justice of Appeal or judge of the High Court in Northern Ireland is not to count as a judge of the relevant court for the purposes of section 2(1) or 3(1) of the Judicature (Northern Ireland) Act 1978 (maximum number of judges) nor as a judge of the [Court of Judicature][18] of Northern Ireland for the purposes of section 9(1)(d) of the 1973 Act (salaries etc.);

   (d) a Circuit judge is not to count as such for the purposes of section 18 of the Courts Act 1971 (salaries etc.);

   (e) a sheriff is not to count as such for the purposes of section 14 of the Sheriff Courts (Scotland) Act 1907 (salaries etc.);

   (f) county court judge of Northern Ireland is not to count as such for the purposes of section 106 of the County Courts Act (Northern Ireland) 1959 (salaries etc.).

(5) If a sheriff principal is appointed a judge of the Court, section 11(1) of the Sheriff Courts (Scotland) Act 1971 (temporary appointment of sheriff principal) applies, while he holds that appointment, as if his office is vacant.

(6) Schedule 4 makes provision about judicial pensions in relation to the holder of a judicial office who serves as a judge of the Court.

(7) The Lord Chancellor or the Secretary of State may by order make such transitional provision (including, in particular, provision for a temporary increase in the maximum number of judges) as he considers appropriate in relation to any holder of a judicial office who has completed his service as a judge of the Court.

(7A) The following paragraphs apply to the making of an order under subsection (7) in relation to any holder of a judicial office listed in subsection (1)(a)—

   (a) before deciding what transitional provision it is appropriate to make, the person making the order must consult the Lord Chief Justice of England and Wales;

   (b) before making the order, that person must consult the Lord Chief Justice of England and Wales.

(7B) The following paragraphs apply to the making of an order under subsection (7) in relation to any holder of a judicial office listed in subsection (1)(c)—

   (a) before deciding what transitional provision it is appropriate to make, the person making the order must consult the Lord Chief Justice of Northern Ireland;

   (b) before making the order, that person must consult the Lord Chief Justice of Northern Ireland.

---

[16] Subsection (4)(a) was amended by the Constitutional Reform Act 2005, s 59(5), Sch 11, Pt 3, para 6(1), (3).

[17] Subsection (4)(a) was amended by the Constitutional Reform Act 2005, s 59(5), Sch 11, Pt 1, para 4 (1), (3).

[18] Subsection (4)(c) was amended by the Constitutional Reform Act 2005, s 59(5), Sch 11, Pt 3, para 6(1), (3).

(7C) The Lord Chief Justice of England and Wales may nominate a judicial office holder (within the meaning of section 109(4) of the Constitutional Reform Act 2005) to exercise his functions under this section.

(7D) The Lord Chief Justice of Northern Ireland may nominate any of the following to exercise his functions under this section—

   (a) the holder of one of the offices listed in Schedule 1 to the Justice (Northern Ireland) Act 2002;

   (b) a Lord Justice of Appeal (as defined in section 88 of that Act).[19]

Parliamentary procedure

19. Statements of compatibility

(1) A Minister of the Crown in charge of a Bill in either House of Parliament must, before the Second Reading of the Bill—

   (a) make a statement to the effect that in his view the provisions of the Bill are compatible with the Convention rights ('a statement of compatibility'); or

   (b) make a statement to the effect that although he is unable to make a statement of compatibility the government nevertheless wishes the House to proceed with the Bill.

(2) The statement must be in writing and be published in such manner as the Minister making it considers appropriate.

Supplemental

20. Orders etc. under this Act[20]

(1) Any power of a Minister of the Crown to make an order under this Act is exercisable by statutory instrument.

(2) The power of the Lord Chancellor or the Secretary of State to make rules (other than rules of court) under section 2(3) or 7(9) is exercisable by statutory instrument.

(3) Any statutory instrument made under section 14, 15 or 16(7) must be laid before Parliament.

(4) No order may be made by the Lord Chancellor or the Secretary of State under section 1(4), 7(11) or 16(2) unless a draft of the order has been laid before, and approved by, each House of Parliament.

(5) Any statutory instrument made under section 18(7) or Schedule 4, or to which subsection (2) applies, shall be subject to annulment in pursuance of a resolution of either House of Parliament.

(6) The power of a Northern Ireland department to make—

   (a) rules under section 2(3)(c) or 7(9)(c), or

   (b) an order under section 7(11),

   is exercisable by statutory rule for the purposes of the Statutory Rules (Northern Ireland) Order 1979.

---

[19] Subsections (7A) to (7D) were inserted by the Constitutional Reform Act 2005, s 15(1), Sch 4, Pt 1, para 278 and the Constitutional Reform Act 2005 (Commencement No 5) Order 2006, SI 2006/1014, art 2(a), Sch 1, paras 10, 11(v). Subsection (4) was amended by the Constitutional Reform Act 2005, s 59(5), Sch 11, Pt 1, para 1(2), Pt 2, para 4(1), (3), and Pt 3, para 6(1), (3).

[20] This section was amended by the Secretary of State for Constitutional Affairs Order 2003, SI 2003/1887, art 9, Sch 2, para 10(2). It was further amended by the Transfer of Functions (Lord Chancellor and Secretary of State) Order 2005, SI 2005/3429, art 8, Schedule, para 3.

(7) Any rules made under section 2(3)(c) or 7(9)(c) shall be subject to negative resolution and section 41(6) of the Interpretation Act (Northern Ireland) 1954 (meaning of 'subject to negative resolution') shall apply as if the power to make the rules were conferred by an Act of the Northern Ireland Assembly.

(8) No order may be made by a Northern Ireland department under section 7(11) unless a draft of the order has been laid before, and approved by, the Northern Ireland Assembly.

21. Interpretation etc.[21]

(1) In this Act—

'amend' includes repeal and apply (with or without modifications);

'the appropriate Minister' means the Minister of the Crown having charge of the appropriate authorised government department (within the meaning of the Crown Proceedings Act 1947);

'the Commission' means the European Commission of Human Rights;

'the Convention' means the Convention for the Protection of Human Rights and Fundamental Freedoms, agreed by the Council of Europe at Rome on 4th November 1950 as it has effect for the time being in relation to the United Kingdom;

'declaration of incompatibility' means a declaration under section 4;

'Minister of the Crown' has the same meaning as in the Ministers of the Crown Act 1975;

'Northern Ireland Minister' includes the First Minister and the deputy First Minister in Northern Ireland;

'primary legislation' means any—

    (a) public general Act;

    (b) local and personal Act;

    (c) private Act;

    (d) Measure of the Church Assembly;

    (e) Measure of the General Synod of the Church of England;

    (f) Order in Council—

        (i) made in exercise of Her Majesty's Royal Prerogative;

        (ii) made under section 38(1)(a) of the Northern Ireland Constitution Act 1973 or the corresponding provision of the Northern Ireland Act 1998; or

        (iii) amending an Act of a kind mentioned in paragraph (a), (b) or (c);

and includes an order or other instrument made under primary legislation (otherwise than by the [Welsh Ministers, the First Minister for Wales, the Counsel General to the Welsh Assembly Government], a member of the Scottish Executive, a Northern Ireland Minister or a Northern Ireland department) to the extent to which it operates to bring one or more provisions of that legislation into force or amends any primary legislation;

'the First Protocol' means the protocol to the Convention agreed at Paris on 20th March 1952;

'the Eleventh Protocol' means the protocol to the Convention (restructuring the control machinery established by the Convention) agreed at Strasbourg on 11th May 1994;

'the Thirteenth Protocol' means the protocol to the Convention (concerning the abolition of the death penalty in all circumstances) agreed at Vilnius on 3rd May 2002;

'remedial order' means an order under section 10;

'subordinate legislation' means any—

    (a) Order in Council other than one—

---

[21] This section was amended by the Human Rights Act (Amendment) Order 2004, SI 2004/1574, art 2(2); the Government of Wales Act 2006, s 160(1), Sch 10, para 56(1), (2), (3), (4); and the Armed Forces Act 2006, s 378(2), Sch 17.

      (i) made in exercise of Her Majesty's Royal Prerogative;

      (ii) made under section 38(1)(a) of the Northern Ireland Constitution Act 1973 or the corresponding provision of the Northern Ireland Act 1998; or

      (iii) amending an Act of a kind mentioned in the definition of primary legislation;

(b) Act of the Scottish Parliament;

(ba) Measure of the National Assembly for Wales;

(bb) Act of the National Assembly for Wales;]

(c) Act of the Parliament of Northern Ireland;

(d) Measure of the Assembly established under section 1 of the Northern Ireland Assembly Act 1973;

(e) Act of the Northern Ireland Assembly;

(f) order, rules, regulations, scheme, warrant, byelaw or other instrument made under primary legislation (except to the extent to which it operates to bring one or more provisions of that legislation into force or amends any primary legislation);

(g) order, rules, regulations, scheme, warrant, byelaw or other instrument made under legislation mentioned in paragraph (b), (c), (d) or (e) or made under an Order in Council applying only to Northern Ireland;

(h) order, rules, regulations, scheme, warrant, byelaw or other instrument made by a member of the Scottish Executive, a Northern Ireland Minister or a Northern Ireland department [, Welsh Ministers, the First Minister for Wales, the Counsel General to the Welsh Assembly Government], in exercise of prerogative or other executive functions of Her Majesty which are exercisable by such a person on behalf of Her Majesty;

'transferred matters' has the same meaning as in the Northern Ireland Act 1998; and

'tribunal' means any tribunal in which legal proceedings may be brought.

(2) The references in paragraphs (b) and (c) of section 2(1) to Articles are to Articles of the Convention as they had effect immediately before the coming into force of the Eleventh Protocol.

(3) The reference in paragraph (d) of section 2(1) to Article 46 includes a reference to Articles 32 and 54 of the Convention as they had effect immediately before the coming into force of the Eleventh Protocol.

(4) The references in section 2(1) to a report or decision of the Commission or a decision of the Committee of Ministers include references to a report or decision made as provided by paragraphs 3, 4 and 6 of Article 5 of the Eleventh Protocol (transitional provisions).

[. . .]22

22. Short title, commencement, application and extent

(1) This Act may be cited as the Human Rights Act 1998.

(2) Sections 18, 20 and 21(5) and this section come into force on the passing of this Act.

(3) The other provisions of this Act come into force on such day as the Secretary of State may by order appoint and different days may be appointed for different purposes.

(4) Paragraph (b) of subsection (1) of section 7 applies to proceedings brought by or at the instigation of a public authority whenever the act in question took place but otherwise that subsection does not apply to an act taking place before the coming into force of that section.

(5) This Act binds the Crown.

(6) This Act extends to Northern Ireland.

[. . .]23

---

22 Subsection (5) repealed by the Armed Forces Act 2006, s 378(2), Sch 17.
23 Subsection (7) repealed by the Armed Forces Act 2006, s 378(2), Sch 17.

SCHEDULES

SCHEDULE 1

Section 1(3)

THE ARTICLES

PART I
THE CONVENTION RIGHTS AND FREEDOMS

Article 2
Right to life

1. Everyone's right to life shall be protected by law. No one shall be deprived of his life intentionally save in the execution of a sentence of a court following his conviction of a crime for which this penalty is provided by law.
2. Deprivation of life shall not be regarded as inflicted in contravention of this Article when it results from the use of force which is no more than absolutely necessary:
    (a) in defence of any person from unlawful violence;
    (b) in order to effect a lawful arrest or to prevent the escape of a person lawfully detained;
    (c) in action lawfully taken for the purpose of quelling a riot or insurrection.

Article 3
Prohibition of torture

No one shall be subjected to torture or to inhuman or degrading treatment or punishment.

Article 4
Prohibition of slavery and forced labour

1. No one shall be held in slavery or servitude.
2. No one shall be required to perform forced or compulsory labour.
3. For the purpose of this Article the term 'forced or compulsory labour' shall not include:
    (a) any work required to be done in the ordinary course of detention imposed according to the provisions of Article 5 of this Convention or during conditional release from such detention;
    (b) any service of a military character or, in case of conscientious objectors in countries where they are recognised, service exacted instead of compulsory military service;
    (c) any service exacted in case of an emergency or calamity threatening the life or well-being of the community;
    (d) any work or service which forms part of normal civic obligations.

Article 5
Right to liberty and security

1. Everyone has the right to liberty and security of person. No one shall be deprived of his liberty save in the following cases and in accordance with a procedure prescribed by law:
    (a) the lawful detention of a person after conviction by a competent court;
    (b) the lawful arrest or detention of a person for non-compliance with the lawful order of a court or in order to secure the fulfilment of any obligation prescribed by law;

(c) the lawful arrest or detention of a person effected for the purpose of bringing him before the competent legal authority on reasonable suspicion of having committed an offence or when it is reasonably considered necessary to prevent his committing an offence or fleeing after having done so;

(d) the detention of a minor by lawful order for the purpose of educational supervision or his lawful detention for the purpose of bringing him before the competent legal authority;

(e) the lawful detention of persons for the prevention of the spreading of infectious diseases, of persons of unsound mind, alcoholics or drug addicts or vagrants;

(f) the lawful arrest or detention of a person to prevent his effecting an unauthorised entry into the country or of a person against whom action is being taken with a view to deportation or extradition.

2. Everyone who is arrested shall be informed promptly, in a language which he understands, of the reasons for his arrest and of any charge against him.

3. Everyone arrested or detained in accordance with the provisions of paragraph 1(c) of this Article shall be brought promptly before a judge or other officer authorised by law to exercise judicial power and shall be entitled to trial within a reasonable time or to release pending trial. Release may be conditioned by guarantees to appear for trial.

4. Everyone who is deprived of his liberty by arrest or detention shall be entitled to take proceedings by which the lawfulness of his detention shall be decided speedily by a court and his release ordered if the detention is not lawful.

5. Everyone who has been the victim of arrest or detention in contravention of the provisions of this Article shall have an enforceable right to compensation.

Article 6
Right to a fair trial

1. In the determination of his civil rights and obligations or of any criminal charge against him, everyone is entitled to a fair and public hearing within a reasonable time by an independent and impartial tribunal established by law. Judgment shall be pronounced publicly but the press and public may be excluded from all or part of the trial in the interest of morals, public order or national security in a democratic society, where the interests of juveniles or the protection of the private life of the parties so require, or to the extent strictly necessary in the opinion of the court in special circumstances where publicity would prejudice the interests of justice.

2. Everyone charged with a criminal offence shall be presumed innocent until proved guilty according to law.

3. Everyone charged with a criminal offence has the following minimum rights:

(a) to be informed promptly, in a language which he understands and in detail, of the nature and cause of the accusation against him;

(b) to have adequate time and facilities for the preparation of his defence;

(c) to defend himself in person or through legal assistance of his own choosing or, if he has not sufficient means to pay for legal assistance, to be given it free when the interests of justice so require;

(d) to examine or have examined witnesses against him and to obtain the attendance and examination of witnesses on his behalf under the same conditions as witnesses against him;

(e) to have the free assistance of an interpreter if he cannot understand or speak the language used in court.

Article 7
No punishment without law

1. No one shall be held guilty of any criminal offence on account of any act or omission which did not constitute a criminal offence under national or international law at the time when it was committed. Nor shall a heavier penalty be imposed than the one that was applicable at the time the criminal offence was committed.
2. This Article shall not prejudice the trial and punishment of any person for any act or omission which, at the time when it was committed, was criminal according to the general principles of law recognised by civilised nations.

Article 8
Right to respect for private and family life

1. Everyone has the right to respect for his private and family life, his home and his correspondence.
2. There shall be no interference by a public authority with the exercise of this right except such as is in accordance with the law and is necessary in a democratic society in the interests of national security, public safety or the economic well being of the country, for the prevention of disorder or crime, for the protection of health or morals, or for the protection of the rights and freedoms of others.

Article 9
Freedom of thought, conscience and religion

1. Everyone has the right to freedom of thought, conscience and religion; this right includes freedom to change his religion or belief and freedom, either alone or in community with others and in public or private, to manifest his religion or belief, in worship, teaching, practice and observance.
2. Freedom to manifest one's religion or beliefs shall be subject only to such limitations as are prescribed by law and are necessary in a democratic society in the interests of public safety, for the protection of public order, health or morals, or for the protection of the rights and freedoms of others.

Article 10
Freedom of expression

1. Everyone has the right to freedom of expression. This right shall include freedom to hold opinions and to receive and impart information and ideas without interference by public authority and regardless of frontiers. This Article shall not prevent States from requiring the licensing of broadcasting, television or cinema enterprises.
2. The exercise of these freedoms, since it carries with it duties and responsibilities, may be subject to such formalities, conditions, restrictions or penalties as are prescribed by law and are necessary in a democratic society, in the interests of national security, territorial integrity or public safety, for the prevention of disorder or crime, for the protection of health or morals, for the protection of the reputation or rights of others, for preventing the disclosure of information received in confidence, or for maintaining the authority and impartiality of the judiciary.

Article 11
Freedom of assembly and association

1. Everyone has the right to freedom of peaceful assembly and to freedom of association with others, including the right to form and to join trade unions for the protection of his interests.

2. No restrictions shall be placed on the exercise of these rights other than such as are prescribed by law and are necessary in a democratic society in the interests of national security or public safety, for the prevention of disorder or crime, for the protection of health or morals or for the protection of the rights and freedoms of others. This Article shall not prevent the imposition of lawful restrictions on the exercise of these rights by members of the armed forces, of the police or of the administration of the State.

Article 12
Right to marry

Men and women of marriageable age have the right to marry and to found a family, according to the national laws governing the exercise of this right.

Article 14
Prohibition of discrimination

The enjoyment of the rights and freedoms set forth in this Convention shall be secured without discrimination on any ground such as sex, race, colour, language, religion, political or other opinion, national or social origin, association with a national minority, property, birth or other status.

Article 16
Restrictions on political activity of aliens

Nothing in Articles 10, 11 and 14 shall be regarded as preventing the High Contracting Parties from imposing restrictions on the political activity of aliens.

Article 17
Prohibition of abuse of rights

Nothing in this Convention may be interpreted as implying for any State, group or person any right to engage in any activity or perform any act aimed at the destruction of any of the rights and freedoms set forth herein or at their limitation to a greater extent than is provided for in the Convention.

Article 18
Limitation on use of restrictions on rights

The restrictions permitted under this Convention to the said rights and freedoms shall not be applied for any purpose other than those for which they have been prescribed.

PART II
THE FIRST PROTOCOL

Article 1
Protection of property

Every natural or legal person is entitled to the peaceful enjoyment of his possessions. No one shall be deprived of his possessions except in the public interest and subject to the conditions provided for by law and by the general principles of international law.

The preceding provisions shall not, however, in any way impair the right of a State to enforce such laws as it deems necessary to control the use of property in accordance with the general interest or to secure the payment of taxes or other contributions or penalties.

Article 2
Right to education

No person shall be denied the right to education. In the exercise of any functions which it assumes in relation to education and to teaching, the State shall respect the right of parents to ensure such education and teaching in conformity with their own religious and philosophical convictions.

Article 3
Right to free elections

The High Contracting Parties undertake to hold free elections at reasonable intervals by secret ballot, under conditions which will ensure the free expression of the opinion of the people in the choice of the legislature.

PART III
ARTICLE 1 OF THE THIRTEENTH PROTOCOL

Abolition of the death penalty

The death penalty shall be abolished. No one shall be condemned to such penalty or executed. [This Part was substituted by the Human Rights Act (Amendment) Order 2004, SI 2004/1574, art 2(3).]

SCHEDULE 2
REMEDIAL ORDERS

Orders

1.—(1) A remedial order may—
    (a) contain such incidental, supplemental, consequential or transitional provision as the person making it considers appropriate;
    (b) be made so as to have effect from a date earlier than that on which it is made;
    (c) make provision for the delegation of specific functions;
    (d) make different provision for different cases.
  (2) The power conferred by sub-paragraph (1)(a) includes—
    (a) power to amend primary legislation (including primary legislation other than that which contains the incompatible provision); and
    (b) power to amend or revoke subordinate legislation (including subordinate legislation other than that which contains the incompatible provision).
  (3) A remedial order may be made so as to have the same extent as the legislation which it affects.
  (4) No person is to be guilty of an offence solely as a result of the retrospective effect of a remedial order.

Procedure

2. No remedial order may be made unless—
    (a) a draft of the order has been approved by a resolution of each House of Parliament made after the end of the period of 60 days beginning with the day on which the draft was laid; or
    (b) it is declared in the order that it appears to the person making it that, because of the urgency of the matter, it is necessary to make the order without a draft being so approved.

Orders laid in draft

3.—(1) No draft may be laid under paragraph 2(a) unless—

    (a) the person proposing to make the order has laid before Parliament a document which contains a draft of the proposed order and the required information; and

    (b) the period of 60 days, beginning with the day on which the document required by this sub-paragraph was laid, has ended.

  (2) If representations have been made during that period, the draft laid under paragraph 2(a) must be accompanied by a statement containing—

    (a) a summary of the representations; and

    (b) if, as a result of the representations, the proposed order has been changed, details of the changes.

Urgent cases

4.—(1) If a remedial order ('the original order') is made without being approved in draft, the person making it must lay it before Parliament, accompanied by the required information, after it is made.

  (2) If representations have been made during the period of 60 days beginning with the day on which the original order was made, the person making it must (after the end of that period) lay before Parliament a statement containing—

    (a) a summary of the representations; and

    (b) if, as a result of the representations, he considers it appropriate to make changes to the original order, details of the changes.

  (3) If sub-paragraph (2)(b) applies, the person making the statement must—

    (a) make a further remedial order replacing the original order; and

    (b) lay the replacement order before Parliament.

  (4) If, at the end of the period of 120 days beginning with the day on which the original order was made, a resolution has not been passed by each House approving the original or replacement order, the order ceases to have effect (but without that affecting anything previously done under either order or the power to make a fresh remedial order).

Definitions

5. In this Schedule—

'representations' means representations about a remedial order (or proposed remedial order) made to the person making (or proposing to make) it and includes any relevant Parliamentary report or resolution; and

'required information' means—

    (a) an explanation of the incompatibility which the order (or proposed order) seeks to remove, including particulars of the relevant declaration, finding or order; and

    (b) a statement of the reasons for proceeding under section 10 and for making an order in those terms.

Calculating periods

6. In calculating any period for the purposes of this Schedule, no account is to be taken of any time during which—

    (a) Parliament is dissolved or prorogued; or

    (b) both Houses are adjourned for more than four days.

7.—(1) This paragraph applies in relation to—

    (a) any remedial order made, and any draft of such an order proposed to be made,—

        (i) by the Scottish Ministers; or

        (ii) within devolved competence (within the meaning of the Scotland Act 1998) by Her Majesty in Council; and

    (b) any document or statement to be laid in connection with such an order (or proposed order).

    (2) This Schedule has effect in relation to any such order (or proposed order), document or statement subject to the following modifications.

    (3) Any reference to Parliament, each House of Parliament or both Houses of Parliament shall be construed as a reference to the Scottish Parliament.

    (4) Paragraph 6 does not apply and instead, in calculating any period for the purposes of this Schedule, no account is to be taken of any time during which the Scottish Parliament is dissolved or is in recess for more than four days.

[This Schedule was amended by the Scotland Act 1998 (Consequential Modifications) Order 2000, SI 2000/2040, art 2(1), Schedule, Pt I, para 21.]

SCHEDULE 3
DEROGATION AND RESERVATION

PART I

[The UK's previous derogations from art 5(1) were repealed by the Human Rights Act (Amendment) Order 2001, SI 2001/1216, art 4, and the Human Rights Act 1998 (Amendment) Order 2005, SI 2005/1071, art 2.]

PART II
RESERVATION

At the time of signing the present (First) Protocol, I declare that, in view of certain provisions of the Education Acts in the United Kingdom, the principle affirmed in the second sentence of Article 2 is accepted by the United Kingdom only so far as it is compatible with the provision of efficient instruction and training, and the avoidance of unreasonable public expenditure.

Dated 20 March 1952. Made by the United Kingdom Permanent Representative to the Council of Europe.

[This Schedule was amended by the Human Rights Act (Amendment) Order 2001, SI 2001/1216, art 4. It was further amended by the Human Rights Act 1998 (Amendment No 2) Order 2001, SI 2001/4032, art 2, Schedule.]

SCHEDULE 4
JUDICIAL PENSIONS

Duty to make orders about pensions

1.—(1) The appropriate Minister must by order make provision with respect to pensions payable to or in respect of any holder of a judicial office who serves as an ECHR judge.

    (2) A pensions order must include such provision as the Minister making it considers is necessary to secure that—

    (a) an ECHR judge who was, immediately before his appointment as an ECHR judge, a member of a judicial pension scheme is entitled to remain as a member of that scheme;

(b) the terms on which he remains a member of the scheme are those which would have been applicable had he not been appointed as an ECHR judge; and

(c) entitlement to benefits payable in accordance with the scheme continues to be determined as if, while serving as an ECHR judge, his salary was that which would (but for section 18(4)) have been payable to him in respect of his continuing service as the holder of his judicial office.

Contributions

2. A pensions order may, in particular, make provision—

(a) for any contributions which are payable by a person who remains a member of a scheme as a result of the order, and which would otherwise be payable by deduction from his salary, to be made otherwise than by deduction from his salary as an ECHR judge; and

(b) for such contributions to be collected in such manner as may be determined by the administrators of the scheme.

Amendments of other enactments

3. A pensions order may amend any provision of, or made under, a pensions Act in such manner and to such extent as the Minister making the order considers necessary or expedient to ensure the proper administration of any scheme to which it relates.

Definitions

4. In this Schedule
'appropriate Minister' means—

(a) in relation to any judicial office whose jurisdiction is exercisable exclusively in relation to Scotland, the Secretary of State; and

(b) otherwise, the Lord Chancellor;

'ECHR judge' means the holder of a judicial office who is serving as a judge of the Court;

'judicial pension scheme' means a scheme established by and in accordance with a pensions Act;

'pensions Act' means—

(a) the County Courts Act (Northern Ireland) 1959;

(b) the Sheriffs' Pensions (Scotland) Act 1961;

(c) the Judicial Pensions Act 1981; or

(d) the Judicial Pensions and Retirement Act 1993; and 'pensions order' means an order made under paragraph 1.

APPENDIX 2

Convention for the Protection of Human Rights and Fundamental Freedoms, as amended by Protocols Nos. 11 and 14, with Protocols Nos. 1, 4, 6, 7, 12 and 13

The text of the Convention is presented as amended by the provisions of Protocol No. 14 (CETS no. 194) as from its entry into force on 1 June 2010.

The text of the Convention had previously been amended according to the provisions of Protocol No. 3 (ETS no. 45), which entered into force on 21 September 1970, of Protocol No. 5 (ETS no. 55), which entered into force on 20 December 1971, and of Protocol No. 8 (ETS no. 118), which entered into force on 1 January 1990, and comprised also the text of Protocol No. 2 (ETS no. 44) which, in accordance with Article 5 § 3 thereof, had been an integral part of the Convention since its entry into force on 21 September 1970. All provisions which had been amended or added by these Protocols were replaced by Protocol No. 11 (ETS no. 155), as from the date of its entry into force on 1 November 1998. As from that date, Protocol No. 9 (ETS no. 140), which entered into force on 1 October 1994, was repealed and Protocol No. 10 (ETS no. 146) lost its purpose.

The current state of signatures and ratifications of the Convention and its Protocols as well as the complete list of declarations and reservations are available at http://conventions.coe.int.

Registry of the European Court of Human Rights, June 2010.

CONVENTION FOR THE PROTECTION OF HUMAN RIGHTS AND FUNDAMENTAL FREEDOMS

Rome, 4.XI.1950

The governments signatory hereto, being members of the Council of Europe,

Considering the Universal Declaration of Human Rights proclaimed by the General Assembly of the United Nations on 10 December 1948;

Considering that this Declaration aims at securing the universal and effective recognition and observance of the Rights therein declared;

Considering that the aim of the Council of Europe is the achievement of greater unity between its members and that one of the methods by which that aim is to be pursued is the maintenance and further realisation of human rights and fundamental freedoms;

Reaffirming their profound belief in those fundamental freedoms which are the foundation of justice and peace in the world and are best maintained on the one hand by an effective political democracy and on the other by a common understanding and observance of the human rights upon which they depend;

Being resolved, as the governments of European countries which are likeminded and have a common heritage of political traditions, ideals, freedom and the rule of law, to take the first steps for the collective enforcement of certain of the rights stated in the Universal Declaration,

Have agreed as follows:

Article 1
Obligation to respect human rights

The High Contracting Parties shall secure to everyone within their jurisdiction the rights and freedoms defined in Section I of this Convention.

SECTION I. RIGHTS AND FREEDOMS
Article 2
Right to life

1. Everyone's right to life shall be protected by law. No one shall be deprived of his life intentionally save in the execution of a sentence of a court following his conviction of a crime for which this penalty is provided by law.
2. Deprivation of life shall not be regarded as inflicted in contravention of this Article when it results from the use of force which is no more than absolutely necessary:
    (a) in defence of any person from unlawful violence;
    (b) in order to effect a lawful arrest or to prevent the escape of a person lawfully detained;
    (c) in action lawfully taken for the purpose of quelling a riot or insurrection.

Article 3
Prohibition of torture

No one shall be subjected to torture or to inhuman or degrading treatment or punishment.

Article 4
Prohibition of slavery and forced labour

1. No one shall be held in slavery or servitude.
2. No one shall be required to perform forced or compulsory labour.
3. For the purpose of this Article the term "forced or compulsory labour" shall not include:
    (a) any work required to be done in the ordinary course of detention imposed according to the provisions of Article 5 of this Convention or during conditional release from such detention;
    (b) any service of a military character or, in case of conscientious objectors in countries where they are recognised, service exacted instead of compulsory military service;
    (c) any service exacted in case of an emergency or calamity threatening the life or well-being of the community;
    (d) any work or service which forms part of normal civic obligations.

Article 5
Right to liberty and security

1. Everyone has the right to liberty and security of person. No one shall be deprived of his liberty save in the following cases and in accordance with a procedure prescribed by law:
    (a) the lawful detention of a person after conviction by a competent court;
    (b) the lawful arrest or detention of a person for non-compliance with the lawful order of a court or in order to secure the fulfilment of any obligation prescribed by law;
    (c) the lawful arrest or detention of a person effected for the purpose of bringing him before the competent legal authority on reasonable suspicion of having committed an offence or when it is reasonably considered necessary to prevent his committing an offence or fleeing after having done so;

(d) the detention of a minor by lawful order for the purpose of educational supervision or his lawful detention for the purpose of bringing him before the competent legal authority;

(e) the lawful detention of persons for the prevention of the spreading of infectious diseases, of persons of un-sound mind, alcoholics or drug addicts or vagrants;

(f) the lawful arrest or detention of a person to prevent his effecting an unauthorised entry into the country or of a person against whom action is being taken with a view to deportation or extradition.

2. Everyone who is arrested shall be informed promptly, in a language which he understands, of the reasons for his arrest and of any charge against him.

3. Everyone arrested or detained in accordance with the provisions of paragraph 1 (c) of this Article shall be brought promptly before a judge or other officer authorised by law to exercise judicial power and shall be entitled to trial within a reasonable time or to release pending trial. Release may be conditioned by guarantees to appear for trial.

4. Everyone who is deprived of his liberty by arrest or detention shall be entitled to take proceedings by which the lawfulness of his detention shall be decided speedily by a court and his release ordered if the detention is not lawful.

5. Everyone who has been the victim of arrest or detention in contravention of the provisions of this Article shall have an enforceable right to compensation.

Article 6
Right to a fair trial

1. In the determination of his civil rights and obligations or of any criminal charge against him, everyone is entitled to a fair and public hearing within a reasonable time by an independent and impartial tribunal established by law. Judgment shall be pronounced publicly but the press and public may be excluded from all or part of the trial in the interests of morals, public order or national security in a democratic society, where the interests of juveniles or the protection of the private life of the parties so require, or to the extent strictly necessary in the opinion of the court in special circumstances where publicity would prejudice the interests of justice.

2. Everyone charged with a criminal offence shall be presumed innocent until proved guilty according to law.

3. Everyone charged with a criminal offence has the following minimum rights:
   (a) to be informed promptly, in a language which he understands and detail, of the nature and cause of the accusation against him;
   (b) to have adequate time and facilities for the preparation of his defence;
   (c) to defend himself in person or through legal assistance of his own choosing or, if he has not sufficient means to pay for legal assistance, to be given it free when the interests of justice so require;
   (d) to examine or have examined witnesses against him and to obtain the attendance and examination of wit-nesses on his behalf under the same conditions as witnesses against him;
   (e) to have the free assistance of an interpreter if he cannot understand or speak the language used in court.

Article 7
No punishment without law

1. No one shall be held guilty of any criminal offence on account of any act or omission which did not constitute a criminal offence under national or international law at the time when it

was committed. Nor shall a heavier penalty be imposed than the one that was applicable at the time the criminal offence was committed.

2. This Article shall not prejudice the trial and punishment of any person for any act or omission which, at the time when it was committed, was criminal according to the general principles of law recognised by civilised nations.

Article 8
Right to respect for private and family life

1. Everyone has the right to respect for his private and family life, his home and his correspondence.
2. There shall be no interference by a public authority with the exercise of this right except such as is in accordance with the law and is necessary in a democratic society in the interests of national security, public safety or the economic well-being of the country, for the prevention of disorder or crime, for the protection of health or morals, or for the protection of the rights and freedoms of others.

Article 9
Freedom of thought, conscience and religion

1. Everyone has the right to freedom of thought, conscience and religion; this right includes freedom to change his religion or belief and freedom, either alone or in community with others and in public or private, to manifest his religion or belief, in worship, teaching, practice and observance.
2. Freedom to manifest one's religion or beliefs shall be subject only to such limitations as are prescribed by law and are necessary in a democratic society in the interests of public safety, for the protection of public order, health or morals, or for the protection of the rights and freedoms of others.

Article 10
Freedom of expression

1. Everyone has the right to freedom of expression. This right shall include freedom to hold opinions and to receive and impart information and ideas without interference by public authority and regardless of frontiers. This Article shall not prevent States from requiring the licensing of broadcasting, television or cinema enterprises.
2. The exercise of these freedoms, since it carries with it duties and responsibilities, may be subject to such formalities, conditions, restrictions or penalties as are prescribed by law and are necessary in a democratic society, in the interests of national security, territorial integrity or public safety, for the prevention of disorder or crime, for the protection of health or morals, for the protection of the reputation or rights of others, for preventing the disclosure of information received in confidence, or for maintaining the authority and impartiality of the judiciary.

Article 11
Freedom of assembly and association

1. Everyone has the right to freedom of peaceful assembly and to freedom of association with others, including the right to form and to join trade unions for the protection of his interests.
2. No restrictions shall be placed on the exercise of these rights other than such as are prescribed by law and are necessary in a democratic society in the interests of national security or public safety, for the prevention of disorder or crime, for the protection of health or morals or for the

protection of the rights and freedoms of others. This Article shall not prevent the imposition of lawful restrictions on the exercise of these rights by members of the armed forces, of the police or of the administration of the State.

Article 12
Right to marry

Men and women of marriageable age have the right to marry and to found a family, according to the national laws governing the exercise of this right.

Article 13
Right to an effective remedy

Everyone whose rights and freedoms as set forth in this Convention are violated shall have an effective remedy before a national authority notwithstanding that the violation has been committed by persons acting in an official capacity.

Article 14
Prohibition of discrimination

The enjoyment of the rights and freedoms set forth in this Convention shall be secured without discrimination on any ground such as sex, race, colour, language, religion, political or other opinion, national or social origin, association with a national minority, property, birth or other status.

Article 15
Derogation in time of emergency

1. In time of war or other public emergency threatening the life of the nation any High Contracting Party may take measures derogating from its obligations under this Convention to the extent strictly required by the exigencies of the situation, provided that such measures are not inconsistent with its other obligations under international law.
2. No derogation from Article 2, except in respect of deaths resulting from lawful acts of war, or from Articles 3, 4 § 1 and 7 shall be made under this provision.
3. Any High Contracting Party availing itself of this right of derogation shall keep the Secretary General of the Council of Europe fully informed of the measures which it has taken and the reasons therefor. It shall also inform the Secretary General of the Council of Europe when such measures have ceased to operate and the provisions of the Convention are again being fully executed.

Article 16
Restrictions on political activity of aliens

Nothing in Articles 10, 11 and 14 shall be regarded as preventing the High Contracting Parties from imposing restrictions on the political activity of aliens.

Article 17
Prohibition of abuse of rights

Nothing in this Convention may be interpreted as implying for any State, group or person any right to engage in any activity or perform any act aimed at the destruction of any of the rights and freedoms set forth herein or at their limitation to a greater extent than is provided for in the Convention.

Article 18
Limitation on use of restrictions on rights

The restrictions permitted under this Convention to the said rights and freedoms shall not be applied for any purpose other than those for which they have been prescribed.

SECTION II. EUROPEAN COURT OF HUMAN RIGHTS

Article 19
Establishment of the Court

To ensure the observance of the engagements undertaken by the High Contracting Parties in the Convention and the Protocols thereto, there shall be set up a European Court of Human Rights, hereinafter referred to as "the Court". It shall function on a permanent basis.

Article 20
Number of judges

The Court shall consist of a number of judges equal to that of the High Contracting Parties.

Article 21
Criteria for office

1. The judges shall be of high moral character and must either possess the qualifications required for appointment to high judicial office or be jurisconsults of recognised competence.
2. The judges shall sit on the Court in their individual capacity.
3. During their term of office the judges shall not engage in any activity which is incompatible with their independence, impartiality or with the demands of a full-time office; all questions arising from the application of this paragraph shall be decided by the Court.

Article 22
Election of judges

The judges shall be elected by the Parliamentary Assembly with respect to each High Contracting Party by a majority of votes cast from a list of three candidates nominated by the High Contracting Party.

Article 23
Terms of office and dismissal

1. The judges shall be elected for a period of nine years. They may not be re-elected.
2. The terms of office of judges shall expire when they reach the age of 70.
3. The judges shall hold office until replaced. They shall, however, continue to deal with such cases as they already have under consideration.
4. No judge may be dismissed from office unless the other judges decide by a majority of two-thirds that that judge has ceased to fulfil the required conditions.

Article 24
Registry and rapporteurs

1. The Court shall have a Registry, the functions and organisation of which shall be laid down in the rules of the Court.

2. When sitting in a single-judge formation, the Court shall be assisted by rapporteurs who shall function under the authority of the President of the Court. They shall form part of the Court's Registry.

Article 25
Plenary Court

The plenary Court shall
(a) elect its President and one or two Vice-Presidents for a period of three years; they may be re-elected;
(b) set up Chambers, constituted for a fixed period of time;
(c) elect the Presidents of the Chambers of the Court; they may be re-elected;
(d) adopt the rules of the Court;
(e) elect the Registrar and one or more Deputy Registrars;
(f) make any request under Article 26 § 2.

Article 26
Single-judge formation, Committees, Chambers and Grand Chamber

1. To consider cases brought before it, the Court shall sit in a single-judge formation, in Committees of three judges, in Chambers of seven judges and in a Grand Chamber of seventeen judges. The Court's Chambers shall set up Committees for a fixed period of time.
2. At the request of the plenary Court, the Committee of Ministers may, by a unanimous decision and for a fixed period, reduce to five the number of judges of the Chambers.
3. When sitting as a single judge, a judge shall not examine any application against the High Contracting Party in respect of which that judge has been elected.
4. There shall sit as an ex officio member of the Chamber and the Grand Chamber the judge elected in respect of the High Contracting Party concerned. If there is none or if that judge is unable to sit, a person chosen by the President of the Court from a list submitted in advance by that Party shall sit in the capacity of judge.
5. The Grand Chamber shall also include the President of the Court, the Vice-Presidents, the Presidents of the Chambers and other judges chosen in accordance with the rules of the Court. When a case is referred to the Grand Chamber under Article 43, no judge from the Chamber which rendered the judgment shall sit in the Grand Chamber, with the exception of the President of the Chamber and the judge who sat in respect of the High Contracting Party concerned.

Article 27
Competence of single judges

1. A single judge may declare inadmissible or strike out of the Court's list of cases an application submitted under Article 34, where such a decision can be taken without further examination.
2. The decision shall be final.
3. If the single judge does not declare an application inadmissible or strike it out, that judge shall forward it to a Committee or to a Chamber for further examination.

Article 28
Competence of Committees

1. In respect of an application sub-mitted under Article 34, a Committee may, by a unanimous vote,
   (a) declare it inadmissible or strike it out of its list of cases, where such decision can be taken without further examination; or

(b) declare it admissible and render at the same time a judgment on the merits, if the underlying question in the case, concerning the interpretation or the application of the Convention or the Protocols thereto, is already the subject of well-established case-law of the Court.

2. Decisions and judgments under paragraph 1 shall be final.

3. If the judge elected in respect of the High Contracting Party concerned is not a member of the Committee, the Committee may at any stage of the proceedings invite that judge to take the place of one of the members of the Committee, having regard to all relevant factors, including whether that Party has contested the application of the procedure under paragraph 1 (b).

Article 29
Decisions by Chambers on admissibility and merits

1. If no decision is taken under Article 27 or 28, or no judgment rendered under Article 28, a Chamber shall decide on the admissibility and merits of individual applications submitted under Article 34. The decision on admissibility may be taken separately.

2. A Chamber shall decide on the admissibility and merits of inter-State applications submitted under Article 33. The decision on admissibility shall be taken separately unless the Court, in exceptional cases, decides otherwise.

Article 30
Relinquishment of jurisdiction to the Grand Chamber

Where a case pending before a Chamber raises a serious question affecting the interpretation of the Convention or the Protocols thereto, or where the resolution of a question before the Chamber might have a result inconsistent with a judgment previously delivered by the Court, the Chamber may, at any time before it has rendered its judgment, relinquish jurisdiction in favour of the Grand Chamber, unless one of the parties to the case objects.

Article 31
Powers of the Grand Chamber

The Grand Chamber shall

(a) determine applications submitted either under Article 33 or Article 34 when a Chamber has relinquished jurisdiction under Article 30 or when the case has been referred to it under Article 43;

(b) decide on issues referred to the Court by the Committee of Ministers in accordance with Article 46 § 4; and

(c) consider requests for advisory opinions submitted under Article 47.

Article 32
Jurisdiction of the Court

1. The jurisdiction of the Court shall extend to all matters concerning the interpretation and application of the Convention and the Protocols thereto which are referred to it as provided in Articles 33, 34, 46 and 47.

2. In the event of dispute as to whether the Court has jurisdiction, the Court shall decide.

Article 33
Inter-State cases

Any High Contracting Party may refer to the Court any alleged breach of the provisions of the Convention and the Protocols thereto by another High Contracting Party.

Article 34
Individual applications

The Court may receive applications from any person, non-governmental organisation or group of individuals claiming to be the victim of a violation by one of the High Contracting Parties of the rights set forth in the Convention or the Protocols thereto. The High Contracting Parties undertake not to hinder in any way the effective exercise of this right.

Article 35
Admissibility criteria

1. The Court may only deal with the matter after all domestic remedies have been exhausted, according to the generally recognised rules of international law, and within a period of six months from the date on which the final decision was taken.
2. The Court shall not deal with any application submitted under Article 34 that
   (a) is anonymous; or
   (b) is substantially the same as a matter that has already been examined by the Court or has already been submitted to another procedure of international investigation or settlement and contains no relevant new information.
3. The Court shall declare inadmissible any individual application submitted under Article 34 if it considers that:
   (a) the application is incompatible with the provisions of the Convention or the Protocols thereto, manifestly ill-founded, or an abuse of the right of individual application; or
   (b) the applicant has not suffered a significant disadvantage, unless respect for human rights as defined in the Convention and the Protocols thereto requires an examination of the application on the merits and provided that no case may be rejected on this ground which has not been duly considered by a domestic tribunal.
4. The Court shall reject any application which it considers inadmissible under this Article. It may do so at any stage of the proceedings.

Article 36
Third party intervention

1. In all cases before a Chamber or the Grand Chamber, a High Contracting Party one of whose nationals is an applicant shall have the right to submit written comments and to take part in hearings.
2. The President of the Court may, in the interest of the proper administration of justice, invite any High Contracting Party which is not a party to the proceedings or any person concerned who is not the applicant to submit written comments or take part in hearings.
3. In all cases before a Chamber or the Grand Chamber, the Council of Europe Commissioner for Human Rights may submit written comments and take part in hearings.

Article 37
Striking out applications

1. The Court may at any stage of the proceedings decide to strike an application out of its list of cases where the circumstances lead to the conclusion that
   (a) the applicant does not intend to pursue his application; or
   (b) the matter has been resolved; or
   (c) for any other reason established by the Court, it is no longer justified to continue the examination of the application.

However, the Court shall continue the examination of the application if respect for human rights as defined in the Convention and the Protocols thereto so requires.

2. The Court may decide to restore an application to its list of cases if it considers that the circumstances justify such a course.

Article 38
Examination of the case

The Court shall examine the case together with the representatives of the parties and, if need be, undertake an investigation, for the effective conduct of which the High Contracting Parties concerned shall furnish all necessary facilities.

Article 39
Friendly settlements

1. At any stage of the proceedings, the Court may place itself at the disposal of the parties concerned with a view to securing a friendly settlement of the matter on the basis of respect for human rights as defined in the Convention and the Protocols thereto.
2. Proceedings conducted under paragraph 1 shall be confidential.
3. If a friendly settlement is effected, the Court shall strike the case out of its list by means of a decision which shall be confined to a brief statement of the facts and of the solution reached.
4. This decision shall be transmitted to the Committee of Ministers, which shall supervise the execution of the terms of the friendly settlement as set out in the decision.

Article 40
Public hearings and access to documents

1. Hearings shall be in public unless the Court in exceptional circumstances decides otherwise.
2. Documents deposited with the Registrar shall be accessible to the public unless the President of the Court decides otherwise.

Article 41
Just satisfaction

If the Court finds that there has been a violation of the Convention or the Protocols thereto, and if the internal law of the High Contracting Party concerned allows only partial reparation to be made, the Court shall, if necessary, afford just satisfaction to the injured party.

Article 42
Judgments of Chambers

Judgments of Chambers shall become final in accordance with the provisions of Article 44 § 2.

Article 43
Referral to the Grand Chamber

1. Within a period of three months from the date of the judgment of the Chamber, any party to the case may, in exceptional cases, request that the case be referred to the Grand Chamber.
2. A panel of five judges of the Grand Chamber shall accept the request if the case raises a serious question affecting the interpretation or application of the Convention or the Protocols thereto, or a serious issue of general importance.
3. If the panel accepts the request, the Grand Chamber shall decide the case by means of a judgment.

Article 44
Final judgments

1. The judgment of the Grand Chamber shall be final.
2. The judgment of a Chamber shall become final
   (a) when the parties declare that they will not request that the case be referred to the Grand Chamber; or
   (b) three months after the date of the judgment, if reference of the case to the Grand Chamber has not been requested; or
   (c) when the panel of the Grand Chamber rejects the request to refer under Article 43.
3. The final judgment shall be published.

Article 45
Reasons for judgments and decisions

1. Reasons shall be given for judgments as well as for decisions declaring applications admissible or inadmissible.
2. If a judgment does not represent, in whole or in part, the unanimous opinion of the judges, any judge shall be entitled to deliver a separate opinion.

Article 46
Binding force and execution of judgments

1. The High Contracting Parties under-take to abide by the final judgment of the Court in any case to which they are parties.
2. The final judgment of the Court shall be transmitted to the Committee of Ministers, which shall supervise its execution.
3. If the Committee of Ministers considers that the supervision of the execution of a final judgment is hindered by a problem of interpretation of the judgment, it may refer the matter to the Court for a ruling on the question of interpretation. A referral decision shall require a majority vote of two thirds of the representatives entitled to sit on the Committee.
4. If the Committee of Ministers considers that a High Contracting Party refuses to abide by a final judgment in a case to which it is a party, it may, after serving formal notice on that Party and by decision adopted by a majority vote of two-thirds of the representatives entitled to sit on the Committee, refer to the Court the question whether that Party has failed to fulfil its obligation under paragraph 1.
5. If the Court finds a violation of paragraph 1, it shall refer the case to the Committee of Ministers for consideration of the measures to be taken. If the Court finds no violation of paragraph 1, it shall refer the case to the Committee of Ministers, which shall close its examination of the case.

Article 47
Advisory opinions

1. The Court may, at the request of the Committee of Ministers, give advisory opinions on legal questions concerning the interpretation of the Convention and the Protocols thereto.
2. Such opinions shall not deal with any question relating to the content or scope of the rights or freedoms defined in Section I of the Convention and the Protocols thereto, or with any other question which the Court or the Committee of Ministers might have to consider in consequence of any such proceedings as could be instituted in accordance with the Convention.
3. Decisions of the Committee of Ministers to request an advisory opinion of the Court shall require a majority vote of the representatives entitled to sit on the Committee.

Article 48
Advisory jurisdiction of the Court

The Court shall decide whether a request for an advisory opinion submitted by the Committee of Ministers is within its competence as defined in Article 47.

Article 49
Reasons for advisory opinions

1. Reasons shall be given for advisory opinions of the Court.
2. If the advisory opinion does not represent, in whole or in part, the unanimous opinion of the judges, any judge shall be entitled to deliver a separate opinion.
3. Advisory opinions of the Court shall be communicated to the Committee of Ministers.

Article 50
Expenditure on the Court

The expenditure on the Court shall be borne by the Council of Europe.

Article 51
Privileges and immunities of judges

The judges shall be entitled, during the exercise of their functions, to the privileges and immunities provided for in Article 40 of the Statute of the Council of Europe and in the agreements made thereunder.

SECTION III. MISCELLANEOUS PROVISIONS
Article 52
Inquiries by the Secretary General

On receipt of a request from the Secretary General of the Council of Europe any High Contracting Party shall furnish an explanation of the manner in which its internal law ensures the effective implementation of any of the provisions of the Convention.

Article 53
Safeguard for existing human rights

Nothing in this Convention shall be construed as limiting or derogating from any of the human rights and fundamental freedoms which may be ensured under the laws of any High Contracting Party or under any other agreement to which it is a party.

Article 54
Powers of the Committee of Ministers

Nothing in this Convention shall prejudice the powers conferred on the Committee of Ministers by the Statute of the Council of Europe.

Article 55
Exclusion of other means of dispute settlement

The High Contracting Parties agree that, except by special agreement, they will not avail themselves of treaties, conventions or declarations in force between them for the purpose of submitting, by way of petition, a dispute arising out of the interpretation or application of this Convention to a means of settlement other than those provided for in this Convention.

Article 56
Territorial application

1. Any State may at the time of its ratification or at any time thereafter declare by notification addressed to the Secretary General of the Council of Europe that the present Convention shall, subject to paragraph 4 of this Article, extend to all or any of the territories for whose international relations it is responsible.
2. The Convention shall extend to the territory or territories named in the notification as from the thirtieth day after the receipt of this notification by the Secretary General of the Council of Europe.
3. The provisions of this Convention shall be applied in such territories with due regard, however, to local requirements.
4. Any State which has made a declaration in accordance with paragraph 1 of this Article may at any time thereafter declare on behalf of one or more of the territories to which the declaration relates that it accepts the competence of the Court to receive applications from individuals, non-governmental organisations or groups of individuals as provided by Article 34 of the Convention.

Article 57
Reservations

1. Any State may, when signing this Convention or when depositing its instrument of ratification, make a reservation in respect of any particular provision of the Convention to the extent that any law then in force in its territory is not in conformity with the provision. Reservations of a general character shall not be permitted under this Article.
2. Any reservation made under this Article shall contain a brief statement of the law concerned.

Article 58
Denunciation

1. A High Contracting Party may denounce the present Convention only after the expiry of five years from the date on which it became a party to it and after six months' notice contained in a notification addressed to the Secretary General of the Council of Europe, who shall inform the other High Contracting Parties.
2. Such a denunciation shall not have the effect of releasing the High Contracting Party concerned from its obligations under this Convention in respect of any act which, being capable of constituting a violation of such obligations, may have been performed by it before the date at which the denunciation became effective.
3. Any High Contracting Party which shall cease to be a member of the Council of Europe shall cease to be a party to this Convention under the same conditions.
4. The Convention may be denounced in accordance with the provisions of the preceding paragraphs in respect of any territory to which it has been declared to extend under the terms of Article 56.

Article 59
Signature and ratification

1. This Convention shall be open to the signature of the members of the Council of Europe. It shall be ratified. Ratifications shall be deposited with the Secretary General of the Council of Europe.
2. The European Union may accede to this Convention.

3. The present Convention shall come into force after the deposit of ten instruments of ratification.
4. As regards any signatory ratifying subsequently, the Convention shall come into force at the date of the deposit of its instrument of ratification.
5. The Secretary General of the Council of Europe shall notify all the members of the Council of Europe of the entry into force of the Convention, the names of the High Contracting Parties who have ratified it, and the deposit of all instruments of ratification which may be effected subsequently.

Done at Rome this 4th day of November 1950, in English and French, both texts being equally authentic, in a single copy which shall remain deposited in the archives of the Council of Europe. The Secretary General shall transmit certified copies to each of the signatories.

PROTOCOL TO THE CONVENTION FOR THE PROTECTION OF HUMAN RIGHTS AND FUNDAMENTAL FREEDOMS
Paris, 20.III.1952

The governments signatory hereto, being members of the Council of Europe,

Being resolved to take steps to ensure the collective enforcement of certain rights and freedoms other than those already included in Section I of the Convention for the Protection of Human Rights and Fundamental Freedoms signed at Rome on 4 November 1950 (hereinafter referred to as "the Convention"),

Have agreed as follows:

Article 1
Protection of property

Every natural or legal person is entitled to the peaceful enjoyment of his possessions. No one shall be deprived of his possessions except in the public interest and subject to the conditions provided for by law and by the general principles of international law.

The preceding provisions shall not, however, in any way impair the right of a State to enforce such laws as it deems necessary to control the use of property in accordance with the general interest or to secure the payment of taxes or other contributions or penalties.

Article 2
Right to education

No person shall be denied the right to education. In the exercise of any functions which it assumes in relation to education and to teaching, the State shall respect the right of parents to ensure such education and teaching in conformity with their own religious and philosophical convictions.

Article 3
Right to free elections

The High Contracting Parties undertake to hold free elections at reasonable intervals by secret ballot, under conditions which will ensure the free expression of the opinion of the people in the choice of the legislature.

Article 4
Territorial application

Any High Contracting Party may at the time of signature or ratification or at any time thereafter communicate to the Secretary General of the Council of Europe a declaration stating the extent to which it undertakes that the provisions of the present Protocol shall apply to such of the territories for the international relations of which it is responsible as are named therein.

Any High Contracting Party which has communicated a declaration in virtue of the preceding paragraph may from time to time communicate a further declaration modifying the terms of any former declaration or terminating the application of the provisions of this Protocol in respect of any territory.

A declaration made in accordance with this Article shall be deemed to have been made in accordance with paragraph 1 of Article 56 of the Convention.

Article 5
Relationship to the Convention

As between the High Contracting Parties the provisions of Articles 1, 2, 3 and 4 of this Protocol shall be regarded as additional Articles to the Convention and all the provisions of the Convention shall apply accordingly.

Article 6
Signature and ratification

This Protocol shall be open for signature by the members of the Council of Europe, who are the signatories of the Convention; it shall be ratified at the same time as or after the ratification of the Convention. It shall enter into force after the deposit of ten instruments of ratification. As regards any signatory ratifying subsequently, the Protocol shall enter into force at the date of the deposit of its instrument of ratification.

The instruments of ratification shall be deposited with the Secretary General of the Council of Europe, who will notify all members of the names of those who have ratified.

Done at Paris on the 20th day of March 1952, in English and French, both texts being equally authentic, in a single copy which shall remain deposited in the archives of the Council of Europe. The Secretary General shall transmit certified copies to each of the signatory governments.

PROTOCOL NO. 4 TO THE CONVENTION FOR THE PROTECTION OF HUMAN RIGHTS AND FUNDAMENTAL FREEDOMS SECURING CERTAIN RIGHTS AND FREEDOMS OTHER THAN THOSE ALREADY INCLUDED IN THE CONVENTION AND IN THE FIRST PROTOCOL THERETO

Strasbourg, 16.IX.1963

The governments signatory hereto, being members of the Council of Europe,

Being resolved to take steps to ensure the collective enforcement of certain rights and freedoms other than those already included in Section I of the Convention for the Protection of Human Rights and Fundamental Freedoms signed at Rome on 4 November 1950 (hereinafter referred to as the "Convention") and in Articles 1 to 3 of the First Protocol to the Convention, signed at Paris on 20 March 1952,

Have agreed as follows:

Article 1
Prohibition of imprisonment for debt

No one shall be deprived of his liberty merely on the ground of inability to fulfil a contractual obligation.

Article 2
Freedom of movement

1. Everyone lawfully within the territory of a State shall, within that territory, have the right to liberty of movement and freedom to choose his residence.
2. Everyone shall be free to leave any country, including his own.
3. No restrictions shall be placed on the exercise of these rights other than such as are in accordance with law and are necessary in a democratic society in the interests of national security or public safety, for the maintenance of ordre public, for the prevention of crime, for the protection of health or morals, or for the protection of the rights and freedoms of others.
4. The rights set forth in paragraph 1 may also be subject, in particular areas, to restrictions imposed in accordance with law and justified by the public interest in a democratic society.

Article 3
Prohibition of expulsion of nationals

1. No one shall be expelled, by means either of an individual or of a collective measure, from the territory of the State of which he is a national.
2. No one shall be deprived of the right to enter the territory of the State of which he is a national.

Article 4
Prohibition of collective expulsion of aliens

Collective expulsion of aliens is prohibited.

Article 5
Territorial application

1. Any High Contracting Party may, at the time of signature or ratification of this Protocol, or at any time thereafter, communicate to the Secretary General of the Council of Europe a declaration stating the extent to which it undertakes that the provisions of this Protocol shall apply to such of the territories for the international relations of which it is responsible as are named therein.
2. Any High Contracting Party which has communicated a declaration in virtue of the preceding paragraph may, from time to time, communicate a further declaration modifying the terms of any former declaration or terminating the application of the provisions of this Protocol in respect of any territory.
3. A declaration made in accordance with this Article shall be deemed to have been made in accordance with paragraph 1 of Article 56 of the Convention.
4. The territory of any State to which this Protocol applies by virtue of ratification or acceptance by that State, and each territory to which this Protocol is applied by virtue of a declaration by that State under this Article, shall be treated as separate territories for the purpose of the references in Articles 2 and 3 to the territory of a State.
5. Any State which has made a declaration in accordance with para-graph 1 or 2 of this Article may at any time thereafter declare on behalf of one or more of the territories to which the declaration relates that it accepts the competence of the Court to receive applications from individuals, non-governmental organisations or groups of individuals as provided in Article 34 of the Convention in respect of all or any of Articles 1 to 4 of this Protocol.

Article 6
Relationship to the Convention

As between the High Contracting Parties the provisions of Articles 1 to 5 of this Protocol shall be regarded as additional Articles to the Convention, and all the provisions of the Convention shall apply accordingly.

Article 7
Signature and ratification

1. This Protocol shall be open for signature by the members of the Council of Europe who are the signatories of the Convention; it shall be ratified at the same time as or after the ratification of the Convention. It shall enter into force after the deposit of five instruments of ratification. As regards any signatory ratifying subsequently, the Protocol shall enter into force at the date of the deposit of its instrument of ratification.
2. The instruments of ratification shall be deposited with the Secretary General of the Council of Europe, who will notify all members of the names of those who have ratified.

In witness whereof the undersigned, being duly authorised thereto, have signed this Protocol.

Done at Strasbourg, this 16th day of September 1963, in English and in French, both texts being equally authoritative, in a single copy which shall remain deposited in the archives of the Council of Europe. The Secretary General shall transmit certified copies to each of the signatory States.

PROTOCOL NO. 6 TO THE CONVENTION FOR THE PROTECTION OF HUMAN RIGHTS AND FUNDAMENTAL FREEDOMS CONCERNING THE ABOLITION OF THE DEATH PENALTY

Strasbourg, 28.IV.1983

The member States of the Council of Europe, signatory to this Protocol to the Convention for the Protection of Human Rights and Fundamental Freedoms, signed at Rome on 4 November 1950 (hereinafter referred to as "the Convention"),

Considering that the evolution that has occurred in several member States of the Council of Europe expresses a general tendency in favour of abolition of the death penalty;

Have agreed as follows:

Article 1
Abolition of the death penalty

The death penalty shall be abolished. No one shall be condemned to such penalty or executed.

Article 2
Death penalty in time of war

A State may make provision in its law for the death penalty in respect of acts committed in time of war or of imminent threat of war; such penalty shall be applied only in the instances laid down in the law and in accordance with its provisions. The State shall communicate to the Secretary General of the Council of Europe the relevant provisions of that law.

Article 3
Prohibition of derogations

No derogation from the provisions of this Protocol shall be made under Article 15 of the Convention.

Article 4
Prohibition of reservations

No reservation may be made under Article 57 of the Convention in respect of the provisions of this Protocol.

Article 5
Territorial application

1. Any State may at the time of signature or when depositing its instrument of ratification, acceptance or approval, specify the territory or territories to which this Protocol shall apply.
2. Any State may at any later date, by a declaration addressed to the Secretary General of the Council of Europe, extend the application of this Protocol to any other territory specified in the declaration. In respect of such territory the Protocol shall enter into force on the first day of the month following the date of receipt of such declaration by the Secretary General.
3. Any declaration made under the two preceding paragraphs may, in respect of any territory specified in such declaration, be withdrawn by a notification addressed to the Secretary General. The withdrawal shall become effective on the first day of the month following the date of receipt of such notification by the Secretary General.

Article 6
Relationship to the Convention

As between the States Parties the provisions of Articles 1 and 5 of this Protocol shall be regarded as additional Articles to the Convention and all the provisions of the Convention shall apply accordingly.

Article 7
Signature and ratification

The Protocol shall be open for signature by the member States of the Council of Europe, signatories to the Convention. It shall be subject to ratification, accept-ance or approval. A member State of the Council of Europe may not ratify, accept or approve this Protocol unless it has, simultaneously or previously, ratified the Convention. Instruments of ratification, acceptance or approval shall be de-posited with the Secretary General of the Council of Europe.

Article 8
Entry into force

1. This Protocol shall enter into force on the first day of the month following the date on which five member States of the Council of Europe have expressed their consent to be bound by the Protocol in accordance with the pro-visions of Article 7.
2. In respect of any member State which subsequently expresses its con-sent to be bound by it, the Protocol shall enter into force on the first day of the month following the date of the deposit of the instrument of ratification, acceptance or approval.

Article 9
Depositary functions

The Secretary General of the Council of Europe shall notify the member States of the Council of:
(a) any signature;
(b) the deposit of any instrument of ratification, acceptance or approval;

(c) any date of entry into force of this Protocol in accordance with Articles 5 and 8;

(d) any other act, notification or communication relating to this Protocol.

In witness whereof the undersigned, being duly authorised thereto, have signed this Protocol.

Done at Strasbourg, this 28th day of April 1983, in English and in French, both texts being equally authentic, in a single copy which shall be deposited in the archives of the Council of Europe. The Secretary General of the Council of Europe shall transmit certified copies to each member State of the Council of Europe.

PROTOCOL NO. 7 TO THE CONVENTION FOR THE PROTECTION OF HUMAN RIGHTS AND FUNDAMENTAL FREEDOMS

Strasbourg, 22.XI.1984

The member States of the Council of Europe signatory hereto,

Being resolved to take further steps to ensure the collective enforcement of certain rights and freedoms by means of the Convention for the Protection of Human Rights and Fundamental Freedoms signed at Rome on 4 Nov-ember 1950 (hereinafter referred to as "the Convention"),

Have agreed as follows:

Article 1
Procedural safeguards relating to expulsion of aliens

1. An alien lawfully resident in the territory of a State shall not be expelled therefrom except in pursuance of a decision reached in accordance with law and shall be allowed:
   (a) to submit reasons against his expulsion,
   (b) to have his case reviewed, and
   (c) to be represented for these purposes before the competent authority or a person or persons designated by that authority.
2. An alien may be expelled before the exercise of his rights under paragraph 1 (a), (b) and (c) of this Article, when such expulsion is necessary in the interests of public order or is grounded on reasons of national security.

Article 2
Right of appeal in criminal matters

1. Everyone convicted of a criminal offence by a tribunal shall have the right to have his convic-tion or sentence reviewed by a higher tribunal. The exercise of this right, including the grounds on which it may be exercised, shall be governed by law.
2. This right may be subject to exceptions in regard to offences of a minor character, as prescribed by law, or in cases in which the person concerned was tried in the first instance by the highest tribunal or was convicted following an appeal against acquittal.

Article 3
Compensation for wrongful conviction

When a person has by a final decision been convicted of a criminal offence and when subsequently his conviction has been reversed, or he has been pardoned, on the ground that a new or newly discovered fact shows conclusively that there has been a miscarriage of justice, the person who has suffered punishment as a result of such conviction shall be compensated according to the law or the practice of the State concerned, unless it is proved that the non-disclosure of the unknown fact in time is wholly or partly attributable to him.

Article 4
Right not to be tried or punished twice

1. No one shall be liable to be tried or punished again in criminal proceedings under the jurisdiction of the same State for an offence for which he has already been finally acquitted or convicted in accordance with the law and penal procedure of that State.
2. The provisions of the preceding paragraph shall not prevent the reopening of the case in accordance with the law and penal procedure of the State concerned, if there is evidence of new or newly discovered facts, or if there has been a fundamental defect in the previous proceedings, which could affect the outcome of the case.
3. No derogation from this Article shall be made under Article 15 of the Convention.

Article 5
Equality between spouses

Spouses shall enjoy equality of rights and responsibilities of a private law character between them, and in their relations with their children, as to marriage, during marriage and in the event of its dissolution. This Article shall not prevent States from taking such measures as are necessary in the interests of the children.

Article 6
Territorial application

1. Any State may at the time of signature or when depositing its instrument of ratification, acceptance or approval, specify the territory or territories to which the Protocol shall apply and state the extent to which it undertakes that the provisions of this Protocol shall apply to such territory or territories.
2. Any State may at any later date, by a declaration addressed to the Secretary General of the Council of Europe, extend the application of this Protocol to any other territory specified in the declaration. In respect of such territory the Protocol shall enter into force on the first day of the month following the expiration of a period of two months after the date of receipt by the Secretary General of such declaration.
3. Any declaration made under the two preceding paragraphs may, in respect of any territory specified in such declaration, be withdrawn or modified by a notification addressed to the Secretary General. The withdrawal or modification shall become effective on the first day of the month following the expiration of a period of two months after the date of receipt of such notification by the Secretary General.
4. A declaration made in accordance with this Article shall be deemed to have been made in accordance with paragraph 1 of Article 56 of the Convention.
5. The territory of any State to which this Protocol applies by virtue of ratification, acceptance or approval by that State, and each territory to which this Protocol is applied by virtue of a declaration by that State under this Article, may be treated as separate territories for the purpose of the reference in Article 1 to the territory of a State.
6. Any State which has made a declaration in accordance with paragraph 1 or 2 of this Article may at any time thereafter declare on behalf of one or more of the territories to which the declaration relates that it accepts the competence of the Court to receive applications from individuals, non-governmental organisations or groups of individuals as provided in Article 34 of the Convention in respect of Articles 1 to 5 of this Protocol.

Article 7
Relationship to the Convention

As between the States Parties, the provisions of Article 1 to 6 of this Protocol shall be regarded as additional Articles to the Convention, and all the provisions of the Convention shall apply accordingly.

Article 8
Signature and ratification

This Protocol shall be open for signature by member States of the Council of Europe which have signed the Convention. It is subject to ratification, acceptance or approval. A member State of the Council of Europe may not ratify, accept or approve this Protocol without previously or simultaneously ratifying the Convention. Instruments of ratification, acceptance or approval shall be deposited with the Secretary General of the Council of Europe.

Article 9
Entry into force

1. This Protocol shall enter into force on the first day of the month following the expiration of a period of two months after the date on which seven member States of the Council of Europe have expressed their consent to be bound by the Protocol in accordance with the provisions of Article 8.
2. In respect of any member State which subsequently expresses its consent to be bound by it, the Protocol shall enter into force on the first day of the month following the expiration of a period of two months after the date of the deposit of the instrument of ratification, acceptance or approval.

Article 10
Depositary functions

The Secretary General of the Council of Europe shall notify all the member States of the Council of Europe of:
(a) any signature;
(b) the deposit of any instrument of ratification, acceptance or approval;
(c) any date of entry into force of this Protocol in accordance with Articles 6 and 9;
(d) any other act, notification or declaration relating to this Protocol.

In witness whereof the undersigned, being duly authorised thereto, have signed this Protocol.

Done at Strasbourg, this 22nd day of November 1984, in English and French, both texts being equally authentic, in a single copy which shall be deposited in the archives of the Council of Europe. The Secretary General of the Council of Europe shall transmit certified copies to each member State of the Council of Europe.

PROTOCOL NO. 12 TO THE CONVENTION FOR THE PROTECTION OF HUMAN RIGHTS AND FUNDAMENTAL FREEDOMS

Rome, 4.XI.2000

The member States of the Council of Europe signatory hereto,

Having regard to the fundamental principle according to which all persons are equal before the law and are entitled to the equal protection of the law;

Being resolved to take further steps to promote the equality of all persons through the collective enforcement of a general prohibition of discrimination by means of the Convention for the

Protection of Human Rights and Fundamental Freedoms signed at Rome on 4 November 1950 (hereinafter referred to as "the Convention");

Reaffirming that the principle of non-discrimination does not prevent States Parties from taking measures in order to promote full and effective equality, provided that there is an objective and reasonable justification for those measures,

Have agreed as follows:

Article 1
General prohibition of discrimination

1. The enjoyment of any right set forth by law shall be secured without dis-crimination on any ground such as sex, race, colour, language, religion, political or other opinion, national or social origin, association with a national minority, property, birth or other status.
2. No one shall be discriminated against by any public authority on any ground such as those mentioned in paragraph 1.

Article 2
Territorial application

1. Any State may, at the time of signature or when depositing its instrument of ratification, acceptance or approval, specify the territory or territories to which this Protocol shall apply.
2. Any State may at any later date, by a declaration addressed to the Secretary General of the Council of Europe, extend the application of this Protocol to any other territory specified in the declaration. In respect of such territory the Protocol shall enter into force on the first day of the month following the expiration of a period of three months after the date of receipt by the Secretary General of such declaration.
3. Any declaration made under the two preceding paragraphs may, in respect of any territory specified in such declaration, be withdrawn or modified by a notification addressed to the Secretary General of the Council of Europe. The withdrawal or modification shall become effective on the first day of the month following the expiration of a period of three months after the date of receipt of such notification by the Secretary General.
4. A declaration made in accordance with this Article shall be deemed to have been made in accordance with paragraph 1 of Article 56 of the Convention.
5. Any State which has made a declaration in accordance with para-graph 1 or 2 of this Article may at any time thereafter declare on behalf of one or more of the territories to which the declaration relates that it accepts the competence of the Court to receive applications from individuals, non-governmental organisations or groups of individuals as provided by Article 34 of the Convention in respect of Article 1 of this Protocol.

Article 3
Relationship to the Convention

As between the States Parties, the provisions of Articles 1 and 2 of this Protocol shall be regarded as additional Articles to the Convention, and all the provisions of the Convention shall apply accordingly.

Article 4
Signature and ratification

This Protocol shall be open for signature by member States of the Council of Europe which have signed the Convention. It is subject to ratification, acceptance or approval. A member State of the

Council of Europe may not ratify, accept or approve this Protocol without previously or simultaneously ratifying the Convention. Instruments of ratification, acceptance or approval shall be deposited with the Secretary General of the Council of Europe.

Article 5
Entry into force

1. This Protocol shall enter into force on the first day of the month following the expiration of a period of three months after the date on which ten member States of the Council of Europe have expressed their consent to be bound by the Protocol in accordance with the provisions of Article 4.
2. In respect of any member State which subsequently expresses its con-sent to be bound by it, the Protocol shall enter into force on the first day of the month following the expiration of a period of three months after the date of the deposit of the instrument of ratification, acceptance or approval.

Article 6
Depositary functions

The Secretary General of the Council of Europe shall notify all the member States of the Council of Europe of:
(a) any signature;
(b) the deposit of any instrument of ratification, acceptance or approval;
(c) any date of entry into force of this Protocol in accordance with Articles 2 and 5;
(d) any other act, notification or communication relating to this Protocol.

In witness whereof the undersigned, being duly authorised thereto, have signed this Protocol.

Done at Rome, this 4th day of November 2000, in English and in French, both texts being equally authentic, in a single copy which shall be deposited in the archives of the Council of Europe. The Secretary General of the Council of Europe shall transmit certified copies to each member State of the Council of Europe.

PROTOCOL NO. 13 TO THE CONVENTION FOR THE PROTECTION OF HUMAN RIGHTS AND FUNDAMENTAL FREEDOMS CONCERNING THE ABOLITION OF THE DEATH PENALTY IN ALL CIRCUMSTANCES

Vilnius, 3.V.2002

The member States of the Council of Europe signatory hereto,

Convinced that everyone's right to life is a basic value in a democratic society and that the abolition of the death penalty is essential for the protection of this right and for the full recognition of the inherent dignity of all human beings;

Wishing to strengthen the protection of the right to life guaranteed by the Convention for the Protection of Human Rights and Fundamental Freedoms signed at Rome on 4 November 1950 (hereinafter referred to as "the Convention");

Noting that Protocol No. 6 to the Convention concerning the abolition of the death penalty, signed at Strasbourg on 28 April 1983, does not exclude the death penalty in respect of acts committed in time of war or of imminent threat of war;

Being resolved to take the final step in order to abolish the death penalty in all circumstances,
Have agreed as follows:

Article 1
Abolition of the death penalty

The death penalty shall be abolished. No one shall be condemned to such penalty or executed.

Article 2
Prohibitions of derogations

No derogation from the provisions of this Protocol shall be made under Article 15 of the Convention.

Article 3
Prohibitions of reservations

No reservation may be made under Article 57 of the Convention in respect of the provisions of this Protocol.

Article 4
Territorial application

1. Any State may, at the time of signature or when depositing its instrument of ratification, acceptance or approval, specify the territory or territories to which this Protocol shall apply.
2. Any State may at any later date, by a declaration addressed to the Secretary General of the Council of Europe, extend the application of this Protocol to any other territory specified in the declaration. In respect of such territory the Protocol shall enter into force on the first day of the month following the expiration of a period of three months after the date of receipt by the Secretary General of such declaration.
3. Any declaration made under the two preceding paragraphs may, in respect of any territory specified in such declaration, be withdrawn or modified by a notification addressed to the Secretary General. The withdrawal or modification shall become effective on the first day of the month following the expiration of a period of three months after the date of receipt of such notification by the Secretary General.

Article 5
Relationship to the Convention

As between the States Parties the provisions of Articles 1 to 4 of this Protocol shall be regarded as additional Articles to the Convention, and all the provisions of the Convention shall apply accordingly.

Article 6
Signature and ratification

This Protocol shall be open for signature by member States of the Council of Europe which have signed the Convention. It is subject to ratification, acceptance or approval. A member State of the Council of Europe may not ratify, accept or approve this Protocol without previously or simultaneously ratifying the Convention. Instruments of ratifi-cation, acceptance or approval shall be deposited with the Secretary General of the Council of Europe.

Article 7
Entry into force

1. This Protocol shall enter into force on the first day of the month following the expiration of a period of three months after the date on which ten member States of the Council of Europe have expressed their consent to be bound by the Protocol in accordance with the provisions of Article 6.

2. In respect of any member State which subsequently expresses its con-sent to be bound by it, the Protocol shall enter into force on the first day of the month following the expiration of a period of three months after the date of the deposit of the instrument of ratification, acceptance or approval.

Article 8
Depositary functions

The Secretary General of the Council of Europe shall notify all the member States of the Council of Europe of:

(a) any signature;
(b) the deposit of any instrument of ratification, acceptance or approval;
(c) any date of entry into force of this Protocol in accordance with Articles 4 and 7;
(d) any other act, notification or communication relating to this Protocol;

In witness whereof the undersigned, being duly authorised thereto, have signed this Protocol.

Done at Vilnius, this 3rd day of May 2002, in English and in French, both texts being equally authentic, in a single copy which shall be deposited in the archives of the Council of Europe. The Secretary General of the Council of Europe shall transmit certified copies to each member State of the Council of Europe

Index

abortion 4.21, 6.16–6.17, 7.231
absolute rights 6.01–6.127 *see also* **life, right to**
  definition 6.01
  extraterritoriality 6.04–6.07
  fair hearing, right to a 7.77
  forced or compulsory labour 6.115–6.116,
    6.120–6.127
  inhuman or degrading treatment 6.55–6.114
  jurisdiction 6.03–6.08
  life, right to 2.26
  limitation on use of restriction on rights 7.592
  public interest 2.26
  retrospectivity 2.26
  slavery and servitude 2.26, 6.115–6.119,
    6.125–6.127
  torture 2.26–2.27, 6.58, 6.62–66
abuse of process 4.05
abuse of rights, prohibition of 7.587–7.590
access to court 7.105, 7.108–7.112, 7.350, 7.398
access to information 1.25, 7.364–7.366, 7.397
access to legal advice 7.99, 7.158, 7.160–7.164
accessibility of law 2.44–2.45, 4.108
adequate time and facilities to prepare a
    case 7.158–7.159
Administrative Court 4.09
administrative law 7.85–7.87
admissibility
  European Commission on Human
    Rights 10.04–10.05
  European Court of Human Rights 9.18–9.54,
    10.06, 10.08
  torture, evidence obtained by 4.38,
    6.74–6.78, 7.77
adoption 7.280, 7.282, 7.478–7.479
adversarial proceedings 7.64, 7.132, 7.143
adverse inferences from silence 7.139, 7.155
adverse possession 8.31, 8.42–8.43
advertising
  party political broadcasts 4.126, 7.376–7.377
  religion 7.403
  tobacco 7.360
agnosticism 7.307
aircraft noise 7.249, 9.46
alcoholics, detention of 7.33
aliens
  elections, right to free 8.106
  political activity of aliens, restrictions on 2.76,
    5.579–7.586
American Society for International Law's *Guide*
    to Electronic Resources for International
    Law 10.02
amicus briefs 4.18

anonymity
  births 7.279
  European Court of Human Rights 9.30
  freedom of expression 7.263, 7.364
  media, anonymity orders and 7.263, 7.364
  private and family life, right to respect for 7.263
  witnesses 7.166–7.167
anti-Semitism 7.362–7.363
appeals
  criminal charges 7.163, 7.171
  EU law 5.17
  fair hearing, right to a 7.163, 7.171, 7.77, 7.105,
    7.135, 7.147, 8.140–8.145
  legal assistance 7.163
  reasons 7.135
  Special Immigration Appeals
    Commission 6.74–6.78, 7.503
appropriate forum 4.07–4.15
armed forces *see also* **Iraq, UK military action in**
  conscientious objection 6.123,
    7.312–7.313, 7.336
  courts martial 7.116–7.118
  forced or compulsory labour 6.123
  freedom of association 7.413, 7.455–7.456
  homosexuals 7.235, 7.499
  inquests 6.46
  investigative duty 6.46
  life, right to 6.46
  manifest one's religion or beliefs, right to 7.336
  private life, definition of 7.235
  thought, conscience and religion, freedom
    of 7.312–7.313
  trade unions, right to form and
    join 7.455–7.456
arrest 7.28–7.30, 7.48–7.51
artificial insemination 7.240, 7.480–7.484
artistic expression 7.357, 7.359, 7.362
assembly, freedom of *see* **freedom of assembly**
assisted suicide 4.104, 6.27, 6.98, 7.230,
    7.232–7.233
association, freedom of *see* **freedom of association**
asylum seekers
  civil rights and obligations 7.92–7.93
  expulsion from and entry into national
    territory 8.125
  inhuman or degrading treatment 4.106, 6.110
  liberty and security, right to 7.45
  proportionality 4.116
  subsistence 4.106, 6.110
atheism 7.307
autonomous concepts 2.14–2.16, 7.179
autonomy 6.61, 7.230–7.232

bad faith 7.593 *see also* good faith
bail 7.51, 7.54–7.56, 7.64
balancing rights
  freedom of assembly 7.414
  freedom of association 7.414
  freedom of expression 7.253, 7.261,
    7.263–7.264, 7.373, 7.379, 7.395–7.396,
    7.400, 7.406
  media 7.253, 7.261, 7.263–7.264
  positive obligations 2.37
  private and family life, right to respect for 7.222,
    7.253, 7.261, 7.263–7.264
  restrictions on Convention rights 2.40
  thought, conscience and religion,
    freedom of 7.348
bankrupts
  detention 7.26
  peaceful enjoyment of possessions 8.49
Beijing Rules (the Standard Minimum Rules
    for the Administration of Juvenile
    Justice) 2.21
beliefs *see* manifest one's religion or beliefs,
    right to; religion or beliefs; thought,
    conscience and religion, freedom of
best practice 1.38
bias *see* independent and impartial tribunals
bibliographic resources 10.18
Bill of Rights 1689 1.06
bill of rights and future of HRA
  Commission on a Bill of Rights 1.52–1.55
  consultation 1.51
  green paper 1.50, 1.54
  proportionality 1.54
  public interest 1.54
  responsibilities, reference to 1.54
bills 3.13, 3.43–3.44
Blackstone, William 1.27
blanket policies 2.64, 7.111, 7.427–7.428, 7.521
blasphemy 2.49
blogs 10.17, 10.26
books 10.20, 10.23
breach of statutory duty 3.22, 3.57, 4.62
bringing rights home 1.24, 1.05, 1.40, 4.01–4.02,
    4.05, 4.131
British and Irish Legal Information Institute
    (BAILII) database 10.25
broadcasting
  access to balanced, informative and pluralistic
    services 7.369
  freedom of expression 7.369, 7.373–7.377
  licensing 7.373–7.377
  party political broadcasts 4.126, 7.376–7.377
Butterworths' Human Rights Cases 10.12

Canada 1.22, 1.29, 7.528
cannabis, criminalization of 7.340
capital punishment *see* death penalty
care arrangements 7.18
care proceedings 7.223

care workers, provisional blacklisting of 3.47, 4.79
Case Law Information Notes 10.16
cases, finding 10.10–10.21, 10.24, 10.26
cautions 7.103
charges *see* criminal charges
Charter of Fundamental Rights of the EU 5.03,
    5.05, 5.11–5.16
  civil partnerships
  contents 5.12
  European Convention on Human
    Rights 1.25, 5.15
  European Court of Human Rights 5.09
  interpretation 2.21, 5.12, 5.14. 5.21
  jurisdiction 5.16
  Lisbon Treaty 5.11
  marry, right to 7.474
  preamble 5.12
  primary law, as part of 5.11
  rights and principles, distinction between 5.13
Charter of Human Rights. Labour Party 1.20
children *see also* education, right to
  abuse 6.96, 7.495
  access to children 7.223
  adoption 7.280, 7.282, 7.478–7.479
  anonymous births 7.279
  Beijing Rules on Juvenile Justice 2.21
  best interests 7.284, 7.286
  biological ties 7.276–7.277
  Children Act 1989 3.40, 7.124
  civil rights and obligations 7.92
  conjoined twins, separation of 6.30
  Convention on the Rights of the Child 1.55,
    2.21, 7.286
  corporal punishment 6.94–6.95, 7.319,
    7.340, 8.78
  DNA, retention of 2.21
  effective remedy, right to an 7.495
  estranged parents and children 7.278
  European Convention on Human Rights 1.25
  family life, definition of 7.276–7.282
  fostering 7.223, 7.280
  identify parents, right to 7.279
  illegitimacy 4.20
  immigration control 7.284, 7.286
  legal proceedings, identification in 7.262
  liberty and security, right to 7.32
  paternity, presumption of 7.281
  prisons, children in adult 6.83
  private and family life, right to respect for 4.106
  protestors' abuse of schoolchildren 6.97
  public hearings 7.124
  same sex partners 7.308, 8.13
  spouses, equal rights and responsibilities
    of 8.156–8.157
chilling effect 4.91, 7.256, 7.372, 7.383, 7.398
citizenship 5.584
civil partnerships 7.275, 7.344, 7.474, 7.590
civil and political rights *see* International Covenant
    on Civil and Political Rights (ICCPR)

civil rights and obligations
  administrative discretion 7.88–7.89
  administrative law 7.85–7.87
  asylum seekers 7.92–7.93
  child maintenance 7.92
  definition 7.79, 7.85–7.87
  determination, definition of 7.79, 7.81–7.84
  employment 7.94
  expulsion/deportation 8.139
  fair hearing, right to a 7.81–7.94, 7.148
  framework of ECHR 2.02
  homelessness 7.93, 7.148
  planning 7.90
  pure public rights 7.89–7.94
  Regulatory of Investigatory Powers Tribunal 7.93
closed shops 7.444
cohabitation 7.270
Coke, Edward 1.27
collective bargaining 7.438, 7.448
comfort clauses 3.26, 7.405
commercial expression 7.357, 7.360, 7.400
committal 7.98, 7.163
Committee of Ministers 2.05, 3.48, 9.37, 9.52, 9.62, 10.07–10.08
common law 1.06–1.11, 1.17, 2.03, 2.43
Commonwealth constitutions 10.02
companies 4.16, 7.353
comparative law 10.02
compensation see also damages
  effective remedy, right to an 7.493, 7.500
  employment tribunals 4.53–4.54
  European Court of Human Rights 9.01, 9.51
  ex gratia payments 4.69
  liberty and security, right to 7.73
  miscarriages of justice 7.152, 8.146–8.150
  peaceful enjoyment of possessions 8.37, 8.50, 8.58–8.59
  proportionality 2.64
compulsory labour see forced or compulsory labour
compulsory transfer of property 8.05, 8.13, 8.36, 8.40–8.41, 8.46, 8.50, 8.58
conditional cautions 7.103
conditional discharges 7.40
conditional fee agreements 7.398, 9.58
confidentiality 7.242, 7.257–7.259, 9.30, 10.09
confiscation 7.151, 7.212, 8.30, 8.53
conjoined twins, separation of 6.30
conscience see conscientious objection; thought, conscience and religion, freedom of
conscientious objection 6.123, 7.311, 7.336
constitutional instrument, HRA as 1.26–1.36
constitutions
  Commonwealth constitutions 10.02
  unwritten constitution, flexibility of 1.17
contempt of court 1.14, 2.48, 7.98
contracting out 3.66, 3.68–3.71
contractual obligations, deprivation of liberty on grounds of inability to fulfil 8.114–8.115
control orders 3.46, 4.83, 7.15–7.16

Convention on the Rights of the Child 1.55, 2.21, 7.286
copyright 8.14
corporal punishment 6.94–6.95, 7.319, 7.340, 8.78
correspondence
  definition 7.296–7.298
  legal privileged correspondence of prisoners 7.297
  legitimate aims 2.53
  prisoners' correspondence, interference with 2.53, 2.64, 7.296–7.297, 7.494
  private and family life, right to respect for 7.296–7.298
  telephone tapping 7.296
costs
  access to courts 7.398
  adverse costs orders 4.91
  chilling effect 4.91
  conditional fee agreements, success fees and 7.398
  declarations of incompatibility 4.89–4.91
  European Court of Human Rights 9.51, 9.54, 9.55, 9.59
  fair hearing, right to a 7.84
  freedom of expression 7.398
  funding 9.55, 9.59
  Jackson Review 7.398
  media 7.398
  peaceful enjoyment of possessions 8.50
court, access to see access to court
Court of Protection proceedings 7.365
courts and tribunals as public authorities 3.19, 3.24
courts martial 7.116–7.118
criminal charges
  access to legal advice 7.99, 7.158, 7.160–7.164
  accusation, right to be informed of 7.157
  adequate time and facilities to prepare a case 7.158–7.159
  appeals 7.163, 7.171
  cautions 7.103
  charges 7.95, 7.103, 7.157
  choice of legal representative 7.160
  classification of offences 7.96
  committal 7.98, 7.163
  conditional cautions 7.103
  contempt proceedings 7.98
  criminal, definition of 7.96
  criteria 7.96
  defence
    adequate time and resources for preparation 7.158–7.159
    effectiveness 7.160–7.161
  definition 7.79, 7.95, 7.102
  delay 7.127
  deprivation of liberty 7.99
  determination, definition of 7.79, 7.81–7.84
  disciplinary proceedings 7.159

criminal charges (*Cont.*)
  disclosure 7.144
  effective participation, right to 7.137
  Engel criteria 7.96–7.99
  equality of arms 7.137, 7.143–7.145,
    7.165–7.166
  expulsion 7.171
  fair hearings 7.76, 7.95–7.104, 7.127,
    7.150–7.170
  free legal assistance 7.160, 7.163
  hearsay 7.166, 7.168
  interpreters 7.169–7.170
  language 7.157, 7.169–7.170
  legal aid 7.99, 7.144, 7.160, 7.163–7.164
  legal representation 7.99, 7.158, 7.160–7.164
  life, right to 7.166
  margin of appreciation 7.166
  nature of offences 7.96
  Parole Board decisions 7.101
  penalty, nature and severity of 7.96, 7.99
  presumption of innocence 7.150–7.155
  preventive measures 7.96
  prison discipline 7.100
  private, right to consult with lawyers in 7.162
  procedural safeguards 7.156–7.170
  proportionality 7.144
  Protocol 7 to ECHR 7.171
  public interest immunity certificates 7.144
  punitive measures 7.96, 7.98
  reasons 7.48–7.49
  rule of law 7.99
  self-incrimination, privilege against 7.138, 7.141
  sex offenders register 7.102
  silence, right to 7.138–7.141
  special advocates 7.144
  specific safeguards 7.137–7.145
  terrorist suspects 7.102
  translations 7.157, 7.169–7.170
  warnings 7.103
  witnesses
    anonymity 7.166–7.167
    life, right to 7.166
    right to examine 7.165–7.167
Criminal Law Review (CLR) 10.22
criminal offences *see also* **criminal charges**
  cannabis, criminalization of 7.340
  convictions 4.05, 7.22–7.25, 8.140, 9.53
  criminal, definition of 7.177–7.179
  delay 7.126–7.127, 7.130
  double jeopardy 8.151–8.155
  enforcement of HRA 4.05
  European Court of Human Rights 9.53
  evidence, exclusion of 4.05
  expulsion/deportation 8.139
  fair hearing, right to a 4.05
  freedom of expression 7.388, 7.400
  homosexual acts 2.59, 4.20
  indictments, quashing 4.05
  international crimes 7.213–7.216

  liberty and security, right to 7.22–7.25
  no punishment without lawful
    authority 7.177–7.179
  precedent 3.34
  prevention of crime and right to life 6.19–6.24
  prosecutions, dismissal of 4.05
  protest, right to 7.435
  remedies 4.05–4.06
  retrials 9.53
  sentences, reduction in 4.05
  stay of proceedings as abuse of process 4.05
  summons, withdrawing issue of 4.05
crucifixes in school, display of 8.82
culture
  human rights culture 1.37–1.48
  margin of appreciation 2.78
  Parliament 1.40
customary international law 7.561

damages *see also* **compensation**
  aggravated damages 4.57, 9.51
  assessment principles 4.57–4.59
  breach of statutory duty 4.62
  causal link 4.57
  comparators 4.64
  costs 4.58
  declarations of incompatibility 4.69, 4.87
  defamation 2.64
  detention 4.60
  discretion 4.57
  enforcement of HRA 4.05–4.06, 4.53–4.70
  EU law 5.24
  European Court of Human Rights 4.57,
    4.63–4.64, 9.51
  exemplary damages 4.57, 7.73, 9.51
  exhaustion of local remedies 4.55
  expenses 4.58
  freedom of expression 7.372, 7.386
  inhuman or degrading treatment 4.66
  judicial acts 3.24, 4.13
  judicial bodies 4.68
  judicial review 4.55, 4.67, 4.68
  jurisdiction 4.53–4.55
  just satisfaction 3.23, 4.05, 4.53,
    4.57–4.58, 4.69
  Law Commission 4.62–4.63
  legal funding 4.65
  liberty and security, right to 4.68, 7.73
  maladministration 4.55
  Mental Health Review Tribunal 4.68
  non-pecuniary loss 4.58, 4.60
  pain and suffering 4.58
  Parliament 4.69–4.70
  pecuniary loss 4.58
  permission 4.55
  personal injuries 4.58
  principles 4.56–4.67
  procedural guidelines 4.55
  proportionality 2.64

psychological damage 4.58
public authorities 4.68
public funding 4.65
punitive damages 4.57, 9.51
quantum, guidelines on 4.56–4.67
restitutionary principle 4.57, 4.59
slavery and servitude 6.127
death penalty
abolition 6.10
death row phenomenon 6.71
derogations 8.161
extradition 6.07, 6.71
inhuman or degrading treatment 6.08, 6.71
life, right to 6.10
protocols 8.127–8.128, 8.161–8.162
reservations 8.161
wartime 8.161–8.162
deaths and near-deaths in custody 6.41–6.46
declarations of incompatibility
appropriate forum 4.11–4.14
control orders 3.46, 4.83
costs 4.89–4.91
county courts 4.11
damages 4.69, 4.87
delay 4.131
discretion 4.75
effective remedy, right to an 4.85, 4.87, 7.500,
7.502, 9.02, 9.27
enforcement of HRA 4.05, 4.71–4.99, 4.131
European Court of Human
Rights 9.01–9.02, 9.27
examples 4.79
fast track procedure 3.14, 4.72, 4.92–4.99
framework of HRA 3.07, 3.14
High Court, transfer of proceedings to 4.11
interpretation 3.38, 3.45–3.47, 4.73
judicial review 4.25
jurisdiction 4.77
notice to the Crown 4.14
parliamentary sovereignty 1.28, 4.72
primary legislation 4.71–4.74, 4.92
procedure 4.81–4.88
public interest 4.89
remedial orders 1.28, 4.72, 4.84–4.86,
4.92–4.99
standing 4.77
striking down legislation 3.14
terrorist suspects, detention without trial of 4.83
torture, return of foreign nationals to face 4.83
transfer of proceedings 4.11
transsexuals, legal recognition of 7.237
victim requirement 4.77
vote, right to 8.101
widows' benefits 3.46
defamation
access to court 7.398
conditional fee agreements, success
fees and 7.398
costs 7.398

criminal sanctions 7.388
damages 2.64, 7.372
freedom of expression 1.15, 7.254, 7.358–7.359,
7.372, 7.388–7.389, 7.398
Internet 7.389
local authorities 1.15
media 7.254, 7.398
political expression 7.358
private and family life, right to respect for 7.254
proportionality 2.64
United States, proof of malice with regard to
public figures in 7.358
defence against criminal charges
adequate time and resources for
preparation 7.158–7.159
effectiveness 7.160–7.161
**deference and discretionary area of
judgment** 4.111, 4.117–4.130
delay
charge and sentence, time between 7.127
declarations of incompatibility 4.131
European Court of Human Rights 9.05
fair hearing, right to a 7.126–7.130
liberty and security, right to 7.43–7.44, 7.52,
7.57–7.63, 7.69
marry, right to 7.464
democracy 1.11, 1.35, 2.09, 7.350, 7.450–7.453
deportation and removal *see* **expulsion/deportation;
extradition**
deprivation of liberty *see also* **liberty and security,
right to**
conditions in prison 6.81–6.84, 6.105
contractual obligations, grounds of inability
to fulfil 8.114–8.115
criminal charges 7.99
damages 4.60
deaths in custody 4.105, 6.41–6.45
definition 7.10–7.19
delay 7.127
deportation 6.105
dignity 6.85
fair hearing, right to a 7.99
habeas corpus 1.06
hunger strikes 6.111–6.112
immigration detention 6.85
inhuman or degrading treatment 6.81–6.88,
6.90–6.91, 6.105, 6.111–6.113
life, right to 4.105, 6.20, 6.25–6.26
mental health 6.86–6.88
minors in adult prisons, detention of 6.83
Scotland 6.84
seclusion of mental health patients 6.86
self-inflicted conditions 6.111–6.113
slopping out 6.84
terrorist suspects 3.46, 4.83, 7.09, 7.53, 7.65,
7.570–7.578
transfers 6.83
war and emergencies, derogations in
time of 7.570–7.578

derogations *see also* **war and emergencies, derogations in time of**
  death penalty 8.161
  fair hearing, right to a 7.78
  framework of HRA 3.27
  legality 2.42
  liberty and security, right to 7.08–7.09, 7.47
  no punishment without lawful authority 7.172
  proportionality 2.73
  restrictions on Convention rights 2.73–2.75
detention *see* **deprivation of liberty; liberty and security, right to; prisoners**
Dicey, AV 1.08–1.11, 1.27
die, right to 4.104, 6.27, 7.230, 7.232–7.233
Digest of Strasbourg Case Law 10.15
dignity 6.61, 6.70, 6.85
disabled persons *see also* **mental disabilities**
  discrimination 7.513
  private and family life, right to respect for 7.225
disciplinary proceedings
  criminal charges 7.159
  fair hearing, right to a 7.159
  freedom of expression 7.392
  opportunity to present case 7.134
  political expression 7.392
  prisoners 7.100
  professional hearings 7.150
  public hearings 7.122
disclosure
  criminal charges 7.144
  equality of arms 7.144
  opportunity to present case 7.132–7.133
  proportionality 7.144
  religion, freedom not to disclose one's 7.309
discretion
  civil rights and obligations 7.88–7.89
  damages 4.57
  declarations of incompatibility 4.75
  deference 1.34, 4.111, 4.117–4.130
  judiciary, politicization of 1.34
  no punishment without lawful authority 7.186
  PACE, judicial discretion to exclude of evidence under 1.15
discrimination and equality *see also* **Equality and Human Rights Commission (EHRC); race discrimination**
  analogous or similar situations 7.516–7.520, 7.532
  armed forces, homosexuals in the 7.499
  birth 7.540
  blanket bans 7.21
  burden of proof 7.518, 7.531
  Canada 7.528
  comparators 7.520
  concept of discrimination 7.516
  disabled persons 7.513
  DNA, retention of 7.515
  education, right to 8.86–8.87
  European Convention on Human Rights 1.25

expulsion from and entry into national territory 8.125
failure to treat like cases differently 7.521
forced or compulsory labour 7.511
freedom of association 7.428
gypsies and travellers 7.506
homelessness 4.42
housing 4.42, 4.79, 4.82
illegitimacy 4.20
immigration rules on marriage 7.523
importance of article 7.504–7.506
indirect discrimination 7.517, 7.522–7.529
international Covenant on Civil and Political Rights 7.508
Joint Committee on Human Rights 8.160
jury service 7.526
justification 7.516–7.517, 7.523–7.525, 7.530–7.546
legitimate aims 7.530–7.535
limited and qualified rights 7.504–7.546
living instrument doctrine 7.538, 7.540
margin of appreciation 7.537–7.545
marital status 7.540
minority rights 7.506, 7.528
nationality 4.79, 4.81, 5.584, 5.586, 7.540
peaceful enjoyment of possessions 8.51
positive obligations 7.517, 7.546
proportionality 7.530–7.531, 7.535–7.536
protected rights or status 7.514–7.515
protocol 8.159–8.160
religion
  margin of appreciation 7.540
  special cases and exceptions 3.81
  symbols 7.528
  thought, conscience and religion, freedom of 7.301, 7.521
Roma children, education of 8.87
scope 7.507–7.515
sex discrimination
  jury service 7.526
  margin of appreciation 7.539, 7.542–7.544
  pensions 7.541–7.544
  state retirement age 7.541–7.544
  welfare benefits 7.543
sexual orientation 4.20, 7.540, 8.13
standard of proof 7.525
state benefits 8.51
state retirement age 7.541–7.544
substantive right, need for breach of 1.25, 7.506, 7.511, 8.159
suspect classes principle 7.539–7.542
systemic discrimination 7.528
technical points 7.520, 7.545
terrorist suspects, pre-trial detention of 5.576
thought, conscience and religion, freedom of 7.521
trade unions, right to form and join 7.428
transsexuals 7.538
victims, standing of 9.21

vote, right to 8.100
welfare benefits 7.543
widows' benefits 4.20
**diseases, detention of persons with
infectious** 7.33, 7.41
divorce in Ireland, ban on 4.20
DNA
children 2.21
discrimination 7.515
Protection of Freedoms Bill 7.244
protest, right to 7.423
retention 2.21, 7.243–7.244, 7.423, 7.515
domestic violence 6.23, 6.34
double jeopardy 8.151–8.155
abolition 8.155
fundamental defect exception 8.154
International Covenant on Civil and Political
Rights 8.151–8.155
Law Commission 8.155
Macpherson Report 8.155
new and compelling evidence 8.155
drugs
addicts, detention of 7.33–7.34
cannabis, criminalization of 7.340
confiscation 8.53
peaceful enjoyment of possessions 8.53
dualism 1.12
duties and rights, relationship between 1.02

EC law see **EU law**
economic rights 1.04, 1.25, 2.02
education, right to 8.60–8.87
access to educational institutions 8.64, 8.69
corporal punishment 8.78
crucifixes in school, display of 8.82
discrimination 8.86–8.87
effective education 8.64
exclusions from school 8.71–8.74
foreseeability 8.83
higher education 8.68–8.69
home schooling 8.67, 8.72
Islamic dress 8.84–8.85
language 8.64, 8.86
liberty and security, right to 7.32
limitations 2.28–2.29, 8.83–8.85
margin of appreciation 8.82
official recognition of completed studies 8.64
positive obligations 2.32, 8.64
private education 8.67
proportionality 8.83–8.84
protocol 8.60–8.87
religious and philosophical convictions of the
parents 8.61, 8.75–8.82
religious education 8.81
reservations 2.71, 8.61
Roma children, discrimination against 8.87
scope of right 8.64–8.74
sex education 8.80
special education 8.73, 8.87

thought, conscience and religion,
freedom of 8.76
effective remedy, right to an 7.490–7.503
armed forces, homosexuals in the 7.499
child abuse 7.495
compensation 7.493, 7.500
declarations of incompatibility 4.85, 4.87,
7.500, 7.502, 9.02, 9.27
deportation 7.498, 7.503
European Court of Human Rights 9.02, 9.27
exhaustion of local remedies 7.500, 9.27
extradition 7.497
extraterritoriality 7.503
freedom of expression 7.367
investigative duty 6.47
judicial review 7.494–7.499
life, right to 6.47
limited and qualified rights 7.490–7.503
national authority 7.501
Parliamentary Commissioner for
Administration 7.494
peaceful enjoyment of possessions 8.37
prisoners' correspondence, interference
with 7.494
remedial orders 4.99
special cases and exceptions 3.76–3.77
Wednesbury unreasonableness 7.496
effectiveness principle see also **effective remedy,
right to an**
access to courts 2.12
European Court of Human Rights 3.54–3.56
fair hearing, right to a 2.12, 7.137, 7.142
implied rights 2.12
interpretation 2.11–2.13, 3.54–3.56
investigative duty 6.37–6.38, 6.47
life, right to 6.37–6.38, 6.47
object and purpose of Convention 2.12
positive obligations 2.13, 2.33–2.34
EHRC see **Equality and Human Rights
Commission (EHRC)**
elections, right to free 8.88–8.112
aliens standing for election, prohibition on 8.106
dishonest statements by candidates 8.107
elections, definition of 8.94–8.97
electoral systems 8.108–8.112
EU law 5.20
first past the post systems 8.109
freedom of expression 7.350, 8.107, 8.111
Gibraltar 5.20
implied limitations 8.90
legislature, definition of 8.92–8.93
legitimate aims 8.89–8.90
limited and qualified rights 2.28
margin of appreciation 8.91, 8.108
necessity 8.90
positive obligations 2.32
presidential elections 8.95
prisoners 1.53, 2.68, 4.86, 8.100–8.101,
9.52, 9.63

EHRC *see* **Equality and Human Rights Commission (EHRC)** (*Cont.*)
  proportional representation 8.108
  proportionality 8.89–8.90, 8.111
  protocol 8.88–8.112
  referenda 8.94
  residence requirements 8.103–8.104
  Sark 8.96–8.97, 8.106
  sit in legislature, right to 8.105
  stand for election, right to 7.350, 8.89, 8.102–8.107
  validity of elections 8.112
  vote, right to 1.53, 2.68, 4.86, 7.350, 8.89, 8.98–8.101, 9.52, 9.63
elective dictatorship 1.18
electronic and online resources 10.02, 10.10, 10.16–10.17, 10.19, 10.24–10.26
emergencies *see* **war and emergencies, derogations in time of**
employment *see also* **forced or compulsory labour; trade unions**
  barring persons from employment without representation 7.223
  care workers, provisional blacklisting of 3.47, 4.79
  civil rights and obligations 7.94
  compensation 4.53–4.54
  dismissal 7.325
  employment tribunals 4.42, 4.53–4.54
  fair hearing, right to a 4.42
  freedom of expression 7.354
  legal representation 4.42
  manifest one's religion or beliefs, right to 7.324–7.325
  religion 7.324–7.325, 7.345–7.348
  state employees, freedom of expression of 7.354
  Sunday working 7.324
  time off 7.324
enforcement of HRA 4.01–4.132
  abstract review of legislation 4.132
  appropriate forum 4.07–4.15
  bringing rights home 4.01–4.02, 4.05, 4.131
  convictions, quashing 4.05
  criminal proceedings 4.05
  damages 4.05–4.06, 4.53–4.70
  declarations of incompatibility 4.05, 4.71–4.99, 4.131
  Equality and Human Rights Commission 4.26–4.28, 4.40–4.52, 4.131
  evidence, exclusion of 4.05
  extraterritoriality 4.101–4.103
  indictments, quashing 4.05
  injunctions 4.05
  Joint Committee on Human Rights 4.132, 10.25
  judicial review 4.05
  jurisdiction 4.04
  just satisfaction 4.05
  key concepts in domestic courts 4.100–4.130

  legality 4.108–4.110
  limitation periods 4.04, 4.29–4.32
  mandatory orders 4.05
  positive obligations 4.104–4.107
  pre-emptive measures 4.132
  pre-legislative scrutiny 4.132
  procedural issues 4.04
  prohibiting orders 4.05
  proportionality 4.111–4.130
  prosecutions, dismissal of 4.05
  public interest litigation 4.04, 4.23–4.25, 4.36–4.39
  quashing orders 4.05
  remedies 4.05–4.06, 4.53–4.99, 4.131
  retrospectivity 4.33–4.34
  sentences, reduction in 4.05
  standing 4.04, 4.16–4.28
  stay of proceedings as abuse of process 4.05
  summons, withdrawal of issue of 4.05
  third party intervention 4.04, 4.35–4.43
  victims 4.03–4.05, 4.16–4.22
engagements 7.269
entrenchment 1.19–1.22, 1.27–1.30
environmental damage
  air traffic over houses 7.249
  environmental impact assessments 7.250
  European Convention on Human Rights 1.25
  margin of appreciation 7.250
  noise pollution 7.249
  peaceful enjoyment of possessions 8.32
  private life, definition of 7.249–7.251
Equality and Human Rights Commission (EHRC) 1.43–1.48
  abolition 2.05
  assessments 4.48, 4.52
  creation 1.39, 1.43–1.45, 2.05
  culture of human rights 1.39, 1.43–1.48
  duties and powers 1.45–1.46, 4.43–4.46
  enforcement of HRA 4.26–4.28, 4.40–4.52, 4.131
  Equality Commission for Northern Ireland 4.48
  equality with human rights, linking 1.44
  Human Rights Inquiry 1.46, 1.49, 4.51
  inquiries 1.46, 4.43, 4.49–4.50
  interpretation 2.06
  intervention 4.26–4.28, 4.35–4.36, 4.40–4.43, 9.46
  investigations 4.48, 4.52
  Joint Committee on Human Rights 4.46
  judicial review 1.46, 4.25–4.28, 4.40, 4.43
  legal assistance 1.46, 4.43, 4.47
  legal policy work 4.43, 4.48
  list of interventions 4.42
  monitoring 4.43, 4.46, 4.48
  Northern Ireland Human Rights Commission 4.48
  own name proceedings 4.25
  pre-emptive role 4.46
  public awareness 1.49

Public Bodies Bill 1.48
public sector duties 4.52
review 1.48, 4.43
Scotland 4.26
Scottish Human Rights
    Commission 1.47–1.48, 4.48
standing 4.18, 4.25–4.28, 4.40–4.52, 4.131
test and illustrative cases 4.27
victims 4.26
equality *see* discrimination and equality;
    equality of arms
equality of arms 7.64, 7.105, 7.107, 7.131, 7.137,
    7.143–7.145, 7.165–7.166
ethics
culture of rights 1.37
freedom of expression 7.400–7.404
public morality 7.400–7.404
EU law 5.01–5.27 *see also* Charter of
    Fundamental Rights of the EU
accession to ECHR 5.17
appeals 5.17
citizenship 5.584
competence 5.05, 5.22–5.23
damages 5.24
direct effect 5.01, 5.06, 5.22–5.23
discrimination 5.584
elections to European Parliament, right of
    Gibraltar residents to vote in 5.20
emanations of the state 5.26
European Communities Act 1972 1.27, 5.01
European Court of Human Rights 5.01, 5.17
European Court of Justice 5.17
European Parliament, members of 5.581
exhaustion of local remedies 5.17
free movement rights 5.19
fundamental rights 5.03–5.16
general principles of law 5.03
interpretation 3.34, 5.01, 5.21, 5.23
judicial review 5.26
legality 2.43
Lisbon Treaty 5.17
Marleasing principle 5.01, 5.22
nationality discrimination 5.584
parliamentary sovereignty 1.27
political activity of aliens,
    restrictions on 5.581, 5.584
proportionality 4.113, 5.24
public authorities 5.26
public interest 5.19
purposive approach to interpretation 3.34
remedies 5.24
representative standing 5.25
standing 5.25
striking down primary legislation 5.22–5.23
sufficiently serious breach of EU law,
    damages for 5.24
supremacy of EU law 5.01, 5.06, 5.22
UK courts, interaction of EU law and
    Convention principles in 5.18–5.26

victim requirement 5.25
European Commission on Human Rights
abolition 10.05
admissibility 10.04–10.05
Decisions and Reports series 10.13–10.15
Digest of Strasbourg Case Law 10.15
European Court of Human Rights 10.04
European Human Rights Reports (EHRR) 10.14
interpretation 10.05
merits 10.10
merits test 10.04–10.05
Protocol 11 2.05, 10.05
research 10.04–10.05, 10.08, 10.10,
    10.13–10.15
websites 10.16
weight of authorities 10.08
*Yearbook of the European Convention on Human
    Rights* 10.15
European Convention on Human Rights *see also*
    framework of ECHR
accession 5.17
before HRA 1.12–1.16
bringing rights home 1.05
Charter of Fundamental Rights of
    the EU 1.25, 5.15
children, rights of 1.25
Council of Europe 2.01
development of UK law before HRA,
    impact on 1.12–1.15
direct effect of treaties 1.12
discrimination provision, parasitic nature of 1.25
dualism 1.12
economic rights 1.25
entry into force 2.01, 10.03
environment 1.25
European Union, accession of 5.03
freedom of information 1.25
gaps in protection 1.25
historical background 2.01
incorporation 1.05, 1.12, 1.17–1.25, 1.28, 1.55
individual right of petition 1.12, 1.18, 2.04
libel, local authorities and 1.15
living instrument, as 1.25
object and purpose of ECHR 2.09–2.10
PACE, judicial discretion to exclude of evidence
    under 1.15
protocols 8.01–8.162
ratification 1.05, 1.12, 1.18, 2.03, 10.03
research 10.03–10.09
self-incrimination, lack of absolute
    prohibition on 1.25
social rights 1.25
statutory interpretation 1.16
travaux préparatoires 10.19
European Court of Human Rights 1.13–1.15,
    5.01, 9.01–9.63 *see also* **standing**
abuse of right of petition 9.36
address 9.10
admissibility 9.18–9.54, 10.06, 10.08

European Court of Human Rights (*Cont.*)
  anonymity 9.30
  applications, making 9.10–9.19, 9.50
  blog 10.17
  businesses 9.46
  Butterworths' Human Rights Cases 10.12
  Case Law Information Notes 10.16
  Chambers 9.08, 9.36–9.40, 9.49–9.50,
    9.52, 10.06
  Charter of Fundamental Rights of the EU 5.09
  Committee of Ministers 2.05, 3.48, 9.37, 9.52,
    9.62, 10.07–10.08
  compensation 9.01, 9.51
  compliance with judgments 9.62–9.63, 10.06
  confidentiality 9.30, 10.09
  convention issues, application must
    concern 9.24
  costs 9.51, 9.54, 9.55, 9.59
  creation 2.05
  criminal convictions, quashing or retrials of 9.53
  damages 4.57, 4.63–4.64, 9.51
  declarations of incompatibility 9.01–9.02, 9.27
  declining to follow jurisprudence, reasons
    for 3.50–3.52
  defendants 9.22
  delay 9.05
  disadvantage, where applicants have suffered
    no significant 9.35
  effective remedy, right to an 9.02, 9.27
  effectiveness, principle of 3.54–3.56, 9.02, 9.27
  electronic library 10.19
  EU law, fundamental rights
    doctrine in 5.09–5.10
  European Commission on Human Rights 10.04
  European Court of Justice 5.17
  *European Human Rights Law Review (EH-
    RLR)* 10.12, 10.24
  *European Human Rights Reports
    (EHRR)* 10.11, 10.24
  execution of judgments 9.62–9.63, 10.25
  exhaustion of local remedies 9.02, 9.25–9.27
  extraterritoriality 9.23
  Factsheets 10.16
  forms 9.11, 9.17
  freedom of assembly 7.408
  freedom of association 7.412
  friendly settlements 9.41, 9.61
  funding 9.55–9.60
  government, communication of admissibility
    decisions to 9.38–9.40
  Grand Chamber 9.08, 9.49–9.50, 9.52, 10.06
  hearings 9.47–9.48
  HUDOC database 10.10, 10.16
  Human Rights Act 1998, amendment of 9.01
  incompatibility of applications with provisions
    of ECHR 9.33
  interim measures 9.13–9.14
  international bodies, examination by other 9.32
  interpretation 3.11, 3.49–3.56, 9.01, 9.08

  interpreters 9.47
  intervention 9.39, 9.46
  investigative powers 9.45
  judges 3.55, 9.08
  judgments
    compliance 9.62–9.63, 10.06
    copies 9.49
    final judgments 9.49
    implementation 9.62–9.63, 10.25
    pilot 9.42, 9.52
    reading out 9.49
  judicial reasoning 3.55
  jurisdiction 9.08–9.09, 9.14, 9.18, 9.23
  just satisfaction 9.51, 9.62
  language 9.47
  legal representation 9.16
  living instrument principle 10.08
  location 2.05, 9.10
  manifestly ill-founded applications 9.34, 10.08
  margin of appreciation 3.49, 10.08
  merits test 9.34, 9.40–9.41, 9.43–9.44,
    10.06, 10.08
  non-governmental organisations 9.20, 9.39, 9.46
  number of cases 9.03, 9.05, 10.01
  official reports 10.10–10.12
  oral hearings 9.47–9.48
  parliamentary sovereignty 9.01
  pilot judgments 9.42, 9.52
  precedent 3.51–3.52, 3.56, 10.08
  private and family life, right to respect for 7.220
  private parties, cases against 9.22
  procedure 9.01–9.63
  proportionality 3.55
  Protocol 11 2.05, 10.05–10.07
  referencing system 10.09
  remedial orders 4.93
  remedies 4.57, 4.63–4.64, 9.51–9.53, 9.62
  replies to applications 9.15
  Reports of Judgments and Decisions 10.10
  research 10.01–10.12
  rules of procedure 9.07
  settlements 9.41, 9.61
  specific action, orders to take 9.52
  structure 9.08–9.09
  substantially the same as previous applications,
    petition is 9.31
  third party intervention 9.39, 9.46
  time limits 9.12, 9.27, 9.28
  trade unions 9.20
  urgent cases 9.13–9.14
  victim requirement 4.19–4.20, 9.19, 9.21
  website 9.07
  weight of authorities 10.08
  workload 9.03, 9.05, 9.35, 10.01
*European Human Rights Law Review
  (EHRLR)* 10.12, 10.22, 10.24
European Human Rights Reports (EHRR) 10.11,
  10.14, 10.24
European Social Charter 2.21–2.22, 7.447–7.449

European Union *see* EU law
evangelism 7.336
evictions 7.293, 8.33, 8.45
evidence
  criminal proceedings 4.05
  double jeopardy 8.155
  enforcement of HRA 4.05
  fair hearing, right to a 7.77
  hearsay 7.166, 7.168
  PACE, judicial discretion to exclude of
    evidence under 1.15
  torture 4.38, 6.74–6.78, 7.77
execution of judgments 9.62–9.63, 10.25
executive
  civil servants, political activities of 4.21
  Ministerial Code, breach of 3.44
  Parliament 1.10, 1.20
  politicization of judiciary 1.31–1.33, 1.35–1.36
exhaustion of local remedies
  damages 4.56
  effective remedy, right to an 7.500, 9.27
  EU law 5.17
  European Court of Human Rights 9.02,
    9.25–9.27
  flexibility 9.26
  formalism 9.26
  framework of HRA 3.25
  funding 9.57
  time limits 9.26
explanatory notes 3.42
expropriation 8.05, 8.13, 8.36, 8.46, 8.50, 8.58
expulsion/deportation *see also* extradition
  assurances 6.104
  asylum seekers 8.125
  civil rights and obligations 8.139
  collective measures 8.125
  conditions in prison 6.105
  criminal charges 7.171, 8.139
  definition 8.136
  delay 7.43–7.44
  discrimination 8.125
  effective remedy, right to an 7.498, 7.503
  EU law 5.07
  external territories 8.124
  fair hearing, right to a 7.80, 7.171
  family life, definition of 7.284–7.285
  freedom of association 7.440–7.441
  future of HRA 1.49
  immigration control 7.284–7.285
  inhuman or degrading treatment 6.71,
    6.99–6.108
  International Covenant on Civil and
    Political Rights 8.133–8.139
  liberty and security, right to 7.18, 7.42–7.44
  mandatory life sentences 6.103
  medical treatment, adequacy of 6.106–6.108
  national security 6.100, 7.498, 8.136
  national territory, expulsion from and
    entry into 8.122–8.125

  no punishment without lawful
    authority 7.198, 7.200
  non-state actors, risk from 6.102
  oral hearings 8.138
  procedural rights 8.133–8.139
  proportionality 8.136
  protocol 8.122–8.125
  public opinion 1.49
  public order 8.136
  representation 8.137
  residence 8.134–8.135
  reviews 8.137–8.138
  Special Immigration Appeals
    Commission 7.503
  terrorist suspects 6.78, 7.569–7.570
  third party intervention 9.21
  torture 1.49, 2.27, 4.83, 6.04, 6.65,
    6.78, 6.101, 7.77
  victims, standing of 9.21
  war and emergencies, derogations in
    time of 7.569–7.570
extradition
  death penalty 6.07, 6.71
  effective remedy, right to an 7.497
  fair hearing, right to a 7.80
  inhuman or degrading treatment 6.71, 6.99,
    6.103, 6.105
  liberty and security, right to 7.43
  national territory, expulsion from and
    entry into 8.123
  torture 2.27, 4.83, 6.04, 6.65, 6.78, 6.101
extraterritoriality
  absolute rights 6.04–6.07
  effective remedy, right to an 7.503
  enforcement of HRA 4.101–4.103
  European Court of Human Rights 9.23
  Iraq, UK military action in 4.102–4.103
  jurisdiction 2.23–2.24, 3.10, 4.42
  liberty and security, right to 7.07
  life, right to 4.103, 6.06
  NATO forces in Yugoslavia, air
    strikes by 4.101, 6.05
  torture 4.103
  war and emergencies, derogations in
    time of 7.559

fair hearing, right to a 7.74–7.171
  absolute right, as 7.77
  abuse of rights, prohibition on 7.588
  access to courts 2.12, 7.105, 7.108–7.112,
    7.350, 7.398
  access to legal advice 7.99, 7.158, 7.160–7.164
  adequate time and facilities to prepare
    a case 7.158–7.159
  appeals 7.77, 7.105, 7.135, 7.147, 7.163, 7.171,
    8.140–8.145
  Beijing Rules on Juvenile Justice 2.21
  care workers, provisional blacklisting of 4.79
  civil proceedings 7.76

fair hearing, right to a (*Cont.*)
civil rights and obligations 2.15, 7.79,
    7.81–7.94, 7.148
composite approach 7.146–7.149
contempt proceedings 7.98
convictions, review of 4.05, 8.140
costs proceedings 7.84
criminal charges 2.15, 7.76, 7.79, 7.81–7.84,
    7.95–7.104, 7.137–7.145, 7.150–7.170
defence
    adequate time and resources for
        preparation 7.158–7.159
    effectiveness 7.160–7.161
deportation 7.80
derogations 7.78
determination, definition of 7.79, 7.81–7.84
disciplinary proceedings 7.159
disclosure 7.144
effective participation, right to 7.142
effectiveness principle 2.12, 7.142
employment tribunals 4.42
equality of arms 7.64, 7.105, 7.107, 7.131,
    7.137, 7.143–7.145, 7.165–7.166
EU law, fundamental rights doctrine in 5.09
evidence obtained by torture 7.77
extradition or expulsion 7.80, 7.171
free legal assistance 7.160, 7.163
freedom of expression 7.350
funding 2.32
general entitlements 7.107
genuine or serious disputes (*contestation*) 7.81
guarantees 7.76
homelessness decisions 7.148
implied rights 2.12
independent and impartial tribunal 7.107,
    7.113–7.121, 7.148
International Covenant on Civil and Political
    Rights 8.140–8.145
interpretation 7.74–7.75
interpreters 7.169–7.170
judicial rehearings 7.149
judicial review 7.147–7.149
juries, reasons and 7.135
language 7.157, 7.169–7.170
legal aid 7.99, 7.105, 7.144, 7.160,
    7.163–7.164
legal representation 7.99, 7.158, 7.160–7.164
    choice 7.160
    effectiveness 7.164
    private, right to consultation in 7.162
life sentences, tariff for 4.79
limited and qualified rights 2.28, 7.74–7.171
necessity 7.106
Northern Ireland 7.588
opportunity to present case 7.107, 7.131–7.134
Parole Board decisions 7.101
positive obligations 2.32
presumption of innocence 7.150–7.155
private parties 3.73

    private, right to consultation with
        lawyers in 7.162
    procedural safeguards 7.156–7.170
    proportionality 7.106
    public hearings 7.107, 7.122–7.125
    public interest immunity certificates 7.144
    quasi-legal proceedings 7.82
    real and effective fair trials 7.105, 7.107
    reasonable time 7.126–7.130
    reasons 7.107, 7.135–7.136
    rehearings 7.149
    review of sentences and convictions 8.140–8.141
    rule of law 7.74
    scope 7.79–7.103
    self-incrimination, privilege against 7.138, 7.141
    sentences, review of 8.140–8.141
    silence, right to 7.138–7.141
    standing 4.16
    terrorists 7.80, 7.588
    torture, evidence obtained by 7.77
    witnesses 7.165–7.177
false imprisonment
    habeas corpus 4.10
    inhuman or degrading treatment 4.10
    judicial review 4.10
    liberty and security, right to 4.10
families *see* **family life, definition of; family, right
        to found a; private and family life,
        right to respect for**
    family courts 4.09
    investigations, family involvement in 6.39
    victims, standing of 4.20
family life, definition of 7.266–7.287
    adoption 7.280, 7.282
    anonymous births 7.279
    asylum seekers, removal of 7.285
    biological ties 7.276–7.277
    civil partnerships 7.275
    cohabitation 7.270
    Convention on the Rights of the Child 7.286
    couples 7.269–7.270
    deportation 7.284–7.285
    dissolving family ties 7.281
    engagements 7.269
    family relationships 7.280
    foster relationships 7.280
    immigration control 7.283–7.287
    marriages 7.268, 7.269, 7.271
    marry and found a family, right to 7.268
    parents and children 7.276–7.282
    paternity, presumption of 7.281
    polygamous marriages 7.270
    proportionality 7.284, 7.285
    same sex relationships 7.267, 7.271–7.275
    transsexuals 7.272
family, right to found a 7.477–7.489
    adoption 7.478–7.479
    artificial insemination 7.480–7.484
    cohabitation, right to 7.488

family life, definition of 7.268
limited and qualified rights 2.28, 7.459–7.460,
    7.477–7.489
medical negligence 7.479
positive obligations 7.484, 7.487–7.489
prisoners 7.481
private and family life, right to
    respect for 7.460–7.461, 7.487
proportionality 7.485–7.486, 7.488
transsexuals 7.489
fast-track procedure 3.14, 4.72, 4.92–4.99
foetuses, right to life of 6.11–6.18
forced or compulsory labour
    absolute rights 6.115–6.116, 6.120–6.127
    discrimination 7.511
    lawyers, pro bono work by 6.122
    military service, conscientious objection to 6.123
    positive obligations 6.125–6.127
    servitude 6.121
fostering 7.223, 7.280
framework of ECHR 2.01–2.83
    civil and political rights 2.02
    Committee of Ministers, creation of 2.05
    economic and social rights 2.02
    European Commission on Human Rights,
        abolition of 2.05
    European Court of Human Rights,
        creation of 2.05
    individual petition, right of 2.02, 2.04
    interpretation 2.07–2.24
    margin of appreciation 2.77–2.83
    Protocol 11 2.05
    public authorities 3.57–3.71
    restrictions on rights 2.40–2.76
    scope of Convention rights 2.25–2.39
    Universal Declaration of Human Rights 2.02
framework of HRA 3.01–3.81
    courts and tribunals, obligations of 3.30
    declarations of incompatibility 3.07, 3.14
    definition of Convention rights 3.09–3.10
    derogations 3.27
    exhaustion of local remedies 3.25
    freedom of expression 3.26
    further effect to ECHR, giving 3.07, 3.09
    horizontal effect 3.20
    interpretation 3.02–3.04, 3.07, 3.11–3.12,
        3.31–3.56
    judicial acts 3.24
    judicial discretion 3.24
    overview of key provisions 3.08–3.27
    parliamentary sovereignty 3.02, 3.07, 3.29
    primary legislation 3.07
    private parties 3.05–3.07, 3.20, 3.72–3.74
    public authorities 3.04–3.07, 3.15–3.22, 3.29,
        3.57–3.71
    remedies 3.23, 3.25
    reservations 3.27
    safeguard for existing human rights 3.25
    secondary legislation 3.07

special cases 3.06, 3.75–3.81
statements of compatibility 3.13, 3.43–3.44
storage of information 7.419
summary of effects 3.07–3.08
thought, conscience and religion,
    freedom of 3.26
victims 3.05, 3.07
freedom of assembly 7.408–7.437 see also
    protest, right to
    balancing rights 7.414
    common law 1.09
    European Court of Human Rights 7.412
    freedom of association 7.408
    freedom of expression 7.411
    legality 7.413
    legitimate aim 7.413
    liberty and security, right to 7.411
    limited and qualified rights 2.30, 7.408–7.437
    necessary in a democratic society 7.413
    obstruction of police or highways 4.10
    overlap with other rights 7.411–7.412
    peaceful assembly 7.415–7.437
    political nature of right 7.408
    positive obligations 7.457–7.458
    private and family life, right to respect for 7.411
    proportionality 7.412
    thought, conscience and religion,
        freedom of 7.411
    trespassory assembly 1.11
    Universal Declaration of Human Rights 7.408
freedom of association 7.438–7.456
    administration of the state, members of 7.414,
        7.455–7.456
    armed forces 7.413, 7.455–7.456
    balancing rights 7.414
    bans or dissolution of associations 7.452–7.453
    closed shops 7.444
    collective bargaining 7.438, 7.448
    definition 7.438
    democracy 7.450–7.453
    discrimination 7.428
    European Court of Human Rights 7.412
    European Social Charter 7.447–7.449
    exclusion or expulsion 7.440–7.441
    financial disincentives offered by
        employers 7.458
    form and join associations, right to 7.409,
        7.439–7.442
    freedom of assembly 7.408
    freedom of expression 7.411–7.412
    hunting bans 7.439, 7.441
    labels 7.442
    legal status to associations, refusal
        to give 7.442
    legality 7.413
    legitimate aim 7.413
    liberty and security, right to 7.411
    limited and qualified rights 2.30, 7.408–7.414,
        7.438–7.456

freedom of association (*Cont.*)
necessary in a democratic society 7.413,
7.450–7.451
non-association, right to 7.443–7.444
overlap with other rights 7.411–7.412
pluralism 7.450–7.451
police 7.413, 7.455–7.456
political associations 7.440, 7.452–7.453
political nature of right 7.408
positive obligations 7.457–7.458
private and family life, right to respect for 7.411
professional bodies 7.445–7.446
proportionality 7.442, 7.444
public authorities 3.16, 7.445–7.446
register associations, refusal to 7.442
scope of the right 7.438–7.442
strike, right to 7.438, 7.448
terrorism, support for 7.452–7.453
thought, conscience and religion, freedom
of 7.411–7.412
trade unions, right to form and join 7.409,
7.428, 7.439–7.440, 7.444, 7.447–7.449,
7.455–7.456, 7.458
Universal Declaration of Human
Rights 7.408–7.409
violence, propagating 7.452–7.454
freedom of expression 7.349–7.407
abuse of rights, prohibition on 7.589–7.590
access to court 7.350, 7.398
access to information 7.364–7.366, 7.397
access to personal material 7.364
anonymity orders 7.263, 7.364
anti-Semitism 7.362–7.363
artistic expression 7.357, 7.359, 7.362
balancing exercise 7.253, 7.261, 6.263–7.264,
7.373, 7.379, 7.395–7.396, 7.400, 7.406
blasphemy 2.49
broadcasting
access to balanced, informative and
pluralistic services 7.369
licensing 7.373–7.377
party political broadcasts 7.376–7.377
children in legal proceedings,
identification of 7.261–7.262
chilling effect 7.256, 7.372, 7.383, 7.398
comfort clauses 3.26, 7.405
commercial expression 7.357, 7.360
common law 1.09, 7.351–7.352, 7.381
companies 7.353
conditional fee agreements, success
fees and 7.398
confidentiality 7.257–7.259
conflict with other rights 7.396–7.399
content of expression 7.362
costs 7.398
Court of Protection proceedings 7.365
criminal sanctions 7.388, 7.400
damages 7.372, 7.386
defamation

access to court 7.398
conditional fee agreements, success
fees and 7.398
costs 7.398
criminal sanctions 7.388
damages 7.372
Internet 7.389
local authorities 1.15
private and family life, right to respect
for 7.254
United States, proof of malice with regard
to public figures in 7.358
democratic process, protection of 7.350
disciplinary action 7.392
effective remedy, right to an 7.367
elections, right to free 8.107, 8.111
emotional suffering, intentional
infliction of 7.257
everyone, definition of 7.353–7.354
ex parte orders 7.405
exceptions 7.373–7.399
fair hearing, right to a 7.350
foreseeability 7.380
framework of HRA 3.26
freedom of assembly 7.411
freedom of association 7.411–7.412
freedom of the press 3.78, 7.262–7.263, 7.361
hate speech 7.363, 7.372, 7.384, 7.387
Holocaust denial 7.363, 7.399
imprisonment for hate speech 7.372
injunctions 7.405–7.407
insults 7.362
interferences 7.370–7.372
Internet 7.377, 7.389
investigative duties 7.367
journalistic sources, protection of 7.361,
7.368, 7.380
legal persons 7.353
legality 2.49, 7.378, 7.380–7.381
legitimate aim 7.378–7.379, 7.382, 7.394
licensing 7.373–7.377
limited and qualified rights 2.30, 7.349–7.407
local authorities 1.15
manifest one's beliefs, right to 7.350
margin of appreciation 2.80, 7.360, 7.382,
7.400–7.404
media 3.78–3.80, 7.351, 7.353, 7.364–7.365
anonymity orders 7.364
broadcasting 7.369, 7.373–7.377
comfort clause 7.405
costs 7.398
Court of Protection proceedings 7.365
defamation 7.398
freedom of the press 3.78, 7.262–7.263, 7.361
injunctions 7.405–7.407
super-injunctions 7.407
medium of communication 7.356,
7.383, 7.387
national security 7.394

necessary in a democratic society 7.378,
  7.382–7.395
non-governmental organizations 7.353
objective of expression 7.387
obscenity 2.49
offensive, shocking or disturbing
  speech 7.362–7.363, 7.399, 7.401
official secrets 7.394
overlap with other rights 7.350, 7.396–7.399
party political broadcasts 5.585, 7.376–7.377
philosophical underpinning 7.349
political activity of aliens, restrictions on 5.585
political expression 7.357–7.358
  defamation 7.358
  definition 7.358
  disciplinary action 7.392
positive obligations 7.367–7.369
potential recipients of information 7.354
pre-notification requirements 7.256,
  7.404, 7.407
prior restraint 7.264, 7.371
privacy 7.350, 7.397, 7.405
private and family life, right to respect for 3.78,
  3.80, 7.253–7.265
private information 7.246
private, proceedings held in 7.365
procedural safeguards 7.367–7.368
proportionality 2.64, 2.65, 4.116, 7.261,
  7.354, 7.377, 7.383, 7.386, 7.388–7.394,
  7.398
protest, right to 7.425
  public interest 7.358
  United States 7.358
protests 7.350, 7.395, 7.412, 7.436–7.437
public figures 7.358
public interest 3.79, 7.256, 7.265, 7.358, 7.360,
  7.385
public morality 7.400–7.404
public order 7.390–7.393
racist speech 7.363, 7.387, 7.589–7.590
receive opinions and information, right
  to 7.354–7.355
religion 7.402–7.403
reporting restrictions 7.262
reputation 7.246
scope of right 7.355–7.366
sensational and titillating reporting 7.256
state employees 7.354
super-injunctions 7.264, 7.407
thought, conscience and religion, freedom
  of 7.350
tobacco advertising 7.360
trade union members 7.354
types of expression 7.357
victims 7.354
vote and stand for office, right to 7.350, 8.107,
  8.111
freedom of information 1.25, 7.364–7.366,
  7.397

freedom of movement 8.116–8.121
  economic welfare 8.119
  EU law 5.07, 5.19
  external territories 8.121
  leave state, freedom to 8.120
  legality 8.117
  margin of appreciation 8.117
  necessity 8.118
  proportionality 8.117
  protocol 8.116–8.121
  public interest 8.119
  restrictions 8.118–8.119
freedom of the press 3.78, 7.262–7.263, 7.361
friendly settlements 9.41, 9.61
fundamental rights doctrine in EU law 5.03–5.10
  accession to ECHR 5.03
  Amsterdam Treaty 5.05
  Charter of Fundamental Rights of the EU 5.03,
    5.05, 5.09, 5.11–5.16
  competence of EU 5.05
  deportation 5.07
  direct effect 5.06
  divergences in interpretation 5.08
  European Court of Human Rights 5.09–5.10
  fair hearing, right to a 5.09
  free movement rights 5.07
  general principles of EU law 5.03
  interpretation 5.08
  self-incrimination, privilege against 5.08
  supremacy of EU law 5.06
  television licences, restrictions on 5.07
funding
  conditional fee agreements 7.398, 9.58
  contributions 9.60
  costs 9.55, 9.59
  damages 4.65
  eligibility 9.60
  equality of arms 7.144
  European Court of Human Rights 9.55–9.60
  exhaustion of local remedies 9.57
  fair hearing, right to a 2.32, 7.105
  friendly settlements 9.61
  Legal Services Commission 9.56–9.57
  means test 9.60
  pressure groups 9.58
  pro bono work 9.58
  Strasbourg legal aid 9.59–9.61
  trade unions 9.58
future of HRA 1.39, 1.49–1.55
  bill of rights
    Commission on a Bill of Rights 1.52–1.55
    consultation 1.51
    green paper 1.50, 1.54
    proportionality 1.54
    public interest 1.54
    responsibilities, reference to 1.54
  deportation to countries where there is risk of
    torture 1.49
  European Court of Human Rights 9.01

future of HRA (*Cont.*)
    Joint Committee on Human Rights 1.50
    press 1.49
    prisoners' right to vote 1.53
    privacy, creation of law of 1.49
    public opinion 1.49
    rebalancing 1.49

gagging injunctions 3.79–3.80, 7.264, 7.407
gaps in protection 1.25
gender reassignment *see* **transsexuals**
Gibraltar residents to vote in European
    Parliamentary elections 5.20
good faith 2.53, 2.67 *see also* bad faith
gypsies and travellers, discrimination
    against 7.506

habeas corpus 1.06, 4.10, 7.61
Hansard 3.42, 10.27–10.28
harassment 7.340
hate speech
    freedom of expression 7.363, 7.372,
      7.384, 7.387
    Holocaust denial 7.363, 7.399
    imprisonment 7.372
    racist speech 7.363, 7.387
hearings *see also* **fair hearing, right to a**
    European Court of Human Rights 9.47–9.48
    expulsion/deportation 8.138
    oral hearings 7.122, 8.138, 9.47–9.48
    private, proceedings held in 7.123–7.124, 7.365
    public hearings 7.107, 7.122–7.125
hearsay 7.166, 7.168
historical background 1.01–1.16, 2.01
Holocaust denial 7.363, 7.399
home, definition of 7.288–7.295
    evictions 7.293
    failure to provide a particular home 7.291
    homes for life promises 7.293
    hospital stays 7.289
    intends to live, where one 7.290
    legitimate expectations 7.291
    offices 7.289
    possession orders 7.292–7.295
    procedural safeguards 7.293
    proportionality 7.293–7.295
    re-establishing home life 7.290
    repossession proceedings 7.294
    second homes 7.289
home schooling 8.67, 8.72
homelessness 4.42, 7.93, 7.148
housing *see also* **home, definition of; private**
    and family life, right to respect for
    destruction of homes 8.48
    discrimination 4.42, 4.79, 4.82
    homelessness 4.42, 7.93, 7.148
    housing benefit 8.12
    hybrid or functional authorities 3.71
    immigration control 4.79

peaceful enjoyment of possessions 8.48
    private and family life, right to respect for 7.224
HUDOC database 10.10, 10.16
Human Rights Alerter 10.22
Human Rights Law Reports – UK 10.21
Human Rights Updater 10.22
hunger strikes 6.111–6.112
hunting ban
    freedom of association 7.439, 7.441
    peaceful enjoyment of possessions 8.34,
      8.44, 8.47
    private life, definition of 7.233
    thought, conscience and religion,
      freedom of 7.308
hybrid or functional authorities 3.60–3.71
    contracting out 3.66, 3.68–3.71
    definition 3.60–3.70
    delegation 3.63–3.64
    housing management functions 3.71
    Joint Committee on Human Rights 3.66, 3.71
    judicial review 3.63
    public interest 3.69

illegality 3.22
illegitimacy 4.20
immigration
    children, best interests of 7.284, 7.286
    control 4.79
    Convention on the Rights of the Child 7.286
    deportation 7.284–7.285
    detention 6.85, 7.46, 7.50
    family life, definition of 7.283–7.287
    Hardial Singh principles 7.46
    housing 4.79
    liberty and security, right to 7.46, 7.50
    marriage 7.253
    proportionality 7.284
    reasons, right to be given 7.50
    Special Immigration Appeals
      Commission 6.74–6.78, 7.503
immunity
    access to courts 7.110–7.112
    blanket immunity 7.111
    fair, just and reasonable test 7.111–7.112
    police 7.111–7.112
    public interest immunity certificates 7.144
    torture, state immunity and 6.66
impartiality *see* **independent and impartial**
    tribunals
incorporation of European Convention on
    Human Rights
    commission, proposal for a 1.22
    common law 1.17, 2.03
    elective dictatorship 1.18
    entrenchment 1.19–1.22
    judiciary, party politics and 1.21
    Labour Party conference 1993 1.22
    notwithstanding clause procedure 1.22, 1.24
    parliamentary sovereignty 1.17, 1.19–1.20, 1.28

party politics 1.18, 1.21
separation of powers 1.17
unwritten constitution, flexibility of 1.17
indefinite sentences for public protection (IPP)
sentences 6.80
independent and impartial tribunals
appearance of impartiality 7.114
composite approach 7.148
courts martial 7.116-7.118
criminal proceedings 7.113
fair hearing, right to a 7.107, 7.113–7.121,
7.148
jury bias 7.119–7.121
legality 7.115
military tribunals 7.116–7.118
separation of powers 7.115
individual right of petition 1.12, 1.18, 2.02, 2.04
infectious diseases, detention of
persons with 7.33, 7.41
information and advice, duty to provide 2.34
inheritance laws 8.31
inhuman or degrading treatment 6.55–6.114
absolute rights 6.55–6.114
agents, responsibility for acts of 6.72
Al Sweady Inquiry 6.91
assisted suicide 6.98
assurances, reliance on 6.104
asylum seekers, subsistence for 4.106, 6.110
autonomy 6.61
Baha Mousa Inquiry 6.91
children in adult prisons 6.83
corporal punishment 6.94–6.95
counter-terrorism 6.74–6.78
damages 4.66
death penalty 6.07, 6.71
definition 6.58, 6.67–6.68
degrading treatment, definition of 6.58
deportation and removal 6.71, 6.99–6.108
detention 6.81–6.88, 6.90–6.91, 6.105,
6.111–6.113
dignity 6.61, 6.70, 6.85
extradition 6.71, 6.99, 6.103, 6.105
false imprisonment 4.10
hunger strikes 6.111–6.112
immigration detention 6.85
indefinite sentences for public protection (IPP)
sentences 6.80
inhuman treatment, definition of 6.58
interrogations 6.69
investigative duty 6.56, 6.88–6.92
Iraqi detainees, allegations of ill-treatment
of 6.91
judicial punishments 6.68
living instrument, ECHR as 6.59
mandatory life sentences 6.79–6.80, 6.103
medical treatment abroad,
adequacy of 6.106–6.108
mental health patients, compulsory
treatment for 6.88

negative obligations 6.73–6.88
non-state actors, risk from 6.102
omissions 4.107
police 6.97
positive obligations 4.107, 6.89–6.113
prevention 6.93–6.98
prison conditions 6.81–6.84
race discrimination 6.70
reasonable punishment of children 6.94–6.95
schoolchildren, protestors' abuse of 6.97
scope 6.58–6.71
Scotland 6.84, 6.86
self-inflicted conditions 6.111–6.113
sentencing 6.79–6.80, 6.103
severity, minimum level of 6.59, 6.103, 6.109
sexual abuse, failure to protect children
from 6.96
slopping out 6.84
state responsibility 6.72
state support 6.109–6.110
subsistence 6.110
terrorist suspects 6.74–6.78
threshold 6.59, 6.103, 6.109
torture distinguished 6.62, 6.68
transfers 6.83, 6.110
vulnerable adults, failure to protect 6.96
warning decisions 6.114
whole life sentences 6.80
injunctions
enforcement of HRA 4.05
freedom of expression 7.405–7.407
super or gagging injunctions 3.79–3.80, 7.264,
7.407
innocence, presumption of *see* **presumption**
of innocence
inquests 6.42–6.46
institutional framework 1.37–1.48
insults 7.362
intellectual property 8.14–8.15
interception of communications
correspondence, right to respect for 7.247
prisoners' correspondence 2.53, 2.64,
7.296–7.297, 7.494
private and family life, right to respect for 1.14,
7.247–7.248
telephones 1.14, 2.47, 7.296
interim measures 9.13–9.14
international bodies, examination of cases by 9.32
International Court of Justice website 10.03
International Covenant on Civil and Political
Rights (ICCPR) 1.04, 8.129–8.158
contractual obligations, deprivation of liberty
on grounds of inability to fulfil 8.114
discrimination 7.253
double jeopardy 8.151–8.155
entry into force 8.130
expulsion 8.133–8.139
fair hearing, right to a 8.140–8.145
interpretation 1.55, 2.22, 8.132

International Covenant on Civil and Political Rights (ICCPR) (*Cont.*)
matrimonial property 8.131, 8.156–8.158
miscarriages of justice, compensation for 8.146–8.150
peaceful enjoyment of possessions 8.02
protocol 8.129–8.158
ratification 8.131
spouses, equal rights and responsibilities of 8.156–8.158
International Covenant on Economic, Social and Cultural Rights (ICESCR) 1.04, 8.02
international law
interpretation 2.20
life, right to 6.28
torture 6.66
war and emergencies, derogations in time of 7.561, 7.563, 7.578
Internet 7.377, 7.389
interpretation 2.07–2.24
ambiguity 1.16
amendment of legislation 3.40, 3.45
autonomous concepts 2.14–2.16
Beijing Rules on Juvenile Justice 2.21
Charter of Fundamental Rights of the EU 2.21, 5.12, 5.14, 5.21
Children Act 1989 3.40
common law 3.12
Convention on the Elimination of All Forms of Racial Discrimination 2.22
Convention on the Rights of the Child 1.55, 2.21
Council of Europe 2.22
declarations of incompatibility 3.38, 3.45–3.47, 4.73
deference and discretionary area of judgment 4.124
dynamic interpretation 2.17–2.19
effectiveness principle 2.11–2.13, 3.54–3.56
Equality and Human Rights Commission 2.06
EU law 3.34, 5.01, 5.08, 5.21, 5.23
European Commission on Human Rights 10.05
European Court of Human Rights 3.11, 3.49–3.56, 9.01, 9.08
European Social Charter 2.21–2.22
explanatory notes 3.42
fair hearing, right to a 7.74–7.75
framework of ECHR 2.07–2.24
framework of HRA 3.02–3.04, 3.07, 3.11–3.12, 3.31–3.56
Hansard 3.42, 10.27–10.28
human rights instruments, recourse to other 2.20–2.22
International Covenant on Civil and Political Rights 1.55, 2.22, 8.132
international law, rules of 2.20
judiciary, politicization of 1.31
jurisdiction 2.23–2.24
limitation on use of restriction on rights 7.595

living instrument, as 1.25, 2.17–2.19
margin of appreciation 2.78, 3.49
natural meaning 3.36
object and purpose 2.08–2.10, 2.12
parliamentary intention 3.36
parliamentary sovereignty 1.28, 3.38
peaceful enjoyment of possessions 8.07
political activity of aliens, restrictions on 5.579
precedent 3.51–3.52, 3.56
primary legislation 3.12, 3.31–3.32, 3.35–3.40, 3.45
proportionality 3.42
public authorities, definition of 3.12
purposive approach 2.09, 3.34
reading down 3.37
reading in 2.12, 3.17, 3.37, 3.39
reservations 2.72
retrospectivity 4.33
secondary legislation 3.07, 3.12, 3.31–3.32, 3.36
standing 3.33
statements of compatibility 3.43, 3.45
statutory provision which breaches ECHR, identification of 3.35
travaux préparatoires 10.19
UN human rights bodies 2.22
UN human rights instruments 2.22
interpreters 7.169–7.170
intervention *see* third party intervention
investigations *see also* investigative duties under Article 2 (right to life)
Equality and Human Rights Commission 4.48, 4.52
European Court of Human Rights 9.45
freedom of expression 7.367
inhuman or degrading treatment 6.56, 6.88–6.92
torture 6.92
investigative duties under Article 2 (right to life) 4.42, 6.09, 6.33–6.47
access to reports or materials 6.40
armed forces, inquests and 6.46
deaths or near-deaths in custody 6.41–6.45
domestic violence 6.34
effective remedy, right to an 6.47
effectiveness 6.37–6.38, 6.47
enhanced investigations 6.45
extraterritoriality 4.103
family involvement 6.39
inquests 6.42–6.46
medical negligence cases, inquests in 6.46
police, independence of 6.38
positive obligations 2.35, 4.105
use of force 6.33–6.47
Iraq, UK military action in
Al Sweady Inquiry 6.91
Baha Mousa Inquiry 6.91
extraterritoriality 4.102–4.103
inhuman or degrading treatment 6.91
international law 6.28

jurisdiction 2.23, 4.102–4.103, 6.06–6.08
liberty and security, right to 7.97
life, right to 4.103, 6.06, 6.08, 6.28
torture 4.103
Ireland
abortion 4.21
divorce, ban on 4.20
irrationality 4.111–4.112, 4.115
Islamic dress
education, right to 8.84–8.85
manifest one's religion or beliefs,
right to 7.322, 7.327–7.331,
7.337–7.338, 7.341

Joint Committee on Human Rights
bill of rights, inquiry into 1.50
bills, scrutiny of 1.42
creation 1.40
discrimination 8.160
enforcement of HRA 4.132
Equality and Human Rights Commission 4.46
execution of judgments 9.73
future of HRA 1.50
hybrid or functional authorities 3.66, 3.71
judgments, implementation of 10.25
judiciary, politicization of 1.33
pre-legislative scrutiny 4.132
reasons 10.25
remedial orders 1.41, 4.92
statements of compatibility 4.132
terms of reference 1.41
vote, right to 8.101, 9.63
journalistic sources, protection of 7.361, 7.368,
7.380
journals 10.20, 10.22
judgments of ECtHR
compliance 9.62–9.63, 10.06
copies 9.49
implementation 9.62–9.63
final judgments 9.49
pilot judgments 9.42, 9.52
reading out 9.49
judicial review
Civil Procedure Rules 4.05
damages 4.55, 4.67, 4.68
declarations of incompatibility 4.25
deference and discretionary area of
judgment 4.120
effective remedy, right to an 7.494–7.499
emanations of the state 5.26
enforcement of HRA 4.05
Equality and Human Rights
Commission 1.46, 4.25–4.28, 4.40, 4.43
EU law 5.26
fair hearing, right to a 7.147–7.149
false imprisonment 4.10
illegality 3.22
intervention 4.40
irrationality 4.111–4.,112

Judicial Review 10.22
liberty and security, right to 7.35
maladministration 4.55
mandatory orders 4.05
private parties 3.73
prohibiting orders 4.05
proportionality 4.11–4.112, 4.116
public authorities 3.22, 3.57, 3.63, 5.26
quashing orders 4.05
standing 4.16, 4.23–4.25
victims 4.23–4.25
Wednesbury unreasonableness 4.112
judiciary
acts 3.24, 4.13
damages 3.24, 4.13, 4.68
democratic dialogue 1.35
discretion 1.34, 3.24
European Convention on Human Rights,
incorporation of 1.21
European Court of Human Rights 3.55, 9.08
executive 1.31–1.33, 1.35–1.36
framework of HRA 3.24
Joint Parliamentary Committee on Human
Rights 1.33
judicial activism 1.32, 1.34, 1.36
parliamentary sovereignty 1.28–1.31,
1.35–1.36
politicization 1.21, 1.28–1.36
reasoning 3.55
statements of compatibility 1.33
statutory interpretation 1.31
jurisdiction
absolute rights 6.03–6.08
appropriate forum 4.10–4.15
Charter of Fundamental Rights of
the EU 5.16
damages 4.53–4.55
declarations of incompatibility 4.77
definition 2.23–2.24
enforcement of HRA 4.04
European Court of Human Rights 9.08–9.09,
9.14, 9.18, 9.23
extraterritoriality 2.23–2.24, 3.10, 4.42,
6.04–6.08
interpretation 2.23–2.24
Iraqi, UK forces in 2.23, 4.102–4.103,
6.06–6.08
military occupations 6.05
jurisprudence, researching *see* **researching human
rights jurisprudence**
jury, trials by
bias 7.119–7.121
Magna Carta 1.06
media coverage 7.121
racism 7.120
reasons 7.135
sex discrimination 7.526

kettling 4.110, 7.411, 7.426

labour *see* forced or compulsory labour
language
  criminal charges 7.157, 7.169–7.170
  discrimination 8.86
  education, right to 8.64, 8.86
  European Court of Human Rights 9.47
  fair hearing, right to a 7.157, 7.169–7.170
  interpreters 7.169–7.170
  translations 7.157, 7.169–7.170
law reports 10.10–10.12, 10.16, 10.20-10.21,
    10.24, 10.26
lawful chastisement 6.94–6.95, 7.319, 7.340, 8.78
Lawtel 10.24
lawyers *see* legal representation
leasehold enfranchisement 8.40
legal funding *see* funding
legal representation
  access to legal advice 7.99, 7.158, 7.160–7.164
  appeals 7.163
  choice 7.160
  committal 7.163
  criminal charges 7.99, 7.158, 7.160–7.164
  deprivation of liberty 7.99
  effectiveness 7.164
  employment tribunals 4.42
  Equality and Human Rights Commission 1.46,
    4.43, 4.47
  European Court of Human Rights 9.16
  expulsion/deportation 8.137
  fair hearing, right to a 7.99, 7.158, 7.160–7.164
  forced or compulsory labour 6.122
  pro bono 6.122, 9.58
  special advocates 7.65–7.66, 7.110, 7.144
Legal Services Commission (LSC) 9.56–9.57
legality
  accessibility of law 2.44–2.45, 4.108
  certainty rule 2.46–2.49
  common law 2.43
  contempt of court 2.48
  derogations 2.42
  enforcement of HRA 4.108–4.110
  EU law 2.43
  freedom of assembly 7.413
  freedom of association 7.413
  freedom of expression 2.49, 7.378, 7.380–7.381
  freedom of movement 8.117
  independent and impartial tribunals 7.115
  interception of telephone calls 2.47
  kettling 4.110
  liberty and security, right to 7.34
  manifest one's religion or beliefs,
    right to 7.334–7.335
  margin of appreciation 2.80
  no punishment without lawful authority 7.174
  Parliament 1.09
  presumption 1.09
  private and family life, right to
    respect for 7.226–7.227
  professional bodies 2.43

protestors 4.110
  restrictions on Convention rights 2.41–2.49
  rule of law 2.42, 2.44
  secondary legislation 2.43
  stop and search powers under
    Terrorism Act 2000 2.47, 4.109
legislation *see also* primary legislation;
    secondary legislation
  abstract review of legislation 4.132
  amendments 3.40, 3.45
  bills 1.42,3.13, 3.43–3.44
  failure to legislate 3.18
  interpretation 3.40, 3.45
  pre-legislative scrutiny 1.10, 1.42, 4.132
  striking down 3.14, 5.22–5.23
legitimate aims
  discrimination 7.530–7.535
  elections, right to free 8.89–8.90
  examples 2.52
  freedom of assembly 7.413
  freedom of association 7.413
  freedom of expression 7.378–7.379, 7.382,
    7.394
  good faith 2.53
  limited and qualified rights 2.31
  manifest one's religion or beliefs,
    right to 7.334–7.335, 7.338
  marry, right to 7.465–7.466
  pressing social need 2.59
  prisoner's correspondence, interference with 2.53
  proportionality 4.116
  protest, right to 7.433
  restrictions on Convention rights 2.41,
    2.50–2.53
  use of lethal force 6.50
legitimate expectations 7.291, 8.05, 8.11–8.12,
    8.18–8.22
LexisNexis online database 10.24
libel, local authorities and 1.15
liberty and security, right to
  adversarial proceedings 7.64
  alcoholics 7.33
  arbitrariness 7.04, 7.34
  arrest 7.28–7.30, 7.48–7.51
  asylum seekers, detention of 7.45
  bail 7.51, 7.54–7.56, 7.64
  bankrupts 7.26
  Bournewood gap 7.39
  burden of proof 7.37
  care arrangements 7.18
  causal connection between conviction and
    detention 7.24–7.25
  challenging lawfulness of detention,
    ability to 7.57–7.69
  charges, reasons for 7.48–7.49
  children 7.32
  common law 1.09
  compensation 7.73
  conditional discharge, deferral of 7.40

conditions of detention 7.72
control orders 7.15–7.16
convictions by competent courts 7.22–7.25
court orders or fulfil legal obligations,
    failure to observe 7.26–7.27
damages 4.68, 7.73
delay 7.43–7.44, 7.52, 7.57–7.63, 7.69
deportation, detention pending 7.18, 7.42–7.44
derogations 7.08–7.09, 7.47
drug addicts 7.33–7.34
education 7.32
equality of arms 7.64
examples of deprivation of liberty 7.12
exceptions 7.20–7.47
exemplary damages 7.73
extradition 7.43
extraterritoriality 7.07
false imprisonment 4.10
freedom of assembly 7.411
freedom of association 7.411
grounds for deprivation of liberty 7.42–7.47
habeas corpus 7.61
Hardial Singh principles 7.46
immigration detention 7.46, 7.50
infectious diseases, people with 7.33, 7.41
Iraq, detention in 7.07
judicial review 7.35
legal certainty 7.34
length of detention 7.51–7.53
life sentences, tariff period in 7.67–7.69
limited and qualified rights 7.03–7.73, 7.594
local authority obligations 7.70
mental disabilities 7.33–7.39
    amenability to treatment 7.38
    Bournewood gap 7.39
    burden of proof 7.36
    care arrangements 7.18
    challenges to detention 7.63, 7.66
    conditional discharge, deferral of 7.40
    Mental Health Review Tribunal 4.10, 4.68
    positive obligations 7.70
    procedural rules 7.21, 7.39
    reasons 7.49
necessity 7.28, 7.39
offender behaviour programmes, access to 7.25
Parole Board 7.58, 7.66–7.69
positive obligations 7.70–7.72
pre-trial detention of foreign terrorist
    suspects 7.09, 7.53, 7.65
preventive detention 7.30
procedural safeguards 7.06, 7.20, 7.48–7.69
proportionality 7.17, 7.27–7.28,
    7.33–7.34, 7.42
protest, right to 7.17, 7.31, 7.411
public hearings 7.64
public interest 7.52
reasonable suspicion 7.29
reasons 7.48–7.50
remand 7.28

restrictions of liberty 7.10–7.11
special advocate procedure 7.65–7.66
Special Immigration Appeals
    Commission 7.65
stop and search 7.13–7.14
terrorist suspects
    control orders 7.15–7.16
    length of detention 7.53
    pre-trial detention terrorist suspects 7.09,
        7.53, 7.65, 7.570
    preventive detention 7.30, 7.575
torture 4.83
war and emergencies, derogations in
    time of 7.570
licensing 5.07, 7.373–7.377
life, right to 6.09–6.54 *see also* **investigative
        duties under Article 2 (right to life)**
abortion 6.16–6.17
absolute rights 2.26
assisted suicide 6.27
conjoined twins, separation of 6.30
crime prevention 6.19–6.24
criminal charges 7.166
death penalty, abolition of 6.10
deaths in custody 4.105
detention 6.20, 6.25–6.26
die, right to 4.104, 6.27
domestic violence, prevention of 6.23
'everyone' 6.11–6.18
extraterritoriality 6.06
fair hearing, right to a 7.166
foetuses 6.11–6.18
Gibraltar killings 6.49
international law, compliance with 6.28
Iraq, UK military operations in 4.103, 6.06,
    6.08, 6.28
lethal force 6.48–6.50
margin of appreciation 6.13, 6.18
medical treatment 6.25, 6.27, 6.30
mental disabilities 4.105, 6.26
natural disasters 6.22
near-deaths in custody 4.42
negligence by state forces 6.31
persistent vegetative state, treatment for
    persons in a 6.27
police 6.21, 6.24
positive obligations 2.35, 4.104–4.105
procedural obligations 4.42, 6.09,
    6.33–6.47
standing 6.53–6.54
suicide 6.20, 6.26–6.27
taking life, prohibition on 6.29–6.32
use of force 6.29, 6.31–6.53
witnesses 7.166
life sentences
fair hearing, right to a 4.79
inhuman or degrading treatment 6.79–6.80,
    6.103
liberty and security, right to 7.67–7.69

life sentences (*Cont.*)
mandatory life sentences 6.79–6.80, 6.103
no punishment without law 7.205–7.209
tariffs 4.79, 7.67–7.69
limitation on use of restriction
on rights 7.591–7.595
limitation periods *see* time limits
limited and qualified rights 7.01–7.595 *see also*
restrictions on Convention rights
discrimination 7.504–7.546
education 2.28–2.29
effective remedy, right to an 7.492–7.500
elections 2.28
fair hearing, right to a 2.28–2.29, 7.74–7.171
family, right to found a 7.459–7.460,
7.477–7.489
freedom of assembly and association 2.30,
7.408–7.456
freedom of expression 2.30, 7.349–7.407
general principles 2.31
in accordance with the law 2.31
interpretation 2.29
legitimate aims 2.31
liberty and security, right to 2.28, 7.03–7.73
manifest one's religion or beliefs,
right to 7.333–7.344
marry and found a family, right to 2.28
marry, right to 7.459–7.476
necessary in a democratic society 2.31
no punishment without lawful
authority 7.172–7.216
peaceful enjoyment of possessions 2.30
private and family life, right to respect for 2.30,
7.217–7.298
proportionality 2.29, 4.111
protest, right to 7.410–7.412, 7.415–7.437
thought, conscience and religion, freedom
of 2.30, 7.299–7.238
war and emergencies, derogations in time
of 7.547–7.578
living instrument principle
discrimination 7.538, 7.540
European Convention on Human Rights 1.25
European Court of Human Rights 10.08
inhuman or degrading treatment 6.59
interpretation 1.25, 2.17–2.19
transsexuals, birth certificates of 2.18–2.19
local remedies, exhaustion of *see* exhaustion of
local remedies
Locke, John 1.07
locus standi see standing

Macpherson Report 8.155
Magna Carta 1.01, 1.06
mainstreaming 1.37
maintenance and further realization of
human rights 2.09
maladministration 4.55
mandatory life sentences 6.79–6.80, 6.103

mandatory orders 4.05
manifest one's religion or beliefs,
right to 7.315–7.344
bullock, slaughter of a sacred 7.340
cannabis, criminalization of 7.340
causal link 7.320
civil partnerships in religious premises 7.344
conscientious objection 7.336
corporal punishment 7.319, 7.340
cremation in open-air 7.321
direct connection between belief and
acts 7.316–7.318
dismissal from work 7.325
effect on others 7.317
evangelism 7.336
failure to accommodate beliefs 7.337
freedom of expression 7.350
harassment 7.340
hold and change beliefs, right to 7.300
interference with manifestation 7.322–7.333
intimately linked acts 7.315
Islamic dress 7.322, 7.327–7.331,
7.337–7.338, 7.341
legality 7.334–7.335
legitimate aims 7.334–7.335, 7.338
limitations 7.333–7.344
margin of appreciation 7.338–7.339
military service, conscientious
objection to 7.336
national security 7.333
necessary in a democratic society 7.334
neutrality of state 7.337
nuisance 7.340
obligations 7.315
prisoners 7.326, 7.340
proportionality 7.334–7.336, 7.340–7.343
proselytization 7.300, 7.327
race discrimination 7.331–7.332
ritual slaughter 7.323
same sex couples, services to 7.342–7.344
Sunday working 7.324
time off 7.324
manifestly ill-founded applications 9.34, 10.08
margin of appreciation
autonomous concepts 6.18
blanket interference 2.82
commercial expression 7.360, 7.400
criminal charges 7.166
culture 2.78
deference and discretionary area of
judgment 4.120–4.122
definition 2.77–2.78
discrimination 7.537–7.545
education, right to 8.82
elections, right to free 8.91, 8.108
environmental damage 7.250
European Court of Human Rights 3.49, 10.08
fair hearing, right to a 7.166
framework of ECHR 2.77–2.83

freedom of expression 2.80, 7.360, 7.382, 7.400–7.404
freedom of movement 8.117
interpretation 2.78, 3.49
legality 2.80
life, right to 6.13, 6.18
manifest one's religion or beliefs, right to 7.338–7.339
necessary in a democratic society 2.80
peaceful enjoyment of possessions 8.04, 8.06, 8.33, 8.39, 8.41
positive obligations 2.39
private and family life, right to respect for 2.82, 7.222
private life, definition of 7.236
proportionality 2.78, 2.80, 2.83
religion 7.402–7.403, 7.540
sentencing 7.201
subsidiarity 2.78
transsexuals, legal recognition of 7.236
war and emergencies, derogations in time of 7.553, 7.555, 7.557
marriage see also marry, right to
divorce 4.20, 8.158
engagements 7.269
equal rights and responsibilities of spouses 8.156–8.158
family life, definition of 7.268, 7.269, 7.271
immigration rules 7.253
International Covenant on Civil and Political Rights 8.131, 8.156–8.158
Ireland, ban on divorce in 4.20
marital status, discrimination on grounds of 7.540
matrimonial property 8.131, 8.156–8.158
polygamous marriages 7.270
race discrimination 7.523
rape 7.183–7.184, 7.216
same sex couples 7.271
transsexuals, legal recognition of 7.237
marry, right to 7.459–7.476
age 7.463
Charter of Fundamental Rights of the EU 7.474
civil law, registration or affirmation of religious marriage by 7.467
civil partnerships 7.475
convenience, marriages of 7.468–7.469
delay 7.464
dissolution of marriage 7.476
family life, definition of 7.268
fees 7.470
formalities 7.463–7.467
gender 7.471–7.473
gender recognition certificates 7.473
legitimate aim 7.465–7.466
limited and qualified rights 2.28, 7.459–7.476
non-nationals 7.462, 7.468–7.470
prisoners 7.465

private and family life, right to respect for 7.460–7.461
proportionality 7.475
regulation 7.463–7.467
religion 7.463, 7.467
same sex couples 7.271, 7.474–7.475
shams 7.468–7.469
stateless persons 7.462
transsexuals 7.472–7.473
Universal Declaration of Human Rights 7.476
materials, finding 10.20–10.28
media see also broadcasting
anonymity orders 7.263, 7.364
balancing exercise 7.253, 7.261, 7.263–7.264
children in legal proceedings, identification of 7.261–7.262
chilling effect 7.256
comfort clause 7.405
confidentiality 7.257–7.259
costs 7.398
Court of Protection proceedings 7.365
defamation 7.254, 7.398
emotional suffering, intentional infliction of 7.257
freedom of expression 3.78–3.80, 7.351, 7.353, 7.364–7.365
freedom of the press 7.262–7.263, 7.361
future of HRA 1.49
gagging injunctions 3.79
injunctions 7.405–7.407
jury bias 7.121
photographs of celebrities 7.255, 7.259–7.260
pre-notification requirements 7.256
prior restraint 7.264
privacy law, creation of 1.49
private and family life, right to respect for 3.78, 3.80
private life, definition of 7.253–7.265
proportionality 7.261
public interest 3.79, 7.256, 7.265
reasonable expectation of privacy 7.255, 7.260
reporting restrictions 7.262
sensational and titillating reporting 7.256
super-injunctions 3.80, 7.264, 7.407
torture 2.27
medical information 7.242
medical treatment
abroad, adequacy of treatment 6.106–6.108
artificial insemination 7.240, 7.480–7.484
compulsory treatment 6.88, 6.106–6.108
deportation 6.106–6.108
family, right to found a 7.479
inhuman or degrading treatment 6.106–6.108
investigative duty 6.46
life, right to 6.46
medical negligence 6.46, 7.479
mental patients, compulsory treatment of 6.88, 6.106–6.108
private and family life, right to respect for 7.225

mental disabilities
  amenability to treatment 7.38
  Bournewood gap 7.39
  burden of proof 7.36
  care arrangements 7.18
  challenges to detention 7.63, 7.66
  compulsory treatment 6.88, 6.106–6.108
  conditional discharge, deferral of 7.40
  damages 4.58, 4.68
  deprivation of liberty 6.86–6.88
  inhuman or degrading treatment 6.86–6.88,
    6.106–6.108
  liberty and security, right to 4.68, 7.21,
    7.33–7.40, 7.49
  life, right to 4.105, 6.26
  Mental Health Review Tribunal 4.10, 4.68
  mental integrity 7.231
  positive obligations 7.70
  procedural rules 7.21, 7.39
  psychological damage 4.58
  reasons 7.49
  slopping out 6.84
  suicide following escape from mental
    hospitals 6.26
  vote, right to 8.99
merits test
  European Commission on Human
    Rights 10.04–10.05
  European Court of Human Rights 9.34,
    9.40–9.41, 9.43–9.44, 10.06, 10.08
military occupations 6.05
military service *see* **armed forces**
Mill, JS 1.07, 1.11
Ministerial Code, breach of 3.44
minority rights 7.506, 7.528
miscarriages of justice, compensation for 7.152,
  8.146–8.150
Modern Law Review 10.22

national security
  expulsion/deportation 6.100, 7.498, 8.136
  freedom of expression 7.394
  manifest one's religion or beliefs, right to 7.333
  opportunity to present case 7.133
  pressing social need 2.60
  public hearings 7.123
  torture 4.83
  war and emergencies, derogations in
    time of 7.567–7.578
nationality discrimination 4.79, 4.81, 5.584,
  5.586, 7.540
NATO air strikes on Yugoslavia 4.101, 6.05
natural disasters, protection from 6.22
necessary in a democratic society *see* **necessity**
necessity 2.41, 2.54–2.68
  access to courts 7.110
  elections, right to free 8.90
  fair hearing, right to a 7.106
  freedom of association 7.413, 7.450–7.451

  freedom of expression 7.378, 7.382–7.395
  freedom of movement 8.118
  liberty and security, right to 7.28, 7.29
  limited and qualified rights 2.31
  manifest one's religion or beliefs, right to 7.334
  margin of appreciation 2.80
  peaceful enjoyment of possessions 8.56
  pressing social need 2.58–2.60
  principles 2.57
  private and family life, right to respect for 7.226
  proportionality 2.54, 2.57, 2.61–2.66, 4.111
  protest, right to 7.424
  reasons, relevant and sufficient 2.57, 2.67–2.68
  restrictions on Convention rights 2.41,
    2.54–2.68
  terrorist suspects, pre-trial detention of 7.575
  use of lethal force 6.48, 6.50
  war and emergencies, derogations in
    time of 7.558, 7.575
negative 'liberty' rights 1.01, 1.03, 1.04, 1.08,
  2.32, 7.222
negligence
  life, right to 6.31
  medical negligence 6.46, 7.479
no punishment without lawful
    authority 7.172–7.216
  autonomous concepts 7.179
  civil proceedings 7.179
  common law 7.183, 7.188
  criminal, definition of 7.177–7.179
  defined in law, offences must be 7.174,
    7.188–7.192
  deportation 7.198, 7.200
  derogations 7.172
  detriment, law construed to court's 7.174
  discretion 7.186
  emergencies 7.172
  foreseeability 7.185–7.187
  general principles of law of civilized
    nations 7.213–7.216
  heavier penalties 7.173, 7.194–7.212
  international crimes 7.213–7.216
  legal advice 7.185
  legal certainty 7.189
  legality 7.174
  life sentences 7.205–7.209
  limited and qualified rights 7.172–7.216
  marital rape immunity 7.183–7.184, 7.216
  penalties
    definition 7.195–7.200
    deportation 7.198
  preventive measures 7.200
  rule of law 7.172
  sentencing 7.201–7.212
  strict liability offences 7.193
  war, derogations in time of 7.172
noise from aircraft 7.249, 9.46
non-governmental organisations (NGOs) 7.353,
  9.20, 9.39, 9.46

Northern Ireland
Equality Commission for Northern Ireland 4.48
fair hearing, right to a 7.588
protest, right to 7.417
terrorist suspects 7.588
war and emergencies, derogations in
time of 7.567–7.568
notwithstanding clause procedure 1.22, 1.24, 1.29
nuisance 7.340, 7.424

object and purpose of ECHR
democratic society, promotion of ideals and
values of 2.09
effectiveness principle 2.12
interpretation 2.08–2.10, 2.12
maintenance and further realization of
human rights 2.09
purposive interpretation 2.09
restrictions, narrow interpretation of 2.10
rule of law 2.09
Vienna Convention on the Law of Treaties 2.08
obscenity 2.49
occupations 6.05
offender behaviour programmes, access to 7.25
offensive, shocking or disturbing
speech 7.362–7.363, 7.399, 7.401
official reports 10.10–10.12
omissions 4.107
online resources 10.02, 10.10, 10.16–10.17,
10.19, 10.24–10.26
opportunity to present case 7.107,
7.131–7.134, 8.25
oral hearings 7.122, 8.138, 9.47–9.48

**PACE, judicial discretion to exclude of
evidence under** 1.15
Paine, Tom 1.02, 1.07
parents and children *see also* **family,
right to found a**
adoption 7.280, 7.282, 7.478–7.479
anonymous births 7.279
artificial insemination 7.240, 7.480–7.484
biological ties 7.276–7.277
embryos, consent to use of 7.239
estranged parents and children 7.278
family life, definition of 7.276–7.282
home births 7.241
identify parents, right to 7.279
private and family life, right to
respect for 7.239–7.341
Parliament *see also* **Joint Committee on Human
Rights; parliamentary sovereignty**
culture 1.40
damages 4.69–4.70
executive power 1.10, 1.20
interpretation 3.36
legality 1.09
Parliamentary Commissioner for
Administration 7.494

protest, right to 7.431–7.432
public authority, definition of 1.28
racism, East African refugees and 1.11, 6.70
scrutiny of legislation 1.10
trespassory assembly 1.11
parliamentary sovereignty
Canadian Charter of Fundamental Rights 1.29
constitutional instrument, HRA as 1.26–1.30
declarations of incompatibility 1.28, 4.72
entrenchment 1.27–1.30
European Communities Act 1972 1.27
European Convention on Human Rights,
incorporation of 1.17, 1.19–1.20
European Court of Human Rights 9.01
framework of HRA 3.02, 3.07, 3.29
incorporation of ECHR 1.28
interpretation 1.28, 3.38
judiciary, politicization of 1.26, 1.31, 1.35–1.36
New Zealand Bill of Rights 1.29
primary legislation 1.28–1.30
public authorities 3.17
remedial orders 1.28
secondary legislation 1.28, 1.30
striking down legislation 1.28–1.29
Parole Board 7.58, 7.66–7.69, 7.101
party political broadcasts 4.126, 7.376–7.377
patents 8.14
paternity, presumption of 7.281
peaceful enjoyment of possessions 8.02–8.59
adverse possession 8.31, 8.42–8.43
bankruptcy systems 8.49
civil and political interests 8.02–8.03
common law 1.09
compensation 8.37, 8.50, 8.58–8.59
conditions provided by law 8.38
confiscation 8.30, 8.53
contributory benefits 8.16
control by state 8.07–8.08, 8.29–8.34
costs 8.50
destruction of homes 8.48
discrimination 8.51
drug trafficking 8.53
economic interests 8.02–8.03
effective remedy, right to an 8.37
environmental laws 8.32
eviction 8.33, 8.45
expropriation 8.05, 8.13, 8.36, 8.40–8.41, 8.46,
8.50, 8.58
fair balance test 8.29, 8.37, 8.45–8.57
foreseeability 8.38
forfeiture laws 8.53
future possessions 8.11
housing benefit 8.12
hunting with dogs 8.34, 8.44, 8.47
inheritance laws 8.31
intellectual property 8.14–8.15
interference with right to property 8.26–8.35
International Covenant on Civil and Political
Rights 8.02

peaceful enjoyment of possessions (*Cont.*)
International Covenant on Economic and
Social Rights 8.02
interpretation 8.07
leasehold enfranchisement 8.40
legitimate expectations 8.05, 8.11–8.12,
8.18–8.22
limited and qualified rights 2.30, 8.36–8.59
margin of appreciation 8.04, 8.06, 8.33,
8.39, 8.41
necessity 8.56
non-contributory benefits 8.05, 8.11–8.12, 8.16
opportunity to present case 8.25
planning 8.31
positive obligations 8.23–8.25
possessions, definition of 8.10–8.22
private and family life, right to respect for 8.48
proportionality 4.117, 8.37, 8.41, 8.49,
8.53–8.54, 8.57–8.58
protocol 8.02–8.59
public interest 8.04, 8.07, 8.39–8.57, 8.59
public law rights 8.16–8.22
squatters 8.31, 8.42–8.43
state benefits 8.05, 8.11–8.13, 8.16–8.17, 8.51
state pensions 8.16–8.17
tax 4.10, 8.29, 8.31, 8.38, 8.52
three rules 8.07–8.08
Universal Declaration of Human Rights 8.02
pensions 7.519, 7.541–7.544, 8.16–8.17, 8.51
**persistent vegetative state, treatment for
persons in a** 6.27
photographs
celebrities 7.255, 7.259–7.260
protestors 7.422
pilot judgments 9.42, 9.52
planning 7.90, 8.31
police
access to courts 7.111
freedom of association 7.413, 7.455–7.456
freedom of expression 4.116
immunity 7.111
independence 6.38
inhuman or degrading treatment 6.97
investigative duty 6.38
life, right to 6.21, 6.24, 6.38
PACE, judicial discretion to exclude of
evidence under 1.15
private and family life, right to respect for 4.106,
7.223, 7.229
proportionality 4.116
statements of compatibility 3.44
threats to private life, information on 4.106,
7.223
trade unions, right to form and
join 7.455–7,456
Police Reform and Social Responsibility Bill 7.431
**political activity of aliens, restrictions
on** 2.76, 5.579–7.586
definition of political activities 5.580

European citizenship 5.584
European Parliament, members of 5.581
freedom of expression 5.585
interpretation 5.579
nationality discrimination 5.584, 5.586
political associations 7.440, 7.452–7.453
political convictions, freedom of 7.305
political expression 7.357–7.358
defamation 7.358
definition 7.358
disciplinary action 7.392
party political broadcasts 7.376–7.377
proportionality 4.116
protest, right to 7.425
public interest 7.358
United States 7.358
political rights *see* **International Covenant
on Civil and Political Rights (ICCPR)**
politicization of the judiciary 1.21, 1.31–1.36
polygamous marriages 7.270
positive 'claim' rights 1.01, 1.03, 1.04, 1.06
positive obligations
balancing exercise 2.37
die, right to 4.104
discrimination 7.517, 7.546
education, right to 2.32, 8.64
effectiveness 2.13, 2.33–2.34
elections 2.32
enforcement of HRA 4.104–4.107
fair hearing, right to a 2.32
family, right to found a 7.484, 7.487–7.489
forced or compulsory labour 6.125–6.127
freedom of assembly 7.457–7.458
freedom of association 7.457–7.458
freedom of expression 7.367–7.369
general theory 2.33
information and advice, duty to provide 2.34
inhuman or degrading treatment 4.105–4.107,
6.89–6.113
liberty and security, right to 7.70–7.72
life, right to 2.35, 4.104–4.105
margin of appreciation 2.39
negative obligations 2.32
peaceful enjoyment of possessions 8.23–8.25
prevent breaches, duty to 2.34
private and family life, right to respect for 2.36,
2.38–2.39, 4.104–4.106, 7.223
private parties 3.73, 9.22
proportionality 2.63
protest, right to 7.458
public authorities 1.37, 3.16
resources to prevent breaches, duty to 2.34
respond to breaches, duty to 2.34
severity of effects of omission 2.38
slavery and servitude 6.125–6.127
possession of property *see* **peaceful enjoyment
of possessions**
possession orders 4.116, 7.292–7.295
precedent 3.51–3.52, 3.56, 10.08

pre-emptive measures 4.132
pre-notification requirements 7.256, 7.404, 7.407
prescribed by law *see* legality
press *see* media
pressing social need 2.58–2.60
  homosexual behaviour, criminalization of 2.59
  legitimate aim 2.59
  national security 2.60
  private and family life, right to respect for 2.58
pressure groups 9.58
presumption of innocence
  civil proceedings 7.150
  confiscation proceedings 7.151
  fair hearing, right to a 7.150–7.155
  miscarriages of justice, compensation for 7.152
  professional disciplinary hearings 7.150
  reverse burden of proof 7.153–7.154
  silence, right to 7.138, 7.155
  suspicions of guilt, expressions of
    continued 7.152
preventive measures 2.34, 7.30, 7.96, 7.200,
    7.427–7.428
primary legislation
  amendment 4.92–4.94, 4.99
  declarations of incompatibility 3.07, 4.71–4.74,
    4.92–4.99
  framework of HRA 3.07
  interpretation 3.12, 3.31–3.32, 3.35–3.40, 3.45
  public authorities 3.15, 3.17–3.18
  remedial orders 4.92–4.94, 4.99
prior restraint 7.264, 7.371
prisoners *see also* life sentences
  artificial insemination 7.240, 7.481
  children in adult prisons 6.83
  conditions in prison 6.81–6.84, 7.72
  correspondence, interference with 2.53, 2.64,
    7.296–7.297, 7.494
  criminal charges 7.100
  declarations of incompatibility 8.101
  discipline 7.100
  early release 4.79, 4.81
  effective remedy, right to an 7.494
  execution of judgments 9.73
  fair hearing, right to a 7.100
  family, right to found a 7.481
  future of HRA 1.53
  inhuman or degrading treatment 6.81–6.84
  hunger strikes 6.111–6.112
  Joint Committee on Human Rights 9.63
  manifest one's religion or beliefs,
    right to 7.326, 7.340
  marry, right to 7.465
  nationality discrimination 4.79, 4.81
  offender behaviour programmes, access to 7.25
  Parole Board 7.58, 7.66–7.69, 7.101
  reasons 2.68
  recall 4.31
  slopping out 6.84
  time limits 4.31

transsexuals, legal recognition of 7.238
voting 1.53, 2.68, 4.86, 8.100–8.101, 9.52, 9.63
privacy
  creation of law of privacy 1.49
  freedom of expression 7.350, 7.397, 7.405
  media 1.49
  private and family life, right to
    respect for 7.219
  public figures 3.74
private and family life, right to
    respect for 7.217–7.298
  access to children 7.223
  access to information 2.36
  anonymity orders 7.263
  artificial insemination 7.480–7.482
  balancing exercise 7.222, 7.253, 7.261,
    7.263–7.264
  birth certificates, deceased father's on
    name of 4.79
  care proceedings 7.223
  care workers, provisional blacklisting of 4.79
  children
    care, in 4.106
    legal proceedings, identification of 7.261–7.262
  chilling effect 7.256
  correspondence, definition of 7.296–7.298
  defamation 7.254
  disabled persons 7.225
  divorce in Ireland, bans on 4.20
  employment without representation, barring
    person from 7.223
  European Court of Human Rights 7.220
  family life, definition of 7.266–7.287
  family, right to found a 7.460–7.461, 7.487
  fostering 7.223
  freedom of assembly 7.411
  freedom of association 7.411
  freedom of expression 3.78, 3.80, 7.253–7.265
  freedom of the press 7.262–7.263
  home, definition of 7.288–7.295
  illegitimacy 4.20
  interception of communications 7.227
  legality 7.226–7.227
  limited and qualified rights 2.30, 7.217–7.298
  margin of appreciation 2.80, 7.222
  marry, right to 7.460–7.461
  media 3.78, 3.80, 7.253–7.265
  medical treatment 2.82, 7.225
  necessary in a democratic society 7.226
  negative obligations 7.222
  peaceful enjoyment of possessions 8.48
  photographs of celebrities 7.255, 7.259–7.260
  police's obligation to inform citizens of threats to
    private life 4.106, 7.223
  positive obligations 2.36, 2.38–2.39,
    4.104–4.106, 7.221–7.225
  pre-notification requirements 7.256
  pressing social need 2/58
  prior restraint 7.264

private and family life, right to respect for (*Cont.*)
prisoners' correspondence, interference with 7.494
privacy 7.219
private life, definition of 7.229–7.265
procedural obligations 7.223
proportionality 2.65, 7.220, 7.228, 7.261
protest, right to 7.423
public interest 7.256, 7.265
reasonable expectation of privacy 7.255, 7.260
reporting restrictions 7.262
respect, concept of 7.221–7.222
same sex couples as a family 4.42
sexual offenders, notification of travel plans requirement imposed on 3.47,4.79
social housing 7.224
super-injunctions 7.264
telephone tapping 1.14, 7.296
terrorist suspects, stop and search of 7.227
transsexuals 2.18–2.19, 4.79
widows' benefits 4.20
zone of interaction 7.229
private information 7.242–7.246
private life, definition of 7.229–7.265
abortion 7.231
armed forces, homosexuals in the 7.235
autonomy 7.230–7.232
die, choice of how and when to 7.230, 7.232–7.233
environmental damage 7.249–7.251
hunting with dogs 7.233
identity 7.232
margin of appreciation 7.236
media 7.253–7.265
mental integrity 7.231
parenthood 7.239–7.241
physical integrity 7.231
police searches 7.229
private information 7.242–7.246
public spaces 7.251
sexuality 7.235
social ties 7.232
surveillance 7.247–7.248
transsexuals, legal recognition of 7.236–7.238
zone of interaction 7.229
private parties
common law 3.73–3.74
European Court of Human Rights 9.22
fair hearing, right to a 3.73
framework of HRA 3.05–3.07, 3.20, 3.72–3.74
horizontal effects 3.73
indirect enforcement 3.73
judicial review 3.73
positive obligations 3.73, 9.22
public figures, privacy of 3.74
private, proceedings held in 7.123–7.124, 7.365
privilege against self-incrimination *see* self-incrimination, privilege against

prohibiting orders 4.05
property, right to *see* peaceful enjoyment of possessions
proportionality
access to courts 7.110
asylum seekers, removal of 4.116
bankruptcy 8.49
bill of rights 1.54
blanket policies 2.64
compensation 2.64
confiscation 8.53
constitutional legitimacy 4.124–4.126
costs 8.50
criminal charges 7.144
damages for defamation 2.64
deference 4.117–4.130
development and application 4.112–4.118
disclosure 7.144
discretion 4.111, 4.117–4.130
discrimination 7.530–7.531, 7.535–7.536
education, right to 8.83–8.84
elections, right to free 8.89–8.90, 8.111
emergencies 2.73
enforcement of HRA 4.111–4.130
EU law 4.113, 5.24
European Court of Human Rights 3.55
eviction 7.293
expropriation 8.58
expulsion/deportation 8.136
fair balance 2.61–2.62
fair hearing, right to a 7.106, 7.144
family life, definition of 7.284, 7.185
family, right to found a 7.4865–7.486, 7.488
forfeiture 8.53
freedom of assembly 7.412
freedom of association 7.442, 7.444
freedom of expression 2.65, 4.116, 7.261, 7.354, 7.377, 7.383, 7.386, 7.388–7.394, 7.398
freedom of movement 8.117
home, definition of 7.293–7.295
immigration control 7.284
implied rights 2.63
institutional competence 4.124, 4.127–4.130
interpretation 3.42
irrationality 4.111–4.112, 4.115
judicial review 4.111–4.112, 4.116
legitimate aims 4.116
liberty and security, right to 7.17, 7.27–7.28, 7.33–7.34, 7.42
limited and qualified rights 2.29
manifest one's religion or beliefs, right to 7.334–7.336, 7.340–7.343
margin of appreciation 2.78, 2.80, 2.83
marry, right to 7.475
media 7.261
necessity 2.54, 2.57, 2.61–2.66, 4.111
peaceful enjoyment of possessions 4.117, 8.37, 8.41, 8.49, 8.53–8.54, 8.57–8.58
police 4.116

political speech 2.64
positive obligations 2.63
possession proceedings 4.116, 7.295
private and family life, right to respect for 2.65,
    7.220, 7.228, 7.261
procedural fairness 2.66
protest, right to 7.424, 7.426, 7.430, 7.433,
    7.435, 7.437
qualified rights 4.111
repossession proceedings 7.294
terrorist suspects, pre-trial
    detention of 7.575–7.576
use of lethal force 6.48, 6.51
war and emergencies, derogations in
    time of 7.558, 7.575–5.576
Wednesbury unreasonableness 4.112, 4.115
proselytization 7.300, 7.327
Protection of Freedoms Bill 7.244
protest, right to
    authorization measures 7.429–7.433
    blanket measures 7.427–7.428
    camps 7.424, 7.431–7.432
    children going to school, abuse of 6.97
    counter-demonstrations 7.420, 7.434, 7.458
    criminal sanctions 7.435
    DNA samples, retention of 7.423
    freedom of expression 7.31, 7.350, 7.395, 7.412,
        7.436–7.437
    Houses of Parliament, protests around
        the 7.431–7.432
    interception of protestors 4.110, 7.31, 7.426
    kettling 4.110, 7.411, 7.426
    legality 4.110
    legitimate aim 7.433
    liberty and security, right to 7.31, 7.411
    limited and qualified rights 7.410–7.412,
        7.415–7.417
    necessary in a democratic society 7.424
    Northern Ireland 7.417
    notification requirements 7.430–7.431
    nuisance 7.424
    Orange Order and Orange Lodges 7.417
    Parliament, protests around 7.431–7.432
    peaceful assembly 7.415–7.437
    penalties 7.435
    photographs of protestors, taking 7.422
    police cordons, keeping 7.17
    Police Reform and Social Responsibility
        Bill 7.431
    political speech 7.425
    positive obligations 7.458
    preventive measures 7.427–7.428
    private and family life, right to respect for 7.423
    private property, assemblies on 7.436–7.437
    proportionality 7.424, 7.426, 7.430, 7.433,
        7.435, 7.437
    public interest 7.425
    public order 7.420, 7.435
    regulation of assemblies 7.429–7.433

scope 7.418–7.423
Scotland 7.417
Serious Organised Crime and
    Police Act 2005 7.431–7.432
spontaneous protests, bans on 7.431
standing 7.418
stop and search 7.422
storage of information 7.419
strict liability offences 7.435
trespass 7.432
victims 7.418
violent assemblies 7.420, 7.435
protocols to ECHR 8.01–8.162
    contractual obligations, deprivation of liberty on
        grounds of inability to fulfil 8.114–8.115
    criminal charges 7.171
    death penalty 8.127–8.128, 8.161–8.162
    discrimination 8.159–8.160
    education, right to 8.60–8.87
    elections, right to free 8.88–8.112
    European Commission on Human
        Rights 2.05, 10.05
    European Court of Human Rights 2.05,
        10.05–10.07
    expulsion from and entry into national
        territory 8.137–8.138
    fair hearing, right to a 7.171
    framework of ECHR 2.05
    International Covenant on Civil and Political
        Rights 8.129–8.158
    peaceful enjoyment of possessions 8.02–8.59
    ratification 8.126, 8.160, 8.162
psychological damage, damages for 4.58
public authorities
    acts 3.15–3.20
    best practice 1.38
    breach of statutory duty 3.22, 3.57
    contracting out 3.66, 3.68–3.71
    core public authorities 3.59
    courts and tribunals 3.19, 3.24
    damages 4.68
    definition 3.06–3.07, 3.29, 3.60–3.70, 5.26
    delegation 3.63–3.64
    direct enforcement 3.21–3.22, 3.57
    emanations of the state 5.26
    EU law 5.26
    failure to act 3.15, 3.18
    failure to legislate 3.18
    framework of ECHR 3.57–3.71
    framework of HRA 3.04–3.07, 3.15–3.22,
        3.29, 3.57–3.71
    freedom of association 3.16
    growth in numbers 1.10
    horizontal effect 3.20
    housing management functions 3.71
    hybrid or functional authorities 3.60–3.71
    institutional framework 1.37–1.38
    interpretation 3.12
    Joint Committee on Human Rights 3.66, 3.71

public authorities (*Cont.*)
  judicial review 3.22, 3.57, 3.63, 5.26
  minimalist approach 1.38
  Parliament 1.28, 3.17–3.18
  parliamentary sovereignty 3.17
  positive obligations 1.37, 3.16
  primary legislation defence 3.15, 3.17–3.18
  private functions 3.58
  proceedings against authorities 3.21
  Public Bodies Bill 1.48
  public functions 3.58
  public interest 3.69
  public nature, functions of a 3.06
  public sector duties 4.52
  quasi-public bodies, growth in number of 1.10
  retrospectivity 4.33–4.34
  Strasbourg proofing 1.38
  time limits 3.21, 4.29–4.30
  vertical effect 3.57–3.58
  victims 3.21
public funding *see* **funding**
public hearings
  Children Act hearings 7.124
  disciplinary hearings 7.122
  fair hearing, right to a 7.107, 7.122–7.125
  judgments, public pronouncements of 7.125
  liberty and security, right to 7.64
  national security 7.123
  oral hearings 7.122
  private hearings 7.123–7.124
  waiver 7.123
public interest
  absolute rights 2.26
  bill of rights 1.54
  declarations of incompatibility 4.89
  enforcement of HRA 4.04, 4.23–4.25,
    4.36–4.39
  Equality and Human Rights Commission 4.25
  EU law 5.19
  expropriation 8.59
  fair balance test 8.45–8.57
  freedom of expression 3.79, 7.256, 7.265, 7.358,
    7.360, 7.385
  freedom of movement 8.119
  groups 4.35–4.39
  hybrid or functional authorities 3.69
  judicial review 4.23–4.25
  liberty and security, right to 7.52
  media 3.79, 7.256, 7.265
  peaceful enjoyment of possessions 8.04, 8.07,
    8.39–8.57, 8.59
  political expression 7.358
  private and family life, right to
    respect for 7.256, 7.265
  protest, right to 7.425
  public interest immunity certificates 7.144
  standing 4.04, 4.23–4.25
  sufficient interest 4.25
  victims 4.04, 4.23–4.25

Public Law 10.22
public morality 7.400–7.404
public opinion and awareness 1.39, 1.49
public order
  expulsion/deportation 8.136
  freedom of expression 7.390–7.393
  protest, right to 7.420, 7.423
public spaces, privacy in 7.251

qualified rights *see* **limited and qualified rights**
quashing orders 4.05
quasi-legal proceedings 7.82
quasi-public bodies, growth in number of 1.10

race discrimination
  dignity 6.70
  East African refugees 1.11
  freedom of expression 7.363, 7.387
  immigration rules on marriage 7.523
  inhuman or degrading treatment 6.70
  jury bias 7.120
  manifest one's religion or beliefs,
    right to 7.331–7.332
  racial hatred 7.589–7.590
  racist speech 7.363, 7.387
reading down 3.37
reading in 2.12, 3.17, 3.37, 3.39
reasonable time, fair hearings and
  charge and sentence, time between 7.127
  civil proceedings 7.126–7.128, 7.130
  criminal proceedings 7.126–7.127, 7.130
  detention 7.128
  final determinations in civil proceedings 7.127
  prejudice 7.129
reasons
  appeals 7.135
  criminal charges 7.48–7.49
  fair hearing, right to a 7.107, 7.135–7.136
  good faith 2.67
  liberty and security, right to 7.48–7.50
  necessity 2.57, 2.67–2.68
  prisoners' voting rights 2.68
  relevant and sufficient reasons 2.57, 2.67–2.68
  remedial orders 4.96
  sparse reasons 7.135
rebalancing HRA 1.49
reciprocity 1.02
referencing system 10.09
referenda 8.94
reform *see* **future of HRA**
Regulatory of Investigatory Powers Tribunal 7.93
religion and beliefs *see also* **manifest one's religion
    or beliefs, right to; thought, conscience
    and religion, freedom of**
  advertising 7.403
  blasphemy 2.49
  crucifixes in school, display of 8.82
  discrimination 3.81, 7.521, 7.528, 7.540
  education 8.61, 8.75–8.82, 8.84–8.85

freedom of expression 7.402–7.403
Islamic dress 7.322, 7.327–7.331, 7.337–7.338,
      7.341, 8.84–8.85
margin of appreciation 7.402–7.403, 7.540
marry, right to 7.463, 7.467
religious education 8.81
religious marriage, registration or affirmation
      by civil law of 7.467
symbols 7.528
thought, conscience and religion,
      freedom of 7.521
remand 7.28
remedial orders 4.92–4.99
   declarations of incompatibility 1.28, 4.72,
      4.84–4.86, 4.92
   ECtHR judgments 4.93
   effective remedy, right to an 4.99
   emergency procedure 4.94, 4.98
   fast-track procedure 4.92–4.99
   Joint Committee on Human Rights 1.41, 4.92
   parliamentary sovereignty 1.28
   primary legislation,
      amendment of 4.92–4.94, 4.99
   procedure 4.94–4.98
   reasons, statements for 4.96
   retrospectivity 4.95
   standard procedure 4.94, 4.96
   subordinate legislation 4.93, 4.99
   time limits 4.97–4.98
remedies see also compensation; damages;
         effective remedy, right to an; exhaustion
         of local remedies; remedial orders
   criminal proceedings 4.05–4.06
   enforcement of HRA 4.05–4.06,
      4.53–4.99, 4.131
   EU law 5.24
   European Court of Human
      Rights 9.51–9.53, 9.62
   framework of HRA 3.23, 3.25
   injunctions 3.79–3.80, 4.05, 7.264,
      7.405–7.407
   interim measures 9.13–9.14
   just and appropriate relief 3.23
   just satisfaction 4.05, 4.32
   mandatory orders 4.05
   prohibition orders 4.05
   quashing orders 4.05
   restrictive attitude 4.131
   super-injunctions 7.407
   time limits 4.32
reporting restrictions 7.262
Reports of Judgments and Decisions 10.10
repossession proceedings 7.294
representation see legal representation
representative standing 5.25
reputation 7.246
researching human rights
         jurisprudence 10.01–10.28
   bibliographic resources 10.18

blogs 10.17, 10.26
books 10.20, 10.23
British and Irish Legal Information
      Institute's database 10.25
Butterworths' Human Rights Cases 10.12
case law, finding 10.10–10.21, 10.24, 10.26
Case Law Information Notes 10.16
Commonwealth constitutions 10.02
comparative law 10.02
Criminal Law Review 10.22
Digest of Strasbourg Case Law 10.15
electronic and online resources 10.02, 10.10,
      10.16–10.17, 10.19, 10.24–10.26
European Commission of Human
      Rights 10.04–10.05, 10.08, 10.10,
      10.13–10.16
European Convention on Human Rights
      jurisprudence 10.03–10.09
European Court of Human Rights 10.01–10.12,
      10.16–10.17, 10.19, 10.24
European Human Rights Law Review
      (EHRLR) 10.12, 10.22, 10.24
European Human Rights Reports (EHRR) 10.11,
      10.14, 10.24
Factsheets 10.16
Hansard 10.27–10.28
HUDOC database 10.10, 10.16
Human Rights Alerter 10.22
Human Rights Law Reports – UK 10.21
Human Rights Updater 10.22
Joint Committee on Human Rights
      website 10.25
journals 10.20, 10.22
Judicial Review 10.22
law reports 10.10–10.12, 10.16, 10.20-10.21,
      10.24, 10.26
Lawtel 10.24
LexisNexis online database 10.24
materials, finding 10.20–10.28
Modern Law Review 10.22
official reports 10.10–10.12
Public Law 10.22
referencing system 10.09
Reports of Judgments and Decisions 10.10
Supreme Court website 10.26
travaux préparatoires 10.19
UK Human Rights Blog 10.26
United Kingdom Human Rights Reports 10.21
Universal Declaration of Human Rights 10.02
websites 10.02, 10.10, 10.16–10.17, 10.19,
      10.24–10.26
Westlaw 10.24
Yearbook of the European Convention on
      Human Rights 10.15
reservations
   death penalty 8.161
   definition 2.69
   education, right to 2.71, 8.81
   framework of HRA 3.27

reservations (*Cont.*)
  interpretation 2.72
  invalidity 2.70
  restrictions on Convention rights 2.69–2.72
  Vienna Convention on the Law of Treaties 2.69
residence
  elections, right to free 8.103–8.104
  expulsion/deportation 8.134–8.135
  vote, right to 8.98–8.99
residual rights, theory of 1.08–1.09
responsibilities and rights, relationship
      between 1.02
restrictions on Convention rights *see also* limited
      and qualified rights
  balancing exercise 2.40
  derogations 2.73–2.75
  destruction of Convention rights 2.76
  improper purpose, using restrictions for an 2.76
  legality 2.41–2.49
  legitimate aim 2.41, 2.50–2.53
  necessary in a democratic society 2.41,
    2.54–2.68
  political activities 2.76
  reservations 2.69–2.72
  rule of law 2.40
retrospectivity *see also* no punishment without
     law authority
  absolute rights 2.26
  enforcement of HRA 4.33–4.34
  interpretation 4.33
  public authorities 4.33–4.34
  remedial orders 4.95
  tax 8.52
right to a fair hearing *see* fair hearing, right to a
right to an effective remedy *see* effective remedy,
    right to an
right to found a family *see* family, right to found a
right to free elections *see* elections, right to free
right to liberty and security *see* liberty and
    security, right to
right to life *see* life, right to
right to manifest one's religion or beliefs *see*
    manifest one's religion or beliefs, right to
right to marry *see* marry, right to
right to silence *see* silence, right to
Rights Brought Home white paper 1.40
ritual slaughter 7.323
Roma children, discrimination against 8.87
royal prerogative 1.08
rule of law
  autonomous concepts 2.15
  criminal charges 7.99
  fair hearing, right to a 7.74
  historical background 1.07
  legality 2.42, 2.44
  no punishment without law 7.172, 7.201
  object and purpose of ECHR 2.09
  restrictions 2.40
  sentencing 7.201

same sex partners
  Charter of Fundamental Rights of
    the EU 7.474
  children 7.308, 8.13
  civil partnerships 7.275, 7.344, 7.475, 7.590
  discrimination 8.13
  family life, definition of 7.267, 7.271–7.275
  manifest one's religion or beliefs,
    right to 7.342–7.344
  marry, right to 7.271, 7.474–7.475
  private and family life, right to respect for 4.42
  religious premises, civil partnerships on 7.344
  services, provision of 7.342–7.344
  thought, conscience and religion,
    freedom of 7.308, 7.590
Sark, elections in 8.96–8.97, 8.106
scope of Convention rights
  absolute rights 2.25–2.27
  limited rights 2.25, 2.28–2.29
  positive obligations 2.3202.39
  qualified rights 2.25, 2.30–2.31
Scotland
  creation 1.47–1.48
  devolved matters 1.47
  inhuman or degrading treatment 6.84
  protest, right to 7.417
  Scottish Human Rights Commission 1.47–1.48,
    4.26, 4.48
  slopping out 6.86
seclusion of mental health patients 6.86
secondary legislation
  framework of HRA 3.07
  interpretation 3.07, 3.12, 3.31-3.32, 3.36
  legality 2.43
  parliamentary sovereignty 1.28, 1.30
  remedial orders 4.93, 4.96
security *see* liberty and security, right to;
    national security
self-incrimination, privilege against
  criminal charges 7.138, 7.141
  EU law, fundamental rights doctrine in 5.08
  European Convention on Human Rights 1.25
  fair hearing, right to a 7.138, 7.141
  samples 7.141
  silence, right to 7.155
  speeding offences, identity of drivers and 7.141
sentences *see also* life sentences
  age at time of conviction 7.202–7.203
  charge and sentence, time between 7.127
  enforcement of HRA 4.05
  extended sentences 7.210
  foreseeability 7.201, 7.203–7.207
  heavier penalties, rule against 7.201–7.212
  indefinite sentences for public protection (IPP)
    sentences 6.80
  inhuman or degrading treatment 6.79–6.80
  licence periods 7.210
  mandatory life sentences 6.79–6.80, 6.103
  margin of appreciation 7.201

no punishment without lawful
  authority 7.201–7.212
  reviews 8.140–8.141
  rule of law 7.201
  whole life sentences 6.80
separation of powers 1.17, 7.115
September 11, 2001 terrorist attacks on the United
  States 7.567, 7.569–7.578
servitude *see* slavery and servitude
settlements 9.41, 9.61
sex discrimination
  jury service 7.526
  margin of appreciation 7.539, 7.541–7.544
  pensions 7.541–7.544
  state retirement age 7.541–7.544
  welfare benefits 3.46, 7.543
sex education 8.80
sex offenders
  criminal charges 7.102
  fair hearing, right to a 7.102
  lifelong registration 7.245
  private and family life, right to
    respect for 3.47, 4.79
  register, inclusion on 7.102
  travel plans, notification of 3.47, 4.79
sexual abuse of children 6.96
sexual orientation *see also* same sex partners
  armed forces, homosexuals in the 7.499
  criminalization 2.59, 4.20
  discrimination 4.20, 7.540, 8.13
  Northern Ireland, criminalization of
    homosexual acts in 4.20
  pressing social need 2.59
sexuality 7.235
sham marriages 7.468–7.469
silence, right to
  adverse inferences 7.139, 7.155
  fair hearing, right to a 7.138–7.141
  innocence, presumption of 7.138
  presumption of innocence 7.155
  self-incrimination, privilege against 7.155
slavery and servitude
  absolute rights 2.26, 6.115–6.119, 6.125–6.127
  damages 6.127
  forced or compulsory labour 6.121
  positive obligations 6.125–6.127
  servitude, definition of 6.118–6.119
  Slavery Convention 6.117
  slavery, definition of 6.117
  trafficking in human beings 6.127
slopping out 6.84
social rights 1.04, 1.25
social ties 7.232
sovereignty *see* parliamentary sovereignty
special advocates 7.65–7.66, 7.110, 7.144
special cases and exceptions
  effective remedy, right to an 3.76–3.77
  framework of HRA 3.06, 3.75–3.81
  freedom of expression 3.78–3.80

  interest groups 3.75, 3.78
  media 3.78–3.79
  private and family life, right to
    respect for 3.78, 3.80
  religious bodies 3.81
  super-injunctions 3.79–3.80
  thought, conscience and religion,
    freedom of 3.81
Special Immigration Appeals Commission
  (SIAC) 6.74–6.78, 7.503
speeding offences, identity of drivers and 7.141
spouses, equal rights and
  responsibilities of 8.156–8.158
squatters 8.31, 8.42–8.43
standing *see also* victims, standing of
  amicus briefs 4.18
  companies 4.16
  declarations of incompatibility 4.77
  enforcement of HRA 4.04, 4.16–4.28
  Equality and Human Rights Commission 4.18,
    4.25–4.28, 4.40–4.52, 4.131
  EU law 5.25
  European Court of Human Rights 4.19–4.20,
    9.19–9.21
  fair hearing, right to a 4.16
  interpretation 3.33
  judicial review 4.16, 4.23–4.25
  life, right to 6.53–6.54
  protest, right to 7.418
  public interest groups 4.23–4.25
  public interest litigation 4.04
  representative standing 5.25
  sufficient interest 4.25
  third party interventions 4.18
state benefits
  contributory benefits 8.16
  declarations of incompatibility 3.46
  discrimination 3.46, 4.20, 7.541–7.544
  inhuman or degrading treatment 6.109–6.110
  non-contributory benefits 8.05, 8.11–8.12, 8.16
  peaceful enjoyment of possessions 8.05,
    8.11–8.13, 8.16–8.17, 8.51
  pensions 7.519, 7.541–7.544, 8.16–8.17
  sex discrimination 3.46, 4.20, 7.541–7.544
  subsistence 6.110
  widows' benefits 3.46, 4.20
state retirement age 7.541–7.544
state security *see* national security
stateless persons, marriage of 7.462
statements of compatibility
  bills 3.13, 3.43–3.44
  framework of HRA 3.13, 3.43–3.44
  interpretation 3.43, 3.45
  Joint Committee on Human Rights 4.132
  judiciary, politicization of 1.33
  Ministerial Code, breach of 3.44
  police 3.44
statutes *see* primary legislation
stay of proceedings as abuse of process 4.05

stop and search 2.47, 4.109, 7.13–7.14,
  7.227, 7.422
strict liability 7.193, 7.435
strike, right to 7.438, 7.448
subordinate legislation *see* secondary legislation
subsidiarity 2.78
subsistence 4.106, 6.110
suicide
  assisted suicide 4.104, 6.27, 6.98, 7.230,
    7.232–7.233
  die, right to 4.104, 6.27, 7.230, 7.232–7.233
  inhuman or degrading treatment 6.98
  life, right to 6.20, 6.26–6.27
Sunday working 7.324
super-injunctions 3.79–3.80, 7.264, 7.407
Supreme Court website 10.26
surveillance *see* interception of communications

tax
  peaceful enjoyment of possessions 4.10, 8.29,
    8.31, 8.38, 8.52
  retrospectivity 8.52
  thought, conscience and religion,
    freedom of 7.310, 7.312
telephone tapping 1.14, 2.47, 7.296
television licences, restrictions on 5.07
territoriality *see* extraterritoriality
  terrorism
    control orders 3.46, 4.83, 7.15–7.16
    declarations of incompatibility 3.46, 4.83
    deportation 6.78, 7.80, 7.569–7.570
    discrimination 5.576
    evidence, admissibility of 6.74–6.78
    extradition 7.80
    fair hearing, right to a 7.80, 7.588
    freedom of association 7.452–7.453
    inhuman or degrading treatment 6.74–6.78
    legality 2.47, 4.109
    length of detention 7.53
    liberty and security, right to 4.83, 5.576,
      7.13–7.16, 7.30, 7.53, 7.65, 7.570
    nationality discrimination 4.83
    necessity 7.575
    Northern Ireland 7.588
    opportunity to present case 7.133
    pre-trial detention 3.46, 4.83, 7.09, 7.53, 7.65,
      7.570–7.578
    preventive detention 7.30
    private and family life, right to
      respect for 7.227
    proportionality 7.575
    September 11, 2001 terrorist attacks on the
      United States 7.567, 7.569–7.578
    special advocate procedure 7.65–7.66
    Special Immigration Appeals
      Commission 6.74–6.78, 7.65
    stop and search 2.47, 4.109, 7.13–7.14, 7.227
    torture 6.74–6.78, 6.92
    use of lethal force 6.49

war and emergencies, derogations in time
  of 7.555, 7.557–7.560, 7.567–7.578
test and illustrative cases 4.27
third party intervention
  amicus briefs 4.18
  enforcement of HRA 4.04, 4.35–4.43
  Equality and Human Rights
    Commission 4.26–4.28, 4.35–4.36,
    4.40–4.43, 9.46
  European Court of Human Rights 9.39, 9.46
  growth in cases 4.36–4.39
  joint interventions 4.38
  judicial review 4.40
  list of interventions by EHRC 4.42
  multiple interventions 4.38
  public interest groups 4.35–4.39
  torture, admissibility of evidence
    obtained by 4.38
  victims, standing of 4.18
thought, conscience and religion,
  freedom of 7.299–7.238 *see also*
  manifest one's religion or beliefs,
  right to
abuse of rights, prohibition on 7.590
atheism and agnosticism 7.307
balancing exercise 7.348
beliefs, range of 7.305–7.307
civil partnerships 7.590
comfort clauses 3.26
conscientious objection 7.311
convictions 7.306, 7.308
deportation 9.46
disclose one's religion, freedom not to 7.309
discrimination 7.301, 7.521
education, right to 8.76
employment in religious bodies 7.345–7.348
everyone, definition of 7.303–7.304
framework of HRA 3.26
freedom of assembly 7.411
freedom of association 7.411–7.412
freedom of expression 7.301–7.302, 7.350
hold and change beliefs, right to 7.300
hunting 7.308
ideas 7.306
legitimacy of beliefs, assessment of 7.313
limited and qualified rights 2.30, 7.299–7.238
military service, conscientious
  objection to 7.312–7.313
neutrality and impartiality of the state 7.313
non-religious beliefs 7.305–7.307
opinions 7.306, 7.308
overlap with other provisions 7.301
political convictions 7.305
proselytization 7.300
same sex couples 7.314
scope of freedom 7.305–7.309
special cases and exceptions 3.81
state activities 7.310–7.314
taxation 7.310, 7.312

time limits
  enforcement of HRA 4.04, 4.29–4.32
  European Court of Human Rights 9.12,
    9.27, 9.28
  exhaustion of local remedies 9.26
  public authorities 3.21
  remedial orders 4.97–4.98
  victims 3.21
time off for religious purposes 7.324
tobacco advertising 7.360
torture
  abroad, torture of terrorist suspects 6.92
  absolute rights 2.26–2.27, 6.58, 6.62–6.66
  declarations of incompatibility 4.84
  definition 6.58, 6.62
  deportation/extradition 2.27, 4.83, 6.04, 6.65,
    6.78, 6.101
  Detainee Inquiry 6.92
  evidence, admissibility of 4.38, 6.74–6.78, 7.77
  extraterritoriality 4.103
  fair hearing, right to a 7.77
  inhuman or degrading treatment, distinguished
    from 6.62, 6.68
  international law, prohibition under 6.66
  investigative duty 6.92
  Iraq, UK military action in 4.103
  liberty and security, right to 4.83
  media 2.27
  mental anguish 6.64
  national security 4.83
  purpose 6.62
  state immunity 6.66
  terrorist suspects 6.74–6.78, 6.92
trade associations 4.21
trade marks 8.14–8.15
trade unions
  administration of state, members of 7.455–7.456
  armed forces 7.455–7.456
  closed shops 7.444
  discrimination 7.428
  European Social Charter 7.447–7.449
  financial disincentives offered by employ-
    ers 7.458
  freedom of association 7.409, 7.439–7.440,
    7.444, 7.447–7.449
  freedom of expression 7.354
  funding 9.58
  right to form and join unions 7.409,
    7.439–7.440, 7.444, 7.447–7.449
  police 7.455–7.456
trafficking in human beings 6.127
transsexuals
  birth certificates 2.18–2.19, 7.236
  declarations of incompatibility 7.237, 7.473
  discrimination 7.538
  family life, definition of 7.272
  family, right to found a 7.489
  gender recognition certificates 7.473
  margin of appreciation 7.236

  marriage 7.237, 7.472–7.473
  prison 7.238
  private and family life, right to
    respect for 2.18–2.19, 7.272, 7.236–7.238
  private life, definition of 7.272, 7.236–7.238
travaux préparatoires 10.19
trespassory assembly 1.11, 7.432
tribunals as public authorities 3.19, 3.24
tyranny of the majority 1.11

UK Human Rights Blog 10.26
UK Human Rights Reports 10.21
United Nations (UN)
  human bodies bodies 2.22
  human rights instruments 2.22
  human rights website 10.03
  international law website 10.03
  interpretation 2.22
United States
  political expression 7.358
  September 11, 2001 terrorist attacks on the
    United States 7.567, 7.569–7.578
Universal Declaration of Human Rights 1.04
  framework of ECHR 2.02
  freedom of assembly 7.408
  freedom of association 7.408–7.409
  marry, right to 7.476
  peaceful enjoyment of possessions 8.02
  research 10.02
unwritten constitution, flexibility of 1.17
urgent cases at ECtHR 9.13–9.14
use of force
  Gibraltar killings 6.49
  investigative duty 6.33–6.47
  legitimate aims 6.50
  lethal force 6.48–6.51
  life, right to 6.29, 6.33–6.53
  necessity 6.48, 6.50
  planning and control 6.49, 6.52
  proportionality 6.48, 6.51

victims, standing of 4.16–4.22
  abortion advice 4.21
  actual victims 9.21
  amicus briefs 4.18
  appropriate forum 3.21
  declarations of incompatibility 4.77
  definition 3.07, 4.19
  deportation 9.21
  discrimination 4.20
  enforcement of HRA 4.03–4.05, 4.16–4.22
  Equality and Human Rights Commission 4.26
  EU law 5.25
  European Court of Human Rights 4.19–4.20,
    9.19, 9.21
  family members of deceased persons 4.20
  framework of HRA 3.05, 3..07
  freedom of expression 7.354
  future, persons may be affected by breach in 4.20

victims, standing of (*Cont.*)
  indirect victims 9.21
  judicial review 4.23–4.25
  just satisfaction 4.05, 4.19
  local authorities 4.22
  political activities of civil servants 4.21
  potential victims 9.21
  protest, right to 7.418
  public authorities 3.21
  public interest 4.04, 4.23–4.25
  third party interventions 4.18
  time limits 3.21
  trade associations 4.21
Vienna Convention on the Law of
    Treaties 2.08, 2.69
vote, right to 8.89, 8.98–8.101
  age 8.98
  declarations of incompatibility 8.101
  discrimination 8.100
  freedom of expression 7.350
  Joint Committee on Human Rights 9.63
  mental health patients 8.99
  prisoners 1.53, 2.68, 4.86, 8.100–8.101,
    9.52, 9.63
  reasons 2.68
  residence requirements 8.98–8.99
vulnerable persons, failure to protect 6.96

war and emergencies, derogations in
    time of 2.73, 7.547–7.578
  customary international law 7.561
  death penalty 8.161–8.162
  deportation 7.569–7.570
  designated derogations 7.564–7.566
  emergency, definition of 7.552
  exigencies of the situation 7.547, 7.549,
    7.556–7.560, 5.575

  international law obligations 7.561, 7.563, 5.578
  liberty and security, right to 7.570
  limited and qualified rights 7.547–7.578
  margin of appreciation 7.553, 7.555, 7.557
  national security 7.567–7.578
  necessity 7.558, 7.575
  no punishment without lawful authority 7.172
  non-derogable rights 7.550–7.551
  Northern Ireland 7.567–7.568
  pre-trial detention of terrorist
    suspects 7.570–7.578
  procedural requirements 7.562
  proportionality 7.558, 7.575–5.576
  September 11, 2001 terrorist attacks on the
    United States 7.567, 7.569–7.578
  territorial scope 7.559
  terrorism 7.555, 7.557–7.560, 7.567–7.578
  threshold requirement 7.552–7.553, 7.572
  treaties and conventions 7.561
websites
  European Court of Human Rights 9.07
  research 10.02, 10.10, 10.16–10.17, 10.19,
    10.24–10.26
***Wednesbury* unreasonableness** 4.112, 4.115, 7.496
weight of authorities 10.08
Westlaw 10.24
widows' benefits 3.46, 4.20
witnesses
  anonymity 7.166–7.167
  criminal charges 7.165–7.167
  fair hearing, right to a 7.165–7.167
  life, right to 7.166
  right to examine 7.165–7.167

Yearbook of the European Convention on
    Human Rights 10.15
Yugoslavia, NATO air strikes on 4.101, 6.05